A House of Kings

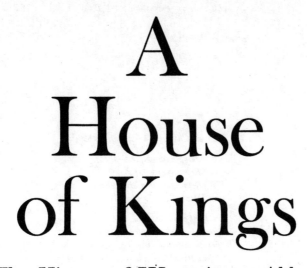

A House of Kings

The History of Westminster Abbey

EDITED BY

EDWARD CARPENTER

ILLUSTRATED

WESTMINSTER ABBEY BOOKSHOP

© *1966, 1972*
The Dean and Chapter of Westminster Abbey

First paperback edition, revised, 1972
Reprinted 1980, 1992
The Westminster Abbey Bookshop
21 Dean's Yard, London SW1

First published June 1966
Second impression September 1966
Third impression December 1966
John Baker (Publishers) Ltd

ISBN: 0 9501018 1 8

Produced on behalf of the Westminster Abbey Bookshop
by A & C Black (Publishers) Ltd, 35 Bedford Row,
London WC1R 4JH.

Printed and bound in Great Britain by
The Redwood Press Ltd, Melksham, Wiltshire

The Queen's Message
to Westminster Abbey

ON the occasion of the 900th anniversary of the Dedication of Westminster Abbey, I join with the Dean and Chapter of Westminster in the thanksgiving which they are offering to Almighty God for the witness to God's Sovereignty and the Gospel of Christ which the Abbey has borne throughout the centuries, both in monastic times and since the Reformation. In particular, I am bound to recall my own Coronation in the great Church which has seen the crowning of so many Kings and Queens since the Coronation of William the Conqueror on Christmas Day, 1066.

I send to the Dean and Chapter my heartfelt good wishes for their work at the present time, and pray that through the years to come Westminster Abbey may serve the cause of Christian unity, inspire our national life, and be a focal point for the spiritual life and aspirations of a great multitude of people.

Foreword

BY THE DEAN OF WESTMINSTER

I COMMEND this book, which has been written by present and past members of the Collegiate Church of St Peter in Westminster and by two independent scholars, to those readers who will be glad that the Abbey's history—so admirably told by Dean Stanley nearly a hundred years ago—has now been retold, in the light of modern research, to those who will rightly be considering the function of Westminster Abbey in Church and State as it enters the tenth century of its history.

Home of a Benedictine Community, whose inspiration is by no means lost; Coronation Church and symbol of the union between Church and State; Monument to the intellectual and cultural history of the nation—the passing of centuries has both enriched and complicated the Abbey's symbolic and practical functions.

What of the future? The Abbey cannot but stand for tradition and continuity, for stability. On the other hand, in a society which is full of change and innovation, its freedom as a Royal Peculiar and its freedom of prophesying a Gospel which claims to be ever new, gives it an opportunity to rise above the dangers of a defunct or irrelevant symbol and to speak its word to our secularized society.

How is it to do this? At the heart of the enterprise there must be a 'household of faith' and a community of prayer. There is a Christian life to be lived in community, out of which the witness comes, in word and action. The Anglican tradition must be deeply understood and faithfully interpreted, yet in the ecumenical setting. The best of our nation's social, cultural and moral tradition must be presented and the nation be reminded of its deepest roots, yet in a setting of a 'plural' and secularized society. The particularity of the Christian faith must be proclaimed but in the setting of an increasing dialogue between the great Religions of the world. We have to grapple with ecumenism true and false, with universalism true and false.

We must hope that this great Church, itself a household word in Christendom and beyond, will be so served by men of faith and wisdom in this era of rapid change that the strategic position of Westminster Abbey will be used not for any kind of selfish Anglican privilege but for the good of the whole Church, for a witness to the Nation, for a humble but convinced contribution to the new Society that is being made out of the old traditions and the new discoveries. *A House of Kings* gives a vivid account of the inheritance into which the Abbey has entered as it seeks to do this.

Meanwhile, the Foundation of our continuing life at Westminster Abbey as we move into its tenth century can only be One who is 'the same yesterday and today and for ever'.

ERIC S. ABBOTT

The Deanery,
Westminster.
February 1966

*　　*　　*

The Dean and Chapter of Westminster are very glad that a paper-back edition of *A House of Kings* is now being made available, and we trust that it will be enjoyed by a great number of our friends from all over the world who visit Westminster Abbey.

Our hope also is that not only the history of the Abbey but its life, worship and witness at the present time will be more fully understood by the readers of this book, for the fact is that since the Abbey's 900th anniversary year, for which *A House of Kings* was produced, not only has the number of visitors to the Abbey increased but the Special Services and the statutory Services have continued to be very largely attended.

While, therefore, all of us are living at a time when it would seem to many that faith is being eroded, Westminster Abbey stands as something of a bastion of the faith, and it is my own belief and prayer that it will continue to do so.

I invite all the readers of this commemorative book to enter, so far as they possibly can, into the authentic spirit of this great church.

ERIC S. ABBOTT

The Deanery,
Westminster
September 1972

Editor's Preface

IT is some thirteen years since *A House of Kings* first appeared as a commemoration of Westminster Abbey's nine hundredth anniversary year. Now that it is to go into a second paperback edition it is inevitable that this should recall Dean Stanley's great achievement in his *Historical Memorials of Westminster Abbey* of a century previously.

Every historical work, no matter how much its author(s) may claim to be objective, of necessity mirrors something of the 'slant' and attitudes of its own day. Neither Stanley's *Memorials* nor *A House of Kings* is any exception to this rule. Stanley wrote in the heyday of nineteenth century liberalism and against the backcloth of an Empire which engendered pride, was evocative of challenge and inspired to mission. The story he tells of the Collegiate Church of St Peter in Westminster finds its place within this ongoing national theme. Both text and footnotes bear witness to his industry and his proper conviction that history ought never to be dull.

A House of Kings was written at a time when account rolls and manuscripts had replaced chronicles and memoirs as primary sources for historical writing. This in itself is indicative of the increasing areas in which the scientific method is now applied. With the publication of a second edition it is natural for the editor to ask himself whether he should contemplate bringing *A House of Kings* up to date. It is indeed tempting to say 'yes' to such a proposition but more mature reflection prompts a more negative answer. Thirteen years is but the twinkling of an eye when set within the context of a work which spans a period of some 900 years. Canon Adam Fox, who died full of years in 1978, tells us that in his contribution he purposely refrained from mentioning any clergyman at the Abbey —with one exception—active during the period of his chapter. He was undoubtedly wise. However, in coming to such a conclusion, a few remarks ought to be made.

If a concluding section were now to be added the author might be tempted to claim that the last thirteen years, under the leadership of Dean Abbott—years consequent upon the

900th Anniversary celebrations with its theme 'One People'—
led to an enlargement of the Abbey's role and its national
significance. But the colder light of a future assessment might
well see this as but a ripple on the river's surface, not disturbing
the main flow of the slow moving current. Distance sometimes
leads to disenchantment with the view. It is true that if *A
House of Kings* were a guide book certain additions would have
to be made. Lord Byron, that wayward but endearing 'Pilgrim',
'half ape half angel', has at long last entered among his peers
into Poets' Corner (see page 247). The mortal remains of Sybil
Thorndike rest under a verse epitaph, the first of its kind for
over two-hundred years. The constitutional relationship
between St Margaret's Church and the Abbey was changed
yet once again under an Act passed through Parliament in
1972.

But an additional chapter bringing the story of the Abbey
up to date—if it is to be included in a historical work—must do
more than add factual information of this kind. It would need
to evaluate what happened during a critical decade to and at
Westminster Abbey within the context of a bewildering
national and international scene—religious, political, social
and economic. To do this, however, would require a more
concentrated treatment of a brief period of years than could
reasonably be given as an addendum to a book such as *A
House of Kings*.

In this epilogue something would need to be said as to the
efforts that have been made to make the link between the
Abbey and the Commonwealth Countries closer and more
personal; to the significance of the increase in Special Services
which reach out into many and diverse areas of the life of the
United Kingdom—and more widely; to the role of this
Collegiate Church in ecumenical enterprise and inter-church
relations, along with its fostering of those eirenical and relief
agencies which in their several ways are endeavouring through
the promotion of justice and goodwill to build up amongst
mankind 'One People'. One would need to ask how far the
Abbey with an incursion of tourists in their millions to the
Abbey—international travel is now an industry—has faced up
to the challenge of this quantitively new problem. Other
questions thrust themselves up. What assessment ought to be
made of patterns of worship in the Abbey; its preaching, more
questing and less dogmatic than hitherto; the use put by the
Abbey to its constitutional status as a Royal Peculiar with the
Sovereign as its Visitor and the opportunity thus given to be

responsibly irresponsible and to tread new paths. Nor could it
fail to mention that at the moment, through the financial help
brought to the Dean and Chapter by the Westminster Abbey
Trust, work of restoration on external Abbey stonework is
being undertaken greater in its extent than at any time since
its reconstruction by Henry III.

Institutions, like people, develop their own personalities
and idiosyncracies. The Abbey across the centuries has lived
its life cheek by jowl with the centres of governmental and
ecclesiastical power. As a consequence it has responded, for
better or for worse, to the environmental pressures brought to
bear upon it, as *A House of Kings* makes abundantly clear.
Indeed the take-over by the House of Commons of the Chapter
House in the latter years of the Middle Ages made it, so one
scholar has asserted, the noisiest monastery in western Europe.

Over long years the Abbey has, at times, identified itself
with its environment almost without remainder; at others, if
rarely, it has brought to bear upon it protest and judgment; at
others it has hovered between the two, too often letting I dare
not wait upon I would. It is, I suspect, within such canons of
criticism that further pages might in the future be added to
A House of Kings—that is when the dust has been allowed to
settle or new dust is borne along fresh winds of change. More
likely, however, as the authors of *A House of Kings* made no
effort to rival or emulate the treatment adopted by Stanley in
his minor classic, so a new group of writers, when the time is
ripe, will bypass *A House of Kings* and proceed to write their
own book in their own way.

In their own way—yes! but the forces of tradition are
strongly formative, particularly in long-continuing institutions
and often defy the most radical of reformers, allowing them
only the transient satisfaction of a pyrrhic victory. Perhaps
this means that change, to be purposeful, must move within
the nature and ethos of the institution itself. To use a not
wholly appropriate metaphor, 'We have but scotch'd the
snake, not killed it: She'll close and be herself'.

No-one knows what Westminster Abbey will be like in
2065–6 and how it will set about its 'vocation of the moment'.
Who knows whether its clerical Dean and Chapter, as at
present constituted, will remain its Governing Body? whether
its worship will have taken into itself forms and insights culled
far more widely than a Western tradition? whether it will have
entered into an apprehension of truth in dimensions at present
only glimpsed at from afar?

The future of Westminster Abbey must depend upon the fate of Western Europe and here prophecy falters and prediction fails. History, under God, is an open system. The doom watchers may be right, but I have a Christian hunch that they will prove wrong. Right or wrong, however, I would indulge the wish that the future author(s) of another History surveying the period 1965–6—2065–6 will be able to testify that even 'in the day when Heaven was falling, the hour when earth's foundation fled' the Abbey upheld contemporaries with a Christian hope and inspirited them with a Christian vision.

EDWARD CARPENTER

March 1979

List of Contributors

The Very Reverend the Dean of Westminster

Dom Hugh Aveling, o.s.b., Ampleforth Abbey

The Reverend A. Tindal Hart, m.a., d.d.

The Reverend E. F. Carpenter, m.a., ph.d., b.d., Canon and Archdeacon of Westminster

The Reverend M. S. Stancliffe, m.a., Canon of Westminster, Rector of St Margaret's, Westminster

The Reverend Canon Adam Fox, m.a., d.d., formerly Canon of Westminster and Sub-Dean

S. E. Dykes Bower, m.a., f.r.i.b.a., f.s.a., Surveyor of the Fabric

L. E. Tanner, c.v.o., m.a., f.s.a., Librarian and Keeper of the Muniments

Sir William McKie, m.v.o., m.a., d.mus., Organist and Master of the Choristers, 1941–63

The Reverend C. Hildyard, m.a., Sacrist

W. R. J. Pullen, m.v.o., ll.b., f.c.i.s., Receiver-General, Chapter Clerk and Registrar

Contents

PART I

WESTMINSTER ABBEY— THE BEGINNINGS TO 1474

By Dom Hugh Aveling, o.s.b.

PART II

THE REFORMATION AND ITS AFTERMATH 1474–1660

By The Rev. A. Tindal Hart

PART III

RESTORATION AND RESETTLEMENT

By The Rev. Canon E. F. Carpenter

CONTENTS

Illustrations

PLATES

ILLUSTRATIONS IN THE TEXT

PART I

Westminster Abbey— The Beginnings to 1474

By Dom Hugh Aveling, o.s.b.

Ampleforth Abbey

1

Fact and Myth

THE SOURCES

LET us imagine that a historian, many centuries in the future and in an age in most ways very different from our own, should set out to reconstruct the life of some Oxford or Cambridge college from 1500 to 2000. His work would start with the buildings (still there, but much altered to other uses) and the surviving college archives. He might well be lucky and have several hundredweight of these—the files of college officials, deeds, lists, memoranda, bills, a few college magazines. Over and above this our historians would labour through the chance survivals of other materials—newspapers, Government records, odd private letters. If we know anything of the realities of historical research, we should not be surprised to hear that his final report would be bulky and reveal an astonishingly close—if very patchy—knowledge of the material side of the college's life, but a depressing failure to bring its inmates to life as credible, sensate, thinking beings, into whose outlooks a reader could enter so much that he could feel he knew them as persons. They would remain curiously alien, cardboard creations, dictionary entries.

Now it does seem that medieval historians mostly have this experience, and the history of medieval Westminster cannot be counted among their few relative successes in reconstruction of an age. On the one hand, Westminster's medieval archives (still extant in quantity in their original place in the buildings) are fuller than those of any other medieval English religious house. A very large proportion of its medieval buildings has survived intact and little altered. Because of the abbey's close proximity to the Palace of Westminster, no monastery figures more in State records and chronicles. Much more than that—since the eighteenth century far more concentrated attention has been paid to Westminster history by experts than to any other medieval monastery. Yet in spite of this at no period in its history does the medieval Westminster community come alive for us as do, for instance, Bury St Edmunds

3

in Abbot Samson's time, Christ Church, Canterbury, in the twelfth (Eadmer, St Anselm, St Thomas Becket), fourteenth and fifteenth centuries, Evesham in the sixteenth century, Rievaulx (St Aelred), St Mary's, York, and Fountains in the twelfth.

It would be quite untrue to say that the documents cast no real light at all on the inner life of medieval Westminster, but the light we do get resembles the hundreds of faint flickers, pin-points and small corners seen from the outer darkness by an observer looking at the thickly-curtained window of a lighted room. Moreover, the glimmers are limited to parts of the curtain—we know extremely little about monastic personalities at Westminster before the thirteenth century, and very little indeed of those of the fifteenth. Such a frustrating situation presents the historians with two different temptations. The first is to rely excessively on the argument from silence (absence of records), to conclude that medieval Westminster always was a house of mediocrities. After all, we could argue, the house was founded late in the golden age of Black monasticism (the seventh to the twelfth centuries) and was at its most prominent from the thirteenth to the early sixteenth—an age when that type of religious life was hardly at its best—with a prominence largely due to the peculiarities of Westminster's geographical position. Again, we could argue that close proximity to the royal Court, civil service and London cannot have made for monastic *quies*.

The second temptation is to rely excessively on arguments from analogy (what we know of other houses and general conditions elsewhere). Precious and indispensable as this type of argument is to historians of obscure periods, it can open the door to every kind of subjectivism in judgement. We can use our historical imaginations far too freely (as John Flete, the fifteenth-century Westminster monk chronicler, put it—*mendaciter et sine causis fingere*). The temptation has special allurements for different types of minds—for the modern Catholic English Benedictine (another Cardinal Gasquet), for Anglican historians bred in the powerful influence of Westminster's still living *genius loci* (unconsciously seeing medieval monks as High Churchmen), for modern academic historians (by training and academic environment disposed and admirably technically equipped to destroy the assumptions of earlier historians and to erect startlingly novel hypotheses and orthodoxies). In this chapter I cannot pretend any ability to draw the dark curtain aside or reveal any really significant new chinks of light, but only to propose the problem briefly and try to sail between the Scylla and Charybdis of the tempters.

In the mid fifteenth century John Flete wrote the best surviving medieval history of Westminster. He was not a historian by vocation (like William of Malmesbury or Matthew Paris) or—so far as we know—university-educated. As an able monastic official, who occupied in turn most of the responsible 'obediences' in the community, he set out to provide them with a brief, business-like compendium of Westminster history, solidly based on archive sources, so as to put beyond cavil the proud claim of the house that it was unique in England, the oldest monastery, from its very origins the *sedes regia* (family monastery of the royal house, coronation church, storehouse of the regalia and other royal treasures, royal mausoleum) —indeed the *caput regni* or spiritual capital. It was also claimed that Westminster was, *par excellence*, a 'little Rome', most directly linked to the Holy See and so most free of all episcopal interference. Flete's critical spirit and technique of references are impressive and show that he had some knowledge of the law. He sticks closely to the extensively quoted letter of existing 'approved chronicles, authenticated writings . . . charters . . . bulls . . .'. The story he tells of Westminster origins is remarkable. The house, he says, was founded in the year 184 by the convert British King Lucius who was in touch with the Holy See and made the house a *sedes regia*—long before the see of London existed. The house was dissolved late in the third century by the Emperor Diocletian, restored in the fifth by a Christian king, again ruined and again restored in 604 by a Saxon king, Sebert, and now consecrated personally and miraculously by St Peter the night before Mellitus, Bishop of London, was due to perform the consecration. Thereafter Westminster was preserved and endowed by a succession of kings, Offa, Ethelstan, Edgar, Canute, Edward the Confessor, and cherished by a line of Popes.

Since the eighteenth century the splendid fabric of this story has been progressively demolished by historians. The main demolition charges were two facts: that the great contemporary sources of early Anglo-Saxon history (the *Anglo-Saxon Chronicle* and Bede's *Ecclesiastical History*) do not mention Westminster, and that all the early charters cited by Flete in evidence were forgeries made in the house between about 1070 and 1215. The dust caused by this demolition has still not settled completely. But we can now, at least, see fairly clearly the small parts of the original fabric which still stand. The Lucius story (as Flete himself seems to feel) was never more than a legend—apparently based on one of Bede's comparatively few mistakes expanded imaginatively. The first extant Westminster historian, Sulcard (*c.* 1070) does not mention it. The fifth-century story only occurs casually and rather out of logical place in Flete's narrative, as if he set little store by it. It even seems that neither he nor other monastic historians were perfectly convinced of the truth of the Sebert story—though the consecration legend seems to have been rooted in English pious folk-lore, and in the mid thirteenth century the monks claimed to have discovered Sebert's grave and translated his body to a more honourable place in the church. Perhaps for Flete—and certainly for Westminster historians before Widmore (in the eighteenth century)—the extant charters of King Offa provided the first really solid ground. But critics are unanimous in judging these spurious.

It is only when we reach the late tenth century that we come in sight of materials left intact by the demolition. It is true that the charters of King Edgar and Archbishop Dunstan, cited by Flete and still extant, are pretty certainly spurious; also an identification of three tenth-century names in Flete's traditional list of abbots with diocesan bishops of the same names and period is little more than a guess. But there do exist three charters (now elsewhere) of some date between 975 and 1020 which mention the Westminster community and are most likely genuine. Hence William of Malmesbury's rather vague description of the Westminster of the 1040s as a little *monasteriolum* housing a mere dozen monks, and the phrase of the *Vita Ædwardi* (Anonymous) 'insignificant in buildings and numbers . . . only a small community . . . the endowments from the faithful were slender and provided no more than their daily bread . . .' do most likely give us a fair idea of Westminster in its earliest days. We are tempted to contrast this with the large, splendid, fashionable Westminster of later centuries. But we ought not to stress the contrast too much. There is no reason why the site—the island of Thorney— should not have housed intermittently hermits or a minster of clerks long before 1000. There was an informality about Anglo-Saxon monachism, and—certainly in 1040–66—great houses such as Evesham had no more than a dozen or fifteen monks.

This was the obscure background to Edward the Confessor's adoption of Westminster. Our evidences for this are three charters (all forged), some thirty of the King's writs (some of them genuine), a brief account apparently all but contemporary (the *Vita Ædwardi Regis*) and the comments of two Westminster historians (Sulcard in about 1076–82 and Osbert of Clare half a century later) together with the reports of archaeologists on the remains of Edward's buildings. Our haul of certain facts from these writings is very small. It was only in the early thirteenth century that any king of England had a stable administrative capital to house a departmental civil service. Before that, royal archives and treasures were distributed unsystematically around a number of strongholds—with Winchester perhaps having a slight predominance.

Kings and their skeleton households and officials travelled incessantly, showing the flag in all the main strategic centres of domains which included tracts of France, and including in the tour a wide variety of royal country houses, the size and importance of which waxed and waned greatly according to the tastes of individual kings. (Indeed, although the Exchequer, and later other departments, settled finally at Westminster in the thirteenth century, kings remained very changeable in their choice of personal residences until quite modern times.)

Anglo-Saxon kings had long been accustomed to the building of monasteries, for a variety of reasons—as a penance, as an act of devotion to a favourite saint, to secure prayers, to secure burial close by the saint, to have a storage place for valuables especially protected by God, to have a loyal centre to which royal lands and jurisdictions could be entrusted. So, for instance, Alfred had built a minster at Athelney to a new, Continental, round design; he had started the monastery at Winchester; Canute had finished Winchester and built Bury out of his special devotion to St Edmund. Thus Edward's action in picking on Westminster, rebuilding it to a Continental pattern—probably to redeem a vow of pilgrimage to Rome—and endowing it quite lavishly with estates in part confiscated from others all conforms to the traditions of his predecessors. It may well be that the new church was a copy of one or other of the Duke of Normandy's foundations at Caen or Jumièges.

It is certain that Edward built a house for himself alongside the abbey. But there was nothing revolutionary in this. His *palatium* at Westminster merely replaced an earlier royal one at Aldermanbury, and was in no way an administrative capital or even a permanent royal residence. The monks of Westminster did not become Edward's confessors and confidants—that place was occupied by his *capella* of (mostly foreign) secular clerks and by the abbots of other monasteries. The building of the new church at Westminster seems to have been a very slow business—as almost always in the Middle Ages. It seems that the old church remained alongside the new, so that even in 1066 the monastic buildings must have looked a higgledy-piggledy group, with the unfinished Choir and Nave towering over a huddle of older parts—the Western Towers and most of the community buildings do not seem to have been completed until well after 1066. A chance scrap of information collected by Leland (the sixteenth-century searcher of monastic libraries) says that Edward imported Exeter monks to Westminster. If this is true it combines with the evidence of the estates (a very artificial creation of bits and pieces in many counties, some apparently not securely conveyed to the abbot by 1066) and buildings to heighten our strong impression that Westminster was an artificial, piece-meal creation. Nevertheless by 1066 it had clearly 'arrived'. The designer of the Bayeux tapestry included a large picture of the church. The Domesday survey rated Westminster seventh in order of income among some fifty English monasteries—a position which it must already have occupied in 1066.

2

1066–1215

AS we have seen, the extreme scantiness of Westminster records before 1065 does correspond with the facts—a late foundation and modest start. Also the Anglo-Saxon charters and writs have introduced us in a small way to what becomes a great and provoking difficulty for the historian of the house's affairs from 1066 to 1215. After 1066 records become more plentiful, but that only multiplies our difficulties in interpreting them, since we now run into what has been called 'the golden age of the forger's art throughout Europe'. Wherever we turn in the secular or ecclesiastical history of this 150 years we run into documents which have been doctored, touched up or completely forged. It is true of the charters, bulls and chronicles of the Black monks, the early Cistercians, the early Augustinian Canons, the Premonstratensians, the cathedral Chapters, and equally true of the records of lay lawyers and administrators.

In the thirteenth century lawyers and judges and popes were forced to work out rule-of-thumb methods for distinguishing true documents from false. By the later seventeenth century the French Benedictine, Jean Mabillon, developed these rules into the science of Diplomatic —as the necessary tool for a modern historian of the early Middle Ages. Diplomatic has since steadily improved its methods of detection, but alone it can tell us little about the genuine documents from which these forgeries were often made, nor can it provide us with any safe touchstone to distinguish classes of forgery—simple errors by careless copyists, innocent but deliberate 'improvement' of existing texts, outright inventions.

Our steadily increasing knowledge of the contemporary background makes it possible to guess at the motives of the 'improvers' and forgers, but leaves the depths of their psychology obscure. The period was one of bewildering changes. In both Church and State, organization and administrative methods were becoming daily more expert and complex. Great landowning corporations, founded in the Dark Ages and geared to work in old-fashioned ways, ran into all the acute difficulties of adaptation. They were forced to produce ever more explicit and detailed title-deeds for all their ancient lands and jurisdictions. Their ancient records must have been defective for this job—defective in quantity due to fires and careless keeping, defective in clarity because they were drawn up in another language (Anglo-Saxon), in out-of-date jurisdictional and legal terms, and at a time when such close scrutiny of deeds was not expected or usual.

The intellectual and academic revolution of the later eleventh and twelfth centuries brought with it an urge to rewrite history, to find justifications in the past for disputed positions taken up in the present (legal, hagiographical). These historians had had a solid classical education with a little logic and perhaps some study of the law; they had a sense of evidence but little idea of historical perspective. Perhaps their classical studies had accustomed them to *pastiche*. Certainly a barbaric combative spirit lay close beneath the surface of most minds, and communal loyalties had a feudal strength and ferocity. Where a corporation felt itself to be fighting for its very life men tended to be ruthless. If we appreciate all this it makes mass tampering with documents more comprehensible. Yet we still wonder at the psychology of good men who could accept knowingly the services of the several consultant-monk forgers engaged at this period by Westminster and many other English and Continental religious houses and Chapters.

With all this in mind we approach the history of Westminster of 1066–1215 with some trepidation. The prominent position into which King Edward had thrust the house meant both hopes and difficulties. It was very closely associated with a defeated cause; Harold II had been crowned in the new church immediately after Edward's death. The house's temporal and ecclesiastical position cannot have been secure. The estates were an artificial collection, dispersed over a dozen counties, hard to supervise and defend against fraudulent bailiffs and aggressive new Norman magnate neighbours, and (or so it seems) not always secured by adequate title-deeds. Also, unlike the great old Anglo-Saxon houses, Westminster had only a very small property immediately round the house and no extensive jurisdictions. The church of St Margaret, alongside the monastery, had already been claimed by the Bishop of London in King Edward's days. Thus in a very direct sense Westminster was vulnerable. It had no long traditions to depend on, and no great saint's shrine to defend it. All hung on the favour of the new kings. William I was careful to stage an impressive coronation in Westminster. But that was a political move. He clearly did not regard the house as his *sedes regia*—he already had one at Caen. What little interest he displayed in patronage of English monasteries was lavished on his new French foundation at Battle in Sussex. The Westminster records (which would clearly, if they could, have pressed to the hilt every scrap of evidence of favour from him) mention only his confirmations of their estates but no contributions to the continuing building operations there. Some have cited Battle charters to prove that William regarded three English churches (his *capella*, Battle and Westminster) as especially under his protection—but there is suspicion that the charters have been 'improved'. In his time Westminster Palace was of comparatively little importance. There is some evidence that he may have contemplated repairing it, but none to counter other indications that he thought of it as no more than one of several main stations on his constant progresses— possibly of less importance to him than Winchester, Gloucester and Abingdon.

In common with most other prominent English monasteries, Westminster received from William by outright appointment and lay investiture a series of Norman abbots, and they introduced a more Continental type of observance, based on Lanfranc's Canterbury Customary. William's first two choices were undistinguished— Geoffrey of Jumièges (soon packed off summarily to Normandy, no doubt for over-violent rule of an Anglo-Saxon community) and Vitalis of Bernay (who only survived a short time and made little impression on the chroniclers). The third choice was Lanfranc's chaplain, Gilbert Crispin of Bec, a monk of great influence and ability. There is little doubt that Lanfranc urged this course because Westminster, in 1083, must have been stagnating.

The years 1087 to 1154 saw Westminster emerge—slowly, indeed, and somewhat painfully—from insignificance and begin to rival great and famous houses like St Albans, Bury St Edmunds, Worcester, Ramsey and the Canterbury and Winchester twin monasteries. To the community it must have seemed a precarious fight to win an ordered security in the midst of a storm of unparalleled difficulties. Their main hopes lay in Gilbert Crispin and the possibility of an unbroken succession of abbots of like ability and influence. That, in its turn, depended on the goodwill of kings. The house's other assets were relatively subsidiary—papal bulls of protection, a large estate, what was still perhaps the finest monastic church in England, the geographical position of Westminster alongside the rising power of London and the Palace, the claim (as yet new and fragile) to be the royal coronation church.

The dangers were real and manifold. As Holy Scripture reminded the monks, the favour of kings is capricious. William II turned out to be that unusual medieval phenomenon, a man not even conventional in his religion, but actually indifferent. Even the forgers thought it inadvisable to attempt to father on him grants to West-minster. Though he seems to have liked the Palace and built a large new hall there, he showed little interest in the abbey. Henry I, in his turn, showed little more interest. He made or confirmed a few small grants to the house, but his real devotion was to the Cluniac monks and his own Cluniac foundation at Reading, where he was buried. He left the abbacy of Westminster vacant four years, while he enjoyed its revenues, and then allowed the house to elect a member of their own community, who proved incompetent. He allowed Westminster Palace to fall into neglect and disrepair.

The reign of Stephen brought to the abbacy one of his illegitimate sons, an association which gave few advantages and many anxieties in the chaos of the civil war. Westminster itself was not sacked by the Empress's men, but considerable outlying parts of the estate suffered. On top of these political dangers came others, as the strong tide of the Gregorian Church Reform movement began, in succes-sively more powerful waves, to wash over and recast the whole organization of the English Church and its relations with the Crown. Basically this movement was a great European religious revival which touched and quickened every side of Christian life. In particular, it brought great benefits to monks, who, by the very nature of their life, were always liable to slip into over-conservatism and laxity. The movement shook them to new life, much increased their numbers and, in many ways, forced them to adapt their lives and outlooks. From the 1130s the new monastic reform of the Cistercians began to establish itself in England. As yet, by 1154, the Black monks in general, and Westminster in particular, seem to have felt few misgivings as they watched these developments in spirituality and observance. Indeed Cistercian abbots became frequent visitors to Westminster, and a row of them could be seen in the refectory there as they stayed overnight on their way to and from their General Chapters at Cîteaux.

But it was otherwise with the jurisdictional and legal sides of the Reform. Although all of these (the much increased centralization of the Church on Rome, the separation of Church courts from lay courts, the revival of episcopal jurisdiction and activity, the revival of regular synods, the attack on lay investiture) were proposed as necessary embodiments of the spiritual principles of the Reform—the deeper Christianization of society—they gave rise both to practical diffi-culties for old-established corporations linked to the Crown and to disagreements on the extent to which they should be carried. The implementation of the Reform programme in these matters took decades and ran into severe opposition from kings and conservatives, lay and clerical.

Westminster found itself often in a no-man's-land, fought over and shot at by both sides. Even when the Reform had finally brought the Crown and society to accept the main lines of the programme, the outcome was—compared with the state of things prevailing to the 1120s—a bewilderingly complex new interrelationship of jurisdictions, papal, episcopal, royal, in the midst of which monasteries had to find their new place.

We can understand why monastic communities took their time to assimilate the new spirit and accept the new order, and why, once they had done so, they still felt the latter a not unmixed blessing. Lastly there was a third type of danger during these years—bankruptcy. Population was increasing markedly, prices and standards of living rising alarmingly, the economic life of the country growing every day more fluid, active and complex. Monasteries like Westminster, with much expanded communities to clothe and feed and heavy building programmes on hand, found it perilously easy to drift into serious debt. Their assets consisted almost entirely of farm land, scattered (in Westminster's case especially) widely, uneconomically and inconveniently over wide areas, and of rents mostly in the form of food 'farms'. The problem was increased by the imposition of knight service on Westminster by William I, with its attendant burden of supporting on the estate between fifteen and twenty-five of these expensive soldiers. At the same time the abbot had become a tenant-in-chief of the king, subject to lay investiture, aids and reliefs, the maintenance of feudal courts, suit of the King's Council and subjection to royal wardship of the monastery's lands during abbatial *interregna*.

During these years other monasteries were universally groping their way towards solutions—separating the abbot's estate from the convent's rigidly, enfeoffing their knights with parts of the estate, attempting to increase the yield of the rest by various methods of close monastic supervision. At every point the essential was superiors who had considerable business acumen, a commanding presence, knowledge of the law, ability to delegate authority successfully. Such men, not very surprisingly, were in short supply in religious houses. In short, peace of mind for monks in the society that was fast emerging, lay in having superiors who were, at one and the same time, spiritual fathers, experts in feudal law, canonists and businessmen. On the whole, when we reflect on this, we are surprised, not at the intermittent periods of poor abbatial rule, dissension in communities and financial troubles, but at the number of able superiors in houses like Westminster over such long spaces of time, and the corporate strength, resilience and ability to learn from experience and the outside world which is so much in evidence.

GILBERT CRISPIN (c. 1083–1117)

Gilbert Crispin, during his long abbacy proved himself the first great superior of Westminster and undoubtedly raised it from mediocrity to rivalry with the top five or six houses in the kingdom, Black monk and Cistercian. It was a remarkable effort, considering —as we have seen—that he got little help from William II or Henry I. Moreover he was an ex-novice at Bec of St Anselm's and his close friend, a friendship cemented again during the months of Anselm's stay at Westminster immediately before he became Archbishop of Canterbury. Both belonged to a rising élite of sensitive and highly intelligent scholars. Gilbert (to judge from the scanty remains of their correspondence) had early acquired the habit of referring questions of every sort to Anselm. Indeed, the spirit of Anselm's training of his young monks and the nature of their training put a premium on lively and thorough discussion and on a kind of free obedience. In other circumstances, this friendship would have been a great stay for Gilbert. But since Anselm's archiepiscopate was one long battle with the king to secure the jurisdictional positions of the Reform, and Gilbert could hardly avoid—on his allegiance—being present as a voting member at most of the baronial Great Councils and provincial or English Church Councils of those hectic years, the friendship must have caused him acute difficulties. Unfortunately there is very scanty evidence of Gilbert's views and even actions during the quarrel. In 1095 he may well have been one of the abbots whom Eadmer says were present at the stormy Council of Rockingham. Eadmer's account of the Council shows the bishops acutely embarrassed and trying to combine allegiance to the king with canonical obedience to the Archbishop. The account does not mention any contribution by an abbot.

In 1102 an English Church Council was held in the church at Westminster and there—not for the first time—Gilbert found himself and his community involved in the struggle for precedence between Anselm and the Archbishop of York. In 1107 the abbot took part in another Church Council which discussed and confirmed a settlement between the Archbishop and the King over lay investiture. The following year he was, with three bishops, sent by the King to Anselm to offer the former's mediation in a dispute with St Augustine's, Canterbury. Here, perhaps, he was picked precisely because of his friendship with Anselm. As for Gilbert's views on the issues of the Reform, we only have two small pieces of evidence. One is a short treatise on the validity of the sacraments administered by simoniac bishops—in which he takes a definite but moderate Reforming line. The other is an undated set of verses imploring

Anselm in exile to return to his English flock, beset by ravening wolves. Here also Gilbert's views are moderate—that the pastoral need for the Archbishop's presence in England outweighed the technical objections to lay investiture.

In the domestic affairs of Westminster Gilbert's ability can be seen in operation almost everywhere. He continued the building of the monastery. He came to grips with estate-administration— though the evidence for this is so fragmentary as to tell us very little indeed about his methods. In 1102 he opened the tomb of Edward the Confessor. This event seems later to have been regarded as a legal 'translation' (enshrining) or tantamount, in the practice of those days, to a preliminary stage of canonization—beatification. Moreover in Gilbert's day men were seeking sanctuary 'at the altar of St Peter and the tomb of King Edward', and receiving certificates to that effect from the abbot. Lanfranc, Gilbert's old master, had been very suspicious of Anglo-Saxon popular canonizations. St Anselm, though on occasion more sympathetic, seems to have shared the suspicion. Perhaps Gilbert felt constrained to make modest concessions to a very local cult of Edward, since the community may well have been still half Anglo-Saxon. He was a Norman of the Normans, as was his prior, Robert, an able man and later abbot of Bury St Edmunds. Anselm's letters to Gilbert contain brief references to troubles with individual monks at Westminster—but not enough detail to suggest reasons.

Gilbert seems to have been mainly responsible for the foundation of dependent priories at Hurley and Great Malvern. This was then the fashionable method of satisfying the onerous spiritual obligations attached to gifts of land to monasteries and of trying to supervise estates at a distance from the mother house. Hurley was a gift of Geoffrey de Mandeville, who had earlier made over to Westminster lands adjacent to the tiny home demesne, so making it a more manageable unit. These priories were made possible by an expansion in numbers—to eighty, if we are to believe a Westminster tradition. Lastly, there is some reason to imagine that Gilbert raised the academic standards of the claustral school. Osbert of Clare—whom we shall soon meet—must have been a monk-pupil there in Gilbert's days. If so his education did Gilbert some credit.

Events after the abbot's death in 1117 must have brought Westminster down to earth sharply and painfully. Its affairs between 1117 and 1154 have lately been subjected to close examination by historians. It is agreed that, either during the four years of abbatial interregnum between Gilbert's death and the election of Abbot Herbert from the community, or early in Herbert's rule, the house fell into grave difficulties. The roots of the trouble may just possibly

lie in unwise actions by Gilbert in his last years, but the lack of a
superior for so long and Herbert's incompetence at least violently
exacerbated it. There were economic troubles—a mounting debt
to Jews, the loss of control of great parts of the estates (perhaps due
to overlong leases at uneconomic rents or to wholesale challenges of
the abbey's title-deeds by lay claimants invading its lands, disastrous
experiments in farming properties to inexperienced monk officials,
insubordination by the abbey's knights). On top of all this there were
dissensions and parties within the community.

OSBERT OF CLARE AND THE THEME OF VIRGINITY

One trouble-maker was Osbert of Clare. He seems to have become
prior first by election—most likely during the abbatial interregnum
of 1117–22. In the latter year he was a candidate at the abbatial
election, but Herbert was elected and Osbert packed off into exile
for a dozen years. During the troubles which followed Osbert moved
miserably as a guest round other monasteries—Ely, Reading,
Pershore, Bury St Edmunds. In about 1134 Herbert recalled him to
Westminster and restored him to the priorship. Once more he was an
unsuccessful candidate, at the election of 1136, when King Stephen
put in as abbot his illegitimate son, Gervase of Blois. Osbert remained prior. A later Westminster tradition implies that Gervase
was another incompetent ruler and that he was deposed by Henry II
in 1154, that an interregnum followed until 1160. It has been
suggested of late that this tradition merely reflects a party view,
and that Gervase was—if we take into allowance the civil strife of
those days—a fairly able abbot, and that he was certainly functioning
as abbot in 1157/8 and probably died in office in 1159/60.

In all this troubled period of Westminster history there are present
factors which we can grasp and appreciate—mismanagement of
business affairs, consequent dissension, personal animosities in the
community. The twelfth century in England was full of character-
istics which we normally associate with the Elizabethans—the striking of extreme and rhetorical attitudes, passionate loves and enmities,
an adventurous spirit. But the part played by Osbert of Clare
remains provokingly obscure. This is true in spite of the fact that
he left behind him over forty voluble letters, half-a-dozen treatises
and several liturgical compositions.

For the first time in Westminster history since Gilbert Crispin we
come across a sizable corner of light in the dark curtain, and meet
a documented personality—only to find that what we discover is
puzzling. An initial difficulty is Osbert's very florid Latin style,
crammed with imagery and tricks of rhetoric. We attempt to push

our way through this stifling curtain of verbiage to reach the man
and the mind behind them. Yet here we run into a more profound
difficulty. Osbert's mind runs around a circle of ideas, mostly common then among English monks of the educated kind. Was this his
whole mental stock-in-trade, did he really and whole-heartedly
believe them or were they a conventional means of expression
covering quite other motives?

In common with numbers of other Westminster monks and a
circle of monastic acquaintances elsewhere, he pressed hard for the
revival of Anglo-Saxon devotions—in particular to Mary Immaculate, St Anne, St Ethelburga, St Edmund of Bury, St Edburga of
Pershore, St Ethelbert, St Edward the Confessor. Lanfranc had
suppressed these and St Anselm—who was, in many ways, the hero of
Osbert's circle of acquaintances—had given them very little credence.
Osbert's first objective was to get the Anglo-Saxon monastic feast
of the Conception of our Lady restored to the calendar in England,
and in that and other ways to promote belief in the doctrine of
Mary's Immaculate Conception.

Preaching played a large part in the campaign, and Osbert
claimed that he got large congregations of monks, clergy and laity to
his sermons in the church and Chapter House at Westminster. He
met resolute opposition, but secured a remarkable partial triumph,
when an English Council of 1129 restored the Conception to the
calendar. It does not seem that the resistance to the feast had much
foothold in the Westminster community, since it was celebrated there
well before 1129. But it may well be true that the doctrine roused
resentment there. Encouraged by all this, Osbert set about rewriting
the lives of his favourite Anglo-Saxon saints. In part this must have
been a solace during his exile—which took him to their shrines—and
in part a literary exercise. But his motive also was to recast the lives
to express clearly certain general themes.

His favourite theme was virginity. In one of his plainest passages
in the letters he says:

This is that chief of all virtues, gem of all good works, which God
made man took to Himself especially at His birth, and in which
alone His worthy and immaculate Mother conceived and bore
Him. . . . Without it other women give birth and merely produce
mortal flesh from corruptible flesh; they bear, I say, what they
conceive, sin out of sin, and they not infrequently have to pay for
their offspring the price of their own lives. But those who bear
spiritual fruit to God do not have to undergo the perils of that
sort of childbirth. In their case the husband who generates is
Himself virgin and the source of virginity, the origin both of the

c

virgin's intention and flesh. . . . These are imitators of her who bore God's Son virginally. So therefore you conceive progeny by Him in such a fashion that you give birth without feeling the corruption of the flesh. . . .

Here we are at grips not only with a literary style strange to us, but with sets of ideas and a way of arguing which are alien to the modern mentality. It does seem, however, that Osbert was trying to express the main great insight of both the Gregorian Reform and contemporary monastic thought—the necessity that a Christian should be utterly converted to God, pure in intention, totally dedicated in mind and body in virgin simplicity. Elsewhere he says that this is a work of Divine grace, a conforming to Christ, a real Passion; Christ's human virginity of heart and body is the source and archetype, but Mary's virginity is the archetype of the purity of the redeemed race, the Church. The redemption is not only from sin in general, but from worldly, superstitious, self-centred and conventional Christianity. The life of all Christians who give up self for God—especially the virgin saints and martyrs and monks and nuns—is a lamp to guide others, and, under God, a source of grace. Scattered through Osbert's writings are clear traces of the idea common in monastic writers—for instance in his master, St Anselm—that monastic virginity and obedience are the surest road to God, and that others only gain Heaven by being fellow-travellers on the same road.

Osbert's view of history was solidly in line with Biblical and Christian tradition; history is *gesta Dei per homines* made evident to the spiritual man, rather than a naturalistic, photographic reconstruction. In fact, English history for the twelfth-century educated man pretty well meant what was contained within the covers of Bede's *Ecclesiastical History*, continued in the same vein and style by imitators like William of Malmesbury.

Two hundred years after Osbert, another Westminster monk, Richard of Cirencester, in his *Mirror of the History of the Deeds of the Kings of England*, was faithfully treading the same path. In his '*Proemium*' to the *Mirror* Richard takes for granted that history is primarily spiritual reading—especially for kings, since: 'Amongst all other Kingdoms under heaven England shines with a special glory from the sanctity of her Kings, by whose merits she is strengthened, by whose prayers she is helped and by whose examples she is inspired to holiness. . . .'

Some of her kings, he says, acknowledging God as their author, gained a return in Heaven for their sacrifices in alms and church-building; others abdicated and gained a hundredfold in Heaven by becoming monks; others abdicated to become life-long pilgrims;

others embraced virginity: 'choosing for the love of Christ to lack heirs on earth so that they might gain an inheritance in heaven', while others gave their lives in defence of their native land and the *respublica* and so reign in Heaven as martyrs, and others, as warriors, left behind them an example of boldness and spirit. Yet history cannot be silent about other kings who were altogether ignorant of Christian truth and served pagan errors.

It was this schematic spiritual interpretation of history which lay behind Osbert and all later medieval chroniclers and writers, enclosing, as within a picture-frame, all their particular nationalisms and political aspirations, their personal loyalties and even their aspirations to be critical historians. The existence everywhere of copies of Bede in itself ensured that the Anglo-Saxon past would always set the tone and standards for judging the later medieval present. We do not therefore require to posit any 'English reaction' to Anglo-Norman rule to account for Osbert's taking for granted everywhere (without much overt comment) that England was converted by virgins, martyrs, monks and holy kings, who endured a Passion from the Devil working among their countrymen. The Old Testament (applied constantly by Osbert as a key to the Providential action of God in the present) illuminated this process of Divine Judgement through suffering and human failure.

The sufferings of England in 1070 and again in the chaos of Stephen's reign, 'when Christ and His saints slept' paralleled the sufferings in the Danish wars. Redemption would always come by the restoration of ruined temples, setting up again the old lamps on their lampstands, done by the *Sacerdotium* (priesthood) and *Regnum* (kingship) renewed. As in the Old Testament, one should be always hoping and never expecting too much, waiting on events and trying to puzzle out their divine significance. Osbert hails the new papal legates (Henry of Winchester and Theobald of Canterbury) in turn with reminders of their vocation to renew the *Sacerdotium*; he looks part-expectantly at Stephen—and perhaps the Empress too—and then at the young Henry II as possible renewers of the *Regnum*, true heirs of Edward the Confessor and the Saxon Royal Martyr, pilgrim and virgin kings.

The real virtue of Edward lay, not in any success as a ruler (contemporaries like Eadmer were frank in seeing little but bad morals and ruined religion in England in his day), but in his virgin, monk-like oblation of himself and his kingdom in faith. Thereby, humanly speaking, he condemned his family and nation to much suffering; but on his deathbed he prophesied (as St Dunstan and a good many other English saints were supposed to have done) the eventual rise of a true heir to unite kingship and priesthood.

Such an attitude in medievals begot simultaneously hope and disillusionment. The miracle stories about Edward the Confessor reflect this attitude. Some sought miracles at his tomb at once after his death—as they tended to do at the tombs of all but the most obviously unlikely English sovereigns—even, according to the Westminster continuer of the *Flores Historiarium*, at the tomb of Henry III where miracles were sought and obtained. Others doubted—like the Westminster monk who was saying five psalms for Edward's soul's redemption from Purgatory until he was forced by a miracle to change his judgement, or the community's opening of the tomb of Edward in 1102 in doubt whether they would find his body corrupt or not.

Osbert set out to campaign for the papal canonization of Edward. He rewrote an existing *Life* of the King to express his ideas—that the hand of God, working through miracles at the tomb which he had experienced; through the discovery of the uncorrupt body in 1102; through the fulfilment of Edward's prophecies of ruin; was demanding that Edward be set up as a lamp at Westminster. Osbert collected a dossier of the miracles and commendatory letters from King Stephen, the legate of Winchester and others, and, in 1139, was allowed to carry them to Rome. The outcome was disappointing, since the Pope put off a decision pending the arrival of more decisive evidence of miracles and a widespread cult in England. As we shall see, the canonization hung fire until 1161, by which time Osbert was most probably dead.

Some modern historians, not surprisingly, are very disinclined to take Osbert's views at their face-value. In the first place they suggest that his devotion to our Lady Immaculate and belief in the Immaculate Conception were really only a personal *attrait* or foible, a 'luxury of devotion', devoid of any solid theological backing in the minds of Osbert and Eadmer of Canterbury, devoid of any widespread support in England then and, *ipso facto*, irrelevant to the main concerns of a Christian life. A great theological revival was slowly coming to birth in Osbert's day. Both he and Eadmer belonged to monastic circles affected by St Anselm, the originator of that revival in England. It is true that they were both far below Anselm in stature as theologians. Patristic learning was primitive and the attributions of texts often wildly mistaken. On the point at issue, the Immaculate Conception, Osbert and Eadmer had against them the immense authority of St Anselm. Also the main weight of twelfth-century theologians—even of those so devout to our Lady as St Bernard and the early Cistercian doctors—was hostile to their views.

On the other hand a solid devotion to our Lady had always

existed in England. The early twelfth century saw both a considerable heightening of that and theological efforts to base it on a revived Mariology—that is, on theology and not on devotional and human feeling. St Anselm himself had been prominent in this. He had taught his pupils to see Mary as holding a position in the economy of Redemption, and had stimulated them to speculate in matters not yet decided by the Church. In fact Osbert, for all his ineptitude, had the courage to follow this lead and not to be intimidated by Anselm's authority; and he made some progress along a theological path which was—it is true, much more due to the writings of his contemporary, Eadmer, than his own—to attract so many others that England by the next century was a stronghold of belief in the Immaculate Conception.

THE CULT OF EDWARD THE CONFESSOR

In the second place, modern historians have suggested that Osbert's cult of Edward the Confessor was a spiritual fraud, motivated by a desire to aggrandize Westminster and exalt Henry II, and sustained by unscrupulous history and forgery. The argument runs as follows: once we cut loose from the versions of later chroniclers and hagiographers and study the contemporary evidence of his reign, Edward appears clearly as a normal Anglo-Saxon king, in no way remarkable for either piety or virtue. It is unlikely that he lived a virgin life. Immediately after his death, although there was a very small local cult of him, real devotion was only shown by some foreign clerks of his *capella*, who wrote a *Vita Ædwardi* wildly at variance with the facts. In effect, having decided that he must be a saint, they wrote a 'saint's life' on the very strict and exceedingly formalized pattern of contemporary hagiography, setting imagination and edification before historical truth. The cult then languished and was almost extinct when Osbert and his party at Westminster set out to revive it. They were most probably motivated simply by nationalistic feeling and a desperate desire to rescue Westminster from her embarrassments by creating what she had hitherto badly lacked—a great shrine, drawing down special royal protection and bringing pilgrims, patronage and prosperity.

It cannot be merely a coincidence that Osbert's lack of compunction in accepting the *Vita Ædwardi* and producing a touched-up version of it was contemporary with the great Westminster forgeries. In his days the community was hiring expert forgers to create or 'improve' a series of bulls and royal charters—thereby endowing Westminster with a past at least as great as that of a Bury St Edmunds and protecting her from assaults on her exemption and estates. In

this work the experts probably used the charters of the great Cape-
tian royal peculiar monastery in Paris, St Denis. In fact this daring
and desperate enterprise succeeded. It succeeded partly because
of the forger's skill, partly because the Anglo-Saxon past was becoming a fashionable interest, and partly because the Pope in 1161 was
in a hurry to conciliate Henry II and undisposed to examine the
evidence closely.

This is a powerful indictment but, as in the case of Osbert's devotion to our Lady, it seems that the prosecution has lighted on valid
grounds for criticism and then exaggerated them out of proportion.
The canonization of saints was much discussed in twelfth-century
England. Lanfranc and the Norman bishops and abbots had treated
Anglo-Saxon popular canonizations severely. St Anselm, on at
least one occasion had disputed with Lanfranc on the question. By
the 1130s papal canonization had been established as a check on
local cults. The argument continued long afterwards—particularly
over the cases of St Bernard and St Thomas Becket. In Becket's
case the sceptics were overwhelmed by a sudden tornado of popular
devotion, of cures and conversions. It seems to have become
generally agreed that, in the complex and delicate matter of recog-
nizing sanctity, there were three factors. The first was the *Advocatus
Diaboli*, the place of critics; the second the positive spiritual reaction
of the faithful, assessed by the authority of the Holy See; and the
third the necessity of some divine intervention or sign. After all, as
Osbert saw clearly, the saints are themselves living messages or signs
from God to a faithless and doubting generation. The naïve but
very real outlook of contemporaries, therefore, in judging whether
particular men were saints and to be set up as lamps and signs
before men, attempted to discover the will and design of God in
history—in the crisis of England, of Westminster, in the advent to
the throne of a king of Edward's lineage, in the crisis of the papal
schism.

We do not know precisely what documentary evidence was produced in Rome in 1139 and 1161; but even if we did, we should still
have to account as extra evidence all kinds of imponderables present
in the minds of contemporaries, popes, cardinals, and Osbert himself. The modern *Advocatus Diaboli* in the cause of the Confessor,
with all his technical and diplomatic equipment, far superior to that
of Osbert or Alexander III, is still very far short of being able to
arrive at the truth. He can suggest multiple reasons for doubt—the
evidence of touched-up documents, the real possibility of strong
material motives, self-deception, superstition. But he cannot get
at or assess accurately the genuine elements underlying the imagin-
ary. The anonymous *Vita Ædwardi* (ostensibly the work of some clerk

of the Confessor's *capella*) for all its hagiographical formalism and exaggerations must have had some basis in reality. It is quite certain that the cult never was widespread, but it existed immediately after the Confessor's death. It cannot have faded out between the 1070s and 1130s, since even the disapproving Norman Gilbert Crispin found it advisable to hold the 'translation' of 1102 and to grant the sanctuary certificates.

HENRY II

The reign of Henry II clearly brought better abbatial government —significantly through the resumption of royal appointments of outsiders. Abbot Laurence (1160–75) came from St Albans and abbot Walter (1175–90) from Winchester. Apart from this, however, there is extremely little solid evidence of interest by the King in the abbey. Perhaps he helped in the restoration of the estates. He attended the translation of St Edward in 1163 and must have listened to St Aelred of Rievaulx's pious and patriotic sermon delivered then. Perhaps the ideal of kingship moved him momentarily. But as an Angevin his first loyalty lay to his ancestral monastery and mausoleum at Fontrevault. In England his monastic building was confined to his penance-churches at Waltham, Witham and Amesbury and additions to Godstow nunnery, the burial place of his mistress. The cult of St Edward was now modestly established in the English calendar as a feast of obligation, with nocturn lessons from the revision of Osbert's *Vita* made by St Aelred at the request of Abbot Laurence. But Becket in his agony invoked only our Lady, the saints of the church of Canterbury and St Denis, and after 1170 his own cult overshadowed all others.

The part played by Westminster in the quarrel between Henry II and Becket was very small. Abbot Laurence apparently had no more desire than Gilbert Crispin to be directly embroiled in such high matters, and, as an abbot, seems to have been left in his obscurity. He certainly was acquainted with Becket. Laurence was a well-educated man, and, in a modest way, something of a celebrity. A scholar of the school of St Victor in Paris, he had returned to be a secular clerk employed by the Bishop of Durham and to enter the monastery of St Albans. He was well-known to St Bernard and related to St Aelred of Rievaulx. Aelred visited Westminster on his way to and from Cistercian General Chapters at Cîteaux. He also visited his friend Gilbert Foliot, a Cluniac monk, Bishop of London and an inveterate opponent of Becket.

There is a story in the *Life and Miracles of St Godric of Finchale* that Laurence visited Durham shortly after his election to Westminster and Becket's election to Canterbury. A Westminster monk in his company paid a visit of respect to St Godric—who knew Laurence—and conversation turned to Becket. The hermit asked the monk to carry to Becket a prophecy that the archbishop would suffer exile but triumph in the end. Laurence himself took the message to Becket. The many pages of the Rolls Series volumes of materials for the life of Becket contain exceedingly few references to Westminster. We do not even know whether Laurence was present at the stormy Great Councils of Northampton and Clarendon. In 1170 the Prince Henry was crowned at Westminster abbey, though Becket excommunicated the bishops who took part. The abbot was untouched, however, and shortly afterwards was among the prelates who wrote to Alexander III to ask for the absolution of Gilbert Foliot. Laurence has left behind him a number of sermons, and no doubt when they find an editor we shall get light on his personality and outlook.

The curtain over Westminster history between 1190 and 1216 is very largely opaque. In 1214 abbot Ralph Papillon was deposed by a papal legate after an inquiry into his misgovernment. Perhaps significantly he was succeeded by the Norman monk of Caen and friend of King John, William de Humez. Otherwise there is little surviving trace of interest in Westminster on the part of Kings Richard and John. The Palace was also neglected. Richard built only two monasteries—in Normandy and Aquitaine. John had as his personal patron St Wulfstan of Worcester and was buried at Worcester, though he had planned a tomb for himself in his one foundation, the monastery of Beaulieu. William de Humez was no doubt an embarrassed spectator of the events of the charter crisis of 1215. A few months after his election in 1214 he had been sent by John as a junior member of an embassy to King Philip of France. In 1216, when Louis of France and the rebel barons held London, a party of them was denied entrance to the abbey and took their revenge by seizing the royal regalia.

3

The Thirteenth Century

AT the death of King John in 1216 Westminster must have appeared a hum-drum Black monk house of comparatively little distinction, probably ranking in popular esteem below such places as St Albasn, Bury St Edmunds, Christ Church Canterbury—and perhaps some Cistercian houses. A historian is also strongly tempted to judge that, in common with all other Black monk houses, it had now reached a watershed in its history. We should imagine that the Black monks now found themselves, as the result of massive changes in Church and State between 1100 and 1216, thrust into an honourable but increasingly insignificant place in society. Changes in relations between Church and State and in the organization of the Church had steadily demoted the great old monasteries; very active secular bishops now dominated the English Church and had replaced abbots as the Crown's main ecclesiastical advisers; the rise, first of episcopal schools, and then of the great *Studia Generalia*, together with the collapse of monastic schools as monasteries ceased to recruit from boys (after about 1150), had much reduced the intellectual prestige of the monastic Order. Added to this, the Black monks of 1216 were dwarfed by the rise in the twelfth century alongside them of new Orders (Cistercians, Augustinian Canons, Premonstratensians, Gilbertines, Carthusians) who now much outnumbered them. Shortly after 1216 the new Orders of the Friars were to enter England and, by their even more massive growth, still further reduce the Black monks to a minority of all religious. Also in general these developments drew vocations away from the Black monks—to the schools as well as to other 'religions'—and tended to make their form of life, in comparison with the others, seem stagnant. So—it might be argued—the two generations of Black monks after 1216 were decisive. They should have faced the challenge of the times, and launched out on bold and sweeping reforms and adaptations; whereas, in reality, they shrank from the challenge and merely made insignificant changes—more forced, willy-nilly concessions to the age than positive reforms—and settled down to a stagnant conservatism for the rest of the Middle Ages, stagnation which inevitably bore its fruit in a late medieval degeneration.

Attractive as this judgement is, it is really a mental structure composed of individual true points, each—like stones in a building—radically squared and simplified so as to produce a symmetrical whole which is a distortion and caricature of the total truth about the Black monks. The rest of the chapter will, in effect, be an effort to demonstrate this. For the moment let it suffice to say that the religious life in the Church is a phenomenon much more like a growing plant than a 'planned society'. To a certain extent the plant is improved and kept healthy by pruning and training and crossing, but the good gardener's planning is based on respect for the natural integrity of the plant, its organic powers of self-repair and growth. Where a gardener attempts to do undue violence, nature has a way of revenging herself by action or reaction.

The various 'new experiments in the religious life' of the eleventh and twelfth centuries—and early thirteenth—reflected this. They were reforms of the religious life as their founders knew it, attempts to return to features of monastic tradition obscured in the immediate past. A deep conservatism informed the most revolutionary-seeming provisions, and, once rooted, the new Orders tended unconsciously to conform to type, while the older Orders, by action and reaction, absorbed an influence from the new. In reading the documents of medieval history we have constantly to pull ourselves up and try to purge our minds of quite modern ideas of progress; the medieval man almost always set his ideals in the past and regarded his present duty as a constant struggle to arrest the decay of change and keep returning to ancient virtue. We may well reflect that this was simply a mental form, a cover for what was, in fact, a very natural process of growth and adaptation to meet new circumstances, and, as such a rather inhibiting and hobbling cover. On the other hand, the conservatism and traditionalism of medieval revolutionaries gave their society stability.

In reality Westminster in 1216, though hardly *avant-garde*, was changing and adapting herself very slowly and not unsuccessfully. The monastic church in 1070 had been the last word in size and modernity. In the twelfth century it had endured at least one serious fire and several repatchings, so that in 1216 it must have seemed worn, battered and old-fashioned. But at least the community had been spared the vain expense of a great Norman or Angevin rebuilding in styles which would, by 1216, have been already outmoded by 'French work'.

We are in the dark about most sides of Westminster economic

organization before the early decades of the fourteenth century, but such few indications as survive suggest that in 1216 it was rather behind the times. This also may well have been a blessing in disguise. Monastic records elsewhere in the twelfth century show that the rapid adoption of advanced systems of estate management brought an appearance of prosperity which enticed communities to build beyond their means. It also led to a multiplication of dependent priories and cells which became eventually a curse; it brought a rigid distinction between the abbot's estate and that of the convent and a multiplication of monk officials dividing between themselves responsibility for the convent's estate. Inevitable as these changes were, the rapid introduction of them brought strains and difficulties which were only resolved as a result of a good many decades of experience. It may well be that houses which took to these measures very slowly, profited from others' mistakes and disasters.

Simultaneously the years since 1066 had seen considerable constitutional changes in Black monk houses. Abbots of greater houses, like Westminster, had become tenants-in-chief of the king and thereby had necessarily been forced to separate their establishments (now baronies) from those of their communities. This had come about very gradually. In 1216 it was still (so far as we can judge from the scanty evidence) rare for Westminster abbots to be involved in royal administrative business. As we have seen, Gilbert Crispin, Laurence and William de Humez had, because of this fact, avoided much trouble during national crises. Unlike other old houses—for instance Bury St Edmunds, St Albans and Peterborough —the abbot of Westminster was not responsible for the burdens of secular administration of wide areas round the monastery. Also the slow process of adjustment to the new position of the abbot was made easier by the fact that the *Rule of St Benedict* and monastic tradition generally were familiar with abbots who might have to rule their monasteries (or groups of monasteries) from a distance. Especially in cathedral-monasteries, but also at Westminster, the spiritual direction and rule of the community was easily devolved on a system of priors (Claustral, 2nd, third). That is to say the 'feudalization' of abbots—like the feudalization of bishops—*could* have disastrous spiritual effects on their subjects, but, in itself, it did not necessarily do so. Moreover, there was much to be said for a system which ensured that abbots should have a voice in royal Great Councils and that monasteries should perform the civic duties incumbent on landowners. The history of Cistercian estate-management (even in its earliest days), the curious knots and self-contradictions into which the theorists among the Friars caught themselves in their radical attack on corporate landowning by religious, the careers in public life of St Bernard and St Hugh of Lincoln (a Cistercian and a Carthusian) all provide us with material for a defence of the basic position of the Black monks.

The gradual separation of abbatial from conventual estate, the multiplication of monk officials administering the convent's, the rise of a sense of conventual solidarity in responsibility and a desire for constitutional checks on abbatial exercise of power—all these features were emerging in Westminster by 1216. It would be an illusion to imagine that such developments were either quite unknown to monastic tradition or essentially alien to monastic *quies*. The accidents of later history have ensured that there is a very heavy preponderance, among surviving monastic documents, of financial and administrative records over directly spiritual ones. The study of charters, cartularies and account-rolls exclusively can lead us unconsciously to imagine that monks were overwhelmingly absorbed in estate business, litigation and electioneering. The chance survival of the *Chronicle of Jocelin of Brakelond* has probably done more than any other publication to fix our image of the medieval Black monk. He was human; he had embraced a vocation which was meant for all men of all types, and was not a specialized, minority, élite vocation. He did not live in a Charterhouse or in the higher degrees of a Mount Athos. His very faults—volubility and anxiety about the business affairs of the house—proceeded in large degree precisely from the fact that most of his time and attention was absorbed in the performance of an exceedingly long and most complicated round of liturgy both in and out of the monastic church.

THE CLAUSTRAL SCHOOL

Our knowledge of the educational standards of Westminster monks in 1216 or at any time before the mid fourteenth century is exceedingly scanty. Up to the mid twelfth century the great majority entered the novitiate very young and the novitiate or juniorate of young monks formed a large proportion of the community and the *schola noviciorum* bulked large in its life. This school was regarded primarily as a *schola disciplinae*, of spiritual and moral training in the monastic life. The young monk had there to learn by heart a very large quantity of Latin—the whole *Rule of St Benedict*, the entire psalter, a mass of liturgical formulae with their chant, the whole ceremonial of monastic life in church, cloister, Chapter, refectory, dormitory. In addition he had to acquire the ability to read Latin fluently in public so that he could take his place as reader in the

refectory, in choir (the nocturn lessons and chapters) and in the
Chapter House (the Rule and Necrology). It was obviously very
desirable that he should know and read this Latin with understanding
—that he should learn the Latin language from a grammarian so
that he could read, speak and write it properly. But he could fall
short of this by acquiring no more than a brushing of Latinity, or
even by acquiring ability to pronounce, read and write Latin without
undertanding it.

There is some evidence that from 1066 into the 70s the claustral
school at Westminster was producing at least some monks with a fluent
Latinity—for instance Sulcard the chronicler. In Gilbert Crispin's
time it is hard to believe that the well-educated Abbot, a product
of the flourishing claustral school at Bec, did not raise standards
at Westminster. Osbert of Clare and his three or four Westminster
monk-correspondents may well have been the products of this
renaissance. Abbot Laurence, as we have seen, was a graduate of
the Paris schools, and must have taken care to improve the teaching
at Westminster. Thus it seems clear that, up to the disappearance
of the claustral school, Westminster generally had grammar teaching, and sometimes the standard—for a few brighter pupils—must
have been quite high. Yet the masters of novices and abbots
never ceased to require from novices a tremendous amount of
sheerly mechanical memory work—a clear indication that (even
when we have made due allowances for monastic conservatism) the
bulk of the entry was still incapable of taking much grammar if
any.

By 1216 the recruitment of small boys was only a memory. The
claustral school now was much smaller, containing only the age
group seventeen to twenty-one. We must presume that at least
some entrants had already spent a few years at grammar schools.
Occasionally—as before the mid twelfth century—*magistri* (graduates
of universities) may have entered the novitiate. The Westminster
Customary of 1266 is not a comprehensive guide to what went on in
this school. It still insists that all novices, whatever their intellectual
capabilities and past schooling, should shoulder the traditional
memorizing. This *disciplina* of obedience is the prime test of the
novitiate, trying novices 'like gold in the furnace'. We gather that
some novices are capable of occupying themselves in reading in
the cloister, while others are incapable and must be kept occupied
in learning to read the Latin of the next day's nocturn lessons or in
manual labour. Latinists must be in a minority, since Norman-
French is the community's vernacular, to be used in conversations
between master and novices, in the 'parliament' (or conferences)
given by the master, in all talk between superiors and monks and

in Chapter. The author of the *Customary* allows that Latin may sometimes be used by superiors, but implies that it is unusual. 'The English idiom' is forbidden. We therefore get an (admittedly speculative) impression that the intellectual attainments of Westminster monks in 1216 (and even in 1266) did not differ markedly from those of their twelfth-century predecessors. But, as we shall see, there were monks who, for a long time, had been thinking that this situation was undesirable and not inevitable. For spiritual reasons they thought higher educational standards essential, and, for lesser reasons, that an up-to-date knowledge of law and logic would be very useful.

In 1216 Westminster was nearing the end of a long and desultory legal battle to secure and stabilize its place in the new order in Church and State. The Westminster twelfth-century bulls and royal charters all seem to have been tampered with, but we are justified in thinking that they merely take an over-idealistic view of a process already in reality well advanced. The legal position of Westminster was being defined clearly as one of relative autonomy. It was one of only half-a-dozen large English Black monk houses to be completely exempt from episcopal authority and interference. In 1216 or not long afterwards, agreement was reached with the Bishop of London and the Pope, and the parish of St Margaret became a peculiar archdeaconry of the diocese under a monastic archdeacon. The house was free of episcopal charges and visitations. The abbot might be blessed wherever he pleased, and could pontificate in his own church. Abbatial elections were now canonically free, though confirmation by the king (with restoration of the baronial temporalities in return for homage) and Pope (by a visit of the elect to Rome immediately after election) was necessary. The house was subject to apostolic supervision through papal legates—who had deposed abbot Ralph Papillon in the special legatine visitation of Westminster in 1214.

In 1216 it was clear that further and more far-reaching measures of papal supervision were pending. The Lateran Council of 1215 had decreed the formation of provincial Congregations of Black monk superiors, with delegated papal authority to legislate in general matters and to carry out regular and systematic visitations of all houses. At the same time diocesan bishops were empowered to visit the non-exempt houses. These decrees had still to be enforced in 1216, but clearly papal action through legates and congregational action by the united body of superiors would offer the Black monks an entirely new hope of mutual help, exchange of views and a positive programme of adaptations and reforms. Many monks must have been part-hopeful and part-fearful about the future.

MONASTIC OBSERVANCE

This brings us to the question of monastic observance in 1216 and of changes in it, either already achieved or in prospect. Of all sides of monastic history this is obviously by far the most important. The spiritual life of monasteries, the Divine Office, private prayer and observance were the centre of Westminster's life. Yet we are, at all periods in the Middle Ages, less informed about them than about almost any other feature of its life. This is due partly to the course taken by the Reformation in the destruction and conservation of monastic records and libraries, and partly to the wearing out of much-used texts and the scrapping of old-fashioned ones by the monks themselves. The surviving texts, moreover, are extremely difficult to interpret. But there is one vital preliminary point which seems to be clear. Historians have absorbed themselves in the differences between the Black monks and the new Orders which arose from the twelfth century onwards and in the far-reaching effect of the various monastic reforms. But all these differences of observance and outlooks—fiercely argued over as they were at the time—when put together still bulk small when compared with the great amount that all religious still had in common down to the end of the Middle Ages.

In spite of all the reforms and adaptations, medieval religious as a whole retained as the dominating centre of their lives the obligation on each community to perform the liturgy in choir. In sheer quantity of daily liturgy (and, commonly, quantity of it sung to note) the ordinary, even quite small, medieval religious house surpassed the standards of even the most liturgical of modern monasteries and far surpassed the great majority of modern religious houses. This liturgical round in fact overflowed from the community churches into every side of the medieval religious' life in the cloister, the refectory, the Chapter House, the dormitory, the fields and on journeys. Their whole life was filled with customary pious gestures and prayers and, indeed, the religious life was identified with taking on oneself the yoke of all this observance and performing it with great exactitude. Though, of course, the many details of observance differed greatly from house to house and Order to Order, this ceremoniousness was a marked characteristic common to all. It seems to have been, before all else, a spirit or impulsion drawing religious to see every act of their daily lives as full of religious symbolism. They were drawn to fix this pious meaning by ejaculations and prayers, which at first were individual and voluntary, and then inevitably became corporate, obligatory observances. Osbert of Clare's works are full of this attitude of mind. Indeed it was there in him and imprinted by his novitiate.

The intricate imagery of his literary style was a fashion, but it fitted the man like a glove. The *Gemma Animae* of a twelfth-century Black monk, Honorius of Autun (probably a pupil of St Anselm at Canterbury), is a useful dictionary of monastic 'ceremonial symbolism'. To our minds, as we read it, the atmosphere is stifling:

CHAPTER 148. OF THE CLOISTER.

The claustral building in the monastery is derived from the porch of Solomon built next to the Temple. In that the apostles all stayed united and went thence together into the Temple to pray and the multitude of believers were of one heart and one mind (Acts IV). In accordance with that example religious live as one in the cloister and thence, by night and day, go together into church to the service of God. Here the faithful, abandoning worldly things, lead a common life in the cloister.

CHAPTER 149. THAT THE CLOISTER IS HEAVEN.

Now the cloister foreshadows heaven (Genesis IV.), and the church Eden, the stronghold of heaven. The fountain of joy in heaven is the font of baptism in the church; the tree of life (crucifix) is in paradise; the Body of the Lord is in the church. The different fruit-bearing trees (of Paradise) are the different books of Holy Scripture (in the cloister cupboard). . . .

The roots of this observance and its holy symbolism however, like those of a tree, can be dimly traced running in all directions. Some came from the strong sacramental sense of Catholics; some came from ancient catechetical methods used with simple and illiterate people; some were inextricably bound up with monastic ways of meditation (the slow, always mouthed and voiced reading of Scripture, Patristic commentaries and liturgical texts); some came from a Neo-Platonism which had, over the centuries, become absorbed into Christian mentality until it was bone of its bone and flesh of its flesh. The idea of the yoke of obedience, the bearing of the burden of observance, the constant use of metaphors taken from agricultural toil or feudal warfare (particularly castleguard) had natural enough origins. The *Rule of St Benedict* used them. The ordinary social surroundings suggested them powerfully. The difficulties which men, drawn from a primitive and overwhelmingly illiterate society, had in coping with the Latin divine Office (even with the help of simple aids to grasping the broad, general sense of the words they were using) drove the metaphors home.

It is not surprising, therefore, that we should find a kind of rhythm in monastic history during the Middle Ages. Liturgy and observances tended to pile up steadily, partly by a natural process and partly as a result of periods of great fervour. Then the sheer weight became unbearable. There followed a reaction and a partial purge. Then the process set in again until the next reform. By the beginning of the twelfth century a reform was overdue. The accumulation of liturgy and observances had become very great. The ordinary Office of the day had become much expanded by the doubling of antiphons and lengthening of lessons. On top of that the day was full of liturgical accretions, once voluntary. There were extra daily votive Offices, the fifteen Psalms said before Matins, the two daily conventual Masses, much intercessory psalmody, litanies and processions. The horarium was so crammed with this that the other traditional features of monastic life—private prayer, spiritual reading, study, work—were almost totally crowded out.

The two main criticisms of this situation were put neatly by St Bernard when he wrote that 'It positively impedes devotion [*affectum*] and, to me, somehow recalls the ancient rites of the Jews'. Thus the sheer weight of liturgy bred dullness of mind and disgust, while the system was held to inculcate an idea that the mere physical performance of the rites was sanctifying. St Bernard insisted that the liturgy must be an offering, free and loving, out of a life rooted in personal, private prayer and penance. This reaction led to the foundation of new Orders which axed the liturgy and observances to make room for the other traditional features of religious life. The Cistercians made room for private prayer and manual labour, the Carthusians for a semi-eremitical life, the Canons Regular for pastoral work and the Friars for study and preaching.

In practice, however, these reforms were an adaptation and adjustment of the old ways rather than a radically new approach. The Cistercians regarded the liturgy—still lengthy for them—as the essential work of monks. They invented lay *conversi* and used lay servants precisely because the choir-monks still had insufficient free time for farm-work to ensure the support of the community. Also the lay-brothers were denied the full name of monks on the grounds that they were not bound to choir office. Ceremonial observances, though simplified, remained normal for Cistercians. The Canons and Friars, by their system of extensive dispensations of individuals from the choir, paid homage to their continued acceptance of the idea that a long liturgy was the primary community duty. Thus the twelfth- and thirteenth-century desire for personal freedom only made its way within the framework of traditional monachism. This was true even of the more advanced humanism of the fourteenth and fifteenth centuries. Late in the Middle Ages the author of the *Imitation of Christ*, however critical of contemporary formalism in religious Orders and insistent on an inner, individual and personal

D

spirituality, could still take for granted the monastic spirit of the eleventh and twelfth centuries. For him the 'service of God' (the traditional phrase for the Office) is the highest and central duty of religion; religious life consists in exact and humble obedience to observances. However necessary it may be to avoid Pharisaism and cultivate interior prayer, the acid test is always the fulfilment of monastic duties: 'It is no small thing to dwell with brethren in a monastery, and to live there without complaint, and to persevere faithfully even to death.' Lastly, the author wholeheartedly accepts the early medieval view that the monastic life is simply the quintessence of the Christian life. There is no salvation or peace of mind except for those who seek God in religious life—that is, in an actual monastic life or a life in the world lived in a monastic spirit.

Considering all this, we should expect to find the twelfth-century monks of Westminster and the other Black monk houses conscious of the wave of criticism of their ways and reacting to it. In France there was a resounding public debate between Peter the Venerable, Abbot of Cluny and St Bernard the Cistercian. As we should expect, the contestants in the end found themselves divided by no great contradictions of principle. Peter admitted that Cluniac houses had distorted the balance of the horarium very excessively and that they were passing through a period of misgovernment and laxity; he carried out reforms to right these matters.

In England there is extremely little evidence of a similar clash (only the affair of St Mary's, York). On the surface, at any rate, relations between Black monks and Cistercians were friendly. Westminster occasionally entertained numbers of Cistercian abbots and— if we interpret the author of the Westminster *Customary* of 1266 rightly—had a kind of alliance of particular friendship with them. Perhaps the relations between St Aelred of Rievaulx and his cousin, Abbot Laurence of Westminster, had something to do with his. Osbert of Clare, when in exile and prior of a dependent house, was warned by the Council of Seniors ruling Westminster (during an abbatial interregnum) not to receive men who had left Cistercian houses. This seems to be additional evidence of a friendly feeling. On the other hand St Anselm had felt the need for adaptations in Black monk ways. He regarded Cluniac ways as far too overbalanced with liturgy, but was content with the observance of Bec where the liturgy, though very long and elaborate, left space in the horarium for a modicum of reading, private prayer and study. He entirely accepted the current idea of monastic life as a labour of exact obedience to observances; indeed, though he admitted that he found it extremely hard, he blamed the fact on his own frailty and late entry into religion. His one criticism of this observance was that monks tended to execute it too mechanically. He thought that the fault lay in the novitiate, where the whole emphasis tended to lie on drilling in physical exactitude and in the memorizing of formulae and actions. To his mind, even considering the very modest intellectual abilities of most novices, it ought to be possible, by a higher level of Latin studies and a more humane treatment, to produce much more spontaneity, intelligent understanding of the liturgy, desire to study, and a more personal and affective kind of private prayer.

It seems very likely indeed that English Black monk houses (non-Cluniac) in the twelfth century were like Bec in general observance; that is to say that the weight of liturgy, though very heavy, was notably more moderate than at Cluny, and there was at least some time for private prayer, reading and study—and even for a modicum of manual labour, confined to writing books and housework. This would, in part, help to account for the apparent absence of a head-on clash with the Cistercians. There are signs that Westminster took to heart St Anselm's criticism.

Osbert of Clare's works contain a series of affective and highly personal prayers, clearly modelled on examples given by Anselm. Osbert's theological and literary work shows that at least individual monks could find time at Westminster for reading and study. But apart from this, we find it hard to generalize about twelfth-century Westminster observance and the spirit of the community. On the one hand there are a few signs that the liturgy lengthened in the course of the century. The number of saints' days (with a longer Office than that of ordinary days) increased notably. We have seen Osbert's part in that development. The daily Office of the Dead may well have come in at this period. The daily Office of our Lady began, apparently, as a private devotion of a purely voluntary kind early in the twelfth century. The Westminster *Customary* of 1266 speaks of the well-established obligation of it—but still mostly to be said privately, out of choir at fixed times by all.

Besides this there were pacts made with other monasteries. William de Humez made one with Bury, binding his monks to extra prayers for Bury's dead. To judge from the *Customary*, this may well have meant that each Westminster monk recited privately a whole Psalter for the soul of each Bury monk who died. This practice obviously also covered Westminster's own dead and lay persons who were her *confratres* and benefactors.

A major change in the horarium was made some time in the course of the century by the transference of the Night Office from 2 a.m. to midnight, thus decisively splitting the night's sleep. But we are left entirely unable to assess how much of the day—or rather any particular

day, since the horarium was so exceedingly complex and variable
—still remained effectively for reading, study and work. This
ignorance about the *proportions* of real life in the Westminster of the
twelfth century and 1216 continues with us when we turn to other
sides of observance. Traditional monastic observance had, built
into it, a thorough-going system of dispensations to apply in cases of
necessity, and these had always been much in evidence. The consequence is that, if we were able to go back in spirit for a day to
Westminster in 1216—or 1150, or 1066—we should be forcibly struck
by an impression of great austerity mingled (to our modern minds)
oddly with humanity. We should be especially moved by the
prodigious amount of church services—in and out of church—and
the midnight Office, of great length and sung almost entirely in the
dark by heart. Yet, on the other hand, we could hardly appreciate
the ameliorating effects on the monks of an entire familiarity with it
all, and of having a mentality so much unlike ours—more habituated
to physical discomfort and pain, tougher, much less introspective . . .
We should soon have to give up the unequal effort of trying to calcu-
late comparatively the strains on such men and moderns. We
should undoubtedly be impressed by the fearful cold of the cloister
and church. The cloister arcades on the open side were still un-
glazed. According to the *Customary* iron chafing-dishes with lighted
charcoal on them were provided by each altar at time of Mass
whenever it might be necessary in winter. We can compare the
practice today in the great unheated monastic churches of places
like Engelberg in Switzerland, where, in winter, the cruets for Mass
have to be kept beforehand in ovens and the priests at Mass must
wear mittens. We might well be bewildered by the silence rules,
with very strict silence in general and yet apparently a deal of talking
at various extremely limited times and places, even more limited
by rules and customs about posture, precedence, language and
manner of address.

There was a very strict rule of enclosure for the community. But
the superiors and more important obedientiaries could make limited
but quite frequent visits to the Palace and London on business. At
least by 1266 seculars were admitted to enclosed places with—to our
minds—extraordinary freedom. Ladies were allowed into the
cloister and refectory on certain very limited occasions, and the
mothers of monks could dine in the Locutorium down the cloister.
Osbert of Clare remarks that he had preached to congregations of
priests, laymen and laywomen in the church and Chapter House.
As we shall see, assemblies of barons and bishops could take place
periodically in the Infirmary or Chapter House and a bishop could
seal a grant in the cloister. But then, I suspect that we should be

continually surprised by the—to our minds—casualness of medievals about their use of churches and holy places. Once more we should find our sense of the fitting at variance with their's, often find them strict where we are lax and lax where we are strict.

A considerable part of the monastic Calendar was occupied by fast days (with rules, to our minds, mostly incredibly strict, yet a few oddly lax) and perpetual abstinence from flesh-meat (not birds) the rule. The ordinary food of the monastery would be, to our taste, very plain and unvarying. The times for meals would be fantastic— especially the long daily fast (through the long morning's liturgy) before a heavy dinner at either midday or 2 p.m. (and in Lent not until 4.30 or 5 p.m.). On the other hand feast days really were feasts, with quite numerous extra dishes—though the feast-day liturgy was extraordinarily long. The sick, the aged and the young were always allowed to anticipate the meals and eat meat, though they had to confess this breach of observance in Chapter as a fault and receive penance.

Monk officials were allowed a limited dispensation from the Office —which they had to make up privately—for necessary business. In the tenth, eleventh and twelfth centuries, in any monastery, we should always be struck by the fact that a section of the community was absent from any particular Hour of the Office. For at least a century before 1216 current medical practice required the com- pulsory monthly bleeding of all the community in the Infirmary. The monks went there in batches, a few at a time, and, for the day or two involved, were treated as sick. Here and there in English monasteries, before 1216 (though we know nothing of Westminster practice then) abbots had also instituted regular 'recreations'. These were dispensations for the community, in batches, to eat meat in a separate *misericordia* room apart from the rest, apparently a day at a time and at periods unknown to us. In the daily Chapter faults against the *Rule* or observance were confessed (or denounced) and penances awarded. In our ignorance of medieval (and monastic) psychology, we should undoubtedly be struck by the strange mixture of ebullience (or even violence) and simple humility—and by the floggings administered on the spot for the graver faults. Puritanism and the public school system had yet to make their deep impress on Englishmen, and in 1216 (and long afterwards) they were noted by the sober French and Germans and Italians as violent, passionate and demonstrative by nature.

With all this dim picture before us, it is almost impossibly hard to judge the spiritual state of Westminster in 1216. By a fixed and traditional habit of mind (to be found in the *Rule* itself) the monks of each generation themselves seem to have believed, not in inevitable moral progress, but in a process of regress. It was a folk-saying among them that the *moderni* could never rise to the standards of the *antiqui patres* or even be persuaded of their ability to do so. 'We are not the men our forefathers were.' Hence the dispensations were traditionally regarded (witness the Chapter procedure we have mentioned) as signs of a culpable weakness. To some extent this extremism proceeded from a naïve over-objectivity, disregarding the subjective element in sin. But it also came from a strong sense that monastic life is a total self-committal and sacrifice, without turning back from the plough. Osbert of Clare puts the point in what is certainly his most eloquent letter, addressed to a monk (presumably of Westminster) who was gravely tempted to flee the monastery: '. . . sic in sancto proposito religiosus circumferebas monachus ut toto tempore vitae praesentis totum teipsum deo redderes holocaustum.'

However, although there was no clash in England with the Cistercians, St Bernard's criticisms of Cluny must have been read at places like Westminster. There are signs (though only documented in the decades after 1216) that the English Black monks were discussing the issues raised—the extent to which they had really distorted monastic tradition, the problem of obeying the *Rule* and, above all, the problem of the letter and the spirit. The new thought in the schools (the rise of logic and a questioning spirit, the slow influx of the naturalistic thought of Aristotle) was perhaps having some effect, though we have no idea how many *magistri* from the schools had entered Westminster. Adam of Eynsham, the Black monk biographer of St Hugh of Lincoln writing shortly after 1216, probably reflects the mind of an average monk of the time. His attitude to monastic life is utterly conventional. Man is born to labour, and the monastic life, the life of full humanity, is essentially a labour of submission and a yoke of martyrdom. We can hear the echoes of Honorius of Autun's Chapter sermon to the monks of Canterbury half a century before:

> . . . we walk in hope in the steps of the saints so that we may merit to reach the company of those whom we rejoice to follow. Let us remember that we have quitted the world to seek our heavenly fatherland, and that we have bent our necks to the yoke of claustral servitude so that we may gain the liberty of eternity. For the observance of claustral discipline is like putting oneself into the fire of a forge, in which the rust of our sins must be consumed and the image of God in our souls reformed. We who are called monks are counted amongst the martyrs if our lives conform to our profession . . . we suffer a daily martyrdom. For enclosure in the cloister, subjection to the Rule, the laying aside of secular clothes,

the yoke of silence, being entirely at the will of another, the frequent fasts, assiduous floggings, vigils, standing through the days' Hours in ceaseless watch, the shame of confession of faults, the bitterness of penances, the public correction before the brethren and bodily punishments, the constant effort to pray, the struggle to read, all these are crucifixions of the flesh. . . .

Yet Adam puts into St Hugh's mouth more naturalistic ideas. There are differences of observance (Carthusian, Cistercian, Black monk) but they exist only because men differ in bodily strength and in temperament. The laity, even though they do not enter religion, can enter the kingdom of God provided they have lived in truth, charity and chastity. Although St Hugh's Carthusian customs forbade meat even to the sick and dying, he ate a little meat on his deathbed in obedience to his doctors and as a sign of his view that common sense should temper observance, and that occasional meat-eating as a recreation ought to be allowed in large non-Carthusian monasteries meant for ordinary men of all temperaments and strengths. It has been suggested that these were only Adam's ideas and not St Hugh's. But there are other indications that this may not be so—for instance St Hugh's admiration for Cluny and his view that life there would have suited him well. In any case Hugh and his chaplain, Adam, were on very friendly terms with Westminster. Hugh had been consecrated Bishop of Lincoln in the Infirmary chapel at Westminster. As he lay dying he sent for the Prior of Westminster to ask for prayers for his soul.

A PERIOD OF CHANGE

The eighty years after 1216 brought great changes to Westminster. The first was the rebuilding of the monastery church by Henry III. The long reign (1216–72) of this remarkable king saw the community involved very closely in his fortunes and the impress of his curious character still remains strongly on the place. His family had no particular interest in Westminster and at the start of his reign there can have been no indication of the way his affections were to fix upon it. As a child he was crowned at Malmesbury—it is true that this was due to the presence of his enemies round Westminster, and his ministers apologized to the abbot. He had ambitions to recover Anjou and Fontrevault, his family monastery (indeed his heart was buried there). His personal piety, like everything else about him, was wide-ranging, capricious and shallow. He was an inveterate pilgrim to shrines, with an especial devotion to our Lord in the Blessed Sacrament, to the Holy Blood of Bromholm and our Lady of Walsingham. His piety was intensely áffective. A monastic chronicler told how, when St Louis pressed on him the need for listening to good sermons at Mass and having a well-instructed devotion, he impatiently brushed the advice aside with the remark that he went to Mass to meet our Lord and not to think about Him.

It is unlikely that the growth of his devotion to St Edward the Confessor was due to any dynastic theories—though it is true that he pressed Matthew Paris (the St Albans monk chronicler) to write a new version of the *Life* of the saint, and there is some evidence that, both at Westminster abbey and elsewhere, some in their minds transferred to Henry the hopes built by Osbert of Clare and St Aelred on Henry II. It is also unlikely that the King's devotion had its root in spiritual direction by Westminster monks. In fact, Henry's confessors seem to have been Dominicans. Nor can he have been carried away by the flowering of a great popular, spontaneous devotion for St Edward. There is no evidence of any such flowering. Such rather unusually widespread signs of the devotion which appear during his reign (Matthew Paris's *Life* and his little prayer to the Confessor, the dedication to St Edward of the conventual church built by the King for the Dominicans at Canterbury, the circulation among pious and aristocratic ladies of various new French verse-lives of the saint) all seem to stem from the King's personal influence on a comparatively small circle of people. On the contrary, it seems that he became (as an inscription in his church entitles him) the 'friend' of the Confessor as the result of a purely personal *attrait* in a way quite typical of his special tastes and complex character.

By the 1220s he was drawn to spend a good deal of time and money on repairs, alterations and additions to the old and now decrepit Palace at Westminster. Perhaps he liked the place; in any case the Exchequer had long been settling down there and needed more room. The exercise of building soon fascinated Henry and drew out latent talents for the arts, and particularly interior decoration of a lavish and exquisite kind. It so happened that Abbot Richard of Barking was then starting to build a small Lady Chapel on to the monastic church—perhaps meant to be a first instalment of a complete rebuilding of the church. Henry began to transfer his interest to the Chapel, to interfere in its design and details, and finally took over entire responsibility for it, using the plant and workmen already assembled on the Palace site.

The decisive point in his attraction towards the patronage of the Confessor came perhaps before 1239/40 when his long-desired first-born son was named Edward. At the same time the King determined to rebuild the monastic church himself on ambitious lines, without sparing cost or trouble in getting workmen and materials. It was to centre on a magnificent shrine (which took twenty years to make). Through all the preoccupations and political crises of the next thirty years, he pressed on with the building. Medieval building was almost always very slow, but the King's perfectionism slowed up operations even more. In 1269 the Apse, Presbytery and Crossing (with the Chapter House) were completed and opened for use. Yet this was only an earnest of the whole; building was in progress to his death in 1272 (when his tomb was unfinished, so that his body lay for some years in a temporary place). Edward I's coronation took place in a boarded up and truncated church. The major part of the Nave was not completed for many years. Henry's new work rose majestically over a huddle of closely-packed buildings, the new Palace Hall, the old Palace buildings, the old monastery, houses of royal and abbey officials and servants. Westminster must have looked, in silhouette, unrecognizable to someone who had known it in 1240.

Obviously these changes thrust the abbey dramatically to the fore and engaged it in far closer association with the royal family than it had known since 1065. But it is not so easy to determine precisely what this new position meant and how far it really benefited the house. Henry's devotion to the Confessor, though showy, was no flash in the pan. His bedroom in the Palace had, on its walls, fine pictures of the coronation of St Edward and the legendary episode of his ring. He meant the church to be his own burial place but it is not so clear that he ever thought of it as a permanent family mausoleum. The regalia were kept in the abbey; but this was nothing new and English kings then and later had a multiplicity of different storehouses for valuables. The monastic church was not his 'parish church' or ordinary place of worship, or his Palace chapel. In this it bore no resemblance, say, to Charlemagne's Palace chapel at Aachen or Philip II's Jeronimite monastic church in the Escorial. Henry appears to have heard Mass daily in an oratory near his bedroom, while his Court was served by at least two other chapels in the Palace, of St Stephen and St John. Indeed the Westminster monks would probably have found it difficult to receive him befittingly, confined as they were, for twenty years before 1269, to makeshift temporary arrangements for worship—most likely in the old Nave.

It would also be wrong to imagine that the King enriched the monastery with great gifts of lands. There is record only of the grant of one manor. At this period relations between the royal government and the monastery became embarrassingly close—on terms of almost domestic intimacy. Abbots Richard of Barking, Richard Crokesley and Richard Ware were all employed by the King on Exchequer business and Barking was, for a time, King's Treasurer and a Baron of the Exchequer. All three were employed as Justices in Eyre to counties as distant as Cumberland, and as members of embassies to Germany, France and Rome.

The new Chapter House was no sooner finished than it was used for occasional meetings of the King's Council. The monastic Refectory served the same purpose at least twice. Official meetings were held in the infirmary chapel and episcopal consecrations took place there. Building operations at the Exchequer blocked the monastic kitchen window. Part of the Royal Wardrobe was kept in the monastery. The *Customary* of 1266 finds it necessary to warn monks how to make due reverence when the King or magnates pass down the Cloister, and takes note of the changing tempo of life in Westminster caused by the King's arrivals or departures. Henry was quite capable of interfering in sacristy matters—for instance the exact kind of lights in the Lady Chapel. He had an irritating habit of importing into the abbey some bishop of his choice to sing the Mass on great feast days. When short of money he tended to make part-pious, part-collecting tours round his favourite shrines and monasteries—Westminster abbey included. At least once, in an emergency, he borrowed for pawn some fine jewellery which he had given to the Confessor's Shrine.

LIMITED PATRONAGE OF HENRY III

None of these phenomena really meant that the King had given the abbey a national status as *caput regni*. They are all readily explainable out of the close physical juxtaposition to the rising centre of royal government (for all its goldleaf and marble, run on a shoestring and chronically cramped for space as it expanded), to a royal habit of using Black monk abbots for administrative tasks (noticeably growing during the fifty years before 1216), and to Henry's personal peculiarities. The relationship of the abbey to the King was surely simply that of ordinary patronage. Black monk houses of secondary rank or less mostly had magnates as patrons and 'founders'—advocates. The monastery had close ties with such families over the years. The magnate protected the interests of the house at law and by his influence; the monks (or Canons) gave hospitality to him and his, stored his valuables and buried his dead—and prayed for the family in life and death. Such relationships were utterly natural and endured on the Continent and among English Catholics after the Reformation to modern times. But a number of the greatest houses of Black monks claimed royal foundation and competed for royal protection. Westminster had particular need of royal influence in repeated legal brushes with Bishops of London in 1221, 1229, 1254 and 1268; in getting the Pope to dispense the house from rules imposed by visiting papal commissioners in 1232; in several violent disputes with the citizens of London and the monastery of St Albans —and above all in the great disputes between the convent and abbot Crokesley in 1251–2. In these crises the King's help was forthcoming.

This profitable patronage had another side to it—trouble for the community. They must have watched the rise of the new church and all that went with it in a mood compounded of pride and alarm. Between 1240 and the end of the reign they endured cramped quarters, incessant hammering and noise from the workmen. Abbot Richard of Barking, striding up the Cloister in his baron's cloak on his way to Exchequer sessions, seems to have had much trust in the new patronage. Before he died in 1246 (and when the contracts for the start of the new work were barely sealed) he commissioned the weaving of a set of great wall-tapestries for the adornment of the new Choir on major feast days. Some of the pictures demonstrated his devotion to our Lady, but most told the story, episode by episode, of the Confessor's life. The moral was pointed by captions. A seventeenth-century antiquarian saw them and noted one caption which claimed that the house was the peculiar favourite of the papacy and the great 'seat of Kings'. But the author of the 1266 *Customary* here and there hints plainly that much of the new patronage was doing monastic observance no good.

Neither the Confessor nor Henry III quite squared with the idealistic vision of some monks of the patron-king. Edward I was no improvement. He was quite prepared to give the Confessor and abbey their due—in a very limited and off-hand way. He had caught his father's devotion to the saint, but in Edward it was conventional. He gave an expensive gold statuette of the Confessor to St Thomas Becket's shrine at Canterbury—but along with one of similar size of St George, the crusaders' patron who was becoming fashionable in England. Edward gave his own name to his heir. His queen, Eleanor, was quite devoted to St Edward and to the Palace of Westminster, and until her death in 1290, the King spent much time there with her and restored his father's improvements. After her death he had built a splendid tomb for her body in the Westminster monastic church and seems to have contemplated making the place a permanent royal mausoleum, with a circle of royal dead round the Confessor's shrine. He also enlarged the Queen's gift of manors to the monastery.

All of this was evidence of real patronage in the grand manner. But in other ways he displayed a disconcerting coolness. He refused repeated requests from the Abbot that he should complete the church and only made very small grants of money and materials for pressing needs. He started, as early as 1270, to put much money and labour into building the new Cistercian house of Vale Royal, meant to be exceptionally large and splendid. The Westminster community must have sought news of the progress of this project with anxiety, and received with mixed feelings the news that he had totally lost interest in the half-finished church, refused all further help and left the wretched Cistercian community to finish it as best they could. After the death of Queen Eleanor he conceived a dislike for residence at Westminster Palace and abandoned it for a borrowed house nearer London. The Palace fell into neglect and suffered a bad fire in 1298. Yet, oddly enough, in 1292 the King put in train the rebuilding of St Stephen's Chapel, meaning to rival St Louis's *Sainte Chapelle* in Paris.

Patronage also meant, as we have seen, influential protection. In Edward's reign the steadily increasing complexity of both secular and ecclesiastical administration and of their bewildering and multiple interpenetration made this all the more pressingly necessary. Richard of Ware and Walter of Wenlock, the two Westminster abbots of Edward's reign, were able men of business and both employed intermittently in royal administration. But it would be quite wrong to read too much into this fact. As the thirteenth century advanced it became more and more evident that only a most exceptionally able abbot could ever expect to play a major rôle in secular or ecclesiastical administration or in politics. The chief places now overwhelmingly fell to professionals trained in the law, career administrators who worked their way up the king's service and ended as bishops. The abbots of monasteries like Westminster were amateurs, however experienced. The Crown (and the Papal Curia) inevitably made use of their services and staff in multiple ways, but simply as auxiliaries to the professionals. It was convenient to keep part of the treasury of the King's Wardrobe in Westminster abbey and to use the abbot's strongroom occasionally to hold the receipts of royal taxes or papal taxes, appointing him a temporary collector. The numerous royal commissions to collect evidence in suits at law drew on a wide list of responsible amateurs and professionals—and any abbot of a greater house was bound to find his name included. Hence a general history of England in the thirteenth century can treat at length of politics and administration without bothering to mention Ware and Wenlock. With all their general ability, both found it essential to fee permanently an informal group of legal advisers—mostly royal Judges and civil servants—since these years were occupied in ceaseless litigation. Indeed, the surviving records of the two abbots consist so overwhelmingly of legal papers that we are in grave danger of imagining that they never had time to concern themselves with anything else. Throughout the records there is little to show that Westminster ever gained from King Edward any extraordinary favours at law.

Almost the entire reign was occupied in a series of acrid disputes with the English Franciscans, beginning with various severe altercations with John Pecham, the Franciscan Archbishop of Canterbury, and continuing with the long-drawn-out case of an apostate Friar received at Westminster abbey. In all this worrying business the King seems to have let affairs take their course. In 1303 there began the dramatic and well-known case of the Westminster abbey burglary. The case is well-documented and has been much discussed, but of late years little has been written on it because, in spite of the documents, important details are obscure and much of the background is unknown.

The accepted facts are startling enough. A portion of the King's treasure kept in the monastery was burgled. Edward ordered an inquiry, as a result of which the abbot (Walter of Wenlock) and forty-eight of the community, together with numbers of monastic servants and a few laymen living in the vicinity of the abbey, were suspected of having a hand in the affair. We do not know whether all the accused were gaoled. It is possible, but, of the monks, all except ten were soon at liberty. Of the ten (who were put in the Tower of London) all were eventually released without trial after periods ranging from two to five years. Half-a-dozen laymen were found guilty of the crime and executed. Two of the monks (one the Sacrist) were especially suspected.

In 1305 Abbot Wenlock was entrusted with royal administrative duties again. Monastic chroniclers, at Westminster and elsewhere, regarded the monks as innocent and traduced and the imprisoned among them as confessors framed by anticlericals. The most diverse of generalizations—about the spiritual state of the community, the Abbot's capabilities, relations between the royal patron and the house, medieval anticlericalism (particularly of Londoners)—have been made about this case.

The crisis produced the most extreme of all conceivable instances where royal patronage was vitally necessary. Medieval Englishmen were passionate and barbaric. The very complications of legal procedure they used were witnesses to the extreme difficulties they had in keeping order and securing justice. Partly owing to their unruliness and partly to the very complexity of the processes, litigation became a passion and its outcome was notoriously uncertain. In practice influence counted greatly. Like so many other acts by King Edward concerning Westminster, his apparently rigorous prosecution of the case and his dropping of the charges against the monks demonstrated the very strictly limited form of patronage which he thought proper. In 1284 shortly after his election as abbot, Wenlock obtained from the King a real, but very limited favour. During an abbatial inter-regnum the goods and lands of the abbacy (not those of the convent) automatically passed into the King's hands. Now Edward, as he said, out of reverence for St Peter and St Edward, and to benefit the souls' health of his father and other relatives buried in the monastic church—and so that Westminster might enjoy as full a liberty as any other church in the realm—granted that the goods of a dead abbot should be handed over intact to his successor. But the King would continue to pocket the issues of the abbatial lands as long as the interregnum lasted.

The second considerable change at Westminster abbey in the thirteenth century was the effect on it of the Congregational reform movement. In 1218/9 the first Canterbury Provincial General Chapter of Black monk superiors met at Oxford. Thereafter the Chapter meetings occurred about once every three years. An abbot of Westminster was elected a President at some dozen Chapters down to 1307. The usual meeting place in this century was at Oxford, but in 1299, 1302 and 1304 (at the height of the burglary case) it was at Westminster. Our knowledge of the impact of the Chapter reforms on Westminster comes from three limited sources. The first is the surviving papers of the Chapters (scattered among the archives of individual monasteries for the most part); the second the Westminster documents of a series of abbatial Constitutions and Legatine visita-tion Injunctions, of 1225, 1227, 1234, 1252, 1269, 1283 and 1287; the third is the sole surviving (and much mutilated) copy of Abbot Ware's Westminster *Customary* begun in 1266.

As we have seen, it is likely that the more educated and active-minded Westminster monks were already discussing the problem of observance in 1216 and reform was much in the air. The thirteenth century, as it proceeded, brought considerable changes in the life of English society at large, a somewhat greater degree of sophistication of thought and material conditions of living (among the better-off classes), a still greater development of the universities and the num-bers of university-trained clerks. Aristotelian thought penetrated the minds of academics much more and brought with it a somewhat more naturalistic attitude of mind. The massive rise of the Friars in England from the 1220s challenged, to some extent, accepted views about the religious life, more than the Cistercians had in the twelfth century. But revolutions are very relative to existing conditions of life and thought; seen in the perspective of later history we are usually more struck by the conservatism of revolutionaries than their novelties. Also the inevitable effect of revolutions is a quite rapid compromise with the establishment.

In general the scanty documents show that the Chapter revolution got off to a slow start in the 1220s. That is not surprising. After all, communities like that of Westminster seem then (and throughout the century) to have consisted overwhelmingly of entrants drawn young from the sons of yeomen on the monastic manors. Thus the intellectuals of Westminster—for instance the community canonists used as proctors to Rome or Convocations—were mostly homebred in their learning. They can only have followed the great debates at Oxford and Cambridge and Paris as spectators. By the 1240s apparently there was increasing ferment at Westminster. It is unlikely that there was a clean division between *avant-garde* learned and conservative *claustrales*. A variety of inchoate positions on a variety of topics must have existed together in flux. The original view of the Roman Curia and of the legates Otho and Ottoboni, who tried to enforce in England reforming decrees of Gregory IX and later Popes, was that abbots should live strictly in community again, and that dispensations in matters of meat-eating, recreation and silence should be restricted to the sick and aged; that abbots should make important decisions only with the counsel and consent of the convent in Chapter; that in each monastery there should be a central 'exchequer' and a single monk manager of all the convent's estates. (These last provisions were devised as a way of confining the handling of money and travel to superintend estates to a very few of each community.) These radical decrees were eventually much watered down in implementation. As we shall see, the reasons for this were mixed.

There is some tenuous evidence that Westminster abbots at first made an effort, if only in token, to implement the decree on their return to the common life of the monastery. The Westminster *Customary* of 1266 implies that abbots would occasionally preside in choir, at Chapter, in the Refectory and even sleep in the monks' dormitory. But thereafter abbots became less involved in community life than ever. Abbot Walter of Wenlock (1283–1307) was no more than an occasional visitor to the monastery on the greatest feasts or other important occasions. He normally moved round his own residences, at Paddington, Denham, Islip (near Oxford) and— most significantly—La Neyte near the monastery. This was admittedly only the final stage of a long and very slow evolution.

If not dictated, it was made very natural, by a number of pressing administrative and economic reasons. The thirteenth century provided a strong economic reason. Great landowners of every kind found that they could no longer maintain their accustomed way of life unless they abandoned letting out demesne and took to farming it themselves. In common with other Black monk superiors, Wenlock combined amateur secular administration and law with 'high farming' management. His voluminous surviving business correspondence deals almost entirely with prices and wages, stock and grain, wool and markets. In fact his time was now so occupied that he could only have become a *claustralis* by letting out his demesne and seeing his income drop and his hardly-won rights suffer. As his twelfth-century predecessors must have realized, short of transferring the whole community to poverty and insecurity on the Farne Islands, or turning Friars, they could not avoid acute difficulties. They were bound to the defence of an inherited situation, and estates given to them in pledge for the performance of duties of prayer. It was therefore a situation which allowed, in practice, little liberty of choice. The writer of the Westminster *Customary* hints pretty clearly that he felt uncomfortable about the situation.

The second set of decrees concerned dispensations. It is very likely that the Westminster community contained younger monks who were, overtly at least, as 'naturalistic' as Adam of Eynsham. Moved partly by the excited feeling of those who sense that all past ways are crumbling, partly by the impulsion of easier living outside the monastery walls, partly (no doubt at second or third hand) by *avant-garde* thought from university circles, they must have said that common sense required meat-eating, regular recreations and holidays, far less stiffness in training and observance. Temperaments differed; they were not by vocation Carthusians or Friars; they were no longer living in the eleventh century. The writer of the *Customary* repeatedly contrasts the unceremonious and lax ways of *moderni* with those of 'the more spiritual' monks and of the old customs. In Chapter he sees the more spiritual scrupulously performing the complex ritual of old days while the *moderni* cut it short brusquely. In the Refectory, alas, the *moderni* will no longer wait outside until the abbot has entered. At the monthly blood-letting you cannot stop the *moderni* chattering. The master of novices has nowadays extra reasons for keeping his charges from all contact with the community and immersed in their *schola* grind. However, he accepts the existence of a *misericordia* for recreational meat-eating. It is probable that he belonged to the majority school of thought at Westminster, who wanted to limit severely dispensations for meat-eating, talk and officials' visits to estates, but who felt that, as things then were, full implementation of papal policy would do more harm than good. This is suggested also by the stormy debate in 1251 at Westminster before the 1249–50 decrees of General Chapter were accepted.

There were many reasons at that time why debate should have been full of altercations. Abbot Richard Crokesley, who presented the decrees as from a General Chapter at which he himself had accepted them, was engaged in a hard contest with the convent over his voice in control of its officials and lands. The decrees contained liturgical alterations hateful to ultra-conservatives. But the main issue then was the decrees on dispensations—in which General Chapter set forward a modified version of the Roman rules, restricting recreations strongly, but giving discretion over them to abbots. This remained official policy for the rest of the century and was most probably the wisest course that could have been pursued.

The third set of Legatine or Roman decrees imposed on abbots the duty of ruling constitutionally. Here the Black monks, on their small stage, debated one of the great problems of their age—how to combine a divinely-given authority with rule by law and consent of the ruled. The problem is set out in the *Customary* in the section on the abbot. The *Rule* and monastic tradition emphasized with enormous strength the authority of the abbot 'who, as vicegerent of Christ, commands all others in the monastery'. Many observances stressed the fact typically in a ceremonial way. Thus, for instance, all stop and bow low as he passes; when the prior and seniors take their places by him, they genuflect and kiss his hand; a monk told to sit by him first kneels and kisses his knees. The writer summarizes the matter: 'Indeed everything in the whole monastery hangs for its ordering on his will.' But he goes on: '. . . but he must neither teach nor order (God forbid) anything contrary to the Lord's precepts, nor attempt to do anything against the approved customs of the monastery without the counsel of the seniors.' Elsewhere, when speaking of the Chapter, the writer says:

> Because the laws and canons are wont to treat superiors gently . . . if the Lord abbot commits a fault against due order, since he is not set over the *Rule* but bound to observance of it he should be gently admonished out of Chapter by one or two of the officials. But if his fault be generally known and necessity seems to call for it (for instance if he falls into a habit of it) the Council of Seniors has the power to draw his attention to it tactfully but openly in Chapter.

Quite apart from any hypothetical influence on the monks of outside constitutional theorists, lay or ecclesiastical, the Westminster community of this time had several strong 'professional' reasons for seeking to put constitutional checks on abbatial power. For one thing, the strict division between their estate and the abbot's, at a period when they had abbots who fancied themselves as 'high farmers', easily led to efforts by abbots to gain control of the convent's estate. There was obvious danger here of upsetting the division line and of establishing precedents which would enable an indebted abbot to save himself at the expense of the convent.

Again, these were years when radical changes were being introduced into monastic life by a General Chapter of abbots (without representation of their communities) and the decrees of General Chapter sent to conventual Chapters with papal authority behind them. It is not very surprising that communities should feel this very unfair and in complete contradiction of the customary rule (and decree of Popes) that no new customs should be introduced without the consent of the conventual Chapter. Hence there is plenty of evidence of brushes between Westminster abbots and the conventus in this century, usually ending in agreements which read rather like treaties. By 1307 the convent had important gains to its credit. It had very long been the Westminster custom that the Prior (the practical, day-to-day superior of the convent) should be elected by the convent and not (as the *Rule* supposed) appointed by the abbot. It was also long before established that neither abbot nor convent might alienate properties without each other's permission. A third ancient and maintained right of the convent, as we have seen, was to approve new customs or the abrogation of old ones. Now also the convent seems to have secured that its main monastic officials should only be chosen by the abbot from a short-list presented by the convent. The abbot was not to impose grave penances or send monks to other houses (as a punishment) except in open Chapter. He was not to remove from office the main officials without the Chapter's consent. Safeguards were established to prevent abbots overstepping the line of division between the two estates. However, much, if not all, of this constitutional achievement was really precarious. The abbot still claimed a 'prerogative' whereby he might, claiming necessity, override much in these checks. The consent of the Chapter could be obtained by the sheer personal ascendancy of an able abbot, with the support of the chief officials. In case of deadlock with the abbot, recourse must be to Rome and the mediation of the king —both precarious measures. Lastly, of course, the convent's supreme difficulty was that great monastic tradition that the abbot was the vicegerent of Christ.

THE RULE OF POVERTY

The last of the Roman decrees concerned poverty. Here the reformers were up against a mass of technical difficulties. The extreme decentralization of the financial and administrative affairs of convents' estates into the hands of a multiplicity of obedientiaries was deeply rooted. As we have already seen, it had grown up as the only possible answer to a number of practical problems. The supreme objection to the reform plan of confining finance and estate management to two or three monks, reducing the other obedientiaries to the rank of minor assistants, was the real danger of making it far easier for the abbot to secure control of the convent's estate. It is significant that the centralization only really came into force in cathedral monasteries—that is to say in places where there was no division of interests between superior and convent.

An incidental disadvantage of the centralization was that it made the fortunes of the convent hang on the ability and integrity of a very few. Monasteries had an exceedingly limited field of choice of business ability. One can understand their reluctance to put all their eggs in one doubtful basket. It appears, therefore, that Westminster implemented the reform very partially indeed. By 1252 obedientiaries were expected to keep, and make an exact annual return of, exact accounts, though we do not gather what sort of audit took place. A single Treasurer for the convent existed in the 1280s and possibly earlier, but few funds were centralized in his hands. The management of estates remained substantially in the hands of the main obedientiaries (and was apparently now restricted somewhat), though the bulk of the work on the manors seems to have been done by lay-stewards for them.

For lack of obedientiaries' account rolls before the end of the century we have no idea how far, if at all, Westminster monks in general received periodical *peculium* (small allowances of money to buy clothes and other necessaries and for alms) at this period. The reformers detested the practice and struck hard at it, but it persisted among Black monks. In fact the handling of administrative funds by monks and the granting to them of occasional permissions to receive and use small sums of money for reasonable causes were, in themselves, compatible with the *Rule*. The danger was that the spirit of poverty would be sapped by a too extensive practice of these things. The best defence here lay in severe limitation and vigilance on the part of superiors.

SHORTENING THE LITURGY

Apart from these papal reform schemes there were others which seem to have derived from the monks themselves and which had a far more profound effect on their lives. These were the curtailment of their liturgy, the simplification of their observances, the extension of monastic studies (both in monasteries and at universities) and a reform of novitiate training. It is significant that reforms imposed on the monks from outside had relatively little effect, whereas their own reforms were better implemented. As we have seen, complaints about the inordinate (and still increasing) length of the liturgy occur in the twelfth century. By the end of it experiments at shortening it had begun on the initiative of individual abbots. Matthew Paris, in his *Gesta Abbatum Monasterii S. Albani*, records with enthusiasm the modest efforts of this kind of Abbot Warin (1183–95).

St Albans then and later was an altogether more literate community than Westminster. Warin was a university graduate late vocation, a physician and classicist of distinction. The atmosphere at St Albans in Warin's day and Matthew's must have been distinctly conservative. Matthew comments that Warin cut away a number of superfluities—extra intercessory psalmody—and shortened some lessons and antiphons. The greatest cut was the halving of the thirty extra Psalms said after Matins from All Saints to Easter: 'which we used to get through, not really as psalmody but with some of us stammering through them and others asleep'.

Matthew says that it was a holy act, so that the Office could be recited with greater devotion and reverence. The same abbot carefully made things easier for those in recreation for blood-letting, while ensuring that they missed little of the Office. In 1249 General Chapter ordered the first small liturgical cuts—partly on the grounds that some monasteries had already enforced them. The main cuts were made at General Chapters in 1277 and 1279. It would require much more study of the evidence than has yet been given to it to determine precisely how far-reaching these changes were. Thus the votive extra daily Office of All Saints, the fifteen extra Psalms before Matins and various intercessions were dropped, other intercessions shortened, the Office of the Dead cut down and the pauses during litanies much reduced. But, on the other hand, a considerable mass of intercessions remained, the communities had still to spend the space of the lost fifteen Psalms before Matins of the day in praying privately or saying part of the Office of our Lady. The votive Office of our Lady was still to be said daily, in or out of choir by all. The whole Office was now to be recited more slowly, with longer pauses at the *caesurae* in the middle of each verse. The two daily conventual Masses remained in place.

It does seem clear that, however dramatic the shortening must have seemed to those used to the old ways, the monks were still very far indeed from having cut the liturgy back to the modest amount given in the *Rule*. Moreover, they were only pruning a fast growing plant. Even as they implemented these decrees saints' days were increasing in numbers (each lengthening the Office of the day), the Westminster community was accepting increased numbers of obligations for private Masses for benefactors' intentions, the new monastic church was going to require a more solemn ritual, and the day of lengthy polyphony was fast approaching.

Resistance to the liturgical changes was brisk, if ultimately ineffective. There was a complete contradiction between reformers who said that the changes would infallibly produce greater *delectatio* in praying the Office, and the conservatives (Archbishop Pecham, the Franciscan, prominent among them), who insisted that the extra psalmody (for instance the fifteen Gradual Psalms before Matins) was essential to 'warm up' the monks' *devotio* for the Office proper. We are in the unhappy position of ignorant spectators of this controversy, since we lack adequate evidence of the mentality and inner prayer-lives of the contestants. One thing is clear, at any rate. Both reformers and conservatives were united in regarding the vocal prayer of the liturgy (and semi-liturgical additions) as far more than simply a holy gesture or penance. To both most of its value before God lay in the degree to which it was the vehicle and expression of what they called *affectio*, *devotio* or *delectatio*—true interior mental prayer.

The writer of the Westminster *Customary* of 1266 gives us some precious examples of this close association of vocal and mental prayer. Speaking of the monks in the dormitory when roused for Matins, he writes:

> Some brethren, when they hear the bell, are accustomed to draw their minds to listen interiorly to God's messenger saying to them 'Behold the Bridegroom comes; go out to meet Him', or perhaps to that terrible voice we shall hear at the Judgment, 'Arise, ye dead who lie in your graves, and run to the Lord's judgment.' Also the brethren, in gratitude for God's mercy in protecting them and setting the holy Angels to guard them in the night, say repeatedly within themselves 'Thanks be to God.' The custom of some brethren is, since midnight is the hour when Christ was born of the Virgin Mary, to say privately 'Blessed be that hour in which Christ was born of the Virgin Mary', and, signing themselves with the sign of the Cross, to say 'In the name of the Father and of the Son and of the Holy Ghost', and then, so as to speak regarding the glory of the Virgin Mary with the eyes of their mind, to add, in the depths of their hearts, 'Hail Mary etc.' Then, diligently and devoutly, with fear and reverence, they begin privately the Matins of our Lady, followed, as in the presence of God, by Matins of All Saints with the suffrages of the saints, commending themselves suppliantly to their prayers. . . .

He remarks that 'most monks' say the Matins of our Lady in this fashion even if it is to follow in choir before Matins of the day. They

count this voluntary repetition as a reparation for their lack of
devotio and attention in choir at any time. Similarly, after Compline
of the day in choir, the monks go to the dormitory, and, standing
facing each other (each at the foot of his bed) they recite Compline
of our Lady. Then, either still standing, or sitting on their beds (or
even lying in them):

> more privately with a better intention and pure heart they can
> pray as each pleases with (as we do) remembrance of our sins
> with weeping, tears, groans or sighs. But let none distract his
> fellows as he does this. But let each give thanks to God, saying
> silently 'I thank Thee, holy Lord, Almighty Father, who hast
> deigned this day to keep me in Thy holy mercy. Grant that I
> may pass through this night clean in heart and body that, rising
> at its end, I may perform Thy service worthily through Jesus
> Christ our Lord.' And while he is lying down, he may say, if he
> pleases, 'Deus in adjutorium etc.', the 'Gloria', then this verse
> 'Keep a guard over my lips, O Lord etc.' . . .

The conservatives at Westminster were to receive at least one other,
lesser shock before the century was out. In 1287 Abbot Wenlock,
from Orleans, sent to the Prior a series of statutes to be promulgated
in Chapter. It is clear that the Abbot had already introduced a new-
fangled way of giving out antiphons which he had first seen (and
much admired) in Rome. The community was unwilling to accept
the change and showed it by their unco-operative manner even in
choir. The Prior was told to be firm and reprimand the chief resisters,
however senior they were. Thus by 1307 Westminster's liturgy, to
the eye and ear of a contemporary monk, was radically changed from
what it had been in 1216. We may reasonably wonder, however,
whether the changes did, in fact, create appreciably larger free
spaces in the horarium for reading and study. We may even wonder
whether Westminster had implemented all of the General Chapter's
cuts in the Office. Half-way through the fourteenth century a
General Chapter decree took note (without disapprobation) of the
fact that the fifteen Gradual Psalms were still being recited, and its
words imply that the practice was not rare.

The modification of observances never appears in General Chapter
decrees, since it was obviously a local matter, concerning each individual abbot and community. We have already noted how the
writer of the *Customary* disapproves of a tendency among *moderni* to
sit light to ancient customs of the house. In his section on the
Chapter he even launches out into a sermonette on the theme:

> For blessed Anselm says that in a monastery where all the least
> customs—that is to say customary gestures, modes of diction and

singing and all other observances of regular discipline—are kept, there order remains inviolate amongst the monks; there is peace amongst the brethren and harmony in Chapter. But where the least excesses grow up and are neglected, there all due order collapses. So those who wish to advance in goodness and monastic perfection ought always to fear transgressions of custom. . . .

In fact we may suspect that, in a curious domestic way familiar to monks of all periods, ancient customs remained in force to the six-teenth century at Westminster with incredible tenacity, though here and there adapted to new conditions. It is perhaps significant that we hear of no major revision of the *Customary* after 1266. The sur-viving copy seems to be of the fourteenth century and may well in-corporate slight contemporary adaptations into the ancient structure.

REVIVAL OF MONASTIC STUDIES

The last of the monks' own reforms of this period was the revival of monastic studies. The reasons given for this by General Chapters were various indeed: to speed on a general revival of fervour, to satisfy the minds of the rising generation, more active and bookish than their forefathers in the habit, to stop the drift of possible voca-tions of educated men, who could not face the memorizing drill of the novitiate and the immense concentration of time and energy on liturgizing to the neglect of reading and study; and to provide in each monastery theologians and canon-lawyers so needed for the defence of the Order. In the 1240s General Chapter was urging that selected monks should attend lectures in theology in the monastery—if necessary from hired secular masters. The *Customary* incorporates this decree but does not otherwise mention lectures in operation at Westminster in 1266. By 1277 Chapter proposed to raise taxes from all member houses for the foundation of a monastic students' priory at Oxford. There was lively resistance (abetted again by the Francis-can Archbishop Pecham) but in 1283, with lay help, St Benedict's, Oxford (later Gloucester College) was actually founded. Abbot Wenlock of Westminster, as one of the two Presidents of the 1288 General Chapter, must have helped in the penning of a Presidential circular asking—rather rhetorically—for better support from the houses of Canterbury Province for this effort to draw the Black monks back to 'the truth of the *Rule* . . . our primitive glory . . .'

Wenlock was generally very active in the matter. He was present at the graduation of the first monk-scholar at Oxford; in 1291 he endorsed a new appeal for funds which made Westminster and St Benedict's the two collecting centres. By 1298 Chapter owed

Westminster a hundred marks expended by Wenlock, most probably in procuring a royal licence in Mortmain for the priory. After all this evidence of the Abbot's concern in the foundation we should expect to find him sending young Westminster monks regularly to St Benedict's from 1283. Yet no one has yet uncovered any evidence of a Westminster student at Oxford before the mid fourteenth century. Moreover the priory was organized oddly. It consisted of a series of monastic cells, built and maintained by several great houses. The students were expected to live in these separate groupings, though subject to a prior appointed by the congregation. Westminster had no cell there until August 1371. We can imagine a variety of good reasons for this slowness to seize the Oxford opportunity. The legislation of General Chapters seems to reflect the difficulties of organizing an academic renaissance in monasteries. Until the number of Oxford-trained monks had grown to appreciable numbers the abbot of a house like Westminster would find it hard to raise the level of the claustral school and so fit a number of young monks to face university courses. Then there was the perpetual difficulty that a considerable majority of entrants to Westminster would never be intellectually fitted, whatever schooling they received, to go to the university. This created an additional reason for caution in shortening the liturgy. It was no use making empty spaces for study and reading in the horarium if the majority of the community could not use the time for those purposes. Quite apart from these reasons for slowness in making use of Oxford, there were others of a more material kind. In 1298 the great fire in the Palace spread to the monastery buildings, destroying the Refectory, Dormitory and much of the Cloister. The community was at sixes and sevens for decades after this as new building went on. In 1303 came the burglary affair, and in 1307 (as we shall see) began the great troubles over Prior Hadham and the debt. Westminster did not emerge into peace and prosperity until after 1350.

We know a little about intellectual standards and aspirations at Westminster in this period. Sub-prior William of Haseley, the probable author of the *Customary*, was a reader with traditionalist tastes. He twice quotes St Anselm's letters, and probably had a copy of St Bonaventure's sermons. Around 1307 an unknown Westminster monk had procured a copy of Matthew Paris's *Flores Historiarium* (which ended in 1265) and tried his hand at a continuation down to 1306. His Latin is distinctly better than Haseley's, but he shows no scholarly interests. He quotes at great length a 'prophecy of St Hildegard' against the Friars and, in dealing with the Westminster burglary, invites his readers to procure a copy of a monastic lament on his imprisoned brethren, *Passio monachorum . . . secundum*

Johannem. These writings and the copious correspondence of Abbot Wenlock, together with the few surviving pre-1307 Westminster obedientiaries' rolls, give us an impression of a solid, utilitarian and homebred scholastic training still prevailing among the house's most literate monks. If this state of things was characteristic of most Black monk houses in the early fourteenth century, we can well understand why (as the records of General Chapters show) no moves had yet been made to change the ancient form of novitiate training, with its memory drill.

There are two other features of life in Westminster in the second half of the thirteenth century which are worth mention: recluses and lay brothers. In 1246 and 1248 there are references to a recluse (or hermit) at Westminster, and Haseley, in 1266, expressly mentions the presence of a fellow-monk as a hermit in a separate cell or *reclusorium*, apparently to the east of the abbey enclosure. We shall see later that this phenomenon in the monastery's life remained in place until the middle of the fifteenth century. It cries aloud for explanations. We find none in other Westminster documents. The eremitical form of religious life in medieval England has yet to find an adequate historian. From the Anglo-Saxon period until the Reformation it remained a constant and well-known feature of English life. St Aelred of Rievaulx, who wrote a treatise on the recluse life for his sister, who had embraced it, even remarks that there was an English proverb that you hear the latest news first at the grill of a hermitage. In fact hermits were popularly sought out as spiritual guides—hence perhaps the placing of the Westminster *reclusorium* outside the enclosure. The existence of hermits in Black monk communities was not common, but nevertheless quite regular throughout the Middle Ages, even at a large monastery like Durham, which was famous for its hermits at Finchale and on the Farne islands. The existence of the Westminster *reclusorium* in the thirteenth, fourteenth and fifteenth centuries should give us additional reason for not being hasty in our judgements of the community's spiritual state. Lay brothers (*conversi*) appear in Westminster documents first in Haseley's *Customary* and can be traced from 1266 to the dissolution of the monastery. It has been suggested that this half-dozen men, living apparently in the precincts of the monastic Infirmary, were no more than pious old laymen and oblates of the house. But Haseley's details seem rather to indicate that they were, in all essentials, much like Cistercian *conversi*—illiterates, taking a vow, wearing the habit and performing manual tasks while substituting the rosary for attendance at the Divine Office. Perhaps, at Westminster and among the Cistercians, *conversi* had deep historical roots and descended from a class of extremely simple and illiterate late entrants into monastic life whom we find in earlier centuries. In any case, the presence of these *conversi* at Westminster reminds us once more of our ignorance of so many features of its life.

In general, therefore, the Westminster abbey of 1307 had evolved considerably, in some respects, since 1216. From outside far-reaching reform schemes and theories of the monastic life (some *avant-garde*, some very reactionary) had beaten against its walls and found support within them. In fact the community had pursued its own way of evolution, accepting some suggestions in part, rejecting others, and taking its time to assimilate what it accepted. The house produced no St Bernard and no St Aelred. Perhaps the older monks were glad that it did not. Saints, they knew, were signs from God and such signs demanded from those surrounding them very hard and bewildering choices.

4

The Fourteenth Century

THERE is, of course, as we all know, no such thing as a normal age in history. Nevertheless the years from 1308 to 1399 in English history were, by any standards, if not abnormal at least unusually full of violent changes and natural catastrophes. There was much political unrest, several short bouts of civil war, the deposition of two kings (Edward II and Richard II), the dragging and drain of the Hundred Years' War (from 1337 onwards), and the great Peasants' Revolts of 1381. In Church affairs there was the catastrophe of the Great Schism of 1378 (lasting to 1409) and the rise of an English, militant heretical movement (the Lollards). Besides this there was the great European famine of 1315–17, the Black Death of 1348–50, 1361–2 and 1369 (which most probably halved the population of the country) and a major economic slump spread over many years of the century. All of these disasters and troubles struck an England which had evolved greatly in population, economic resources and sophistication of life since 1066. Society was at once more vulnerable, more sensitive and more capable of rapid recuperation than it had been in 1066. The life of Westminster abbey reflected this pretty exactly.

Between 1307 and 1349 the community endured a great many troubles. In 1307 they were still living (as they were to do for the next forty years) in a patched and only partly rebuilt monastery, when a violent dissension broke out between Abbot Wenlock and his Prior, Reginald Hadham. The Prior was deposed but appealed to the Holy See. The case was decided in the Prior's favour by 1308, but Wenlock had died and the reinstated Prior presided over a very heated abbatial election. When Richard of Kedington was elected, a minority of some eighteen monks, supported by Hadham, appealed to the Holy See. The papal judges at Avignon did not reach a verdict until 1310. They accepted Kedington, but made his accession as abbot dependent on an independent inquiry by King Edward II. Kedington emerged from this inquiry as abbot, but the community's troubles were only beginning. The Abbot was not a success as an

59

administrator and, at his death in 1315, left a large debt. By this time the great European famine was raging, a considerable part of the estates was mortgaged to pay debts to Avignon lawyers, and the King's officers had distrained other manors.

Kedington's successor, William of Curtlington, was elected promptly and without trouble. It is likely that his financial abilities commended him to the community. In fact he seems to have been unable to solve the house's economic difficulties. Famine conditions and rising prices brought on most large landowners an acute crisis, which was usually weathered temporarily by radical changes in estate management—passing from 'high farming' to letting out demesnes on long leases with high entry fines and low annual rents.

It was only natural that the community should have looked to their patron, Edward II, for help in this emergency. Robert of Reading, Westminster's monk-chronicler of the reign, seems to reflect with brutal directness the community's reaction to what they felt was shameful neglect of them by the King. He stole from them (apparently mostly during the abbatial interregnum of 1308–10) the tithes of Droitwich, the abbatial house of La Neyte and a part of the Abbey Garden itself. His officers entered on other Westminster lands, claiming debts due to the King. His favourite, Piers Gaveston, had a hand in the dissensions within the community. While the abbey was struggling on unaided, the King was spending money wholesale in restoring Westminster Palace, and his workmen there interfered with the monks and brawled with them. At the Council of Vienne in 1311 the Friars mounted a heavy general criticism of Black monk life, so that General Chapter had hastily to levy a tax on monasteries and dispatch proctors to Vienne to defend the Order.

Yet at this time, and throughout his reign, the King and royal family were ostentatious in their support of the Friars. Edward built the Dominicans a large friary beside his favourite house at King's Langley, and a Franciscan church in London became the fashionable burial-place for the Court. It is therefore hardly surprising that Reading hardly has a single good word to say for the King and is wholeheartedly on the side of the baronial Opposition. Looking back on this, we can see that this foolish and eccentric King (in many other respects, quite apart from his treatment of the abbey, violently disliked by many contemporaries) probably did express his spleen against the monks, whom he knew to be friendly with the Opposition and acidly hostile to the Dominicans (witness Reading's pages of scurrility about them).

Edward III was regarded by the community much more favourably. The Westminster monk, Richard of Cirencester, writing the

'*Proemium*' to his *Speculum Historiale de Gestis Regum Angliae*, perhaps shortly after 1376 (a work which he seems to have left four-fifths uncompleted), then felt so optimistic as to venture the judgement that: '. . . you will hardly or rarely find amongst the kings of England any one who did not, in his lifetime, do some praiseworthy and virtuous deed . . . '. The inscription on Edward III's tomb expresses the same optimism in an equally conventional way:

> Here [lies] the glory of England, the flower of
> past kings and the pattern for those to come.

If Edward II had been, in some important respects, a throw-back to Henry III, Edward III was a weaker version of Edward I—the other type of that family. So the abbey could expect to receive a limited royal patronage once more—limited and conventional.

Even after his accession, Westminster monks felt for years that the semicircle of 'roials', lying suppliantly in their tombs round the Confessor's shrine, was never going to be made a reality. The tombs of Henry III, Edward I, Eleanor of Castile, with help from the Valences and King Sebert's tomb (shifted in 1308) still only filled a third of the space available. The monks even sent to beg the body of Edward II, in vain. John of Reading, the monk who continued the Westminster *Flores* for this period, said darkly that the Queen-Mother, Isabella of France (an unpleasant woman, dead in 1358), had been promised to Westminster but appropriated in death by the London Franciscans (of whose Order she was, in fact, a tertiary). However, after burying some of his numerous children elsewhere in the church, Edward III made up his mind to complete the ring. He buried Queen Philippa of Hainault in it and intended to lie beside her himself. Edward had images of the Confessor carved or painted in several places in the Palace and in London. Also on the credit side of this patronage were favours—small ones—granted to abbots Langham and Littlington, in whose time the abbey became distinctly more closely related to the Court than at any time since 1265.

Unfortunately there was a debit side to the balance. There was nothing even remotely exclusive about it. If anything the royal family were more often visitors to St Albans abbey than to Westminster, and the Black Prince's main devotion was to Christ Church, Canterbury, where he founded a chantry and was buried. The King was interested in church building. Yet his money and interest went, not to Westminster abbey, but to the foundation of large and impressive colleges of canons at St Stephen's (which he completed) and St George's, Windsor, where he increasingly chose to reside. The truncated church at Westminster and the unfinished monastery stood, throughout the reign, as mute reproaches to the caprice and ingratitude of kings—or so the monks thought, and they were, no doubt, not mute. Richard of Cirencester's hints are robust. Moreover the cult of St Edward the Confessor was as far from popularity as ever. At Canterbury the yearly offerings at St Thomas Becket's shrine are reckoned to have averaged about £300–400 during the fourteenth century. At Westminster the offerings at the Confessor's shrine increased after 1300 to a peak in the 1350s and then declined again. Even so, in 1354 they only amounted to £30—about half of the total offerings at the various shrines in the monastic church.

In 1333 Abbot Curtlington was succeeded by Thomas of Henley, whose good management made possible a modest start on the cloister 'new work'. But his successor, Simon of Bircheston (1344–9), left behind him in the community's memory only a picture of mismanagement and favouritism. His rule ended abruptly in the first onslaught of the Black Death. In 1349 the abbot and twenty-seven of the monks died of the plague. Moreover, although mortality does not seem to have been very evenly spread over England (thus St Albans abbey lost forty-nine monks and Christ Church, Canterbury, only four), Westminster must have suffered considerable dislocation of her estate system by deaths among her servants and tenants scattered over so wide an area of England. If this disaster had happened two centuries earlier, it might well have forced the survivors of the community to disband, at least for a time, and recovery would have been slow. Yet there is every sign that, so far from 1349 marking the start of decades of misery for the community, it opened a half-century of great vigour and relative prosperity—a complete contrast to the years 1307–49. There must be some general economic reasons for this astonishing reversal of fortune, since much the same story (though perhaps less dramatic and sudden) is told by the records of a good many other religious houses and of the country at large. Yet Westminster undoubtedly owed a great deal to Simon Langham (abbot 1349–62) and his successor, Nicholas Littlington (1362–86).

SIMON LANGHAM'S ADMINISTRATIVE GIFTS

Langham was an extremely able administrator. He started his abbacy with a debt of some £2,500 and was compelled to sell numbers of the abbey's valuables in order to pay the legal expenses of his accession. Yet in his twelve years of office he paid off the entire debt, bought a number of manors for the convent and was able to complete the building of the Cloister. Besides this, as we shall see later, his reforming hand was felt in every part of the community's life. Flete treats him with reverence as the true 'second founder' of the house. That view was most probably the result of hindsight—especially of his lavish patronage of the house after 1362. We have a contrary opinion from one of his monks, John of Reading the chronicler, who frankly disliked him as dictatorial and ambitious. There is little doubt that he was dictatorial—in the sense that the crisis of 1349 and his own temperament enabled him to put an end to the long period of 'constitutional monarchy' at Westminster. Henceforward the community tended to be ruled by what we can describe as 'monarchy somewhat tempered by oligarchy'—a small oligarchy of chief obedientiaries working closely with, and under, the abbot, and excluding the rest from a voice in the details of estate administration. But Flete's account of Langham's methods stresses his diplomacy—that he repressed unruly individual officials (including his first prior, Benedict of Chertsey) but was careful of the corporate rights of the community and treated men like Chertsey, after their fall, with consideration. This account fits in with what we know of Langham's later career as a distinguished diplomat in the service of the Roman Curia at Avignon. As for the charge of ambition, we know that his departure from Westminster for a bishopric in 1362 must have been a severe shock to the community. He had been appointed Treasurer of the Exchequer in November 1360—the first abbot for almost a century to hold a prominent post in royal administration. In March 1362 he became Bishop of Ely—apparently provided to the see by the Pope, in agreement with the King. The see was not an important one and its cathedral was served by a Black monk monastery. But one can understand monks at Westminster viewing this sudden desertion of the house with suspicion, especially since the circumstances were all concealed from them. Also Langham's later career was one of extraordinarily rapid promotion. In February 1363 he moved from the Exchequer to become Lord Chancellor, and in July 1366 was Archbishop of Canterbury. His tenure of the Archbishopric was brief. In September 1368 the Pope made him a Cardinal and he left England for the service of the Papal Curia—according to the chroniclers to the fury of the King, who had not been consulted. Meanwhile the community had elected as Abbot Langham's Prior, Nicholas Littlington.

Able manager as Langham was, his promotions cannot have been simply a reward for very exceptional ability and push. In fact there was a notable tendency at the time to reverse the course of royal policy and appoint religious (even men of very indifferent ability) to administrative office and bishoprics. There is a parallel shift in papal policy and Langham was not the only English religious to be made a

Cardinal at that time. Similarly it was probably no isolated accident
that Littlington was one of the very few Westminster abbots of noble
birth—it is extremely probable that he was a member of the De-
spencer family and so related to Edward III.

About this time there began a definite invasion of the higher ranks
of the ecclesiastical hierarchy by men of noble birth. It has been
suggested that this reflected at least two movements at work among
their class—the start of 'bastard feudalism' and the spread of a new
wave of religious devotion. Littlington was apparently an older
man than Langham, and even before 1350 had made use of his
standing to win royal favours for his house—particularly the vital
one of remission of the king's right to take the profits of the abbatial
estate during *interregna*. The abbot's rule saw the culmination of the
wave of prosperity begun in 1350. His achievements were striking—
even if we admit that some were started before his time. He certainly
built a large addition to the Nave of the monastic church (though it
was far from finished in 1386), the Abbot's house (in the monastery),
alterations and additions to most parts of the monastery. The abbey's
patronage of artists (producing a number of good painters within the
community itself) dated from Henry III, but in quantity and quality
the artistic adornment of the church, Cloister and Chapter House
reached a peak in Littlington's time. The sedilia paintings and the
superb Majesty in the Chapter House were most likely in place
already in 1362, but Littlington added paintings round most of the
Cloister walls (a Crucifix—presumably of the Five Wounds—with our
Lady and St John, and the history of the house), on the Nave walls,
and in the Abbot's Hall. The Apocalypse painting was made in the
Chapter House. It was probably Littlington who glazed the Cloister
arcades with stained glass. Chantries were rising fast in the church,
all elaborately painted. If St Stephen's chapel in the Palace was then
the finest-painted church in England, Westminster must have been a
close rival. As we move around its church—and especially the
Cloisters—today it is hard to imagine the blaze of bright colours they
must have presented by 1386. Littlington also seems to have added
to the vestments, plate and illuminated choir-books of the church—
particularly his magnificent great Missal. His time saw a distinct
increase in gifts to the church. He acquired for Westminster the
Canterbury *camera* at Gloucester College, Oxford (the old St Benedict's priory). He bought a number of manors. He successfully
defended the sanctuary rights of the shrine. Needless to say there
were members of the community who viewed these developments
with distaste—particularly among the seniors—and some laid charges
of mismanagement against him. In 1362, nevertheless, Westminster
had been one of the triumvirate of leaders of the Black monks, with

Bury St Edmunds and St Albans; by 1386 the other two were forced to yield the abbot of Westminster precedence in Parliaments.

RICHARD II'S DEVOTION TO THE CONFESSOR

This achievement was due (after Littlington's ability and influence) to two main causes. The first was the generosity of Cardinal Langham. At Avignon a mass of benefices had descended on him by papal provision. From his English benefices (a deanery, three canonries and three archdeaconries) he gave for the 'new work' at Westminster a lump sum of £4,000 in gold and £200 a year. He had founded a Carthusian monastery in France, but, at his death in 1376, was still able to bequeath to Westminster (in cash, vestments and books) £7,800. Thus the house probably received some £14,000 from him. Princely as this donation was, it could not rival the £50,000 spent by Henry III on the church. Without some other patronage than Langham's, Littlington could not hope to complete his building plans. This is where the second cause came in—King Richard II. With a curious regularity, the royal blood, after Edward III, reverted to a king of the same general type as Henry III and Edward II. Richard was a pious man and took very seriously indeed his vocation to follow the Confessor in spirit. William of Sudbury, a Westminster monk, dedicated to him a treatise on the Regalia of England, to prove that they derived from King Alfred and not the Confessor—a question which, Sudbury says, interested Richard deeply. The Wilton Diptych shows the King with his patrons, our Lady, the Confessor, St Edmund the King and martyr and St John the Baptist. An anonymous Westminster monk chronicler (*Polychronicon* ix) gives us a lively picture of the King's visits to the abbey. We see Richard in 1381, at the height of Wat Tyler's peasant revolt, riding to the abbey and kneeling before the shrine of St Edward to pray 'since human counsel had altogether failed'. His attendants, in arms, shoved each other aside in anxiety to get to the shrine to offer, tears streaming down their cheeks. They must have known that, shortly before this, the rebels had burst into the same church, dragged the warden of the Marshalsea from his clutch on the pillars of the shrine, and murdered him outside. 'And,' says the chronicler, 'God's help did not fail to answer their devout prayers and the merits of the glorious St Edward'—Richard, with unusual presence of mind, faced the mob and the rising fizzled out.

We see the new Queen, Anne of Bohemia, coming to be crowned. The monk agrees with the common English judgement that she then seemed a bad bargain—'so great a sum paid for so little a scrap of humanity'. In the following years we hear of occasional visits by the

F

royal couple to the conventual Mass at great feasts, or visits by the King to pray at the shrine. They lived mostly at Sheen and we get the impression that Richard's appearances in the monastic church were very occasional all his life. But by the 1380s he seems to have decided to keep the feast of the Translation of St Edward as Henry III had done. So we hear that his practice was to go in a public procession, barefoot, with the monks to Charing Cross and back the day before the Vigil of the feast. He attended first Vespers of the feast with his whole *capella* of clerks, taking the Bishop of London to act as celebrant. At midnight he and the *capella* came to Matins, retired to bed, then rose for the procession and High Mass, followed by a dinner—at least once with most of the community in the abbot's new house. When in the monastic church at the Office or Mass he usually sat in choir (as did the Queen). Also by now a ritual had been devised for his visits to the shrine. He was met at the monastery gate by the community in copes with incense, dismounted, put off his crown, kissed the Gospel book, and followed the community into the church, as they sang the responsory *Agnus in altari*. He knelt on the marble steps of the high altar of St Peter while they sang the antiphon *Salve jubente*. After the Prayer for the King, he passed to the shrine and prayed as they sang the antiphon *Ave, sancte rex Edwarde*. Having made his oblations, he retired—unless he meant to hear Mass at the shrine altar. If we remember the great carving of St Edward on the front of St Stephen's opposite, the pictures of the saint round the church and monastery, the King's (probably votive) portrait in the church, the silent ring of 'roials' round the shrine, Richard's formal quartering of the Confessor's arms with his own, the royal device high up in the church, the King's growing habit of going to the saint before all decisions in crises, of making his followers repeatedly swear support on the shrine, his appointment of Thomas Merke (a monk of Westminster) as Bishop of Carlisle, we get a stifling sense of hieratic, staged dedication to an unreal ideal.

But (even allowing for Richard's own incipient unbalance and over-dramatizing) we are being unhistorical. He really believed it, as Becket had believed and Osbert of Clare and St Louis and count-less other medievals. Even Richard of Cirencester's schoolboy Latinity and childlike Anglo-Saxon history only muffle the real strength and nobility of an ideal. Moreover, although they thought it historically true in most of its details, the historical truth was only incidental; the main pattern was not Henry III or the Confessor or Alfred, but our Lord—*Agnus in altari*. That meant suffering and human-seeming defeat, even by a king's own lower self. Richard II even tried to get Edward II canonized—and it is likely that this was only a symptom of his absorption in his ideal. There are two other facts which perhaps indicate his growing devotion to St Edward. From 1377 the abbey spent years in successful litigation to secure a nominal recognition that St Stephen's and its Chapter lay under the abbot's jurisdiction. The King does not seem to have raised a hand to defend St Stephen's, the royal chapel. Similarly he later appointed Littlington's successor to a board of visitors of St George's Chapter at Windsor, the other royal chapel. These may be accidents, but in such an atmosphere it is likely that they were not.

When we have assimilated all this we shall not be surprised to hear that Richard proved to be a poor financial backer of the abbey's 'new work'. It has been calculated that he subscribed, in all, £1,685 for this, gave a ring worth £100 to the shrine, and left lands worth £200 a year (actually, it turned out, only £125) for his and the Queen's anniversary. So he ranks far below Langham as a contributor.

Abbot Littlington seems, at any rate by the end of his life, to have been wholly of a mind with the King. In old age, hearing of a threat of French invasion, he decided in Chapter to put himself and two stout monks in armour and take the field, armed with the ring of St Edward, but was prevented by his infirmities. His successor as abbot in 1387, William of Colchester, was not King Richard's own choice. Colchester had twelve years of subjection to the final, fullest intensity of the King's idealism. In 1397 the St Albans conspiracy (in which a Westminster monk—either the Prior or a recluse—was involved) and the autumn Parliament (which the Abbot must have attended) began Richard's attempt to crush his political critics, with executions and oaths. In 1399, on his foolish visit to Ireland he took Abbot Colchester with him. The Abbot thereafter was in the thick of the revolution, was one of the Commissioners sent by Henry of Lancaster to Richard in the Tower to get his abdication. While Bishop Merke—then and later apparently a close friend and collaborator of the Abbot's—was sticking up for Richard in Parliament, Colchester was joining those who voted for the King's separation from his companions. The Abbot took part in the coronation of Henry IV. Yet in the following month he was (if we are to believe the scanty records, made questionable by political bias) plotting with some of Richard's followers entrusted to him by Henry as prisoners, and in January 1400 was arrested and sent to the Tower, but acquitted in February and released.

The only reference to the revolution by a Westminster monk is Roger Cretton's bald, brief chronicle of the deposition-abdication without comment. As for Richard's body (buried at King's Langley after his murder), Henry V moved it to the prepared site by the shrine at Westminster. Perhaps Colchester had a hand in drawing up the very odd inscription, which merely says that the King was 'overcome by Fate' and several times insists on his prudence—'prudent in mind like Homer'; also there is no reference to St Edward (apart from the shields of arms), but a prayer to St John the Baptist ('save him who was devoted to you') and a picture of the coronation of the Blessed Virgin. It is unfortunate that the line of Westminster chroniclers gave out with Flete, who was writing in Colchester's time, too close to the revolution and whose purpose, in any case, precludes politico-religious comment.

LIFE WITHIN THE ABBEY OF WESTMINSTER

The dark curtain over Westminster history gives us especially little light on the internal life of the monastery between 1307 and 1399. The depressive effect of this, combined with an obsessive desire to discover the causes of the Protestant Reformation, has led historians to imagine that the community now slithered into an inevitably deepening slough of stagnation and laxity. As we have seen, thirteenth-century Black monks were caught up in the early stages of a process of organic evolution, adapting and reforming the organization of their lives. By 1307 this was taking shape as an organization rather raggedly cobbled together from 'regular observance', kept by all at various times and in various parts of the monastery (a liturgy still exceedingly long, elaborate observances, strict communalism in cloister and dormitory, massive memorization of liturgical texts, continual abstinence and silence, very sharp and paternalistic discipline), and a regime of Dispensations allowed to most at various other times and places (recreations from Office, abstinence and silence, study in universities, Chapter 'constitutional government'). The mixture was typical of human institutions—particularly those old and traditionalistic—at a time of rapid transition. It was typical that the monks who lived in it were torn in mind between pangs of conscience and justification of the coming order of things. It was typical also that the situation made discipline harder to enforce. But, all the time, lying athwart the old order and the new, there was the peculiar administrative-economic set-up of 'separated abbots' and obedientiaries with their rigidly departmentalized finance. It made the adaptation far more difficult; but no one could see how it could be uprooted.

After 1307 the congregational system evolved. Attendance at Chapter by abbots was poor. But this proved a blessing, since it brought thither university-educated choir monks as their proctors, active in discussions, visitations, as envoys to the Roman Curia. We get an impression that this fact, combined with the steady ferment in the universities of critical ideas on the religious life, and three major crises in the century, helped to create and keep alive a *foyer* of Black monk discussion, opinion and writing, seeking to adjust their new order and to justify it to the world and their own consciences and intelligences. Some of the stream of Black monk writing on this (by Uthred of Bolton, Adam Easton, Bishop Brinton) has been explored by scholars. More remains unstudied. But some day, no doubt, we shall learn that Westminster university-monks (like Thomas Merke, Simon Langham, William Sudbury) were vocal in the discussion. The first crisis came in 1311, when, at the Council of Vienne, the Friars (after full warning, and before proctors of the English monks) criticized the Black monk set-up bluntly and skilfully. Lively discussion brought Benedict XII's *Summi Magistri* code for the monks in 1336. Abbot Thomas Henley presided at the Chapters of 1338–40 which debated this, kept the authentic copy at Westminster and supervised the proctors sent to Rome. The result was the Congregational Statutes of 1343, revised under Abbot Littlington's presidency in 1363—all very realistic and quite successful efforts to adjust the new organization, while freely admitting that 'separate abbots' and the obedientiary system were an insoluble difficulty. In the 1370s came the third crisis fomented by Wycliffe. His sweepingly radical attack on the religious life as such grew to some extent out of a personal quarrel with the Black monks in which Westminster played a large part. It was Cardinal Langham who ousted Wycliffe from a Black monk college at Oxford. The first condemnations of Wycliffe's theses at Rome seem to have proceeded from the dispatch thither by Abbot Littlington (at Cardinal Adam Easton's request) of copies of Wycliffe's texts got from Westminster monk students at Gloucester College.

WESTMINSTER OBSERVANCE

What was Westminster observance like at this period? We can only guess, using faint scraps of surviving evidence as our guides—rather like trying to reconstruct a faint and much perished medieval wall-painting. In the first place the abbots, in spite of Littlington's interesting move in building the Abbot's House in the monastery, remained strangers to the daily life of the monastery. General Chapter was very alive to the undesirability of this, but no one could see how it could be altered. However an abbot like Colchester obeyed Chapter decrees; he seems to have lived simply (in the midst of much architectural and ceremonial splendour) and his household consisted of secular clerks and laymen, not monks.

Langham had a special devotion to the Carthusians, and Colchester made a compact with the London Charterhouse for their

prayers and for keeping with solemnity the Translation of St Edward.
After Langham's time Westminster abbots seem to have escaped
permanent office in the royal government. We gather that obedientiaries were better ordered after 1349. Chapter and the ordinary
monk ceased to be informed about details of business, the old business
wrangles there seem to have ceased, affairs being managed by the
abbot and a small committee of officials, while the bulk of the worry
and travelling on convent estate business was confined to the Convent
Treasurer and Monk Bailiff. Until 1349 the giving of dispensations
was apparently rather arbitrary. It seems that Langham, in obedience to General Chapter, put order and a communal discipline into
them.

So far as we can see, the new system amounted to this: the choir
monk kept ordinary observance during the penitential seasons and
days; at other seasons he was allowed certain fairly regular days of
recreation. These days were staggered, so that at least half the choir
monks were on regular observance when the other half were on
recreation. Recreation allowed of fixed degrees, but basically seems
to have meant a day in which the monk ate meat at two meals in the
misericord (with talking after a short silence with public reading) and
was excused attendance at the night Office, but not the day Hours.
Recreation could occasionally mean a feast, or a week's holiday at
Denham, or a visit home for a wedding or deathbed. Obedientiaries
and students were allowed restricted absences from parts of the
Office where necessary. It is likely that Langham also put order into
the system of 'allowances'. This (though it had roots in the past) was
peculiar to the times and we find it hard to understand how they
could have tolerated it. In fact, however, it was very deeply en-
grained in their lives, tied up a hundred ways with contemporary
methods of administering large institutions, and surrounded with
safeguards of a practical and ideological kind. The point seems to
have been that supplying a body of men with necessities was a
complex business before the days of bulk manufacture and market-
ing.

A wide variety of bequests and funds were earmarked (through
lands and contracts) to deliver specific services, often in return for
masses and prayers. The Cellarer supplied 'commons'—the basic
regular observance food ration. Various other officers each supplied
'pittances' and 'exennia'—the other foods and clothes, some daily
necessities, others seasonal. This left out of account certain com-
modities which were necessary for some monks at certain times—
particularly spices (very expensive, and the market supply fluctuat-
ing), books, illuminating materials, the rarer medicaments. Considering (as the Westminster chroniclers lament) contemporary

inflation, it was often decided to divide some funds in cash among the community rather than promise regular supplies in kind. Thus, in many houses (though apparently never at Westminster) clothes-money was given and monks forced to eke it out in buying their own. At Westminster, parts of Queen Eleanor's Fund and Richard II's were earmarked to provide each monk with an annual allowance—by the 1390s about £4 a year. Besides this priests received occasional allowances of a few pence from funds for mass foundations. General Chapter insisted that this must not be regarded as *peculium*—property—but regularly accounted for to the superior and its spending sub-jected to restrictions. What was it spent on? Part went in spices, ink, quills, paint, and—for the educated—part in books (extremely expensive and passed on eventually to the house Library), part in procuring indults from the Roman Curia for personal spiritual favours. Still, clearly some monks accumulated money, which either passed to the house at their death or was spent in adornments of the church—particularly numerous in Littlington's time.

The rigours of life at Westminster were alleviated in other ways. Littlington seems to have glazed the open sides of the Cloister and provided a work room for students. There appeared a set of separate *camerae* (cells) for senior obedientiaries and *stagiarii* (old monks, in-capable of sustaining full regular observance). After 1343 educated novices were freed from a part of the burden of memorizing liturgical texts, and, in consequence, the night Office was now no longer recited in the dark. Efforts were made to provide various kinds of work for the community. From the 1340s more monks were sent to Oxford. Very few of these (Thomas Merke, William of Sudbury) were allowed to stay long enough there to acquire a bachelor's degree in theology. Indeed, the aims of the abbots in sending men to the university were strictly limited: to maintain in the house a modest supply of men sufficiently instructed in theology and canon law to defend the house and Order, to supply good preachers, and to im-prove the standard of teaching in the monastery. Ripe scholars were hardly needed to accomplish this; moreover, bachelors' and doctors' courses at Oxford were extremely long (and therefore expensive), and a long life under Oxford conditions was hardly good for the monastic spirit of the average man.

The abbot, from his house at Islip, could exercise some supervision over the two or three Westminster monks who formed the usual complement of the house's *camera* at Gloucester College. They were set under religious obedience to the senior Westminster student—who ought to be a priest. Normally they recited the Office, heard Mass and received the sacraments only in the little *camera* chapel, but attended Office in the choir of the College chapel with the monk-

students from other *camerae* on feast days. They received allowances
to buy books and necessaries and had two holidays a year—at
Steventon, a Westminster manor. They were required to preach to
the people there and at Westminster, when summoned back for that
purpose. Once back in the monastery, the university monk very soon
became a junior obedientiary and was employed as a proctor to
General Chapters or even to Avignon and Rome; he was set to teach
and preach, and, if he wished, could write. William of Sudbury
produced *tabulae* (highly systematic synopses) of St Thomas's *Summa
Theologica* and Nicholas of Lyra's Biblical commentaries—surely for
lectures in the house, in the cloister, or study-room. As we have seen,
the writing of chronicles never ceased at Westminster during the
century—though we have no evidence that the writers were university men. Besides this, superiors had to find occupations for the
non-university monks (the great majority)—men who were doubtless
better-educated and several degrees more sophisticated than their
eleventh- and twelfth-century predecessors. Fortunately Westminster
had had a 'school' (or so it seems) of able painters since William of
Westminster in Henry III's time. The growing use of books (in
choir, in the monastery, at the university, through Langham's bequest) begot a 'school' of copyists, binders and repairers. Then there
was always sacristy work (now increased), obedientiary's jobs, and
the work involved in the constant building.

LITURGY AND NEW DEVOTION

There is no doubt that the monastic liturgy remained very long, and
that it now began to increase again, by an inevitable process of
accretion. From General Chapter decrees we gather that the
Gradual Psalms remained in a good many houses (before Matins),
the Office of our Lady was universal, as were the Penitential Psalms
after Prime (with the litany and long prayers), rows of commemorations after each Hour, the *Psalmi Prostrales* daily in Lent, the singing
of antiphons twice-over on feasts, processions, the weekly Maundy,
the daily Chapter and Collation, two sung conventual Masses every
day and the daily sung Lady Mass. To this were now added the great
antiphons of our Lady after Compline (1343), the use of polyphonic
singing, daily sung Masses at the chantries, an elongation of the rite
of the Mass (as private prayers became parts of its structure). As
Chapter cut down the calendar at one end, they added to it at the
other—for instance votive Offices of St Benedict. But the impact of
all this on the community was much eased by dispensations, more
variegated works, a freer spirit, the fact that the Lady and chantry
Masses were only attended by the celebrants and a rota of a few

singers. The foundation of the Almonry school in this century perhaps provided, by 1399, a choir of boys for these 'rota Masses'.

What of the spiritual life and prayer of the monks? It is commonly said that, by now, a widespread 'devotio moderna' was growing up quite apart from monasteries—and, indeed, hostile to their liturgical formalism. But this seems a great over-simplification of a very complex movement. It is more likely that this devotion had its roots in the writings of twelfth-century monastic reformers like St Anselm and St Bernard. Its spirit of intense criticism of monastic formalism, its insistence that God is attained in any walk of life solely by inner discipline and prayer—all this arose from the internal struggles of monks. The first products of this new devotion were monastic before they spread to those outside—an affective devotion to our Lady (her joys and sorrows), the Passion, the Sacred Heart, the Blessed Sacrament; the private use of the traditional monastic semi-liturgical prayers (the Gradual and Penitential Psalms, Litanies, the Office of our Lady); and lastly the fusion of both in compositions for private use like Matins of the Compassion of our Lady, or long, highly affective and personal private prayers to be used at Mass by both priest and people. Two laymen (both connected with Westminster abbey) made long and pious Wills in 1415—King Henry V and Henry, Lord Scrope. The Wills are a compendium of the forms of the new devotion as it had grown up in the fourteenth century. It is based on the use of private prayer books (listed by Scrope) which absorbed the reader's mind into a set of spiritual exercises as he attended Mass and the Office—so, for instance that he concentrated on seeing each part of the Mass as representing a stage in the Passion. An anonymous monk of Westminster, in his *Versus Rhythmici de Henrico Quinto*, could therefore rightly describe the King at Mass: 'while he heard Mass the cell of his mind was tight shut (*illum clam cellula claudit*); sweetly he implores and then devoutly prays . . .'. Indeed Henry imposed his devotions on the Westminster liturgy by the elaborate form he gave to the services he required from the monks serving his chantry. There were to be three Masses daily at it (the first during Prime, the second apparently during Terce, and the third to start after the Gospel was sung at the community's High Mass). He could not prevent one Mass a day being controlled by the Church's calendar, but the other two were to be votive Masses, arranged in a complex order to follow his favourite devotions. But it would be wrong to regard Westminster abbey as a fortress captured for the new devotion by Henry V. The Westminster community itself (witness the *Customary*) had long been going the same way of its own accord. There are four other pieces of evidence of this. The first is the long, private prayers given to the celebrant in Littlington's

Westminster Missal. The second is the wall-paintings—actually offered by individual members of the community. The third is the presence among Langham's bequest of books (amidst the canon law and scholastic theology) of a *Cloister of the Soul*, a *Mariale* (meditative prayers on her Joys), and sets of the works of St Anselm and St Bernard. The fourth is sympathy among the monks for the eremitical life. This was shown by Langham's and Littlington's patronage to the Carthusians, and by the existence (in the midst of the community in the old *reclusorium* and a new one by the Infirmary) of one or even two hermits at a time between about 1375 and 1450. These recluses certainly gave spiritual direction to pious lay people (including Richard II) and—we should expect—both witnessed to, and forwarded, an impulse towards a more intense 'interior living' among their brethren.

By chance we have two important outsiders' views of the abbey at this period. William Langland, the author of the *Vision of Piers Plowman*, was most probably educated at an almonry school at Westminster's daughter priory of Malvern. He spent much of his life within a very few miles of Westminster abbey, and the *Vision* shows that he had a devotion to St Edward the Confessor. It also contains at least a dozen passages of reflection on monastic life. Geoffrey Chaucer, who was very familiar with Westminster, and was, for a time, a keeper of the Palace, in 1399 leased from the abbot and convent a house in the monastic garden by the Lady Chapel, and, at his death in 1400, was accorded the (then rare) privilege of burial in the abbey church. In the *Canterbury Tales* he includes a monk whose first choice of a story is *The Life of Edward the Confessor*. Here then are obviously two highly perceptive judgements of the community. But when we have meditated on what they say, we end with a strong impression that it tells us more of their own minds than of the spiritual state of the abbey.

Langland seems to have been a clerk in minor Orders (and a married man), earning his bread by 'singing for souls'—helping out in parish churches at Requiem Masses and Dead Offices. He revered the liturgy and saw in it, not a mechanical act but a sharing in the Word and prayer of Christ with interior devotion. He feared life in the world. To him, if there be heaven on earth or 'ease in . . . spirit', it lies only in monastic life or the life of a Winchester College or New College. But why? For his mind the core of 'religion' lies in literal obedience to an ancient (early medieval) Rule, *districtio ordinis* ('for the love of our Lord living in strictness', few occasions of sin because of the narrow restriction to the cloister, constant labour, ceaseless supervision by 'many sturdy spirits to spy on my doings', floggings, penances), the labour of 'travailing in prayers'. Therefore he regarded travelling obedientiaries, 'allowances', 'separate abbots' and all dispensations as of the Devil. He prophesied that 'the King and his Council' would forcibly put an end to them. In the same way he detested speculative Scholastic theology and academic freedom in the universities. His ideal of a school was old in St Anselm's day— *non plus sapere quam oportet*, grammar and scripture only, floggings (spare the rod . . .) and strait old-fashioned discipline. Such reactionary traditionalism (allied with a profoundly Christian mysticism) probably represented the dominant note in the outlook of all pious men (monks included) throughout the Middle Ages. But it was not the only note.

Chaucer was a very different kind of man and temperament—a lay courtier, a fashionable poet, an amateur of French Courtly Love and the rising Italian Humanism of Petrarch and Boccaccio. He was so much an entertainer and his verse so often mannered or *pastiche* that we find it very hard to penetrate to the man beneath. Perilous erections of cards have been built up by theorists on his treatment of the monk-pilgrim. All that is quite certain is that, though well-read in his religion (when such reading was 'clerkly' of its nature), he was, by his whole life and mind, a layman. The dominant note of tradition was there but muted—especially in his *Retractation* and last days at Westminster (in spirit, if not in fact, he 'died in the habit'). His modernity and Humanism could see the difficulty of adaptation for religious ('he let go by the things of yesterday . . .')—after all Chaucer was having the same difficulties himself on his own level. But he has no real answer to the problem—not for himself, and certainly not for religious.

5

The Fifteenth Century to 1474

ABBOT COLCHESTER ruled until 1420. Perhaps because of his political past, the abbey received very little attention from Henry IV, who chose to be buried at Canterbury. However, Henry V was anxious to resume foundership and patronage of Westminster abbey. The monk author of the *Versus Rhythmici*, writing before Henry's death, lists enthusiastically the fruits of his patronage, and (clearly in expectation or hope of far more) salutes him as the equal of King Sebert and St Edward—a greater benefactor than Henry III or Richard II. The author invites monks to say extra prayers for Henry after each Hour of the Office of our Lady. In fact the patronage was modest—an express, public acceptance of the office of protection, the moving of Richard II's body to its place by the shrine, 1,000 marks to the Nave 'new work', a chantry, £100 a year in land, the restoration of some stolen relics (perhaps lifted by Henry IV in 1400 when Colchester was arrested), gifts of a few vestments, some protection in two law-suits, royal approval of an effort to secure a papal remission of the expensive obligation of an abbot-elect's journey to Rome and subsequent visits *ad limina*.

Yet the King's devotion fell very far short of that of Henry III and was perhaps less than that of Richard II. In his Will made in 1415 he only mentions St Edward once—in the middle of a short Litany of his patrons. His chantry is to be dedicated to our Lady of the Annunciation and All Saints. He describes its site without any reference to the Shrine of St Edward—'amongst the tombs of the Kings in the place where the relics of the saints were formerly kept'. The immense list of votive masses to be said after his death and at the chantry covers all his devotions but includes none of St Peter, St Edward or St Benedict. In fact his chantry imposed a serious burden on the monks. Its 'private liturgy' was almost set up in opposition to the community's. Henry fixed the hours of the chantry Masses—especially the third one, to coincide with the community High Mass so that the two Consecrations would come rapidly one after the other

1 Grant of land at Aldenham, Hertfordshire, from Offa, King of Mercia, to the monastery at Westminster. Date A.D. 785.

2 Funeral of Edward the Confessor, showing the only known representation of the Abbey built by him. From the Bayeux Tapestry.

3 Coronation of a king and queen, from the *Liber Regalis*, late fourteenth century.

4 Richard II. The earliest known painting of a British monarch, which hangs in the Nave.

6 Chantry Chapel of Abbot Islip, d. 1532.

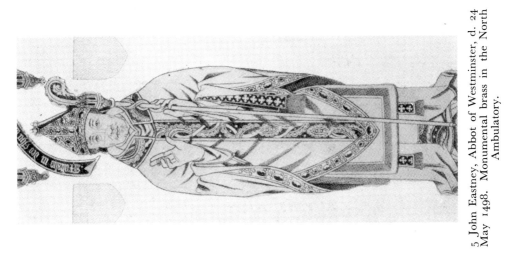

5 John Eastney, Abbot of Westminster, d. 24 May 1498. Monumental brass in the North Ambulatory.

7 Lease from the Monk Warden of the Lady Chapel to Geoffrey Chaucer, the poet, of a house near St Margaret's Church. Date Christmas Eve, 1399.

8 The colophon of William Caxton who printed and published at the Sign of the Red Pale in Westminster Almonry. His advertisement of 1477–8 reads: 'If it plese ony man spirituel or temporel to bye ony pyes [rules for priests on adjusting the Office according to the variable date of Easter] of two and thre comemoracions of Salisburi use enprynted after the forme of this present lettre whiche ben wel and truly correct/late hym come to Westmonester in to the almonesrye at the reed pale and he shal have them good chepe.'

9 Page recording the issue of clothing to monks at Westminster. The column headings reading from left to right are: *habitus* (habits); *stragule* (bed coverings); *staminis* (shirts of linsey-woolsey); *femoralia* (breeches); *pellis alluta* (leather leggings[?]); *calige* (hose); *pedule* (slippers). From the Monk Chamberlain's Roll, 1507–8.

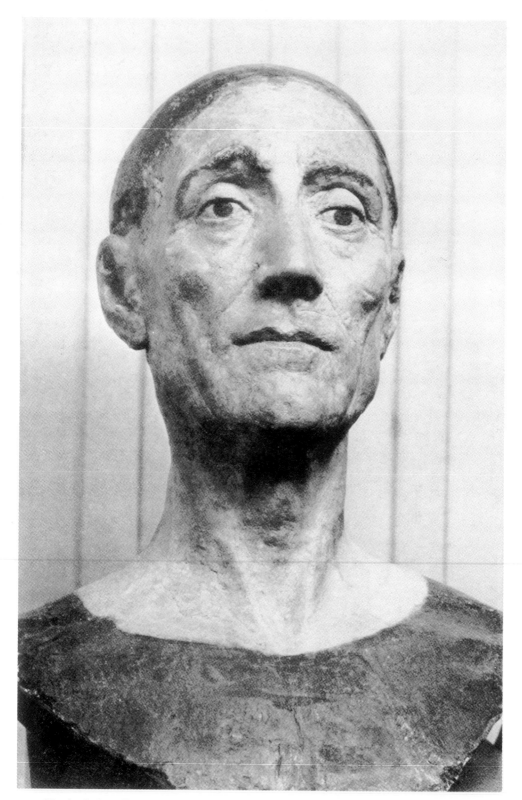

10 Head of the effigy carried at the funeral of Henry VII, d. 1509. From his death mask.

11 Henry VII's Chapel from a painting attributed to Canaletto, *c*. 1740.

12 St Matthew wearing spectacles.

13 St Wilgefortis or Uncumber. A woman of
exceptional beauty, her beard answered her
prayers for protection against the attentions of
men.

14 Carved stone head of Abbot John Islip, d. 1532.

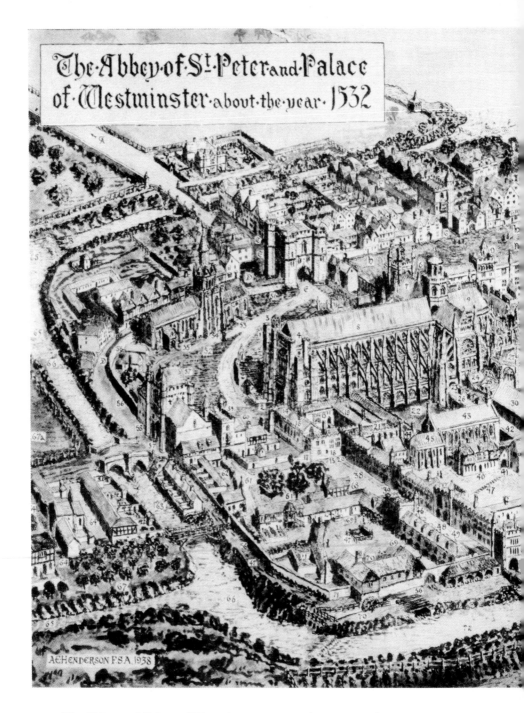

The Abbey of St. Peter and Palace of Westminster about the year 1532

15 The Abbey and Palace of Westminster, *c.* 1532. A reconstruction drawn by the late A. E. Henderson, F.S.A., based on information in the Abbey Muniments.

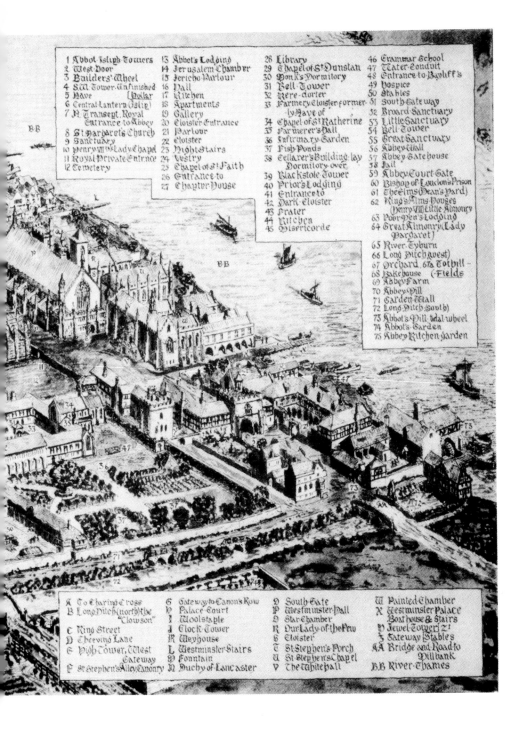

1 Abbot Islip Towers
2 West Door
3 Builders' Wheel
4 S.W. Tower Unfinished
5 Nave [Pollar
6 Central Lantern (Islip)
7 N. Transept, Royal Entrance to Abbey
8 St Margaret's Church
9 Sanctuary
10 Henry VII's Lady Chapel
11 Royal Private Entrance
12 Cemetery
13 Abbot's Lodging
14 Jerusalem Chamber
15 Jericho Parlour
16 Hall
17 Kitchen
18 Apartments
19 Gallery
20 Cloister Entrance
21 Parlour
22 Cloister
23 Night Stairs
24 Vestry
25 Chapel of St Faith
26 Entrance to
27 Chapter House

28 Library
29 Chapel of St Dunstan
30 Monk's Dormitory
31 Bell Tower
32 Rere-dorter
33 Farmery Cloister, formerly Nave of
34 Chapel of St Katherine
35 Farmer's Hall
36 Infirmary Garden
37 Fish Ponds
38 Cellarer's Building, lay Dormitory over
39 Blackstole Tower
40 Prior's Lodging
41 Entrance to
42 Dark Cloister
43 Frater
44 Kitchen
45 Misericorde

46 Grammar School
47 Water Conduit
48 Entrance to Bayliff's
49 Hospice
50 Stables
51 South Gateway
52 Broad Sanctuary
53 Little Sanctuary
54 Bell Tower
55 Great Sanctuary
56 Abbey Wall
57 Abbey Gate house
58 Jail
59 Abbey Court Gate
60 Bishop of London's Prison
61 The Elms (Dean's Yard)
62 King's Alms Houses (Henry VII Little Almonry)
63 Poor Men's Lodging
64 Great Almonry (Lady Margaret)
65 River Tyburn
66 Long Ditch (west)
67 Orchard, 67a Tothill
68 Bakehouse (Fields
69 Abbey Farm
70 Abbey Mill
71 Garden Wall
72 Long Ditch (south)
73 Abbot's Mill tidal wheel
74 Abbot's Garden
75 Abbey Kitchen garden

A To Charing Cross
B Long Ditch (north) the "Clowson"
C King Street
D Thieving Lane
E High Tower, West Gateway
F St Stephen's Alley Canonry
G Gateway to Canon's Row
H Palace Court
I Woolstaple
J Clock Tower
K Weighouse
L Westminster Stairs
M Fountain
N Duchy of Lancaster
O South Gate
P Westminster Hall
Q Star Chamber
R Our Lady of the Pew
S Cloister
T St Stephen's Porch
U St Stephen's Chapel
V The Whitehall
W Painted Chamber
X Westminster Palace Boat house & Stairs
Y Jewel Tower (?)
Z Gateway Stables
AA Bridge and Road to Millbank
BB River Thames

16 Henry VII. Bronze effigy from his tomb, designed by Torrigiani.

17 Obsequies of Abbot Islip, from the *Obituary Roll of John Islip*. The only known representation of the interior of the Abbey in pre-Reformation times. It shows the High Altar with the Abbot's funeral hearse.

18 Monument in St Benedict's Chapel to Dr Gabriel Goodman, Dean of Westminster, d. 1601.

—for the benefit of 'those flowing into the church to hear Masses'. (It was perhaps because of this distraction during the Office and High Mass in choir that in 1441 the community built the solid screen to cut off the High Altar from the shrine-space behind it.) The King's gifts to the 'new work' were large enough to tempt the monks to carry on, but far too small to pay for more than a single bay of the Nave. In fact Henry's care for monastic building was spent else-where—in founding the Bridgettine house of Syon and the Charter-house of Richmond.

These foundations went with an evident impatience with the Black monks and an intention of forcing on them (as Langland had pro-phesied) a strict reform. At Henry's demand a General Chapter waited on him in 1422 in the Westminster Chapter House. There he proposed a detailed list of reforms. Of recent years on the Continent (speeded up by war conditions and the collapse of regular life in many monasteries there) quite numerous model centres of monastic reform had appeared. In organization and spirit they were very much the children of their age. Abbots and abbacies there were generally far more secularized than in England. Therefore the logical step was taken of separating the abbacies entirely from the communities and organizing the latter in more or less strait sub-jection to a tight congregational rule. Allowances in money were abolished and the obedientiary system reduced to little, estate matters passing to the control of lay stewards—an easier matter now, since 'high farming' was again out of the realm of economic possibilities. The liturgy was cut back with extreme violence—in some cases by jettisoning the monastic Office and taking to the short Roman curial Office. The horarium was filled in with long periods of study, reading and semi-liturgical 'exercises' of prayer of the kind made fashionable by the 'devotio moderna'. The double regime of regular observance and dispensations was, to a large extent, abolished, in some reforms (of élite houses) by a communal return to the major part of the regular observance, in most by a compromise observed simultaneously by all. Henry V certainly had some acquaintance with French versions of this reform and made abortive efforts to persuade the Celestines (who belonged to the severer wing of the reform) to make a foundation in England. The presence of a Carthusian with the King and as his advocate of reform at the West-minster Chapter is a further indication of the King's mind.

The royal reform scheme amounted to a literal observance of the papal Statutes of 1336. The Chapter must have been well aware of Continental methods. Abbot Colchester had been an indefatigable traveller abroad. As a young monk in 1378 he had been in Rome at the time of the fatal papal conclave. In 1409 he had been one of

Henry IV's ambassadors at the Council of Pisa, and again in 1414–17 at the Council of Constance—which had discussed the new monastic reforms at length and launched them in Germany. As we have seen, the Westminster monks were on friendly terms with the Carthusians. They even had a mysterious link with both the King and the Bridgettines, through William Alnwick. Alnwick was apparently a monk-hermit of Westminster and, on occasion, the King's confessor. He had also left Westminster for a time to act as confessor to the Bridgettines of Syon.

It would seem therefore that the discussions of reform at the Westminster Chapter of 1422 were well-informed. They were certainly inconclusive. The King's contributions—to judge from the very few documents of the affair—were negative and almost military. The Chapter committee (of university-monks) simply defended the monks' right of self-determination. The Presidents, while typically paying homage to the doctrine of the Golden Age of monachism and modern degeneracy, and frankly admitting the weak points of contemporary Black monk organization, insisted on the necessity of a humane and positive approach to reform. Some historians have seen this answer as full of pusillanimity and laxity. On the contrary, when read in its medieval context, and in the wider context of monastic history, it is a humble, realistic and impressive judgement.

But the debate was cut short almost immediately by the King's death. There followed the minority of Henry VI, with its mounting political tension, culminating in the Wars of the Roses. Most of this difficult period coincided with a very bad patch in the Westminster community's history. At the abbatial election of 1420 choice was very limited, since disease carried off Colchester and at least a dozen other monks in one year. Richard Harwden, the new abbot, seems to have made very little impression indeed on the records and resigned his abbacy—probably because of debts and misgovernment—in 1440. Nicholas Ashby, his Prior, was an able man and would probably have become abbot if he had not been made Bishop of Llandaff shortly before the abbatial election.

KIRTON'S FAILURE

The successful candidate—helped out by a papal bull of provision—was Edmund Kirton. He had spent almost all his monastic career away from Westminster at Oxford, first in a long doctorate course, and then for six years as Prior of Gloucester College. His rule of Westminster very soon proved disastrous. In 1444 Henry VI secured a special Chapter visitation of the house. Kirton was suspended from

office and charges of gross immorality and mismanagement hung
over his head. Several obedientiaries were removed from office and
a number of monks exiled to other houses. The community limped
on in grave debt. Kirton was not finally ousted until 1463. His
successor, George Norwich—also apparently put in by papal provision—proved totally incapable and was forced to resign in 1467.
By that time the house was well over £2,000 in debt. At Norwich's
death in 1469 Dr Thomas Milling was elected. He was perhaps the
best university scholar Westminster produced. Italian Humanism
was beginning to have an impact on English ecclesiastical circles.
Milling, together with Abbot Whethamstede of St Albans and Prior
Selling of Canterbury formed the pioneers of the movement among
the Black monks. He was apparently a man of much energy and
ability and both paid off the debts and restored the community to
order—but was made Bishop of Hereford in 1474.

Our knowledge of Westminster observance and spirituality in the
fifteenth century is exceedingly small. On the one hand there is the
evidence of the line of monk-hermits to about 1450 (the start of
the real troubles), the Bridgettine connexion early in the century, the
gradual flowering of the 'chantry liturgy', the definite appearance of
the boys' song-school and choir, the devout Humanism of Milling.
Henry VI was very possibly rather more friendly towards the community than we might gather from his intervention of 1440 (in a
brief, general order to reform) and his absorption in building his
colleges at Eton and King's. There is some evidence that he planned
a tomb for himself in the monastic church and his forces in France
certainly took into battle two standards—of St George and of St
Edward.

On the other hand the black smear of the troubles of 1444–67 lies
across the Westminster picture. To some these were an inevitable
collapse of a community wholly demoralized already by the loss of its
monastic spirit. But that judgement seems very exaggerated. Another dose of reform and adaptation was as overdue in 1474 as it had
been in 1216. Baroque monasticism was on the horizon. As ever, the
Black monk plant was stubbornly slow in its reactions to these waves
of influence and enthusiasm. Pending the discovery of information
about the troubles of 1444–67, it is very arguable that they bear the
typical marks of a natural disaster (like that of Osbert of Clare's
days). In 1478 Edward IV wrote to the Pope saying that the house
was 'much decayed because of civil war and floods'. A combination
of three bad abbots, heavy debts, the endemic plague of that century,
the impact of widespread civil disorder and 'bastard feudalism'
would have brought most monasteries to total ruin before 1215. The
sudden revival of Westminster under Milling and Eastney, Edward

IV's appointment of Milling to his Council and a bishopric, his Queen's devotion to the house—all of this reminds us of the past.

Finally we must return to our original question—*was* medieval Westminster a house of respectable (on the whole) mediocrities? Was it merely a mute stage, across which so many great and holy men moved (St Anselm, Lanfranc, St Aelred, St Thomas Becket, St Hugh of Lincoln, William Langland, Chaucer, Caxton, to name a few)? The ultimate answer, of course, cannot be given by any historian, since it depends on imponderables—the inner devotion of hundreds of outwardly undistinguished *claustrales* (or obedientiaries, or superiors), the effect of the unceasing liturgy from the tenth century (so appreciated by Henry III, Richard II, Henry V before Agincourt), the physical austerities accepted (which, however mitigated, still would make any modern, however religious, wilt). We should hazard a guess that medieval Westminster, with all its human ups and downs and failures, still performed a specially difficult vocation—not that of Cistercians, Cathusians, Bridgettines, St Bernards, Beckets, but, in its own way, as necessary: to remind English kings, courtiers, civil servants, Westminster lawyers (so suspected by Langland) and Londoners, with all their evident inconstancy, of the *unum necessarium* for the ordinary man. Chaucer seems to have seen that in the end. Thomas Merke, the courageous monk and Bishop of Carlisle, wrote to his friend, Abbot Colchester, what may well be the best epitaph on the whole medieval Westminster community:

> . . . For they see your steadfastness [*soliditatem*],
> which is a rare virtue in these modern days,
> and, because of it, look to you especially.

APPENDIX TO PART I

(I) THE MONASTIC HORARIUM

BENEDICTINE monastic life, lived for so many centuries at Westminster abbey, is, of course, very far from being merely an interesting but dead relic of a remote past. It continues vigorously today in many monasteries all over the world. At least one reason for its vigour and powers of resistance to disaster is that, in all centuries (both medieval and modern), it has combined an unchanging rigidity of general structure with a very great flexibility in details. The history of the monastic horarium (i.e. daily timetable) witnesses vividly to this fact. Thus if you took, at random, any period in Westminster's medieval history, you would find it quite impossible to compile a complete daily timetable unless you produced a small library of notebooks, full of tables and rules—because there would be so very many variants for different classes of seasons, feasts, fasts, occasions, classes of monks. If you then consider that these variants themselves changed often in the course of history, you can understand why those who write descriptive books on medieval monasticism in general invariably make their chapters on the horarium brief and vague.

Nevertheless it is possible to give, in table-form, a rough idea of the general lay-out of a medieval Westminster monk's average day.

The night Office began his day. Until the thirteenth century this started some time between 1.30 and 2.30 a.m. (depending on calculations of season, etc.). Thereafter it started at midnight. At some early periods it may well have been placed in the evening of the previous day—on a few great days in the year, when the Office would be exceedingly long (about three hours or more). Depending on the calendar, this night Office might take as little as one and a quarter to one and a half hours, or as much as over two and a half. During this time the monks were sometimes seated, sometimes reclining (half-standing, half-seated on *misericords* or narrow ledges projecting out from the underside of their seats—tipped up), sometimes standing. The great bulk of this Office (itself divided into two parts, Matins and Lauds) consisted of protracted psalmody to a simple, meditative tune with distinct pauses. But there were also parts sung to fine and elaborate plainsong melodies, and other parts recited in a very low voice without note.

Prime, a comparatively short service of the same character, lasting

perhaps a little over thirty minutes, followed at about 6 to 6.45 a.m.
Until the thirteenth century monks stayed in church or cloister,
meditating privately during the fairly short period between the end
of Lauds and Prime. Thereafter they retired to bed in the interval
(now very much longer) and so, in fact, their night's sleep was always
broken in two by the night Office.

The Morrow Mass followed Prime, usually after an interval of perhaps
three-quarters of an hour, during which the priests of the community
said their private Masses, served by the others. One of these Masses,
at the altar of our Lady, was often sung by a choir of monks. The
Morrow Mass was the first of two daily 'conventual' (community)
sung Masses and lasted about three-quarters of an hour.

The Chapter followed this immediately, the monks passing in procession from the church to the Chapter House, where they seated themselves in order of seniority round the walls. There followed—not
always in this order—(i) the announcement of notices for the day,
deaths and anniversaries of friends, the names of those appointed to
various duties for the day; (ii) the reading of a commentary on the
Gospel for the day at Mass; (iii) an address by the abbot on some
feature of monastic or spiritual life; (iv) if necessary, an orderly
discussion of the business of the monastery; (v) 'the Chapter of
Faults'—a sort of general 'self-criticism' by the community of their
monastic observance (not—at any rate directly—their sins), in which
superiors reported the mistakes and faults against due order of
monks, monks voluntarily confessed their failings and the abbot
awarded penances.

Work followed the Chapter—a period lasting an hour or as much as
two and a half hours used for a multiplicity of jobs, classes and
studies, chores of housework, administrative work, artistic work by
specialists.

The Sung Mass—the second, and more important and solemn, community Mass—followed, usually preceded and followed by Terce,
Sext and None (hours of psalmody) so that the whole lasted over an
hour.

Dinner followed. Although a good many monks at all periods—
especially the young and old—were allowed a small snack, usually
after the Chapter, Dinner was the only major meal in the monastic
day. It began at some hour between 11.30 a.m. and 2 p.m.

Work. A second period of work followed—usually until about 3 or
3.30 p.m. In the heat of summer a short siesta was allowed after
Dinner.

The rest of the day was variously arranged. But its constants were: (i) the service of Vespers, which lasted rather over three-quarters of an hour; (ii) attendance at the public reading of a spiritual book; (iii) *Supper*—a light meal, reduced in penitential seasons to a drink— at around 4.30 to 5.30 p.m.; (iv) Compline—the last service of the day, ending with visits to altars to pray and with the solemn singing of a seasonal hymn to our Lady (e.g. the *Salve Regina*). The monks retired to bed at an hour calculated to give them some eight hours of (broken) sleep—that is, in the later Middle Ages, around 7 or 8 p.m.

The whole of this timetable fitted exactly the natural rhythm of a primitive and agricultural society, living by sun-time. Modern Benedictines universally have moved their whole timetable on— retiring later (about 9 or 9.30 p.m.) and rising later (at times ranging between 4 and 5.30 a.m.). The late medieval tendency to simplify and shorten the very great length of the services has gone much further in modern times. Thus, for instance, the Morrow Mass has universally disappeared, and Chapters often occur weekly, not daily.

(II) THE OBEDIENTIARIES

This was a monastic name for monks who had committed to them 'obediences'—that is offices which had attached to them not only duties in the house, but the administration of a part of the monastic estates. This latter provided the 'obedientiary' with a revenue to supply the goods needed by his duties. At Westminster, as every-where else in monasteries from the twelfth century, the numbers and subdivisions of these jobs tended to multiply. The existence of a multiplicity of offices in a monastic community is inevitable and healthy. Thus modern Benedictine houses have Procurators, assistant Procurators, Junior-Masters, Auditors, Sacristans, head-masters, etc., in profusion. In large communities this inevitably produces some degree of division of financial administration, and— as medieval monks discovered—this needs limiting to prevent the officials becoming too absorbed in business. The chief Westminster 'obedientiaries' were:

1. *The Cellarer*—a sort of general Bursar.
2. *The Granger.* 3. *The Gardener*—his assistants.
4. *The Chamberlain*, who provided clothing, shoes, etc.
5. *The Refectorer.* 6. *The Kitchener*, who ran dining-hall and kitchen.
7. *The Pittancer*, who administered legacies left to provide treats for the community on great feast days.

8. *The Domestic Treasurer*—an accountant and auditor.
9. *The Monk-Bailiff*, who generally administered the estates.
10. *The Wardens*, who administered particular funds—e.g. Queen Eleanor's manors, St Mary's Chapel endowments, various churches belonging to the house.
11. *The Almoner*, who administered poor-relief.
12. *The Infirmarer*, who cared for sick monks.
13. *The Sacristan*, who was responsible for the upkeep of the church fittings.
14. *The Precentor*, who looked after choir-books and music.

There were, from time to time, other 'obediences'—for instance *Warden of the New Work* (responsible for the finances of new building operations), and there were monastic offices to which no funds were attached—the Prior, Sub-Prior and his assistants, Archdeacon, Novicemaster, Guestmaster, etc.

PART II
The Reformation and its Aftermath
1474–1660

By The Reverend A. Tindal Hart, M.A., D.D.

6

Abbot Islip and the Funeral of the Middle Ages

AFTER BOSWORTH

IT is of absorbing interest to speculate on what might have happened had Henry Tudor rather than Richard Plantagenet fallen on Bosworth Field. The Tudor was practically the last serious Lancastrian claimant to the throne of whom the Yorkists had reason to be afraid; while Richard himself, who was not yet thirty-three years old, by a second marriage possibly this time with some foreign princess, could well have fathered a long line of Yorkist kings.

After Bosworth, Richard, no less than Henry, must needs have devoted himself to curbing the over-great powers of the feudal aristocracy; to erecting a strong national monarchy based upon the loyalty of his own household, an efficient civil service and a compliant Parliament; and to building up those very policies in the economic and financial fields that his great brother Edward had so successfully pursued, and which in the event were largely taken over by his successors. There is in fact little doubt but that some sort of kingly despotism, tempered on the one hand by the growing power of the House of Commons with its fingers on the taxation money-bags and the increasing prestige of the Common Law on the other, would have emerged under the Plantagenets, as it certainly did in the case of the Tudors and Stuarts. What it might be harder to believe in or to visualize would have been such a violent break with the papacy and the wholesale plunder of the Church as were so successfully and cynically engineered by Henry VIII and Thomas Cromwell.

Richard was indeed a child of the Renaissance, and sufficiently Puritan at heart to study Wycliffe's English New Testament; yet neither he nor any of his successors was in the least likely to approach the problem of the sixteenth-century Church in the spirit of the Welshman. Reformation from within in line with the demands of the Oxford Reformers or the ideals of Thomas Wolsey, rather than a drastic Cromwellian purgation from without, would have been more in keeping with Plantagenet traditions. Moreover, as one peers into the mists of 'what might have happened', it is possible to glimpse the outlines of a shadowy Plantagenet dynasty as the ally of Spain and a champion of the Counter-Reformation in Europe: helping to exploit the wealth of the New World, while coercing the Protestantism of the Old; helping to win the Thirty Years War for Catholicism; and ultimately climbing off the back of a declining Spain and Holy Roman Empire into very much the same kind of leadership in Europe that Louis XIV aspired to at the beginning of the eighteenth century.

At Westminster the Yorkist sympathies of his immediate predecessors would have insured for Abbot Islip the royal patronage. Richard had already proved himself the lavish founder of chapels, colleges, chantries and hospitals; his coronation was one of the most spectacular that the Abbey had yet witnessed; and his first wife lay buried within its walls. He had moreover endowed the convent with 'an egle of gold garnysshed with perles and precious stones in which is inclosed the precious relique called the Ampule'; and it is credibly reported, although never proved, that he himself had received from the Yorkist abbot Eastney St Edward's sceptre a week before he was actually made king. Is it then beyond the bounds of reason to suppose that Henry VII's Chapel could still have arisen to house a Yorkist dynasty; while so much that was lost, the Confessor's own shrine and a host of other irreplaceable medieval beauties, might well have survived into our own day? Furthermore Islip would not have been the last abbot to continue the enlargement and beautification of the Abbey; and we should certainly not have had to wait until the eighteenth century for the present far from satisfactory West Front. These things were not to be. Bosworth Field decided once and for all not only that England was to become Protestant, but also that Westminster Abbey would soon be dissolved, stripped of most of its wealth and much of its loveliness; and in its present reconstructed status as College and peculiar, stand forever as the sadly mutilated shell of its former splendours.

But it is now high time that we left the realms of fantasy for those of hard fact.

THE RULE OF JOHN EASTNEY

On the day that Bosworth was lost and won John Eastney ruled at Westminster. He had been elected abbot in August 1474 after first serving the abbey as Prior, Sacrist, domestic treasurer and warden of the *Novum opus* ('New Work'); and like his predecessor was a Yorkist, although playing little or no part in public life. He had, none the less, personally entertained Elizabeth Woodville when, with the little

Duke of York, she had fled to Westminster for sanctuary in 1482; and welcomed her back to the abbot's house, Cheynegates, after her restoration to the full rights of Queen-Dowager in 1486. The house was leased to her for forty years; yet within a few months she had once again suffered a turn of fortune's wheel, and retired to end her days in the abbey of Bermondsey. However, in the palmy days of 1479 she had shown her gratitude by securing to the abbey a royal charter for endowing the new Chapel of Erasmus with the rents from the manors of Cradley and Hadley in Worcestershire. In this Chapel two monks daily sang masses for the souls of Edward IV and his queen, whose anniversaries were further celebrated by a distribution to the poor of 240 pennies. Any residue remaining from the rents, after these tasks had been duly accomplished, was divided among the monks themselves.

Eastney, whose main preoccupation had always been the fabric of the church, retained, even when he became abbot, the important officers of Sacrist and Warden of the *Novum opus* in his own hands— an example to be imitated by his successors—and vigorously carried on the construction of the Nave where Abbot Millyng had left off. John Felix later wrote of him: 'In his care for the House of Israel he provided that the building of the minster should go forward; so that both the vaultings of the new work, that is, both the higher and the lower vaultings, together with the great window over the west door, were fully completed while he was yet alive.'

To Eastney in fact, during his twenty-six years as warden of the new work, we owe not only the roofing of the Nave and most of the vaulting, which is its chief glory, but also the great west window and the flying buttresses and battlements; much of which he paid for out of his own pocket. In all he spent something like £4,400 on the 'new work', and at his death left a deficit of £600, which the next abbot, George Fascet, made good as an act of piety for his predecessor's soul. Fascet, a man of means, likewise gave further large sums, totalling about £10,000 in terms of our present inflated currency, towards the continued prosecution of the building.

Eastney, the Yorkist, had naturally been somewhat out of favour with the new king, Henry VII, at whose coronation the Yeomen of the Guard appeared for the first time, and where the Lancastrian bishops of Exeter and Ely took the place of their Yorkist brethren of Durham and Bath and Wells. Neither was Henry a friend to the 'sanctuary men', for whom Eastney was responsible; and when the King learned in the autumn of 1492 that twelve convicts had escaped from the abbot's prison at Westminster, he took the opportunity of mulcting the abbey of a thousand marks, the last instalments of which were not paid off until 1497.

Eastney's reign is memorable in other ways. He obtained from the Pope an indulgence whereby, as happened after his own election, future abbots-elect were exempted from visiting Rome for their confirmation upon the payment of one hundred florins. At the same time the monks of Westminster were granted the privilege of being ordained to the priesthood upon reaching the age of one and twenty.

It was Eastney too rather than Islip, as Stow believed, who patronized William Caxton. Caxton, whose father lived in Westminster, was connected with the London mercers; and first came to set up his printing press within the precincts of the Abbey, where a relation, Richard Caxton, was a monk, in 1476. From then until 1500 he, and later his assistant and successor Wynkyn de Worde, occupied a shop near the Chapter House. It was not until 1482/3 that he took over premises in the Almonry itself and set up his famous sign of the Red Pale there, while still retaining his original establishment. Another shop later rented by him may have been either under the Chapel of St Edmund or that of St Nicholas, thus giving rise to the well-known term 'chapel' in the printing trade. No doubt one of the reasons why he originally settled near the Chapter House was the presence there of Parliament. This ensured him a constant flow of wealthy customers, possibly even of royalty itself, passing close to his door. The first books printed here are described as 'emprynted by me William Caxton in thabbey of Westminster'; but after the removal to the Almonry they were simply designated 'at Westminster'. Caxton himself exhorted his friends 'to come to Westmonester in the Almonestrye at the reed pale'. Eastney, himself a man of learning who collected ancient manuscripts, had in his capacity as Sacrist first let the shop to Caxton; later he provided him with additional accommodation at the Almonry; and finally, as abbot, allowed him to adorn Chaucer's grave with a leaden tablet complete with epitaph. They seem to have been close friends; for in the Prologue to *Eneydos* the printer tells us that it was 'my lord abbot of Westmynster [who in 1490 had shown him] certayn evydences wryton in olde englysshe for to reduce it in our englysshe now usid. And certaynly it was wreton in such wyse that it was more like to dutche than englysshe. I coude not reduce ne brynge it to be understonden.'

But, alas, there is little evidence that the monastery itself ever made any use of this new invention; and certainly it never honoured the great printer in any way. He died in 1491 and lies buried not in the Abbey but at St Margaret's.

WESTMINSTER'S CLAIM AS BURIAL PLACE OF KINGS

King Henry VI had been a regular visitor to Westminster Abbey; and, after rejecting a suggestion that his father, Henry V, might be moved a little to make room for his own tomb with the words: 'Nay, let hym alone, he lieth lyke a nobell prince, I wolle not trouble him', eventually had his burial place marked out with a pick for him by the abbey mason, John Thirske, between the tomb of the Confessor and that of Henry III. Some twenty years later Henry was murdered in the Tower and his body hastily buried at Chertsey Abbey. However, he would not lie quiet in his grave. The story ran that miracles were being wrought at his tomb; so Richard had him moved to Windsor; but the tales continued to grow in volume and e'er long a cult of the saintly Henry sprang up, spread and flourished in all parts of the country, particularly in the East and North. 'Images of him were set up in the churches and lights burnt before them. New gilds were founded in his honour.' The crafty Tudor decided therefore to cash in on the sanctity and popularity of his Lancastrian predecessor. He made it known that he intended to secure his uncle's official canonization and to build a shrine-chapel at Windsor for the housing of his body. Immediately both the abbeys of Chertsey and Westminster decided to contest Windsor's claim to the royal corpse; and early in 1498 the latter petitioned the King *pro corpore beati viri Henrici Sexti*. At the subsequent judicial inquiry before the Lord Chancellor and Privy Council Westminster was represented by George Fascet the Prior and John Islip the Monk-Bailiff, who had been a member of Gray's Inn since 1492. Windsor's strongest argument lay in the actual possession of the body, which was regarded as nine-tenths of the law; Chertsey's in its brutal removal from their precincts, although it was unkindly alleged by his enemies that the Abbot himself had assisted at its exhumation with his own fair hands; but Westminster alone could show that she had been Henry's own choice. Furthermore it was pleaded that this Abbey had long been the burial place of kings—conveniently forgetting the recent cases of Edward IV and Richard III—and, since the Palace was so closely and clearly associated with the convent, Henry might even be considered a parishioner. Eventually judgement was given at Greenwich on 5 March 1498 in favour of Westminster; and during the following May Abbot Eastney died. He was succeeded by Fascet, who promptly agreed to pay the King £500 to cover the expense both of the necessary papal licence and also 'for the removal of the illustrious King Henry VI from Windsor to the monastery of the Blessed Peter, Westminster'. The money was paid over and the licence was granted; but apparently the translation never took place, despite Widmore's assertion, based on Stow's evidence, that it did. Even he, however, was forced to admit: 'in what part of the church the body was deposited I have not discovered'.

Henry VII had originally secured leave from the papacy to dissolve the two small religious houses of Mottesfont and Luffield in order to erect 'a stately monument' to the saint at Windsor. Now, on applying for his canonization, he obtained fresh grants for the dissolution of these and other houses for building a chapel at Westminster instead. In his Will drawn up in 1509 the King re-asserted his intention 'right shortely to translate . . . the bodie and reliques of our uncle of blessed memorie King Henry VIth'; but the Pope was demanding so exorbitant a price for the canonization that it shocked the parsimonious soul of the Tudor to its very depths. He therefore decided to delay it, along with the removal of the body to Westminster, until the new shrine was ready. Before that had come to pass Henry VII was dead, and his successor, whose title to the throne was much more secure than that of his father, never showed any real interest in the canonization, and harboured very different ideas in his mind respecting the Chapel. It was, of course, quite impossible for the abbey to shoulder all the expense alone; and so the translation of the royal corpse was tacitly abandoned. What became of the splendid tomb, for which Henry VII had paid sixty pounds to a certain Master Esterfelde to construct for his uncle, is now anybody's guess. None the less the building of the Chapel itself continued and prospered.

When George Fascet was elected to the abbacy he was already a chronic invalid, and soon found himself compelled to retire permanently to the convent Infirmary, where he died in September 1500. During his brief tenure of office he had continued his predecessor's policy of retaining the Wardenship of the *Novum opus* in his own hands, but was unable to do more personally than to give it a most welcome financial fillip. The actual supervision of the renewed building of the Nave fell upon the shoulders of the prior, John Islip, who also acted as abbot during Fascet's long illness.

JOHN ISLIP ELECTED ABBOT, 1500

On 27 October 1500, however, his labours were rewarded when the forty-odd monks then present in the Chapter House unanimously elected him abbot, *per viam Spiritus Sancti*; and Dr Richard Rawlyns preached upon the text: 'Instead of thy fathers thou shalt have children, whom thou mayest make princes.' Islip himself accepted this honourable but arduous post with genuine reluctance, being 'unwilling to resist the divine will' and 'at the urgent request of the Chapter of the said monastery and its proctors'. He was installed the following 25 November, and afterwards gave a banquet to the whole of the convent which cost him £4. 13s. 7d. The very next Christmas Day he feasted his monks once again at his manor house of Neyte, but for nearly double that sum. The menu for this gargantuan meal has been preserved and reads as follows: 'Two oxon 13s. 4d. each, 17 sheep at 1s. 6d. each, nine pigs at 2s. each, 27 geese and 23 capons.' The dessert alone ran to £2. 6s. 8d., a very large sum for those days. John Islip was born on 10 June 1464, at the little village of Islip in Oxfordshire, whose manor had been conferred on Westminster by its founder, Edward the Confessor. We know more of him than of most of his immediate predecessors, since from 1492, when twenty-eight years of age, he kept a diary in which he also incorporated some details of his earlier life, although he tells us little of his parents and family beyond the undoubted fact that in 1496 he was paying 13s. 4d. quarterly for the board and education of a sister, Agnes; and, at the same time, provided her with shoes and gaiters for a further shilling. It has indeed been suggested that he was a bastard of the Giles family; but this is based on nothing more than the knowledge that as abbot he founded a chapel at Westminster dedicated to the saint of that name. In all probability he received his earliest education from the chantry priest of his native village, who introduced him either to some monastic official or possibly to the Abbot himself while on a visit to the manor, as a promising candidate for the cloister. Islip entered the monastery on 21 March 1480 under the auspices of Abbot Eastney, who was responsible for bringing him to Westminster in the first place, and was to prove his good friend, ultimately exercising the deepest influence on his character and career. For six years—the usual period of the novitiate was seven—he studied under the novice master, was professed and finally ordained priest in his twenty-second year.

He celebrated his first mass on 1 January 1486. This celebration was one of the four most important occasions in an ordinary monk's life, the other three being: his first appearance as a junior, his first day as president in the refectory, and his death. It was the custom at the time to send one out of every twenty of the Westminster monks to Gloucester Hall (now Worcester College) in Oxford, where quite a number of them proceeded to degrees in divinity. In 1499 the convent also started a connexion with Buckingham College (now Magdalene) at Cambridge, when a certain Thomas Gardener, after two years' residence as 'scolaris studens Oxon', appeared in the monastic treasurer's accounts as 'studens Oxon et Cantebrig'; and by 1533/4 there were several more 'studentes Cantabrigie'. Henry VII, out of

various estates he had given to the monastery, paid for the maintenance of at least three such Cambridge students; while the known
preference of his mother, Lady Margaret, Countess of Derby and
Richmond, one of Westminster's most lavish benefactresses, for the
University of Cambridge, would have further helped to modify the
previous addiction to Oxford. None the less it was to the Oxford
scholars that the monastery still turned for its preachers on Palm
Sunday and Good Friday, the two principal days of the year for
sermons in Benedictine houses. Islip himself did not receive a
university education. Possibly by the end of the fifteenth century it
was considered more profitable from the point of view of monastic
administration to be trained as a common- rather than a canon-
lawyer.

In 1487 he became Eastney's domestic chaplain, a recognized
monastic springboard and a post approximating to that of a modern
bishop's secretary, which was designed of course to prove a searching
test of his abilities and capabilities. Such a chaplain must always be
'polite, discreet and pleasant, especially to strangers'; and forever
seek, as the main link between them, 'to foster the love of the
abbot to the convent and that of the convent to the abbot'. His professional duties would also entail the celebration of masses in the
abbot's private chapel, and the general regulation of his household.
Other offices were now quickly showered upon him in preparation for
the highest; which included those of Sub-Almoner, whose main
responsibilities lay with the children of the Almonry and the song-
children, the wardenship of the manors and churches, the treasury-
ship, and the post of the abbot's own receiver and cellarer, all of
which, except the last, he resigned upon his election as prior in 1498.

Probably the most interesting was that of the wardenship of the
manors and churches, since they necessitated regular tours of the
various monastic properties and appropriations belonging to Westminster. Attended by a substantial retinue he would ride from one
country manor to another, usually spending a night at each, collect
the rent and inspect the church, chantry chapel or other religious
buildings. Such travels had their dangers; and Islip recorded in his
diary a tale told him many years later by a guest, Richard Dolande,
one Sunday night at the Abbot's table. It dealt with a murderous
assault on an abbey official at a lonely inn, which in its details
closely resembled that of the famous attack on Gerard and Denys
by 'the abbot' and his band at the Burgundian roadside auberge, as
described by Charles Reade in *The Cloister and the Hearth*. The
servants of the priest in question, while stabling their horses, discovered two corpses under the straw; but the innkeeper's wife spun
a convincing story and the travellers retired uneasily to bed. In the

middle of the night the landlord, with a gang of eleven men, broke into the priest's bedroom and threatened him with instant death. However, he secured permission first to shrive his servants, who were sleeping elsewhere; and together they rounded on their foes, fought desperately, drove them off, and went unharmed on their way. Islip could easily have been that man, as he well knew, and so he used thoughtfully to provide his servant, Robert Seston, with arrows at a cost of 3d.

HENRY VII's LADY CHAPEL

This year [wrote Stow in *The Annales*] the chappell of our ladie, above the east end of the high altar of Westminster Church with also a taverne neere adioyning called the white rose, were taken downe: in the which place or plot of ground, on 24 January 1502/3, the first stone of our Lady Chappell was laid by the hands of Joh. Islip abbot of the same monastery, sir Reginald Bray, knight of the Garter, Doctor Barons master of the Roles, doctor Wall chaplaine to the king, master Hugh Oldham chaplaine to the Countess of Derby and Richmond the king's mother, sir Ed. Stanhope knight and divers other.

Ten years later the whole structure was complete, apart from the bronze effigies of Henry VII and his queen, which Peter Torrigiano had been commissioned to make. In his Will, drawn up on his death-bed, Henry explained his reasons for building this chapel: it was first to honour the Virgin, on whose 'high Aultre' would stand 'the greatest image of Our Lady that we now have in our Juelhouse', together with 'a crosse of plate of gold upon tymber to the value of C lb'; secondly, as a tomb for himself, his queen and his descendants; and finally as an honourable resting place for his saintly uncle, Henry VI, a project never realized. He ordered it to be 'painted, garnished and adorned in as goodly and rich a manner as such work requireth and as to a king's work apperteyneth'. Expense was no object. Henry himself gave £3,000, paid in instalments, followed by another £5,000 in his Will. This last was mainly for the furnishings. The Lady Margaret likewise poured out her wealth upon 'oure chapell of Westminster'. In all, according to Holinshed and Stow, the total cost was in the region of £14,000, a vast sum for those days.

The Tudor had expected to be buried in a black and white marble tomb, garnished with bronze statues and the kneeling effigies of his wife and himself, which would stand in 'a closure of metall in manner of a chapell [i.e. a chantry] itself established in the myddes of the same chapel before the high aultier'. But his son and successor 'mis-liked' the plan, relegated his father and mother to the east end, and buried them in a sepulchre designed not by the Englishmen, Ymber, Drawswerd and Vertue, but by the Florentine, Peter Torrigiano, who accepted the contract in 1512 and completed the work some six years later. For this he was paid £1,500. It is said that Henry VIII wished to preserve the central position in the Chapel for himself and appropriate the whole building to his own memory rather than to that of his sire. With this end no doubt in view he commissioned Torrigiano to construct an even larger tomb for himself at a cost of £2,000. It was never finished; and in the event Harry lies with his favourite wife, Jane Seymour, at Windsor. None the less Torrigiano did go on to build the altar and also the tomb of Margaret of Richmond. Hacket later described his creations as looking 'like ye work, not of moderns, but of Bezaleel'. It is not known for certain who was the architect of Henry VII's Chapel. Very possibly it was Robert Vertue, the King's senior mason and the designer of Greenwich Palace. William Bolton, Prior of St Bartholomew's, Smithfield, was the master of the works, and Abbot Islip acted in the capacity of general supervisor of the whole operation. Henry had written in his Will: 'We will that . . . the said chapel be decked and the windows glazed with stone, images, badges, and "cognaissaunts" as is by us readily devised and in picture delivered to the Prior of St Bartholo-mew, master of the works of the said chapel.'

One of the consequences of pulling down the old Lady Chapel was the exhumation of Henry V's queen, Katherine, who lay buried there. Her wooden coffin, wrapped in lead from the roof, was placed on the floor in her husband's chantry chapel, where it re-mained on view for the next two hundred and seventy-four years.

Besides contributing lavishly towards the building and furnishing of their chapel, Henry VII and his mother provided funds for its maintenance. Three new monks were added to the foundation for the express purpose of saying weekly masses in the chapel, who had to be either bachelors or doctors of divinity from Oxford or Cam-bridge. Furthermore on the King's anniversary every priest in the convent was expected to say a mass of requiem, including special collects, and every lay brother recite the psalter of David or our Lady. These celebrants were well paid; and fees were also given 'to the lords chancellor and treasurer, to the chiefs of the law, to the lord mayor, the recorder and sheriffs of London', provided they attended these celebrations. Any surplus was distributed in the prisons. Besides Westminster some nineteen other monastic and collegiate foundations performed similar devotions in return for similar fees. The expenses of all these devotional and charitable

works, including an almshouse for thirteen poor men established at
the abbey, were met from the proceeds of a number of dissolved
religious houses, which amounted to at least £21,000. Lady Margaret, who died in the Abbot's House on 29 June 1509, also endowed
a chantry for herself, where from Easter 1505 a weekly mass was said
for the good of her soul, for which the celebrant received 3s. 4d. Her
Will ordered the abbot to 'make in the chapel a convenient tomb,
and one altar or two in the same chapel for two chantry masses there
perpetually to be said'.

In startling contrast with this new Lady Chapel, which he was
building with all the glorious elaborations and fan tracery of the
fashionable perpendicular style, Islip continued and finished the
Nave in accordance with that severely plain Norman plan first
drawn up in the thirteenth century; thus preserving the unity and
harmony of its whole length. Hacket wrote of him that 'he enlarged
the length of the church at his own cost', implying that Islip alone
was responsible for the Nave, which he had paid for out of his own
pocket. This was quite untrue. The cost was borne by the funds
of the *Novum opus*, and Islip was only finishing off what Eastney,
Fascet and their predecessors had begun. None the less his was
certainly 'the glory of its completion'.

During his thirty years wardenship of the *Novum opus* he spent
£3,500 on this work. It was slow work, since he was engaged on so
much other building besides, which included, in addition to the
Lady Chapel, the Jericho Parlour and other chambers in the
courtyard of Cheynegates, the chantry chapel known as the Jesus
Chapel where he now lies buried, and the reconstruction of the
Chancel at St Margaret's, Westminster, which cost £191. 11s. 1½d.
Most of this last sum was found by the abbey, although the parishioners did contribute among them some £30. The work on the
Nave fell into four main periods: from 1500 to 1506 Islip finished
the roofing and vaulting; from 1506 to 1510 he glazed the windows
and washed the walls; during the next six years the floor was paved
and the second storey of the North Tower prepared to receive its
bells; and finally from 1524 to 1548 he had those stone screens carved,
bearing his rebus, that originally divided the chapels from one
another under the Western Towers. The Nave itself was now
complete; but the Abbot continued to press on with the Towers,
overspending his income and dying before he could finish them. In
Islip's Obituary Roll, indeed, the Towers are shown as perfect; but
this was no more than wishful thinking. They had in fact to wait for
Hawksmoor and the eighteenth century for their building.

The Jesus Chapel, which was ready two years before his death, contained both upper and lower compartments, whose furnishings and

H

decorations were profusely adorned with the Abbot's arms. It boasted 'a payer of organys with a corten of lynen cloth to cover them'.

After Islip's death in 1532 all work on the Abbey practically came to an end. The last entry in the Sacrist's roll reads: 'Item for paynted peeces sett in the west wyndowe and some coloryd glass in other wyndowes . . . xiid.'

ISLIP'S GOOD STEWARDSHIP

At the time of his election as abbot the convent was in serious financial difficulties. There were the royal subsidies to be paid annually and a 5 per cent. tax on the incomes of the various monastic offices; tithes were decreasing alarmingly and a payment of 50s. from the royal exchequer to provide the candles at Edward I's tomb ended in 1497, not to be renewed until 1514; and, perhaps most disturbing of all, the offerings at the different altars had dropped from a total of £48 in 1496 to a mere £36 four years later. However, Islip was not discouraged and firmly refused either to economize or to reduce the monastic duties. In fact the number of masses increased during the early period of his rule, 48,000 'breads' were purchased between 1500 and 1504, and there was a considerable outlay on the repair or renewal of vestments, lamps and ornaments. His courage was more than justified. The rents from the Westminster properties rose, the offerings at the burials of Henry VII and his mother amounted to at least £170 and the oblations at the subsequent coronation of Henry VIII and Katharine of Aragon totalled another £47.

The Tudor's funeral, like that of his wife six years earlier; was a solemn and sumptuous affair. 'On the 9 of Maie [wrote Stow] he was brought to Paules with many knights and gentlemen and 1,000 torches, and from thence on the next morrow conveied to Westminster, and there buried in the new chappell which he had caused to be builded with the charges of 14,000l on the 11 of Maie.' Islip and Henry VII had been close friends. They worked amicably together in drawing up the plans for the new chapel, for the canonization of Henry VI, and the translation of his body to the abbey. The King was frequently to be found at Cheynegates or Neyte, where he was sumptuously entertained. In 1501, for example, the abbot's Steward noted that 'the Kingis grace dyned at Cheyngate', when, because it happened to fall on a meatless Friday, the cost was kept down to 17s. 4d. Even so the feast was made as splendid as possible with wine and strawberries (3s. 8d.), a barrel of strong ale (2s.) and a 'potell of wyne for to Sowse ffysche wt' (4d.). Henry was also supplied with some of the famous Westminster marrow-bone puddings. The 1501 household accounts record: 'ii marybons for ii podyngis for the Kyng' (2d.).

The King for his part regularly sent the Abbot two tuns of choice wine per annum. As a further mark of his esteem he appointed Islip treasurer of the Savoy Hospital, which was then being built; and at one time, 1512, there was as much as £10,000 in sealed money-bags lying within the Chapter House. Three years later, after rendering a full account of his stewardship, the Abbot withdrew from this particular task. Certainly his links with Henry's son and successor were never as close and intimate as they had been with his father; and although, unlike his immediate predecessors, Islip played some part in public affairs during this reign, yet he remained sufficiently in the background and on the fringe of important events both in Church and State to escape the destruction that engulfed so many who were more deeply involved. By so doing he probably saved Westminster from the utter ruin that befell other equally great and ancient abbeys. The King indeed always found him a faithful and willing servant, and employed him in a number of minor capacities. As a Privy Councillor and in the House of Lords he was active in forwarding the royal policies; in the legal field he became trier of petitions for the whole realm, dealt with the cases of poor men in the Star Chamber, and was on the Commission of Peace for Middlesex; and he was nominated a member of some minor diplomatic missions. He met the Scotch ambassadors in 1516; some four years later helped to 'enterteign' the French envoys at Westminster, when he took them on a conducted tour of Henry VII's Chapel and the Savoy Hospital; and he was one of those privy councillors sent to visit the Princess Mary at Richmond, who reported: 'she is right merry and in prosperous health and state, daily exercising herself in virtuous pastimes'. The Abbot presented her with some of his famous marrow puddings.

In 1522 Islip, together with his brother abbots of Bury, Canterbury and Bermondsey, was in attendance on Cardinal Wolsey at Dover in order to greet the arrival of the Emperor Charles V. Other public duties undertaken by the Abbot of Westminster at this time included the collection of a loan from Middlesex for the French War in 1524, membership of the Commission for Sewers in an area stretching from East Greenwich to Gravesend, and the fitting out of a warship, the *Kateryn Fortileza*, to assist in the blockade of Brest—a striking illustration of the fact that a sixteenth-century abbot was expected to do a great deal more than simply to pray and worship, and direct the religious exercises of his own particular monastery.

In the matter of Henry VIII's divorce no one could have been more accommodating. As a lawyer he was primarily concerned with the legality or otherwise of Pope Julius II's original dispensation that had permitted the marriage between Henry and his brother's widow; and which now, in agreement with the eight so-called impartial universities, Islip and his fellow lawyers declared to be null and void. Furthermore he was one of those who set their signatures to a petition from the House of Lords requesting Pope Clement VII to pronounce a divorce 'if it can be granted with justice'. Wolsey employed him to do some legal research into the documents; and he was present in Court when, under a papal commission issued to cardinals Wolsey and Campeggio, the King and Queen were cited to appear before them on 31 May 1529; and again on the following 18 June when Katharine attended in person to protest. Indeed at this stage in his career he was so much in the royal favour that in July Henry suggested to the Pope, who stood in mortal dread of the Emperor's wrath, that he should allow the Archbishop of Canterbury and the Abbot of Westminster, 'a good old father', finally to determine the matter. But Islip's fortunes and those of his convent were very largely bound up with Wolsey's, with whom he had long been on the closest and friendliest of terms.

WOLSEY

Wolsey had originally been introduced to Islip by Sir Reginald Bray, a favourite of Henry VII, whose chaplain Wolsey then was. From then onwards they worked very closely together until the Cardinal's downfall. They were, for instance, both deeply concerned about the economic revolution that was turning so much cultivated land into pasture, causing unemployment and depopulation, and reducing rents, tithes and money values generally. Westminster, in particular, could ill afford such losses. The royal exchequer was all the time pressing very hard upon the abbey for loans and grants for the French Wars; and Islip personally, like the Archbishop of Canterbury, had to contribute a loan of £1,000, besides his full share of the annual grant levied upon the whole spirituality of the kingdom. On the other hand a princely loan he had himself made to the Earl of Shrewsbury out of the kindness of his heart, showed every appearance of becoming a bad debt. The Earl would send him an annual present of venison, but no money!

The Cardinal and Abbot were likewise agreed on the need to suppress the alarming growth of heresy; while at the same time anxious to reform both the monasteries and the secular clergy. In 1525 Islip was deputed by Wolsey to inquire into the affairs of Glastonbury Abbey, where he secured the election of the Cardinal's nominee, Richard Whiting, in succession to Abbot Bere. Later as Visitor to the London and Midland district of the General Council of the Benedictines he displayed an equally commendable reforming zeal; and when eventually he became its President in 1527 instructed the Abbot of Gloucester to conduct an investigation into the affairs of Malmesbury, where there had recently been something very like a rebellion of the monks against their head. Neither was he averse to similar visitations in his own monastery of Westminster, although, of course, it was exempt from all but papal jurisdiction.

On 15 November 1515 Wolsey's cardinal's hat was borne through London, attended by the Lord Mayor and aldermen on horseback and the City Guilds on foot, to Westminster Abbey, where it rested on the high altar until the following Sunday, when a ceremony took place 'as I have not seen the like', wrote Cavendish, 'unlesse it hath bin at the coronation of a mighty prince'. Three archbishops, eight bishops and eight abbots assisted at the service; while eighteen temporal lords, led by the Dukes of Norfolk and Suffolk, conducted the Cardinal back to York Place afterwards. John Colet, Dean of St Paul's, preached the sermon on the not inappropriate subject of humility. Cardinals, he reminded his audience, like Christ, came not to be ministered unto but to minister; and added 'whosoever shall exalt himself shall be abased'. However, on this splendid and auspicious occasion it was not the Cardinal but the Archbishop of Canterbury who was humbled, since it was noticed that as Warham passed down the Nave of the Abbey no cross was borne before him; and never again was so carried in Wolsey's presence. The new Cardinal on the other hand insisted on walking behind two of them, one to mark him as a cardinal and the other as an archbishop. But a semblance of decency was more or less observed while Wolsey 'lay grovelling' before the High Altar and the Archbishop pronounced the final prayers and benediction. He then rose and had the hat placed upon his head.

After he became legate in 1518 Wolsey made a visitation of Westminster, although no trace of this nor subsequent visits of his remain among the abbey muniments. In February 1521/2 he summoned all the Benedictine abbots and priors to meet him in Chapter at Westminster in order to discuss the reformation of their houses. Then, according to Polydore Vergil, *pour courager les autres*, the Cardinal again visited the convent with a great show of severity that was only relaxed after a sufficiently high bribe had been forthcoming. Be this as it may, it must have been about this date that an amazing document came into his hands, which was to be the harbinger of much that later delighted the eyes and ears of Thomas Cromwell's

Royal Commissioners and, whether true or false, supplied the King with the ammunition he needed to shoot down the monasteries.

Its author, one of the Westminster monks, is unknown by name, but his grievances cover the years around 1518 when William Mane was prior; and his petition is entitled: *A Supplicacon of a monk of Westm' to ye beshop of Rome*. He had, apparently, been accused by the Prior of robbing him of 'lii lib of plate'. Mane took his complaint to the abbot then 'lyeng at Hendon'; and subsequently the defendant, according to his own version, 'was ffet owt of my chamber by Dane John Chorysshe then being his chaplain which brought me unto the prior, which prior commandyd me unto ward in a sertayn chamber where I dyd contynue withowte bed ... untyll the commnyg hom of the Abbot'. He stoutly denied the charge and claimed that he had the plate 'by the deth of my father'; but had to remain in prison while the prior tried to provide 'dew prove thereof'. This he was quite unable to do; whereupon

they beyng ashamed of the sayd slander the abbot cam unto me and sayd Brother A.B. wyll you put this matter unto my handis and I promise yew I shall se yow have a great mense made. And forbycause I was under his obedience I was content so to do, but as yet I had never nothyng but toke by that means a great and greavous sykenesse, at which tym of sycknesse it cam unto my lot to syng the chapter masse, but beyng dyseasyd durst not nor could not take it upon me, but yet wt compulcion he cawsyd me to do it, so it fortuned the sayd day at masse at the Gospell tyme by the reason of sycnesse so takyn to be so sycke that I sownyd at the Auter where at they were fayn to cut my gyrdell to revyve me, so that after masse as sone as I cam in to the revestery I was compelled to vomyt. . . . And after that toke a sycnesse which held me iiij yeres. And where as ther is a howse cawlyd the farmary to kepe syck men in to the which ther is a lowyd i lib by the yere to be put to that use ... every oon beyng sycke iijd by the day wt sertyn fagottis and other thyngis, your sayd suppliant had neither but lay at his owne cost utterly to his undoyng and to the poverysshement of his ffriendis ... But uppon a malyciouse mynd the pryor that now is informyd the abbot so that he sayd openly at the chapter that I was a gret dysoymaler and was no more syck than his horse. Yet he dicharged me there. And so after incontenant wt sutche small comfortis as I had and purchased of my ffrendis I did send for Mr Doctor Yarkeley, doctr. barlet Doctr. ffreman mr Grene Mr Pawle which opynly did prove me to be infected with dyvers sycknesse whereof the lest were able to kyll a Ryht strong man, the Abot heryng of thys comanydy me to ly in

the subchamber and there I lay iii quarteris of a yere and vi weekis
without anny succoure of the howse . . . but had utterly peryeshed
but for my ffrendis.

He concluded this pathetic account of his sufferings by demanding
papal bulls instructing the convent, upon pain of excommunication,
to appoint him to the first vacant benefice in its gift, which must be
worth at least £20, and to give him his portion and monk's pension;
but also to allow him to retain his stall in the Choir and his voice
in the Chapter elections. What Wolsey thought of this particular
effusion is not recorded; but because of a number of such complaints,
admitted by Islip in general terms during some correspondence with
the Cardinal, it is probable that Wolsey visited the abbey for a third
time in 1525. The Abbot himself was an equally ardent reformer,
who conducted visitations at a number of Benedictine houses. At
Malvern, for example, he actually took the drastic step of suspending
the Prior. However, it was not only the regulars whom the Cardinal
and Abbot wished to see disciplined. When Convocation was summoned by the Archbishop of Canterbury to meet at St Paul's on 20
April 1523, Wolsey as legate ordered the clergy to transfer themselves
to Westminster Abbey, where, together with their brethren from the
northern province, they must appear before him in a place and under
a jurisdiction exempt from Warham's authority in order to discuss
their own Reformation. Hall wrote of this episode:

and in this season the Cardinall by his power legantyne dissolved
the convocacion at Paules called by the Archebishop of Cantor-
bury, and called hym and all the clergie to his convocacion to
Westminster, which was never seen before in England . . . whereof master Skelton, a merry poet, wrote,

> Gentle Paule, laie doune thy sweard
> For Peter of Westminster hath shaven thy beard.

In actual fact St Paul's Convocation continued to sit and act until
Parliament had been dissolved; while it is extremely doubtful
whether Wolsey's ever met at all. Certainly there is no record of any
attempt to reform the secular clergy.

In 1526 Islip was appointed by Wolsey to search for heretics
among the Hanseatic merchants; and eventually the Abbot presided
at a trial in his own Chapter House over Hans Ellerdope, who was
accused of having one of Luther's works in his possession. He was
acquitted on the ingenious plea that since he could not read Latin he
had never studied the book in question, which, as he had found it in
someone else's house, he dared not burn, for fear of destroying
another's property. A more famous trial, again in the Chapter

House, before Wolsey himself, was that of Thomas Bilney, which is described at length in Foxe's *Book of Martyrs*; and during the last two years of his life Islip took part in further examinations at the Consistory Court of St Paul's that resulted in the burning of two heretics, Richard Bayfield, an ex-monk of Bury, and John Tewkesbury, a leather seller.

THE WESTMINSTER SANCTUARY

On another matter the two friends were not so well agreed. Islip was a zealous defender of the rights of the Westminster sanctuary, which Wolsey felt were being abused. Sanctuary for treason was not abolished until 1534, and that for debt lingered on to 1623; with the inevitable result that it became a continual source of trouble-making. A good example of this was seen in 1487, when it was rumoured that Henry VII had been defeated at Stoke, and the abbey muniments recorded:

> those who by reason of their crimes enjoy the privileges and immunities of Westminster, being of the opinion that after the commission of any nefarious crime soever they would have the free privilege of returning to that san[c]tuary ... took up arms for the purpose of plundering the houses of those whom they knew to be in the field with us and mustered in a body for the commission of crime.

After the murder of Richard Hunne in the Bishop of London's prison, known as the Lollards' Tower, a case that aroused violent anticlerical feelings throughout the country, one of his gaolers and presumed murderer, Charles Joseph, fled to Westminster for sanctuary; and in 1527 Stubbs, Wolsey's financial agent, gives us an interesting account in a letter of an outbreak of sanctuary men from Westminster with the avowed object of attacking York Place and killing Thomas Cromwell. Another enemy of the Cardinal's, who took refuge there, was the merry poet, Skelton, who had satirized Wolsey's attempts at sanctuary reform in the lines:

> *For all privileged places*
> *He breaks and defaces*
> *All places of religion*
> *He hath them in derision.*

But during the last few years of his life the poet came to terms with the Cardinal and wrote on his side. He lies buried in St Margaret's Church.

No wonder, then, Wolsey was bitter against the sanctuary men;

but it does not appear, legate *a latere* as he now was, that he was ever able to do much about them. He tried to persuade Islip to administer an oath whereby they would swear not to commit either treason or felony inside or outside the sanctuary; but the Abbot coldly informed him that such an undertaking would infringe the very privilege of sanctuary itself. The Cardinal retired baffled, which led his critics to include this proposed reform of 'the abusions of sanctuaries and franchised places' among the many things he had 'begun within the realm' and either 'not finished or else left as dangerous precedents'.

Apart from the sanctuary Islip was also responsible for the Gate-house Prison, which at one time or another housed some very famous men. This was usually profitable, unless prisoners escaped, when the abbot was liable to a very heavy fine.

As Islip had enjoyed the fruits of Wolsey's friendship, so he found himself entangled in his downfall. The statute of Praemunire, which was used against the Cardinal, seemed equally likely to entrap the Abbot.

> Nevertheless [ran one of the accusations] John Abbot of the monastery of St Peter Westminster little weighing the said statute, verily indeed setting it at naught, scheming and seeking after the said Cardinal in all his evil deeds, joined himself to him in a fuller and more extravagant use of his said powers and pretended lega-tine authority, and took him as his guide and almost as his tutor and gradually undermined the laws of this realm and at last almost extinguished the same, with the result that the aforesaid Cardinal bore himself the more loftily and insolently in his legatine state and dignity. Upon a day at Westminster the said Abbot submitted himself to the Cardinal and accepted and approved the several legatine faculties and professed obedience to the same cardinal and promised it by a binding oath. And also he promised him the annates of his exempt monastery right up to the Feast of the Annunciation, 20 Henry VIII, and caused him to be paid in full at Westminster. And so the said Abbot abetted the said Cardinal in his contempt of the king.

None the less Henry graciously extended his pardon to this minor offender, the 'good old father'; although at the same time he took the opportunity of plundering the abbey of its houses in Whitehall, where his new palace was rapidly going up, in exchange for the far less valuable Priory of Poughley in Berkshire. Thomas Cromwell, who had by now transferred his allegiance and services from Wolsey to the King, became closely associated with Islip in the details of this transaction. Together they paid out £1,100 as compensation to the evicted Whitehall tenants; but Cromwell, as always, did not neglect his own opportunities, and by 1531 the convent had been enveigled into paying him an annual bribe, 'a fee granted to him for the term of his natural life'. For his part the Abbot was at least partially restored to the royal favour, and during his last two years held the office of royal chaplain. He died in his manor house of Neyte on 12 May 1532, where his body lay in state for four days. It was then carried to Westminster Abbey escorted by his monks and followed by such a multitude of Londoners that his train stretched from Neyte to Tothill Street, filling the whole roadway between Chelsea and the Abbey. The Abbot of Bury officiated both at the burial in the newly built Jesus Chapel and at the mass of requiem the following day, when the sermon was preached by the Bishop of Croydon. The ceremony has been described as follows:

> The Dirige began, solemnly sung by the said monastery, and divers Diriges done in other places of the church; which being done with the other ceremonies, the morners with thother departid unto a place over the Chappell of the defuncte, where was prepared for them spiced breade, suckett, marmylade, spiced plate, and dyversse sourts of wines plentie. And in the mean ceason they of the Churche did burye the defuncte in the said Chappell of his buyldynge. . . . Then in the choir underneath the herse was made a presentation of the corpse covered with a cloth of gold tyshew . . . which being done every man departed for that night.

It was truly the funeral of the Middle Ages; for Islip, *felix opportunate mortis*, was not three days in his grave before Convocation had agreed not to enact canons without the royal consent, and on the very day of the burial Sir Thomas More, one of the Abbot's oldest and closest friends, relinquished the Great Seal. It was the beginning of the Reformation.

Islip's obituary roll, the brief in which his death was to be announced to other monasteries, was probably decorated by Holbein in person. It contains some exquisite drawings, the most interesting of which is that of the Abbot himself surrounded by flowers characterizing the chief spiritual and theological virtues. In his right hand he holds the lily of piety, while his left grasps the rose of love. 'We see him,' wrote Stanley, 'standing amidst the "slips" or branches of the bower of moral virtues, which, according to the fashion of the fifteenth century, indicate his name.'

Islip's motto had been, 'Seek peace and ensue it.' It was, perhaps, his principal characteristic.

7

Dissolution and Revival

THE last days of the abbey were unpleasantly squalid and quite unworthy of the traditions of so great a convent. Islip's death was followed by a long vacancy, during which John Fulwell, the confidant and right-hand man of the late Abbot, ruled the monastery. He had celebrated his first mass in 1508/9, and was appointed Treasurer, Monk-Bailiff and Archdeacon in 1528. As Islip's chaplain he had busied himself with the furnishings of Henry VII's Chapel, and as Archdeacon had conducted an inquiry into the boundaries of St Botolph's parish in Aldersgate; while he further attracted notice as a member of the deputation that officially waited upon Henry VIII in order to notify him of the Abbot's death. He was also Thomas Cromwell's friend and spy; and, as such, wrote to him on 16 October 1532: 'all things within the sanctuary, as well within the monastery as without, are in due order, according to the advertisement you gave me when I was last with you in London. At your return I trust you shall not hear but that we shall deserve the king's most gracious favour in our suit.' Judging from this letter Fulwell was confidently expecting that his not inconsiderable services would be rewarded by the abbacy. In this he was grievously disappointed; and had to rest content instead with the promise of the Priory of Worcester as soon as it should fall vacant, which did not in fact occur until after his death in 1535/6.

He never entered the King's mind as Islip's successor at Westminster; for Henry was thinking solely in terms of a man utterly servile to himself, a stranger to the convent, who could be relied upon to pave the way for its easy surrender. Such a prelate was eventually found in William Benson or Boston, an obscure monk of Peterborough, who as a Cambridge University doctor had already voted against the validity of Henry VIII's marriage to Katharine of Aragon; and was later to tell his prisoner, Sir Thomas More, when the latter declared it to be against his conscience to acknowledge the Royal Supremacy, 'that he had cause to fear that his mind was erroneous, when he saw the Great Council of the Realm determine contrary to his mind, and therefore he ought to change his mind'.

For three hundred years, ever since the death of William Humez in 1222, the convent had chosen its own abbot out of its own Chapter; but now a total stranger was to be thrust upon it, and one moreover whose sole interest in his new home was to reap whatever personal advantage might accrue to himself from his exalted position. His very preferment reeks of simony. Immediately after his installation he paid over the large sum of £661. 13s. 4d. to Cromwell, then Keeper of the Royal Jewels, and to Sir William Pawlet, Controller of the King's House; the balance of which, some £500, he secured by the mortgaging of the three best monastic manors belonging to the abbot's portion.

Boston took oath as Abbot of Westminster in the Court of Chancery on 12 May 1533 between the hours of nine and ten in the morning, to perform all the duties appertaining to Henry VII's foundation; so his reign may be said to have commenced from that date. Yet from the very first, as his correspondence fully discloses, he bound himself hand and foot to the chariot wheels of the King's new Vicar-General. Cromwell was appointed to various offices within the monastery, including those of Janitor, Keeper of the Gatehouse Prison and Steward. He was also granted, along with Anne Boleyn, her father, Sir Thomas, Sir Thomas Audley and William Butt the court physician, the advowsons of rich abbey livings: and his orders for the gradual and subtle disintegration of the convent from within were faithfully, if not obsequiously, carried out. These last empowered Boston to seize upon and concentrate all the chief reins of government within the abbey, and the administration of its property without, in his own hands; to encourage his monks to absent themselves from the monastery for an indefinite period, thereby giving them a taste for freedom and worldly pursuits: 'ad honestam animi et corporis sui recreationem'; and to welcome noble ladies to his house and table. The abbot and convent were also freed from the obligation to read or even attend the divinity lectures delivered at the greater festivals and on the royal anniversaries.

Some two years later Cromwell's Commissioners, Dr Thomas Legh and Dr John ap Rice, unlikeable in their narrow-minded legalism but reasonably impartial, visited the abbey and found it above reproach. It was, however, in the Westminster Chapter House that the House of Commons finally listened to the Commissioners' indictment of the monastic system as a whole, and perused their report, the famous two-volumed *Liber Regis*, which, written on vellum and adorned with painted miniatures, was the work of one of the Westminster monks.

Boston continued to do his best to play into the royal hands. 'A kind of paralysis seems to have fallen on the monastery with his election,' wrote Westlake. 'Account rolls if written at all were left untotalled, unbalanced and unaudited.' During September 1533 he assisted at the christening of Princess Elizabeth and was active in helping to administer the oath accepting the new succession; but shortly afterwards, in an undated letter, he is to be found writing to Cromwell beseeching him to secure his release from the arduous duties of Abbot of Westminster, which seemed likely both to shorten his days and imperil his soul, 'by reason of divers most grievous diseases'. Cromwell was unable to oblige him; and so he remained, a pliant instrument, first to impoverish and ultimately to destroy the abbey altogether. The chief count against him on the former score is an agreement he made with the King in 1536 whereby, in return for the dissolved daughter Priory of Hurley and other lands in Berkshire, Henry received the important London manors of Hyde, Ebury, Todington and Neyte, together with Covent Garden, the advowson of Chelsea church and a good deal more property in Westminster itself. This had certainly been a profitable exchange from the Henrician point of view; and Boston continued to veer conveniently with the royal wind. He subscribed to the Articles of 1536 and again to the famous Six in 1539, was present at the christening of Prince Edward in 1537, and signed the document declaring the nullity of the King's marriage to Anne of Cleves. Once only did he make any sort of stand, when as Abbot of Westminster he successfully defended the rights of sanctuary at St Martin-le-Grand and defeated all the attempts by the Corporation of London to restrict them.

Westminster abbey finally came to an end on 16 January 1540 in the Chapter House, where Boston and twenty-four of his monks signed the Deed of Surrender. On that day, alas, although 'no breath of scandal had touched it' and the Commissioners' comperta had ostentatiously gone out of its way to vindicate the convent's way of life, the monastery was a mere shadow of what it had once been under John Islip.

No official documents have survived for the last four years of the abbey's life; but there is one interesting set of private accounts, those of Boston himself. They go to show that the last but one abbot of Westminster was spending these years feverishly feathering his own nest and that of his relations, including a married sister, nephew and nieces.

Of the monks who signed with their Abbot, probably not more than fourteen had been at Westminster with Islip. Only one novice, Robert Barnard, had entered the convent in Boston's time, so the remainder must have come from other, already dissolved houses. Some of the older men, no doubt, like Thomas Elfryd who later in his Will asked to be buried by the South Door of the church, which he described as 'sometyme the procession waye', must have resented the change. Others, including the new importations, were probably apathetic; while the Abbot himself, the Prior, Dionysius Dalyons, who had been installed in 1536, and their yes-men were alone enthusiastic.

The King received everything down to the last farthing; for it would have been treasonable as well as illegal to keep back any of the treasure. The annual value of the monastery at the date of its dissolution has been variously estimated. Speed in his *Chronicle* (edn. 1623) gave the figure as £3,977. 6s. 4d.; but Sir William Dugdale's *Monasticon Anglicanum* reduced this by £500. In any case it was a goodly prize, quite apart from the mass of treasure derived from the Confessor's shrine alone. This last had already been raided under a general order issued by the Vicar-General in July 1536, to remove all shrines, relics and images from churches and cathedrals, of which Boston took full advantage. The golden feretory was melted down and the fabulous offerings of centuries seized in order to satisfy Henry's greed, while the saint's body was secretly buried either in the floor of his Chapel or elsewhere in the church. Only the tumbra or substructure remained, together with the altar at the west end of the shrine, which continued in use until the dissolution, when it too disappeared.

WESTMINSTER IS MADE A CATHEDRAL WITH ITS OWN BISHOP

For nearly a year the great abbey lay, officially at any rate, empty and desolate. 'Whether,' wrote Westlake, 'there was any kind of continuity between the old and the new foundations cannot be determined. It is not even possible to say if services were being carried on in the cathedral church.' None the less there is reason to believe that the Dean and Chapter had some kind of unofficial existence before 17 December 1540, when the King by Letters Patent erected Westminster into a cathedral consisting of a bishop, a dean and twelve prebendaries. Henry had himself drawn up a list of bishops for the new sees in 1539, and opposite Westminster he wrote the word 'HILBY'; but at first it looked very much as though Richard Sampson, formerly Wolsey's chaplain and now Bishop of Chichester, would be translated to this see. He actually was offered it, or at least anticipated such an offer; since, according to Marillac, he formally 'took possession of it with all solemnity'. His triumph, however, was short lived; for on 1 June 1540 he found himself in the

Tower, and Thomas Thirlby was appointed in his room. Boston, or Benson as he now called himself, reverting to his family name, became Dean; the prior and five of the monks who had signed the surrender, prebendaries; and the remaining six stalls were filled by Simon Heynes, Dean of Exeter, John Redman, Archdeacon of Taunton, Dr Anthony Bellasis, Rector of Hartlebury, and Drs William Bretton, Edward Layton and Gerald Carleton. Of the remaining monks: four were appointed Minor Canons, four more were elected students on the royal foundations either at Oxford or Cambridge, and the rest were pensioned off, each man receiving from £6 to £10 per annum. The town of Westminster itself was granted the title of City.

Thirlby has had a bad Press. He has been accused of being a willow bending before every breeze; a Catholic under Henry, a Protestant during Edward VI's brief reign, a persecuting papist high in favour with 'Bloody Mary', and of attempting unsuccessfully to revert to his Henrician position when Elizabeth ascended the throne. Above all, he was condemned as an ingrate of the very worst type, the careerist deliberately biting the hands of those who had fed him, and climbing to wealth and power regardless of principle or the claims of friendship and loyalty. Cranmer, who had the highest regard for him, secured for Thirlby the bishopric of Westminster and, when that was dissolved, the see of Norwich. Nothing, in the Archbishop's eyes, was too good for him. 'Insomuch' [wrote Ralph Morice, Cranmer's secretary] 'that it is come into a common proverb that Dr Thirlby's commendation of anything of my Lord's was a plain winning or obtaining thereof.' No wonder then when he repaid the debt by helping Bonner to degrade the Archbishop, albeit he did it 'with tears', claiming that 'had it not been the express command of the sovereigns whose orders he could not deny, no worldly reasons would have made him do it', he was forever damned in the eyes of Cranmer's friends. As Morice later wrote to Day the printer in 1565: 'He abused his [Cranmer's] singular benevolence with overmuch ingratitude.' 'He complied,' declared Strype, 'with King Edward's proceedings all his reign, and so he did with Queen Mary's during her's, being then translated to Ely.'

Such a picture is a caricature. Thirlby was able to serve four successive sovereigns with complete loyalty because he did so as a civil servant and a diplomat rather than as an ecclesiastic. He was fortunate, too, in that during the three major crises of his career he was overseas. His latest biographer, Dr Shirley, writes:

Had he been at home in 1547 when King Henry died, it is hard to see how he could have avoided prison or obscurity in the reign which followed. On the occasion of Edward's death in 1553 it is highly probable he would have followed the example of Cranmer, signed the proclamation of Lady Jane Grey as Queen, and thus condemned himself to idleness or worse during Mary's reign. Again, when Mary Tudor died, he might well have been involved in more active opposition to the new Queen had he not again been occupied overseas in his country's service.

Judged by modern standards his episcopal labours at home certainly left much to be desired; but as a churchman he was consistency itself. From the start he championed Henry VIII's position of orthodox Catholicism, but without the papacy; publicly opposed the Prayer Books of 1549 and 1552; and was finally deprived by Elizabeth because, despite every inducement to do so, he refused to make even an outward show of conformity by attending the new Anglican services. 'I am determined,' he said, 'to keep inviolate the faith of the Catholic Church.' These surely were the words of an honest man. He was consecrated the first Bishop of Westminster by Bonner of London and Ridley of Rochester (Cranmer still being in retirement after Cromwell's disgrace and execution) on 20 January 1540/1; when by charter he was also granted Cheynegates, the abbot's house, as a residence, together with the then glazed walk of the cloister and two other houses in Dean's Yard, Calbege and Black Stole. At the same time he was allocated furnishings and various other pickings from different parts of the monastery, such, for example, as the hangings of Arras work in the Jerusalem Parlour and a considerable number of books. The new diocese comprised the whole of Middlesex, excluding Fulham; and its bishop received an income per annum ranging from £804 to £586, which was derived from the lordships and manors of Hendon, Hampstead, Frith, Newhall, Northolt, Greenford, Hanwell and Downbarnes in Middlesex, besides properties in Buckinghamshire, Hertfordshire, Essex and Worcestershire. He likewise received eleven advowsons in London, and others ranging over sixteen counties. Benson, as the new Dean, moved into the Prior's House, now Ashburnham House, which was also furnished out of surplus monastic stock. The remainder was either sold, given away to the poor and needy or burnt.

THE ESTABLISHMENT OF THE NEW CATHEDRAL

By a patent of endowment dated 5 August 1542 the Dean and Chapter were granted £2,164 yearly from the dissolved monastic estates, plus a further £434 from those of eight other great houses. Out of this, however, £266. 13s. 4d. had to be paid away in stipends to ten professors and twenty students at the Universities of Oxford and Cambridge. A grammar school was erected upon the new foundation, containing a master, an usher and thirty-nine scholars, which was the beginning of Westminster School as we know it today; although there had already been monastic schools of a sort for novices and singing-children prior to the dissolution. Indeed as early as the reign of Edward III a salary had been paid by the Almoner to a schoolmaster, who styled himself: *magister scholarium pro eruditione puerorum grammatoricum.*

The rest of the new establishment consisted of twelve Petty Canons, twelve lay singing-men, ten choristers, the Choirmaster, a Gospeller and Epistoller, two sextons and 'twelve poor men decayed in the King's service', i.e. almsmen.

One of Benson's last acts as Abbot had been to arrange with John Whyt and John Saunders, bell-founders of Reading, for the recasting of the third and fourth bells 'of the rynge of the said monastery' on 3 November 1539; but almost his first as Dean was to grant William Glastoke the lease of the rectory of St Botolph's in Aldersgate for seventy years at £12. 3s. 2d. per annum, on condition that he provided 'wine, wax, singing bread, and a mete and hable priest to celebrat and mynyster wt in the said churche'. This set the tone for subsequent leases, which were sometimes granted up to eighty years at a stretch and on exceedingly easy terms to friends of the King such as Sir Richard Rich, Chancellor of the Court of Augmentations.

Chapter minutes began to be kept on 3 March 1542, being entered at first in a grocer's ledger, and continued unbroken until 24 September 1556, when the secular Chapter was dissolved and the monks restored. The very first item was characteristically enough concerned with the sale of some of the abbey's remaining silver plate: 'Plate sold to alter ye Quire ye dark Entry, etc.' Eleven days later provision was made for the cathedral services: 'It is ordeined and decrede yt every day there shalbe thre masses sayd within the churche. . . . And the petye cannons wt ye deken and subdeken to say ye sayd masses by curse and to begyn of monday next enswyng.' Furthermore, the canonical Hours were to be observed and absentees fined at the rate of a penny or halfpenny per service. 'It is decreyd,' ran another minute, 'yt sermones shud be mayd every Sonday'; and it was laid down that £40, 'beside the waxe', was to be expended on the obit of King Henry VII.

The Master of the Choristers, who was housed over the Almonry, was made responsible for the

whole governing of the choristers, to teache them, to provide them for meate and drink and to se them clenly and honestly apparailed

I

in all things [but] if any of the prestes or syngyng men go forth of
the quere and there tary forth any space wtout licence then his
negligence to be countid an absence although he cum in agayne
afore the ende of the service.

Originally it had been agreed that each prebendary was to 'kepe
the chapter by course or to gyve iiijd for his course to another man
yt kepith it for him'; but the new statutes of 15 December 1545,
increased that sum to a shilling; and moreover declared that 'touching ye sermones every man to do it hymself in his course or to
get one of ye company to doo it for hym if he may or elles sum other
able man under payne of vis, viijd'. Every prebendary resident
either in London or Westminster must 'dayly be present in ye
quyre at mattens masse or evensong . . . upon payne to lose xiid';
preach at least one quarterly sermon or face a fine of ten shillings;
receive Holy Communion weekly; and regularly attend the fort-
nightly meetings of the Chapter unless prevented by sickness or
'lawfully letted'. Absentees from such Chapter Meetings could be
mulcted five shillings. The Dean and each member of his Chapter
were expected 'to be given to hospitality' and 'to kepe xxi dayes
together hospitalitie in his owne house'. None the less the real
problem remained of finding enough prebendal housing to go round
and thus stop absenteeism and provide a quorum at Chapter meetings. For many of the old monastic buildings had either been pulled
down or become the property of private individuals. In this connexion it is of interest to note in passing that on the very day of Henry
VIII's death the Commons sat for the last time in the Chapter
House, which then became the Public Records Office.

At such a time of change and decay it was not at all easy for the
prebendaries to find themselves houses, and this difficulty was
frequently used as an excuse for pluralism as well as absenteeism.
Gradually the position improved as the leases of old dwellings
within the precincts fell in and new ones were built. Even the great
Duke of Somerset was refused Vaughan House in Dean's Yard,
which he greatly coveted, on the grounds that it was a prebendal
house and contrary to the statutes to let it to an outsider. Further, in
order to encourage residence the Chapter decided in 1546 that of
those obeying the rules and keeping '2i days of hospitality in his
owne house', the Dean was to get '20 bushells of wheate' and 'every
prebend to have tenn bushell of wheat'. The disobedient, on the
other hand, would not only lose their corn, but have the mortifi-
cation of seeing it go to their more law-abiding brethren.

The new cathedral quickly found that its income, particularly in
view of the growing inflation of the currency, was not sufficient to

meet all its commitments. 'By reason of ye greate fall of money,' runs a Chapter minute, 'soe as there is not mony to pay ye servants of the Church, plate bee presently sould to pay them.' Other valuables were also sold, but for very different reasons. On 14 January 1549 the Chapter 'determined that the tow lecternes of latten and candelstyckes of latten wythe angells of copper and gylte and all other brasse latten belle mettell and brasse shal be solde by Mr heynes Treasourer bycause they be monymentes of Idolatre and supersticyon'.

The only surviving member of the original six ex-monk prebendaries, Humphrey Charity, who had by now reverted to his paternal name of Perkins, refused, to his great credit, to sign this minute. However, he was quickly over-ruled by the Dean and eight other prebendaries, and the destruction, official and unofficial, continued. One of the more noteworthy desecrations took place during January 1546 when robbers broke into the Abbey under cover of darkness and stole the brazen plates and silver head from the monument of King Henry V.

Benson, it must be admitted, was much more conscientious as Dean than he had ever been as Abbot. He constantly resided, was business-like and kept his prebendaries up to the mark; besides proving himself to be a zealous champion of his new cathedral. His chief enemy in this latter respect was the Protector Somerset, who, according to Peter Heylyn in *Ecclesia Restaurata*, called the church of Westminster to 'a sober reckoning' for the sacriligious manner in which, for profit, it had permitted the destruction of the College of St Martin-le-Grand.

> The Lord Protector [wrote Heylyn] thinking it altogether unnecessary that two cathedrals should be founded so near one another; and thinking that the Church of Westminster (as being of a late foundation) might be best spared, had cast a longing eye upon the goodly patrimony, which remained unto it, And being then unfurnished of a house, or palace, proportionable unto his greatness, he doubted not to find room enough, upon the dissolution and destruction of so large a fabric, to raise a palace equal to his vast designs. Which coming to the ears of Benson . . . he could bethink himself of no other means to preserve the whole, but by parting for the present with more than half of the estate, which belonged unto it. And thereupon a lease is made of 17 manors, and good farms, lying almost together in the county of Gloucester, for the term of 99 years; which they presented to the Lord Thomas Seymour, to serve as an addition to his manor of Sudely: humbly beseeching him to stand their good lord and

patron, and to preserve them in fair esteem with the Lord Protector. Another present of almost as many manors and farms,
lying in the counties of Gloucester, Worcester and Hereford,
was made for the like terms to Sir John Mason, a special confident
of the Duke's: not for his own, but for the use of his great master.
. . . And yet this would not serve the turn, till they had put into the
scale their manor of Islip. . . . By means whereof the deanery was
preserved for the later times. . . . Thus Benson saved the deanery,
but he lost himself: for, calling to remembrance that formerly he
had been a means to surrender the abbey, and was now forced
on the necessity of dilapidating the estate of the deanery, he fell
into a great disquiet of mind, which brought him to his death
within few months.

This account, to say the least of it, is highly inaccurate. It is
probably true that Somerset had some vague idea of demolishing the
Deanery and its precincts, using the stone for the building of Somerset House; and it is even conceivable that he had designs on the
Abbey itself. But it is extremely unlikely that he intended these
threats as anything more than a lever for extorting concessions. On
15 June 1547 the Dean and Chapter granted him twenty tons of
Caen stone, 'if so much can be spared'; and at the same time paid
his steward a yearly fee, ostensibly to help them with 'their dekayed
lands'. As regards the manors, Islip was certainly handed over for a
rental of £51. 19s. 4d. per annum, and fourteen others besides.
Benson died the same year, 1549, and his end may well have been
hastened by the knowledge of these and other surrenders and spoli-
ations; although it has also been attributed to frustrated greed,
'since,' wrote Widmore, 'his great concern seems to have been the
possession and enjoyment of a large income'.

RICHARD COX CONTINUES THE DESTRUCTION OF THE ABBEY POSSESSIONS

The next Dean, Richard Cox, who was Tutor and Almoner to
Edward VI and a violent Protestant, continued with the work of
appeasement and destruction. A Chapter minute of 1550, for example, declared: 'It is decree by Mr Deane and the Chapter that
Mr Thomas ffyssher servaunte to my Lord Somersettes grace shall
have a lease of the parsonage of Shorham and Otford for terme of
LXXXXIX yeres.'
Cox, another of Cranmer's favourites, had been from the first an
ardent reformer, and helped to compile both the Prayer Book of
1549 and the first English Ordinal of 1550. While Vice-Chancellor

of Oxford from 1547 to 1552 he greatly encouraged the admission of such foreign divines as Peter Martyr, Stumphius and John ab Ulmis; and, as one of the seven royal Visitors of 1549, 'swept the schools and colleges with the most destructive zeal, confiscating and converting funds, altering statutes, destroying books and manuscripts with unsparing fury'. Nicknamed 'the cancellor of the university' he now turned his reforming zeal upon his new cathedral: ordering the defacing of all the old Service Books, so that none but the new Prayer Book could be used, and largely destroying the Library. 'The business was to call out all the superstitious books, as missals, legends, and such like, and to deliver the garniture of the books, being either gold or silver, to Sir Anthony Aueher.'

Apart from the alienation of many of its broad lands to the greedy Seymours, the Abbey also suffered much from the depreciation of money and the heavy surrender of property to Henry VIII in 1544 and again in 1546 in order to buy its release from the obligation of paying the stipends of the King's university students and professors. No wonder Benson and his Chapter had then tried to recoup themselves by selling or leasing their possessions in the Collegiate Church of St Martin-le-Grand; and now, under Cox, further sacrifices must be made. Chapter minutes of 1550 and 1551 run as follows:

> Decreed that certeyne plate remaynyng in the vestre be solde by Mr deane, Mr heynes and Mr perkyns for to bear the charges of the alteration and removing the queer, And for the alteracion of the dark entre and the college great gate. . . . As the cathedrall churche of Westminster hath had suche losse by the late fall of the monye that at this present ther ys not mony ynough in the Treasorers handes to pay the charges of this next our Ladye day quarter, yt ys therefore decreed by Mr deane and chapiter that certeyn plate and stuff shalbe furthe withe sold to make monys whearwithe to pay the ministers and other officers wages and other charges not presently to be borne.

About the same time Cox tightened up discipline in the Chapter itself. Prebendaries were expected to wear no more and no less than the surplice and hood 'at Mattens in the Quyor or communion tyme or evynsong'; they should keep at least twenty-one days residence, besides twelve more in each remaining quarter of the year; attend the Saturday Chapter meetings regularly; and, when in residence, receive the sacrament once a week. A number of old officials were dismissed, including John Moulton, who was originally Steward of the Abbot's Household before Benson had made him the Chapter's business agent, and John Markcant, a singing-man, 'because he hathe usyd hym selfe byseley ralyngly and sedycyously by castyng bylles agaynst Scrosse and slanderyng of Roche'.

A new broom sweeps clean, and the new and radically-minded Dean was minded to make a clearance of the old-fashioned conservatives. In May 1550 he had written to Bullinger: 'I think all things in the Church ought to be pure and simple, removed at the greatest distance from the pomps and elements of this world. But in this our Church, what can I do in so low a station? I can only endeavour to persuade our bishops to be of the same mind with myself.'

LONDON ABSORBS THE SEE OF WESTMINSTER

One such bishop was his own diocesan, Thomas Thirlby, who was a stout supporter of the ancient ritual. Thirlby had been very largely an absentee bishop, being employed by the Crown on a succession of diplomatic missions abroad, and leaving the practical administration of his diocese in the capable hands of the Archdeacon of Middlesex, Richard Eden. When at home he probably lived in the Abbot's Bower at Hendon rather than at Cheynegates; and had vigorously opposed Edward VI's first Prayer Book. Cox, and Ridley, the new Bishop of London, were determined to get rid of him and dissolve his see, which could then be reunited to its mother diocese. Accordingly the bishopric of Westminster was suppressed by Letters Patent on 29 January 1550; and the following February it was announced that Ridley would in future be Bishop both of London and Westminster. Finally, two months later, Thirlby was kicked upstairs into the see of Norwich; while Westminster was formally incorporated into London. It is of interest to note that a special Act of Parliament had then to be passed preserving the Abbey as a separate cathedral within the diocese of London, but retaining its Henrician charter. 'The seyd syte and the late cathedral church of saynte Peters Westminster,' stated the royal writ directed to Sir John Mason, clerk of Parliament, 'shall from henceforthe be and remayne for ever a cathedral church and episcopal see to the Bishop of London for the tyme being.'

The episcopal patrimony, which had already been impoverished by the granting of long leases on easy terms and the nepotism of its late incumbent—he had given the bailiwick of Ashwell for life to his brother—was carefully divided up. Thirlby himself acquired a little of it on the cheap; more was exchanged for inferior London manors; and some was applied to the repair of St Paul's Cathedral, thereby occasioning the byword: 'robbing Peter to pay Paul'. Ridley himself took over the profitable convicts' prison; and the bishop's palace passed into the hands of Lord Wentworth, the Lord Protector's cousin, who was eventually buried in the Islip Chapel, Miles Coverdale preaching the funeral sermon. Other henchmen of the Duke, according to Heylyn, also took full advantage of their opportunities. 'Most of the lands,' he wrote, 'were invaded by the great men of the court.' Thus the bishopric of Westminster ignominiously disappeared within ten years of its original creation.

Dean Cox, who attended the Duke of Somerset on the scaffold, saw at least one greedy enemy of the Abbey off the stage; but he was unable to resist, even if he had wished to do so, yet another in the shape of 'the Kynges commyssyoners for the gathering of ecclesiasticall goodes', who descended upon Westminster like vultures in May 1553 and demanded a complete inventory of all its remaining plate, vestments and other goods. Everything was taken, with the gracious exception of 'ii Cupps wythe covers all gylte; one white sylver pott; iii herse clothes; xii cussins; on carpeet for the Table; viii staule clothes for the quyre; iii pulpitt clothes; a little carpett for Mr Deanes staulle; ii table clothes'.

THE MARIAN REACTION

But retribution was only just round the corner. Mary Tudor succeeded her brother on the throne the following July; and a month later Dean Cox was arrested in connexion with Northumberland's plot, cooling his heels for some weeks in the Marshalsea Prison. Deprived of all his preferments he fled abroad after his release, and resided at Frankfurt, where as part author of the 1552 Prayer Book he led the opposition to John Knox.

Hugh Weston, one of Mary's chaplains, reigned at Westminster in his stead. He was a noted controversialist and reckoned one 'of the best preachers and orators of his time'; but his strong Catholic views had been the cause of his ejection during the previous reign from the Lady Margaret Professorship of Divinity at Oxford and his imprisonment in the Fleet. The new Queen found him a useful and faithful friend. He donned armour and was prepared to fight for her against Sir Thomas Wyatt with his sword; while at the same time confuting outstanding Protestants like Philpot, Latimer, Ridley and Bradford with his tongue. He was ultimately to preside over Cranmer's trial.

At Westminster the new regime ushered in many changes. Nine out of the twelve prebendaries, including Alexander Nowell and Edmund Grindall, were deprived and escaped overseas. In the Chapter Minute Book against the names of the three survivors has been written in a later hand: 'Turncoats.' Nowell was succeeded as

Headmaster of the Grammar School by the flogger, Nicholas Udal
from Eton. Six reliable Catholics, described as 'new prebendaries
of the Romish persuasion', were appointed; and the new Dean
proceeded to enforce law and order with a heavy hand. 'Whereas,'
ran a Chapter minute of 1553, 'ser Hamonde pryste dyd breake
John Wode's head being one of the clerkes wt a pote he was
commandyd to ye gate house for the space of iii days by Mr deanes
comanddement and pade Jon Wode for the healinge of his heade
xis by the decree of Mr deane and the chapter.' He had also to
pay a forty shilling fine! About the same date it was 'ordered that
any of ye petty cannons, schoole master usher or any of ye clarkes
pentionares or any other who are in Commons doe call any other
knave or other contumelious reproch he shall be fined 12d to ye
Commons'.

The Abbey was carefully cleaned and aired against the Queen's
coronation: 'Item,' records one of the Treasurer's accounts, 'for
goodwyffe Wyllet and mother syllybarne for makyng cleane Kyng
H. the VII's tombe wt sope and watr II days, iis. . . . Item. for dyvse
penyworth of coles for the perfumyms of the quenes graces crownes
and the coronacyon day kopyns in fyre for the sencers, vid.' The
coronation itself was performed by Gardiner of Winchester 'without,'
as Matthew Parker later commented, 'any express right or precedent'; while the sermon was preached by Day of Chichester.
Mary, terrified apparently lest the holy oil had lost its power during
the interdict and King Edward's chair its sanctity, since its occupation by her Protestant half-brother, obtained a freshly blessed supply
of the former from the Bishop of Arras, and an entirely new chair
sanctified with the benediction of Pope Julius III. It is, however,
extremely doubtful whether she had the temerity to make use of
the latter during the traditional ceremonies of unction and coronation, which had been so long associated with its venerable predecessor. It now stands in Winchester Cathedral, where no doubt
it played its part in the Queen's wedding.

Despite the Marian reaction the papacy had been compelled to
accept the dissolution of the monasteries as a *fait accompli* and leave
their possessions, untroubled, in the hands of the lay despoilers.
None the less the Queen herself was determined on some kind of
restitution. To her great joy in the middle of March 1555 sixteen
Benedictine monks appeared at Court in their habits, led by Dr
Feckenham then Dean of St Paul's and one of the Queen's confessors. They all vehemently asserted their determination to renounce
their clerical preferments and re-enter the monastic life. So every
effort was now made to restore at least a few of the old religious
houses; and it was not long before the royal eye had fallen upon the

Abbey of Westminster. Already there had necessarily been many changes under Weston, although there is no precise record of the kind of worship he instituted there. Certainly he had not been idle. A store of weapons had been laid in at the time of the Wyatt rebellion; and some of the gunpowder and arrows were later used to 'destroy the pigeons in the church'. The great and little organs were overhauled and repaired; and the Lord Chancellor was called in 'for the deprivation of the prebendaries being married within the church'.

Henry Machyn wrote in his diary for 8 August 1553, concerning Edward VI's funeral, 'at ys bereing was the greatest mone mad for him of ys deth as ever was hard or sene, boyth of all sorts of pepull, wepyng and lamentyng'. Now a very different ecclesiastical atmosphere prevailed at the Abbey; and a year later on 12 November 1554 the diarist was recording how the new King and Queen 'rod into Westmynster chyrche to the masse of the Holy-gost'. At the end of the same month he described in detail how the High Mass of the Order of the Golden Fleece was sung there in honour of the reconciliation with Rome. 'The sam nyght,' he went on, 'my lord cardenall [Reginald Pole] cam to the courte, and whent to the chapell with the Kyng, and ther Te Deum songe.'

The faithful Weston was meanwhile being used by the Queen to head the numerous processions, which marched through London to petition the Almighty to grant her the gift of a child; and, indeed, his very last appearance as Dean of Westminster was in such a procession on 27 January 1554/5, 'carehyng the blessyd sacrement'. For some time now Mary had made it plain that she wished him to vacate the Abbey and thus prepare the way for the return of the Benedictines; but Weston was not playing ball. 'He appeared,' Heylyn remarked, 'very backward in conforming to the Queen's desires . . . partly out of a dislike he had for the project (he being one that never liked the profession of monkery) and partly out of an affection which he had to the place, seated so opportunely for the Court and all public business.' He prevaricated and dragged his feet; but by 1556 had agreed to resign his Westminster Deanery in exchange for that at Windsor. He was not allowed long to enjoy his new dignity. Cardinal Pole, who greatly disliked him, took advantage of his fall from grace to prosecute the Dean for immorality. It was given out that he had actually been surprised in the very act of adultery during August 1557; was hastily deprived of all his preferments and imprisoned in the Tower. His Protestant enemies, whom he had once taunted with the phrase 'you have the Word, and we have the Sword', naturally greatly rejoiced in his downfall. John Banks, informing Henry Bullinger in March 1554 of the execution of the Duke of Suffolk, which Weston attended, had already referred to him as 'a swine out of the herd'; and now after his disgrace, John Jewel, regaling Peter Martyr with many tales of Catholic immoralities, wrote: 'You have before heard respecting Weston. But why, say you, do you make mention of such persons? Simply that you may learn by what judges it was thought fit that Cranmer, Ridley and Latimer should be condemned.'

THE MONKS RETURN TO WESTMINSTER

On 27 September 1556, the secular Chapter was finally dissolved; a fact recorded only by a contemporary scribble at the end of the Register Book, since the deed of resignation itself has not survived. Nearly a month later on 20 November the monks re-occupied the abbey. The very next day, Machyn noted in his diary, 'was the new abbot of Westmynster putt in, docthur Feckham, late dene of Powelles, and xiiii noo monks shorne in; and the morow after the lord abott with ys coventt whentt a prossessyon after the old fassyon in ther monkes wede'.

Pole, as papal legate, drew up the statutes for the new monastery, which laid down that the abbot was to be freely elected by his monks for a three-year period on the Italian model. No *congè d'élire* or Royal Assent was required, and the Queen had no power to impose her authority upon the convent. Feckenham himself was consecrated by Bishop Bonner of London, when he 'dyd wher a myter'; mass was sung by Nicholas Heath, Archbishop of York; and the newly made Abbot preached the sermon. The following Sunday 'the abbot of Westminster went a procession with his convent; before him went all the sanctuary men with cross keys upon their garments, and after whent iii for murder'. One of these last was a Westminster scholar 'that kyld a bigge boye that sold papers and pryntyd bokes with horlyng of a stone and yt hym under the ere in Westmynster Hall'.

The original monks were soon joined by a dozen more; and eventually some fifty were professed and became members of the community during its brief life; many of them from Gloucester College, Oxford, which had now entered upon the last decade of its existence.

On the whole it was a well-educated body, comprising men with a real sense of vocation, who had abandoned comfortable, secure and well-paid jobs in order to re-enter the monastic life. Feckenham, for instance, was a learned man, who originally had been professed at Evesham Abbey, and imprisoned under Edward VI because of his strong Catholic views. Now he was to prove himself one of the most formidable and persuasive of the champions of the Old Faith. Mary sent him to try and reclaim both Princess Elizabeth and Lady Jane Grey in their respective prisons. He was successful in advocating clemency on behalf of the former; while the latter, taking his hand on the scaffold, exclaimed: 'God will requite you, good sir, for your humanity to me.'

In March 1554 he had been appointed Dean of St Paul's, a dignity he gladly relinquished at the Queen's prompting in order to re-enter the monastic life.

Little, indeed, is known of the day-to-day routine of the restored abbey. Feckenham of course had often to absent himself from Westminster on the Queen's business, since he was in great demand as a popular preacher, a formidable confuter of heresy and an eloquent speaker both in Parliament and Convocation. He also helped to refound other religious communities, and served on several royal commissions. His Prior, William East, was then left in command at the convent which numbered Sigebert Buckley among its monks. As an old man this last survivor from the Marian abbey could, in conversation with Father Augustine Baker, only recall one memory:

> They rose at midnight, they did eate flesh, that at the refection in the refectory they satt face to face on both sides of the table being fowre to every messe as they do in the innes of court; that at supper they had so in common betweene every fowre, first a dish of cold sliced powdred beefe, and next after a sholder of mutton rosted. I do not remember what post past they had, but it is likely they had cheese and perhaps allso an apple or two or peare.

As Baker later commented in his *Memorials*, 'it seemed a fare somewhat heavy for digestion to them that rise at midnight to me, who had lately before only experienced the monastick fare of Italy'. Certainly this isolated memory does not smack of an austere, secluded body of men, deeply versed in the spiritual life, who were dedicated to silent prayer, diligent study and fasting. The new monks, it must be remembered, were men of the world, some of whom had previously held important posts in the Church. They, like their Abbot, were much in demand as preachers or disputers with heretics. They had a school on their hands; students to be prepared for the secular priesthood as well as novices for the cloister; prisoners to exhort and if possible reclaim; and the sick of the neighbourhood to be visited, particularly in times of plague. There was much else too that took them away from and outside of the narrow round of the contemplative life and the regular worship of the abbey. One secular matter at least no longer concerned them, namely the management of their properties and the collection of their revenues. These last were now left in the very capable hands of the layman, John Moulton, who had returned to the abbey in the capacity of its Receiver-General and Auditor. The income he handled, some £2,064 gross, was of course far smaller than the pre-dissolution figure; although it included a very substantial augmentation contributed by the Queen herself. Furthermore, as a first call upon these funds, pensions had to be paid to the deprived dean and prebendaries, a school of some forty boys and two masters maintained, and a dozen almsmen provided for.

Feckenham, like his predecessors in the abbacy, vigorously defended the convent's right of sanctuary in the House of Lords against some growing criticism of its abuse. For this purpose he suddenly and dramatically produced a Charter of Edward the Confessor's, together with its confirmation by Pope John XX, which had literally been picked up in the street by one of Cardinal Pole's servants where a child was playing with it, 'as by miracle'. Machyn recorded the names of several murderers who took refuge at Westminster during Mary's reign, including a son of Lord Dacre 'for kyllyng of one master West squwyre', and another man who in February 1556/7 'was . . . wypyd a-for the crosse for murder'. These were probably the last to benefit from the abbey sanctuary; but debtors continued to reside there under very strict conditions. In 1558, for instance, Stow declared that a certain Geffray Raineman 'brought into Sanctuary nine cloths, the owner whereof was Thos. Bradley Clothier. Whereupon a letter was sent from the Lords of the Council to the said Abbot [Feckenham] to deliver those cloths, taking first bonds of him to be answerable to all such as should make claim by order of the laws to the said cloths.'

FECKENHAM RESTORES THE SHRINE OF EDWARD THE CONFESSOR

Feckenham is chiefly remembered today for his restoration of the Confessor's shrine. Already on the anniversary of St Edward's death, 5 January 1555, 'there was sett up the scrynne at Westminster and the aulter with dyvers juelles that the quene sent thether'; and as soon as the Abbot was installed he set to work replacing the shrine and restoring the body from its secet to its traditional resting place. The actual ceremony of restoration was described by Machyn as follows:

The xx day of Marche was taken up at Westmynster agayn with a hondered lyghts kyng Edward the confessor in the sam plasse wher ys shryne was, ytt shalbe sett up agayne as fast as my lord abbott can have ytt don, for yt was a godly shyte [sight] to have seen yt, how reverently he was cared from the plasse that he was taken up wher he was led [laid] when that the abbay was spowlyed and robyd; and so he was cared, and goodly syngyng and senssyng as has bene sene, and masse song.

A month later the Duke of Muscovy, after attending the celebration of mass in the abbey and dining with the Abbot, was taken on a conducted tour of the newly completed shrine: 'And after dener,' wrote Machyn, 'he came into the monastery and went up to se sant Edward's shryne nuw set up and there saw all the plasse thrugh.' Feckenham's shrine was necessarily very different from the original. The golden feretory had gone forever, and St Edward's remains had been re-interred in a cavity hollowed out of the substructure itself. A brand new inscription took the place of its mutilated thirteenth-century predecessor, which contained no allusion to King Henry III, but merely confined itself to a simple eulogy of the Confessor and terminated with Feckenham's own initials:

OMNIBUS INSIGNIS VIRTUTEM LAUIBUS: HEROS: SANCTUS EDWARDUS, CONFESSOR, REX VENERANDUS: QUINTO DIE JAN. MORIENS 1065. SUPER AETHERA: SURSUM CORDA. I.F.

The substructure had been so badly hacked about by the Henrician vandals that the very best that Feckenham could do was to repair the frieze, build a new cornice and fill up the many holes with plaster. He then painted and gilded it overall with what might well, at first sight, pass for mosaic work. On top, in substitution for the golden ark and its mass of jewellery, he erected a two-storeyed wooden structure with a gabled roof, composed of wainscoted oak, and probably of foreign design. The whole operation was of necessity hastily and clumsily carried through; but it has survived the passage of time and still stands as a memorial to the last abbot's zeal and devotion.

In 1557 Feckenham persuaded Lord Wentworth to give up Cheynegates in exchange for the manor of Canonbury in Middlesex; and here, at the Abbot's old house, he revived something of the tradition of his predecessors for maintaining a large establishment and entertaining on a lavish scale.

The ancient monastic system whereby each obedientiary entered up his own accounts was allowed to lapse; but the offices themselves, notably those of Sacrist, cellarer, chamberlain, Treasurer and Steward, were still filled; and despite its very substantial commitments to the deprived, the school and almsmen, and for the observance of Henry VII's obit, the convent succeeded in living well within its income. Indeed, it was able to divide a dividend of about £200 among its forty odd monks, in addition to paying the choir and a host of minor officials, servants, cleaners, etc.; while, at a cost of £167. 7s. 6d. per annum, maintained the full Catholic ritual in divine worship both within the abbey and St Margaret's.

The Queen and her husband were constant visitors at the abbey. 'The xxvii day of May (1557),' wrote Machyn, 'the wyche was the Assensyon day, the kynges and quens grace rod into Westmynster with all the lordes and knyghtes and gentyllmen, and ther graces whent a prossessyon abowt the clowster, and so they hard masse.' Public processions became a regular feature of the revived abbey; when with every possible adornment of splendour and ceremonial the monks endeavoured to excite the interest, awe and affection of the populace. Feckenham himself, magnificent orator as he undoubtedly was, strove desperately in sermon after sermon at St Paul's Cross to win over the masses not only to an acceptance of the Old Faith, but to a ready acquiescence in the restoration of the religious communities. This he failed to do. The sermons fell on deaf ears and the monks of Westminster, like all Mary's reactionary activities, remained suspect. They were accused, for instance, of behaving in an unseemly manner after the funeral of ex-Queen Anne of Cleves, who was buried in the Abbey on 3 August 1557. It was true that on this occasion the Abbot 'mad a godly sermon as ever was mad', Bishop Bonner 'song a masse in ys myter', and she was carried to her tomb 'with a herse-cloth of gold wyche lyys over her'; but some nineteen days later 'was the herse of my lede Anne of Cleves taken down at Westmynster the wyche the monkes by night had spoiled of all welvett cloth, armes, baners, penselles, and all the majesty and valens, the wyche was never sene-a-fore so done'.

THE ABBEY'S CLAIM TO FUNERARY FURNISHINGS

The whole question of the ultimate ownership of the hearses in Westminster Abbey was a sorely vexed one. Among the Abbey muniments is a paper entitled: *Ancient proofs and precedents of the right of the Church to Hearses, etc.* This document is dated 1568 and quotes the case of Anne of Cleves, when her hearse was awarded to the convent; and, on appeal by the Heralds to the Privy Council, 'sentence given with the Church against the Heralds'. A decision which was reversed in 1568 after the funeral of Lady Catherine Knowles, despite a violent protest by the Dean and Chapter 'at the delyverye of the furniture of my Lady Knowles herse to ye harolds by the Duke of Norfolk's order'.

'The xxi day of Marche [1558],' recorded Machyn in his diary, 'was the Paskalle for the abbay of Westmynster mad ther, the master and wardens of the wax chandlers with xx more at the makying, and after a grett dinner.' The provision of this gigantic Pascal candle, that weighed some three hundred pounds, for the use of the Confessor's shrine, set the seal on its restoration. And not a moment too soon: for the end of the monastery itself was now in sight.

At 6 a.m. on 17 November 1558, Mary Tudor passed to her final rest, and 'all the churches in London did ring, and at night [men] did make bonfires and set tables in the street, and did eat, and drink, and make merry for the new queen'. Mary was buried in the Abbey on 13 December with all the lengthy solemnity and splendour of the ancient rite; and when at last 'my lord bysshope of York . . . had made an end, all the trumpets bluw a blast'. For his sermon Bishop White of Winchester had taken as his text Eccles. IV. 2 and 3: 'Wherefore I praise the dead which are already dead more than the living which are yet alive. Yea, better is he than both which hath not yet been'; and occasioned great offence by quoting certain other texts in the course of his address, such as: 'a living dog is better than a dead lion', and 'Mary hath chosen the better part'. He also denounced the 'wolves coming out of Geneva' and the suggestion that Elizabeth might revive the title of the Supreme Head of the Church. He ended on a solemn note of warning to all those who still stood for the Old Faith: 'And now it only remaineth that we . . . look and provide for ourselves and, seeing these daily casualties of death, gather our faculties and put ourselves in a readiness to die.' Subsequently the Bishop was summoned before the Privy Council and placed under house arrest.

DAWN OF THE ELIZABETHAN ERA: DISSOLUTION OF THE ABBEY

Cardinal Pole, the abbey's greatest friend, died at Lambeth Palace within twelve hours of Mary's passing, and while the City churches were still resounding to the strains of the TE DEUM LAUDAMUS. To Mary's pathetic appeal to preserve the Catholic faith intact, Elizabeth had returned a soothing and non-committal reply; but it would in fact have been quite impossible for her to do so in the face of the almost universal revulsion against the Marian regime that now set in. Feckenham and his monks were doomed from the very start of the new reign, and Elizabeth could not have saved them even if she had wished to do so. She had certainly not forgotten that she once owed her life to the Abbot, and when in accordance with ancient custom he visited her prior to the coronation, it is reported that he was offered the archbishopric of Canterbury. Fuller thus described the rumoured interview in his *Church History of Britain*:

> Queen Elizabeth coming to the Crown, sent for Abbot Feckenham to come to her, whom the messenger found setting of elms in the orchard of Westminster Abbey. But he would not follow the messenger till first he had finished his plantation, which his friends impute to his being employed in mystical meditations: that as the trees he then set should spring and sprout many years after his death, so his new plantation of Benedictine monks in Westminster should take root and flourish, in defiance of all opposition. . . . Sure I am those monks long since are extirpated, but how his trees thrive at this day is to me unknown. Coming afterwards to the Queen, what discourse passed between them they themselves know alone. Some have confidently guessed she proffered him the Archbishopric of Canterbury on condition he would conform to her laws, which he utterly refused.

He is likewise credited with rejecting a suggestion that the monastery should be allowed to continue, provided he and his monks would acknowledge the Royal Supremacy and 'celebrate the divine offices and mass in the new manner'.

The coronation on 15 January 1558/9 followed the old rite, with only a few minor alterations. The Litany, for instance, was said in English, and the Epistle and Gospel in both Latin and English. The Bishop of Carlisle, who officiated, was the only member of the episcopal Bench present; but he was supported by Feckenham and his monks clad in mitre and copes. At mass the Host was elevated as of yore, whereupon the offended Queen withdrew into her private room or 'traverse'.

Shortly afterwards Elizabeth returned to the abbey for the opening of Parliament; but as the Abbot and his Chapter in full canonicals came forward to greet her, bearing torches and proffering incense and holy water, she exclaimed angrily: 'away with those torches, for we see very well'. Encouraged by the royal mood Dr Cox, the preacher, grasped the opportunity of attacking the Catholics for their burning of Protestants. Feckenham remained undaunted and undismayed. He spoke and voted against the Acts of Supremacy and Uniformity in the House of Lords, where he also strongly opposed the dissolution of the revived monasteries and disputed courageously on behalf of the Old Faith.

'The xii day of June,' wrote Machyn, 'the frers of Grenwyche whent away. The xiii day of July the frers blake in Smythfield went away. The iiii day of July the Thursday, the priests and nuns

of Syon went away, and the Charter-howse. The abbott of Westmynster and the monks was repreyd [deprived].'

The actual dissolution of the abbey, which took place on 10 July
1559, passed off smoothly and amicably enough. Alexander Nowell,
newly returned from abroad, wrote on 28 May 1559: 'the most
part of the monks of Westminster have changed their coats already'.
By this he meant no more than that they were giving up their habits;
for none ever conformed. Commissioners, appointed to inquire
into the financial condition of the abbey, reported that all was well
and there had been no obstruction. Feckenham in particular could
hardly have been more co-operative; even after he had been committed to the Tower. 'The xx day of March,' recorded Machyn,
'was sent . . . master Fecknam, the last Abbott of Westmynster, to
the Towre.' In return the monks were allowed to retain the contents
of their chambers; and were found a small dividend out of the
pawning of various articles of church plate, which the Abbot and
his Receiver-General pledged to a London alderman for £40, but
never redeemed. Feckenham likewise discharged the monastery's
debts that amounted to £309. 10s. 8½d. Some three years later, on
4 April 1563, he conveyed by deed to the then Dean, Gabriel
Goodman, all the church's goods still in his possession. These
consisted mostly of vestments, including a large number of copes,
which had been made over to him at the dissolution on the understanding that they would no longer be required. At the same time
he supplied some valuable information in relation to certain abbey
lands then on lease, 'which could not otherwise have been easily
discovered'.

It is not part of my purpose to pursue Feckenham into his various
confinements. It is enough to say that after being quartered on a
number of church dignitaries, among them Dean Goodman who
treated him very kindly, the last Abbot of Westminster was imprisoned in Wisbech Castle, which had become a sort of concentration
camp for Roman Catholic priests. Here he died and was buried in
the local churchyard. 'Tradition relates,' declares Professor Knowles, 'that he was enabled to receive the Viaticum devoutly shortly
before his death.'

His monks were scattered far and wide. Some fled abroad, others
quickly found their way into prison and one at least became a
fellow of his old Oxford college. John Langdon in 1561 and Hugh
Phillips some fifteen years later were indicted for saying mass in
Essex and London respectively; while William Feckenham, probably
a relative of the Abbot, was in Newgate prison in 1586. The best
known and longest lived of them all was Robert Sigebert Buckley,
who was confined almost continuously from 1582 until his death on

K

22 February 1610. A year previously, in a declaration signed by him as a blind man on 15 December 1609, he received two Cassinese monks, who had secretly entered the country, into the Westminster profession; and, as the last survivor of that community, transmitted to them 'all the rights, privileges, pre-eminence, honours, liberties and favours, which the monks professed and dwelling in the same monastery [Westminster] have in former times enjoyed'. Thus in the eyes of the papacy at least, the nucleus of a new English Congregation had been created, ready and able to take over the inheritance of the past if and when James I or any of his successors should return to the Old Faith.

APPENDIX TO PART II CHAPTER 7

The Coronation of Edward VI

At nine of the clock (20 February 1546/7) [recorded Strype] all Westminster choir was in their copes, and three goodly crosses before them; and after them other three goodly rich crosses, and the King's chapel with his children, following all in scarlet, with surplices and copes on their backs. And after them ten bishops in scarlet with their rochets and rich copes on their backs, and their mitres on their heads, did set forth at the west door of Westminster towards the King's palace, there to receive his Grace: and my Lord of Canterbury with his cross before him alone, and his mitre on his head. And so passed forth in order, as before said. And within a certain space after were certain blue cloths laid abroad in the church-floor against the King's coming, and so all the palace, even to York-place.

A stage had been set up in the cathedral, where 'the King's Majesty's chair-royal stood'; and Edward, after being welcomed into the Abbey by Bishop Thirlby, was 'borne . . . between two noblemen', carried on to it, and shown to the people on each side by Cranmer, who demanded of them: 'Sirs, here I present unto you King Edward, the rightful inheritor to the crown of this realm. Wherefore all ye, that be come this day to do your homage, service and bounden duty, be ye willing to do the same?'

The reply came in a thunderous roar of voices: 'Yea, Yea, Yea.' The service as a whole was abridged; but the unction was carried out with all the usual care: 'My Lord Archbishop kneeling upon his knees, and the King lying prostrate upon the altar, anointed his back.' The crown was placed on his head by the Archbishop and the Duke of Somerset; and a Bible was also presented to him. No sermon was preached; but Cranmer made 'an excellent' speech on the Royal Supremacy. He warned the bishops not to seek to encroach upon the prerogative; 'the wiser sort,' he suggested, 'will look to their claws and clip them. . . . Your Majesty is God's Viceregent and Christ's Vicar within your own dominions, and to see, with your predecessor Josias, God truly worshipped; and idolatry, the tyranny of the Bishops of Rome banished from your subjects, and images removed. These acts be signs of a second Josias, who reformed the Church of God in his days.'

8

Westminster College:
Elizabethan and Stuart Times

THE NEW FOUNDATION

AFTER the dissolution of the monastery the abbey stood empty for nearly a year. Then, on 12 May 1560, Elizabeth signed the Charter of the new foundation; a month later William Bill was installed as its first Dean; and on 30 June he was joined by twelve prebendaries. The new Collegiate church, thus created, consisted, according to Stow, of a Dean, twelve prebendaries, an upper master and usher for the school, and forty scholars, 'besides ministers, singers and organists, ten queristers and twelve poor soldiers'. Elizabeth was in fact very largely restoring her father's original foundation of 1540; and like him she particularly interested herself in the liberal education of youth and the welfare of old servants of the Crown. She sought especially to foster the connexion between 'the three Royal Colleges' of Westminster, Christ Church, Oxford, and Trinity, Cambridge, by providing that scholars from the first should be elected to scholarships and fellowships at the other two. Stanley indeed went so far as to declare that Westminster possessed a collegiate constitution, with the Dean in the position of 'Master' and the prebendaries as 'fellows', who all dined together at 'high-table'; while below them sat the junior members of the body. 'So largely,' he wrote, 'was the ecclesiastical element blended with the scholastic that the Dean, from time to time, seemed almost to supersede the functions of the Head Master. In the time of Elizabeth he even took boarders into his house. In the time of James I . . . he became the instructor of the boys.'

Heylyn, writing some time after the event, accused the Queen of robbing the abbey of its best lands, before conferring the rest upon the Collegiate church. This was not true. Everything was handed over intact; and the new foundation got off to a good start. Of the twelve prebendaries, Humphrey Perkins had long served the abbey in a variety of capacities. He first entered it as a novice in 1517/18 under the name of Humphrey Charity, said his first mass in 1523/4, and was installed as seventh prebendary on 17 December 1540. In 1545 he became treasurer. 'Mr dr Perkyns,' runs the Chapter minute, 'to be tresorer for this yere to take ye money of ye receceyuer and see ye laying of it up in the cheste therto apointed.'

Three years later he was instituted to the benefice of St Margaret, New Fish Street. Now once again he returned to Westminster as its second prebendary, and was elected Sub-Dean the following year. He died on 17 November 1577. Two other restored prebendaries were Alexander Nowell, who had been made Dean of St Paul's, and Richard Alvey, the greatly beloved 'Father Alvie', who as Master of the Temple was responsible for Walter Travers' appointment there as Reader, and so indirectly for the famous battle of Canterbury versus Geneva that produced Richard Hooker's *Ecclesiastical Polity*. Among the newcomers were William Barlow Bishop of Chichester, Edmund Scrambler Bishop of Peterborough, William Downham Bishop of Chester and Gabriel Goodman prebendary of Chiswick in St Paul's Cathedral and the protégé of Sir William Cecil, whose chaplain and secretary he had once been. Camden referred to the last as a man 'of singular worth and integrity, and a particular patron both of me and my studies'.

GABRIEL GOODMAN—A LITERARY DEAN FROM WALES

On the death of William Bill, barely a year after his appointment, Goodman, to many people's surprise, was installed in his room as Dean on 25 September 1561.

During his short tenure of office Bill had taken considerable pains in drawing up the College statutes, which his successor greatly enlarged and improved upon; but they never received the seal of royal confirmation. Consequently Westminster Abbey continued to be governed in accordance with the provisions of the Royal Charter, supplemented by ancient custom, until the present day; although in practice the unconfirmed statutes were also strictly enforced. Under them daily prayers were said at 6 a.m. in Henry VII's Chapel, which were followed by a lecture on Wednesdays and Fridays; while the daily services were sung in the Abbey chancel 'at usual hours', i.e. 'upon Sundays from eight to eleven in the forenoon; upon Wednesdays and Fridays, and other Holy Days, from nine to eleven; at other days to begin at nine until almost eleven. And in the afternoon service to begin at four and to continue until five, or after five.'

A sermon must be preached each Sunday either by the Dean, a prebendary or some official substitute; but the first of these must preach in person at least four times in the year: at Christmas, Easter,

Whitsunday and All Hallows. During their term of residence the prebendaries were bound to preach in their course or provide an acceptable *locum tenens*; otherwise they were liable to a fine of a pound per Sunday. The Eucharist was to be celebrated at least once a month and on all the greater festivals, when the whole of the resident Chapter, together with 'four of the clerks and four of the almsmen' were expected to communicate on each occasion. 'For the not doing thereof,' ran a Chapter minute, 'the Deane to forfeit iiis and iiiid, everie of the prebendaries iis, every prieste xvid, every singing man xiid, and every beadman iiiid.' The almsmen, incidentally, were each given 'a peny-a-piece . . . towardes his offeringe' before attending Communion; and they were all expected to be in their places at the daily services.

Every Saturday after Matins, the Dean and one of the resident prebendaries would call the whole of the College before them, when 'the Chaunter of the Church, in the Books of Perditions, doth shew the default of such as were absent, or negligent in the week before'. Under William Bill the Dean had dined by himself at one table and the four resident prebendaries together at another; but Goodman insisted upon their all sitting side by side at the one high table, ship-shape and college-wise, with the rest of the College eating below them and subject to their lynx-eyed invigilation.

The Dean, of course, was expected to exercise a general supervision over the whole of the College; but under him the Sub-Dean would 'oversee the good order of the Church and House'. The Archdeacon dealt with the ecclesiastical jurisdiction; the Treasurer, Receiver-General and Steward of the Household were jointly responsible for the administrative and financial side of the New Foundation; and 'the Master of the Singing boys has his house and other due allowances for himself and ten children, whom he is charged to bring up in song, for the daily service of the Church'. Westminster School itself was given a curriculum very similar to that of Eton and Winchester; and about a tenth of all the College revenues were allocated to its upkeep.

Goodman was always extremely anxious to get these statutes ratified and confirmed by the Crown, and to this end bombarded Lord Burghley, the Archbishop of Canterbury and the Queen herself with numerous petitions. In 1577, for example, after there had been some trouble with the prebendaries over residence and preaching, he raised the matter strongly with his old patron. 'He was bold,' he told Cecil, 'to send his honour a brief declaration of the orders used in the government of the College by Dr Bill, and him, since the last erection: that it might please him to confer the same with the statutes, and to consider thereof as he should think good.' The Dean and prebendaries, he further contended, ought to preach themselves as often as possible and avoid employing deputies except under extraordinary circumstances. They should be present in church 'to pray, as their most bounden duty was, for her majesty, being their founder'. The trouble lay in the continuing chronic shortage of prebendal houses that encouraged both absenteeism and plurality. None the less he concluded his petition on a pacific note: 'I beseke your honour that there may be that moderation used which shall be most convenient for all respects. Hitherto I and the company, I thank God, have agreed very brotherly, and with great quietness, as any company, I hope: I would be sorry, if seeking to better things, dissension should grow, or unquietness.' Burghley was sympathetic enough; but, in the event, nothing was ever accomplished since 'it seems not well-pleasing to some of the prebendaries, choosing rather to have been left more at their liberty'.

In 1586 the Dean put forward yet another memorandum on the subject, this time especially designed to catch the Queen's eye. Herein he listed all the prebendaries by name, other preferments held by them and which of them were married. No doubt he included the last item of information in the knowledge of Elizabeth's known dislike of a married clergy, and her determination to exclude them at least from cathedral and collegiate precincts. In some attached notes he also referred to an alarming infection of the Chapter by Puritanism. 'Some,' he wrote, 'come not in their habits, nor to preach in the church, because they have not subscribed unto the articles sent unto us by my Lord of Canterbury, in Her Majesty's name. Howbeit they have their whole living as others have.'

During Goodman's incumbency some forty prebendaries were installed; but most of these were nonentities or worse. One of the first and worst was John Hardyman, a fanatical iconoclast, who succeeded during April 1561 in destroying a number of altars in the Abbey, including that in the Confessor's Chapel; when, according to Strype, Queen Mary's 'dyvers juelles' disappeared forever. Fortunately his misplaced zeal was not approved of in official quarters, and he was deprived of his prebend before the year was out. On the other hand Richard Bancroft joined the Chapter in 1587 and Lancelot Andrewes some ten years later. The Chapter minutes recommence on 5 July 1560, 'Acta Decani et Capituli Ecclesiae Collegiatae beati Petri Westm' a quinto die Julii anno 1560, and at first were primarily concerned with enforcing the new statutes. But in 1563 it was decided 'that the plate of the house being thold fasshion by the discretion of Mr Deane and two of the prebendaries altered and chaunged into a better form, so that the same do conteyne the weighte and fynesse of ounces of thold plate'.

Goodman himself presented the College with a 'newe nest of sylver bowles'; and from time to time further plate was given or purchased. In 1568, for example, John Keylle, a goldsmith, received £40. 0s. 7d. for 'one bason and ewer pcell gilt waying fower score ix ounces iii quarters . . . for a lyvery pott pcell gilt waying fyfty one score one quarter'; and three years later Mr Green, another goldsmith, was paid £15. 16s. 'for a silver pott pcell guylt prepared for communion'. The cost of this last item was partly met out of the sale of the silver 'that cam of the burning of certen coapes at vs the oz.'. These copes presumably formed part of the large number bequeathed to Goodman by Feckenham, some of which were also used for covering cushions and chairs. Thomas Holmes, an upholsterer, for example, was paid £6. 8s. 7d. for 'thaltering of certain coapes into quisshions chaires, etc.'. Once indeed when Queen Elizabeth visited the Abbey at the opening of Parliament the Chapter decided that 'a canapie shalbe made of the best copes that are remaining in the vestry if the stuff will serve'.

One of the features of Goodman's incumbency was the large amount of repair work carried out in the Abbey church, particularly to the bells and organ. He himself gave two bells to Westminster, which are still in use. He likewise proved a strong disciplinarian. Clerks, who were in the habit of slipping quietly out of church during the sermon, found to their chagrin that they must now 'be presente at the sermon from the begynning tyll thend on the sundaies upon the payne of iiiid for every defaulte therin'; while each member of the Chapter, who possessed a key to the common garden, could be fined up to ten shillings for any damage caused by him either deliberately or by negligence. In June 1567 there was trouble in the servants' quarters, which was sternly dealt with. 'If anie servaunte,' it was decreed, 'either of Mr Deane or of anie of the prebendaries . . . or any College servaunte shall by fighting, quarrelling or any unseemlie maner' so misbehave himself within the confines of the precincts, then, after due warning, he would be expelled. If, however, relying upon his own master's support, he should refuse to leave, he could be further fined £10, payable either to the Dean or to the prebendary directly involved in the dispute. This decree was strictly enforced. John Ligett, for instance, a servant of Prebendary Yonge's, who by his 'quarrellous behaviour and fighting hath bene sclanderous unto the College', was so expelled the following September and refused permission to return. At the same time a proclamation was 'fastened on the church dores for the avoyding of brawles, frayes and quarrells in the church'; no unusual occurrences in Elizabethan churches.

LIFE IN THE COLLEGE

The Westminster muniments for this period contain some interesting and curious glimpses into the life of the College, of which space permits only a few examples to be quoted: We see Prebendary Thomas Brown at Wheathamsted on College business in 1573 buying 'breade for ye college nagg' and tipping 'ye curitis [courteous] mayde which made cleane youre bootes whilst youe preached'; Dean Goodman 'keeping courts at Southbenflete', where one item on the account sheet ran as follows: 'Item, geve unto you [the Dean] when you played [cardes] with Mrs Apellton [the Rector's wife], 2*s*. 4*d*.', which was repeated a few days later at Bassingbourne: 'Geven to youe to play at cardes there on Thursday at nyght, xiid'; and finally the sad story of Robert Allen, the Chapter Clerk, who 'fledd away the second of November 1570, and not knowing where he was the Deane and prebends entered his chamber and tooke out all ye leases and in his absence ye Chapter was unserved'.

From September 1568 onwards an ominous word appeared again and again in the Chapter minutes: 'plague'; and henceforward it was not easy to find a quorum for Chapter meetings, although Dean Goodman himself stood nobly by his post.

Three years later it was laid down by the Chapter that a prebendary had the right to invite 'any bishop, deane or other worthy mane being a preacher', to give a sermon or a lecture in the Abbey during his absence, provided always that the Dean was given five days' notice. By 1573 this provision had been amended to secure a decanal veto, which was considered necessary in order to exclude either Catholic reactionaries or extreme Puritans from usurping the Abbey pulpit; and he was further empowered to substitute a preacher of his own, to whom the discomforted prebendary in question had to 'paye . . . six shillings, eight pence'.

The chronic shortage of prebendal houses, noticeable in Benson's day, still remained unsolved, due partly to the destruction of so much old monastic building, and partly to the letting on long leases of most of the surviving dwellings in the precincts to laymen. A Chapter minute, dated 31 January 1580/1, summarized the present position succinctly and suggested a possible remedy:

For as much [it declared] as every prebendarye of this Collegiate Churche of Westminster have not in the Close belonginge to the sayde College a howse solye to himself to inhabit in like as the late prebendaries of the late Cathedrall Churche of St Peter of Westminster heretofore there had and enjoyed and are forced thereby to dwell two of them in one house. And by that occasion few of them are there resydent for anie longe tyme, and thereby unwillinge to take upon them the excutinge of anie office of Treasureshippe, Stewardeshippe or other belonginge to the said Collegiate Church. It is therefore . . . decreade that no lease . . . hereafter shalbe made of anie of the sayde late prebendaries howses . . . untill suche tymes that everye of the prebendarys . . . have solye to himself one howse there to dwell in.

The Dean and prebendaries were also forbidden, under heavy penalties, to lease any of their present houses to outsiders, or indeed any other buildings in the Close except those obviously unsuitable for church purposes. 'Further,' the minute continued, 'no prebendary hereafter shall suffer anie woman beinge not his wife, mother, child or servaunte nor anie other person to inhabbyte the said houses . . . nor shall suffer any wasshinge or laundrye to be used in anie of the said howses or any parte therof.' This last proviso presumably did not apply to the resident prebendary's own family!

In 1587 the College Library was re-equipped with shelves, desks and many new books, besides a new Librarian in the person of William Camden. 'Mr Camden,' the Chapter decided, 'usher for the tyme present . . . shall be keper of the said librarie, who shall have a care to kepe cleane, order and dispose, and safelie preserve the same, and for his paynes there imployed, shall have yearlie xxs.' Four years after this minute had been penned, the library was re-housed in more spacious surroundings: '3 December 1591. decreed . . . that the old dorter, and great rome before it, shalbe converyed th'one to a librarie, thother to a schole for the Q. Schollers.'

William Camden certainly owed much to the Dean's patronage. For Goodman had not only been responsible for his appointment as usher under the then Head Master, Edward Grant, and to a prebend in 1575, but finally secured him the head-mastership itself in succession to Grant in 1592. Five years later, and much to the indignation of many influential people, Camden became Clarenceaux King-at-Arms, 'he being but a schoolmaster'. The Dean also generously assisted him with his magnum opus *Britannia* by defraying his research expenses. This work it was said was written 'to awaken the interests of his countrymen to the history and beauty of the English countryside'. Sixteen Latin verses composed by Goodman and extolling the virtues of its author were prefixed to the first edition.

In 1600 Camden wrote the first official guide-book to the Abbey, and presented an especially fine copy to the Queen.

Dean Goodman, who enjoyed at Westminster and far beyond it the reputation of a lover of peace, one that 'agreed very brotherly with great quietness', and 'a right good man indeed of singular

integrity and an especial patron of literature', was particularly kind
to scholars from his native Wales. In 1588 William Morgan stayed
at the Deanery while he was seeing his Welsh Bible through the
Press, and gave one of the first copies to his host. Many other
promising young Welshmen, too, flocking into London in the wake
of the Tudors, found their way into Goodman's household. Thomas
Meredith, for example, became the Dean's Secretary, a post he held
from 1565 to 1576; when he was advised by his father not to trade
too heavily upon his master's good nature. 'Good sone,' he wrote,
'pest not yr mayster's house with strangers of yr countrey.' The
fewer the better in fact, lest the younger Thomas might have to share
the Dean's favour with a horde of newcomers. This bit of advice
was further reinforced by a number of gifts, which Meredith senior
thought Goodman might find acceptable:

> two cases of trensshers, with a paier of wodden knyves . . . and
> they are m'ked with ii letters 'G', signifieing Gabriell Goodman,
> and I praie yr Mr most heartlie to accept them in good pte, and yf
> I had better things that might be convenientlie carried I wold
> present it to his worshippe [One such 'thing' was a Welsh harp,
> for which Mr Meredith had paid ten shillings; but, alas] since the
> harpe came home to myne house, a knave, which is my ser-
> vaunt . . . took her awaye . . . to plaie upon and did put the
> harpe in some moystie place that the bewtie and faireness be
> gone.

Another leading literary figure of this period associated with the
Abbey was Richard Hakluyt, the father of English geography, who
had been a Westminster scholar. He returned to the College as a
prebendary at the beginning of the seventeenth century, where for a
brief period he became its Archdeacon. The Chapter minute recorded: '4 December 1604, it is decreed that Mr Hakluyt shalbe
Archdeacon for this next yeare.'

Probably Goodman's principal material contribution to Westminster during his incumbency was the securing to the College of the
manor house attached to his own St Paul's prebend of Chiswick. This,
with an eye to the ever increasing plague epidemics in London, he designed as: 'a place convenient in the countrey whereunto the youth
of the Gram. schole of Westm' may resorte and be instructed in good
literature, wth as little loose of time as may be, in time of sicknesse or
at other convenient and necessary times.'

That end was achieved only after some ingenious sleight of hand,
whereby the manor was first leased to the Abbey's Receiver-
General for ninety-nine years in 1570; then, within a couple of
months, conveyed to the Dean and Chapter; and finally re-let to one

Thomas Childe, apart of course from the house itself which the College retained for its own use. And long after the prebend had passed into other hands, the Dean and Chapter of Westminster continued as the perpetual tenants of what was to become generally known as 'College House'. Goodman planted a row of elms there, some of which were still flourishing at the end of the eighteenth century; and it was utilized as a summer residence for the school and members of the Chapter, as well as a refuge in times of plague and sickness.

For some unexplained reason Goodman never acquired a bishopric, although both Archbishops Parker and Whitgift, besides his patron, Lord Burghley, were anxious to secure him one. It has been suggested that Elizabeth's favourite, the Earl of Leicester, was the real nigger in the wood-pile, a Puritan who distrusted a churchman so closely associated with the Court of High Commission and the *via media* of Anglicanism. Consequently the Earl threw the whole weight of his influence against the Dean's promotion, and thus prevented the elevation of this 'most upright man' to the episcopal Bench. He is none the less thankfully remembered today both in his native place of Ruthin and at Sydney Sussex, Cambridge, as a founder of their respective Colleges; the appointment to the Wardenship of the former being still vested in the Dean and Chapter of Westminster. He last signed the Chapter Minute Book on 12 May 1601, and died the following year. He lies buried in St Benedict's Chapel at the Abbey, his monument portraying him as kneeling on a cushion, clad in doctor's robes, with a book open on a desk in front of him.

Goodman held and deserved the reputation of being 'a restorer rather than a devastator'. During his forty years' reign he set the new College on its feet and jealously guarded its rights and privileges. His personal pleading before the House of Commons secured the rejection of a Bill to abolish sanctuary for debt, although for the future all sanctuary men were to be obliged to take a stringent oath that they would not knowingly defraud their creditors; and their residence in the precincts was to be 'only for the safe-guarding of their own bodies'. They were also subjected to a much more severe discipline, and were expected to be instantly obedient 'to Mr Dean, to Mr Archdeacon and to other officers'.

The Dean was equally vigorous in defending the rights and liberties of the Abbey in other directions. For example, he declined to allow the Canterbury Convocation to meet in the Westminster Chapter House until he had procured from the Archbishop an unequivocal declaration that 'no archbishop or bishop could exercise any ecclesiastical jurisdiction in it, without leave of the dean for the

time being'. On the other side of the ledger it must however be recorded that he zealously promoted his own relations: Godfrey
Goodman was made Registrar of the Chapter for life, and Thomas
Goodman became 'searcher of ye College'. Furthermore he was
something of a spendthrift. Among the Abbey muniments are
certain letters written by Dr Grant, one of the prebendaries, accusing
the Dean of gross extravagance and wasting the College's substance.
Certainly Goodman's 'borrowings' are a regular feature of the
Treasurer's account-books for this period.

THE INCUMBENCY OF LANCELOT ANDREWES

He was succeeded as Dean in July 1601 by the famous Lancelot
Andrewes, who later became Bishop of Winchester and the author of
Preces Privatae, one of the great Anglican devotional treatises of the
seventeenth century. He had been a close friend of the Goodmans
and a great favourite of Sir Robert Cecil, now High Steward of
Westminster. Hitherto, as prebendary, he had been something of an
absentee attending only thirteen Chapter Meetings, out of a possible
thirty-three, between 1597 and 1601; but he was always present on
important occasions, such as the funerals of Lord Burghley and
Edmund Spenser; and he had served as Treasurer during the year
1597/8. Now as Dean he was to set an excellent example of attendance to duty.

His appointment was a popular one, and his short incumbency
comparatively successful. Hakluyt, Camden and Thomas Ravis, the
Archdeacon, were his closest friends in the Chapter; while his
brother, Nicholas, succeeded Goodman as Registrar. The four prebendaries installed during his reign were all first-class men: William
Barlow, preacher and historian; Richard Hakluyt, the geographer;
Adrian de Saravia, Hooker's confessor; and Christopher Sutton,
whose sermons and devotional writings were to become extremely
popular with the early Tractarians.

At his first Chapter Meeting on 3 December 1601, Andrewes
secured the appointment of an 'usher of the hall' to keep order among
College servants, who apparently were in the habit of selling their
'bevers', i.e. the college allowance of food and drink, to outsiders. In
future anyone caught so doing would have 'the same bever taken
away . . . and given to the poor'. The following year it was the turn
of the Petty Canons or singing-men to be disciplined. Up till then
they had largely pleased themselves about their attendances in the
choir, 'by means whereof divers tymes greate inconvenience hathe
insewed, all the voyces of one part being absent at once'. However,
from now onwards their comings and goings would be watched very

carefully and the rules strictly enforced 'as is the use in Paules'. This last turn of the screw was the sequel to some acrimonious correspondence between the High Steward, Sir Robert Cecil, and the Dean and Chapter over one, John Heathman, who desired 'a singing-man's place' and emoluments, but objected to having to perform any duties. Not unnaturally the Chapter refused to sanction this appointment, since, as they pointed out, not only would the choir be 'impaired with the discontinuance of any voice', but others might well be encouraged to follow his example.

Queen Elizabeth was buried in the unmarked grave of her sister Mary, after a funeral sermon not by Andrewes as Stanley believed, but by Anthony Watson, Bishop of Chichester. Later James I caused a stately monument to be raised over them both, containing the inscription:

REGNO CONSORTES ET URNA, HIC OBDORMINUS ELIZABETHA
ET MARIA SORORES, IN SPE RESURRECTIONIS.

This generous act, according to a letter from Viscount Cranborne to Sir Thomas Lake, dated 4 March 1605, finally scotched the prophecy 'that no child of Henry VIII should be hansomely buried'. 'The lively draught of it,' wrote Fuller, 'is pictured in every London and in most country churches, every parish being proud of the shade of her tomb; and no wonder when each loyal subject created a mournful monument of her in his heart.'

The year 1603 found bubonic plague again raging in London, which caused more than 33,500 deaths in the metropolitan area alone; while at St Giles in Cripplegate, where Andrewes was still Vicar despite Richard Neile's demand that he ought to resign and hand the living over to him, one out of every three in the population died. There were some 2,879 burials; but the Vicar was not present to take them, nor could the Dean be found in his Abbey. However, he returned in time to assist at the coronation of James and his Queen, which, shorn of the usual procession, was held on 25 July 1603. It followed the old ritual of the *Liber Regalis*; and Andrewes, in the capacity of 'abbot', opened the royal garments for the anointing, held 'the oyle in a little goulden ladell', and finally 'closed the loopes again'. He also helped to array the King in his supertunica, hose, sandals and gloves, and placed the sceptre in his hands. Eventually, in the rôle of Dean, he received back the regalia into his custody. Immediately afterwards he fled back to Chiswick; and a Chapter minute of 27 July 1603, declared: 'the College shall break up and ye Commons be dissolved from tomorrow at Night', the dissolution to continue until 7 October or to such time 'as it shall please God to cease his visitation'.

In actual fact this particular exodus lasted for more than four months. Safely at Chiswick Andrewes preached a sermon ascribing the plague to men's sins in general and to the 'wanton inventions' of the Puritans in particular. Whereupon Henoch Clapham retorted with *An Epistle discoursing on the present pestilence, touching what it is, and how the people of God should carrie themselves towards God and their neighbour*, which taunted the Dean for running away from his post. Alas, such frank speaking landed the author in prison, from which he was not released until 1605.

Back once again at Westminster Andrewes started to build up a store of raw materials for the repair of the fabric. 'Item,' ran a Chapter minute of 3 December 1603, 'that provision be made of lead, stone, timber and other necessaries towards the reparations of the fabricke of the church, yearely to the value of forty pounds, layd up in the storehouse, not to be imployed without consent of the deane.' Consequently at his resignation in 1605 Hacket believed that he had 'left a place truly exemplarily collegiate in all respects, both within and without, free from debts and arrearages, from encroachments and evil customs'. This was only partially true. He indeed left the Abbey free of debt and added considerably to the amenities of the Deanery; but other collegiate buildings were bequeathed to his successor in a sad state of decay, and he expected the Chapter to compensate him for his 'stuffe' at Westminster and Chiswick, besides paying for the wainscoting that he had installed in the Dean's Lodging.

Andrewes's incumbency is chiefly remembered for the great interest he took in Westminster School. For when one of his successors, John Williams, asked Hacket, who had been a scholar in the school under Andrewes, about 'the discipline of Dr Andrewes'; the latter replied: '. . . how strict that excellent man was to charge all masters that they should give us lessons out of none but the most classical authors; that he did often supply the place both of headmaster and usher for the space of the whole week together and gave us not an hour of loitering time from morning to night.' He used, or so it was reported, to examine the boys' exercises himself and held a tutorial three or four times a week at the Deanery for some of the older scholars from 8 a.m. to 11 a.m. Hacket continued: 'He never walked to Cheswick for his recreation without a brace of young fry, and in the wayfaring leisure had a singular dexterity to fill those narrow vessels with a funnel . . . all this he did for boys without any compulsion of correction; nay I never heard him utter so much as a word of austerity among us.' Widmore added this testimony: 'He frequently sent for the uppermost scholars and spent whole evenings purely in instructing them.'

His reign at Westminster was likewise noteworthy for the commencement of a tradition whereby the Dean regularly preached a sermon at Court on Good Friday. Not that Andrewes was ever a real courtier. Witty, saintly, extraordinarily learned, an outstanding preacher, he went to Court, where he was a favourite of King James, simply to 'deliver his Master's message' and, unlike his successor, was never obsequious to royalty. There is the well-known story of the two ex-Deans of Westminster, Andrewes and Neile, standing by James's chair, when the King said to the latter: 'My Lord, cannot I take my subject's money without all this formality in Parliament?' Neile promptly replied: 'God forbid, Sir, but you should; you are the breath of our nostrils.' A similar question to Andrewes at first elicited the evasive answer: 'Sir, I have no skill to judge of parliamentary causes.' James, however, would not be put off in this way and pressed his point. 'Then, Sir,' retorted the Bishop, 'I think it lawful for you to take my brother Neile's money, for he offers it.'

RICHARD NEILE'S CROWDED FIVE YEARS

His successor at Westminster, Richard Neile, was certainly of a very different calibre. Both men had been befriended by Goodman, and each owed the Deanery to the favour of a Cecil; but there all similarity began and ended. Neile, a Westminster boy under Camden and no great scholar, would, as the son of a tallow-merchant, in all probability have found himself apprenticed to a bookseller in St Paul's churchyard, had not Goodman out of the kindness of his heart secured him in 1580 one of those scholarships at St John's, Cambridge, which had recently been founded by Lady Mildred Burghley. In recognition of this benefaction Neile himself, while Dean of Westminster, used regularly to send two or three scholars to the University at his own expense. At Cambridge he came under the patronage of the Cecils, was appointed their chaplain, and eventually secured the Deanery from their hands.

Neile may have been a clumsy courtier and a poor scholar; but he was a very much better business-man than Andrewes had ever been. He put the collegiate estates and accounts in order, repaired Henry VII's Chapel and mended the wax effigies of the kings. A document dated 1608, which has recently come to light among the Abbey muniments, sets forth his achievements in detail. These included the restoration of the High Altar from its table-wise position in the centre to the east end of the church, and its adornment and beautification. His next most notable accomplishment was the completion and railing-in of Anne of Cleves's magnificent marble tomb. His five years' decanate was in fact crowded with every kind of activity, from building and repair work, and the increasing of the revenues, to the refurnishing of the church, the overhaul of the charters and registers, and innumerable acts of charity. He entertained at the Deanery on a lavish scale, and for this purpose both enlarged the house itself and constructed 'for the deanes use a large stable sufficient to receave 14 or 16 geldings', besides a coach-house and other outbuildings costing £100.

Neile, like Goodman and Andrewes, was not averse to the practice of nepotism. His eldest brother, William, a layman, became a sort of general factotum at the Abbey; and his step-brother, who was in orders, received first the fat Abbey living of Islip in 1609 and ultimately succeeded to a prebendal stall. The Dean also arranged a lodging for his mother within the College precincts; and, at his very last Chapter Meeting, procured a grant to his wife of a small pew behind the pulpit, which she might occupy whenever she happened to be at Westminster. At the same time he secured for himself a key to one of the Choir pews. Indeed, it would not be very long before the whole question of the right of the Dean and Chapter to appropriate pews in the church for their private and personal use was to flare out into open conflict under Dean Williams.

Despite all the Dean's economies and business acumen, life within the College was not easy, let alone luxurious. On 2 and 3 May 1608 a memorandum was entered in the Minute Book, which declared: '. . . that in regard of the greatness of extraordinary expenses this yeare, it is agreed that the household shalbe dissolved the week after the election for twoe months.'

But by the end of the same year things were little better:

> In regard that this yeare is likely to be an extraordinary yeare of expenses [ran a Chapter minute of 7 December] by reason of the dearth of all things, it is agreed that the deane, subdeane, stuard and treasurer shall take such order as they shall thinke good for moderating of expenses and forebearing of some suppers weekely for ourselves as may stand to the credite and profite of the house.

Some of the servants, too, were continuing to give trouble; so it was decided 'that the backe dore of the Kitchin shalbe kept shut'. The perennial problem of finding sufficient prebendal houses to go round loomed larger than ever. In February 1607 it was noted 'that Mr Sutton [Christopher Sutton] is and hath longe tyme bene destitute of a prebends howse'. He was struggling hard, but not very successfully, to wrest one from Thomas Goodman; and, in the meanwhile, 'shall have and enjoye that howse which is now voyde by the

L

death of doctor Bonde'. Should, however, he finally fail in his efforts to oust Goodman, which appeared highly probable, then 'the junior prebendarie . . . shall sustain the wante of a howse'.

Neile, that 'wise and wary man', was appointed to the bishopric of Chichester in 1608, but allowed to retain his Deanery in commendam. Two years later he went to Lichfield and resigned Westminster; but not before he had made William Laud his chaplain, introduced him to the King and procured him a prebend in the Abbey.

The next Dean, George Mountain, was something of a buffoon. As chaplain to the Earl of Essex he had fought at Cadiz, where, Fuller declared, he 'showed such personal valour that out of his gown he would turn his back on no-man'; and it was said his amusing conversation at Court won for him the Deanery of Westminster in 1610. His seven years of office were chiefly memorable for the burials of Prince Henry and Arabella Stuart, and the translation to the Abbey church of the remains of Mary, Queen of Scots, from her temporary resting place in Peterborough Cathedral. The popular Prince's funeral in 1612, when Archbishop Abbot preached a sermon lasting two hours on the text: Psalm XXCII. 6–7: 'Ye are gods . . . but ye shall die like men and fall like one of the princes', was attended by some 2,000 mourners; but that of the unhappy Arabella, who died mad in the Tower some three years afterwards, was conducted secretly by night, her body being 'brought at midnight by the dark river from the Tower' and laid to rest 'with no solemnity'. It was far otherwise with Mary Stuart, whom her son James honoured with a monument as costly and elaborate as that which covered her old rival, Queen Elizabeth. 'I hear,' said Demster, 'that her bones, lately translated to the burial place of the Kings of England at Westminster, are resplendent with miracles.'

Funerals in the Abbey during the early part of the seventeenth century were often unnecessarily ostentatious. A particularly pompous one was that of Sir John Grimes, a favourite of Sir George Villiers (soon to be created Earl of Buckingham) on 20 April 1616, which so scandalized the inhabitants of London and Westminster that 'the people in mockery buried a dog in Tothill Fields'. It is also remembered as the occasion when two of the eleven remaining copes, together with various altar hangings, were stolen and never recovered.

The reigning favourite, Robert Carr, Earl of Somerset, was married to Frances Howard, the divorced wife of the Earl of Essex, in Westminster Abbey on 30 December 1613, when Mountain preached 'in commendation of the young couple'. Two years later, by one of those little ironies of which history is so full, the Earl was committed to the safe-custody of the Dean before being sent to the Tower, charged as an accessory with his wife to the murder of Thomas Overbury.

THE SERVICE FOR THE HOUSE OF COMMONS

Elizabethan Parliaments had usually opened with a service and sermon in the Abbey, which the Queen attended with her Court. But in 1614, reacting against the Gunpowder Plot and a general relaxation of the penal laws against recusants, the House of Commons decided to go one better and hold a corporate Communion there before the session commenced. However, in view of Mountain's pronounced High Church opinions—he was not averse, for example, to the erection and adoration of images—they eventually decided 'for fear of copes and wafer-cakes' to attend St Margaret's instead. 'This,' declared Mr Fuller, one of the movers of the resolution, 'is the best means for love. Difference in faces but unity in Faith.' The names of the communicants were to be recorded and 'whosoever shall not then receive, shall not after be admitted into the House, till he have received'. There was no sermon in 1614; but in 1621 when Sir James Perrott moved a similar resolution and Dr Usher was nominated as the preacher, the Dean and Chapter objected. John Chamberlain wrote to Sir Dudley Carleton on 20 February 1620/1: '. . . the dean sent them a mannerly message by three or four of the greatest prebends, that they should be welcome to either of those places [i.e. the Abbey or St Margaret's]; but seeing they were both under his care, he would take care to provide them an able preacher.' The Commons, he firmly pointed out, had no right to choose their own preacher, especially 'a strainger, ther beinge a deane and 12 learned prebends who would be ready to do their best service'. The angry Commons thereupon appealed to James, and threatened that if Usher was not allowed to preach they would by-pass both the Abbey and St Margaret's and go to the Temple Church. The matter caused some stir and many rumours were afloat. Joseph Mead told Carleton: 'It was on foot for the dean of Westminster, Dr Williams, to preach, and not Usher; but with some ado, they say, Usher still continues.' In the event the King brought pressure to bear on the Dean and Usher was allowed to preach in St Margaret's after all. Mountain, an ambitious but lazy Dean, of whom Heylyn wrote: 'one that loved his own ease too well to disturb the concernments of the church', did not remain long at Westminster. In 1617 he became Bishop of Lincoln and resigned his Deanery; although he continued to rent one of the prebendal houses for his own use when in attendance at Court. His subsequent career, based on the proverb:

'Lincoln was, and London is, and York shall be', finally brought him to the northern archbishopric. Charles I, who did not like him, probably had someone else in mind when the see fell vacant in February 1627/8. None the less Mountain captured it by a witticism. He secured an audience with the King and told him: 'Hadst thou faith as a grain of mustard seed, thou wouldst say unto this mountain be thou removed, and be thou cast into the sea [see].'

Robert Tounson, one of the royal chaplains, succeeded him at the Abbey in the teeth of an all-out attempt by the Archbishop of Spalato to secure the Deanery for himself. Tounson was perhaps one of the least attractive of deans. 'A person,' wrote Widmore, 'of graceful presence and an excellent preacher'; but pompous, officious and wanting both in manners and learning. It was during his tenure of office that the Chapter decided:

> Commons not to be dissolved, nor law suites to be begun, but by consent of a chapter, nor expenses in building [but necessary], above fortie shillings. The virgirs and other officers to execute their severall offices, and dew respects to the Deane and Prebendaries according to former tymes. All unnecessary hangbies [sic] to be dismissed . . . no servants, nor strangers, to be admitted into the buttery or sellar nor to bring his friends to the buttery hatch.

The Dean further forbade 'ladies in yellow ruffs to be admitted into his church'.

RALEIGH'S COURAGEOUS LAST HOURS

Tounson's dealings with Sir Walter Raleigh, both during the night before his death and on the scaffold itself, left much to be desired. Raleigh spent the last hours of his life in the Abbey Gatehouse Prison, where he composed the famous couplet:

> *Cowards may fear to die. But courage stout,*
> *Rather than live in snuff, will be put out.*

Such courage, alas, earned a rebuke from the Dean, who came to visit him there as an official comforter. 'When,' he later wrote to Sir Justinian Isham, 'I began to encourage him against the fear of death, He seemed to make so light of it that I wondered at him. . . . I said he was a happy man. But if it were out of an humour of vain glory or carelessness or contempt of death, or senselessness of his own estate, he were much to be lamented.' Tounson had not forgotten Raleigh's reputation as an atheist, or his poem, 'The Lie'.

Say to the Court it glows
And shines like rotten wood,
  Say to the Church it shows
  What's good and doth no good.
If Church and Court reply,
Then give them both the lie.

But now the white-haired old admiral courteously turned away the Dean's wrath by asking how could he 'die with cheerfulness and courage, except he were assured of the love and favour of God unto him'. Tounson withdrew and his place was taken by Lady Raleigh, who remained until midnight; then some time in the early hours of the next morning Sir Walter wrote out anew an old love-poem of his, to which he added his postscript of faith. This was afterwards found between the leaves of his Bible.

Even such is Time! that takes in trust
Our youth, our joys, our all we have,
  And pays us but with earth and dust:
  Who in the dark and silent grave,
When we have wandered all our ways,
Shuts up the story of our days.
  But from this earth, this grave, this dust,
  My God shall raise me up, I trust.

Towards dawn Tounson returned and gave him the sacrament; but was surprised and disgusted still to find his prisoner so 'very cheerful and merry'; and worst of all vigorously protesting his innocence. 'I told him,' he informed Isham, 'that he should do well to advise what he said [i.e. on the scaffold] . . . the hand of God has found him out, and therefore he should acknowledge the justice of God.'

Raleigh took no notice of this censure, and continued 'very cheerful'. He ate a hearty breakfast, and in defiance of the King's opinions enjoyed a pipe of tobacco. On the way to the scaffold in Old Palace Yard, accompanied by the Dean, he presented an old bald man with his lace night-cap, saying: '. . . for thou hast more need of it now than I', in obvious imitation of Sir Philip Sidney's action at Zutphen. His speech, which gave no comfort to the Government, won the hearts of his auditory and helped in no small degree towards the undoing of the Stuarts. It changed men's minds, including that of Sir John Eliot, who wrote afterwards: 'Our Raleigh gave an example of fortitude such as history could scarcely parallel.' Furthermore he made a pious end, forgiving his enemies and asking God's pardon. Even the Dean admitted: 'He was the most fearless of death that ever was known, and the most resolute and confident;

yet with reverence and conscience.' However, right at the end the freedom of his mind again re-asserted itself. Asked whether he would wish to lie with his face turned towards the East of Our Lord's Resurrection, he replied: 'So the heart be right, it is no matter which way the head lieth.'

The only other event of importance during Tounson's incumbency, which terminated in 1620, was the funeral of Queen Anne, who was a professed papist and had refused to communicate at her coronation. None the less she regularly attended Anglican services; and she was now buried in the Abbey on 13 May 1619 with the full Anglican rite. Archbishop Abbot preached the sermon from the text: Psalm CXLVI. 3, 'For when the breath of man goeth forth he shall turn again to the earth: and then all his thoughts perish.'

At St Margaret's, which was then under the Dean and Chapter's exclusive jurisdiction, Tounson is remembered for his generosity in handing over the fees he received from its parishioners in return for dispensations to eat meat in Lent, to the overseers of the poor. His widow and fifteen children were perhaps not so appreciative, since when he died in 1621 as Bishop of Salisbury he left them almost entirely destitute.

9

Dean Williams

BUILDER AND BENEFACTOR

JOHN WILLIAMS, the favourite of James and the Marquis of Buckingham, had long had his eye on the Abbey, since it could provide him with a convenient lodging in London near Whitehall. Even before a vacancy had occurred, we find him writing to Buckingham on 12 March 1619/20 suggesting that 'by your happy hand' I might be 'transplanted from Salisbury to Westminster'. He added with refreshing candour, 'for being unmarried and inclining so to continue, I do find that Westminster is fitter by much for that disposition'. His words bore fruit and he was installed at St Peter's as Dean on 12 July 1620, in his thirty-ninth year, holding that office for the next twenty-four years, despite promotion first to the bishopric of Lincoln and then to the northern primacy, and in the face of every effort by Archbishop Laud and Charles I to get rid of him. He was, indeed, to become one of the College's greatest benefactors and an outstandingly colourful figure in its long history. He began by spending some £4,500 of his own money, in addition to what he already found in the fabric fund, on restoring first the south-east end of the Abbey, and then the great buttresses on the northwest side; adorning the latter with statues, including one of Abbot Islip, whom he greatly admired. Within doors he converted 'a waste room', i.e. the monks' old parlour, into 'a goodly library', which, wrote Hacket, 'he model'd into a decent shape, furnished it with desks and chairs, accoutred it with all utensils, stored it with a vast number of learned volumes' to the tune of some £2,000, and persuaded many of his wealthy friends to contribute on an equally generous scale. Williams's Library, which is still one of the Abbey's greatest possessions, contains the Dean's own full-length portrait, which, looking down upon it from the east end and, clad in the traditional ruff and wide-brimmed clerical hat, surveys his creation with that sly, bland smile 'which must often have disconcerted his enemies'.

Williams, like Andrewes before him whom in so many ways he strove to imitate, took an especially deep interest in the school.

He was assiduous [declared Hacket] in the school, and miss'd not sometimes every week, if he were resident in the College, both to dictate lectures to the several classes and to take account of them. The choicest wits had never such encouragement for praise and reward. He was very bountiful in both, and they went always together, scattering money, as if it had been dung, to manure their industry. And seldom did fail, no not when he kept the Great Seal, to call forth some of them to stand before him at his table, that in those intervals of best opportunity, he might have account of their towardliness; which ripen'd them so fast, made them so prompt and ingenious, that the number of the promoted to the universities, which swarm'd out of that stock, was double for the most part of those that were transplanted in the foregoing election.

He added four more scholars to the Elizabethan foundation, who were to be 'distinguish'd from the rest in their habit of violet coloured gowns'; established two additional fellowships at his old Cambridge College of St John's for the exclusive benefit of these same 'bishop's boys'; and finally secured from the King the grant of the patronage of a number of rich Crown livings to which they could ultimately succeed. Thus from the cradle to the grave he provided for his 'elect'.

Another passion of the new Dean's was music, and he helped both to encourage and improve this side of the College's life. In possession of a fine tenor voice himself with which he frequently sang the service, he made every effort to procure 'the sweetest music both for the organ and for the voices of all parts, that ever was heard in an English Quire'. At the same time he and his Chapter made provision for the better housing and increased remuneration of the Precentor, the Librarian, the organist and the choir. It was resolved, for example, on 31 July 1622:

> ... that Mr Frost, now chaunter of our Collegiate Churche in consideration of the new building of a kitchine to the chaunters house wch was a work of necessitie, the old kitchine being so ruinous that it must be pulled down and new builded, shall have a lease of fortie yeares, at the next chapter, of the said kitchine, and as much of the little garden now in the occupation of the said chaunter, as shall be thought convenient by two of the prebendaries. It is farther also decreed at this present chapiter, that the librarye keeper shall have besides the olde allowance he haith alreadye of 20s per annum, a new allowance of £8 per annum to be accruinge out of those two houses within the College Close lately demised to John Packer Esquire and Thomas Ashbury Esquire.

Nearly three years later on 27 January 1625 the same Librarian, Richard Gouland,

> ... in recompence of his pains [had his stipend further raised to £20, and also] shall have and enjoy a diet at the Deane and pre-bendaries table: together with all raites, proffits and comodities to his place belonging. [In addition he might inhabit] that roome betwixt the lybrary and the schoole, wch we do by this present act assigne to him, or his deputy, or deputies, and to their successors in that office forever.

The next year it was the turn of the organist and choir:

> [£40 was to be paid] by the treasurer of this church to the petty canons and singing men of this church, together with the organist if he have not a singing man or petticannon's place, and twenty pounds allso yearly ... to be paid by the said treasurer to the Master of the choristers for the bettering of the apparrell and diett of the said coristers, as shall be approved by the treasurer of the said collegiat church for the tyme beinge.

Finally, a memorandum of 3 May 1631 recorded the care taken for the adequate housing of all the singing-men:

> One of the tenements and back yard in the great Almery [it declared] late in the possession of Abraham Beck, and now pur-chased of him by the Colledge, is assigned over unto Mr Thomas Day, one of the singing men of our church and his successors. So as all the 16 singingmen ar now by the care and charges of the Deane and chapter provided of houses.

Another matter that concerned the Chapter about this time was the housing of the curate at St Margaret's. The late Dean, Tounson, had apparently leased to his wife the minister's usual dwelling place together with the small tithes and oblations of the parish church. It was therefore decreed in April 1624 that this curateage, 'commonly called the Ancars house' was to be handed over to the 'curate for the tyme being' and enjoyed by him 'without any rent or molestation from the said Mrs Tounson or her assignes: and that the said Mrs Tounson shall give assurance to the deane and chapter for the per-formance of this covenant'.

It is of interest to note in passing that Williams himself was in the habit of granting extensive leases of Abbey property to his friends, particularly to his patron the Duke of Buckingham, under the most favourable terms.

The hospitality and magnificent display indulged in by the new Dean quickly became a bye-word. He entertained his distinguished guests on the most lavish scale in the Jerusalem Chamber, which he had entirely repanelled at his own cost; and he was equally generous to his prebendaries 'by the hospitality of his table', thereby extinguishing a debt of some £300 which they had run up on the College. His enemies, however, did not scruple assiduously to spread the report that he had found the money for his extensive repairs and new work upon the Abbey 'out of the diett and bellies of the prebendaries, and revenues of our said churche and not out of his own revenues'. This lie was indignantly nailed by the Chapter in 1628: 'And for ourselves,' they declared, 'we do testify every man under his owne protestation, that we ar neither the authors nor abettors of any such injurious report, untruly uttered by any meane man wth intension to reflect uppon his Lordshipp.'

Williams, indeed, could usually count upon the willing support of a substantial majority in the Chapter—this particular minute for example was signed by nine of them—although there was a small minority, led first by Laud and then by Peter Heylyn, who bitterly opposed him. In 1621 he succeeded Bacon as Lord Keeper and in the same year was consecrated Bishop of Lincoln in Henry VII's Chapel by a former Dean, Bishop Mountain of London, assisted by the Bishops of Worcester, Ely, Oxford and Llandaff, acting under a commission from the Archbishop. Such a commission was demanded and obtained because he entertained scruples about submitting himself to the hands of Archbishop Abbot in Lambeth Chapel, hands which had so recently been stained with the blood of a shot gamekeeper. Williams, in fact, was hoping that this and other protests would persuade James to depose the Primate and elevate his favourite to the vacant archiepiscopate. 'For the king,' he wrote to Admiral Buckingham on 27 July, 'to leave virum sanguineum, a man of blood, Primate and Patriarch of all his churches is a thing that sounds very harsh in the Old Courts and Canons of the Church.' James, however, was not to be bullied and Abbot kept his place until his death in 1633, when he was succeeded not by Williams but by Laud. Williams was no Arminian or High Churchman; and when he heard that the House of Commons, presumably because of their expressed dislike 'of copes and wafer cakes', again intended to by-pass the Abbey for their corporate Communion, he went out of his way to assure them that they would 'find no wafer cakes, copes or candles, nothing but the plain though seemly service of the Reformed Church'. This was not strictly true as both wafer cakes and copes were still in regular use at the Abbey. 'Though there was no necessity,' recorded John Cosin, 'yet there was a liberty still reserved of using wafer-bread, which continued in divers churches of the kingdom, and Westminster for one, till the seventeenth of King

Charles'; and as will shortly be seen, when the Dean himself entertained the French ambassador the choirmen were vested in copes. None the less Williams was apparently sincere in his readiness to drop both on this occasion, provided the Commons for their part would select as their preacher one of the Abbey prebendaries. This they refused to do and once more made their Communion at St Margaret's.

WILLIAMS AND LAUD

From the first the relations between Williams and Laud were strained and uneasy, particularly as the latter's star was quickly rising and would shortly eclipse that of the Dean. Yet it was Williams who secured his rival his first bishopric of St David's and helped him to find a prebendal house in the Abbey precincts.

The thorny problem of the prebendal houses was still acute. At a Chapter Meeting on 4 May 1621 the Dean signed a minute promising to do everything in his power to secure such a house 'for Dr Laud . . . the which he is dispossessed of'. This was none other than the dwelling leased to a certain Mr William Man for the use of the ex-Dean, Bishop Mountain, by Laud's predecessor in the prebend, Dr Bulkeley. Mountain had spent considerable sums upon it and normally resided there while in attendance at Court. So it was decided at a further meeting on 4 December to pay the bishop £200 in compensation, half of which would be found by Laud, £30 by the Chapter itself 'and the remainder . . . my Lord Keeper is pleased to lay downe for the present'. It was also agreed that Laud's successor should repay him £30 under the terms of a new ruling by which 'every successor afterwards shall abate the said sum by a third part in every succession'.

In May 1631 prebendal housing was once again on the agenda. Prebendary John Wilson's home had become so dilapidated that he was compelled, at his own expense, partially to rebuild it. The cost amounted to £173; so the Chapter resolved that his successor must re-imburse him to the tune of two-thirds of that sum: 'and so from time to time the prebendaries succeeding one another in that house, shall receive the sum, so paid by him to his predecessor, deducting still the third part thereof, until in time all the monies laid out in the building shall be fully discharged'. A year later, when Prebendary Wemys received Prebendary Price's house, the minutes confirmed that 'the prebends in their seniority, if they will, may succeed in the houses of the prebend as they shall be void, reserving the house of him that last changeth, to the succeeding prebend that is to be admitted'.

But to return: Laud did not in fact immediately occupy his new

prebendal home, preferring to remain with Bishop Neile at Durham
House in the Strand; and only moved into the Abbey precincts
during January 1623, when his chaplain's apartments were required
for the French ambassador-extraordinary, who had brought over
Prince Charles's bride, Henrietta Maria. But it was in the Close that
he drew up the coronation service from which Williams was to be so
humiliatingly excluded. This particular prebendal dwelling was
to have an interesting history, since it was here that Richard
Steward, who took it over in 1638, held, in his capacity of Pro-
locutor to the Canterbury Convocation, those extraordinary
sessions that continued after the Short Parliament had been dissolved. It was here, too, outside its back door, that the remains of
John Pym and other Commonwealth leaders, disinterred and cast
out of the Abbey at the Restoration, were ultimately buried.

When in 1624 negotiations were afoot for Charles's marriage with
Henrietta Maria of France, Williams assiduously applied himself to
the study of French, as indeed he had previously done to Spanish.
He sumptuously entertained the French envoy, Villoclare, in the
Jerusalem Chamber and also took the ambassador and his suite to a
service in the Abbey, where with Orlando Gibbons at the organ and
the choir vested in gorgeous copes, 'the sweetest voices' sang anthems
for their pleasure. Special copies of the Prayer Book in French were
presented to the guests; but it was noted, with concern, that Villoclare himself remained covered throughout the entire proceedings,
and left his book behind him 'as if he had forgot it'. Afterwards he
told King James that the Dean 'had given him small content in a
long argument vext between them, for he had preached to him till he
was weary to hear his divinity'. Williams had better fortune with a
French abbé, who visited Westminster at Christmas that same year
and remarked on 'the decency' of the service and its ceremonial.

As long as James lived the Dean continued to bask in the sunshine
of the royal favour; but he was no longer *persona grata* with Buckingham or the heir apparent, who, unlike the shrewder James, had taken
William Laud to their bosoms. Buckingham, although at one time
anxious to marry Williams off to one of his kinswomen, had grown
to dislike his ostentatious style of living and believed that he had
been working against him in Parliament; while Laud, of course, was
particularly anxious to humiliate and if possible eliminate a dangerous rival for the primacy. The Lord Keeper in fact had actually
told Buckingham at the time of Abbot's disgrace and possible deprivation: 'His Majesty hath promised me upon my relinquishing
the Great Seal, or before, one of the best places in the church'; which
request 'was one means, if not the chief, of his [Abbot's] affliction'.

James died on 27 March 1625, after receiving the last sacrament at

Williams's hands. The Dean preached his funeral sermon, which lasted a couple of hours and was modelled on Fisher's oration at the burial of Henry VII. The text was taken from 2 Chronicles IX. 31: 'Solomon slept with his fathers and he was buried in the city of David his father', and the preacher declared that the wisdom of James and Solomon 'match'd well together'. There was no mention of Rehoboam! The sermon was later published under the title of *Great Britain's Solomon*. James himself was interred in a coffin designed by Inigo Jones; but no monument was erected over his grave.

WILLIAMS FALLS FROM FAVOUR

Immediately after the funeral Williams was deprived of the Great Seal. Sir John Suckling, who gleefully performed this task, told Buckingham: 'This is a due disgrace to one who had been unthankful and unfaithful to his Grace and may the like misfortune befall all such as shall tread in his hateful path and presume to lift their heel against their maker.' 'The occasion of this . . . the loss of the Lord keeper's place,' wrote John Chamberlain to Joseph Mead, 'was (besides some things that passed at the last sitting of Parliament) a plain piece of counsel his lordship gave my lord duke at Salisbury; namely that being as then general both by sea and land, he should either go in person, or stay the fleet at home, or else give over his office of admiralty to some other.'

The Dean for his part cringed: 'Most gracious Lord,' he petitioned the Duke in January 1625/6 on the subject of the forthcoming coronation, 'I do humbly beseech your Grace to crowne so many of your Grace's former favours and to revive a creature of your owne, struck dead onlye with your displeasure . . . turne me not over to offer my prayers at newe aulters.' Buckingham's reply was to get the Dean excluded altogether from taking part in the coronation service. Instead he was expected to nominate Laud as his deputy. 'The coronation,' Chamberlain informed Sir Dudley Carleton on 19 January 1625/6, 'holds on Candlemas day . . . the late lord keeper, as dean of Westminster, being to perform certain ceremonies at that solemnity, is commanded to substitute the bishop of St David's for his deputy'.

This was too much; and Williams merely presented a full list of the prebendaries to the King for him to choose from. Charles naturally chose Laud and commissioned him to draw up a new and more purely Anglican service. In point of fact this out-Romaned the ancient rite, since unction was performed *in forma crucis*, the coronation oath altered to make it 'more advantageous to the King and less beneficial to the People', and the prayer, omitted from the time of

Henry VI, was reintroduced asking that the King might have 'Peter's keys and discipline and Paul's doctrine', and declaring him to be 'the mediator between the clergy and the laity'. Wise after the event, people remembered that Charles was clothed in white satin, the ominous colouring of a sacrificial victim, and that Bishop Senhouse of Carlisle, who preached the sermon, had taken the funeral text: 'I will give thee a Crown of Life.' He himself incidentally died almost immediately afterwards of the black jaundice. Another ill-omen, later recalled by Baxter, was an earthquake that occurred while the ceremony was being performed. 'It was about two oclock in the afternoon,' he recorded, 'and did affright the boys and all in the neighbourhood.'

Laud acted throughout in the capacity of Dean of Westminster, and at the end of the service received back the regalia into the Abbey's custody.

> The coronation being ended [wrote Heylyn] his majesty going in his robes to Westminster Hall, did there deliver them to Laud . . . together with the crown, septre and the sword called Cortena, to be laid up with the rest of the regalia in their old repository; which he receiving from the king, returned into the Abbey church, offered solemnly on the altar in his majesty's name . . . and so laid them up.

Some months later in the early morning of Trinity Sunday 1626 Laud, still in residence at his prebendal house, ordained Nicholas Ferrar to the diaconate, and afterwards celebrated Holy Communion at Torrigiano's altar, which had hitherto stood unused since the founding of the College. It was now generally supposed that Williams would have to leave the Abbey. The King had already ordered him to withdraw into his diocese; and Chamberlain reported to Joseph Mead in 1626/7: 'the bishop of Lincoln . . . is forbidden to preach his turn at Whitehall, and is therefore gone back into Lincolnshire.' A little later Beaulieu told Sir Thomas Pickering: 'you have heard also, how the bishop of Lincoln, being come hither upon some pretended occasion concerning his deanery of Westminster, was commanded and forced upon a sudden to depart.' This he was able to do with a clear conscience since in a Chapter minute of 27 January 1625/6 his residence had been dispensed with for the time being:

> It is concluded at this present Chapiter [runs the entry] that the right honourable and right reverend Father in God the Lord Bishop of Lincolne our honourable Deane having urgent occasions to be absent from his Deanery for one twelvemoneth following,

shall be dispensed with all, and that tyme of absence is consented unto for his lordshipp, by the whole chapiter, and commanded to be registered in this chapiter Act. His Lordshipp being likewise dispensed with all to supply any or all his courses and daies of preaching, by a sufficient deputy to be appointed by his Lordship.

Already during James's reign, or so it had been rumoured, Williams had offered to give up his deanery to John Preston, the famous Calvinist Master of Emmanuel College, Cambridge, who was pressing Buckingham to persuade the King to sell the lands belonging to Deans and Chapters in order to pay the royal debts, on condition that he abandoned this suggestion and 'would busie himself no more' in trying to ruin the Church. Now in November 1625 Dr Francis Dye, Chancellor of Salisbury, hinted to Secretary Conway 'that, on the changes consequent on the late Lord Keeper's leaving the deanery of Westminster, the writer may have the deanery of Sarum or Rochester or at least of poor Lichfield'; while the Dean of Rochester went further still and actually proposed himself as the new incumbent of the Abbey, 'if there be a probability of a vacancy'. Certainly both Charles and Laud would have been only too glad to see the back of one whom they regarded as an ecclesiastical monster: 'a perfect diocese in himself', bishop, dean, prebendary and parson. As early as 1621 John Chamberlain had complained to Sir Dudley Carleton: 'The Lord keeper hath gotten the deanery of Westminster in commendam during the time he shall continue bishop of Lincoln, beside his parsonage of Walgrave in Northamptonshire and a good prebend of that church, attached to the bishopric of Lincoln forever.' Since then, of course, the Dean's fortunes had taken a turn for the worse; and now he inquired of Lord Cottington what he should do 'to get his peace with the king'. His lordship replied uncompromisingly: 'His Majesty did not like that he should be so near a neighbour to Whitehall, but would be better contented if he would part with his deanery.' This he flatly declined to do. 'To relinquish his deanery,' Hacket declared, 'he was utterly deaf unto it; whosoever ask'd it was a hard chapman, but he did not stand so much in need of his ware, to grant him his price.' 'Into which,' said an enemy, 'he shut himself fast, with as strong bars and bolts as the law could make.'

Meanwhile Laud, who had been appointed to Dr Bulkeley's prebend in 1610, but not formally installed until some ten years later, proceeded to make himself as big a nuisance to the Dean as possible within the Abbey and its precincts, attacking the simplicity of the services and intriguing among the Chapter. It was his hand, for example, behind the muniment of 1625 which reads: 'For setting up the cross rayles at the high altar and putting in bars in them', and when he finally retired upon being elevated to the see of London in 1628, he left his chaplain and future biographer, Peter Heylyn, behind him to carry on the fight. Williams for his part wisely spent most of his time at Buckden; and was only at the Abbey when his presence was absolutely essential.

It was about this time that the controversy over pews flared up again in the Chapter. Under Dean Neile ten 'several large pewes of strong wainscott' had been erected in the Choir at a cost of over £36, for the use of 'the better sort'; while in 1606 the Prebendal Stalls themselves had been repaired in order to enable their occupants to 'sitt together, halfe on one side and halfe on the other side, every one sittinge accordinge to his dignity and degree, the subdeane still keepinge his ancient place'. Near the pulpit stood 'a great pew' with a portrait of Richard II hanging over it, which the prebendaries often appeared to prefer to their own seats; possibly because it was more convenient for hearing the sermon. Williams, however, claimed this last as his own exclusive property, and refused to allow any but the nobility to sit there with him. Such high-handed conduct was strongly resented by some members of the Chapter, and in particular Peter Heylyn, who had already been refused institution to a living by the Dean on the grounds that the benefice in question was in his gift and not that of the Crown. Eventually the malcontents drew up a charge of thirty-six articles against Williams, which led to the setting up of a Royal Commission to investigate the whole matter. Headed by Laud it visited the Abbey in 1635, but nothing could be proved; and a further petition some twelve months later was equally unproductive. The most that the prebendaries could secure was a ruling re-affirming their right to sit in the 'great pew', where 'none should sit there with them but Lords of Parliament and Earls' eldest sons, according to the ancient custom'.

A few years later a Chapter minute of 31 December 1639, dealt with the thorny question of seating for the prebendaries' wives.

> Whereas [it was resolved] there is a pew erected in the church for ye wives of ye prebendaries, it is ordered and agreed that whatsoever rules and orders shall be made by Mr Subdeane [Robert Newell] and ye Deane of Chichester [Richard Steward] . . . for regulating of ye pews shall punctually be observed for all time to come. And in meane season shall no-one sitt there but the wives of the prebendaries.

Insults continued to be heaped on Williams's head. He was forbidden to take his seat in the House of Lords in 1626, and only restored two years later at the express request of Parliament.

Chamberlain wrote to Mead on 28 March 1628: 'the lord arch-bishop returned from his confinement on Tuesday last to Lambeth, and goes to Parliament, as also the bishop of Lincoln.' It was during this Parliament that Williams said in the House of Lords: 'hence-forth neither hope of greater preferments, nor fear of the loss of what he presently enjoyed, should make him do or speak against his conscience.'

The King was making difficulties over the appointment of a new High Steward of Westminster, the Earl of Montgomery, who was also Lord Chamberlain. Conway wrote to the Dean on 12 September 1628: 'The grant sent with a blank to be filled by his majesty for the Stewardship of Westminster was presented to the king. He is not satisfied with it, because putting in a name after it is sealed, makes it void in law, whereof the king conceives the bishop is not ignorant.' As usual Williams grovelled and promised to procure another patent 'if six prebendaries can be found'. But, on hurriedly calling the Chapter together on 19 September, only five could be mustered, who decided that 'as soone as six prebendaries shall be in towne' the patent would again be sealed and delivered to the Lord Chamber-lain. Meanwhile a provisional patent was made out and sent to him.

Despite the gross insults showered upon him by the Duke, the Dean continued to fawn upon Buckingham and eventually claimed that there had been some sort of reconciliation. Certainly he ex-pressed what appeared to be genuine regret at the latter's murder; for writing to the Earl of Holland, Buckingham's 'dearest friend' on 29 August 1628, he declared himself to be 'as sorry for the Duke's death as if he had received his favours only without any mixture of his displeasure'.

'RARE' BEN JONSON'S EIGHTEEN INCHES OF ABBEY GROUND

Ben Jonson was born in Westminster, where he had been educated under William Camden of whom he wrote:

> Camden most reverend head to whom I owe
> All that I am in arts and all I know.

He returned to die in the Abbey precincts. His stepfather, Thomas Fowler, may possibly have been Surveyor to the Dean and Chapter in 1572 and responsible for the fabric of the church. Ben entered the same profession, but could not endure it and went a-soldiering to Flanders instead. Now in his old age he took up his abode in 'a little house' close to the Abbey, 'under wch', Aubrey tells us, 'you passe as you go out of the churchyard into the Old Palace'. Here, surrounded by his books, Ben spent the last twelve years of his life, most of

M

them in dire poverty. It is, however, pleasant to be able to record that when he was finally struck down by paralysis, the Dean and Chapter sent him £5. '19 January 1628/9. Given by Dr Price to Mr Benjamin Johnson in his sickness and want with consent of Dr Price, Dr Sutton, Dr Grant, Dr Holt, Dr Darell and my Lord of Lincoln's good likinge, signified by Mr Osboldston. 5l.' He died on 6 August 1637 and was buried in the church. The story runs that Ben once asked Charles I for a favour. 'What is it?' demanded the King. 'Give me eighteen inches of square ground.' 'Where?' 'In Westminster Abbey.' He was buried standing upright under 'a pavement square of blew marble' with this inscription: 'O Rare Ben Jonson', 'wch,' wrote Aubrey, 'was done at the chardge of Jack Young, afterwards Knighted, who walking there when the grave was covering gave the fellow eighteen pence to cut it'. Those are reputed to have been the words with which the populace greeted his play *Bartholomew Fair* on its opening night.

LAUD CONDEMNS DEAN WILLIAMS

In 1637 Archbishop Laud at last succeeded in getting Williams condemned in the Star Chamber on a treason charge. As early as 1628 he had laid information against the Bishop for saying 'the Puritans are the king's best subjects . . . the Puritans will carry all at last'. This was construed as 'publishing false News and Tales, to the Scandal of his Majesty's Government: and for revealing of Counsels of State, contrary to his oath as a Privy Councillor'; but as long as Noy remained Attorney-General Laud could make little headway. He continued none the less to press on with the matter and stirred up his agents, particularly that odious little attorney, Kilvert, to produce new evidence. In 1635 Williams was given a chance to compromise by buying his pardon with £4,000 and surrendering his Deanery. The offer was rejected, along with another one allowing him to retain Westminster but pay £8,000. He was then accused of saying that 'he held the Deanery of Westminster by as good a right as his Majesty held his crown'; and his prebendaries were stirred up to petition against him for 'sundry grievances'.

Eventually the Dean was brought to trial on 11 July 1637 when he was charged with subordination of perjury and tampering with witnesses. Laud, of course, sat as President of the Court; and after some nine days Williams was condemned and sentenced to a fine of £10,000 and imprisonment in the Tower; but he again declined to accept his release on the condition of giving up all his preferments and retiring to one of the Irish bishoprics.

Because of the Dean's enforced absence two royal commissions, one in November 1637 and the other in February 1638/9, were set up, which granted to the Sub-Dean and prebendaries the right to hold Chapters and perform all the necessary business of the College during Williams's confinement. The Sub-Dean at that time was Robert Newell; but the real power at Westminster during this three-year interregnum was wielded by Peter Heylyn, Laud's chaplain and future biographer. One of his first acts was to persuade the Chapter to sequester the Dean's dividend and allowances, and use them for the upkeep of the church and the payment of its debts; but he also found himself facing some considerable discontent, not to say disorders, both within and without the precincts. In 1637 there was the petition of Prebendary Gabriel More to the commissioners complaining that 'by our local statutes every prebend has his peculiar stall, according to which he is to have his precedence, which is denied to petitioner. By the same statute, all materials for repair of prebendaries houses are to be allowed by the College, which is likewise denied to petitioner.'

Outside, the London apprentices, fanatically Puritan and always ripe for mischief, were giving even more trouble than usual, since they were being joined by 'dissolute persons, who abound in Westminster and the suburbs'. The Trained Bands had to be called out on Shrove Tuesday 1638 and a number of heads were broken. Meanwhile in the very Cloisters of St Peter's church itself Henry, Viscount Newark, and two of his friends, beat up an enemy of their's, Philip Kinder.

A petition from the Sub-Dean and prebendaries in February 1637/8 reported to the King that when, in view of these and other disorders, and in strict accordance with 'ancient and laudable custom', they had caused the gates of the Close to be locked at 10 p.m., 'some of the inhabitants pretending a late liberty of free ingress and egress at all hours have thereupon attempted to break down the gates and have assaulted a servant of the petitioners'. Charles immediately replied confirming their right to shut the gates and warning 'the inhabitants . . . not to presume to disturb "this court" or offer violence to the servants of the College upon pain of severe punishment'. Such conflicts, of course, were the harbingers of the coming troubles.

In February 1638/9 Williams was again arraigned before the Star Chamber for libel. Some letters had been found among his papers at Buckden from his friend and ally, Prebendary Osbaldeston, then Headmaster of Westminster School. These were dated January 1633 and were thought to refer to Laud as 'the little Urchin' and 'the meddling Hocus Pocus', although Osbaldeston strongly denied it. His denial was brushed aside and the Dean was convicted upon the extraordinary statement of Lord Coventry that 'if the letters were in a band-box [where they were found] that was a publishing of them'. He was fined a further £8,000 and returned to the Tower. Meanwhile Osbaldeston, standing unobserved at the back of the court, heard his own savage sentence read out: imprisonment; to have one ear nailed to the pillory in Palace Yard and then to stand before his own scholars in Dean's Yard and have the other similarly treated; and finally to be fined £10,000. Hastening home to his study he burnt his papers; and, before going into safe hiding, left the following note on his desk: 'That if the Archbishop enquire after me, tell him, I am gone beyond *Canterbury*.' This last seemed to imply that Osbaldeston had fled abroad, whereas in reality he lay concealed for three years 'from the cruelty of the Tyger' in Drury Lane.

Williams's enemies refused to leave him alone in the Tower. Pressure continued to be brought to bear upon him to resign his preferments, and every kind of scurrilous tale was industriously spread abroad.

> He never [wrote Heylyn maliciously] went into the Chapel of the Tower, where he was imprisoned to attend the Divine Service of the Church or hear the sermon there, or receive the sacrament, as all other Protestant prisoners had been used to do: but kept himself only to his private devotions, to which his nearest servants were not often admitted: which whether it gave the greater scandal to the protestants, puritans or papists, it is hard to say.

The Dean for his part complained to the Earl of Arundel in October 1640:

> The Tower . . . is . . . from a fair palace and quiet aboad, turned of late to a fort or citadel, and become so full of soldiers and that kind of dirge or noise, which is most adverse and contrary to retired thoughts and the disposition of a student; so that as I have been sequestered for above these three years past from the company of the living, so am I now bereaved from any conversation with the dead, and kept close prisoner from men and books in effect, untill such time in the evening as these people are withdrawn into their private huts and cabins.

A servant of his had got into trouble with the warders, one of whom while drunk insulted the Bishop. 'I could not,' wrote Williams, 'possibly understand him, and therefore he might easily misunderstand me, and in consequence thereof misreport me.' It was certainly a difficult position. However, in November 1640, after the Long Parliament had met and the Queen had pleaded his cause, the Bishop was released and again took his place in the House of Lords as the acknowledged leader of the episcopal Bench, some six of whom conducted him back in triumph to the Abbey, where he once m ore officiated as Dean. 'More honoured,' declared Heylyn bitterly, 'than ever any of his order, his person looked upon as sacred, his words deemed oracles.' It happened to be a day of humiliation, when Heylyn himself was preaching on the appropriate subject of charity and moderation, but with some 'irritating innuendoes' that aroused the Dean's wrath. Sitting in his favourite pew under the pulpit, Williams knocked thereon loudly with his staff, interrupting the preacher and calling out: 'No more of that point, Peter'; to which Heylyn suavely replied: 'I have a little more to say, my Lord, and then I have done.' Afterwards the Bishop, who now constituted himself the censor of all opinions aired in the Abbey, demanded to see the sermon.

He was virtually the Head of the Government; advised Charles to sign the Earl of Strafford's death warrant; became chairman of an Ecclesiastical Committee set up to restore order in public worship; and ordered the Communion table at St Margaret's to be moved into the centre of the Nave to placate the House of Commons, who were again proposing to make their corporate Communion in that church.

> Two members of this House [reported Sir Robert Harley] were required to repair to the Reverend Dean of Westminster, to give him an Intimation of this House, that it was desired the Elements might be consecrated upon a Communion-Table standing in the Middle of the Church, according to the Rubrick; and to have the Table removed from the Altar: he gave the Answer to One of the Members, that was intreated to go unto him, That it should be removed, as it was desired by this House; with this further Respect to the House, that, though he would do greater Service to the House of Commons than this, yet he would do as much as this for any Parish in his Diocese, that should desire it.

The Ecclesiastical Commission met either in the Dean's Lodgings or else in the Jerusalem Chamber, where they were lavishly entertained by their host; but nothing emerged from their deliberations, and they were 'scattered about the middle of [May] 1641 upon the bringing in of a Bill against Deans and Chapters'. Williams's short-lived flirtation with the Puritanical House of Commons was over. He became Archbishop of York in November, being allowed to retain his Deanery for three years as some compensation for the spoliation he had suffered and to give him time to find another London home, when he led the opposition to another Bill proposing to deprive the bishops of their seats in the House of Lords and all their temporal powers. Instead he put forward counter-proposals of his own for the reform of episcopacy and the Church Courts.

RIOTS AT WESTMINSTER

It was then that the London apprentices took a hand in the game, crowding round the coaches of the bishops on Monday, 27 December 1641, as they drove into Palace Yard, and shouting 'No bishops! No Popish Lords!' Williams himself was hustled; and, his Welsh temper aflame, tried to seize one lad, but was immediately set upon by the rest and roughly manhandled. He was rescued with difficulty. The same day there was a further scuffle with the mob when the unpopular Colonel Lunsford drew his sword in Westminster Hall. This, we are told, 'being noised a great crowd of apprentices came to Westminster', where, apparently, they surged about the Abbey and the Houses of Parliament, vociferously condemning the bishops and supporting the Commons, but dispersed without doing any damage. The next morning, 28 December, however, they were in an uglier temper, after hearing that some of their number had been detained and were to be examined in the Abbey before the Archbishop. There was a rush for the great West Door to cries of 'let us pluck down the organs, let us deface the monuments! No bishop, no king!'; a panel was broken in and the mob were only kept out of the church by the resolute action of the Abbey staff, assisted by the Westminster boys and some gentlemen with drawn swords. The leader of the insurgents, Sir Richard Wiseman, was slain by a tile hurled from the battlements; and later buried in pomp by the London apprentices, who made a collection among themselves for this purpose, 'as if he had deserved well of his country'.

Captain Robert Slingsby writing to Sir John Pennington on 30 December thus described the incident:

> I cannot say we have had a merry Christmas, but the maddest one that ever I saw. . . . The Archbishop of York was beaten by the 'prentices the same day as he was going into the Parliament. The next day they assaulted the Abbey to pull down the organs and altar, but it was defended by the Archbishop of York and his servants with some other gentlemen who came to them; divers of the citizens were hurt, but none killed. . . . The officers of the army, since these tumults, have watched and kept a court of guard in the Presence Chamber, and are entertained upon the King's charge. A company of soldiers is put into the Abbey for defence of it.

The last precaution is further reflected in the Abbey account books, where the following item is recorded: 'Item. Given to certayne Captaynes by the Deans appointment for defending the Church Cs. Item. Paid to Mr White and Mr Smyth for powdr and shot CXXIIIs. Purchase of muskets, pikes and pestols XXXVl—VIs—VId.'

When Williams next met the King, the latter congratulated him upon his successful defence of the regalia; whereupon the Dean is reported to have replied: 'Please, Your Majesty, I am a true Welshman, and they are observed never to run away until their generals do first forsake them. No fear of my flinching whilst your Majesty doth countenance our cause.' A cool thrust at Charles's own transparent moral cowardice. The Commons naturally were not so well pleased; and taking advantage of an ill-advised petition by Williams and other 'too-hasty bishops', complaining that they were unable to attend Parliament for fear of their lives, and hence no Act passed in their absence was valid, Pym moved for their impeachment for high treason. And it was not long before that stormy petrel, the Archbishop of York, found himself back in the Tower in company with Archbishop Laud. Hacket believed that they met within its walls and were reconciled; but probably the Puritans were nearer the truth when they alleged that Williams had said to his erstwhile rival: 'Ift please your graceless grace my little Lord, you know that I ever hated papistry from the beginning; for which cause you caused me to suffer a long time imprisonment.'

In May 1642 he was released on bail; but promptly fled to join the King in Yorkshire and to arrange for his own enthronement there. He never saw London or Westminster Abbey again.

10

The Abomination of Desolation

AFTER the flight of Dean Williams to the north, the College fell on evil days. For the rest of the year 1642 the Chapter, under Robert Newell, succeeded in maintaining their position and in carrying on the Abbey services; but early in 1643 the blow fell. Then a Parliamentary Committee was set up, under the chairmanship of Sir Robert Harley, in order to demolish 'the monuments of superstition and idolatry in the Abbey Church and the windows thereof'. The Treasurer's accounts record their work:

> 1644. April 19. Receipt for vis by Thomas Gastaway, from Sir Robert Harley for taking down the High Altar in Henry VII's Chapel.
>
> 1644. May 21. Henry Wilson ffreemason. Working in taking downe the Altar in Henry VII Chapel. Item. for rassing out the painted images, £7–16–0.

This altar, of course, was Torrigiano's work, which except on possibly one occasion had stood there unused since Mary's reign. Keepe described it as 'admirable and unequalled for its curiosity'; Bruno Ryves as 'a curious Touchstone, a rarity not to be match'd; and Dart as 'a brazen altar, artificially wrought and gilt with gold . . . the work of Peter, a painter of Florence'. Under it lay the body of King Edward VI, that most Protestant of monarchs; but this fact did not in any way deter Harley, who 'breaking into Henry VII's Chapel, pulled down the altar stone which stood before the goodly monument of that King' and 'brake it into shivers'.

The lovely Chapel windows were likewise subjected to the 'cleaning out of the pictures', which were taken to Harley's own home and then disappeared forever; while a year later Sir John Rutland received a total sum of £40 to replace them with white glass. At the same time the beautiful thirteenth-century floor was grievously mutilated; and what remained of Feckenham's hundred copes burnt, their gold and silver ornaments being melted down and sold for the benefit of the poor Irish. On 2 June 1643 a motion was put to the Commons 'that the Dean, subdean and prebends be enjoyned and required to deliver to Sir Henry Mildmay and Mr Marten, the keys of the treasury where the Regalia are kept; and that they may search that place and report to the House what they find there'. It was negatived by fifty-eight votes to thirty-seven. But the very next day a similar question, in a slightly different form, was carried by one vote; and it was finally resolved: 'That the locks of the doors where the Regalia are kept in Westminster Abbey shall be opened, notwithstanding any former order made; and search made there, and an inventory taken of what things are . . . and presented to the House.'

Either the Chapter did not possess, or refused to deliver up, the keys, with the result that the doors of the ancient chapel, known as the Chamber of the Pyx, where the regalia were stored, had to be forced. Then occurred the famous scene in which George Withers 'noted for a bad poet' was dressed up as royalty, with a crown on his head and the sceptre in his hand, and walked 'in great scorn and mockery about the room and the cloysters'. Heylyn wrote of him in *Aerius Redivivus*: 'Who being thus crown'd and royally array'd (as right well became him) first marcht about the room with a stately garb, and afterwards with a thousand apish and ridiculous actions exposed those sacred ornaments to contempt and laughter.'

For the moment they were restored to their 'great iron chest'; but shortly afterwards removed once again and this time sold.

The last meeting of the Chapter was held on 25 May 1642, when the minutes were signed by Robert Newell, Peter Heylyn and five other prebendaries; and very soon a gradual exodus of the Abbey staff began.

In the summer of 1643 two companies of soldiers were quartered in the church. Here they amused themselves by breaking down the altar rails and burning them; then smashed the organ to bits and pawned its pipes 'at several ale-houses for pots of ale'. They clad themselves in the choir surplices, and 'in contempt of the canonical habit ran up and down the church. He that wore the surplice was the hare, the rest the hounds.' Forms were placed around the Communion table and the soldiers took their meals there, smoking their pipes and drinking ale to their hearts' content. They also, according to the muck-raking Dr Ryves supported by the testimony of Peter Heylyn, used the Abbey for the vilest and filthiest of purposes, 'introducing their whores into the church' and 'laying their filth and excrements about it'. Dr Ryves's evidence, however, is suspect. He gasps with horror at the 'prophanations' of an ignorant and debauched soldiery; yet he himself, presumably a gentle cultured

Christian, is scarcely behind them in the coarseness of his tastes and uncharitableness of spirit. Speaking of John Pym's burial in Henry VII's Chapel on 13 December 1643, when Prebendary Osbaldeston officiated and Stephen Marshall preached the sermon, he demanded that this great Parliamentarian's 'vulgar lowsy ashes . . . should be buried with the burial of an ass . . . and cast forth beyond the gates of the city'—the mean kind of revenge actually wreaked upon them by the Laudians after the Restoration.

On 21 August the acting Sub-Dean and his few remaining colleagues were ordered 'to grant the use of the pulpit on sundays in the afternoon to such lecturers as the Commons should appoint'; and this intrusion into the Abbey's worship not unnaturally hastened the departure of the Chapter, until by the end of the year none were left excepting Lambert Osbaldeston, who had now emerged from hiding and was high in favour with the Puritans. It was not long either before the Precentor, Minor Canons, Choristers and Lay Vicars followed them into the wilderness.

PURITAN INTERVENTION IN THE ABBEY SERVICE

Early in January 1643/4 a committee was appointed consisting of sixteen M.P.s, to whom four others were quickly added. Their job was 'to enquire into the state of the [Abbey] church'; and one of their first reforms was to substitute, from 28 February onwards, a daily morning 'exercise' for Matins and Evensong. This was held from 7 a.m. to 8 a.m. and conducted in turn by seven carefully selected Presbyterian divines, including Dr Staunton, Stephen Marshall and Philip Nye, who were also allocated prebendal houses belonging to the absentee prebendaries.

Meanwhile the Westminster Assembly of Divines was meeting, first in Henry VII's Chapel and later in the Jerusalem Chamber, where they drew up the Directory of Public Worship, the Longer and Shorter Catechism, and the famous Westminster Confession of Faith. Here took place those fierce disputes between the English Selden and the Scottish Gillespie; and here, too, Herle, Rector of Winwick, delivered his philippics against the bishops. 'For five years, six months, and twenty-five days, through one thousand one hundred and sixty-three sessions,' wrote Stanley, 'the Chapel of Henry VII and the Jerusalem Chamber witnessed their weary labours.' One of their principal enactments was to approve the Solemn League and Covenant, carry the document 'with tears of joy' into Henry VII's Chapel on 16 August 1643, and sign it eight days later in St Margaret's Church. By 22 April the following year 'all persons who belong to, or had dependence on this church' (i.e. the Abbey) were ordered to sign it. Osbaldeston and two Minor Canons, Hutton and White, did so. The rest had presumably all gone and their whereabouts were unknown; although it was credibly reported that two of the prebendaries, Drs Moore and Wemys 'sculk up and downe' in the vicinity; that Drs Wilson and Killigrew were 'at Oxford', and Dr Howard was languishing 'in prison'. Against the Head Master's name, the famous Richard Busby, was inserted the one word, 'sickly'.

At the same time it was decreed that all the brass and iron in the Chapel should be taken down and sold; an order which fortunately was never carried out.

The story of the Abbey plate during this period is an interesting and curious one. A minute of the Parliamentary Committee on 28 March 1644 recorded: 'Plate of ye College carried into one of ye vaults of ye Church and there buried.' But in April it was all dug up again and part of it melted down to pay the College servants and those very workmen who were engaged on the orgy of destruction. The remainder perished the following autumn when, as Widmore informs us, '9 October. two of the [Committee] members were ordered to inform the House what superstitious plate was in the place where the regalia were kept, that it might be melted down and sold, and the produce employed to buy horses.' The destruction went on. Neile's High Altar disappeared, together with those thirteenth-century tapestries of cloth of Arras that had adorned the Choir. A plain wooden table replaced the altar: '1 July,' ran a Treasurer's voucher for 1643, 'One Table for the Communion in the Abbey, £5.' As for the tapestries, they were first taken to the House of Commons, but eventually sold. There is an interesting item among the Receiver's accounts for 29 September 1658, which may possibly refer to some of them: 'Received from Francis Allen Esq. in full of the price of foure peeces of Tapestry Hangings sold him by order of the Governors, £20.'

The Choir and Nave of the church were now filled with pews, so arranged that they all faced the central pulpit. 'From this pulpit,' wrote Westlake, 'came the denunciations of Stephen Marshall, chaplain of the parliamentary Army, and many others whose sermons were characterised by length rather than charity.' The carpenter's plan showing the allocation of these pews is still extant. 'Lord' Bradshaw, who now occupied the Deanery on a long lease, sat on the south side, opposite that formidable royalist, Mr Busby.

In [God's] *Ark over-topping the World's Waves,* John Vicars gives an eye-witness account from the Puritan stand-point of the remarkable changes that had taken place in the Abbey:

...in the most rare and strange alteration of the face of things in
the Cathedral Church of Westminster. Namely that whereas
there was wont to be heard, nothing almost but roaring boys and
squeaking organ pipes, and the cathedral catches of Morley, and
I know not what trash; now the popish altar is quite taken away,
the bellowing organs are demolisht, and pulled down, the treble,
or rather trouble and base singers, chanters or inchanters driven
out; and instead thereof, there is now set up a most blessed orthodox preaching ministry, every morning throughout the weeke,
and every weeke through the whole yeare a sermon is preached
by most learned grave, and godly ministers, of purpose appointed
thereunto, and for the gaudy, guilded crucifixes, and rotten
rabble of dumb idols, popish saints and pictures, set up and placed,
and painted thereabout, where that sinfull singing was used: now
a most sweet assembly, and thicke throng of God's pious people,
and well-affected, living teachable saints there is constantly and
most comfortably, every morning to be seen at the sermons.

John Vicars, for one, would most heartily have approved of a payment made to Thomas Stevens and others about this time, 'for
taking down the angels in the Abbey and cleansing out pictures'.

THE FABRIC UNDER THE GREAT INTERREGNUM

None the less, despite their many detractors ancient and modern, the
Parliamentary Committees and finally the Board of Governors, who
controlled the affairs of the Abbey during the Great Interregnum,
did much both to preserve and repair the fabric of the church itself
and the Royal Tombs, and to conserve and increase the revenues
of its estates.

'Never,' wrote Dr Armitage Robinson, 'were the finances of the
Abbey more carefully handled than by these eminent laymen: every
item of expenditure was noted, every voucher kept.' Among them
is a receipt recording that on 14 October 1645 Richard Troc, a
painter, received ten shillings 'for the gelding of the work that was
broken downe in the freeze over the communion table' and 'for 36
yards of whitting over the presse where the kinges and queenes
stand in King Henneries Chapell.' There is also the bill of Thomas
Symons, the London goldsmith, who made the Governors' seal for
£25. This depicted on one side the House of Commons and on the
other the Great Porch of the Abbey church. Furthermore there is
ample evidence to show that the prebendal houses were kept in
excellent order. 'Lord' Bradshaw, for instance had a lot of work
done on the Deanery.

19 Dr Alexander Nowell, Head Master of Westminster School, afterwards Dean of St Paul's, d. 1602. He was a keen angler, 'was the author of the Shorter Catechism and the inventor of bottled beer'. From a print after the painting in the Bodleian Library, Oxford.

VIVat. VInCat. Regnet,
ELISABETHA,
AngLIæ FranCIæ aC HIbernIæ
RegIna,
FIDeI DefenfatrIX
HenrICI 8i Regis F,
Anno regnI sVI XXXVII

20 Queen Elizabeth I. From the painting in the Deanery of Westminster Abbey. Painted
1594–5.

21 Silver die of the Common Seal of the Dean and Chapter of Westminster, made after the Restoration of Charles II.

22 Funeral cortège of Queen Elizabeth I, showing her funeral wax-effigy laid on the top of her coffin.

24 William Laud, prebendary of Westminster, 1621–8; afterwards Archbishop of Canterbury. Beheaded 1645.

23 William Camden, Head Master of Westminster School, 1593–9, and afterwards Clarenceux King of Arms, d. 1623. Author of the *Britannia* and of the first Abbey guide-book.

25 The neglected Shrine of Edward the Confessor as it appeared to the illustrator of Ackermann's *History of Westminster Abbey*, published in 1812.

30 The crowning of James II, from Sandford's *History*.

31 Thomas Sprat, Dean of Westminster and Bishop of Rochester, d. 1713; with his son Thomas Sprat, prebendary of Westminster, 1713–20. From an engraving by I. Smith after M. Dahl.

32 The North Front of Westminster Abbey painted to show the effect of a spire and cupola, but also showing the houses on the North side, usually omitted from drawings of the time, *c.* 1740–5.

33 Francis Atterbury, Dean of Westminster and Bishop of Rochester, 1713–23. Died in exile 1732. Engraving by H. T. Ryall after the painting by Kneller in the Bodleian Library, Oxford.

34 Zachary Pearce, Dean of Westminster and Bishop of Rochester, 1756–68, d. 1774. From the painting in the Vestry of St Martin-in-the-Fields.

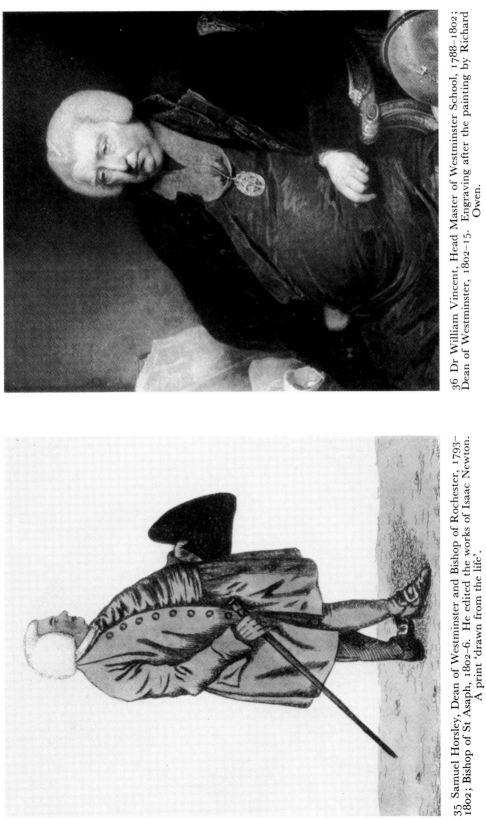

35 Samuel Horsley, Dean of Westminster and Bishop of Rochester, 1793–1802; Bishop of St Asaph, 1802–6. He edited the works of Isaac Newton. A print 'drawn from the life'.

36 Dr William Vincent, Head Master of Westminster School, 1788–1802; Dean of Westminster, 1802–15. Engraving after the painting by Richard Owen.

37 The Great Hall ('School') of Westminster School, showing the apse called the 'shell' which gave its name to the class taught at that end. In this room the entire school was taught until 1882. Lithograph by C. W. Radcliffe, *c.* 1845.

38 Great Dean's Yard, a print from the same series as that above.

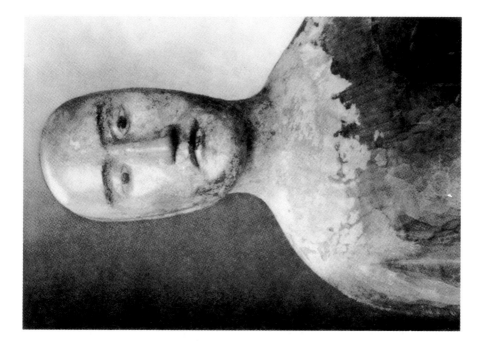

39 The Abbey Effigies are a legacy from the days when a funeral effigy was placed on the coffin in state funeral processions. They were usually made from death masks. (*Above, left to right*) Queen Anne of Bohemia, wife of Richard II; Queen Elizabeth of York, wife of Henry VII; Henry VII; Queen Anne (of Denmark), wife of James I; Queen Catherine (de Valois), wife of Henry V.

40 Head and shoulders of wooden funeral effigy of Edward III. The face was carved from the death mask.

41 Wax effigy of Admiral Lord Nelson, modelled by Miss Catherine Andras. The clothes belonged to Nelson.

42 Wax effigy of Charles II, showing the clothes worn under the Garter robes. The face is a life mask.

43 The Altar Screen erected by Benjamin Wyatt and Bernasconi in 1823 to replace Wren's classical Altar Piece.

44 Wren's classical Altar Piece, originally designed for the Chapel in Whitehall Palace, erected in the Abbey *c.* 1706. The remains now constitute the Altar Piece of the parish church at Burnham-on-Sea, Somerset.

46 R. Chenevix Trench, when Archbishop of Dublin 1864–84; Dean of Westminster 1856–64. Engraving by J. Richardson Jackson after the painting by George Richmond.

45 Rev. William Buckland, D.D., F.R.S., when Canon of Christ Church. Afterwards Dean of Westminster, 1845–56. Engraving by Samuel Cousins after the painting by Thomas Phillips, R.A.

An ordinance of both Houses of Parliament on 18 November 1645, set up another committee consisting of eleven lords and twenty-two commoners, to govern the College; since, it was stated, 'the present Dean and Prebends (except only Mr Lambert Osbolston) have deserted their charge or are become delinquents to the Parliament'. The houses in the precincts, apart from any already allocated to the regular preachers and lecturers, were let out to trustworthy Parliamentarians like Alexander Pym, who occupied the prebendal home of Richard Steward. And later lists of tenants recently discovered among the Receiver's accounts for 1654–6 and 1659 disclose that although Lambert Osbaldeston and Richard Busby continued to live respectively in the Great and Little Cloisters, most of the other dwellings there had been leased to strangers; while a number of the Governors themselves resided in Dean's Yard.

Richard Busby had been appointed to the head-mastership of Westminster School in January 1640 at a Chapter Meeting held on the twenty-first of that month. 'Mr Richard Busby,' it was resolved should be given 'the office and roome of Schoolemaster with his house and lodgings thereunto belonging. Fee per annum £20.' His courageous opposition to Puritan rule is of course well known; but he wisely tempered it with diplomacy. For if it is true that he caused his boys to pray for Charles I on the very day of his execution, regularly conducted the forbidden Prayer Book services under his own roof, and boldly retained the title of 'King's Scholars'; he was also wise enough to know which side his bread was buttered. Thomas Hearne spoke of him as 'a Complyer and a time server' and 'of much less Judgement than Mr Camden'. He slyly wriggled out of his obligation to take the Covenant by feigning sickness, accepted the Engagement and permitted the school to attend the lectures and sermons of the Presbyterian divines at the Abbey. None the less Robert South, a pupil in Westminster School at the time, declared: 'Thanks be to God they were never our teachers'; and the Puritans themselves were not slow to recognize in the school a hot-bed of sedition. 'It will never be well with the Nation,' said John Owen, Dean of Christ Church, 'till Westminster School is suppressed.' 'He knew,' commented Sargeaunt, 'that Busby was in the winter of his discontent and always hoping for the grass-hoppers.'

TACIT RESISTANCE TO THE NEW SERVICES

By an Act of Parliament in September 1649 the affairs of the College were finally put into the hands of fifty-six Governors, who ran it, including the stipends of the preachers and lecturers, for £1,900 per annum. One of their first actions was to station a corporal and nine soldiers in the Abbey church of a Sunday to keep order and suppress hecklers. They must have had a busy time. On 26 December Captain James Straghen wrote to the Governors demanding the payment of a shilling per Sunday that had been promised to each of 'those souldiers that shall attend in ye Abby Church Westmr on the Lords Daie to restraine the noise that is made in the time of Divine Service'. He continued: 'I was comanded be my mayor on the last Lords day to send myn musketeers and an ofischer to west minster abey and ther to contenew fron seven oclock in the morning until the afternoon sermon was ended and to keepe the peopell from making disturbance in sermon time: and if any dide make aney to bring them to the maine gaurd at Whitehall.' One of the preachers in particular must have caused them a lot of trouble. This was Mr Bridock, who received permission to preach in the Abbey from the Governors despite the violent opposition of Strong, the famous independent divine, who threatened to refuse 'to suffer such a person to preach in his pulpit'. However, he was overruled and Bridock held forth amid a great deal of noise. His sermon was later declared to be of unsound doctrine, to have given 'much dissatisfaction', and indeed 'was little less than popery'.

But it was not only the official preachers who were causing dissatisfaction. Instructions had to be issued to the 'officers of the Church' to put a stop to 'the unlawful meetings of idle persons at night in the Abbey . . . and upon examination of such suspicious persons as they shall there finde to carry them before a justice of peace to be proceeded agst accordins'. Trouble, indeed, was piling up on every side, from Busby and his school down to the 'common scolds wthin the citty and libertie', for whose punishment the Governors were compelled to order 'a new cucking stoole', and the thief Nicholas Asaby, who 'having not the fear of God before his eyes', stole the lead from the church roof. Within the Abbey itself Cornet Day was caught in September 1656 'dispersing a seditious paper' and was imprisoned in Windsor Castle; while the very next February thirty or forty men 'hired a house near the Abbey in Westminster' in order to shoot at Oliver Cromwell 'as he went from the Sermon to Parliament'. Cromwell had been installed as Protector in Westminster Hall instead of the Abbey, whose choir none the less sang at the ceremony, which partook of the nature of a coronation.

Despite all the revolutionary changes that had taken place since 1640 the Abbey church continued as of yore to be the burial place of kings, or of those who might wish to be kings, and of the great ones of the realm. Lord Cranfield was interred there on 14 August 1645 'with funeral pomp according to his degree . . . being accompanied by divers of the nobility and several members of the House of Commons,

who followed to the Abbey in coaches'. In November 1650 Thomas
May was laid to rest in 'the south-side of the choir . . . the whole
charge not to exceed £100'. Henry Ireton, who died in Ireland of
the plague during the autumn of 1651, was also honoured with a
sumptuous Abbey funeral. Among the Westminster muniments is a
petition from 'two officers of the church', who demanded their share
of his funeral draperies, i.e. 'the blacke of the pulpitt and quire'.
Some two years later a certain William Wright was paid £120 for
his tomb, which the designer very much hoped would be 'to the
good contentment of your Highness [i.e. Oliver Cromwell, Ireton's
father-in-law] and the most skilful beholders, and to the well-
deserved fame of the said lord deputy'.

Admiral Blake was yet another Cromwellian to be buried 'among
our princes in Westminster' at a cost of £550. These magnificent
obsequies no doubt encouraged the loyalty and zeal of other Repub-
lican commanders. Finally, some little time after his private interment in Henry VII's Chapel, a magnificent public funeral was
organized for Cromwell himself, which was so expensive that it
ruined his son and successor, Richard. But as this 'the joyfullest
funeral that ever I saw,' in the diarist Evelyn's opinion, 'wound its
way into the church on 23 November 1658, strictly guarded to
prevent the crowd of people', a Westminster scholar, Robert
Uvedale, leapt between the legs of one of the soldiers and snatched
a satin banner, known as the Majesty Scutcheon, from off the bier.
The hearse, declared the Surveyor of the fabric when petitioning
to have it taken down, 'had been of great profit to the monument
keepers'.

So, as the preachers raved and ranted, and one after another the
leaders of the Commonwealth and Protectorate passed to their
temporary resting place within her walls, St Peter-in-Westminster
watched and waited for better days.

PART III

Restoration and Resettlement

By The Reverend E. F. Carpenter, M.A., PH.D., B.D.
Canon and Archdeacon of Westminster

11

Rehabilitating Elizabeth's Charter

CAVALIERS AND PRESBYTERIANS COMBINE

WHEN Oliver Cromwell died on 3 September 1658, the anniversary of a day significant in his personal history, the nation was deprived of the one directing will which could have kept the Commonwealth in being at least a little longer. The constitution which the Protector left behind him, in so far as it differed from that of the Stuarts, differed for the better. But there was a paramount factor in the total situation which came to mean everything.

Traditional patterns of government can persist simply by reason of a human inertia which is resistant to change. Non-traditional forms can persist only if they are 'broad based upon the people's will', or are maintained through the power of the sword. In fact it was the Army which kept Cromwell in power. His death left the Army leaderless, with the consequence that there was the grim prospect of anarchy round the corner. Thus the constitutional opposition which resisted and finally liquidated Charles now united with his supporters in a common concern to restore order and a settled government.

In the existing situation, this could only mean a return of the monarchy. So it was that Cavaliers and Presbyterians worked together to bring about the Restoration, after Monck had marched down from Scotland and declared for a free Parliament. The populace was on his side; for the mass of the people had grown weary of a standing army, and were suspicious of all eccentric forms of religious zeal. The monarchy and a rural aristocracy, the Church of England and its settled parochial system, these were all old-established institutions and the nation was now prepared to welcome their return. By the time that Charles issued his declaration from Breda on 4 April 1660, his cause was nearly won: and before he caught sight once more of the white cliffs of Dover on 26 May, and entered into London on the 29th in a riot of enthusiasm, he had already been declared king.

Constitutional theory now assumed that though he had been a

wanderer over Europe since the battle of Worcester, thus gaining experience the hard way, his reign legally began on that tragic day, some eleven years earlier, when his father perished on a scaffold in Whitehall. The passionate desire of his supporters, who had themselves grown bitter by suffering, united in the demand that the clock should be put back; and this necessarily meant, among other things, the restoration of the established Church to its unique position as the one Church of the nation. The result was the Act of Uniformity, passed by a fanatical Parliament whose royalism disturbed even Clarendon and Charles. Under its terms all episcopally-ordained ministers were to go back to their old cures: and where, through death, there was no one to return, only those ministers who secured episcopal ordination and subscribed to the Book of Common Prayer, were to continue in office.

It was inevitable, therefore, that the restoration of the Collegiate Church of St Peter in Westminster, a royal foundation, and the home of coronations, should constitute a strong priority. The Charter of Queen Elizabeth must be made a reality once again.

Only four out of twelve prebendaries had survived the rigours of the Commonwealth to enter once again into their old inheritance. They were Peter Heylin (1600–62), disciple of William Laud and a zealous defender of Charles I; John Lang; William Heywood; and Matthew Nicholas, soon to become Dean of St Paul's. The first task to be undertaken was to re-establish the governing body. It was done rapidly. Within a fortnight of the Restoration, though the actual date is not recorded in the Installation Book, Charles nominated John Earle (1601–65), author of the *Microcosm*, to the office of Dean. The choice was not unexpected, for he had served both as Clerk to the Closet and Chaplain to the exiled Prince and won his complete confidence. 'A most humble, meek but cheerful man, an excellent scholar and rare preacher; I had the honour to be loved by him, he marrying me at Paris, during his Majesty's and the Churches Exile'—so comments John Evelyn.

Nominations to the rest of the Chapter soon followed—Henry Killigrew (1613–1700) a former Chaplain to the King's Army (5 July); Walter Jones; John Doughty; Richard Busby (1606–95) redoubtable Head Master of Westminster, who prayed for Charles I in the school on the very day of his execution, was to carry the ampula at the coronation of his son, and to stand with his hat on in the King's presence lest his authority in the school should be weakened; John Sudbury (14 July); James Lambe (23 July); David Michell (25 July). The Chapter was finally completed with the installation of Francis Walsall on 1 September.

A great many tasks now awaited the newly restored Dean and

Chapter—the revival of daily worship; the repair and cleaning up of the church and precincts; the recovering of properties and rents given to the College under the Elizabethan Charter; the re-establishment of local government in Westminster.

In one particular matter the Dean and Chapter acted with discretion and, considering the passions of the time, with a large measure of charity. There was no sudden or violent expulsion of John Rowe, appointed preacher in 1654, or his congregation. Thus when John Evelyn attended worship in the Abbey on 1 July, there was 'a good sermon by a stranger but no Common Prayer yet'. John Rowe preached his farewell sermon to his own flock on 23 September. It was a dramatic occasion, such that Pepys felt he must not miss, nor was he disappointed. The reader caused some amusement by 'desir[ing] of God that He would imprint his word on the thumbs of our right hands, and on the right great toes of our right feet'. During the preachment, Pepys records, 'some plaster fell from the top of the Abbey that made me and all the rest in our pew afraid, and I wished myself out'.

In spite of this tolerance to John Rowe, it is clear that the regular worship of the Church of England, according to the Book of Common Prayer, was being introduced as rapidly as possible. The strategic position of the Abbey made this necessary, and the Treasurer's accounts early show an expenditure of £120 on the organ, £29. 8s. 0d. on books for the choir, £41 on a silver verge and communion plate.

On 4 October 1660 Dr Accepted Frewen (1588–1664), Bishop of Lichfield and Coventry, was translated to the Archbishopric of York and the Abbey was used for the confirmation, rather than St Mary-le-Bow, possibly to give the occasion more significance. Many bishops in their robes attended. 'Lord! at their going out,' comments the indefatigable Pepys, 'how people did most of them look upon them as strange creatures and few with any kind of love or respect.'

At the Restoration, only nine diocesan bishops remained, and it was therefore necessary, if the Church of England were effectively to revive its traditional order, for this deficiency to be made up straight away. To do this on 28 October, five bishops were consecrated, in Henry VII's Chapel, to the sees of London, Lincoln, Worcester, Salisbury and St Asaph.

At the end of the year came the 'ill fated consecrations' of four Scottish bishops. Isolated instances of consecration went on to the beginning of the next century.

Of more pathetic interest, yet equally indicative that the Abbey's peculiar status was once more becoming a reality, were two royal funerals.

The Stuarts were not a long-lived race and the King's younger brother, Henry Duke of Gloucester, had hardly returned in triumph to Whitehall than he died of the smallpox. He was buried in the Abbey in September. His sister, Mary, who had made the journey to England 'to congratulate the happiness of her brother's miraculous restitution' also died from smallpox on Christmas Eve. Almost her last request was that her body should lie 'next the Duke of Gloucester my own dear brother'. This wish was respected and at nine o'clock in the evening of 29 December, in the presence of the Duke of York as chief mourner, and after a torch-lit procession from Somerset House, she was buried in the vault of another Mary of even more tragic memory—Mary, Queen of Scots.

The old order was returning. Indeed in mid October, so Samuel Pepys records, the Church service was being read in the Abbey; but 'very ridiculously', and, on one occasion, with a 'poor cold sermon' by one of the prebendaries. Maybe the diarist missed the warmth of independent worship, particularly since there was as yet little or no music. The latter, however, was on the way; for when Pepys attended on 30 December, there was 'great confusion of people that have come to hear the organ'.

A musical tradition, once interrupted, cannot be restored in a day, as many cathedral institutions discovered after the Second World War. So with the Abbey at the Restoration, the whole musical foundation needed to be rebuilt. Fortunately there was a vigorous musical interest at the time, by no means confined to what is often called 'sacred' music. As early as July 1660, Pepys, so critical at this time of the Abbey, records after a visit to the Royal Chapel in Whitehall: 'Here I heard very good music, the first time that I ever remembered to have heard the organs and singing-men in surplice in my life.' (Pepys was sixteen when Charles I was beheaded.) That the Dean and Chapter of Westminster moved with some rapidity to secure adequate music can be seen from the following Chapter minute, dated 18 December 1660, which refers to Christopher Gibbons (1615–76), appointed organist at the Restoration and the son of a more famous father:

... ordered that the Backe doore of the Organ Loft bee shutt up and that the Organist come into the quire att the beginning of prayers in his surpliss and betake himselfe to his stall till towards the end of the psalmes [except on festival dayes when the Responds are to be performed with the Organ] and then to go upp the stayres leading from the quire to the organ and perform his duty. And [it] is further ordered that neither the Organist nor any other permit any person to bee in the Organ Loft during the time of divine service and that the Organist and the blower keep themselves private and not expose themselves to the view of the people during their stay in the Organ Loft.

The Organ Loft has often since been a focal point for emotional and even physical disturbance!

It is not easy to trace, in detail and chronologically, the precise order in which the musical foundation was re-established. From the time of the Restoration, a clergyman named William Hooper seems to have officiated as a Minor Canon. What is certain is that in February 1661, Philip Tinker was installed as' Chaunter'. Three singing-men survived from the pre-Commonwealth Choir and returned to take up their old duties. Gradually their number was increased, and they were brought up to their full complement of twelve, when, on 16 February of this same year, four more were installed. There were at first no boys, which made it necessary at times for the adult voices and organ to be augmented by a cornet. John Hill the cornet player was paid £4 as late as 1664. But the boys were soon back again, ready and rehearsed for the coronation of Charles II on St George's Day, 1661, to which great event we must soon turn.

Before the coronation could take place, however, a fanatical royalism demanded a ritual orgy which neither King, nor Dean and Chapter, so we may charitably hope, really desired.

On 8 December 1660, the House of Commons ordered that the bodies of the three chief regicides—Cromwell, Ireton and Bradshaw—interred at the east end of Henry VII's Chapel, should be 'taken up, drawn on a hurdle to Tyburn, there to be hanged up in their coffins for some time and after that buried under the gallows'.

This dreadful ritual was performed to the letter. The Speaker of the House of Commons, with his retinue, solemnly attended in the Abbey on 26 January, while the three bodies were dug up and taken to the Red Lion Inn to await their removal to Tyburn. On 30 January, the anniversary of the death of the Royal Martyr, the grim business at Tyburn was carried out. Those who were witnesses of this nauseating scene could not easily forget it, though even the kindly Evelyn was able to read into it the working out of a divine Providence.

This day [he writes] (ô the stupendious, & inscrutable Judgements of God) were the Carkasses of that arch-rebell *Cromewell, Bradshaw* the Judge who condem'd his Majestie & *Ireton,* sonn in law to the Usurper, draged out of their superbe Tombs (in Westminster among the Kings) to *Tyburne* & hanged on the Gallows there from

9 in the morning til 6 at night, & then buried under that fatal and ignominious Monument, in a deepe pitt: Thousands of people (who had seene them in all their pride & pompous insults) being spectators.

The heads of the regicides were hoisted on poles set above Westminster Hall where they remained many a year. Indeed they were still there twenty years afterwards when they were joined by the head of Sir Thomas Armstrong, implicated in the Rye House Plot of 1684.

Later in the year some twenty-three less distinguished leaders of the Commonwealth were by royal order disinterred and ignominiously cast into St Margaret's churchyard.

CORONATION OF CHARLES II

The Abbey thus being purged of its major defilement, events now moved on steadily towards Charles's coronation on 23 April. The mood of the nation demanded that it should be both traditional and magnificent. The Dean and Chapter complied with the general temper, and copes with vestments were made at a cost of £103. 7s. 2d. There were, however, complications. The ancient regalia for the most part had been broken up and it was some thirty-six years since a coronation had been staged. Doubt as to the correct procedure led to many disputes over rights and privileges, Northumberland and Ossory quarrelling over the insignia, the King's footmen and the barons of the Cinque Ports over the canopy. Every effort was made to emphasize tradition and to bear witness to the continuity of those English institutions which the Commonwealth had interrupted but not destroyed. Thus the King, reviving an ancient custom, rode to Whitehall the day before in procession from the Tower, 'the Lond[on] Militia lining the ways, & the severall Companies with their Banners & Loud musique ranked in their orders: The Fountaines runing wine, bells ringing, with Speeches made at the severall Triumphal Arches'.

The ceremony inside the Abbey on St George's Day was indeed splendid. Several contemporary accounts survive, though Evelyn's, taken in the main from *The Kingdom Intelligencer* of 29 April, is an excellent documentary but dull and uninspired. Samuel Pepys had to content himself with a seat in the North Transept, and only managed to achieve this somewhat lowly station by squeezing himself behind Sir John Denham, the poet. His account, however, is more lively, and has the added advantage of being somewhat shorter. High up as he was, he looked down upon:

. . . the Abbey raised in the middle, all covered with red, and a throne (that is, a chair) and footstool on the top of it; and all the officers of all kinds, so much as the very fiddlers, in red vests. At last comes in the Dean and Prebendaries of Westminster, with the Bishops, (many of them in cloth of gold copes) and after them the Nobility, all in their Parliament robes, which was a most magnificent sight. Then the Duke and the King with a sceptre (carried by my Lord Sandwich) and sword and mond [orb] before him, and the crown too. The King in his robes, bare-headed, which was very fine. And after all had placed themselves, there was a sermon and the service; and then in the choir at the high altar, the King passed through all the ceremonies of the Coronation, which to my great grief I and most in the Abbey could not see. The crown being put upon his head, a great shout began, and he come forth to the throne, and there passed through more ceremonies: as taking the oath, and having things read to him by the Bishop; and his lords (who put on their caps as soon as the King put on his crown) and bishops came, and kneeled before him. And three times the King-at-Armes went to the three open places on the scaffold, and proclaimed, that if anyone could show any reason why Charles Stewart should not be King of England, that now he should come and speak. And a General Pardon also was read by the Lord Chancellor, and medals flung up and down by my Lord Cornwallis, of silver, but I could not come by any. But so great a noise that I could make but little of the music; and indeed it was lost to everybody.

The mood of fanatical royalism which came to a peak at the time of the coronation did not suddenly die. On 29 May, the anniversary of the King's triumphal return, Peter Heylin, now Sub-Dean, who when a thunderstorm broke over London on the evening of 23 April exclaimed that 'the Ordinance of Heaven is answering the Ordnance of the Tower', preached in the Abbey before a large and representative congregation. Taking as his text a verse from the Psalms, 'Blessed be the Lord for he showed me his marvellous kindness in a strange city', he began by comparing Charles with David much to the detriment of the latter. 'As his [Charles's] Birth was higher, so his Fall was lower, and his afflictions so much greater; and the more insupportable because he was more tenderly bred and less able to bear them.' David, when driven out of his own country, at least had Moab and Gath to repair to; but as for Charles 'never was partridge flown at with a swifter wing by a well train'd Falcon, nor game more nobly followed, by the fiercest Hounds, than this poor Prince was chased by these mighty Hounds'. Yet Providence did not forsake his sacred person, for the Prince's sufferings were vicariously borne on behalf of his people 'whose tears he put into his bottle; whose stripes he bore in his own body, and whose calamities did more afflict his righteous Soul than his own misfortunes'. Now he was returned to his Royal city 'not with any army to besiege it, to smite it with the edge of the sword . . . but as a Prince of Peace, as the Son of David, to bring the glad tidings of Salvation to all his Subjects, to put an end to all the miseries of his people and to restore them to that peace and happiness, which they have forfeited by pride and weakness, by disobedience to his Person and distrust to his Promises'.

Could preacher say more? Yet at least we may pay Charles the compliment of supposing that when he read this sermon—he was not present in the Abbey—he permitted himself the luxury of a smile!

Yet it was this same temper of uncritical royalism which in the following year in the Act for the Uniformity of Public Prayer required that all clergy should forswear 'taking up arms against the King and disclaim the Solemn League and Covenant'. Obediently on 1 July 1662 those present at a meeting of the Dean and Chapter of Westminster duly made the appropriate declaration, the Dean adding that he 'heartily subscribed'; and another that he did so 'most willingly'.

Consecration of bishops, royal funerals, days of commemoration, a coronation—these were all great and, in their distinctive ways, colourful occasions. But not all aspects of the life of the Abbey were equally dramatic; for these ceremonies came at a time when the Dean and Chapter were patiently endeavouring to restore the integrity of their own community.

The Collegiate Church of St Peter in Westminster was governed by a Charter, which constituted its trust deed, and was given to it by Queen Elizabeth in 1560. As to its statutes (see pp. 133–5, 452) these had never received the Royal Assent, so that their validity or legal authority was doubtful. Consequently their main function was to serve as a guide in interpreting the Charter. In practice, a great deal of collegiate life was controlled by custom, but for custom to be authoritative continuity is essential; and it was just this continuity which had of late been violently interrupted. The fact that the newly appointed Dean soon went off as Bishop of Worcester, and Nicholas Matthew to the Deanery of St Paul's, and that Peter Heylin died in 1662, could not have made things easier. Yet the Chapter meetings of the time reflect, in detail, here a little, there a little, the slow process of re-establishment. There was much to attend to. In February 1664, for example, a Royal Letter was secured to reinforce the custom that vacant prebendal houses should be offered to the prebendaries in order of seniority.

The Dean and Chapter, in discharging many of their responsibilities—the upkeep of the building, the administration of their vast estates, the lordship of the manor of Westminster—depended upon their lay officers, prominent among whom were the High Bailiff, the Receiver-General, the College Surveyor, the Chapter Clerk and the Clerk of Works. These equally had to be restored to their offices or new appointments made. Thus when Richard Busby was made Treasurer soon after his nomination to a prebendal stall in 1660 he worked with the newly elected (7 July 1660) Receiver-General, John Oakley. The duties of the latter could not have been easy. The legal position in respect of the Abbey estates, as all others, was deemed to be unambiguous, namely that they now reverted to their original owners, or lawful heirs. A legal right, however, is not always the same thing as an actual possession or receipt of rent. This sobering fact is reflected in the early meetings of the Chapter after the Restoration. On 7 July 1660 it was ordered that Thomas Symonds collect the rents belonging in Westminster and the City of London to the Dean and Chapter. Of a similar nature is the minute passed in October that any person who 'gives notice . . . [of] money, goods or utensills' belonging to the College was to be rewarded up to 4% of their value, and (a few months later) that the Dean, Sub-Dean and Treasurer should constitute a sub-committee to 'recover rents and profits'. The suggestion is plain, that there were many people who were defaulters to the Dean and Chapter. Appointments to other lay offices soon followed—constables, coroners and clerk of the markets.

The Abbey and its precincts also needed attention, for the particular kind of religious zeal characteristic of the Puritans did not include a concern for the care of churches. To these men the aesthetics and architecture of buildings did not seem spiritually relevant. For this reason it was, perhaps, fortunate that many great ceremonies took place so soon after the Restoration, for these necessitated the introduction of some measure of decency.

Thus among the first acts of the Dean and Chapter was an order for a cradle and pulley to hoist up a workman to 'Cleanse all ye Rooffs and windowes of the Churche And Henry the 7th Chappell'. The condition of the Cloisters also left much to be desired and a Beadle of the Sanctuary was appointed early in 1661. His assignment was no sinecure. One of his duties was to prevent boys playing or lingering about in the precincts: and to see to it that 'no vagrant beggars or wandering persons bee suffered to pretend to sell any fruit or other wares in the Cloysters, And that none . . . carry any burdens through the Church'. He must also 'take care that no filthy refuse be [dumped] near any of the Church Walls . . . and that noe dunghills bee made in the dean's yard'.

The intention was a general tightening up all round. Thus John France, the gardener, was forbidden to sell any fruit, or make for sale any 'Tartes, pyes . . . or Custards'. The College Surveyor and the Clerk of Works were given the embarrassing responsibility of getting 'laystalls and dunghills' removed from Tothill Fields, which came under the jurisdiction of the Dean and Chapter. Such orders did not immediately solve the problem. Dirty cloisters, beggars and dunghills remained a nuisance for many years, and in 1669 garbage was still being dumped in Dean's Yard up against the windows and walls of the School Dormitory—a 'scandall' with which the Clerk of Works was asked to deal. People continued for a long time to convert the church into a thoroughfare, carrying their 'Burdens' and allowing their dogs to stray into the Choir. A peremptory Chapter resolution (11 January 1682) enjoined that this must cease: and another porter was appointed to carry this order into effect.

Nuisances of this kind long continued and it would be tedious to repeat the same complaints across the years—of butchers carrying meat through the Abbey on market days, even during divine service 'to ye great Scandall and offence of all sober Persons'; of idle boys daily hanging about the Cloisters 'to play at Cards and other Play for money who are often heard to curse and swear'. Charles Caldwell, the College Beadle, was given an additional £10 per annum in 1710 to induce him to be 'tough', but he does not seem to have been much more successful than his predecessors. One helpful decision the Dean and Chapter did make at this time. It was to rail in Dean's Yard and simply to proceed at law against those who continued to dump rubbish there. But to return.

On 30 November 1662 John Earle was consecrated Bishop of Worcester. Among his last acts was to preside at three funerals which attracted a great deal of public attention. The first was that of the once brilliant 'Queen of Hearts', Elizabeth, Queen of Bohemia, the only surviving daughter of James I. Contemporary taste demanded the macabre. Her body was accordingly carried at midnight along the Thames from Somerset House to the Abbey, a procession of lighted barges, draped in black cloth following the coffin. Prince Rupert, later to be laid by her side in Henry VII's Chapel, was the chief mourner.

The two other funerals were of bishops—Henry Ferne of Chester, and Brian Duppa of Winchester, both of whom had ministered to Charles I during the dark days of his imprisonment.

Earle's own consecration as bishop on St Andrew's Day was certainly a notable occasion. Dr Henry Bolton, prebendary, preached an 'excellent discourse' on 'the various Guifts in the Church of Christ, & of their use'. The dinner which followed—so John Evelyn reports

—was 'one of the most plentifull & magnificent . . . that in my life I ever saw; it cost neere 600 pounds, as I was assured: & here were the Judges, Nobility, Clearg[i]e & Gent[lemen] innumerable this Bishop being universaly beloved for his gentle & sweete disposition'. It gave the diarist a particular satisfaction that when he left, the Bishop 'brought me to the Cloysters in his Episcopal habite'.

THE DECANATE OF JOHN DOLBEN

Dr Earle was followed in the Deanery by John Dolben (1625–86) who was installed on 31 December 1662. His reign was a long one for he presided over the Abbey some twenty-one years. In 1666, upon the death of John Warner, he was nominated to the bishopric of Rochester, which, by royal warrant, he held in commendam with the Deanery, the first to do this since the time of Dean Neile. By such pluralism an impoverished bishopric was provided with an income and a London house; which accounts for the fact that eight of his successors assumed this double responsibility. Dolben was consecrated a bishop in Lambeth Chapel on 25 November by the Archbishop of Canterbury.

Manuscript evidence for Dolben's regime is scanty, but all that one learns of him from his contemporaries is favourable. Himself an Old Westminster, taught by the formidable Busby, now his colleague on the Chapter, he was already familiar with the Abbey scene: and as a student of Christ Church he had interrupted his studies to support Charles in the field, receiving wounds at Marston Moor and the siege of York. While at Oxford he maintained the Church of England service along with Fell and Allestree. With his powerful connexions, for he was related through his mother to Lord Keeper Williams and to Dr Sheldon through his wife, his promotion to the Deanery of Westminster could not have come as a surprise. It is to his credit that upon entering the responsibilities of his office he recognized that priority must be given to long overdue repair on the building itself. Thus at his first Chapter he secured the passing of a resolution 'to make the fabrick of the Church an equal share with the prebendaries in their dividends'. Such dividends (we shall return to the subject later; see p. 258) came from fines due upon the sealing of leases on Abbey property, and the above resolution laid it down that each prebendary, equally with the fabric fund, should have one-fifteenth of the total, the Dean having two. In the early days of the Restoration a considerable revenue came from this source, and many later Chapter meetings were almost exclusively concerned with the granting and sealing of leases. Because of Dolben's concern for the building, South said of him: 'That Christ

Church, Oxford, stands so high above ground, and that the Church of Westminster lies not flat upon it, is his Lordship's commendation.'

Dolben is said to have stoutly maintained the extra-diocesan status of the Abbey against the claims of the Bishop of London: and in the House of Lords to have exercised great authority. The Dean undoubtedly enjoyed a contemporary reputation as a preacher, and the story is that he took to performing extempore after a gentle reproach from Charles II for being glued to his manuscript. So efficient did he become in this freer style that on one occasion when a preacher was taken suddenly ill in the course of his sermon after having suggested a threefold division of his subject, Dolben took over, and followed the same scheme. Such prowess won the following tribute from Dryden, later to be buried in Poets' Corner:

> *Him of the Western Dome whose mighty sense*
> *Flows in fit words and heavenly eloquence.*

Dolben's early military training seems to have left its mark upon him. Certainly he acted in character when the Great Fire broke out in 1666. William Taswell, a Westminster schoolboy, later Rector of Newington, writes of Dolben that he 'collected his scholars together in a company, marching them on foot to put a stop, if possible, to the conflagration. I was a kind of page to him, not being of the number of the King's Scholars. We were employed many hours in fetching water from the back side of St Dunstan's Church in the East where we happily extinguished the fire.'

The City of Westminster entirely escaped damage: but it had suffered severely in the previous year from the ravages of the Plague, which swept off some three hundred of its inhabitants. Nor was the Abbey community spared, though the boys of Westminster School sought safety by migrating up the river to Chiswick. Some of its victims were buried in the precincts, for example Tom Chaffinch, one of the King's pages, who a few hours before his death, so rumour had it, was 'playing at tables'. When Sir William Killigrew was buried in July 1665, only the Chanter Tinker Junior, Haywood, Hughes, Ambler and Shorter were present, the rest of the choir being absent because of the Plague. These hardy members who remained in town decided to share out the 'monument money' (see p. 252) among themselves, carefully recording, however, that absent members, if they subsequently objected to this procedure, would be reimbursed. The following entry from the Precentor's book gives a vivid, if somewhat sad picture, of these days:

In the year 1665 by reason of God's Visitation by the plague of pestilence, no wax lights or Tallow candles were used in the

Church, but the Service was dayly performed by daylight by Mr John Tynchare[sic], one of the Petticanons, and by him alone from the beginning of July to almost the end of December. Two of the lay vicars, Thomas Corry and Richard Ambler died during the visitation and both were buried in the Precincts.

The records of the Chapter Meetings for this period show that if Dolben's tenure of the Deanery was in some respects undistinguished, its length of years helped to give stability to the newly re-established College, and allowed custom to reassert itself. This is reflected in Chapter decisions at the time. A few examples must suffice.

On 27 April 1675 the prebendaries agreed to get rid of the tenants in their houses and not to re-let; the hanging of washing in College Garden was restricted to areas near the walls (7 November 1668); the Abbey bells were ordered to be rung on four 'public days' throughout the year—the anniversary of the coronation; 29 May; 5 November; and Queen Elizabeth's birthday—(the Duke of York's birthday was added on 15 July 1684); the holding of an Audit Dinner was revived in 1683, and an expenditure up to £5 upon it authorized. A King's Almsman found pawning his gown was to have his pay stopped!

Burials in the Abbey, which had once again become a regular part of its life, continued under Dolben: and they may be seen as reflecting the history of Britain at this time. Among those interred were some naval officers who 'dyed in his Majesties service against the Dutch'; two of the Duke of York's sons; contemporary poets—Abraham Cowley (buried next to Spenser and near Chaucer), Sir William Davenant and Sir John Denham; the grand architect of the Restoration, George Monck, Duke of Albemarle, whose armour, after a chequered history, survives in the Abbey Museum; members of the Hyde family—some twenty-three of them—including the most illustrious of them all, the Earl of Clarendon (1609–74); Sir Edmund Berry Godfrey, whose murder led to the mendacity of Titus Oates; Isaac Barrow, a mathematician as well as a distinguished divine; and Prince Rupert.

Dolben, as we have seen, was at Westminster during a period which was devoted, in the main, to consolidation and resettlement. His portrait, still in the Deanery, shows those contemporaries to be right who said that he was 'very comely but grown too fat'.

Dolben was succeeded, on his translation to the Archbishopric of York, by one of the prebendaries, Thomas Sprat, who was installed on 21 September 1683, and held the Deanery till 1713. He became Bishop of Rochester in 1684.

Sprat's term of office saw the end of Charles II's reign, and the unconstitutional and Romanizing policy of James II, leading to the Revolution Settlement of 1688, under William and Mary. He lived to enjoy the spacious years of Queen Anne, when the Church of England, in spite of internal division between Whig and Tory, basked in the sunshine of royal favour.

Before turning to Sprat's work as Dean, a word must be said of his most distinguished colleague, Robert South (1634–1716). South, witty, caustic, irrepressible, was an Old Westminster of whom Richard Busby once remarked that he saw 'great talents in the sulky boy'. He caught the eye of Charles II, when in a sermon in the Abbey he referred to Oliver Cromwell as 'a bankrupt, beggarly fellow . . . entering the Parliament House with a threadbare torn cloak and greasy hat and perhaps neither of them paid for'. The King is said to have burst into laughter, exclaiming to Rochester: 'Odds fish Lory, your Chaplain must be a bishop, therefore put me in mind of him at the next death.' The next death, however, was his own, and South remained a prebend of Westminster till the end of his life, attending services in the Abbey with devotion and regularity for over fifty years, though not without occasional somnolence. It is perhaps ironic that on the death of Sprat in 1713, South was offered the Deanery, but wisely recognized that he was now too old. 'Such a chair,' he said, 'would be too uneasy for an old, infirm man to sit in,' and he held himself much better 'satisfied with living upon the eavesdropping of the Church than to fare sumptuously by being placed at the pinnacle of it.' As a theologian South could be devastating in the frankness, and sometimes in the ruthlessness, of his criticism. Typical was his attack on the author of *Treatise upon Death*, William Sherlock, whom in his *Animadversions* he bluntly accused of Tritheism.

South died on 8 July 1716 and was buried under his stall in the Choir near to his old preceptor, Richard Busby. The captain of Westminster School recited an oration.

JAMES II AND THOMAS SPRAT

To return to Thomas Sprat. He had not long been Dean when Charles II unexpectedly expired on 6 February 1685, apologizing for being an 'unconscionable time a dying' and commending Eleanor Gwyn to the charity of his friends with the words, 'Don't let poor Nelly starve.' Charles's funeral—he had, through the initiative of his brother, the new king, become a Roman Catholic on his deathbed —took place at night, though it is quite untrue that it was without ceremony of any kind. (Evelyn writes that it was all done 'very obscurely'.) What is true is that James, in his *Memoirs*, felt it necessary to apologize for its somewhat restrained character on the grounds that this was 'more comfortable with that Christian humility which even Princes may not dispense with.' James himself attended the interment together with members of the Privy Council and such peers as were in town. Charles was buried in a new vault in the southern aisle of King Henry VII's Chapel, where he was to be followed by Mary, William and Anne, with her numerous but tragically short-lived children. No inscription was placed over their graves till the time of Dean Stanley in the nineteenth century. Perhaps the effigy used at his funeral and now in the Undercroft Museum is a more characteristic memorial to the Merry Monarch!

James was not really unpopular at his accession. Indeed many of his subjects were prepared to give him the benefit of the doubt and to wish him well. Prominent among these was Dean Sprat, who found great reassurance in James's early declaration at the Council table that he would maintain the Protestant religion as by law established. So great was the comfort thus given him that he hastened to pass it on to his colleagues at ten o'clock in the evening on the very day it was given.

James's coronation took place on St George's Day, 1685, but the new monarch's Roman allegiance necessitated a truncated version of the ancient liturgy. In particular, the Communion service, within which the central ritual is framed, was entirely omitted. John Evelyn's somewhat reserved comments probably represented the general feelings of an apprehensive nation. 'Having been present at our late King's Coronation,' he writes, 'I was not ambitious of seeing the Ceremonie.'

The preparations for the coronation later led to a curious incident which occurred on the day that the ill-advised Duke of Monmouth landed on these shores. The incident began when a plank which fell upon St Edward's Shrine broke a part of Abbot Feckenham's feretory, and placed temptation in the way of a singing-man, with antiquarian interests, Charles Taylor by name. What followed is best told, more or less, in his own language. Finding a hole in the coffin, '. . . about six inches long and four inches broad', he inserted his hand, and 'turning the bones which I felt there, drew from underneath the shoulder bones a Crucifix richly adorned and enamelled, and a gold chain twenty-four inches long the which I immediately showed to my friends, they being as much surprised and as much admired the same as myself'. Eventually, after an interview with the Dean, on 6 July, Taylor was ushered into the royal presence 'and being no sooner introduced to his Majesty's closet (when I had the honour to kiss his Royal hand) but upon my knees I delivered them with my own hands to him, which his Most Sacred Majesty was pleased to accept with much satisfaction'.

It seems never to have occurred to James that he ought to return

o

these relics to the shrine forthwith; though he did order that Edward the Confessor's coffin should be enclosed in another, each plank of which was to be 'of an extraordinary strength and goodness, two inches thick and cramped together with large iron wedges'.

Doubt has often been cast on the accuracy of the above story, but calm assessment of the available evidence convinces of its substantial truth. Both John Evelyn's *Diary*, in which he records his own conversation with the King on this subject at Winchester, and Simon Patrick's *Autobiography*—he was a prebendary at the time—make scepticism so unreasonable as to be almost absurd.

As to the subsequent history, or present whereabouts, of the cross and chain there is, however, most certainly room for considerable doubt. Dr Perkins believes that the last authentic information about them is to be found in the Will of Mary of Modena, wife of James II, dated 12 August 1702, which requires them to be passed on to 'James III'.

What is certain about this incident is that no one comes out of it very well!

If James II was not unpopular when he ascended the throne, he soon lost this initial goodwill. His twin ambitions—to encourage Roman Catholicism and increase the power of the throne—were pursued at the same time. This proved disastrous for both, the more so as he remained undeterred by that final caution which disinclined his brother 'to go on his travels again'.

Thomas Sprat's position as a convinced supporter of the monarchy, and yet an equally convinced Anglican High Churchman, could not have been easy. Thus when James II set up an Ecclesiastical Commission in 1686 to try Henry Compton, Bishop of London, for refusing at the King's orders, to inhibit John Sharp, Vicar of St Giles-in-the-Field, Sprat consented to serve; but when the Commission, under the ill-famed Judge Jeffries, proceeded to suspend the Bishop, he withdrew. Equally characteristic, when a royal command required the reading of the Declaration of Indulgence, which gave liberty to Roman Catholics and Dissenters contrary to the law of the land, the Abbey was one of half-a-dozen churches in London which complied. Sprat, maybe somewhat unfairly, gave it to one of the Minor Canons, but when the latter began to read, so writes a contemporary, 'there was so great a murmur and noise in the Church that nobody could hear him; but before he was finished there was none left but a few prebends in their stalls, the Choristers and the Westminster Scholars'. When the Abbey bells were rung on the acquittal of the seven Bishops, the Dean peremptorily silenced them.

Thomas Sprat could not have welcomed the 'Glorious Revolution' with such whole-hearted enthusiasm as, for example, did his colleague Simon Patrick, who through his friend Thomas Tenison, then Vicar of St Martin-in-the-Fields, was early apprized of it. Nevertheless he did not follow Archbishop Sancroft into the ranks of the Nonjurors, but assisted at the coronation of William and Mary on 11 April 1689, when, owing to the refusal of the former to become his wife's 'gentleman usher', a new Coronation Chair, now in the Undercroft Museum, had to be made. Of this ceremony John Evelyn writes: 'Much of the splendour of the proceeding was abated by the absence of divines who should have made it up, there being but as yet 5 Bishops, 4 Judges (no more at present, it seems sworn) and severall noblemen and greate Ladys wanting.'

The religious settlement proved in many respects as difficult as the political, and Thomas Sprat agreed to serve on a commission, appointed by William, the real if not ostensible purpose of which was to propose alterations to the Book of Common Prayer to accommodate the Dissenters. The Commission, which consisted of ten bishops, six deans and six professors, held eighteen sessions between the dates 3 October to 18 November in Jerusalem Chamber. Thomas Sprat welcomed them as host, but from the outset he questioned the legality of the Commission, and never attended after the first meeting.

Reference to Jerusalem Chamber may serve to remind us that from 1689 until its prorogation in 1717, the bishops of the Upper House of Convocation met in Jerusalem Chamber, largely because of the comfort of a blazing fire, while the Lower House assembled in Henry VII's Chapel. These years were a period of great dispute between the two houses, some of the worst wrangles taking place in what was then called the Organ Room, which led into the Chamber.

Thomas Sprat's somewhat ambiguous position exposed him, at this time, to an unscrupulous attack, which must have been most disturbing and unpleasant so long as it lasted, and could well have proved the end of his career. The reference is to the so-called 'Flower-Pot Conspiracy'. The circumstances were as follows.

Two prisoners in Newgate confessed themselves members of an 'Association', the object of which was to restore James II to the throne. Certain prominent names, Sancroft, Marlborough, Salisbury, together with a forged signature of Sprat, were discovered on a paper found in a flower-pot in Sprat's episcopal residence at Bromley. The Dean was arrested, his house searched and only after strenuous exertions was he able to clear his name. He did so, however, and so remained safely at the Deanery, to oppose the impeachment of Sacheverell (1710) and to die in his bed at the ripe age of seventy-eight.

Sprat was not only an ecclesiastical figure, for he was well known and respected both in literary and scientific circles. He wrote an appreciation of Cowley and drew up the inscription on his monument in the Abbey. He was also instrumental in securing Dryden's burial in Poets' Corner. His own prose style was excellent and of his *History of the Royal Society*, Dr Johnson writes that it was 'one of the few books which selection of sentiment, and elegance of diction, have been able to preserve, though written upon a subject flux and transitory!'

The lexicographer little knew!

The most significant activity at the Abbey during Sprat's stay in the Deanery was the setting in hand the vast task of repair on the stonework of the church, a matter which will be dealt with in a subsequent chapter. It was Sprat, again, who at the suggestion of William Sancroft, Archbishop of Canterbury, instituted Holy Communion every Sunday after Morning Prayer. For the most part the emphasis during his regime was on securing decency and order both within the Church and outside, often in small ways. Thus a correct procedure was agreed, on 12 January 1686, for approving Chapter minutes. More dignity was insisted upon when the prebendaries entered the Choir. The King's Scholars were to stand up with the singing-men to bow to the altar, and to make a reverence to the Dean and Chapter. The prebendaries were to have cushions in their stalls. All the College officers, and this included the Lay Vicars were to communicate at least three times a year. Each singing-man was to have his own candle in the Choir.

Improvements were also made to the organ by Mr Schrider, in particular bringing it down half a tone in conformity with St Paul's and other 'modern' instruments. This meant changing eight to nine hundred pipes. The opportunity was taken to convert the draw-stops from iron into wood, and to provide a new keyboard.

Of a different character, was the preoccupation of the Chapter with the College water supply which reached a crisis in 1707. As a permanent solution, it was decided to lay down leaden pipes to convey water from Hyde Park. As a temporary expedient one named Thomas was paid two guineas for making Thames water available.

A matter which gave some anxiety to Chapter in 1709 arose out of an Act of Parliament 'for avoiding Doubts Touching the Statutes of diverse Cathedrals and Collegiate Churches'. The question at issue was whether this Act in any way affected the Westminster Abbey statutes, which for various reasons were regarded as of doubtful legal validity. The matter was important, and it was decided to consult James Montague, the Attorney-General, and Sir Edward Northey. Their opinion was emphatic—that the Act of Parliament applied only to the foundations of Henry VIII, and not to an Elizabethan foundation such as Westminster Abbey. The latter's statutes remained after the passing of the Act precisely as they were before.

Thomas Sprat died at Bromley on 20 May 1713. After Dr South had declined the Deanery, Francis Atterbury, Dean of Carlisle and of Christ Church, Oxford, was appointed almost immediately. He was installed as Dean of Westminster on 16 June; and consecrated to the see of Rochester at Lambeth on 5 July. No contemporary ecclesiastic was better known throughout the country, or had more thoroughly identified himself with the fortunes of the High Church party. Strongly anti-Erastian, he had with inadequate historical scholarship, championed the rights of the Lower House of Convocation against the claims of an Upper House dominated by Whig bishops. Though he had taken the oaths to the Government at the time of the 'Bloodless Revolution', his Toryism in the end went beyond an active assertion of the rights of the Church and a nostalgic toast to the 'King over the water'—but to this political treason we shall have to return.

Atterbury's character and temperament were as divisive as his opinions. No one could deny his brilliance nor the magnetism of his presence. Though affectionate in friendship he was of that company who, wherever they go, involve themselves in emotional conflicts with their colleagues, while seeing themselves as defending the rights of their office. At Carlisle and Oxford there was constant strife and general unsettlement.

Atterbury came to Westminster no stranger to its scene. Indeed Dr South remembered him as a scholar in the school, remarking on his appointment that he had now lived to see 'a gentleman who was born in the very year that he was made one of the prebendaries of the Church appointed to be the Dean of it'. In spite of his controversial past, the new Dean was at first received warmly. On 7 July 1713 the Chapter ordered: 'That the Deanery be repaired and made fit for his Ldp's Reception and a new Roome built according to his Ldp's desire.' The College porter was given a new gown 'made agreeable to his Ldp's livery'—an exceptional and unconstitutional sign of favour. Atterbury was empowered to change the College plate in his use 'into such fashion as his Ldp shall desire', the result being a beautiful tureen and laver still in possession of the Dean and Chapter.

The pattern of what had happened elsewhere, however, was not long in asserting itself at the Abbey, though maybe not in quite such an extreme form. Within a matter of months the Chapter became divided. Tendencies towards this, indeed, always exist in corporate bodies; and early in the eighteenth century they were reinforced by politico-religious struggles of the day. The coming of Atterbury had the effect of heightening existing tensions. The irony of it was that, like most people, Atterbury found it easy to give counsel to others which would have been helpful if he could have applied it to himself. An instance of this came when, in a letter to Jonathan Swift, Dean of St Patrick's, Atterbury wrote: 'Upon the whole, the best advice I can give you is, whatever your powers are, by statutes or usage, not to insist on them too strictly, in either of the cases mentioned by you, unless you are very sure of the favour and countenance of your Visitor.'

Atterbury's desire—and his instincts led him the same way—was to increase his own authority as Dean: but at Westminster, he was faced with an initial quandary. When presiding over Carlisle he had done his best to write down the statutes because the Dean was given more power under the Charter. At Westminster, however, the reverse was the case. It was the statutes, since they reserved all *graviores causae* to the Dean unless specifically assigned to the Dean and Chapter, which enhanced the decanal authority the more: but it was these very statutes which had been declared of 'doubtful validity'. Whether tempted to do so or not, Atterbury wisely decided not to reopen this question.

His first contretemps after coming to Westminster was with the Vestry of St Margaret's Church, but here the Chapter were solidly behind him. This unanimity, however, did not last long. The Chapter minutes clearly show the tendency for certain prebendaries to vote with Atterbury—Michael Evans, an Old Westminster, appointed his Sub-Dean, though fifth in order of seniority; Dr Broderick; and Dr Sprat, son of the former Dean; and for others to vote against him—Bishop Bradford, Dr Lynford and Dr Gee. The disposal of Abbey preferment was a frequent occasion for this division to assert itself, and in this respect a minute from a Chapter Meeting of 4 August 1716 may be quoted in full, as typical of other similar occasions:

My Lord the Dean proposed the filling of Islip Parsonage, vacant by the death of Dr. South. Dr. Dent named Dr. Broderick for it as the Senior Prebendary that desired it, and some disputes arising thereupon, voting was proposed and agreed to. Dr. Barker the junior Prebendary began and voted for himself. Dr. Watson, Dr. Cannon, Dr. Bradford, Dr. Gee and Dr. Lynford voted for Dr. Barker. Mr. Archdeacon Sprat, Dean Kimberley,

Dr. Broderick, Dr. Dent, Dr. Sub-Dean Evans and my Lord the Dean voted for Dr. Broderick. Then my Lord the Dean proposed the filling of the Archdeaconry of Westminster, likewise vacant by Dr. South's death. Dr. Dent and Dr. Gee were severally named for it. Dr. Barker, Dr. Watson, Dr. Cannon, Dr. Bradford, Dr. Gee and Dr. Lynford voted for Dr. Gee. Mr. Archdeacon Sprat, Dean Kimberley, Dr. Broderick, Dr. Dent, Mr. Sub-Dean Evans and my Lord the Dean voted for Dr. Dent; whereupon his Ldp declared Dr. Broderick duly elected to the Parsonage of Islip and Dr. Dent duly chosen Archdeacon of Westminster.

Ironically, owing to the subsequent refusal of one prebendary to sign the instrument of presentation, the nomination to Islip lapsed after six months to the Bishop of Oxford who presented his own Chaplain, Dr Pye!

The two most serious clashes, however, came over the election of the High Steward; and the building of a new dormitory for Westminster School in College Garden.

It was the custom for the High Steward to be elected by the Dean and Chapter on the nomination of the Dean, the High Steward being the senior lay officer of the Collegiate Body and representing it in the civil administration of the borough—a kind of very superior mayor. In reality, however, he exercised his authority through a deputy. The first three High Stewards after the foundation of the College in 1560 were members of the Cecil family. They were followed by Lords Rochester and Buckingham. The vacancy in 1715 occurred through the unhappy circumstance of the flight of the Duke of Ormonde to France in order to join James in exile. At a Chapter Meeting on 6 September the Dean read out the Duke's resignation, whereupon the patent was cancelled, and he immediately nominated to the Chapter the Earl of Arran, brother to Ormonde, and his successor in the Chancellorship of Oxford. Three prebendaries immediately opposed this nomination and promptly withdrew from the meeting. Atterbury then 'expressly' asked the remaining prebendaries one by one for their opinions, three of whom declared their consent, the fourth desiring to be excused voting either way. Frequent entreaties failed to persuade the absentee prebendaries to return, and no progress could be made for want of a quorum. The more Whig, or at least the less positively Tory elements in the Chapter, now began to canvas for Thomas Pelham-Holles, Duke of Newcastle, but in vain. On this issue Atterbury was not to be withstood, and managed to get his own way. At a Chapter on 8 February 1716 the nomination of the Earl of Arran was approved on his casting vote, the aged South—it was almost his last act—declaring himself 'heart and soul' for the Dean's nominee. The patent was then formally drawn up. Six prebendaries, however—Dent, Gee, Cannon, Lynford, Bradford and Wake—signed the following statement which was entered in the minutes: 'We whose Names are underwritten do hereby declare and enter our dissent from and protestation against the above written order.'

It may, perhaps, be not unfairly suggested that a more eirenical person would have gone out of his way, in his capacity as Dean, to find someone *persona grata* to the whole Chapter. As it was, in spite of the oath of secrecy by which members of the Chapter are bound, the noise of these 'goings on' at Westminster soon got abroad and a satirical broadsheet appeared at Oxford which could hardly have been welcome to any of the immediate participants in this Collegiate squabble.

The second cause of dissension, long-drawn-out and involving litigation, arose from the proposal to build a dormitory for the Queen's Scholars of Westminster School on the west side of College Garden on the site of the Orchard. In this unhappy controversy there can be no question but that Atterbury was right and his opponents wrong: yet again a less aggressive personality might have achieved the same purpose without fuss and unsettlement. To be fair to the Dean, it must be remembered that political division added to personal antipathies.

The subject of this dispute may be briefly introduced. In 1710 Edward Harris, an Old Westminster and physician to the Queen, left £1,000 to the school to build a new dormitory. The money, as Sir Christopher Wren advised, was obviously inadequate for this purpose, so the Dean and Chapter obtained a Decree in Chancery empowering them to spend this money on repairing the existing Dormitory, the old monastic granary on the west side of Dean's Yard. In April 1713 the Chapter ordered Mr Dickinson, on instructions from Sir Christopher Wren, to prepare plans and to set the work in hand.

Meanwhile Dean Sprat died, and Atterbury arrived. The new Dean took stock of the situation and immediately recognized the great advantages of the original scheme, that is of a new dormitory on the Garden site. At his instigation, Sir Christopher Wren's plan was resurrected and revised by Richard Boyle, third Earl of Burlington (who reconstructed Burlington House), the Head Master of Westminster School, Dr Friend (with whom, and with his brother John, Atterbury's relations were excellent) agreeing. On 7 January 1714 the Dean and Chapter approved this reversion to the original intention, at the same time expressing the hope that fresh donors would be forthcoming to supplement Sir Edward Harris's bequest.

For the time being, however, the scheme hung fire because of lack of funds—the estimated cost was £5,000—with the result that on 8 December 1718 the Dean and three prebendaries waited on the King in an endeavour to secure royal support. They were not disappointed. George I proved sympathetic and subscribed £1,000, to which £500 was added by the Prince of Wales. The new dormitory had at last become practical politics, and it was only at this stage that rumblings of discontent in the Chapter began to be heard. Worse still the Head Master of Westminster School seems surprisingly to have withdrawn his support. At a meeting of Chapter on 29 December 1719 Atterbury managed to gain approval for the new site, but Drs Bradford, Gee and Lynford insisted that their opposition be recorded. These dissidents, however, were not prepared to let the matter rest with only formal protest. They now filed a Bill in Chancery alleging that College Garden belonged as a freehold right to those prebendaries whose houses fronted on to it. To this allegation Atterbury replied, perfectly properly, that the ownership of the Garden was vested in the College as a corporate body and no person had any individual rights in it whatever. Also the new building would be too far away to interfere with air or light, and would prove a great benefit to the school, for whose welfare the Dean and Chapter were responsible.

The evidence on both sides having been heard, the Lord Chancellor, on 20 June 1720, referred the question of freehold rights to King's Bench; which Atterbury countered by getting the cause removed to the House of Lords on the grounds that it was charitable. The Upper House thereupon demanded a written statement from each prebendary, giving his personal views on the proposed dormitory in the College Orchard. Once again, as expected, the Chapter was equally divided; and as before a majority was only secured by the Dean's casting vote. When the matter was finally voted on in the Lords the scheme was approved by twenty-eight votes to twenty-six and accordingly went forward.

In this unhappy controversy, it must be admitted that, together maybe with less worthy motives, Atterbury showed a genuine concern for the College as a whole; while the opposing prebendaries, in the main, sought to protect their own private interests.

The Dean, however, must not be judged solely within the context of controversies on Chapter. During his period of office the repair and restoration of the North Front and the rose window went steadily forward; and it is not fair to blame him for later criticisms of this work. 'The smile of the old . . . shone as it were through an ungraceful veil,' is Professor W. R. Lethaby's assessment; and Dean Stanley condemns Atterbury for 'complacently watching the workers as they hewed smooth the fine old sculptures over Solomon's Porch'.

At public ceremonies, Atterbury's presence was dignified and imposing. He was a forceful, cogent and attractive preacher, indeed somewhat of an orator. Though he could not have greeted the accession of George I with enthusiasm, as for example did that convinced Whig the aged Archbishop Tenison, he yet played his part admirably, even going to great personal pains to ensure that the intricate ritual of the coronation was carried out with propriety.

The Dean also played a leading part in the elaborate funeral of the Duke of Marlborough in 1722, for which the Abbey Organist and Master of the Choristers, Dr William Croft, composed his moving setting of the opening sentences of the Burial service. Yet it was the funeral of his friend, Joseph Addison, which affected Atterbury most. Bishop Newton relates in his *Autobiography* that his grief was only too evident in his manner of conducting the service. Certainly the Deanery at Westminster, during his period of office, was open house to many leading literary figures, among whom Addison (the creator of Sir Roger de Coverley, himself a distinguished visitor to the Abbey!) must have been included.

ATTERBURY'S DOWNFALL AND EXILE

As Atterbury's tenure of the Deanery was stormy, so was his manner of leaving it. His sudden departure was the result of his active allegiance to the 'King over the water'. At first his Jacobitism was romantic and nostalgic rather than actively treasonable. He does not seem to have been implicated in the abortive rebellion of 1715, though in a closely-argued pamphlet he pleaded courageously for clemency to the rebels, and was said to have been prepared to proclaim James III at Charing Cross! 'Never was a better cause,' he cried, 'lost for want of spirit.' There can be no question, however, that he later corresponded with the Old Pretender and was involved, in 1722, in a plan for invasion. Through the treachery of the Earl of Mar, news of his treason reached the ears of Walpole, who cunningly at first held his hand. A curious story, which there seems no reason to doubt, relates that this astute Whig politician, realizing that he now had Atterbury completely in his power, waited secretly on him at the Deanery. The purpose of this clandestine meeting was an indirect compliment at least to the Dean's ability; for Walpole was anxious to avoid, if possible, so intelligent an exile being available to direct from France the counsels of the Old Pretender. He therefore set out to bribe him with the next offer of the Bishopric of Winchester and a pension of £5,000 per annum. The Dean, who was totally ignorant of the interception of one of his letters, declined. He might have refused anyhow: though enemies claimed that it was a matter of 'faith unfaithful kept him falsely true'.

The downfall of Atterbury was now inevitable. On 24 August 1722 he was arrested in his Deanery, hustled off to the Cockpit, not even being given time for his servant to shave.him; and after an hour taken in his own coach to the Tower. The story of the passing through Parliament of a Bill to exile him, and of his own brilliant but not entirely disingenuous defence in the Upper House, lie outside the scope of a history of Westminster Abbey. That the Government was nervous of the possible consequences upon the clergy of his arrest is certain, for superficially it seemed a re-enactment of the trial of the Seven Bishops in 1688, and the so called 'persecution' of Sacheverell in 1710. To prevent such comparisons *A Letter to the Clergy of the Church of England on occasion of the Commitment of the . . . Bishop of Rochester to the Tower* was written hastily by Zachary Pearce, himself destined to be a future Dean of Westminster. The author began by reminding his countrymen that Atterbury was accused of 'Designs and Actions allow'd by all to be wholly foreign to his Function'. Yet even if the Dean's 'designs' had achieved their object of bringing over the Old Pretender this would not have led to peace, for the majority of Englishmen would then have bent their energies to eject the son as they had in fact refused to allow the return of the father. Zachary Pearce concluded, after some fierce references to the 'Hatchet' and the 'Halter', with these words addressed to the exiled Dean: 'The greatest reproof, which we can afford you as your last Farewell, will be that beautiful Apostrophe which Virgil has us'd upon mentioning the punishment of a Trayter against the State of Rome. *At tu dictis, Albane, maneres.*'

The sudden removal of their chief left the Chapter with mixed feelings: but it must be allowed that as a corporate body they behaved well. Of course the business of the Abbey had to go on. To ensure this Atterbury, on 27 April 1723, appointed his consistent supporter Michael Evans, Sub-Dean, as his 'true and lawfull Proxy . . . during my absence from the . . . Church'. The following day the Chapter ordered that the Dean be applied to so that 'all Books, Papers and Writings, which concern the State of the Collegiate Church [be put] into the hands of Mr. Lowe, Chapter Clerk'. The securing of these documents, together with the 'monies' in the dormitory account amounting to the sum of £1,320. 13s. 6d., was embarrassing and long drawn out. This was not so much because of any obstructive tactics on the part of Atterbury as the difficulty experienced by his secretary in straightening out the Dean's affairs. The Chapter on its part grew restless and on 8 June 1723 took notice that 'several applications to the Bishop of Rochester for books and papers in his possession had led to no result'. They therefore ordered 'that Mr. Lowe go this afternoon and acquaint his Lp that if the said Books and Papers be not without delay delivered up to him, the said Mr. Lowe, They think themselves obliged to take such proper steps, as they shall be advised in order to recover them'. In addition to his retaining the books and dormitory money, the Chapter took grave exception to Atterbury's appropriation of the furnishings from the last coronation, as well as the pall used at the funeral of the Duke of Marlborough—all which 'did of right belong to the Dean and Chapter'. The Chapter later decided, on 7 December 1723, that any persons nominated by Atterbury 'to any College servants place', without the approval of Chapter, be discharged from their office, after being paid up to date.

Meanwhile the Act of Parliament which exiled Atterbury—supported in the Lords by his episcopal colleagues on Chapter—deprived him of all his offices as from 1 June, and required his departure from the country by 25 June. It is to the credit of the prebendaries of Westminster that between 17 and 31 May, the Chapter met no fewer than six times so that Atterbury might have his share of fines due on the renewal of leases. Indeed, the Chapter met on the eve of his deprivation to guarantee his share of a fine which had not yet been fixed, though for his benefit the lease was sealed.

And so this period of strain was finally brought to an end on 16 June, when Atterbury left England never to return, taking leave of his friends, says Macaulay, 'with a dignity and tenderness worthy of a better man'. Whether any members of the Chapter—maybe the Sub-Dean—bade him farewell as he stepped on board H.M.S. *Aldborough* we do not know. Certainly there is no extant reference to their being present. What we do know is that the former Dean was deeply moved when a group of Westminster Scholars, who had just been elected to university, called on him in the Tower, not long before his departure. One of them, Thomas Newton, later Bishop of Bristol, recalled how Atterbury quoted from Milton:

> *The world is all before me, where to choose*
> *My place of rest, and Providence my guide.*

Perhaps they gave him a progress report on the new dormitory which he was destined never to see.

Atterbury lived nearly ten years in exile, dying on 4 March 1732 (N.S.), in Paris. He remained avid for Westminster news, and his son-in-law Dr Morice, who retained the office of High Bailiff, did his best to keep him in touch. He lived long enough to hear that the new dormitory was in use. Upon his death, his body was brought back to England, and after delay in the Customs and a night in the workmen's lumber room in the Abbey, was buried 'in a decent and private manner', on 22 May. He was interred in a family vault where his wife already lay, 'at the west door . . . as far from Kings and Kaisers as the space will admit of'.

12

Deans and Chapters

THE exile of Francis Atterbury marked the end of an age. His downfall was due to a deeply felt conviction that devotion to the Church of England demanded of him a political allegiance elsewhere than to the Hanoverians. His Toryism looked back to the days of Archbishop Laud, when the Stuart monarchy was the defender, *par excellence*, of the Ecclesia Anglicana, from foes both within and without. During Atterbury's years of influence, the political disputes in Parliament between Whig and Tory had their repercussions inside Convocation, in the struggle between the Lower House, predominantly Tory, and the Upper House, predominantly Whig. But as the eighteenth century got under way, passions cooled, and the extreme religious strife of the former century began to look almost indecent. Even clergy in the parishes, most of whom were Tory and High Church, began to settle down contentedly into the 'happy establishment in Church and State'. Though they might retain a deep respect for the diminishing number of high principled Non-jurors, they had no real desire to upset the Revolution settlement, thereby forswearing the solid benefits it had brought to them. In taking as his watchword *'quieta non movere'* Sir Robert Walpole had his finger on the pulse of the nation.

The temper of the eighteenth century, moreover, as it pursued its way, became increasingly secular and rational. Though the Deists lost the formal battle against such relative giants as William Law and Joseph Butler, what they stood for subtly insinuated itself into the psychology of more orthodox members of the Church of England. The emphasis now was on an 'essential Christianity', on good works and practical philanthropy rather than on doubtful doctrines and divine decrees. The typical clergyman of the age was Parson Woodforde: it was the Evangelicals and Methodists who constituted a minority. Compared with the preceding century, the Church of England in the eighteenth is without history: its story can be told independently of what happened in the seats of power at Whitehall.

Its political involvement was peripheral rather than central, though an older attitude lingered, particularly as we have seen in the Non-juring schism.

Westminster Abbey, the political colour of whose clergy, with exceptions, was mildly Tory though stoutly Hanoverian, shared the general spirit of the times. On the whole, they were not particularly distinguished either for religious zeal or theological learning. Rather they felt themselves at ease in Zion; thanked God for their restored inheritance, and settled down easily into the social and political calm of the day. The preoccupations of the Dean and Chapter became domestic. It was the period which saw the proliferation of monuments around the Abbey's walls—some of the finest; many an elaborate if unruly funeral; the revival of installation services of Knights of the Bath; the Handel Memorial Festival; the continuing repair of the fabric, beginning with the North Front and Western Towers, and ending, in the nineteenth century, with the restoration of Henry VII's Chapel. As the years went by the Abbey increasingly became a place for the sightseer on a visit to London, attracted not so much by the majestic beauty of the building, as the unique collection of tombs and statuary. Throughout these spacious years in the eighteenth century there was a preoccupation with money and rights of property in the deliberations of the Dean and Chapter which was not entirely due to the necessity of maintaining a large building. At the end of this era, which may be taken as extending to the accession of Queen Victoria, the Abbey stood on the eve of transformation. With the Reform Parliament of 1832 the winds of change began to blow; and their final effects, some years later, were to go a long way towards changing the pattern of its corporate life.

Such general observations suggest that so far as this section of the history of Westminster Abbey is concerned, the chronological method pursued so far will prove less helpful: and that it will be better to deal successively with various aspects of the continuing life of the College.

For this reason it may help to say something of eighteenth- and early nineteenth-century Deans, and the constitution of the Dean and Chapter as a body corporate in perpetual succession.

DOMESTIC CULTIVATION

Francis Atterbury was a national figure, so politically dangerous that he was exiled: but such a national status cannot be claimed for any subsequent Dean up to the time of Queen Victoria's accession, with the possible exception of Horsley. This decline in status was not simply due to successors being less able or of less colourful personality. Rather it was that times had changed, and religious loyalties were less divisive or politically significant. Ecclesiastics were therefore no longer of necessity caught up in national affairs.

After Atterbury's fall, the Government understandably acted rapidly in the appointment of a new Dean, for it was politically important that the office should not be left vacant longer than was absolutely necessary. Thus immediately upon Atterbury's deprivation, indeed while he was still in England, Dr Samuel Bradford (1652–1731), Bishop of Carlisle, was installed as his successor. It was not an exciting choice, for Bradford was what might be described as a 'safe man'; but authority may well have thought that the Collegiate Church had had excitement enough during the last few years. Bradford was already well known in the precincts where he had been a prebendary for some fifteen years; and was generally regarded as kindly and peace-loving.

Perhaps it was the memory of former conflicts which inclined the Chapter, when it met on the day of the Dean's installation, to decide that 'to avoid all disputes the allowances, payments and privileges of the Dean be set down in writing'. During Bradford's period of office, the installation services of Knights of the Bath were revived and he became the first Dean ex-officio of the Order. (See p. 222.)

Bradford was followed, on his death in 1731, by Dr Joseph Wilcocks, Bishop of Gloucester. While the latter was at the Deanery, a period of no less than twenty-five years, he applied himself conscientiously to his duties so long as his health lasted. He was regular at Chapters, and diligent as a diocesan bishop at Rochester to which he was translated.

At one time he could have moved to the archbishopric of York: but declined with the remark: 'Though my wife be poor, I must not think of changing her for one more opulent.' Wilcocks's years of office coincided with great developments in the appearance of the Palace of Westminster. After numerous unsuccessful attempts going back to the reign of the first Elizabeth, vested interests were forced to give way and in 1738 Westminster Bridge was built. The old Woollen Staple was destroyed, and Bridge Street, Great George Street and King Street replaced the old alleyways. Six unsightly houses around the Abbey were swept away and Dean's Yard enclosed. It is to the credit of the Dean, and it certainly made things easier, that he was sympathetic towards these contemporary trends. On his monument in the Abbey and his portrait in the Deanery, as well as in Canaletto's painting, the Western Towers, completed in his regime, appear prominently. Wilcocks died in 1756.

His successor in the Deanery was Zachary Pearce (1690–1774), an Old Westminster, sometime fellow of Trinity College, Cambridge, and best known as a classical scholar, in particular for his edition of Longinus. His preferment to the Deanery of Winchester in 1739, and to the bishopric of Bangor in 1748, came through the patronage of George Parker, second Earl of Macclesfield. He was also a favourite of the intelligent Queen Caroline. While bishop of his Welsh diocese, Pearce preached in 1749 in the Abbey before the House of Lords on the anniversary of Charles I's execution. His sermon was not without interest. Beginning with the customary denunciation of the 'shocking crimes' perpetrated in a rebellion which was not the 'necessary result of self defence', he yet went on to condemn the conduct of Charles I as 'grievous', since by his 'Methods of Proceeding, the Liberty of the Subjects in some cases, and their Property in others, was render'd more uncertain'. In such a situation opposition to the royal policy became 'commendable', and a 'duty'. The tragedy was that those who properly resorted to it did not know 'when to desist'.

Pearce's appointment to the Deanery of Westminster, and his translation to the see of Rochester, was in some respects curious. High preferment in the Church of England often is. In 1755, Pearce was with Archbishop Thomas Herring at Lambeth, when the latter on acquainting him with Wilcocks's illness, asked: 'Will you accept of his Bprck and ye Deanery of Westm[inster]?' Pearce's reply was an emphatic negative, on the grounds that his father's estate had now come to him and that in two years' time he wished to retire from his bishopric of Bangor into private life. The Archbishop, somewhat surprised, replied: 'I doubt whether the King will grant it, or that it can be done!' Herring, however, undeterred, pressed Rochester and the Deanery upon him on two subsequent occasions, and this, together with additional pressure from the Duke of Newcastle, finally induced him to give way.

The bicentenary of Queen Elizabeth's grant of the Charter in 1560 fell during Pearce's tenure of office: and it is indicative of the domestic character of life at the Abbey during the eighteenth century that the celebrations of this 'Jubilee' were entirely private, and confined to one day. They may be briefly described.

On 3 June, at ten o'clock, all members of the Collegiate Body assembled in College Hall. They then proceeded, two by two and in order of seniority, into the Choir where Purcell's TE DEUM was performed, together with one of his anthems. Zachary Pearce preached at this morning service, but no one present could have described his sermon as exciting. In it he considered the virtues of Queen Elizabeth as a person, as a monarch, as the 'author' of the Reformation in

P

England and as the foundress of the Collegiate Church. He concluded with these words:

> Let us all remember, constantly and faithfully, to put in practice everything which our several duties require; with grateful hearts for the benefits which we enjoy, and a strong desire to make those benefits our own by our behaviour, that what was gratuitous in the giver, may be merited and (in some sort) earned by the receivers. Thus, *as her own works sufficiently praise her in the gates*, we shall be able, in the way which she herself wished, to *give her* likewise of *the fruit of her hands*.

Morning Prayer ended, they returned to College Hall, where one of the King's Scholars delivered a typical eighteenth-century oration. 'We are here met together to commemorate our Foundress,' he began. 'T'was for the Honour of God, and the Liberties of mankind she engaged; and no wonder, therefore, that Heaven was on her side; in which case all the might and malice of the World shall miscarry, and means in all human appearance the most improbable shall prosper.' Then followed some English verse recited by the boys, after which at 1.45 p.m. 'the whole Company sat down to a Dinner in the Hall, the Dean, Prebendaries, and upper Officers of the Church being at the Upper End of the Hall; the Minor Canons, Gentlemen of the Choir, Singing Boys and inferior servants of the Church on the Eastern side of it, the King's Scholars on the West side, and the Almsmen at a Table placed in the middle'.

At 4.30 p.m. they went back into the Choir for Evensong, and another of Purcell's anthems was sung. This over, all were dismissed, except the Dean and Chapter who proceeded into Jerusalem Chamber for a Chapter Meeting. Perhaps they had already worked off their post-prandial somnolence in the church!

In view of his earlier hesitation, it is not surprising that, after some years at Westminster, the classically minded, kindly but now aged scholar-Dean, should seek to resign his dual preferment. The resignation of a bishopric, however, was, without precedent. To commend such a unique procedure, he sought in 1761, an audience with George III, and in making his request took the liberty of quoting the words of an officer to the German Emperor: 'Sir, every wise man would at the latter end of his life wish to have an interval between the Fatigue of Business and Eternity.' The King proved not unfavourable, but unhappily the matter got bogged down in party politics: so that while he was able to resign the Deanery in 1768, he was forced to hold the bishopric of Rochester till his death some six years later. Saying good-bye to Westminster led to an effusion in verse:

From all Decanal Cares at last set free
(I would that freedom still more perfect be)
My Sun's meridian, How long past and gone
And Night, unfit for Work, now hastening on.
In Life's late Evening, thro' a light of day
I find me gently tending to decay.

The editor of Longinus would probably have done better in Latin.

Among Zachary Pearce's papers in the Library at Westminster Abbey is a document which he received the evening prior to the interment of the Duke of Cumberland in Henry VII's Chapel on 9 November 1765. It ran as follows:

> Two ladies present their respectfull compliments to the Dean of Westm^r, & would take it as a singular favour if his Lordship would break through the usual Forms observed on these solemn occasions, & permit them to walk & sing in ye Procession. They were once too intimately connected with his late Royal Highness. They have remarkably fine Voices; are at present sincere Penitents and earnestly wish to offer this last Tribute of Tenderness & Respect to his Memory.

Zachary Pearce notes that he refused the request.

Those acquainted with Westminster affairs could not have been surprised when Pearce was followed by his friend, also Sub-Dean, Dr John Thomas (1712–93), though it could have given little satisfaction to another aspirant—Prebendary Thomas Wilson. Certainly the former had not hesitated to let his predecessor know that he would welcome such preferment, as the following extract from a letter to him makes plain:

> Few people indeed have so much reason to wish for a long continuance of your Lordship's health as I have; as well from a grateful sense of past favours, as from the many kind assurances of the satisfaction it would give You to see me succeed to an Office which it has been your intention to resign. Do not imagine my good Lord, that I say this from any impatience in myself, but, as you were pleased to desire me to let you know when there appeared any prospect of success, I think it my duty to acquaint your Lordship, that a friend who has long wished to serve me, now writes me word that he thinks himself so well with the present Minister as to make no doubt of obtaining his favour.

In fairness to Thomas, this letter needs to be read against the background of common practice in the eighteenth century.

Immediately upon his appointment, Thomas had extensive repairs done to the Deanery—he called them his 'extravagant folly'—at a cost of some £800. The Chapter seems to have concurred in this verdict, for they insisted on the new Dean paying the major part of the expense.

Promotion from within the Chapter, though this had happened frequently in the past, undoubtedly led to difficulties, as Thomas himself was forced to recognize. Thus after the funeral of George III's mother (15 February 1772) he confessed to 'fatigue', not due to disputes with the Lord Chamberlain, as all too often happened, but to 'the most uncivil opposition from my own Brethren to the Dean's right of having any more power over the Royal Vaults or of getting tickets for the Chapel than the Prebs have'. He himself might have thought differently a few years earlier!

John Thomas was certainly a man of integrity and cultivation. Passionately fond of music, and in his earlier days no mean performer, he was a connoisseur of painting and an erudite antiquarian. Also a numismatist he left behind him a collection of rare coins. He showed his liberality in supporting the abolition of Roman Catholic disabilities.

It was during his tenure of the Deanery and on his initiative that a new Choir was built (see p. 239); and also, in 1784, that the great Handel Memorial Festival took place. Other musical festivals followed in 1785, 1786, 1787 and 1791, the latter being the significant occasion when those present, taking their cue from the King, rose up as one man when the 'Hallelujah Chorus' was sung. Thomas's later years were handicapped by severe physical infirmities, which led to his retirement to Bromley. Thus he was unable to attend Chapter, and thereby forced to neglect his duties at the Abbey. It became necessary to secure a means of sealing documents without his signature.

Thomas's successor, Samuel Horsley (1733–1806) was almost certainly the most distinguished Dean since Atterbury. His interests were wide, for he was a Fellow and sometime Secretary of the Royal Society (leaving the Society after a dispute in 1783/4); and a member of the Jacobin Club which met at the Essex Head. He engaged in a long controversy with Joseph Priestley on the doctrine of the Incarnation; edited the works of Sir Isaac Newton; and spoke in the House of Lords against the Peace of Amiens. He was also a keen mathematician.

Horsley was not entirely unknown at the Abbey prior to his appointment as Dean, for in 1793 he preached the Anniversary sermon on 30 January before the Upper House. The occasion was felt to have a special significance since only a few days previously Louis XVI had been guillotined in Paris, and Marie Antoinette was in grave peril of a similar fate. Taking as his text Romans XIII. 1, Horsley's sermon began with an admirably reasoned attack on Rousseau's fictional state of nature. In the spirit of Burke, he maintained that 'civil society . . . always implies government . . . the condition to which God originally destined man'. Turning to the contemporary situation, Horsley roused his hearers to a pitch of excitement, as with great passion he inveighed against:

> the horrible example which the present hour exhibits, in the unparalleled misery of a neighbouring nation, once great in learning, arts and arms, now torn by contending fashions; her government demolished, her altars overthrown, her first-born dispoiled of their birthright, her nobles degraded, her best citizens exiled, her riches, sacred and prophane, given up to the pillage of sacrilege and rapine, atheists directing her councils, desperadoes conducting her armies, wars of unjust and chimerical ambition consuming her youth, her granaries exhausted, her fields uncultivated, famine threatening her multitudes, her streets swarming with assassins filled with violence, deluged with blood.

As Horsley entered upon this passage the whole congregation sprang to its feet and remained standing—a gesture of spontaneous feeling maybe unique in the Abbey and only to be compared with what happened at the Handel Memorial Festival.

During his years at Westminster, Horsley's main interests seem to have centred on the Choir and the welfare of its members. He was largely responsible for increasing the incomes of the Minor Canons, the Organist and Lay Cerks: and when he left in 1802 to become Bishop of St Asaph, the Precentor presented him with an address, expressing the deep gratitude of the whole musical foundation for his care and concern. When he died some four years later, the Abbey Choir in force attended his funeral at Newington Butts— a tribute from professional musicians that speaks volumes.

Horsley came near to being a national figure. William Vincent (1739–1815) who followed was a local and Westminster man, who had from his earliest years lived most of his life in the precincts. Appointed an 'usher' of the School in 1761, he became Second Master ten years later, Head Master in 1788, a Canon of Westminster 1801 and Dean the next year. Though somewhat of an authority on ancient geography, and enjoying the distinction of having some of his Latin verses translated by the poet William Cowper, his interests really centred on the 'College'—'the sole object of his affections' as his memorial tablet fittingly says. This was made the more easy as he was not appointed Bishop of Rochester. His great achievement was to tackle with energy the long task of restoring

Henry VII's Chapel. The extent of his preoccupation and concern can be seen in his note-book detailing the day-to-day work on the fabric. He also found time to analyse John Flete's Latin *Chronicle* of the monastery of St Peter's, Westminster, and to write an account of Widmore's labours in the library.

Vincent was succeeded by John Ireland (1761–1842) that great benefactor to Oxford, who rose to high preferment the hard way, being the son of an Ashburton butcher. From Oriel College, where he went as a Bible clerk, he later became Vicar of Croydon and Chaplain to Lord Liverpool. He was appointed a prebendary of Westminster in 1802, Sub-Dean 1806 and Dean some ten years later, which office he retained till his death. In all, he was Dean for some twenty-six years, but his infirmities led to his residing during his last years at Islip, of which he was Rector. For this reason, though he officiated at the coronations of George IV and William IV, he was unable to attend that of the girl queen Victoria. It has been said of Ireland's tenure of office, maybe a little unkindly: 'Had it not been, indeed, for the graves and monuments of those statesmen, philanthropists and other men of mark whose names were "scratched on the Abbey stones" during Ireland's time, the years of his rule would have been wholly uneventful.' The reference is to such men as Castlereagh, Canning, Warren Hastings, Grattan, Rennell, Telford and Zachary Macaulay.

Dean Ireland was essentially an eighteenth-century clergyman who lived long enough to feel the winds of change blowing around him. They were destined to get rid of many of the institutions he cherished.

CONSTITUTIONAL REFORMS WITHIN THE COLLEGE OF WESTMINSTER

During the eighteenth century the Dean and Chapter, as a corporate body, met usually twice a month, though there were occasional breaks. According to the statutes—the legal validity of which was doubtful—each of the twelve prebendaries was required to reside for some four months during the year. Had this been observed, it would have meant that at any one time four members of the Chapter were resident in the precincts. In practice, however, it had not worked out this way, since 'it appears that each prebendary took on himself the service of a separate month', which released him from close residence during the rest of the year. For those who held other preferments, this arrangement was indeed convenient. This customary procedure was given legal authority by the Crown in 1745 in a Supplementary Order allocating one month absolutely to a prebendary, without any 'concurrent' residence by his colleagues.

At a meeting of Chapter held the same year on 24 April, the method of fixing these separate months of residence was laid down. The year was to begin in December, the choice of months was to be made in order of seniority (such seniority to be reckoned according to the date of appointment); and the rota was to be drawn up not later than 14 November. After this date, prebendaries might still change their periods of residence but only by mutual agreement. Fines were fixed for absence, 13s. 4d. for each day. Some prebendaries in their old age became very negligent in their attendance, the more so as resignation was then unheard of. Thus Dean Zachary Pearce wrote to Thomas Wilson: 'I must desire of you not to think of leaving to me the business of providing a Prebendary to attend the services in the Abbey during your absence. . . . If you do not provide Dr Ballard, Dr Blair or Dr Fowler (if in town) to assist you, it will be a heavy disgrace to us if no Prebendary is to be seen for days together.' The Dean was under obligation to attend service in the Abbey on sixty-one days throughout the year, these days being left entirely to his discretion, except when he was required to preach.

An arrangement of this kind, though all prebendaries had houses within the precincts, did not encourage a large attendance at meetings of Chapter. Usually there were not more than some four or five present: though on really crucial issues, such as the erection of the new dormitory in College Garden, votes were canvassed by letter. Yet Chapter business could be impeded by the difficulty of getting together the required quorum of six members, which for the sealing of documents must include the Dean. The latter requirement grew to be a real problem in 1793 when Dean Thomas, already in his eighties, became a semi-invalid and was no longer able to attend Chapter. Something had to be done, so resort was made to the Visitor, and the result was a Royal Letter of 20 May 1793 giving authority for the College Seal to be attached, in exceptional circumstances, without the Dean's signature.

The need to secure a quorum could impede the business of Chapter. An attendance of six during the summer months when prebendaries were for the most part in the country and some on 'progress' was not easily secured. To ease this situation, the Visitor was asked to rule that the Dean and four prebendaries should be adequate. The reply to this request was surprisingly reassuring, namely that a former Royal Letter had already dealt with this point.

But still the problem of securing an adequate attendance at Chapter, as distinct from a quorum, remained unsolved. In April 1817 a more venal remedy was sought by linking up attendance at meetings with the sharing out of dividends, since 'it is highly expedient that a more full and effectual attendance of the Members of

Chapter should be secured for the transaction of business'. Thus on 30 April the following resolution was passed: 'Ordered that, in future, before any Dividend is made to the Dean and Chapter at large the sum of Eighty Pounds (the Fabrick dividends being first deducted) shall be taken out of the whole sum and divided in the usual proportions, among the members of the Chapter who may be present.'

The Dean, however, on reflection, declined to be placed on an equality with the prebendaries in this way, and at a meeting of the Chapter on 31 July, he made a personal statement to the effect that the order must be understood as implying that:

... when any Dividend is made the Dean's Dividend of two fifteenths and the Dividend of one fifteenth shall first be taken out of the whole sum to be divided; that the sum of Eighty Pounds shall then be taken out and divided in equal proportions amongst the Prebendaries who shall attend the Chapter; and that the remainder shall be wholly divided among the attending Prebendaries and those absent in equal proportions.

Changes in the constitution of Chapter, however, were to be brought about independently of the wishes or initiative of its members. The Reform Parliament of 1832 turned with zeal, and with the yard-stick of a practical assessment, to take stock of the institutions of government—local as well as national. The Church of England could not expect to escape scrutiny and in 1832 there were set up 'Commissioners appointed to enquire into the state of the Established Church with reference to Ecclesiastical duties and revenues'. The implication was unmistakable—that something was rotten in the state of Denmark.

The story of the Commission, and its great work of reform which, with the Evangelical and Oxford Movements, 'saved' the Church of England, lies outside the scope of this book though it will be commented on in a subsequent chapter. Suffice that its activities were first felt at the Collegiate Church when in February 1835, the Commissioners gave it as their opinion that it was 'highly expedient that an arrangement be made by which the stall at Westminster now vacant may be made permanently instrumental to the spiritual care of the Parish of St Margaret's'. The custom hitherto had been for the Dean and Chapter to appoint an incumbent, usually from their own number. The new procedure would transfer the nomination to the Crown, through its attachment to a prebendal stall. After consideration, the Dean and Chapter (17 February 1835) 'cheerfully assent[ed]' to the plan of the Commissioners, and agreed to surrender to the Crown the appointment of the minister to St Margaret's 'with the view of the cure of souls becoming permanently attached to the vacant stall'.

The first rector of St Margaret's under the new scheme was Henry Hart Milman, poet, historian and divine, later a most distinguished Dean of St Paul's.

If the suggestion from the Commissioners relating to St Margaret's found ready acquiescence, at least officially, from the Dean and Chapter, this was certainly not the case when the Commissioners put forward a further plan which affected members of Chapter more nearly; namely to reduce the number of prebendaries from twelve to four.

The immediate reaction of the Dean and Chapter (30 March 1836) was one of grave alarm, and they drew up a vigorous protest in which they expressed themselves as 'constrained by a sense of duty to represent to the Commissioners (which they do with all respect) that with so small a number of Prebendaries, the Divine Service cannot be performed, either with convenience to the Officiators themselves or with benefit to the Publick'. Indeed it was a matter of deep regret that the original provision for four prebendaries, jointly resident at the same time, had been dispensed with in 1745 under a Royal Letter. Certainly the results of this dispensation had been unfortunate and if the new proposals for reducing the number of the Dean and Chapter became law these ill effects would be increased 'for the health of a single Prebendary will scarcely sustain him in the effective daily service of three successive months'. At least six prebendaries were required, and two of these ought always to be resident.

The Dean and Chapter also followed up this memorial with a petition (12 October 1836) to the Crown—there were three vacancies on the Chapter at the time—asking that if the proposed scheme were to be put into effect, then a quorum might remain, as at present, at 50 per cent. of their membership, which in these new circumstances would reduce it to two! This request was granted on 20 October 1836.

The alarm, however, proved to be a false one, though the reprieve was only temporary. The reduction of the prebendal body did take place but not until 1842 when its number was fixed at six, as a subsequent chapter of this book relates.

Westminster Abbey was not alone in feeling the force of the new movement for reform. Its status, however, as a 'royal peculiar' served in some ways as a temporary protection, and the Dean and Chapter preferred to put their trust here rather than to associate themselves publicly with other capitular bodies who felt their vested interests equally threatened. Thus when a meeting of 'delegates' was called to

Coventry through the initiative of its Dean and Chapter, the Abbey declined to send a representative ostensibly because the Dean and four prebendaries were absent from the meeting when it was discussed!

PRIVILEGES OF A ROYAL FOUNDATION

One of the most highly cherished privileges of the Dean and Chapter was their relationship to the Sovereign as Visitor; and because of this, their exemption from any episcopal or archi-episcopal control. As they put it on one occasion, they were 'particularly happy' to be under the 'King's immediate and peculiar Inspection and Jurisdiction'. The Abbey, they never tired of repeating, was a 'royal foundation', both in respect of its founder Edward the Confessor, and its Elizabethan Charter of 1560. This status gave them the right to present loyal Addresses on the accession of the Sovereign; and to mark significant occasions in the life of the royal family in a similar way. Thus within a period of some seventy years, seventeen Addresses were presented to members of the royal family.

It would perhaps be unfair to criticize successive Deans and Chapters for the fulsome flattery which characterizes most of these Addresses. Exaggerated language of this kind was regarded as a proper token of respect, and when directed to the royal family was expressive of a general loyalty to the Revolution settlement. These documents have some interest as reflecting the spirit of a naturally conservative institution wedded to the preservation of 'our happy establishment in Church and State'. A few quotations and comments may therefore be offered.

Frequent were the Addresses sent to George III beginning with that on his accession, in which the Dean and Chapter professed themselves 'particularly happy . . . that in virtue of our respective Stations we shall be present and assisting when on some solemn day the Imperial Crown of these Realms shall in our Church be placed on Your Majesty's Sacred Head, with the united Approbation and Acclamations of all your People'. After an attempted assassination, a memorial assured him that his 'personal safety and the public welfare' were 'inseparately united'. Indeed, so the Dean and Chapter wrote on another occasion, if 'the dark designs and outrageous attempts of treason' had been successful 'the happiness of our country had been extinguished, Your Throne overturned, our Constitution subverted and our national Church laid in ruins'. When expressing their heartfelt thanks for the restoration of George III's reason, the implication was that the sins of his people had brought upon him this 'dreadful affliction'.

Such artificial sentiments must, of course, be read against the background of the French Revolution and the spread of Jacobinism.

It may be added here that the Dean and Chapter, at the time of the celebration of the Jubilee of the Hanoverian accession on 1 August 1814, reluctantly declined, on account of 'the danger', an application by Sir William Congreve, inventor of the Congreve Rocket, to illuminate the Towers: but they did agree to erect stands from which to see the fireworks in the Parks, at the same time taking all necessary precautions for preventing 'danger or mischief' to the Abbey.

Less excusable, in its extreme terms, was the Address in 1818 to the Prince Regent—the first gentleman in Europe as well as its greatest cad—which concludes with these words: 'That Your Royal Highness may be spared to a Nation which has the satisfaction of seeing your virtues more and more developed on every great and trying occasion is our sincere and earnest prayer.' It would be unfair to ask the real grounds for this satisfaction. Perhaps the Address should be read in conjunction with the leading article which appeared in *The Times* on the occasion of George IV's death.

On one occasion the precise form of an Address seems to have led to some division of opinion on Chapter. The reference is to one drawn up by Dr Ireland, approved by the prebendary in residence and sent to George IV in January 1821. It began by professing the strong attachment of the Dean and Chapter 'to the happy constitution of these Your Majesty's Dominion in Church and State' and went on:

> We declare, therefore, against the Infidel and the Scoffer, that we humbly bless God for the revealed Religion which his Providence has caused to be established among us. . . . We declare against the Slanderer of our Civil Institutions, that we fondly cherish them, because they have extended to us a larger measure of freedom and security than any other Nation can boast.

At a subsequent meeting the question was raised as to whether Addresses ought to be sent in the name of the Dean and Chapter without the express concurrence of its members. In order to 'protect' the Dean from any charge of 'irregularity' it was agreed that in future absent prebendaries should be sent the proposed Address before it was finally dispatched.

This last Address needs to be read alongside a petition which the Dean and Chapter sent to Parliament on 6 March 1821, 'against the further indulgences proposed to be granted to the Roman Catholics by the Bills now pending in the House of Commons'. In very forthright terms they wrote:

Your Petitioners beg to state that the Roman Catholics of these Dominions have already obtained by law that measure of Christian toleration which allow to them the free and open exercise of their religion; and to this have been added many other indulgencies. But when, not content with these grants, they claim to be admitted to Offices of public trust and power they make a demand as your Petitioners humbly think, contrary to the nature of our Constitution and highly dangerous to our Protestant Establishment in Church and State.

Moreover, Roman Catholic states did not themselves allow a similar liberty, and a religion 'so intolerant in its nature cannot be safely entrusted with political power'.

Such a petition—a similar one was drawn up in 1822—placed the Dean and Chapter on the side of conservative opinion, and against the emergent liberalism of the age. It reads strangely today.

The regular expressions of personal loyalty to the throne, from which quotations have been made, did not, however, go along with any obsequious attitude to the King's servants. Far from it. Here the Dean and Chapter determined to stick up for their rights, as for example upon the occasion of the funeral of Princess Caroline in 1758.

The contretemps which then developed began with a letter to the Dean from the Lord Chamberlain instructing him to deliver up the keys of Henry VII's Chapel to the Board of Works so that the latter might 'open and close the Royal Vault in which Queen Caroline was to be interred'.

No instruction could have touched the Abbey authorities at a more sensitive point. The Dean—Zachary Pearce—immediately returned the letter to the Lord Chamberlain, since the Dean, by virtue of his office, was guardian of the Royal Sepulchres, and the customary procedure, in a matter of this kind, was to request him to order that a vault should be opened.

This firm stand led to a meeting with the Lord Chamberlain in the Deanery on 4 January, in the presence of the Surveyor of the Fabric; and the result was that the Lord Chamberlain asked the Dean to order the workmen to open the vault. At the same time he promised to send a letter to this effect later in the day couched in the usual form. The Lord Chamberlain was as good as his word and the letter duly arrived.

Funerals frequently led to irritating disputes between the various authorities concerned. Particularly was this the case with the interment of the Prince of Wales on 13 April 1751, when as soon as the ceremony was over, and in spite of former agreements, the Lord Chamberlain seized the pall and with the help of the Guards carried it away. We cannot linger over the intricacies of this dispute: its importance is that it led the Dean and Chapter to draw up a long document maintaining their absolute rights in Henry VII's Chapel. It was true, they admitted, that Henry VII had built it as a private burial place for his family; and that the Dean, as an act of courtesy, requires the parties applying to him for an interment to obtain royal assent. Yet there could be no question whatever but that under the Charter of Queen Elizabeth there was granted to the College, without any reservation whatever, 'the whole Church and all the Chapels'.

The Charter was certainly unambiguous on this point; but the Dean and Chapter realistically recognized that there were occasions, in particular coronations, when they could only claim customary rights. This applied, for example, to the seating arrangements for their families and friends. Corporate memories are long: and it was the contention of the Dean and Chapter that they had suffered an injustice at the coronation of George III which they determined to put right at that of his son. Thus when in 1820 the deputy Earl Marshal signified that he would need all the Choir and the vaulting above the Choir and transepts to seat the royal guests, the Dean and Chapter decided on a formal petition to the Sovereign which they sealed on 15 June. The petition concluded as follows:

> The Dean and Chapter are most happy that His Majesty makes choice of their Church, above all others, for the place of His Coronation. They only pray that the Ceremony may be performed without prejudice to their ancient and acknowledged privileges and without the entire exclusion of them and their families in favour of Strangers, from the Choir of their own Church which the Royal Charter of Foundation has munificently and legally conferred on them for ever . . . The Dean and Chapter humbly make this representation to His Majesty in discharge of the duty they owe to themselves and their successors. They do it also as an especial duty to His Majesty himself, that He may graciously condescend to protect those rights and privileges which originally descended from the Crown, and to grant to the Dean and Chapter those advantages which they have enjoyed at former Coronations.

The petition, however, was not successful, and the Dean and Chapter had to be content with putting their families in the Muniment (record) Room.

The coronation of William IV provided a further opportunity for the Dean and Chapter to try to secure redress of grievances. On this occasion they drew up a memorial which they personally sent to the Earl Marshal. They based their case for better accommodation on

ancient and invariable custom', according to which up till the
coronation of George III, 'three inter-columnial spaces' or bays in
the Choir were set apart for their use. Their present allocation of
seats, they protested, led to great 'inconvenience', to say nothing of a
'very distant and imperfect view of the ceremony'. The Dean and
Chapter were confident that the Earl Marshal would make it
possible for their friends and families to view the coronation in a
'commodious manner'.

If this was a genuine as distinct from a wishful confidence, then it
was certainly misplaced. The retort of the Earl Marshal was curt,
for he began by remarking that 'an appeal to his courtesy should
have been unnecessary'. The simple fact was that 'the increased
demands for accommodation in the Abbey' made acquiescence with
the request of the Dean and Chapter impossible—and that was all
there was to it.

THE ORDER OF THE BATH

Perhaps something ought to be said of the revival, during the period
under review, of the installation services of Knights of the Bath. The
Dean of Westminster was made *ex-officio* Dean of the Order, and
Henry VII's established as its Chapel. The first installation of the
reconstituted Order took place in 1725.

The preparations for this colourful, if somewhat archaic ceremony,
presented great difficulties in spite of the fact that they were wisely
set in hand early. Not only was the precise order of the service a
matter of some debate: but there were also delicate negotiations
with officials of the Order on matters of finance and seating. The
Dean and Chapter were concerned, as always, that their immediate families should have a good view of the ceremony which,
after all, so they alleged, was being staged in 'their Abbey': while
they were equally determined that other members of the collegiate
body should be able to use the occasion to supplement their incomes.
Thus on 8 June 1725 the Chapter ordered that scaffolding should be
erected over the West Window of the Chapel for their own families,
and that the Receiver-General, Registrar and Surveyor should be
given permission to build stands outside the Abbey on the north side
for their private benefit. Similar facilities were also granted to the
lay clerks, the library keeper, cellarer, butler, cook, scullion and other
officers. Another Chapter order gave permission for members of
foreign embassies to assemble in Jerusalem Chamber before the
ceremony of installation.

This service was the first of a series which has continued, with
intervals, to the present day. Such an association with the Order of

the Bath has brought colour into the Abbey, not only through the banners and armorial bearings permanently on display in Henry VII's Chapel, but in the splendour of the pageantry at the installations themselves. Yet it must be admitted, on the debit side, that throughout the eighteenth century these occasions led to a great deal of bad feeling between the Dean and Chapter and the College of Heralds, as well as, on occasions, with the Board of Works. Moreover, the erection of scaffolding—this applies equally, of course, to coronations and funerals—was the cause of a great deal of physical destruction to the building. Thus after the first installation, the Dean and Chapter on 7 November 1726, felt it necessary to apply to the Board of Works to make good the damage caused by them in Henry VII's Chapel. On a later occasion, in 1732, the Chapter took legal opinion over a dispute with the Board of Works concerning the erection of scaffolding.

It would be tedious to relate in detail these conflicts of interest which persisted throughout the eighteenth century. Again in 1744 there were squabbles over the perquisites, between the Lord Chamberlain, the Board of Works and the Chapter. The usual custom was for the Regalia to be kept in the possession of the Great Wardrobe and released, as required, for the use of the Dean and Chapter upon a warrant from the Crown.

Allocation of tickets was another very fruitful source of disagreement. Doubtless a great deal of heartburning lies behind the succinct Chapter Order of 22 May 1761, that the Receiver-General should draw up a special account of the 'several Circumstances of the Installation'.

Of course these disputes must be placed within the context of an age renowned for resort to litigation, for its insistence upon rights in particular of property and for controversy in collegiate and ecclesiastical institutions. Energies which in former years were poured into the discussion of predestination and doubtful doctrines were now drawn off into domestic quarrels. At least the latter did not lead to the persecution of heretics!

Reference has earlier been made to the colour which these services of installation brought into the Chapel, not least through the permanent legacy of banners and armorial bearings. In the nineteenth century these began to be a problem.

In 1832, anxiety was expressed by members of the Order as to whether there was sufficient space to allow the practice to continue. The Sovereign, as Head, commanded that the matter should be looked into. As a result, the Dean of the time, John Ireland, accompanied by the Duke of York, and two members of the Order, went round the Chapel and a report was presented to Chapter on 23 May.

On the whole it was reassuring. There was ample space for laying up the banners of Knights Grand Cross 'the only thing requisite being to suspend the new Flags a little above, or a little below, the present Flags in the intermediate spaces'. Also with some alterations, which included the addition of another row of stalls on each side of the Chapel (still leaving an aisle of some twenty-two feet), room could be made for the requisite number of armorial brasses. The banners of the Knights Commanders, for which there was no room in the Chapel, had been relegated to the Choir of the church, but this had led to difficulty, particularly at coronations. It was proposed to remedy this by hanging them from iron rods between the columns. Fortunately the Knights Companion had no banners!

Not all this report, however, was implemented. It only remains to add that the services of installation were discontinued in the nineteenth century to be revived in 1913.

LIFE IN THE PRECINCTS AND THE SCHOOL

Within the precincts of the Abbey, across the centuries, there lived a domestic society over which the Dean and Chapter presided. Much of this history, in the nature of the case, has left no memorial behind it. Doubtless every household had its own individual story, but rarely are we given a glimpse of it. Simon Patrick, prebendary of Westminster, later Bishop of Chichester and Ely, relates in his *Autobiography* with real pathos a domestic tragedy which must have frequently happened in many a family across the years—the death of his little daughter, Penelope, on 20 September 1687, 'of very great beauty—very lovely in our eyes, and grew every day more delightful'. 'It was no small difficulty,' he writes, 'to keep my wife from being overcome with grief. But I upheld and comforted her, as she did me as well as we were able. And the Psalms of the day suited us admirably, the first being very mournful, and the next exceeding joyful, teaching us to say "Bless the Lord O my soul and forget not all his benefits".'

If the life of the Abbey community could be told by those who served it faithfully though in humble capacities the picture which emerged might take on a different perspective from that which finds place in this book. Who can tell which view is more significant or more true, that which was seen from the Deanery or the Porter's Lodge? The fact is that the records, for the most part, are silent as to what the glaziers, the plumbers, the carpenters, the masons, some of whose names remain scratched on the windows or incised into the stone of the building, thought of the Collegiate Church of St Peter in

Westminster. To them, doubtless, Atterbury's Jacobitism mattered less than his degree of understanding of their own personal problems and difficulties. What, we wonder, for example, were the reactions of the group of Quakers who in the seventies of the eighteenth century met in a house 'in the Close of this Collegiate Church'?

Often the Chapter minutes hint, with irritating if suggestive brevity, at 'old far-off unhappy things and battles long ago'. What personal tragedy was it which led to the 'gross frauds' of Mr Jackson the baker; to the insolvency of Mr Merest, the Receiver-General, who in the throes of bankruptcy defaulted to the Dean and Chapter for a sum of over a £1,000? What was the precise 'misbehaviour' at the coronation of George III for which kindly Dean Pearce removed Mr Fidoe, as from Lady Day 1762, of all his employments in the church? Doubtless often a dismissal, and there are many such recorded in the Chapter minutes, has behind it some domestic tragedy and led to subsequent poverty and unemployment.

What, one wonders, were the reactions of the clergy wives to the ambitions and mutual relations of their husbands? Did differences on the Chapter, during the stormy 'reign' of Francis Atterbury, have their repercussions among the ladies? Was it due to internal quarrels that the Dean and Chapter, in 1749, appointed a sub-committee to consider 'how to make room in Pews in the Abbey for the Dean and prebendaries' "families"; and at the same time to provide accommodation for their servants'? The solution arrived at was, perhaps, the normal one for those days; that servants were not really expected to attend 'Choir Services' but 'early morning prayers' conducted by the Minor Canons—and they were early!

Westminster School, of which the Dean and Chapter till 1868 were the Governing Body, has always occupied a unique and intimate place within the life and affections of the 'College'. The Head Master, Master of the Scholars, and the scholars themselves, were members of the foundation. The eighteenth century and the years immediately following were in many respects a halcyon period for the school. During this time it numbered among its *alumni* Lord Mansfield, William Cowper, Jeremy Bentham and Lord John Russell. No school had a higher reputation for scholarship.

So far as the School was concerned the Abbey served the purposes of a Chapel. Such a deployment presented problems then as now. In July 1821 the Head Master requested that the town boys might sit in the western end of the Choir for 'their more effectively hearing Divine Service'. The Dean and Chapter approved but let it be known that in doing so they entertained 'the firmest expectation' that the Head Master and Under Master 'will regularly attend the Church; together with a sufficient number of the Ushers to maintain

Q

an effectual inspection and control of the conduct of the Boys, while attending Service'.

The Election Dinner, held on the day of the election of Westminster boys to Christ Church, Oxford, and Trinity College, Cambridge, was an annual event which now and again gave members of the Chapter some anxiety. In 1736 they solemnly recorded in the minutes that there were 'Great Exceedings in the Article of Wine at the late Election'. Amplifying this statement they go on to complain of 'too great a quantity of common Wines [and a] greater use of French wines than had been customary'. The Steward—that is the prebendary responsible for hospitality—was therefore requested to prevent this excess in the future; and in order to secure this, it was ordered that French wine should not be served except at 'the upper part of the High Table', and then only when called for by the Dean.

A tendency to drink to excess long continued to occupy the minds of the Chapter, and it was probably not only economy which prompted them to keep an eye on money spent for this purpose. In 1782 a gratuity of £21 was given to the Butler, Joseph Thorne, in appreciation of his having effected a considerable economy. It seems, however, that this led to complaints from the Scholars. Hence the passing of a resolution which ordered that since it had been found from the College Butler that the quantity of beer regularly charged to the use of the College, viz. 170 Hogsheads per annum was much greater than was really wanted, 'the Butler do always take care to supply the Scholars with as much Beer as they shall desire without any limitation but that he likewise take care as a part of the proper duty of his Office as Butler that no more be charged on account of the Scholars than they shall really have consumed'.

The Election Dinner was certainly no meagre affair, as can be seen from the Dean and Chapter in 1793 paying to the College Cook £78. 9s. 6d. for expenses he had incurred. Translated into modern money values we can reasonably deduce that they dined well!

Doubtless some domestic history lies behind the decision, taken in June 1812, that the ordering of provisions be taken out of the hands of the Cook and be transferred to the Steward.

School and Abbey, at this period, were almost one and indivisible: but intimate relations of this kind, as in most families, easily lead to stress and strain, particularly when they are lived out cheek by jowl. The precincts of Westminster were no exception. In practice much depended on the temperaments of Dean and Head Master—their mutual understanding and forbearance.

The most serious clash with the School during the eighteenth century arose in a dispute between a prebendary, Thomas Wilson (1703–84), a son of the saintly Bishop Wilson, and the Head Master, Dr Markham. The circumstances were as follows: Wilson, who became more eccentric and irascible as he grew older, 'purchased Mrs French's house adjoining the Old Dormitory and also the Lord Bishop of Norwich's interest in the two houses in Dean's Yard fronting it'. The intention was to repair the former and demolish the two latter to form a garden: but Dr Markham had other views. In 1756 he put forward a scheme to Chapter to demolish this property in order to enlarge Dean's Yard and thus provide more boarding accommodation. On 28 May, Chapter approved this with one dissentient—Thomas Wilson. The rage of the aggrieved prebendary now knew no bounds. He published a vituperative pamphlet *A Review of the Project of Building a New Square at Westminster, Said to be for the Use of Westminster School*; fought an unsuccessful legal action against Dr Markham; and finally migrated to 6, Little Cloister, which had been let during the years 1749 and 1755 to the Moravian minister and evangelist Count Zinzendorf.

It must be admitted that another Head Master, Dr Smith, not a very distinguished one, did not entertain excessively kind feelings towards the Dean and Chapter, if the following extract from Boswell's *Journal* may be taken as typical:

Mrs. Stuart has a great deal of humour. She gave me a most characteristical anecdote of an English pedant, Dr. Smith, the present Headmaster of Westminster School. Lady Percy and she were going to see the procession of the Princess of Wales' funeral, and were to have places in Dr. Blair's, one of the prebendaries of Westminster, from whose windows they could see it well. There was so great a crowd that they could not get their carriage forward to Dr. Blair's. So they stopped at Dr. Smith's door, sent up their names, and begged leave only to walk through his house to Dr. Blair's. They heard him answer the servant, 'It cannot be. I will not let them go through; I'll do nothing to oblige the Dean and Chapter'. It would seem that there had been some quarrel between him and the Dean and Chapter. But his thinking of that and conducting himself sternly with a view to it while two pretty, young, agreeable ladies were waiting with impatience for the simple favour of being allowed to pass through his house, and could not reasonably be supposed to have any connection with the Dean and Chapter, was truly ludicrous. They persisted in their request till at last Dr. Smith himself came downstairs and opened his backdoor saying: 'Well, you may go through. But remember, 'tis not to oblige the Dean and Chapter'.

But Dr Smith must not be taken as representative of a century which saw such great Head Masters as Thomas Knipe, Robert Freeman, Dr Nicholl (under whom Warren Hastings was admitted to the school), and William Vincent. On the whole relations between Abbey and School were cordial and co-operative.

Reference earlier to the boys of Westminster School attending the Abbey for their service leads us to notice that for a short time they were not the only young people to worship collectively in the Abbey. The Governors of the Westminster Free School in Orchard Street petitioned the Dean and Chapter to allow them to hold a service on Sundays at dinner time. The Chapter gave permission but insisted that this must be regarded as 'temporary and experimental'. It required that the Dean must appoint the officiating minister; that the scholars must use Prayer Books and Psalters; and that the service be held in the north choir aisle.

13

The Church

THE most weighty responsibility which fell upon the Dean and Chapter was the upkeep of the building. But the problem after the Restoration was not simply to maintain it, but to undertake major repairs which were the legacy of centuries of neglect on stonework and roofs. There were particular reasons, so Sir Christopher Wren maintained, which had made the Abbey vulnerable in this way. 'The pride of a very high roof raised above reasonable pitch is not for duration, for the lead is apt to slip.' Nothing now could be done about these 'original faults in the first design'. Yet even more disastrous was the choice of materials. The Norman builders liked their own Caen stone, and in England had chosen Reigate as the best equivalent. Certainly this stone was easy to work, as it could be sawed like wood; but it took in water and the effect of frost across the centuries had been to make it peel off to a depth of some four inches. Also the use of Norman chestnut with oak had proved to be unwise.

That the Abbey was in a bad condition was generally recognized at the time. The extent of the damage it had suffered was revealed to the Dean and Chapter in a report which was drawn up in January 1696. As this document has only recently come to light it may be worth quoting in full:

We whose names are under writin have by an Order from ye Right Reverand ye Dean and Chapter veued and surveyed ye Collegiate Church and Chapell of Westminster and do finde ye Wants of Repairing to be so grate and all jitts parts so very defective that unles Speedy Care be taken they will require a much grater Charge.

The Severall Roofes of Which are in a very bad Condition Both as to ye Lead and timber.

All ye Windows are very defective as well in ye Iron as ye Stone and Glass.

The Buterises and buting Arches wth ye Parapatt Walls and ye Gratest part of ye Ashlier Worke of ye Church is in A very Bad Condition.

All ye flooers over ye Side Isles being Wholy decade and Alsoe the Arches under them much out of Repair ocationed by ye decadency of ye Roofe over ye Same.

The Wants of Reparing this and ye other Roofs is a grate Reason of ye Many defects.

And if not timely prevented Will be ye Cause of Much More so that it may be of ill Consequence to delay itt much longer.

The Sum Proper to Answer these Repares will Amount too thirty on thousand Nine hundred and fifty pounds at ye Least.

Estimated January, 1696

By   Mr. Will Meades   ⎱ . . . Surveyers
       Mr. Sam^{ll} Clothier ⎰

       Mr. Jeffes   ⎱   . . . Carpenters
       Mr. Warden ⎰

       Mr. Smith   ⎱   . . . Masons
       Mr. Tuffnell ⎰

       Mr. Clarke   . . . Plumber

JAMES BROUGHTON

The enormous estimated cost of this work of restoration was, of course, quite beyond the resources of the Dean and Chapter. Indeed it was their constant complaint that under their Elizabethan foundation no proper endowment had been given them to deal with capital expenditure on the building. In other words they had inherited a decayed church with no resources to repair long-outstanding damage. True, Dolben had secured the allocation of one-fifteenth of the fines incurred on the renewal of leases for this purpose, but such monies were wholly inadequate to deal with repair work on a vast scale. This income had achieved only minor holding operations, in particular on one of the rose windows.

Fortunately a new source of revenue now unexpectedly came the way of the Dean and Chapter, maybe on the prompting of Dean Sprat, certainly through the good offices of Charles Montague, Chancellor of the Exchequer, an Old Westminster. Using his position and influence he secured that the sixth of a duty levied on coal by Act of Parliament should be used on the repair of the Abbey. It was hoped that this might come to some £3,000 per annum.

This Parliamentary grant made major works of repair to the building practical politics, and encouraged the Dean and Chapter to create another office.

A College Surveyor already existed in the person of James

Broughton, whose oversight extended throughout the whole of the precincts. The Dean and Chapter now decided to appoint a Fabric Surveyor, whose attention would be specially directed to the church itself. Here one name stood pre-eminent: and it must have been a great satisfaction to the Chapter when, on 11 March 1698, they were able to announce the appointment of Sir Christopher Wren to this new office. He held it till his death on 23 February 1723, at the advanced age of 91.

Sir Christopher was by no means unfamiliar with the building, since some years earlier (6 January 1690) he had told Dr South that the general condition of the fabric was 'crazy' (a favourite word with him), so much so that it was difficult to tell what to set about repairing first. Indeed, he said, it would cost £1,800 per annum for twelve years simply to prevent the building falling down within the foreseeable future.

Under Wren's expert direction, and during Sprat's period of office, work was now set in hand. Wren's initial problem—and he fully realized its critical nature—was to decide upon the choice of stone. After considerable thought, he elected for Burford from Oxfordshire, which was conveniently brought up the river. Owing to the inaccessibility of the north side of the Abbey, Wren concentrated his attention on the general repair of the stonework on the south, which included the buttresses in Cloister Garth, and the Chapels.

At the time of Sprat's death in 1713, Wren reckoned that of necessary repair on the stonework, about one-third had been completed. He intended now to open up the roofs, to deal with the 'very ruinous' rose window, and then to begin to tackle the north side. He was hoping that the latter, being partially protected by houses, might be in a better condition than the south side. But these same houses, with their 'privies and cellars' extending right up to the walls, made it difficult to set up scaffolding or to bring in materials. Yet if these works could but be carried through successfully, then the Abbey would be preserved 'for ages to come'.

Wren, however, was not content with 'necessary repairs'. Though he was now 80 years of age, he could not forbear making three suggestions with respect to 'a proper completing of what is left imperfect'. They were:

(1) The erection of a 'lofty spire' as originally intended, 'which will give a proper grace to the whole fabric, and the west end of the city which seems to want it'.

(2) The finishing the two Western Towers.

(3) The making of the North Front more magnificent.

For these three projects—the enthusiasm in an old man is admirable
—Sir Christopher had already prepared drafts and models.

We may note in passing, that, though numbers two and three
have been achieved, the first still awaits (much needed?) implementation.

PARLIAMENT HELPS THE FABRIC FUND

Wren's general schedule of work continued under Atterbury, though
in 1728 the Parliamentary Grant ceased. If work was to be resumed,
more money was essential, and this could only come from the same
source. Thus on 9 March 1731 a formal petition was sent to Parliament, the terms of which are not without interest.

At the time of the dissolution of the monasteries, so the petitioners
complained, the church was left 'in many parts unfinished': and
since those days time had taken its toll upon the external stonework
making the building 'exceedingly decayed and ruinous'. Nor, under
the Charter granted by Queen Elizabeth, had the property been
adequately endowed either with 'fabric rents' or other emoluments
for the purpose of maintaining the building.

> Your Petitioners therefore humbly hope that so great and good
> a Work carried on and so far advanced by the Aid of former
> Parliaments will by the like assistance in the present auspicious
> Reign be happily perfected and this Venerable Pile wherein the
> Remains of the Royal Family, the Nobility & Chief Gentry of
> these Realms, are Deposited which is Honoured with the Corona-
> tion of our Kings; & is appropriated by Royal Authority for the
> performance of the Religious Offices and Ceremonies of the most
> Hon. Order of the Bath will be esteemed a public Concern, and
> be at length finished according to its Noble and intended
> modell.

Parliament was not unsympathetic. Indeed it entertained a
'good disposition . . . towards the Petition', but let it be known that
the condition of a grant must be an undertaking not to renew the
leases on, and eventually to pull down, the houses (including two
prebendal residences) which clustered around the north side of the
Abbey. The Dean and Chapter solemnly accepted this condition,
and Parliament allocated a grant of £4,000, the understanding being
that such payments would be annual. On 12 June 1733 Nicholas
Hawksmoor (1661–1736), who had already gained considerable
experience of the building, was appointed 'Chief Surveyor of Works'
with Thomas Hinton as his assistant.

Work was set in hand, but in March 1735 a further petition was presented to Parliament, since the grant had been discontinued on the grounds that the two prebendal houses, under the immediate control of the Dean and Chapter, were still undemolished. Parliament also wished to be convinced that the resources of the Abbey were as limited as they had been given to understand.

As to the first point, the Dean and Chapter assured Parliament that the two houses would be vacated, and no new life interest in them created. They were as good as their word. Orders were given for demolition, and Lord Ashburnham's house in Little Dean's Yard was purchased for the two prebendaries, Parliament making a grant in compensation of £1,000.

Ashburnham House deserves special mention. It was situated on the site of the Prior's House and was built by Inigo Jones and decorated by Sir James Soane. After Lord Ashburnham ceased occupation, it received, in 1712, the King's Library, and, in 1730, the library of Sir Robert Cotton. In 1731 a disastrous fire broke out in the precincts, and Dr Friend, Head Master of Westminster School, long retained vivid memories of a man in his dressing-gown, a book clutched under his arm, escaping from the blazing house. The man was none less than the celebrated Richard Bentley, Master of Trinity, the great classical scholar: and the book the Alexandrian manuscript of the New Testament, which after a temporary sojourn in the Old Dormitory found its way in 1751 to the British Museum.

As to the second point that Parliament had raised, the Dean and Chapter provided a complete statement of moneys coming to them from funerals and monuments, which revenue alone was available for the purposes of repair. This showed that between the years 1731–7, the receipts amounted to £1,487. 2s.; that is independently of the fees that went to Abbey personnel, which were also listed. In addition the Dean and Chapter provided an exact statement of all moneys expended from their own corporate funds on the church and College, during the same period. They amounted to £4,170. 9s. 10d.

The petition was successful and till 1741, with some interruptions and renewed petitions, the Dean and Chapter received £4,000 per annum from Parliament. Work was resumed. As a result the Western Towers, conceived by Sir Christopher Wren, carried forward by Hawksmoor, were finally completed by James. They now constitute, perhaps, the most familiar view of the Abbey.

Yet fundamental work of restoration, due to past neglect, was not yet complete. As the century drew to a close, the condition of Henry VII's Chapel became more and more ruinous. References to its plight appear frequently in the minutes of Chapter. In

August 1793 James Wyatt (the Surveyor) was asked to consider the releading of the roof: and in April of the following year Mr John Armstrong was questioned concerning its re-timbering. A few years later the repairing of the windows was undertaken at a cost of £200 each.

While these works were going on a ruinous fire occurred on 9 July 1803, due to the negligence of a plumber working in the roof with a brazier of lighted coals. In a short time the Lantern, which Wren for reasons of economy had roofed in with timber rather than stone, was ablaze. Hardly any precautions against fire then existed in the Abbey, and it seemed at one time as if the roof might be a total loss. John Carter, later appointed Clerk of the Works, who was an eye-witness, has left behind a description of this 'horror' in his own highly coloured prose. 'Burning timbers of the roof, and groins [wood] tumbling down in dreadful crash; wide spreading flames, clouds of smoke, rivers of water, all combining to express on each fearful bystander, the sensation that some universal disaster was near its fatal crisis.' As it happened, it was the oil cloth of the chiaroscuro paintings, put there some thirty years earlier, which by containing the draught, prevented the spread of the conflagration.

The greatest damage was to the North Transept, and the Dean and Chapter estimated the total loss at some £4,000. As a safety measure for the future the Chapter ordered that when plumbers were employed in the church or College buildings, the Clerk of Works must always send a man with an express direction to take care of the fire during the time they were absent from their work. A pan of copper was to be provided for the plumbers' grate.

At the same time the Clerk of Works, William Miles, was dismissed, and Edward Glanvill appointed to succeed him.

The fire meant that the available resources of the Dean and Chapter were now strained to the uttermost. It must, therefore, have been particularly galling when Dr Vincent, the Dean, received through the Speaker a letter from the House of Commons, couched in somewhat reproving terms, and written on 28 November 1803. It began abruptly as follows:

Upon consulting the Journals of the House of Commons, I find that the Dean and Chapter presented a petition in the year 1738 for a Grant of Money towards repairing and finishing the Abbey wherein they stated amongst other things 'That the Ten Houses on the North side of the said Church usually leased out like other Tenements had been by Act of Chapter in the year 1731 debarred from any further Renewal with intent to pull them down for the security and ornament of the said Church as soon as they should come into their hands by the Expiration or sooner determination of the Leases'.

It was upon the 'faith' of this promise that money had been granted to the Dean and Chapter by Parliament. Yet some seventy years after, the north side of the Abbey was still encumbered with many of these old houses, the leases of which it was understood expired at Christmas. Were not the Dean and Chapter pledged now to pull down these houses 'for the security and ornament of the Church'? 'I have no doubt,' the Speaker wrote somewhat severely, 'that they will see the propriety of not disappointing the just Expectations of Parliament in this respect when they consider the liberality which they have formerly experienced in their application for public Money and the possibility of future occasions arising when they may find it necessary to make similar applications'. The Speaker concluded by remarking that he was well aware of the great loss to the Chapter caused by the recent fire and the 'cheerfulness with which they are disposed to defray those Expenses out of their own Funds'. Yet, 'to keep faith with Parliament is superior to all other considerations'.

It was not difficult for the Dean and Chapter to see the point: particularly since they were on the eve of making another application for a grant and doubtless news of this had already reached the ears of the Speaker. Indeed Dr Vincent was told that Lord Grenville had been heard to say in connexion with Henry VII's Chapel: 'Why don't they apply to Parliament?' The Chapter met, and an agreed letter in reply to the Speaker was drawn up. It began by assuring him that the houses in St Margaret's Churchyard would be pulled down before Lady Day. No tenant, in fact, had had his lease renewed, but held his house at a rack rent 'subject always to the requisition of Parliament'.

The Chapter were as good as their word: for in June of that year it was ordered that the ground should be levelled.

The intervention of the House of Commons shows that there was a quickened interest in the appearance and amenities of the Palace of Westminster, a fact which is indicated in the setting up of a Committee of both Houses in 1806 for 'the improvement of the approach to the Houses of Parliament'. It was as a result of a request from this committee that the Dean and Chapter agreed to lower the height of the plinth at the east end of the Chapel. Spurred on by this new interest, the Dean now addressed a Memorial concerning Henry VII's Chapel to the Lords of the Treasury, which body referred it to the 'Committee for the Inspection of the Models for National Monuments'. The financial core of this 'Memorial', which came from Wyatt, stated baldly that necessary repairs would amount to at least £14,800 and ornamental work to £10,400.

The ground having thus been prepared, the Dean and Chapter now petitioned the House of Commons (20 June 1807) 'for an Allowance of public money for the repair and support of Henry VII Chapel'. In this document they confessed frankly that the condition of this 'most beautiful specimen of Gothic architecture now remaining in this Kingdom and perhaps in Europe' was one of 'decay' and that its general appearance was 'ruinous'. Out of their own limited resources, they had in the last thirteen years spent some £1,198. 2s. 11¼d. on repair of the roofs, but to restore the 'exterior facing' of the building demanded an expenditure 'to which their resources are inadequate'. Fortunately the essential structure was sound, which meant that if only the repair of the stonework could be tackled the fabric would be preserved from 'further injury'. Based on their Surveyor's estimate, they petitioned for an initial grant of £2,000, and subsequently for £1,000 per annum until the work of restoration was completed.

Once again the application proved successful, and soon the work of repair, under Wyatt's direction, was set in hand. The Committee for the Inspection of Monuments recommended that Bath stone should be used, except for the sills of the windows for which they suggested Hopton Wood stone. An unhappy difference between Dr Vincent, the Dean, and the rest of the Chapter over the payment due to Mr Gayfere, a sub-contractor, led to an unfortunate exchange of letters with the Treasury. On the other hand no praise is too high for the pertinacity with which the Dean successfully resisted the efforts of the Committee to restrict repairs to those which were essential to the security of the building. His technique was simply to order the work to be carried on—and Parliament fell into line.

Thus the Chapel of Henry VII was preserved in its beauty for posterity, the sum granted by the Treasury often exceeding an annual figure of £3,000. In all, the Dean and Chapter received between the years 1807 and 1822 sums amounting to £42,028. 14s. 3¼d. This vast project may be said to have been finished when the Dean and Chapter petitioned the Lords of the Treasury on 4 March 1823 for £499. 18s. 3d. 'to make good the Excess of the Expenditure in the completing the restoration of King Henry VII Chapel beyond the Estimate in 1822'.

References to the Chapel now became less frequent: though there was a sudden scare when it was feared that the Chapel might be 'rated' under an Act of Parliament concerned with the paving of Regent Street. A memorial was presented to the Lords of the Treasury—but fortunately the anxiety proved to be groundless.

The work on the Abbey, just described, was in the main designed to preserve the building from decay and ruin. We now turn to projects of a different character.

The origin of the first is curious. It begins with James II and the magnificent Royal Chapel which he built in the Palace at Whitehall, specially for the use of his Roman Catholic wife, Mary of Modena. No expense was spared. Great contemporary artist-craftsmen such as Verrio, and Reni Cousen were employed upon its embellishment. Central in the Chapel was an altar-piece, constructed according to a specification which required 'clean white marble, free from vents, with pilasters of white well veined marble and columns of purple rance, the shafts of both to be in whole stones and the work adorned with Statues and other Sculptures'. The design was by Sir Christopher Wren in association with Grinling Gibbons and Arnold Quellin. The result was a fine classical three-tiered altar, so fine indeed that it even won the grudging admiration of that convinced Protestant member of the Church of England, John Evelyn.

Yet neither music nor magnificence preserved the Chapel in its former glory once James had fled ignominiously to France. The Chapel became derelict and a few years later the altar-piece was dismantled and shipped down the river to Hampton Court. Sir Christopher Wren, however, did not forget the work of his own hand. In 1706 he persuaded the Dean and Chapter that the altar-piece would fittingly adorn Westminster Abbey. The result was a petition to the Queen through Sidney Godolphin, the Lord High Treasurer, which led to a Royal Warrant dated 21 February 1706, granting the altar-piece to the Dean and Chapter. The cost proved to be considerable, and the placing of the altar in position undoubtedly caused great damage to the Sanctuary. Abbot Ware's fine pavement was in part destroyed and the steps of the ancient altar greatly damaged. Also, since the new altar-piece was concave in form and immense in size, the two wings inevitably concealed a portion of the sedilia to the south, and the tomb of Crouchback to the north.

This intrusion of a classical masterpiece into an essentially Gothic building has been roundly condemned by subsequent generations, not least by Dr Jocelyn Perkins, though he admits that its 'general effect must have been imposing beyond words'.

In the Abbey, however, the altar remained for over a hundred years. 'It was a mistake to have erected it in the first instance in the Abbey,' comments the same writer; 'but it was a still greater mistake to remove it in favour of the worthless trash which now came to take its place.'

This 'worthless trash' was introduced as a result of the coronation of George IV in 1820, in preparation for which Wren's creation had of necessity to be bundled out of the building because of its height, and in order to secure easy access into St Edward's Chapel. Indeed, coronations, generally, were a time of upheaval, and this together with money coming to the Dean and Chapter from them, often stimulated the desire to make changes. It is interesting to note that some parts of Wren's altar are preserved in the parish church of St Andrew, Burnham, in Somerset, and its four principal figures are probably those in College Garden within the precincts of the Abbey.

Mr Benjamin Wyatt now held the office of Surveyor, in succession to his father: and on 17 July 1820 he received instructions from the Chapter (which he may have prompted, for this is how things usually work in corporate bodies) 'to prepare a Plan for new modelling the Choir and restoring the Altar on the Model of the Confessor's Chapel as soon as the Coronation is over'.

THE HIGH ALTAR

The coronation, so vividly described by Sir Walter Scott and during which the new King had to be revived by smelling salts, being safely over, the Dean and Chapter returned to their project of installing a traditional gothic altar. Thus a Chapter minute of 20 July 1821 instructed the Surveyor to prepare a design 'from such materials as now remain, and can be collected of the Antient Altar, with a view to the restoration of the Antient Design as soon as the Church is cleared of the scaffolding, instead of replacing the more modern altar which was taken down on the occasion of the Coronation'. It was the coronation money, which with the dividends, made the scheme possible. Early in his preparations, Wyatt made the important, some may think calamitous, decision to consult Bernasconi who had gained a great contemporary reputation for his imitative work in plaster and cement. A contract with him was entered into on 29 May 1823, by which work was to be done up to a cost of £1,200, the Chapter again describing the whole project as 'the restoration of the Antient Altar', though it is clear that not much of the ancient altar had been found. Truth is sometimes stranger than fiction; and it is surely one of the ironies of architectural history that a young boy of fourteen, later destined to destroy every trace of the labours of Wyatt and Bernasconi, should have witnessed the 'demolition' and 'the reconstruction'. He was none other than Gilbert Scott, and he confesses that at the time the transformation gave him 'extreme delight'.

The new altar that eventually emerged in 'artificial stone' was indeed in many respects an imitation of the ancient one in that the moulding and the canopies were strictly copied. There was, however, a significant difference in that the volettings which on the original were of different designs, here were all uniform. Bernasconi's contribution was to provide an arcade of panelling, surrounded by a quantity of tabernacle work, stretching over the whole width of the Presbytery, except where two new gothic oak doors—they cost £51. 10s. 0d.—admitted to the shrine. Fifty yards of blue Persian carpet used at the coronation helped to complete the 'decor' of the Presbytery.

There can be no doubt that Wyatt and Bernasconi undertook their work at a most unfortunate time. A new enthusiasm for Gothic was indeed being born, but it had not yet acquired the necessary taste and discipline to give the 'revival' articulation and meaning. Also the very materials which Bernasconi employed gave flatness to his work thereby robbing it of effective relief. Maybe it was providential that this new creation in its turn did not last long.

THE CHOIR

We now turn to a third project and for this purpose we must go back to the middle years of the eighteenth century. It may be best introduced by a quotation from the Chapter minutes of 22 March 1763 to the effect that the sum of £1,161. 3s. 4d. remaining in the Receiver's hands since the late coronation 'be laid out in the Alterations intended to be made in the Choir, Agreeable to such Plans as shall hereafter be approved of the Dean and Chapter'.

This brief resolution may seem somewhat surprising, since at that time there still existed the original thirteenth-century medieval Choir, which as Dr Jocelyn Perkins writes, though 'far from rivalling in beauty the sumptuous stalls of Amiens, or even those of our English Chester and Windsor . . . [yet] could claim a superiority in age of nearly two-and-a-half centuries'. If the Chapter resolution is symptomatic of the eighteenth-century lack of appreciation for gothic architecture, its ostensible purpose was to secure a set of choir fittings easily removable on such occasions as coronations. This needs a little explanation.

The woodwork in the Abbey Choir Stalls backed on to solid stonework, and the whole extended so far eastwards as to block off the two Transepts. For great ceremonies this could present a problem: and it was perhaps understandable that the Dean and

Chapter should wish to do something about this, and that the Surveyor, Henry Keene, welcomed the opportunity of designing new stalls. The expense of such a project, however, proved considerable; and Dean Zachary Pearce, preoccupied at this time with promoting his retirement, doubtless lacked the energy to go forward. The proposal, therefore, hung fire, until in 1768 Zachary Pearce was succeeded by his Sub-Dean, John Thomas who, judged by contemporary standards, was a man of taste and cultivation. The new Dean, in taking over his office, was already wedded to a revolutionary scheme for moving the Choir eastwards, indeed within the confines of St Edward's Chapel. The following letter, written to Zachary Pearce in 1770, makes his position clear:

> In our return from Norfolk I purposely came round by Ely and Cambridge to see the effect of removing the Choir of the Cathedral to the upper part of the Cross beyond the Nave, having long entertained a similar idea in regard to that at West[minste]r:—And, tho' the work is not yet finished and cleaned off, there was enough done to convince me of the beauty and propriety of the alteration. I am nevertheless aware of some objections that will lay against the execution of such a plan at the Abbey, tho' I flatter myself with being able to answer all that are material, except that of expense; which however could not answer to much more than they have laid out at Ely, a place remote and little visited, whereas our Church is in the very centre of public Concourse and Observation. I wish this, or still better motives, may rouse us to do something becoming our engagements.

Thomas's enthusiasm led to the reopening of the matter at a Chapter Meeting on 20 May 1773. As a result, the Dean consulted the Abbey Surveyor, Henry Keene, as well as James Essex (who was responsible for the 'destruction' of the medieval Choir at Ely) and James Wyatt (who was to 'restore' Salisbury Cathedral and later become Surveyor of the Abbey). They were specifically asked to give their opinion as to the 'Propriety of erecting a new Choir in the Eastern Part of the Abbey from the Nave to the upper End of Edward the Confessor's Chapel'. Things were now moving, and on 8 December, 'Our Surveyor' was ordered to lay before the next Chapter 'all such Plans, Papers etc. relative to the removal of the Choir to the East End of the Church, together with such Alterations and Improvem[en]ts in its present Situation as have been already prepared or may be thought proper for those purposes'.

It would take too long to describe what followed in any detail. Three schemes in all were submitted to Chapter, and finally, after much heartburning, the least ambitious of the three was accepted.

If the Dean's original scheme, the removal of the Choir to St Edward's Chapel, had been fully implemented it would have meant the destruction of the fifteenth-century altar screen, even the removal of the Confessor's Shrine and the 'huddling up the royal monuments to the body of the Church or the Transepts'. This would in fact have made the Abbey more suitable for the great congregational services which take place in it today; though less fitting for choir offices. For some time, this project hung in the balance, but it was finally turned down by two votes, the Dean being in the minority, at a meeting of Chapter on 19 January 1774 (absent members confirming the decision). At the next Chapter, the debate centred on the second scheme—'whether it is the sense of the present Chapter that the Screen at the Entrance of the present Choir, with the Monuments against the same be removed, and that the Entrance into the Choir be advanced one Inter-Columniation nearer the Altar Eastward and the Organ be placed at the East End of the Choir'. This proposal, put forward by the Dean, would have considerably reduced the length of the Choir: but though it was carried through Chapter by a majority of two votes, this decision was reversed by the absent members.

It now seemed as if a stalemate had been reached so far as Chapter was concerned: particularly as the professional advisers, Keene, Wyatt and Essex continued to press for 'the removal of the present Skreen and Organ Loft and forming a new Choir above the Transept so as to include Edward the Confessor's Chapel therein'.

Finally, however, on 6 May 1774, a very full Chapter once more rejected the architects' advice, since 'it could not for several reasons be carried into action'. At the Dean's suggestion they agreed to a mediating proposal of his own 'for advancing the new Intended Stalls half an inter-Columniation before the inner Front of the present Organ Loft and for erecting and disposing the Seats, Pews and Pulpit in such manner as to render the whole more decent and convenient than at present'.

No second thoughts now intervened, and by 21 July the contract had been signed with Mr Keene. In January of the following year preparations for the work were set in hand, permission being given to enclose an area in the North Crossing for materials, and to make a rubbish dump in St Margaret's churchyard. In addition to the work on the Choir, it was decided to replace the tapestries either side of the altar with Flemish oak wainscoting and to fill the four spaces in the 'Dome now boarded . . . with Chiaroscuro painting on Oil Cloth'.

On 22 May the church was shut, and the daily offices for the time being abandoned; one service only being held in 'the forenoon on Sundays in Henry VII Chapel till the Choir was finished'.

R

The result of this project was the complete destruction of the medieval Choir, the reduction of the stalls from sixty-four to thirty-four and the cutting off of the transepts by two flimsy screens. Brayley describes the new Choir as 'imitation Gothic' and agrees that 'though intended to correspond with the general style of the building displays many variations from the true principles of pointed architecture'.

Dr Perkins's language is characteristically less moderate. In its general details, he writes, the scheme was 'beneath contempt', though he allows its overall plan to be 'impressive'. A judgement offered in 1966 may well, perhaps, be a little more cautious, even if it is still hard not to condemn the loss of medieval woodwork.

14

Funerals and Monuments

FUNERAL DISORDERS

THE eighteenth century, in keeping with its macabre interest in churchyards, was the age of many spectacular funeral services in the Abbey, together with the proliferation of monuments.

The most 'sumptuous' funeral—to quote Dean Stanley's description—during the regime of Dr Bradford, the successor of Francis Atterbury, was probably that of William Congreve (1670–1729). A monument to his memory was erected at the west end of the Nave, at the expense of Henrietta Godolphin, Duchess of Marlborough, who herself wrote the epitaph, commemorating the 'happiness and honour' which she had enjoyed in 'her intercourse'. 'Happiness perhaps,' snorted Sarah, her formidable mother 'but not honour!'

Often such services, however, left much to be desired.

True they were often grand occasions, to which the public flocked the moment the doors were opened, but this in itself made effective control almost impossible. Also there was frequent bad feeling and controversy between the various officials involved. Typical was the funeral of Queen Caroline, wife of George II, in December 1737.

On this occasion the Chapter decided that three of their number who were 'themselves personally insulted' during the ceremony should wait upon the Earl Marshal. They were to insist that his Lordship 'take effective care that the satisfaction that shall be made to the parties concerned may be as public as the offence', the complaint being that it was his own Secretary who had misbehaved himself.

The three prebendaries duly waited upon the Earl and were received with the words: 'Gentlemen, all I can say is, that I have done with him which is all the satisfaction I can give.'

This unhappy incident was finally closed when on 26 January 1738 Hutcheson, the Secretary, in most contrite mood, attended Chapter, and promised never to repeat his fault. Their honour vindicated in an appropriate manner, the Dean and Chapter then magnanimously requested the Earl to restore his Secretary to office.

Queen Caroline's funeral, unfortunately, was by no means unique in its somewhat unseemly character. That of George II, on 11 November 1760—the last monarch to be buried in the Abbey—was no better, even if the contemporary account written by that sophisticated gossip, Horace Walpole, loses nothing in the telling:

> When we came into the Chapel of Henry VII all solemnity and decorum ceased, no order was observed, people sat or stood where they could or would, the yeomen of the guard were crying out for help, oppressed by the immense weight of the coffin; the bishop [Pearse] read sadly and blundered in the prayers; the fine chapter 'Man that is born of a woman' was chanted not read, and the anthem besides being immeasurably tedious, was more fit for a nuptial than a funeral.

An unbelievable scene occurred in 1765, when Pulteney, Earl of Bath, patron of the Dean (Zachary Pearce), was interred. What happened on this occasion lingered long in the memory of a young schoolboy who had the excitement of witnessing it:

> The ceremony [he wrote later] which was by torchlight [took place] opposite the tomb of Edward I in the aisle below. I stood with many others on the tomb. The crowd and confusion was so great that several gentlemen, thinking it necessary to defend (for their own and the company's safety) the stairs into the Chapel of the Confessor, not only drew their swords but tore down the oak canopy above Edward's memorial to convert it into weapons. In such state it now [1817] remains.

Perhaps the worst example of disorder occurred in 1776 at the burial in the family vault of Elizabeth Percy, Duchess of Northumberland. On this occasion the whole front of St Edmund's Chapel, on which a number of men and boys had managed precariously to perch themselves, suddenly collapsed. The result was indescribable. Iron, stonework and timber, upwards of three tons in weight, came crashing down. A report in the *Annual Register* runs:

> The confusion and uproar that ensued may be more easily conceived than described. Numbers had their limbs broke or were otherwise most terribly hurt. This accident put an effective stop to the ceremony, the Dean and his attendants, after resting the body in St Edmund's Chapel, were obliged to withdraw for some time, upon which the crowds, thinking no more was to be seen, thought proper to disperse so as to give the Dean an opportunity of going through the service between one and two o'clock about two hours and a half after the body entered the Abbey, and even

now it was interrupted by frequent cries of 'murder' raised by such of the sufferers as had not been removed.

The Dean and Chapter cannot be entirely exonerated from all blame in connexion with these disgraceful incidents. By building scaffolding for their families and friends, and allowing various officers to do this for 'perks', they encouraged a belief that these solemn services were great social spectacles—which, of course, they were. Also the whole ritual of a river caravanserai, torchlight processions and midnight interments excited popular imagination and made control more difficult.

With the close of the century, however, greater decorum began to prevail: and burials at night were prohibited.

PROLIFERATION OF MONUMENTS

More important in long-term effects upon the building was the myriad of monuments which were erected during the eighteenth and nineteenth centuries.

The practice did not begin then. St Peter's Church, when a Benedictine monastery, was a place of burial, and not only for kings. Their families, their courtiers and friends in the course of time began to cluster around them. The Abbey never became a private mausoleum for monarchs as St Denis's for the kings of France or the Escurial for the monarchs of Spain. True it is that the recumbent effigies of the early days seem more in character with the worshipful nature of the building, and less redolent of human pride, than the post-Reformation monuments, increasingly perpendicular, even gesticulating. Of great significance was the fact that sixteenth-century doctrine by insisting on only one altar in a church made the apsidal Chapels of Henry VII, already used for burials, no longer necessary for their primary purpose. The burial of the young Duke of Buckingham, friend and companion of Charles I, created a disastrous precedent, so that increasingly these Chapels became filled with monuments and the stonework hacked about to get them in.

The eighteenth century certainly inherited an unfortunate tradition, and it began badly with what some have described as a 'monstrous', others a 'magnificent', erection to the memory of John Holles, first Duke of Newcastle (1662–1711). On this colossal monument, the sculptor–architect, James Gibbs, is said to have been prepared to base his claim to immortality. Certainly his allegorical figures 'Prudence' and 'Sincerity'—the latter lost her left hand at the coronation of George IV—have served to encourage a like extravagance in others, thus devouring much needed space.

Less destructive, though equally prominent, north and south of the entry to the Choir, were the (now familiar) monuments to James, Earl of Stanhope (d. 1721), a general in the war of the Spanish Succession, and Sir Isaac Newton (1642–1727) whose body before interment lay in state in Jerusalem Chamber.

Mention, perhaps, ought to be made of the monument to Sir Godfrey Kneller (1646–1723), described, a little unfairly, as that 'spoilt and pampered painter of Court beauties'. In all, some ten reigning sovereigns sat to him. To his friend, Alexander Pope, Kneller declared almost with his last breath: 'By God, I will not be buried in Westminster Abbey, they do bury fools there.' He had his posthumous way, and was interred in his own garden at Twickenham. A monument, however, was another matter, and a request from his wife to re-erect the one originally placed in the church at Twickenham was approved by the Dean and Chapter on 6 March 1726, a fee of twenty guineas being charged. Rysbrack, the Flemish sculptor, was commissioned, and Pope contributed an epitaph, which he confessed to being 'the worst thing I ever wrote'.

To be fair to the Dean and Chapter they did their best, at times, to prevent damage to the building through the erection of monuments. Thus the original site of General Monck's monument was abandoned because it would 'necessarily deface or hide some of the curious workmanship' in an east window of Henry VII's Chapel (1 March 1739). The minutes of Chapter explicitly stated, in respect of a monument to Lady Mountrath in the Holles Chapel, that the projection must be kept within a prescribed limit. The pity is that such regulations were not more general, particularly where the Bath and Wolfe monuments were concerned.

INSCRIPTIONS

Permission for Abbey burial or memorialization was, of course, by no means automatic, though the principle of selection was neither rigid nor clearly defined. During the eighteenth century it was granted by the Dean and Chapter. By and large the latter were more concerned with the wording of inscriptions than the aesthetics or size of the monument. Over this matter a careful watch was kept; and to ensure this the Chapter ordered, on 6 February 1727, that none should be cut on any memorial until the exact wording was approved. As refusals to bury or memorialize were not, like acceptance, entered into a register, it is difficult to provide exact evidence in this field. Three cases, however, may be quoted which are doubtless typical of others for which no evidence remains.

The inscription proposed for the memorial of Thomas Thynne of

Longleat (1648–82), 'Tom of Ten Thousand' reputed the greatest rake in town, and murdered by Königsmark, his wife's suitor, was turned down. A large vacant space on his memorial still bears inelegant witness to this refusal.

Anne Oldfield (1683–1730), a celebrated actress who distinguished herself in the parts of Cleopatra and Calista, lies buried in the Abbey near the entrance to Samaria at the west end of the Nave. When, however, one of the Churchills made application for the erection of a monument in her memory, Dean Bradford on 6 February 1730 reported to Chapter that he felt so strongly on this matter that he could neither support the application nor even bring it before his brethren for discussion. The Chapter were unanimously behind the Dean, though in order to safeguard their own rights they regularized the matter by recording their own refusal on 7 July.

An application for a monument in the Cloisters to the memory of the Rev. J. Henley (1692–1756), known as Orator Henley, was also refused. The proposed inscription ran as follows: 'In memory of ye reverend Mr. John Henley M.A. of St. John's College, Cambridge, Author of ye Universal Grammar, and a great Orator in his time: who contradicted all Religious Sentiments contrary to Reason. He was a Rationalist and Defender of Reason for few there were of his Opinion in ye time he lived.'

But more significant than the refusals is the wide tolerance shown in the choice of those to whom permission was given for burial or memorialization. Though Byron has not yet found a niche within the Abbey in Poets' Corner, yet profligates and sceptics have secured entry. Often and wisely, the Abbey authorities have recognized genius, and trusted to the larger hope. National and religious prejudice have been successfully overcome. Older restraints which demanded that tombs be placed east and west were ignored. Even the location in the Abbey of some memorials has a pathetic human interest—Addison preferring to rest alongside his loved Montague rather than in Poets' Corner: and Atterbury at the west end of the Nave 'far from Kaisers'. Equally interesting are some of the omissions—worthies who unexpectedly are not in the Abbey. Burke confessed to preferring burial in a country churchyard and among his family (as did Sir Winston Churchill): and Samuel Johnson said of Abbey burial that it was peculiarly fitting for great men (such as himself), who have no bond elsewhere.

But what, we may ask, apart from the obvious claim of residence in the precincts, were the customary criteria determining the process of selection? No easy answer is possible. High social rank was certainly one of them. Great distinction in the arts of peace and war was another. But there was no 'policy' to restrict burial to any particular category, although a large monument to an obscure person with no pretensions to distinction of any kind would not have been contemplated. English society in those days was relatively small. Everybody knew everybody else, that is if he moved within the charmed circle which, in a matter of this kind, *was* England. Egalitarianism and Tom Paine were not yet.

THE COSTS OF AN ABBEY BURIAL

One requirement, however, in respect of Abbey burial, was taken for granted. Those who sought it must be able somehow or other to pay for it. The privilege was not 'gratis'.

This point is significant, for the Dean and Chapter were undoubtedly concerned to secure the fees which came to them through burials and monuments. They wanted burials and they wanted monuments because they wanted money. Evidence for this is clearly provided in a discussion which took place in Chapter on 14 January 1746, when anxiety was expressed that though applications for memorials were numerous, it was becoming increasingly difficult to accommodate them in the church: and this at a time when the Parliamentary Grant had been discontinued (see p. 233) and the Abbey would 'stand in more need than ever of monument money to be laid out on our Repairs.' Fortunately, that is from the point of view of the Chapter, there seemed an obvious solution now that St Margaret's churchyard, formerly exposed to 'dogs and swine and other nuisances', was enclosed. This increased decency now made it possible for burials which customarily took place in the Cloisters—those of domestic servants, for example—to be transferred to the churchyard. Hence a resolution was passed, unanimously, that in future the '2 Cloysters great and small, & covered ways leading thereto be regarded as part of the Church'—that is so far as memorials and fees were concerned.

The fees in question were by no means inconsiderable, certainly not when translated into modern monetary values; though they remained very largely unchanged after they were fixed in 1717 until the nineteenth century. These charges fall into two categories, those which went personally to members of the Collegiate Body allegedly 'for services rendered', and those which were paid into corporate funds. Also a distinction was made between burial with a grave, and the erection of a monument.

As to the first, for a burial in the church, the Dean received £2: and there was a graduated scale down to the organ blower's and Beadle's five shillings. For a burying in linen there was a fine of £2. 10s. which was allocated to charity. In addition, and still included in this personal category, there was a carefully worked out scale based upon social differentials. A peer under the rank of duke paid to the Dean £18; Sub-Dean £6. 10s.; Chanter £5; two vergers £4; porter £2; and twelve Almsmen £4. 16s.—in all a grand total of £40. 16s. A duke gave a further £9. 12s. to the Almsmen.

We now turn to the second category, the fines which went to the fabric fund. These fines, again, were carefully graded, a duke or archbishop paying £50, an earl or bishop £40; and so on down the hierarchy.

These various charges, taken together, came to a fairly considerable figure. Three particular examples may be quoted from the early nineteenth century:

For the Bishop of Carlisle £130. 17s. 2d. (1827); William Wilberforce (a 'Choir Funeral', a 'bricked Grave' and a 'Grave Stone') £129. 17s. 6d. (1833); the Earl of Chatham £130. 17s. 2d. (1835).

Not all charges were as high as these, the lowest recorded for the period 1827–36 being £26 11s. 10d., which was usual for the more plebeian.

The above list of charges relates to burial—that is to the funeral service, the interment and the grave. For monuments a special fine was exacted, usually considerable in its amount. In the same period—from 1827 to 1836—these varied from £250 for George Canning to £120 for Dr Thomas Young, physician and Egyptologist.

The privilege of Abbey burial or memorialization could often be bought. Even when it was earned by national distinction executors or friends were charged the customary rate: except that when the monument was what is described in the Chapter minutes as a 'public one'—that is commissioned by Act of Parliament—the customary fine to the fabric fund was waived. It could occasionally be waived in other circumstances. When, for example, a memorial to William Shakespeare was first mooted in 1726, the fine was fixed at twenty guineas; but when an elaborate monument was erected over thirty years later at public expense, no fine was demanded. Twenty-five pounds, however, was charged on Handel's memorial.

POETS' CORNER

Mention of Shakespeare may serve to remind us that it was during the seventeenth and eighteenth centuries that the Poets' Corner received many of its most illustrious 'sons', and that its unique character in this respect was increasingly established. It is said that a few days before his death, Samuel Johnson asked his executor, Sir John Hawkins, where he would be buried. 'Doubtless in Westminster Abbey,' was the reply. Whereupon, writes Boswell, he 'seemed to feel a satisfaction very natural to a Poet'. And so it happened that on 20 December 1784 Samuel Johnson was in fact laid to rest in Poets' Corner 'attended by a respectable number of his friends, particularly such of the members of the Literary Club as were in town'. But there was no choir, no anthem 'merely what is read over every old woman that is buried by the parish'—so wrote Charles Burney in a letter to Dr Parr. Some care, however, was taken, for Dr Taylor, an old schoolfellow of distant Lichfield days, conducted the service. Yet the Dean and Chapter were certainly criticized for the somewhat slovenly way in which the ceremony was carried out. William Smith of Canada, at the time living in London, reflected popular sentiment when he wrote:

> Dr Samuel Johnson's funeral was this day about 1 o'clock, no great pomp. He was buried near Garrick in poets' corner, Westminster Abbey. He died about a week ago at his house, Bolt's Court, Fleet Street, in his 74th year. It seems generally agreed that he was a man of bad manners but good morals, so the clergy concur for his attachment to Revelation. . . . The paper of this morning [25 Dec.] censures the Dean and Chapter of Westminster for taking £54 for Dr. Johnson's grave in the Abbey and the Service. The additional charge is for music and lamps when nothing but the common service was performed, and in full day 1 o,clock of a sun shiney day. Everything is a high charge in this country, nobody is ashamed to take money.

The list of those interred or memorialized in Poets' Corner during this period is a long one: but there was no absolute principle that the South Transept should be confined to poets and literati in general. As late as 1767, permission was given for a monument to the memory of Mrs Mary Hope, 'wife of John Hope Esq' to be erected in the second aisle to the left of 'Mr Handel': and for a Mrs Pritchard, whose memorialization was 'desired by members of the nobility', to have a place next to Shakespeare, if no other site could be found for her.

There can be no question but that this proliferation of monuments has led to a unique collection of statuary to which all the great sculptors of the day contributed. It has also changed the character of the building, in particular the impact which it makes on the visitor as he first enters. To Francis Beaumont, in the seventeenth century, the Chapels spoke of mortality as the common lot of men. Joseph Addison, in a most moving passage in the *Spectator*, confessed that as he contemplated the monuments he was reminded of 'that great day when we shall all of us be contemporaneous, and make our appearance together'.

To the sightseer on a visit to London, these monuments together with the wax effigies to which the singing-men added the figures of William and Mary; Queen Anne; Queen Elizabeth (to mark the Jubilee in 1760) and Lords Nelson and Chatham; and also the wooden models of the fifty new churches ordered to be built by Parliamentary Grant early in the eighteenth century—these were a great attraction, one of the sights of the town, more worth seeing than the building itself. Doubtless something of what Beaumont and Addison experienced moved visitors, even if they lacked the facility to articulate what they felt. Boswell confesses that among the tombs he was 'solemn and happy'.

'UNMEANING MARBLE'

Even so, the statuary came in for occasional criticism, both because of the damage it inflicted on the building and its incongruity with the architecture of the church. Horace Walpole, with his accustomed modesty, claimed the credit for persuading Zachary Pearce not to ruin Aymer de Valence's fine tomb in order to make way for Wilton's 'disfiguring cenotaph to Wolfe'. If this is true, he did well: though on the debit side candour compels the admission that it was the same Horace Walpole who secured permission to erect a statue of his mother in Henry VII's Chapel.

Oliver Goldsmith deplored that so much space should be occupied by monuments, in particular by works of Roubillac, creator of the remarkable memorial to Mrs Nightingale which John Wesley, among so much 'unmeaning marble', found so affecting. 'Alas! alas! cried I, such monuments confer honour, not on the great men but on little Roubiliac.' In his *Citizen of the World* Goldsmith accused the Dean and Chapter of being motivated in this matter by desire for fees and admission charges. This accusation was well founded. When Garrick's wife, in 1822, was interred in her husband's grave two of her friends were refused admittance, being told that they could come back later, and on paying sixpence at Poets' Corner, view the waxworks.

EARLY ADMISSION CHARGES

This charge for admission, ostensibly to see the monuments, models and effigies, often gave rise to criticism, the more so as the way it was worked demanded that the Abbey be kept closed to the public during the day, to be opened, apart from the times of divine worship, only on the payment of admission money.

This custom went back a long time, even to the grant of the Charter in 1560. Originally the right to levy fees was farmed out by the Dean and Chapter in return for a handsome payment. Some forty years after the Restoration, the Dean and Chapter decided to abandon this procedure and to transfer the right to collect fees to the Choir, in return for which its members were required to maintain and keep the monuments clean. Later, in practice, the Treasurer of the Abbey arranged for the cleaning to be done and charged the cost against the receipts for admission.

The admission fees, for those days, were by no means small and steadily increased across the years. In 1697 they were fixed at 3d.; in 1723 with the acquisition of the models they were raised to 6d.; in 1799 to 9d. and after Lord Nelson's effigy was added they were made up to: to view the tombs in Henry VII's Chapel, 6d.; for seeing the models 3d., the wax figures and North Crossing 6d.; the west end 6d. plus 2d. as a gratuity for the 'tomb shewer'—in all 1s. 11d. In practice, the tomb-shewer was seldom content with his permitted gratuity but 'would throw himself on the kindness of the company'. It is not surprising that there were constant complaints against such importunity, and these finally led the Dean and Chapter to abolish gratuities altogether, at the same time increasing the total admission charge to 2s., which was divided as follows: 9d. for admission to the South Transept; 1s. 3d. to the Chapels, the North Transept, the west end and the models. To avoid misunderstanding, at Poets' Corner and at the 'tomb station', a notice was ordered to be prominently displayed on which the exact fees were stated and the following words added:

> The Persons who are employed to shew the Church being sufficiently remunerated are strictly forbidden to demand or accept any further sum from the Public; and it is requested that if there should be any cause for complaint, a report be made to the Dean or in his absence to the residentiary Prebendary, whose name and address may be known at the Porter's Lodge.

At the same time as these new regulations were drawn up, the Chapter decided that one-eighth of the money so received should be equally divided between the three tomb-shewers, who were employed throughout the whole year. The remuneration of the 'extraordinary shewers' (i.e. those employed only during the summer months) was left to the discretion of the gentlemen of the choir.

In spite of these revised charges, criticism at the closure of the Abbey and the payment of admission fees to enter the church continued. Letters of complaint began to appear in the newspapers, in particular in *The Times* and *Morning Herald*. The Minor Canons and singing-men let it be known that they bitterly (and understandably) resented that their 'inadequate' incomes should be supplemented in this 'disgraceful manner'.

The matter was now becoming a public issue. Parliament—it was expressive of a contemporary mood—became interested, and as the result of a letter from Stephen Lushington, an eminent civilian and Member of Parliament for Ilchester, the Dean and Chapter on 29 May 1823 drew up a detailed statement of the position as they saw it. First, they protested, they must maintain their 'absolute right' to appoint 'to the offices or places of keeping and shewing the monuments of the Abbey and the receipt of the emoluments arising from them'. The monuments did not belong to the public, who therefore could claim no right of free access to them; and this applied equally to those erected by Parliamentary grant. Indeed the latter entailed a great loss to the Dean and Chapter, particularly to the fabric fund because no fine was levied upon them. The only right of admission which could be legally demanded was to attend public worship: and for this the Abbey was always opened. 'No sacred place indeed can be free from profanation or injury,' so the Dean and Chapter argued, 'unless precaution be taken of thus shutting the doors. These evils were fully experienced by the Abbey, till the thoroughfare was lately stopped. The Monuments were defaced and broken; and the Tradesmen of the neighbourhood carried their Wares through the Church, as a shorter way to the Cloisters.' At that time there were constant complaints outside and in Parliament that the monuments were dirty. Now they were being cleaned by a new method, but if they were to remain clean, it was essential to maintain order in the Abbey, and to close it as a thoroughfare. Parliament could not have it both ways.

The force of this argument was somewhat weakened by the offer that if Parliament were willing to provide a regular allowance, then the Dean and Chapter, consistent with their rights and privileges under the Elizabethan Charter, would be prepared to consider a 'more easy admission of the Publick'.

The Dean and Chapter, however, were obviously uneasy, and on 6 May 1825 the fees charged for admission at Poets' Corner were reduced to 3d. and this sum gave entry into the Nave. The rest of the church could be viewed for 1s. To work this new system a permanent addition of two extra staff were added.

The Dean and Chapter, however, had to tread warily, for the Minor Canons and singing-men depended upon this source of revenue for supplementing their income. Collectively some £1,400 a year came from this source. Wisely the decision was made that if receipts now fell below this figure they would be supplemented from the Chapter's own dividends.

Certainly the Minor Canons—there were six of them—and the singing-men could not be ignored in this matter, the more so as their claims were vigorously championed by the Precentor, the Rev. Dr W. Dakins, later principal Chaplain to the Forces, and founder of the Royal Military Chapel at Wellington Barracks. He took the opportunity of drawing up a Memorial which certainly lacked nothing in forthrightness, and, we suspect, was seen not only by the Dean and Chapter. It was disgraceful, so he maintained, that the Minor Canons and singing-men should not receive an adequate salary out of corporate revenues. If this were done, as it ought to be, then the public could be charged 9d. or a 1s. and shown the monuments by a qualified guide, it being understood that this money went towards the cleaning—at the moment there was only one old lady dusting the pavement—and repair of the church. The Precentor concluded by announcing his intention to resign his office—but at a time convenient to himself. It did not become convenient until some twenty years later.

The matter, however, was not yet disposed of, and this general background of criticism, encouraged Mr Joseph Hume, radical Member of Parliament for Middlesex, who never tired of attacking the Establishment of the Church of England, to raise the question again in the House of Commons. The result was that the Dean and Chapter, in March 1826, were required to lay before the House an 'account of the sums charged . . . for admission of each visitor to view the public monuments in the Abbey. Also the total amount received for the last five years.'

In their reply, the Dean and Chapter, perhaps a little disingenuously, scored a technical point by saying that they were unable to provide the required information since no separate charge was made for seeing the 'public' as distinct from the 'private' monuments. What they were able and willing to do was furnish the House with the total receipts over the last five years.

These figures constitute a rough guide to the number of people who went as visitors round the Abbey. They were as follows: £648. 11s. 11d.—1821 (a low figure because of preparations for the coronation); £2,317. 9s. 3d.—1822 (a large figure doubtless because of interest aroused by the coronation); £1,664. 13s. 9d.— 1823; £1,529. 0s. 5d.—1824; £1,585. 1s.—1825.

These returns did not satisfy Mr Hume and he moved in the House that the Dean and Chapter now be asked to lay before it 'the charter of Elizabeth, under which [they] by their own showing, derived title to the disputed fees'. Nothing, however, came of this, Mr Robert Peel protesting that 'it was rather a discouraging return for the readiness' with which the requested information had been provided.

Still, the House of Commons was left not content and it was probably because of this, together with public pressure and the opposition within the Abbey, that the payment of the Minor Canons and Lay Vicars was separated altogether from admission fees. Henceforward the Dean and Chapter decided to provide £1,400 per annum out of corporate funds: while at the same time they fixed the salary of tomb-shewers at 25s. per week, and superintendents at 30s.—no small figure when we remember that the wage of an agricultural labourer at the time was about 8s. Even so, Parliament remained critical, and the matter was taken up again some eleven years later.

15

Pounds, Shillings and Pence

WAGES AND PERQUISITES

THE references to admission charges, and their use to supplement the incomes of the Minor Canons and lay clerks, shows that the Dean and Chapter inherited a financial system under which various officers drew their emoluments from particular perquisites allocated to their offices. There was no one overall system. Thus the singing-men also received money from what was known as the 'almonry rents'.

Yet the overriding problem confronting the Dean and Chapter during the eighteenth century was not primarily how to pay the prebendaries and their own officers, but how to find money to meet large capital expenditure on the repair of the building. This problem was not due to inflation. On the contrary, prices throughout the eighteenth century remained fairly stable. The Dean and Chapter bought beef at 9d. a lb. in 1819, and 6d. in 1836. Inflation set in during the Napoleonic Wars and the agricultural depression which followed. Rather the Dean and Chapter ascribed their financial plight to the fact that Queen Elizabeth had made no provision in 1560 for restoration work on the building itself, though she had entrusted to them properties in the cities of London and Westminster and vast estates in eighteen counties in the southern half of England. True, under its trust deed the Dean and Chapter acquired a large annual income through the rentals and fines from estates vested in them as a corporate body. This endowment was expected to cope both with annual expenditure on incomes for the personnel of the College, a large 'labour force'; and on normal repair and upkeep of the buildings in the precincts. On the whole, this expenditure did not greatly vary, but during the period which followed the French Revolution, members of the Collegiate Body began to feel the pinch, and those who were sufficiently organized made their voices heard. Thus on 12 March 1794 the Chapter received 'A Memorial of the Chanter and Minor Canons praying for an Augmentation of their Stipends'. The petition was successful. An increase of £20 per annum was granted, but opportunity was taken to regulate their period of waiting and use of deputies—regulations, it may be noticed, which the Dean and Chapter later complained had been 'construed' by some of the Minor Canons 'into a permission of perpetual absence from their duty'.

Applications for increases of stipend, within corporate bodies, particularly when successful, usually serve 'pour encourager les autres'. It was therefore not surprising that two years later (24 February 1796) a similar approach was received from the 'Organist and singing-men or Lay Clerks'. These applicants proved to be equally fortunate, £12 per annum being added to the Lay Clerks' salary. Once again, however, the conditions of service were tightened up, it being expressly required that to qualify for this increase, they must be present at least fifty times during their month of waiting and twice on Sundays. The same increase was granted to the Organist and Master of the Choristers (whose salary was again dealt with on 27 February 1815). A strict rule as to the use of deputies was also laid down, a subject to which the Chapter returned on 6 June 1816, since the former regulations had been misunderstood and abused—so the Chapter alleged. A deputy, they now insisted, must be: 'a singer in the same class of voice with the lay Clerk in whose stead he attends and of [as] good and effective a voice as the person whom he represents.'

Nothing succeeds like success. A former increase, coupled with the financial difficulties created by the Continental war, encouraged the Minor Canons to try again. In May 1807 the Precentor laid another Memorial before the Dean and Chapter, basing their claim for an increase on 'the Pressure of the Times and the deteriorated Value of Money'. This request, however, was flatly rejected, maybe because the Minor Canons unwisely linked their demand for an increase of salary with a claim to share the patronage of the Dean and Chapter, from which, 'unprecedented in any other College or Cathedral', they were unjustly excluded. To prejudice their own case even further, they added a complaint against the condition of their houses!

It is symptomatic of the social structure of the age that there is no record of any such request ever coming from the vergers, the carpenters, masons or labourers—or any other class of worker in the pay of the Dean and Chapter. The time of the trade union and organized labour was not yet; and the fear of unemployment was ever present. If an approach was ever made, doubtless it was informal and personal.

S

THE COLLEGIATE CHURCH AS LANDLORD

The moneys to keep the Abbey going year by year came, as suggested earlier, from rents and fees. The Dean and Chapter had therefore public as well as private interests in husbanding their resources as well as they could. The custom was for some of their number to go regularly on a 'progress' to various of their estates, usually in the summer. Often these progresses proved a very lucrative affair and helped to swell the dividends. Thomas, in a letter to Zachary Pearce from the country on 16 September 1767, writes of 'the very extra^y success my brethren have had in their progress'. In 1791—and there is no reason to assume this was exceptional—the 'Fines and Perquisites of the Courts' from a progress which began at Wheathampstead and Harpenden and ended at Steventon and Bagnor came to £1,643. 8s. 7½d. This would almost certainly have worked out at £100 for each prebendary. Fines on the renewal of leases were usually fixed at about £1 less than the annual value of the estate. It was therefore beneficial to the Dean and Chapter to abolish life interests altogether. Thus as early as 20 December 1709 they decided, wherever possible, to convert leases for life into tenure for a term of years, preferably fourteen. Such a conversion had a double advantage. First it made possible increased rents—though this could not always be effected particularly as prices remained stable—and, more certain, frequent fines. Throughout the eighteenth century the minutes of Chapter Meetings read like the deliberations of a company dealing in landed estate. It was not exceptional for as many as a dozen leases to be sealed in a single morning. As we have seen, the custom was to divide the 'fines' among the prebendaries, one-fifteenth each, the Dean having two- and one-fifteenth going to the Fabric Fund.

At the beginning of the nineteenth century a question arose as to what precisely were the rights of the prebendaries in this distribution. Was such a right inheritable? Counsel's opinion was sought (2 April 1806), when the ruling given was that there were no individual rights: that the fines came to the corporate body as a whole, and that until these fines were distributed by order of Chapter no individual member had any claim to them.

The administration of their far-flung estates was, for the Dean and Chapter, a constant preoccupation, until the time that they surrendered them in the nineteenth century. Such possessions made the Dean and Chapter more than landlords dealing with tenants, although this was a predominant factor in their relationship. These estates also involved them in responsibilities for local government, that is, in the appointment of parish officials, in the repair of bridges and the upkeep of highways; in the preservation of common rights against encroachments and enclosures.

Such responsibilities undoubtedly brought the Dean and members of Chapter into touch with the life and problems of the countryside.

This administration certainly deserves a more detailed treatment than is possible in this work; since all that can be attempted here is a brief general picture with a few typical examples of the nature of this oversight.

To preserve their rights meant constant vigilance. Thus, on 16 May 1729, an ejectment order was sought at the Hertford Assizes against a Mr Slater for his 'encroachment' upon Harpenden Common. Similar instances abound. On one occasion Sir Samuel Huddyer was brought before Chapter (8 April 1767) to receive a reprimand for his constant nibbling of land owned by the Dean and Chapter in Kingston. The following minute (11 May 1789) has a real breath of rural England about it and may be taken as typical of others: 'Ordered to mark and number with White Lead and Oil the Timber fit to be preserved on Miss Lewis's Leasehold Estates at Hodford and Cowhouse in Middlesex. And also to mark, measure and value thirty six Oaks cut down by Miss Lewis's Tenant and now lying on the Common near Cowhouse.' At Chapter on 18 December, £600 was paid in for this timber, though it was expressly laid down that it was not to be moved till there was a frost 'which may enable it to be carried off without materially damaging the land'. Timber was a most valuable commodity, and the Dean and Chapter, as great landowners, husbanded it carefully. On 13 May 1802 Chapter noted that since the 110 feet of oak required for rebuilding the mill at Islip (the birthplace of Edward the Confessor) 'turns out some of it rotten and defective', the bailiff of the manor 'set out . . . such further quantity as will make good the said allowance made 21 April, 1801'. With understandable prudence, it was strictly enjoined that the decayed timber should be returned to the bailiff 'and accounted for by him'.

The eighteenth century witnessed great strides in farming techniques, though such progress was often purchased at the cost of enclosure leading to eviction and consequent loss of common rights. Regularly the Dean and Chapter were called on to give consent to Acts of Parliament which affected their own property. On 5 June 1801 they approved Bills for draining Wildmore and West Fen in the County of Lincolnshire, and a week later for the enclosure of Dinewich in Berkshire. Many again were the canal companies who approached the Dean and Chapter for the purchase of their land, as for example those of the Grand Junction (9 July 1811); and Ashby-de-la-Zouche (16 November 1815). The same happened with the

railway companies, as their tracks began to thread their way through
rural England in the 1830s. This new (and most civilized) form of
transport led to a large number of Parliamentary Bills; so much so
that the Dean and Chapter engaged Messrs Blake & Co., law
agents, to keep a watching brief and ensure that none of these
affected their rights. When they did, appropriate action was taken,
as in the case of the railways from Birmingham, Bristol and Cheltenham in 1837. No objection was made to a Bill promoted by the
Great Western Railway Company in January 1834.

The ownership of landed estates, with the consequent acquirement
of manorial rights, often meant appointing officers charged with
local responsibilities. Sometimes such officers were guilty of various
misdemeanours. For example, on 22 February 1791, a firm line was
taken with Daniel Tidd, Bailiff of Wheathampstead, who through
'inability' due to illness, was grossly in arrears in paying over his
quit rents. The Dean and Chapter (rather toughly) dismissed him
from his office, and let it be clearly known that if he did not reim-
burse them, he would be brought to Court. After an unhappy
exchange of letters they initiated proceedings in August.

Local responsibility often entailed keeping an eye on roads and
highways. This may be illustrated from what proved an irritating
charge—the upkeep of Pershore bridge in Worcestershire. Between
the years 1812 and 1834 there are no fewer than nine separate
references to this troublesome care. In 1812, the Dean and Chapter
agreed to undertake essential repairs, but refused to contribute
money for a scheme to widen the road. This decision, however, was
not very acceptable to local opinion. A few months later a meeting
was held in the Angel Inn at Pershore, when, in spite of the Chapter's
unco-operative attitude, plans were drawn up for 'widening and
amending the small bridge', and the 'further Arch and wall of the
Great Bridge'. In making this decision, the meeting assured the
Dean and Chapter that these improvements would not add to the
annual cost of upkeep. Perhaps this was true, but in 1820 some
£288. 1s. 10½d. was spent on necessary repairs.

This bridge—it was not the only one, Islip had another—proved a
constant drain on Abbey resources, so much so that the Chapter did
their best to get out of responsibility for its maintenance. A means of
doing this seemed to be offered when a Turnpike Bill came before
Parliament. The Dean and Chapter sent in a petition, 'in consequence of the great public traffic and travelling on and over the
bridge and increased wear and tear', that it might be made 'a Public
County Bridge or that the Dean and Chapter be by any other means
relieved of the charge and care of the said Bridge and the road over
the same'. Messrs Blake & Co. did their best (February 1822)—but

the time of deliverance was not yet. As late as October 1834, the Dean and Chapter were still paying out money for its repair.

Responsibilities for their estates made it important for the Dean and Chapter to have accurate information concerning them. In the middle of the eighteenth century (15 May 1755) the Registrar was required to draw up a *New Standard Book* of all the lands and estates in the ownership of the Dean and Chapter.

Years later it was decided that in future when their lands were surveyed full particulars should be recorded—the annual value independent of repairs; the condition of the buildings, listing the repairs for which the tenant was responsible; the average yearly expense to the Chapter of their maintenance; together with any exceptional reasons which would justify a departure from the usual mode of settling fines.

One of the most important duties devolving upon the Dean and Chapter in their oversight of these scattered estates was the nomination of over twenty parish priests. The link with these livings—independent of their interest as property owners—was often close and intimate; particularly when held by one of their own prebendaries. The custom was for such a prebendary to reside in his parish during the summer, and employ a resident curate for the rest of the year.

Chapter minutes abound in the record of financial help given to such livings. For example, ten guineas were provided for 'the schoolmaster' at South Benfleet for teaching poor children; £20 for sufferers in a fire in Godmanchester; ten guineas for distribution among the poor in Stanford in the Vale because of lack of work and general distress in the village; £10 to provide a barrel-organ for the Church of St Mary, Malden, on condition that the parishioners contributed the rest; an interest-free loan for the Vicar of Pershore to assist him with a law case to recover his tithes. And so on!

At a time when many parish priests suffered great poverty and lacked the capacity of Goldsmith's vicar, to become 'passing rich with forty pounds a year', the Dean and Chapter tried to do what they could for their own parsons. Concern for the Rector of St Brides, Fleet Street, made the Dean and Chapter refuse consent to an Act of Parliament affecting the parish unless the parishioners increased the stipend of their incumbent from £180 to £200 per annum (6 May 1819) a fairly large sum for those days. Nor was this simply a gesture, which 'passed the buck' over to the parishioners; for in 1832, the Chapter decided that they must do the same for all the incumbents of their livings. On 9 February a circular letter was sent to them for details as to their total salary, the sources from which this came, together with the population of their parish at the last census. On their part, the Chapter undertook to raise all stipends up to £200 per annum, 'such augmentation to take place when the Incumbent of each is resident in the Parish and performs Morning and Evening Service on Sundays'. In cases where non-residence was due to there being 'no glebe house proper for a clergyman', then steps were to be taken to build one. The circular letter revealed that there were some five livings—Malden, Alconbury, Otford, Eckington and Mathon— which the Dean and Chapter had to augment to attain the required sum.

16

The City of Westminster

WITH the City of Westminster the relations of the Dean and Chapter were intimate and many sided. This arose from the ecclesiastical jurisdiction which they exercised; their responsibility for local government as Lords of the Manor; and their position as a vast owner of property.

As to their ecclesiastical jurisdiction this extended over the parishes of St Margaret's and St John's, Smith Square (created in 1728); and the Chapels in Duke Street, the Broadway, Queen Street, and Neway.

Here again the Dean and Chapter were jealous of their rights; and this meant eternal vigilance, to the extent of firmly rebuking the churchwardens of St Margaret's on one occasion for felling trees in the churchyard without capitular permission. In June 1759 a visitation was held by the Dean, Dr Zachary Pearce, and as a result the names and degrees of all the clergy who officiated in these churches, together with a complete list of their services and times of sermons, were entered into the Chapter Book. This showed that most of them held a monthly Communion after Morning Service (Duke Street Chapel held two, but owing to the smallness of the congregation was dispensing with the second); two services on Sunday; and prayers on Wednesday and Friday. Four churches conducted daily prayers, the Broadway Chapel at 9 a.m. and 3 p.m.

As we have seen, the responsibilities of the Dean and Chapter in the City of Westminster were not confined to the oversight of certain churches. They had responsibilities both as Lords of the Manor and as property owners. In both capacities the Dean and Chapter were presented with many problems.

Property rights in the Cities of London and Westminster were being forced to give way to the need of a rapidly growing population, for bridges over the Thames, more streets and new buildings. The civic requirements of Westminster were indeed rapidly outgrowing the simple administrative structure deriving its authority from the Dean and Chapter. Increasing complexity indeed demanded a more specialized and trained personnel. As it was, until 1899, the titular head of the City of Westminster was the High Steward, who was nominated to his office by the Dean and Chapter. The post was usually held by a nobleman and was regarded as a very honourable one. Effective power, however, lay in the High Bailiff, also appointed by the Dean and Chapter, and in the Court of Burgesses. It is recorded of Dean Dolben that on one occasion he summarily removed from office a member of the latter august body for unseemly conduct in church. It was, moreover, the Dean and Chapter who appointed such lay officers as the Coroner of the City, together with the Clerk of the Markets. Their Chapter Clerk swore in the constables.

To preserve this traditional system of local government from encroachment by officers of other authorities was never easy. Thus far back in 1726 the Dean and Chapter became alarmed at the Clerk of the Markets of His Majesty's Household taking upon himself to exercise jurisdiction within the precincts. Counsel's opinion was sought, and as a result the High Constable was instructed to refuse to execute any writ emanating from this quarter. This was by no means an isolated instance of an attack on their rights and status. On 25 March 1771 the Dean and Chapter protested to Parliament that the Bill for 'embanking' the Thames by Durham Yard invaded their privileges as Lords of the Manor of Westminster; and what was worse did so by assuming such privileges to be vested in the Aldermen and Commonalty of the City of London!

The Dean and Chapter were very jealous of their status on public occasions. The funeral of Lord Nelson, who, going into action, cried 'Victory or Westminster Abbey' but was buried in St Paul's, led to some bad feeling. The circumstances were as follows:

On 3 January 1806, in connexion with the State procession, the usual orders appeared in the *London Gazette* for regulating traffic in the streets of Westminster; but the Government had done this 'without any notification to the High Steward', which omission 'highly interfered with the jurisdiction and Ancient Privileges of the Dean and Chapter of the Collegiate Church of St Peter, Westminster, their High Steward and their Burgesses Court, and in their Governance and the good ordering of the City and Liberty of Westminster'. The Marquis of Buckingham, the High Steward, personally protested with vigour and successfully, to Lord Spencer, Secretary of State.

The fruits of this timely intervention were seen when the Secretary of State in a letter to Lord Buckingham at the time of William Pitt's funeral on 22 February, acknowledged the jurisdiction of the Dean and Chapter in these words: 'I have received his Majesty's Commands to notify [the route of funeral] in order that you may in conjunction with the Court of Burgesses take such measures as may be most advisable in Execution of the powers vested in you by

Law for removing all annoyances and maintaining the Peace in the different Streets of the City of Westminster upon that Day.'

Not everyone was so sensitive to their feelings in a matter of this kind as Lord Spencer—certainly not the Lord Mayor of London, who on 9 November 1816 processed publicly, on returning from the Court of the Exchequer, through the streets of the City of Westminster, without so much as a 'by your leave' from the Lord High Steward, now Lord Sidmouth. The latter, on hearing of it, immediately protested against this 'pretension' and gained his point. Once again the Dean and Chapter expressed to the Viscount their 'just sense of the obligation conferred upon them'. For this initiative they assured him that they would 'ever retain a full sense of the obligation conferred upon them by his constant defence of their privileges and immunities'. To express their gratitude the Dean waited on him in person.

An embarrassing responsibility which weighed heavily upon the shoulders of the Dean and Chapter was their ownership of the ancient Gatehouse Prison situated at the entrance to Tothill Street, which across the centuries had confined so many illustrious if tragic inmates, and where Raleigh spent the last night of his life. One of its two rooms was used by the Bishop of London for convicted clergy, and the other became the public prison for Westminster. The condition of the building in the eighteenth century was frightful, so much so that it was bitterly criticized by Dr Johnson; and the Dean and Chapter themselves admitted that it had become 'less fit for the secure Detention of Prisoners', particularly since an increase in Westminster's population had led to an increase of crime. In March 1768 an official approach came to the Dean and Chapter from Sir John Fielding (of Wilkes fame) and other Justices of the Peace of the City of Westminster acquainting them with their intention of applying to Parliament for the erection of a new prison in Tothill Fields. A meeting between the Chapter and the Justices took place in the Deanery, when the 'human and laudable intentions of the justices was approved'. When the Dean and Chapter met on 3 March it offered to provide a suitable site. The scheme unfortunately hung fire and in 1774 a careful survey of the Gatehouse Prison was undertaken by the Dean and Chapter in order to decide finally whether the building was beyond repair. The report condemned it once and for all and in July 1776 Chapter ordered that the prison be pulled down, together with the adjoining almshouse. The scheme for rebuilding in Tothill Fields was at last set in hand, and King George III gave a donation of £500 towards it (3 June 1778). The Dean and Chapter continued to have an oversight of the new prison, though there was some doubt as to precisely how far their responsibility

extended. As late as March 1819 the Justices of Westminster petitioned the Dean and Chapter to appoint a new keeper, which led the
latter to seek Counsel's opinion as to whether this responsibility really
devolved upon them. It was not for some years yet that this link
with the Abbey was finally broken.

With the return of the Reform Parliament in 1832 the structure of
local government came under review. In 1834 an Act of Parliament
deprived Lords of Liberties of some of the emoluments which they
had hitherto enjoyed through the levying of fines. This legislation
affected the Dean and Chapter as Lords of the Manor of Westminster
since it led to a loss of income for their High Bailiff. Fortunately in
this case they were able to take advantage of a clause in the Bill
which provided for compensation.

This Act, however, was but a prelude to others which were to
follow. Two years later came another inroad upon the powers, and
consequently the emoluments, of the High Bailiff under the Westminster Small Debts Act. The promoters of the Bill, in the House of
Lords, did offer to allow the Dean and Chapter to nominate the four
officers who were to serve and execute the process of the Court set up
under the Bill; but this did not alter the basic fact that the general
effect of this piece of legislation was to limit the traditional scope and
exercise of the office of High Bailiff.

Its ramifications led to prolonged discussions at Chapter. The
High Bailiff, one Arthur Morris, resigned because he felt that his long
association with the Dean and Chapter might prejudice any efforts to
maintain the rights of his office. A successor, Francis Smedley, was
appointed, but his inheritance proved a pale imitation of that of his
predecessors. The simple truth was that one method of local government was on the way out, and another on the way in.

Nor were problems connected with local government the only
ones that pressed heavily upon the Dean and Chapter in the City of
Westminster. Others came from their rôle as vast owners of property.
Thus a proposal, in 1734, to build a 'theatre or playhouse' upon an
estate belonging to the Dean and Chapter in St Martin-le-Grand
drew forth a vigorous protest, and the instruction:

> That our Solicitor enquire into the Truth of the said Report, &
> signifie to our Tenants there, that the Chapter have determined, to
> the utmost of their power, to oppose & discourage such Desyn; as
> well by insisting on a strict performance of the Covenants in their
> several and respective Leases, as by refusing to renew any Lease
> that shall be assumed with a View to promote a project of that
> kind.

This was a matter on which Dr Wilcocks felt keenly.

According to their lights the Dean and Chapter endeavoured to preserve some of the amenities of the City of Westminster. For example, when in 1803, John Jones, an enterprising plumber, was given permission to occupy some waste ground east of Dean Street, it was expressly laid down that he must not use it for 'any manufacturing, slaughtering or boiling house, forge or melting house for metals or any trade or profession that can or may be deemed unhealthy or any way offensive'.

In June 1837 Messrs. Blake & Co. were consulted as to how to abate the 'excessive nuisance' arising from two chimneys erected by the Westminster Gas & Coke Company Limited.

One of the Dean and Chapter's most embarrassing responsibilities, and it remained so throughout the eighteenth century and beyond, was their oversight of Tothill Fields, then unenclosed. To local, and not only local, residents this large open space of some ten acres served as an almost free-for-all recreation ground; and as such always a potential source of disturbance. In 1737 the Dean and Chapter received a complaint from the Head Master of Westminster School that the King's Scholars, who were accustomed to 'take the air' in the fields, had lately been 'interrupted' by horse riding. A peremptory order was given to the Field Keeper that this 'horse play' must cease forthwith, except at St Bartholomew's time when the School was on holiday. Almost inevitably, in line with current practice, the Dean and Chapter came to the conclusion that to preserve any semblance of order in Tothill Fields they must be enclosed: and in July 1777 the Chapter decided to petition Parliament to this end. At the same time, notices of this intention were posted on the doors of St Margaret's and St John's, Smith Square. The scheme, however, for the time being miscarried.

Complaints therefore continued to come in to the Dean and Chapter. In November 1796 they decided to see for themselves: and the Dean accompanied by two prebendaries walked round the Fields and drew up a list of nuisances and encroachments. There were numerous instances of the latter: and just over a year later formal notice was served upon all such offenders ordering them to pull down the railings they had erected. If they failed to comply, the Dean and Chapter would themselves see that it was done.

As late as 1815 the Fields remained unenclosed and a problem. The prospect of their being used as a fairground made the Dean and Chapter take fright. Special constables were sworn in, and posters erected in Westminster and in the 'small villages in the outskirts' to prevent people assembling on the Ten Acres, Tothill Fields, under the pretext of holding a fair. For undertaking these precautions the Chapter Clerk was reimbursed £19. 18s. 6d.

So the problem of maintaining order in Tothill Fields persisted until it was enclosed little by little and used for building. Its last remains are to be seen in Vincent Square ('Up Fields') the sports ground of Westminster School.

Increased building in the City of Westminster urgently demanded more streets, and it was for lack of these that the value of property in Westminster undoubtedly had depreciated. Such streets became even more necessary after the building of Westminster Bridge. In 1777 the Dean and Chapter, together with other property owners in the parishes of St Margaret's and St John's, Smith Square, sent a petition to Parliament calling attention to the 'ruinous' condition and reduced value of many houses in Smith Street, Marsham Street, St Peter's and Tothill Street due to 'the want of those streets having commodious and safe communication with each other and with the other parts of the said City and Liberty'. This petition finally led to 'An Act to enable the Dean and Chapter of the Collegiate Church of Saint Peter in Westminster to open a street from the South End of Long Ditch to the North End of Smith Street.' The enterprise was a considerable one and led to the pulling down of much old property.

This particular development scheme was promoted by the Dean and Chapter. Others, not so promoted, were sometimes viewed with grave suspicion.

The building of Westminster Bridge (1738–50) and Vauxhall Bridge (1808) caused the Dean and Chapter many a headache. Both involved the surrender of Abbey land, and in respect of Westminster Bridge the destruction of the old fish market, which, however, the Dean and Chapter succeeded in transferring to a new site in 1750. As to Vauxhall Bridge they petitioned Parliament in May 1808 to defer approval of the plans until the rights of the Collegiate Church as property owners were safeguarded. Their point was accepted, and the Act required that the road to be built giving access to the bridge from Tothill Fields must be restricted to the width of eighty feet.

The Dean and Chapter, however, were not so successful when it came to the rebuilding of Westminster Hospital.

When the Commissioners of the Treasury submitted plans for its erection on the north side of the Abbey, the Dean and Chapter registered their strong opposition. The reasons for their objections were two-fold.

First, because a hospital, so near the Abbey, might create 'alarm in the minds of parents, and prevent them from placing their sons for education in the Royal School of Westminster'. Secondly, because the erection of a large building on the proposed site was architecturally undesirable. The position of the Church of St Margaret meant that only from the north-west could the whole extent of the

Abbey be seen; and this view would now disappear if the hospital were built where planned. Such a deprivation would be particularly unfortunate since the Dean and Chapter had not long ago been engaged in restoring the north side to its original splendour.

The objections of the Chapter, however, were over-ruled.

A further cause for alarm came in 1837 when in 'A Report for the Improvement of the Metropolis' it was suggested that the immediate precincts of the Abbey would be 'materially affected by pulling down Jerusalem Chamber and adjoining buildings'. A deputation was sent to Mr Alderman Wood, promoter of the Report. Suffice to say that though the adjoining buildings have gone, Jerusalem Chamber remains to this day.

PART IV
Victorian Chapter

By The Reverend M. S. Stancliffe, m.a.
Canon of Westminster, Rector of St. Margaret's, Westminster

17

The Age of Reform

1837—1864

THIS section has a strictly limited aim: to draw a sketch of Westminster Abbey during the reign of Queen Victoria as seen chiefly through the minutes of the meetings of the Dean and Chapter between March 1837 and January 1901. These minutes fill eight folio volumes, each of over 500 pages, and they have been largely unexplored—partly because successive Deans and Chapters have not thought it right to make public in a hurry what their immediate predecessors had sworn (at their installations) to keep secret, and partly because both historians and their public have hitherto shown much more interest in the pre-Reformation monastery than in the post-Reformation Collegiate Church. And it is not only the difficulty of getting the more recent age into perspective that deters the would-be historian of Victorian Westminster Abbey; he cannot but be daunted by the sheer quantity of evidence to be sifted. The accounts of particular officers and of numerous funds, architects' reports, Parliamentary debates, law reports, reports of a dozen royal commissions, service papers, volumes of sermons, newspaper reports—these are only a few of the sources which, in addition to the Chapter minutes, will have to be examined before the full history can be written.

The Chapter Books are for the most part easy to read, being written in good black ink in a fair copperplate hand; and the language itself is reasonably easy to follow. It requires some knowledge of property law; it needs no knowledge of theology. A few changes in spelling are noticeable: words like 'colour' and 'labour' and 'honour', for instance, are non-u as in North America today; and there are some unusual words like 'messuage', 'heriot', 'shackage', 'noctuary' (opposite of diary), 'deputation' (in the sense of a document issued under seal appointing a gamekeeper), 'tent' wine, and coco-nut 'Bump' (a proper quantity of which the Sub-Dean on 11 March 1846 was requested to provide for the choir).

Before coming to the Chapter minutes themselves it may be useful to recall briefly the general situation in which the Chapter found itself in the early years of Victoria's reign, and to remind the reader of the nature of the Chapter and of the institution of which it was the governing body. With only a few exceptions, the type of clergyman who had been appointed to a Westminster Canonry in the first three decades of the nineteenth century was neither theologically significant nor spiritually energetic; but he was widely unpopular— unpopular with the Dissenters who resented the privileges and endowments of the Established Church and unpopular with many Anglicans as well on account of the unequal distribution of those privileges and endowments. While, for instance, more than half of the 4,000 curates (upon whom fell the brunt of the work of the Church of England) received less than £60 per annum, the Bishop of Winchester had an annual income of some £50,000 and in 1805 Archbishop Moore of Canterbury had died a millionaire.

Change, however, was in the air. In their different ways both the Industrial Revolution and the French Revolution were making themselves felt, and, while the railway system of England was being created and Darwin was voyaging in the *Beagle*, Parliament reformed first itself, and then much else besides—including the Established Church. This Church was, at the same time, producing within itself men, movements and measures of reform. It was not, however, the thinking of the Evangelicals or of the Oxford Movement which made itself immediately conspicuous in the meetings of the Dean and Chapter of Westminster. What the Chapter Books reflect most clearly are the reforming measures of Parliament, such as were the Act to restrict the more enormous forms of pluralism, the Act to provide for the payment of tithes in cash instead of in kind, and the motion to set up a Royal Commission to investigate Cathedral and Capitular Churches. Above all there was the Act to bring into existence the Ecclesiastical Commissioners—two archbishops, three bishops and four laymen—who then and subsequently were given far-reaching powers to take over the control of the Church's endowments, to distribute its revenues more fairly and to make some provision for the spiritual welfare of the England that was emerging as a result of the Industrial Revolution.

I pass the magnificent church which crowns the metropolis, and is consecrated to the noblest of objects, the glory of God, and I ask of myself in what degree it answers the object. I see there a dean, and three residentiaries, with incomes amounting in the aggregate to between £10,000 and £12,000 a year . . . I proceed a mile or two to the east and north-east, and find myself in the midst of an immense population, in the most wretched state of destitution and neglect, artisans, mechanics, labourers, beggars, thieves, to the number of at least 300,000. I find there, upon an average, about one church and one clergyman for every 8,000 or 10,000 souls; in some districts a much smaller amount of spiritual provision.

So Charles Blomfield, Bishop of London, and the virtual creator of the Ecclesiastical Commission. He was writing of St Paul's, but *mutatis mutandis* he might have been writing of Westminster—and with as much justification if not more. And the fact that the Collegiate Church of St Peter Westminster was royally peculiar did not avail to delay or lessen the impact of reform upon the Chapter meetings held in the Jerusalem Chamber. A door had been opened which no man could shut, and the consequent draught not only blew a great deal of paper about but also stimulated the men concerned to take increasingly violent exercise if they were not to catch their death of cold. Had Darwin at this time chosen to study the Canons of Westminster instead of orchids and earthworms he would have been led to his same conclusions about the survival of the fittest. What the Chapter Books show is a species of Christian minister, congenitally resistant to change, giving way to a new breed which positively welcomed the invigorating gale. It is not perhaps without significance that the author of the 'Ode to the North East Wind' was appointed a Canon of Westminster in 1875, but lest anyone should suppose that by that time hardness was all, it is as well to add that three years later Mr Disraeli nominated to a Westminster Canonry the author of *Eric, or Little by Little*.

THE OLD ESTABLISHMENT AND SOME NEW MEN

An earlier chapter in this book has described how, in the second year of her reign, Elizabeth I founded, on the site of the Benedictine monastery of St Peter, a college or collegiate church of one Dean and twelve prebendaries, priests, there for ever to serve Almighty God,

> and to the intent: *that* true Religion and the true Worship of God, without which we are either like to Brutes in Cruelty or to Beasts in folly, may . . . be restored . . . reformed and brought back to the primitive form of genuine and brotherly sincerity . . . *that* the Documents of the sacred Oracles . . . and pure Sacraments of our salutary Redemption may be administered . . . *that* Youth, who in the Stock of our Republick like certain tender Twiggs daily encrease, may be liberally trained up in usefull Letters to the greater Ornament of the same Republick *that* the Aged, destitute of their Strength, . . . may be suitably nourished and LASTLY *that* offices of

Charity to the Poor of Christ, Enlargements of Ways, Reparations of Bridges, and all other offices of every kind of Piety may be from thence shewn forth to all places that are destitute of them and be dispersed far and wide to the Glory of Almighty God and to the common Utility and Happiness of our Subjects.

For the carrying out of these all-embracing objects both near and far Elizabeth put the Dean and prebendaries in possession of the abbey church and all the conventual buildings (with the exception of the Chapter House, which remains under the control of H.M. Minister of Works to this day); she made over to them manors, lordships, lands, tenements and other hereditaments in London and Westminster and in eighteen counties in the southern half of England; and she gave them a set of statutes in which she prescribed the composition of the college, its body of officers and servants, their duties and stipends and the rules by which their lives were to be governed. In addition to the Dean and prebendaries the statutes provided for

six Minor Canons, 12 Lay Clerks, 10 Choristers, a teacher of the Choristers, two Schoolmasters, 40 Grammar School boys, 12 Alms-men—and [among others] 2 vergers, four bellringers, a Chapter Clerk, Auditor, High Steward, a Proctor for lawsuits, 3 Butlers, 3 Cooks, 2 Porters, one of whom shall be a barber, a Groom, and one for cleaning the waterpipes and roof of the Church.

The Chapter responsible for the government of this establishment in 1837 was still as prescribed by Elizabeth I, but by recent action of Parliament and the Ecclesiastical Commissioners, resisted at the time and resented for many years after, there were to be no new Canons appointed until preferment or death had reduced the number to six, the emoluments attaching to the vacant stalls being appropriated elsewhere to the raising of existing clerical stipends and the endow-ment of new incumbencies. Of the five Deans who presided over the diminishing Chapter between 1837 and the appointment of Stanley in 1864 three can be mentioned with brevity: John Ireland was a sick man, and died in 1842 at the age of 81; Thomas Turton left to be Bishop of Ely after only three years; Samuel Wilberforce followed, but was appointed Bishop of Oxford after only eight months at Westminster.

The two other Deans deserve longer notice, though the first of them, William Buckland, was only effectively Dean for a bare four years. Early in 1850 he fell ill, and at the Chapter Meeting on 3 February the Sub-Dean took the chair by virtue of a letter from the Royal Visitor in which it was stated that 'the Dean has humbly repre-sented to Us that his illness makes his attendance if not impossible yet

in the highest degree distressful to him'. Though Buckland remained
Dean until his death six years later he never again attended a
Chapter Meeting. And this was undoubtedly Westminster's loss, for
Buckland was a man of wide learning and vigorous powers who in the
short period of his active decanate made a lasting mark.

> *Endued with superior Intellect,*
> *He applied the Powers of his Mind*
> *To the Honour and Glory of God,*
> *The advancement of Science,*
> *And the welfare of Mankind.*

This inscription on his monument (it was composed by the
Sub-Dean) was not undeserved. First Professor of Geology and
Mineralogy in the University of Oxford, Fellow of the Royal Society,
Trustee of the British Museum, member of over fifty scientific
societies in the British Isles, on the Continent and in North America,
he was a Canon of Christ Church when Peel nominated him Dean of
Westminster. His most famous published work was his *Bridgewater
Treatise*, 'Geology and Mineralogy considered with reference to
Natural Theology', a contribution to the great debate then going on
between churchmen and geologists. But he was no narrow specialist
in his scientific interests; Faraday, William Harcourt and George
Stephenson as well as the geologist Murchison were his friends, and
he published articles on such diverse subjects as artesian wells, new
manures, Roman and Celtic remains, potato disease and 'the
Temporary Suspension in the Growth of Fleas'. As some of these
titles suggest, his scientific interests were by no means academic, and
the Abbey was to benefit from his understanding of stone as the
precincts from his interest in sanitation.

> As Mr. Cundy, the builder, will testify, Dr. Buckland looked very
> sharply after the masons when repairing Westminster Abbey, or
> any other of the collegiate buildings in which he had any interest,
> examining the various kinds of cements, the blocks of building
> stone, the means adopted to repair and keep in order the regal and
> other monuments, and taking special care that no faulty bits of
> stone were used.

One is tempted to speculate how relations between religion and science
might have developed had Buckland's health lasted another fifteen
years. Almost his last public appearance was to preach in the Abbey
on 15 November 1849, being a 'National Day of Thanksgiving to Almighty God for the Removal of the Cholera'. He brought all his knowledge and experience of water supplies and sewage disposal to bear
upon the elucidation of his text, 2 Kings v. 13: 'Wash and be clean.'

Buckland's successor was Richard Chenevix Trench, so that the scientist was followed by the man of letters, and the author of works on fossils and fleas by the author of a number of volumes of poems and a life of Plutarch, to say nothing of Trench on the *Miracles* and on the *Parables*, on the *Study of Words*, on *English Past and Present*, and on the *Synonyms of the New Testament*. A regular correspondent of F. D. Maurice and John Sterling, and an acquaintance of Coleridge, Carlyle, Wordsworth and Tennyson, Trench was much influenced by Samuel Wilberforce whose chaplain he had been and from whom he chiefly derived his High Church principles. After eleven years as Professor of Divinity at King's College, London, he was appointed Dean (when still under 50) by Lord Palmerston in 1856, and a clergyman wrote: 'It is very gratifying, indeed, to find such claims as yours recognised. With a few such chiefs and leaders, our establishment will at least perish honourably, and not die in a ditch of nepotism and imbecility.'

The ditch of nepotism was not, in fact, quite dry—one of Trench's first acts was to present his son Francis to the desirable Abbey living of Islip; but he might have kept it for himself, as Buckland had done to the day of his death. However, with Trench as Dean—he held the office for seven years before becoming Archbishop of Dublin—there was no question of imbecility nor of the establishment perishing, at Westminster at all events. It was Trench who persuaded the Chapter to take the step which more than any other made Westminster Abbey the force it was to be for the next sixty or seventy years (see infra p. 295).

So much for the Deans who presided over the meetings which the Chapter Books under consideration record. Of the Canons easily the most important, if not the most learned, was the remarkable the Rev. and the Rt. Hon. Lord John Thynne, D.D. The 3rd son of the 2nd Marquis of Bath and of Isabella, the 2nd daughter of the 4th Viscount Torrington, this nobleman became Canon and Sub-Dean in 1831. He owed the appointment to the Dean, and when he had been safely installed Ireland is reputed to have said: 'Now I can go to bed.' Then aged 33, Thynne remained Canon and Sub-Dean for fifty years. He was also rector of Kingston Deverill in Wiltshire (until 1836), of Street in Somerset (until 1850), and of Blackwell in Somerset (until 1872). When in due course of canonical seniority he became entitled to occupy Ashburnham House as his official residence he provided £1,000 out of his own pocket for the considerable repairs and alterations he felt to be necessary. He also had a country seat near Bedford, and the Treasurer's accounts of 1842 include the payment of 10s. to the porter for his journey to Bedfordshire to tell the Sub-Dean that Dean Ireland was dead. Thynne was one of those rare men who are content (perhaps we should say, who can afford to be content) to be permanently second-in-command—and do the job superbly, neither shirking responsibility when it must be taken, nor resenting it when the time comes to surrender their power again. Not only was he acting Dean during five interregna, but he was also in charge throughout the whole period of Buckland's illness. And at all times he was ready to undertake whatsoever the Chapter asked of him. And it was not only that he undertook to provide coco-nut bump for the choir, to confer with the physicians attending patients in the precincts during a typhoid epidemic (May 1848) or to obtain estimates for, and see to the execution of, this or that work in the church or the precincts; it was Lord John Thynne who corresponded delicately with the Ecclesiastical Commissioners and who drafted diplomatic replies to the questionnaires of the Commission inquiring into the Revenues and Management of the Cathedrals and Collegiate Churches. His fellow Canons paid him a pretty compliment when, after the six years of Buckland's illness, they wrote a letter to the new Dean which is recorded in the Chapter Book and which still reads warmly today:

Very Reverend Sir,

We the undersigned Canons of this Collegiate Church, in congratulating you on your appointment to the highest position in it, feel persuaded that you will participate in our sentiments of affectionate regard and respectful gratitude to one who has been for many years our Sub-dean, and who under special circumstances has been called upon in difficult and eventful times to discharge the duties of the Dean.

In the honorary performance of these functions the Reverend Lord John Thynne, D.D., has rendered great public services to this Chapter and Church; and we may be permitted to express our belief that by his judicious and efficient administration, he has made the task of government more easy to yourself, who by Divine Providence are now set over us.

We trust you will concur with us in the desire that this declaration of our sentiments may be recorded in the Chapter Book of our Collegiate Church.

With our earnest and united prayer that the Divine Blessing may rest upon you in all your endeavours to promote the welfare of our ancient and Religious Institution,

                    We have the honor to be
                    Very Reverend Sir
                    Your faithful Brethren and Servants . . .

Of the six signatories of this letter in November 1856 only two had been members of the Chapter nineteen years before, and one of these, W. H. E. Bentinck (Westminster and Christ Church) had been a Canon for forty-seven years and was to go on for eight years more. The other five, like the Sub-Dean, were pluralists, being parish priests in Westminster, Kent, Essex and Berkshire. In addition to Bentinck, the Westminster, Thynne was an Etonian and Christopher Wordsworth a Wykehamist; the other four were from country grammar schools or had been privately educated. Three were Christ Church men, two were Trinity, Cambridge, and one was Trinity, Dublin. One of them had a son who was a Minor Canon.

These statistics give some indication of the way the wind had been blowing in the previous nineteen years. Of the ten Canons in 1837, four were Etonians, three were Westminsters, and Harrow and Charterhouse had one each. Five were Christ Church men, one was Trinity, Cambridge, one was Trinity, Dublin. But the most significant change lay in the fact that back in 1837 no less than four were pluralists in a big way. Two were bishops (Hereford and Gloucester), one was Dean of Ripon and one was Archdeacon of Stow in the Diocese of Lincoln. A few months earlier there had been a third bishop.

CHAPTER BUSINESS AND ESTATE MANAGEMENT

What do the Chapter Books themselves reveal of how these men sought to fulfil the objects of the Royal Founder? Space does not allow of a chronological answer, and in many ways this is regrettable, for without immersing oneself in the stream of history and allowing oneself to be carried along with those who made it, it is not easy to temper one's judgement with understanding. It is fascinating to see how one little item of Chapter business, recorded shortly and almost casually, turns out to be a grain of mustard seed from which ramifications spread through the following months and even through the years. On 16 March 1837 the Chapter discussed the possibility of improvements on the north side of Dean's Yard, and ordered that the opinion of Counsel should be taken. For the next twenty years the subject engages the Chapter's attention repeatedly: permission to rebuild is obtained, money is found, plans are prepared; a Surveyor resigns and a new one is appointed; new plans are prepared, are approved and tenders invited; then demolition begins, and the neighbours complain; building starts, falls behind schedule, is speeded up until finally George Gilbert Scott's Sanctuary Buildings are finished and the Archway Entrance (complete with the heads of Victoria and Albert) is opened on 1 January 1854. Meanwhile rents have been fixed, and the houses let. But that is not the end of the story, for soon Messrs Lee and Bolton are complaining of a defective chimney and Mr Bonamy Dobrée wants a coal cellar. Not all items of Chapter business have so lengthy a story as this, of course, and some have but one short sharp mention. There was a Chapter Order of 20 January 1858, by which the Clerk of the Works, who had reported an offensive smell proceeding from a vault in the South Transept, was instructed to open up the vault, lay fresh lime and cover with dry rubbish (the word being used in its original and proper sense of 'rubble'). That, fortunately, was the end of that.

The first Chapter Meeting of 1837 was not held until 7 March, and one of the Acts of that Chapter was to confirm 'the several Acts, Matters and things done and ordered' at the twelve Committees of Chapter which had been held since the last full Meeting on 6 December—an indication of the difficulty of getting a quorum when so many members held other cures outside London. The business transacted on 7 March (and on the three subsequent dates to which this meeting was adjourned) was thoroughly typical, though not exciting. The Chapter sealed nine leases and one conveyance of lands and tenements in Westminster, Oxfordshire, Leicester, Middlesex, Huntingdonshire, Hertfordshire and Worcester; they sealed a Petition to both Houses of Parliament against part of the Bill for the improvement of the River Severn Navigation; and they sealed a power of Attorney to Job Smallpiece to act as their agent at meetings for the Commutation of Tithes. They discussed the canal at Ashby-de-la-Zouche, the shortage of timber for the repair of farms and farm buildings on their Suffolk estates, and a letter from the Rector of Harpenden about the working of the Tithe Commutation Act in his parish. They ordered 'that a Dividend be now made'. They discussed Mr Clarke's wrongful possession of the porter's apartments. They gave provisional consent to the Bishop of Hereford's request that in addition to his own house in the Little Cloister he might occupy the vacant prebendal house next door and that a communication be opened between the two houses. They required the Surveyor to obtain an estimate for the repaving of Poets' Corner, and ordered that 'the fires for heating the water for warming the [School] Dormitory be discontinued at old Lady Day and begin at old Michaelmas Day'. They appointed the Bishop of Hereford and Mr Milman to be a committee to direct the alterations in the doors and locks of the Library. Further, since this was the annual Audit Chapter, they examined, approved and signed the accounts of the Treasurer and the Steward, noting that the Treasurer had in his hands £2,447. 8s. 6d., and that the Profits of Courts had amounted to £1,653. 18s. 9d. The mulcts, fines imposed by the Dean and Canons upon themselves for failure in attending at Divine service during

their period of Residence (at 6s. 8d. per service), had amounted to
£60. 13s. 4d. in the past year. £12 13s. 4d. being deducted for the
several prebendaries in attendance, there remained for the Poor
£48. They ordered the payment of £1,854. 11s. 9d. out of the
Fabric Fund for workmen's bills, for materials, for the wages of
mechanics and workmen, and for the repair of one of the Bays of the
church by an outside contractor; and they ordered the payment of
£1,093. 18s. 7d. to solicitors for law business. The Dean continued
Lord John Thynne as Sub-Dean, and the Dean and Chapter continued Mr Milman as Treasurer, Dr Bayley as Steward, Dr Causton
as Archdeacon and the Bishop of Hereford as Term Lecturer.
Finally it was ordered that £5,000 of the balance of the moneys
standing in the Treasurer's name should be laid out in Exchequer
bills.

Typical, but not exciting—unless you happened to be immediately
concerned both as a director and a shareholder of this corporation—
for that is what the Dean and Canons were, directors and share-
holders whose work in Chapter largely consisted in the management
of property for the fulfilment of the pious intentions of the founder,
in accordance with the law of the land, and in the furtherance of the
pecuniary interests of themselves. And it has to be admitted that the
last was often first, and the first last. The management of property—
this was their chief work so far as the Chapter Books are concerned.
None of the Abbey estates were in the North or West, so that the Dean
and Chapter were not fortunate enough to have coal and other
mineral assets to enjoy (there is suppressed excitement beneath the
Chapter minute of 11 November 1857, which records the reported
discovery of iron ore on Abbey land at Westbury in Wiltshire, and a
little later one of the Canons and the Receiver-General travelled
down to Wiltshire to investigate. The expenses of their journey are
recorded on a sheet of the notepaper of the hotel at which they spent
the night, and amounted to £7. 10s.). But though the Dean and
Chapter had no mining royalties and though Westbury never became a Scunthorpe or a Corby, there was plenty of compensation in
the shape of the extensive properties in the City of London, Kensing-
ton, Paddington and above all in Westminster, which the Church
Commissioners hold today. Outside London their manors and other
estates were scattered throughout the Midlands. The greatest acre-
ages were in Oxfordshire, Worcestershire and Berkshire, but there
were also holdings, some of considerable extent, in Kent, Middlesex,
Herefordshire, Essex, Suffolk, Norfolk, Lincolnshire, Rutland,
Leicester, Bedford, Buckinghamshire, Wiltshire and Gloucestershire.
Once or twice a year a Progress was made; that is, by Chapter Order,
certain members of the Chapter went on a tour of inspection of some

of the manors, lunching with local incumbents and other worthies. In 1859 it was ordered that the Progress should go to Steventon, Islip, Binholme, Mathon, Longdon, Plaistow and then to Oakham. Those going to Huntingdon and Bedford the previous year were instructed to consider and determine on the erection of a pound for the Manor of Offord Cluny. In 1852 those who went on the Progress to Worcestershire were Mr Frere (Treasurer), Mr Jennings (Rector of St John's) and Dr Causton (Rector of St Margaret's and Steward); they were particularly instructed to visit and report on the site of the proposed gas-works at Pershore.

In the first summer after his installation as Dean, Trench went on the Progress to Wiltshire and Gloucestershire, and wrote to his wife from the Plough Inn, Cheltenham, on 30 July:

> We have had two very fine days, and have been pleasantly, I hope usefully, employed. We stopped yesterday at Swindon; turned off to see a property lately purchased by Dean and Chapter, where many things had to be looked to, and where we saw an old woman who was veritably a hundred and three years old. She was rather blind, but otherwise in full possession of her faculties, and rather vivacious than otherwise. After three or four hours at this estate, we returned to Swindon, and came on here by a later train; dined and slept, and to-day have made two expeditions in different directions to properties at five and eight miles distance from this; seen many things with our own eyes of which we shall be much better judges now than if we only knew them by report of others; lunched amongst the Cotswold hills with a gentleman who wants us to sell him a property of which he is now our tenant, and who, of course, treated us to his best; and have just returned here, where we entertained two or three of the neighbouring clergy to dinner.

But for the rest of the time, all was managed from the Jerusalem Chamber and from the Chapter Office next door. Bailiffs and other agents collected the rents and saw to the execution of Chapter decisions on the spot, but the decisions themselves were the Chapter's which had to be consulted before a single tree was cut down. And this explains why so much Chapter time was taken up with buying and selling land, fixing rents, renewing leases, taking legal action against encroachments, negotiating for enclosures, repairing bridges, negotiating with Turnpike Trusts over the widening of roads. Now that tithes had been commuted tithe-barns began to fall into decay— and twenty years later, in the 'fifties, the Chapter was being asked for permission to pull them down and put their materials to other uses. Tenants wrote asking for timber with which to repair their houses, their cowsheds and their cartsheds, their gates and fences. Only the Dean and Chapter, on the report of the local forester, could give the order for felling the necessary trees. Not a little time was spent in 1851.on the subject of the mill at Wheathampstead when its waterwheel came to pieces, and still more time was spent throughout the whole period in dealing with problems created by the growth of the railway system. To begin with the Chapter resolutely opposed almost every Parliamentary Bill by which this and that little railway company sought the necessary powers and proposed a line which would run across Abbey property. Later, after taking careful advice, the Chapter were more ready to make hay while the sun shone: in December 1850 they learned with satisfaction that the Windsor, Staines and South Western Railway had paid £801. 14s. 3d. for 9 acres, 3 rods and 21 perches at Yeovenny, and that the Buckinghamshire Railway had paid £500 for just over 2 acres at Islip. In June 1852, £1,536. 0s. 8d. from the Oxford, Worcester and Wolverhampton Railway Company and £1,136. 6s. from the South Western Railway Company were invested in 3% Consols. At the last meeting of 1865, on 16 December, the Chapter were concerned with ten different companies, including the East London, the Metropolitan and St John's Wood, the North Metropolitan, the Metropolitan and District, the Ross and Tewkesbury, the Hemel Hempstead, London and North Western, the Andover, Radstock and Bristol, and the Northampton and Banbury Junction Extension railways.

Meanwhile, and nearer home, as London spread, the Chapter were developing for building purposes their estate at Belsis, known today as Belsize Park, and they were in constant negotiation for the sale of properties to such bodies as the Commissioners for the Improvement of the Metropolis, the Westminster Improvements Commission, the Commissioners for Public Baths and Wash-houses, the Metropolitan Commissioners for Sewers, and the Downing Street Improvement Commissioners.

And so on and so on—and all the time, from rents and dividends, from sales and from the fines for renewals of leases, the income flowed in; and six or seven times a year the Chapter ordered 'that a Dividend be now made'. When allowance had been made for certain outgoings—property tax, agents' salaries, surveyors' and solicitors' fees—the remainder was divided into fifteen equal shares: two for the Dean, one for each Canon and one for the Fabric of the Abbey. Up to 1853 the amounts are not recorded, but in that year, and under pressure from the Ecclesiastical Commissioners, new arrangements were made, £2,000 were to be put aside quarterly for current expenses, and the dividend (made in October, January, April and July) was henceforth regularly recorded in the Chapter Book. From Michaelmas 1854 to Michaelmas 1855 the total dividend was £20,056; in 1859–60 it was £32,895 and in 1864–5 it was £30,056. One-fifteenth of that last is approximately £2,000—so that one can understand that the Dean and Chapter did not take kindly to the Ecclesiastical Commissioners' proposal that future Deans and Canons should be paid fixed annual incomes of £2,000 and £1,000 respectively. But the time was at hand when the Commissioners would have their way.

MATERIAL IMPROVEMENTS IN CHURCH AND PRECINCT

However, the Dean and Chapter were more than landowners, and while no picture of Chapter business would be true that failed to make it clear that property management was a major item on every agenda, it was by no means the only item nor always the most important. There were matters concerning the fabric and furnishing of the Abbey itself, and the upkeep of the buildings in the precincts; there was the Library and the School and the Choir School (which came into being at this time); there were the benefices of which the Dean and Chapter were the patrons; and there were what Elizabeth in the Charter called 'offices of every kind of piety to be shewn forth to all places that are destitute of them and to be dispersed far and wide to the Glory of Almighty God and the common Utility and Happiness of our Subjects'. And although, for reasons to be explained later, only a small part of what might be called the Abbey's contribution to the life of the Church and the nation finds a mention in the Chapter Books, there was such a contribution.

In 1837 the Abbey Surveyor was Edward Blore, whose chief monument is the present Choir. The desirability of rearranging the Choir 'as a means of affording more accommodation for the congregation on Sundays' had been under discussion for a number of years, but it was not until November 1844 that the Chapter finally approved Blore's far-reaching plans to lower the whole of the Choir by some three feet, to remove the screens separating the Choir from the transepts, to move the organ and to put in new stalls and pews. There were certain further delays, but once Buckland had been installed as Dean the work went ahead rapidly and the new Choir was first used on Easter Day, 1848. Though the 'exact copy in the best yellow brass of the Lectern in St. George's Chapel, Windsor', was not yet ready, 'proper cushions, hassocks and books' had been furnished in accordance with a Chapter order of the previous February. The Dean's sermon 'on the occasion of the Re-opening of the Choir and the Application of the Transepts to the Reception of the Congregation'

was subsequently published by John Murray and a note explained
that

> . . . the new arrangement affords more space for persons attending
> Divine Service to sit and hear and see the officiating ministers than
> could be obtained in the Nave. The Choir, including the space
> under the central tower with the two Transepts, will hold about
> 1,600 persons:

The Choir	600
N. Transept	500
S. Transept	500
Total	1,600

The entire Nave could not accommodate so large a number.

But in the sermon itself the Dean was very properly less concerned
with the Abbey's new interior than with the revolutions abroad and
the Chartist riots at home, and a paragraph from it is worthy of
quotation:

> The God of Nature has determined that moral and physical in-
> equalities shall not only be inseparable from our humanity, but
> co-extensive with His whole creation. He has also given com-
> pensations co-ordinate with these inequalities, working together
> for the conservation of all orders and degrees in that graduated
> scale of being which is the great law of God's providence on earth.
> From the mammoth to the mouse, from the eagle to the humming-
> bird, from the minnow to the whale, from the monarch to the man,
> the inhabitants of the earth and air and water form but one vast
> series of infinite gradations in an endless chain of inequalities of
> organic structure and of physical perfections . . . So also there
> never was and, while human nature remains the same, there never
> can be, a period in the history of human society when inequalities
> of worldly condition will not follow the unequal use of talents and
> opportunities originally the same. . . . Equality of mind or body,
> or of worldly condition, is as inconsistent with the order of Nature
> as with the moral laws of God. . . .

It would be incorrect to say that Blore's pre-occupation with the
new Choir meant that he neglected the building as a whole; in the
Chapter minutes of the decade 1837–47 there are repeated references
to the repair of buttresses and parapets, as there are references to the
filling of the rose window in the South Transept with coloured glass
and to the repair of 'the window in the Consistory Court damaged by
the late stormy weather' (March 1842). Nevertheless it appears that
Blore was not always as careful of the fabric as he might have been.
At the Audit Chapter in February 1847 he reported that the saddle

stones of the flying buttresses were in a very dilapidated state. The Chapter ordered that work be started at once, that £300 per annum be laid out on the necessary restoration, and that Blore get delivery by June 1st of a sufficient quantity of Anson stone (for use in that same year and) 'of the same quality as that used in the Houses of Parliament'. What the Chapter Book does not record is whether Blore was asked why, at the previous Audit Chapter, he had reported the building 'to be in a sound state'!

But Blore was getting old, and in February 1849 the Dean and Chapter accepted his resignation but 'not without expressing the satisfaction received from his valuable services for so many years . . . a connection alike honorable to him and conducive to the advantage of the Dean and Chapter'. That same day, 14 February, and in Blore's room, the Chapter appointed George Gilbert Scott, 'the said George Gilbert Scott to have the salary of £10 a year for the duties of his office and £10 a year more for checking the tradesmens' Bills'. Three weeks later the Chapter had a report from the new Surveyor 'that the eastern portion of the Abbey was in a decayed and dangerous state', and orders were instantly made for the affected parts to be shored up and the work of restoration to be put in hand. Three weeks later again there was a further report from Scott about the condition of the buttresses and other repairs calling for immediate attention, and once again it was necessary to order further shoring up and the most urgent repairs to be started. And so it goes on—for the rest of his life Scott and Chapter were kept busy by the decayed state of the outside stonework. In between times, and when he was not occupied with his new Sanctuary Buildings and his other works throughout the country, Scott was designing, for instance, a platform for the Lectern, new pews, a new pulpit, a grill for Queen Philippa's tomb, new altar rails. In February 1853 the Chapter instructed him to consider a Mr Smith's 'suggestion of consulting some eminent chemists about means to prevent the decay of stone, and if commended, that the means be tried on the pinnacles and parapets, but with the especial exception of the use of any fire for dissolving or melting or preparing the applications to be used'. Three months later the Chapter ordered 'that the trial of Mr Smith's preparation for preserving stone be tried on one of the Towers under the direction of the Sub-Dean'. Presumably the experiment seemed successful; at all events the Chapter Books contain many references to 'induration' of the stonework from that time onwards.

Reference was made earlier (see p. 253) to the criticisms voiced in Parliament at the admission charges levied on visitors entering the Abbey other than at the time of divine service. This critical attitude did not suddenly cease, and again, on 5 April 1837, following a

debate in the House of Commons, the Dean and Chapter were
required to make a return of fees and charges for burials and monuments, and the receipt of moneys for showing the tombs. The Dean
and Chapter replied in almost identical terms as some eleven years
earlier, and their returns were largely the same. The end of the
older system, however, was in sight, and in May 1841 the Chapter
ordered that in future no charge should be made for admission to the
Abbey, but that those wishing to view the Nave and the North
Transept should pay 3*d.*, and those wishing to view the Royal Chapels
should pay an additional 3*d.* Times of opening and closing were laid
down, and the Chapter ordered 'that lithographed Plans of each
Chapel describing the Monuments be placed on large Boards in each
Chapel for the information of Visitors, so that the attention of the
Guides be not too much distracted from their charge of protecting
the Monuments'; 'that numerous boards be placed about the Abbey,
requesting Persons not to touch the Monuments'; and 'that all
Sticks, Whips, Umbrellas and Parasols be required to be left at the
door of the entrance'.

From then on until 1865 there are periodic references in the
Chapter Book to the fines required for monuments, thus:

> An application having been made to the Subdean to place a
> monument to the poet William Wordsworth in the Abbey in —
> to occupy a space of about — in height by — in breadth and pro-
> jecting —, and the Subdean having approved the situation and
> given leave for its erection on the payment of the fine required
> which is £200 including the half burial fees ORDERED that the
> amount of the fine be communicated to J. D. Coleridge Esq.

But such entries become fewer and fewer. There were only two
monuments erected in the decade 1856–65, as against eighteen in
1827–36; and the number of funerals was likewise less, eleven as
against twenty-three. But the Chapter Book is innocent of the growing discussion going on outside about the propriety of adding to the
Abbey's collection of what Pugin called 'incongruous and detestable
monuments' and 'cumbrous groups of pagan divinities'. The Ecclesio-
logical Society called for the removal of 'the revolting monuments
and wax dolls', and Scott, in 1853 and again in 1863, drew up
schemes for a new memorial cloister or Campo Santo on Millbank.
There is no reference to any of this in the Books. But it would be
wrong to infer that the Dean and Chapter cared for none of these
things; it was the Sub-Dean who, in the years of Buckland's illness,
first invited Scott to make proposals for new accommodation for
monuments.

Before leaving this subject it should be said that while, as has been

shown, fees for burials and fines for monuments went to the maintenance of the fabric, the money paid for admission was applied 'for
such ornamental improvements of the Abbey and buildings belonging thereto as do not fall within the ordinary repairs of the Fabrick'.
But what was 'ornamental' it was for the Dean and Chapter to
decide—and some of their decisions were strange. The purchase of
Prayer Books and alms dishes, the gilding of organ-pipes, the provision of altar rails—these are understandable. But it is surprising to
find that this fund was used to provide a gratuity for a Clerk of the
Works on his retirement, still more surprising to read that on
23 September 1851 the Chapter ordered the payment of £3. 7s. out
of the Ornamental Fund 'for a slate slab for the Urinal at the West
end of the Abbey'.

  Lighting (by candles and oil lamps), heating (virtually nil, but by
Chapter Order of 16 December 1851 'Sheepskin ruggs' were 'to be
supplied for the Canons' stalls in the Abbey who keep residence in
Winter'), the insurance of the Abbey for £10,000 at 1s. 6d. per cent.
(2 May 1860), organs and clocks, lightning-conductors and choir
music, misbehaviour by attendants, misbehaviour by the public—
all these and many other subjects find their place in the Chapter
Books. But we leave the Abbey itself for the time being. Nor does
space allow us to linger in the Precincts, to see books being added to
(and borrowed from) the Library occasionally, to watch the painting,
in rotation, of the Canons' houses, the macadamizing of the carriage-
way in Dean's Yard, the pulling down of the Dean's Brewhouse and
the building of a new Chapter Office on the site, the planting of
trees, the repaving of the Bishop of Gloucester's stables, the inspection
of chimneys that smoke and the replacement of chimney pots that
have been blown down, the mowing of grass, the spreading of
manure, the placing of 'a *chevaux de frise* like that in Buckingham
Palace Garden' on the wall, the planting of 'Box for edgings and
Taroes'. There is not space to show Buckland's expertise being
brought to bear upon the increasingly frequent failure of the College's
water supply (which came by private conduit from Hyde Park), nor
should we wish to be there when (after an outbreak of typhoid fever
and on Buckland's initiative) cesspits were cleaned out, faulty pipes
dug up and a whole new drainage system laid down. This was done
in the summer holidays 1848, and life must have been unbearable
for a time; there were no Chapter Meetings between 23 August and
4 October, and it was subsequently ordered that Mr Turle, the
Choirmaster, be paid £20 'on account of his expenses in removing
his family from the Cloisters during the executing of the New
Drainage'. Gordon, in his life of Buckland quotes the Report of the
Metropolitan Commission of Sewers:

U

During the cleansing of the Westminster Abbey precincts, in the autumn of 1848, four hundred cubic yards of foul matter had been removed from the various branches of the ancient sewers, which were obliterated and filled up with earth. An entirely new system of drainage by pipes alone was then substituted, and not a single case of failure had been discovered by careful examinations made weekly ever since the new pipe-drainage had been laid down.

The relationship between the Chapter and the School during this period is a study in itself, but the gist of the matter is as follows. For two centuries, while the income from the Dean and Chapter's estates had been steadily increasing and there had been a regular dividend of the profits several times a year, virtually nothing had been done for the grammar school which was part of the College, and by the 1830s the position had become scandalous. Certain improvements followed complaints being made to the Prime Minister in person, and while Buckland was actively Dean and Liddell was Head Master a good deal was done to make life more tolerable for the boys—though there was much prejudice to be overcome, including that of the boys themselves. Buckland saw to it that better food was provided in College Hall and also appointed a new college cook. But when this cook produced an innovation in the shape of puddings, he had them thrown at his head. But then Buckland fell ill and retired to Islip for the rest of his life, and for the greater part of the 'fifties little further was done until the public and Parliamentary discussion began which resulted in the appointment in 1861 of a Royal Commission 'to inquire into the Revenues and Management of Certain Colleges and Schools, and the studies pursued and instruction given therein'. The Dean and Chapter now roused themselves and a whole series of Chapter Orders were made to improve accommodation and so on. After the summer holidays of 1860 two letters were received which were ordered to be entered in the Chapter Book. One was from the Head Master expressing the gratitude of himself and his colleagues 'for the real and great improvements which have been made in the Vacation'. The other ran as follows:

The Captain and Queen's Scholars of Westminster present their compliments to the Very Reverend the Dean of Westminster, and beg to assure him on his return to Town of their entire appreciation of the improvements which he has been the means of bestowing upon the School.

They wish therefore to express a deep sense of gratitude to the Dean and Chapter for their late kindness in carrying out so many and extensive changes, so well calculated to increase the many comforts which they previously enjoyed.

The Queen's Scholars do not presume to pronounce an opinion on the question of the removal of the School feeling quite confident that the Dean and Chapter will do whatever is best for their happiness, but they do express a firm hope that whether they stay at Westminster or in the lapse of years few or many remove to another spot they may by their conduct prove themselves not altogether unworthy of the liberality of the Dean and Chapter.

Further improvements followed, including the allocation of 280 guineas annually out of Chapter funds towards raising masters' salaries and the provision of a covered playground, but it was too little and too late to repair the neglect of two centuries, and in 1868 by the provisions of the Public Schools Act the school became practically independent of the Dean and Chapter. It is impossible to acquit successive Deans and Chapters of gross neglect or to see how the Royal Commission could have recommended anything different, though it may be remarked that for the whole period from 1837 to his retirement in 1864 the least effective member of the Chapter was himself an Old Westminster (Bentinck, whose attendances at Chapter were very rare and who is only mentioned throughout the years in connexion with repairs to his house and as having provided the money to build Holy Trinity Church, Bessborough Gardens).

WIDER CONCERNS

The boys at Westminster were not, however, the only 'tender Twiggs' to receive some nurture, albeit so little, from the Dean and Chapter, for the minutes contain many references during these years to the making of grants towards the building of national schools (and of residences for the school masters and mistresses)—from Knightsbridge and Hendon to Godmanchester and Hinckley, from Swaffham to Westbury, from Malvern to St Margaret's, Westminster. There was an annual subscription to the National Society, and a donation of £300 to it in 1844, and in 1849 £20 were voted towards the cost of founding a school in Adelaide 'on the principle of a collegiate school'. Frequent contributions were also made towards the repair and restoration of existing churches and the building of new churches—£1,000 for St Matthew's, Westminster (1844), £50 for the Lady Chapel at Pershore (1845), £300 for the enlargement of the district church at Haverstock Hill (1852), £25 for the repewing of Godmanchester (1852), to mention only a few. Not all appeals were answered however; the Chapter declined (October 1861) to aid the repair of the damage done to St Mary's Church, Malden, by 'electric fluid'.

Subscriptions and donations of a different nature were also constantly being made. There was, for instance, an annual subscription of ten guineas to the Middlesex Clergy Widows and Children and another of five guineas to the Society for the Protection of Life from Fire. In the first six months of 1837 £10 was given to the father of a boy run over and killed by Dr Wilson Philip's carriage, £10 to the unfortunate driver of the cab, £10 towards the relief of the present distress among the poor at Hinckley, £10 for the sufferers in Wheathampstead 'in the failure of the collector of the St Alban's Savings Bank', £20 'to the subscription raising for the destitution in the Highlands and Scotch Islands'. This last, however, was exceptional; the general rule was that assistance to schools, churches and the relief of distress should be restricted to parishes on the Dean and Chapter estates and of which they were the patrons.

There were other ways, however, in which the Dean and Chapter may be said to have contributed in a wider fashion to the Church and the nation. Most of these were of a negative kind, and took the form of opposition, either by indirect means or by direct petition, to Bills before Parliament. Again and again one reads that the dissent of the Dean and Chapter be signified from this and that—and not only from this or that railway or metropolitan improvement scheme, but (for example) from a new Divorce Bill (1857) and from a Bill to enable a man to marry his deceased wife's sister. Particularly sad reading is made by the Humble Petition to the House of Lords (July 1857) against the admission of Jews to Parliament, on the grounds 'that the paramount duty and the noblest work of Government is the maintenance of True Religion, and that these are incompatible with the extension of Legislative Privileges and Functions to those who make it part of their Religion to affirm that Christianity is false'. It is equally sad to read the Memorial to the Queen 'on the occasion of a Papal Brief appointing a Romish Ecclesiastic with the Style and Title of Archbishop of Westminster'. Such intolerance and sectarianism occasionally showed itself in other ways too. When in October 1851 a ninety-nine-year lease was being negotiated with a Mr Land who wished to develop Belsize Park, the Chapter expressly added a stipulation 'effectually to prohibit any building to be used for the purpose of the Roman Catholic Religion whether Ecclesiastical, Collegiate or otherwise'. At another Chapter Meeting two months later this was extended to prohibit 'the use of any building as a chapel or meeting house for any congregation of people dissenting from the Church of England'.

Rather more pleasant reading is afforded by the Loyal Addresses offered to the Queen from time to time, but they are not of any great significance except as reflecting the nation's enthusiasm at the opening of her reign and the cooling of that enthusiasm as time went on. In the first six years of her reign the Dean and Chapter addressed her six times. They congratulated her on her Accession (and on the same day condoled with the Queen-Dowager whom they described as 'a memorable instance of female excellence'); they congratulated her on her marriage 'with a Prince not only esteemed for his private virtues and personal accomplishments, but descended from a house distinguished for the most eminent services towards the Protestant faith'; they congratulated her on the birth, first of a princess and then of a prince, and in 1841 and again in 1842, on her deliverance 'from the wicked and atrocious attempt upon Your Majesty's valued Life'. It was not until 1858 that they congratulated her again (on the marriage of the Princess Royal); and in 1861 they condoled with her on the death of Prince Albert, ending with a prayerful paragraph which begins with the theologically revealing sentence: 'We earnestly pray that He Who has been pleased to send this sorrow will impart also the best comforts of His grace.'

PUBLIC WORSHIP AND THE SUNDAY EVENING SERVICES

But to return to the Abbey itself, it was through the worship and preaching therein that perhaps the greatest contribution was made to Church and nation. Unfortunately, with a notable exception to be described below, there is very little about this in the Chapter Books. The statutory services of Morning and Evening Prayer went on day after day, there were two sermons on Sunday, and lectures in Lent; the first Sunday of every month was Sacrament Sunday. In their return to the Commissioners for inquiry into the State of Cathedral and Collegiate Churches, a copy of which was entered in the Chapter Book on 21 February 1855, it is said:

> The Dean and Chapter of Westminster are deeply sensible of the great importance of maintaining the Choral Service in a manner becoming its sacred character and the noble edifice in which it is celebrated, and the appreciation of it is manifested by the crowded congregations every Sunday little if at all short of 2,000.

One important innovation had been made eight years before when, on 9 June 1847, the Chapter ordered 'that there be an Early Celebration of the Lord's Supper on such Sundays in the month as it has not been customary heretofore to celebrate the same, Provided that the average number of communicants shall not be less than seven for one year . . . and the Subdean is requested to see to the attendance of the Minor Canons'. Though the numbers attending were small for many years the required average was comfortably reached, and there was never any question of bringing the experiment to an end.

Special services, as distinct from these statutory and regular services, were (and are) the responsibility of the Dean alone; he did not need to consult the Chapter unless some extra expense was involved. So there is little in the Books, for instance, about the consecration on St Peter's Day, 1847, of four bishops for South Africa and Australia, a service of considerable significance for the revival of the missionary work of the Anglican Church—and nowhere does there appear any reference to such events as the Crimean War (though the Treasurer's audited account for 1857–8 includes 5s. for 'Forms of Prayer for use of the Abbey on the Fast Day on the occasion of the Indian Mutinies').

But there was one exception to the Chapter Book's ignorance of special services, and this deserves more detailed notice. The story begins with a Chapter Order in February 1851:

> In reference to the circumstance that a great number of foreigners may be expected to visit England and a letter received from the Royal Commission for the Management of the Great Exhibition that is to take place in May next ORDERED that the arrangements for the Public Admission to the Abbey and the providing of Guides for that purpose be referred to the Subdean, the Treasurer and the Steward: that notices in French and German be prepared; and that there be an additional service at half past six or seven o'clock in the evening on the Sundays during the continuance of the Great Exhibition; and that £200 be set aside for the expenses and remuneration of those whose attendance and services will be required.

A week or two later the Sub-Dean reported that he had 'met with two respectable persons to act as interpreters in the Abbey on the occasion of the approaching visit of Foreigners at the Great Exhibition'. The Chapter agreed to their being paid 26s. a week, and approved the expenditure of £6. 5s. for tickets 'for the deposit of Sticks and Umbrellas of Visitors to the Abbey'. The services were duly held and were a marked success, but the Chapter set its face resolutely against repeating them, and gave their reasons to the Commissioners inquiring into the State of Cathedral and Collegiate Churches. In the return entered in the Chapter Book in February 1855 they say:

> Her Majesty's Commissioners are pleased to allude to the additional services celebrated on Sunday evenings at 7 o'clock during the summer months of the year 1851 and to add the

suggestion that 'perhaps it might be resumed'. Before Her Majesty's Commissioners come to any conclusion upon this point the Dean and Chapter of Westminster feel it due to themselves to observe in correction of the statement contained in the report, that there are already 3 Services in Westminster Abbey daily (at 8, 10 and 3) and that on every Sunday there is scarcely the space of 2½ hours between 8 a.m. and 5 p.m. during which the Church is unoccupied, the Servants being on duty above seven hours in the day.

For the permanent addition of a fourth service on every Sunday during the summer months no little additional strength throughout the establishment would be required, and considerable expense would be incurred. Without speaking of the additional duty which would devolve upon the Dean and Canons whose office it is to preach, additional Minor Canons, Lay Vicars and Choristers would be necessary who must be remunerated for their services.

It is true that the experiment of an Evening Service at 7 o'clock was tried with great success and good effect in 1851, a year of more than ordinary excitement, but the Dean and Chapter were then indebted to many for friendly assistance . . . but feel . . . it would be unreasonable to expect permanently such aid. . . .

Having stated these facts for the consideration of H.M. Commissioners the Dean and Chapter will only add that they trust they shall never be found unwilling to exert themselves for the spiritual edification of those who may attend Divine Service in Westminster Abbey.

There the matter rested for the moment—but not for long. At the end of 1856 Trench was installed Dean, and the following summer he wrote to his wife from Cuddesdon: '. . . There are calls on all sides since Exeter Hall has been opened, "Why not the Abbey?" I heartily wish we could do something even this year, and am very much inclined to try.'

He did, and with success. No doubt he had informal discussions with other members of the Chapter, and on Sunday, 22 November, five men were employed (at 2s. each) to count the persons attending the morning and evening services. On 3 December the Chapter agreed to the Dean's proposals, and the following Order was made:

ORDERED that there shall be a Sunday Evening Service in the Nave of the Abbey for six months from the first Sunday in January: the Service shall be the usual evening Service with a Sermon, the Dean to make arrangements for the Preachers and to communicate with the Chapter thereon from time to time; and that the Dean, the

Subdean, the Treasurer, the Steward and Dr. Cureton be a Committee to make the arrangements.

The Committee had only four weeks in which to do what was necessary—and that was considerable. But a choir was got together, gas-lighting was installed, £244 worth of carpenter's work was done, £141 worth of matting was bought; three policemen were hired and a large number of chairs from the Crystal Palace; in addition, Psalm 100 was printed on large posters which were then mounted on calico, roughly framed and, on the day, hung up on the Nave pillars. The Dean himself preached on the first occasion, and his peroration was as follows:

One word, my brethren, in conclusion. Christ gave us a token of His Kingdom, that in it the Gospel was preached to the poor. There are some of these poor here present. Would they were many times more numerous! Let me say, in my own name and in the name of my brethren, a word to them. It is this. Others we cannot hinder from coming here; but it is you that we had chiefly in our eyes when this service was designed. The fact that you are poor, that you are humble, it may be meanly clad, only makes you the more welcome to us. Tell your friends and neighbours the same; bring them here with you. Bring not those who are church-goers already, for there is little gained in this; but bring, if you can, the ignorant, the careless, and the profane. You sometimes complain that the rich shut you out from the churches. If you would come here in such numbers as to shut out them from the evening service of this Abbey, we should only be the better pleased, and should thank God that the purpose for which these services were commenced—namely, the preaching of the Gospel to the poor—was in the act of being fulfilled.

The next Sunday it was the Lord John Thynne's turn, and he preached on the vision of Habakkuk, and said:

We have taken the prophet for our example. We have watched, we have prayed for a right direction and a wise decision; and now, brethren, we essay to fulfil the command which the prophet received. We have determined to throw the doors of this house of God open for a fourth time every Lord's day, in the hope that they who, for reasons best known to themselves, cannot make it convenient to come within the sound of the generous gospel of peace at other times, may at this hour be persuaded to accept the invitation which is heartily given them to come within these sacred walls, and there receive the message which the Lord, Who came to redeem them out of bondage, and to enlist them in to the service of their merciful God, has left for their comfort and encouragement through life.

In a letter to his son written during the following week the Dean wrote:

Many of our arrangements last Sunday were a manifest improvement on those of that preceding: the pulpit far better placed, against a pillar; the amount of the draught and cold air much diminished by addition of curtains; more chairs, more matting, and perfect order and quietness in the admission of the people. This I know as an eye-witness and on the same authority I can say that the number of poor, meanly, shabbily dressed people was very large, much larger than on the first occasion. The sermon, admirably delivered, was a plain and earnest and solemn inculcation of some fundamental Gospel truths. The Psalm was not so well known to the people, and the effect of it not so grand. Altogether we have very much to thank God for, and, with His blessing, this may be the beginning of a great work.

It certainly was, and Sunday after Sunday the congregation of two thousand came, filling the Nave to capacity. More Psalms (1, 15, 104, 148), an evening hymn and Luther's hymn were printed to be mounted on more calico and hung up on the pillars, and 2,000 chairs were ordered. One thousand came from the Crystal Palace Company and 1,000 (very improbably) from M. Obert in Paris at the price of 2s. 6d. per chair delivered to Westminster. The services ended, as planned, at the beginning of July, but in the late autumn the Chapter decided that they should start again on the first Sunday in January, and at Dr Wordsworth's suggestion they ordered another 100 chairs 'similar to those in use at St Paul's' and that small hymnbooks should be provided—the first time the word 'hymnbook' appears in the Chapter Books. Thereafter the services were held every year from January to the end of June, and in July the Dean and Chapter would reward the voluntary choir with a dinner. Among the Treasurer's papers is preserved the bill for the dinner for thirty-eight on 20 July 1859, and it is reminiscent of Parson Woodforde at his most expansive:

> 4 Dishes of Turbot and Salmon and Lobster Sauce
> 4 Tureens of Soup
> 1 Haunch of Mutton, etc.
> 1 Edgebone of Boiled Beef
> 1 Forequarter of Lamb
> 1 Fine York Ham, glazed and garnished
> 4 Roast Fowls

> 2 Boiled Fowls
> 1 Large Pigeon and Rump Steak Pie
> 2 Dishes of Lobster Cutlets
> 2 Geese, Stuffing, etc.
> 2 Ducklings, ditto
> 1 Plum Pudding with Custard Sauce
> 1 Cabinet Pudding with Custard Sauce
> 2 Dishes of Lobsters
> 4 Apricot and Raspberry and Currant Pies
> 4 Moulds of Jellies
> 4 ditto of Blankmange
> 2 Salads, dressing, etc.
> 2 fine framed Cucumbers
> 2 dishes of French beans
> 1 ditto of new carrots
> 6 ditto best Potatoes
> 4 ditto Peas
> With Sauces (various), Brown Bread and Butter, Cheese,
> cakes and choice fruit, the total bill was £20. 7s.

Equally monumental, though in a different way, was the gigantic pulpit of magnesia limestone and grey Derbyshire marble which was erected in the Nave in 1862. Designed by Scott, it bore the inscription:

THIS PULPIT IS PRESENTED TO
THE DEAN AND CHAPTER OF WESTMINSTER
BY A FEW FRIENDS IN GRATEFUL COMMEMORATION OF
THE OPENING OF THE NAVE FOR PUBLIC WORSHIP AND PREACHING,
JANUARY, 1858.

As men say, the Dean and Chapter had certainly started something. The chief credit must go to Trench, but it was Stanley who reaped the harvest and made that pulpit one of the most significant in the land by inviting to it men of great gifts whom the Canons would neither have dared nor desired to invite. The following is entered in the Chapter Book, 25 June 1864:

The Dean having this day communicated to the Chapter a list of Preachers selected by him for the Special Evening Services in the Abbey for the ensuing month and that list containing the name of one of the contributors to a volume entitled 'Essays and Reviews' which has been unanimously censured by the Bishops of the Church of England in 1861 and subsequently severely animadverted upon by many of the Bishops in their Charges to the Clergy of their respective Dioceses as containing doctrines repugnant to the received Faith of the Church the Canons in Chapter assembled unanimously represented to the Dean their belief that such a selection would create distrust in the minds of the great majority of the members of the Church as well as deter many eminent persons from rendering assistance at the Special Services in Westminster Abbey they therefore respectfully requested the Dean to cancel the selection of the writer so connected with the said Volume and the Dean having declined to accede to their request or to pledge himself not to select as preachers other contributors to the said Volume the Canons feel it their painful duty to record their remonstrance and to disclaim all responsibility in the selection of Preachers at such Special Services.

Stanley is supposed to have said: 'You are acting entirely according to your sense of duty in doing as you do. I am acting from the same sense of duty in insisting on his name. You may sign the protest; but there is one thing you cannot do, and that is, make me quarrel with you for doing so.'

In any event, no more was heard of the matter. The objectionable George Frederick Temple preached—and so subsequently did F. D. Maurice and Benjamin Jowett, and that Nave Pulpit was established as one of the finest ornaments of the Anglican Church for the next fifty years.

18

The Reign of Dean Stanley
1864—1881

IF the credit for the inauguration of the popular Sunday evening
services should go to Trench, it was Trench's successor who saw to
the reaping of the harvest and who more than any other single
individual was responsible for making Westminster Abbey what it
is to-day in the eyes of the multitudes who visit it. On any reckoning
Arthur Penrhyn Stanley must be accounted one of the great Victor-
ians. Born within a few months of the battle of Waterloo he was 48
when he came to Westminster and already had behind him a rich
experience which his background, education and natural gifts had
made possible for him. His father became Bishop of Norwich, his
father's eldest brother was the first Lord Stanley of Alderley, and his
idol as a boy and young man was Thomas Arnold whose pupil he
was and whose biographer he became (when still in his twenties).
He was at Oxford from 1834 to 1851—stirring years in the University
—first as an undergraduate at Balliol and then as a Fellow of University College; and after seven years as a Canon of Canterbury he
returned to Oxford as Regius Professor of Ecclesiastical History.
Strong in the head, stronger still in the heart—'we believe that your
generosity rather than your judgement links you with Mr Maurice
and Mr Jowett', wrote Liddon—an eloquent speaker and a stylish
and prolific writer (he had already published eleven major books
when he became Dean and was a frequent contributor to such journals as the *Quarterly* and *Edinburgh Reviews*) he involved himself in
many of the Church, State and university controversies of the time,
inclining towards the liberal side in each case and always seeking to
win tolerance and understanding for those whose views seemed outrageous to traditionalists and dogmatists. As Pusey put it in a
letter, 'You seem to me to take every opportunity of committing
yourself to anyone who does not believe as others.' Perhaps his
broadmindedness owed something to his having the inclination and

47 Victoria Street in the making, September 1851. View from the fields near what is now Ashley Place, showing the Abbey rising above the slums and the new street running into the 'countryside'. In the background is the Victoria Tower under construction.

48 Choral Marriage of the Rev. Arthur Thynne with Miss Kendall, Westminster Abbey, 9 July 1859.

49 View of the Abbey showing the South Transept and Chapter House before and after restoration.

Photographs presumably from the Victoria Tower at different stages of its construction.

53 Queen Victoria seated in the Coronation Chair at her Jubilee Thanksgiving Service, 21 June 1887.

54 The Funeral of Lord Tennyson, 1892.

55 Livingstone's Grave, 1873.

56 The Rev. Lord John Thynne, Canon and Sub-Dean, 1831–1881.

57 Dr George Granville Bradley, Dean of Westminster, 1881–1902.

58 Charles Gore, photographed when he was a Canon of Westminster, 1894–1902.

59 Robinson Duckworth, Canon and Sub-Dean, 1875–1911.

60 J. Armitage Robinson, Dean of Westminster, 1902–11; Dean of Wells, 1911–33; Lord High Almoner, 1906–33.

61 Herbert Edward Ryle, Bishop of Winchester, 1903–11; Dean of Westminster, 1911–25. After the painting by William Carter.

62 Adam Fox, formerly Canon of Westminster, 1941–63. From the painting by John Wheatley, A.R.A., at Magdalen College, Oxford.

63 Herbert Hensley Henson, Canon of Westminster, 1900–12; Bishop of Durham, 1920–39; d. 1947. Drawing by Aidan Savage.

64 'A British Warrior Unknown by Name or Rank'.
Vigil at the grave, 20 November 1920.

65 Bomb débris before the High Altar, 12 May 1941.

66 Her Majesty Queen Elizabeth II unveiling the commemorative stone to Sir Winston Churchill after the Battle of Britain Service, 19 September 1965. On the far right are twenty of the pilots who took part in the battle twenty-five years previously.

67 The 1953–4 Appeal. One thousand balloons released in Dean's Yard carrying 'Thank You' messages on reaching the target of one million pounds. 24 May 1954.

68 The late Sir Jacob Epstein beside his bust of William Blake after the unveiling in Poets' Corner by Sir Geoffrey Keynes. 24 November 1957.

69 Eric S. Abbott, Dean of Westminster. 1959–74.

70 The North Front and Henry VII's Chapel from an aquatint in R. Ackermann's *History of Westminster Abbey*, published in 1812.

the means to travel widely. He was the first Dean of Westminster of which it could be said that there was scarcely a country in Europe and the Near East which he had not visited at least once, and the man who was now to preside over Chapter meetings in the Jerusalem Chamber was already familiar with Jerusalem itself, as he was with Moscow and Constantinople, Cairo and Mount Athos. In 1862 he was chosen to accompany the Prince of Wales on a six-months' tour of Egypt, Palestine, Syria and Asia Minor; this was the beginning of an intimate and lifelong friendship with the Queen and her family, and also led to his marriage to the Lady Augusta Bruce, daughter of the Earl of Elgin. Stanley received and accepted Palmerston's offer of the Deanery on 8 November 1863; he married the Lady Augusta quietly in the Abbey on 23 December (her father had died the previous week), and he was installed on 9 January 1864. The Archdeacon, Canon Christopher Wordsworth, conscientiously absented himself. A traditional High Churchman, he was more than suspicious of Stanley's orthodoxy and believed that his writings were wanting in loyalty both to Holy Scripture and the Church and likely to undermine men's faith. He had accordingly published a pamphlet protesting against Stanley's appointment and had preached against it from the Abbey pulpit. It was typical of Stanley that he should have written to his wife: 'Perhaps it [Wordsworth's sermon] is to be answered by a calm reply, certainly by an invitation to dinner at the first opportunity.'

Wordsworth's protest was not the only matter to cause Stanley disquiet, and for a short time he had doubts about the usefulness of his move from Oxford to 'that Church of Tombs' (the phrase was his own in a letter to his bride shortly before their wedding). Describing his first meeting with the Canons immediately after his installation he wrote:

> I confess that I felt no elation, nothing but depression, at the prospect before me. It seemed to me as if I were going down alive into the sepulchre.
>
> I had a long conversation with Lord J. Thynne, very courteous and sensible, but opening a vista of interminable questions of the most uninteresting kind, for the discussion of which I felt totally incapable. I repeat that, as far as the actual work of the Dean is concerned, it is far more unsuited to me than that of a bishop. To lose one's time in Confirmations is bad, but to lose it in leases and warming-plans is worse.
>
> However, the deed is done, and my useful life I consider to be closed, except so far as I can snatch portions from the troubles of the office.

STANLEY'S AIMS AND ACHIEVEMENTS

But revealing as the paragraph is, it should not be taken over-seriously as an indication of Stanley's view of what lay before him. He had been much struck and inspired by a phrase in the oath he had taken at his installation, that he was 'set there for the enlargement of the Christian Church', and it became his first aim to make Westminster Abbey more and more 'the centre of religious and national life in a truly liberal spirit'. History had made the building 'the seat of royalty and the cradle of liberty' (the latter phrase a reference to the use of the Chapter House as the meeting place of early Parliaments), and Stanley conceived it as his task so to order what was done in the Abbey as to bring out as clearly as possible what its fabric and monuments showed it to be, the visual embodiment of the national Church. Though no Dean has done more to underline that the Abbey is a 'Church of Tombs' Stanley himself saw each tomb not so much as a dumb relic of a dead past but as the eloquent mouth of one who being dead yet speaketh. It was one of Stanley's achievements to enable those stones to sound and thus to bring alive to his contemporaries the lives and examples of all those who in so many ways had helped to make the national Church and to create the Christian nation. Within only four years of his coming to the Deanery he had written his encyclopaedic *Historical Memorials of Westminster Abbey* which is still an essential book of reference for anyone who wants to understand the Abbey. From time to time the Chapter Book witnesses to his interest in tombs and tablets and in making the Abbey an expression in stone of the national Church: in June 1867, for instance, it minutes the receipt of a letter from the Home Secretary sanctioning 'the erection of a Record to mark the spot where lie the remains of Elizabeth Cromwell, Mother of the Protector, Admiral Blake and others, whose bodies have been buried in Westminster Abbey and were disinterred by a Warrant of the Secretary of State, bearing the date "the 9th September 1661" '; in March 1871 the Chapter agrees to the expenditure of £30 'on the repair of grave slabs in the North Transept'; in November 1875 to 'placing a Tablet in the Abbey to the memory of John Wesley' (at a fine of £200). At the end of his life Stanley was still making the stones speak, and his last sermon was the fourth in a series (unfinished) preached on Saturday afternoons in the summer of 1881 and in the first of which he declared his intention was to take

> . . . from those who are commemorated in this Abbey some one or two persons for each of the Beatitudes who may give us something of a glimpse of what is meant by the 'pure in heart', by the 'merci-

ful', by the 'poor in spirit', by the 'peacemakers', by those who 'hunger and thirst after righteousness', and those who are persecuted for 'righteousness' sake'. If I can raise your minds to the appreciation of such virtues, if I can do this in any way so as to produce an impression upon you that we have something in life worth striving for, and that this Abbey, by its various examples, has something worth teaching, I shall not have spoken in vain.

Commemorating the good and great of the past was one thing, burying the good and great of the present was another; and Stanley strongly supported the increasing reluctance of his immediate predecessors to sanction burials in the Abbey. For one thing, the space still available was by now very limited and Stanley estimated that there was further room for no more than one hundred. He needed to be convinced of strong public support before consenting to an Abbey burial—in the case of Rowland Hill he felt himself obliged to allow public demand to override his personal judgement—and whereas there had been 169 burials in the last twenty years of the seventeenth century, there were only fifteen during Stanley's time. Of those, David Livingstone's was attended by the largest crowd ever known on such an occasion, and that of Charles Dickens took place secretly at 9.30 a.m. in the presence of only a dozen mourners. This last aroused great disappointment, both to the public at large and to the members of the Choral Foundation in particular, and the Precentor wrote in his book of 'Special Services Fees':

Read Service throughout. Organ for Introit—Interlude—and the Dead March at end. N.B. Mr. Dickens' wish that his Funeral shd. be strictly private was adhered to. Only the Dean, 2 Canons, the Precentor, 2 Minor Canons, the Receiver and Chapter Clerk (with the Clerk of Works) being present. No Fittings given, or worn by Mourners. *This* extraordinary and exceptional.

Little was done in Stanley's time to forward the idea of building an extension to the Abbey to house the monuments of the nation's great men. At the Sub-Dean's request Gilbert Scott had produced in 1853 a design for a 'wide and lofty Cloister' running from the Chapter House to Great College Street behind the houses in Abingdon Street, and in 1863 he put forward a still more ambitious scheme for a national Campo Santo. The estimated cost—well over half a million pounds—put the scheme out of court, and during Stanley's time statues, busts and tablets continued to be erected in the Abbey though the problem of diminishing space was always in the minds of himself and the Chapter. They found a very temporary solution for it in the form of a number of memorial windows (twenty-one between 1860 and 1890) and five floor brasses. It was not until after Stanley's death that the idea of a new building was revived. Throughout the 'eighties the subject was under public discussion, various plans were put forward, and in 1890 a Royal Commission was appointed to

> inquire into the present state of the Abbey of Westminster as regards the facilities which it offers for providing for the interment, and otherwise preserving the memory, of the most illustrious of our subjects, in the manner which has been customary for many centuries; and to hear evidence, and to consider plans for providing at the Abbey or elsewhere, an additional place for memorials, should such a provision appear necessary.

The Commission put forward two good schemes, and there was immense public debate for several years. But Parliament could not make up its mind and all came to nothing; the problem remains unsolved to this day. (An excellent account of the problem and the various designs put forward by Scott, Pearson and others is given in an article 'Imperial Valhalla' by A. D. C. Hyland, in the *Journal of the Society of Architectural Historians*, October 1962, Vol. XXI, No. 3, pp. 129–39.)

Though Gilbert Scott and his successors were disappointed of their hopes in this matter, better success attended the Abbey's concern for the Chapter House which the Government had been using for centuries as a Public Record office. Scott had persuaded the authorities to allow him to investigate what lay behind the cupboards and shelves, the gallery, staircase and false ceiling with which the building's interior had been masked for so long. In his *Gleanings from Westminster Abbey* he gives a steel plate illustrating the interior as it then was and a description of it as it had been originally; and he concluded: 'Let us hope that the Government will recollect the conditions of five centuries back,—that they should keep the building in repair, and that they will give it up to the Chapter, with a restoration fund proportioned both to the extent of the dilapidations and the merits of the building.' Scott persuaded Trench to take the matter up with the authorities, and later found an enthusiastic supporter in Stanley, who succeeded in rousing the support of so strong a body of informed opinion that he was able to obtain a government grant for the completion of the Chapter House's restoration. But the Chapter House remained in the Government's possession, though Stanley extracted agreement to his suggestion that it should be open to the public. The suggestion is made in a letter from Stanley to Gladstone dated 3 February 1872, a copy of which is preserved in the Chapter Book, and in it the Dean asks the Government to consider

> that there should be some one stationed there, Policeman or Guard of some kind, to protect the more delicate parts of the building from the injury to which they would inevitably be exposed by the free admission of the Public, including (as this must of necessity be the case in London) mischievous boys, eccentric or crazy persons, and relic hunters. Our staff of Guides is so completely occupied in the other parts of the Abbey that we have none to spare for the purpose—and as the Chapter House is still in the possession of the Crown its preservation necessarily devolves on the Government.

Though it could be argued that Stanley's enthusiasm for the Abbey's stones had the effect of perpetuating and hardening the public's idea of it as a national mausoleum, he himself never lost sight of the fact that his overriding concern was to make the Abbey 'the centre of religious and national life in a truly liberal spirit'. This fact is fully documented in G. W. Prothero's *Life and Letters of Dean Stanley* (the two volumes are most readable, and make excellent bedside books for those with a taste for ecclesiastical Victoriana; included is Stanley's account of the only dream he considered worth recording, that he had been elected pope and had discussed at the Athenaeum the vexatious question of what name he should take!), and it is sufficient here to recall briefly that he invited clergymen of all shades of opinion to preach in the Abbey (though Pusey, Keble and Liddon felt bound to refuse to occupy the pulpit to which such 'rationalists' as F. D. Maurice and Benjamin Jowett were also invited), and that he inaugurated a series of annual missionary 'Lectures' and in this way brought in Freechurchmen and laymen to speak in the Abbey. This last experiment was altogether too far in advance of the times, and although the lecturers included Max Müller and a Moderator of the General Assembly of the Church of Scotland it was viewed with little warmth even in liberal and Freechurch quarters, and the lectures were discontinued after seven had been given.

Much more fruitful was the encouragement Stanley gave to the use of the Abbey for 'special services'. Before his time the Abbey had known few special services beyond marriages and funerals, an occasional consecration of bishops and a still more occasional coronation. Even the celebration of the 800th Anniversary of the Confessor's Foundation of the Abbey on 28 December 1865 was confined to choral Morning Service (Matins to the third collect, followed by Holy Communion with sung responses to the Ten

x

Commandments and the Creed sung to Turle in D), with the festive excitements confined to an introit with words by Archdeacon Wordsworth and the music by the niece of the late Canon Temple Frere, a commemorative sermon by the Dean, and the singing of the 'Hallelujah Chorus' by an augmented choir (with the assistance of one trumpeter and an extra organ blower). A luncheon was given in the Jerusalem Chamber and College Hall (at a cost to Chapter funds of £18. 11s. 4d.) and Evensong followed at 3.0 (MAGNIFICAT and NUNC DIMITTIS to Cooke in G, and the anthem 'Cry aloud and shout' by Croft). Altogether a very modest celebration, but a large congregation attended the Morning Service, and an even larger one the service on Christmas Day the following year, which Stanley arranged as a commemoration of the 800th anniversary of the coronation of William the Conqueror.

These were not strictly speaking 'special services', but from 1867 onwards records begin to appear of 'Festival of the Church Missionary Society in the Nave', 'Service for the Church of England's Lay Helpers' Association', 'Special Service on Ascension Day in the Nave at 7 p.m.', 'Service for the Bishop of London's Fund', and so on. Provided that the sponsoring organizations were missionary in aim and non-partisan in spirit Stanley encouraged the use of the Abbey for such services, and in 1870 there were four in the month of May alone. In the following month there was another special service of a different kind when Stanley arranged what a later generation called 'a corporate communion' for members of the body of scholars appointed to revise the Authorized Version of the Bible, on the occasion of their first meeting. Stanley's invitation was accepted by all the members, but since some were Freechurchmen and one a Unitarian Stanley was widely criticized and certain sections of the religious Press exploded with odium theologicum. Four years earlier Stanley had provoked a similar outburst—on that occasion by *refusing* to allow the Abbey to be used for a special service for the Pan-Anglican Synod of 1867, on the grounds that the Synod was likely to be used for an illiberal condemnation of Bishop Colenso. Another 'bold innovation' for which Stanley was strongly criticized was the performance of Bach's St Matthew Passion in the Nave in 1871. The Passion was sung in the course of Evensong (Part I in place of the Psalms, Part II after the Dean's sermon), and one church newspaper produced the following report:

The Dean of Westminster, on the evening of Maundy Thursday, gave a grand performance of Bach's Passion Music in the Abbey, by way of counterpoise to such devotions as the Reproaches, the Three Hours, and the Stations. The result was exactly what might have been expected. The church was crammed, and the audience—congregation would be a misnomer—was very much the same as at any other concert. Dean Stanley, of course, took the opportunity of airing his peculiar views as to the Atonement, the chief purpose of which, he seemed to think, was to furnish artists of all kinds, not to say graphic writers, with subjects.

But those who so moaned were a small minority, the experiment was repeated in the following year, and it was not long before the Abbey's example was being copied in cathedrals and other churches all over the country.

Meanwhile, and partly as a result of the Dean's many-sided efforts and the publicity given to some of them, the Abbey became more and more an attraction for sight-seers; in June 1868 the Chapter sanctioned the appointment of an extra attendant on Saturdays during the summer season, and Stanley estimated the number of visitors on Easter Monday 1870 to have been 9,000. The Dean himself delighted to show visitors round, and enjoyed doing this for a Thames lighterman as much as for the Queen of the Sandwich Islands (though he later recalled that of all the distinguished visitors she was 'the one who expressed the greatest interest in the Abbey'). From Easter 1870 onwards the whole of the church was open to the public on Mondays free of charge; Stanley would have liked it to have been open free every day of the year, but recognized the need to charge for admittance to the Royal Chapels in order to pay the staff needed to guard the building. Then, as now, the church even more than the Chapter House required protection against 'mischievous boys, eccentric or crazy persons, and relic hunters'.

STANLEY IN CHAPTER AND THE NEW SACRARIUM

While Stanley was thus increasing the Abbey's stature and fame in the eyes of the world at large, what was happening within the little world of the precincts, at the Chapter meetings, and in the offices of such officials as the Receiver-General and the Clerk of Works? Nothing that Stanley did to make the Abbey a greater church lessened the responsibilities of the Canons or the work of administration; rather the reverse, not only because new ventures entailed more work but chiefly because Stanley himself was not much help when it came down to the minutiae of mundane existence. He groaned that the discussion of 'leases and warming plans' was a waste of time. One sympathizes, but also suspects an element of self-excuse. Even his admiring biographer admitted that 'he never quite appreciated the difference between eighteenpence and one-and-eightpence', that

> a Dean possessed of greater financial capacity would undoubtedly have arranged for better terms for the Abbey when its property was transferred to the Ecclesiastical Commissioners, and that a Dean more qualified to deal with practical details of business would not have allowed Westminster School to become possessed of a portion of the Abbey property, the loss of which clouded and embittered the last few months of his life.

Not that it should be concluded that Stanley had nothing to contribute to Chapter meetings. He was presumably not uninterested in the state of the Deanery stables, which matter was referred to the Sub-Dean at Stanley's second Chapter, upon which the Sub-Dean had recommendations to make the following month, and which was again referred to the Sub-Dean five months later. And certain matters which engaged the Chapter's attention in the following years reflect Stanley's particular interests: the calendaring of the muniments; the restoration of the portrait of Richard II (the Chapter Book contains a copy of the letter in which George Richmond described how the cleaning of the picture had been done); the state of the 'gurgoyle [sic] at the S. corner of the Dean's Library'; the arrangements for 'Illumination on Tuesday 27th instant, being the day of National Thanksgiving for the restoration to health of H.R.H. the Prince of Wales' (February 1872); the borrowing of Prayer Books belonging to the Abbey for use by the Dean himself when officiating at the marriage of the Duke of Edinburgh to Her Imperial Highness the Grand Duchess Marie Alexandrovna of Russia at St Petersburg in March 1874; the return by the University of Oxford of two marble pillars standing at the entrance to the Ashmolean Museum, and originally forming 'two of the pillars supporting the Altar at the head of Henry VII's Chapel'. Stanley was a man who was impatient of what he called 'the materialism of the Altar and the Sacristy', but he interested himself keenly in the restoration of the Sacrarium and of the Screen behind the High Altar, seeing to it that Armstead's figure of Moses looked towards the statesmen in the North Transept and that of David towards the Poets' Corner (Prothero describes the erection of these figures as Stanley's 'one piece of ritualism'); and on 9 May 1870 the Chapter recorded their grateful thanks to the Dean and Lady Augusta Stanley 'for their kind, appropriate and costly gift of Porphyry for the circles in the pavement in front of the Altar'.

The restoration of the Sacrarium and the rebuilding of the Altar

Screen had been occupying the attention of the Chapter and the Surveyor for a number of years before Stanley came to the Abbey. Scott's designs for new rails for the Sacrarium were accepted in April 1856, but things moved slowly until 1862 when the following minute was made:

> The Report of the Subdean of his conference with Mr. G. Gilbert Scott on the subject of the Reredos and Altar Table . . . being considered ORDERED that Mr. Scott's plan for restoring the Reredos to a certain line in Marble and Alabaster be adopted, and that Mr. Poole's estimate for the same be referred to Mr. Scott for examination—and that Mr. Scott be requested to prepare a plan for a new Altar Table in cedar, using the present black Marble slab adding to the length and width of the same by Mosaic work—the works to be done accordingly and the expense to be paid from the Ornamental Fund.

Thirteen months later (22 July 1863) the Chapter approved the estimates for the Reredos, Altar Table 'and general restoration within the Altar Rails', but ordered 'that no new Cartoons be furnished but Leonardi [sic] de [sic] Vinci's representation of the Last Supper to be adhered to'. When Stanley arrived the work had begun—there appeared to be enough money after the Second International Exhibition of 1862 had brought exceptional numbers of visitors to the Abbey—and in March 1865 an agreement was sealed between the Dean and Chapter and Mr Antonio Salviati whereby the latter agreed 'to make in enamel mosaic a picture of the Last Supper to be placed on the Altar Screen' for £550. Two years later it was agreed that Armstead be paid £70 for designs 'for the fourteen subjects on the frieze of the Altar Screen', and a fortnight later the Chapter ordered 'A Report on the Expenditure of the Ornamental Fund' to be entered in the Chapter Book.

This report was drawn up by the Sub-Dean on his relinquishing the office of Treasurer, and shows that in the thirty years of Thynne's stewardship of this Fund a total of £22,000 had been spent on the restoration of the interior of the central part of the Abbey—£8,761 on the reconstruction of the Choir, £3,320 on stained glass, £1,026 on the organ, £380 on the pulpit, £882 on the Lantern, £1,488 on the Screens, £568 on the Sacrarium and £4,838 on the Reredos. (The same document also records that the figures on Scott's archway entrance into Dean's Yard, including the busts of Queen Victoria and Prince Albert, cost £882. 8s. 11½d.) The Sub-Dean's report is not however to be taken to mean that the work on the Sacrarium and Reredos was finished. In February 1868 the Chapter was ordering that 'the framework of the altar-piece be proceeded with before all else'; Armstead was still working at his figures (he was to be paid £375 for Moses, St Peter and St Paul in March 1870); and it was not until Easter Day 1873 that Stanley was able to preach a sermon in which he said that it is meet and right and our bounden duty, to give thanks to God at all times and in all places . . .

chiefly on this day, when we have brought to its desired completion the work which has been wrought out with such loving care by those who planned and by those who executed it. . . . We, God's humble servants, entirely desire His fatherly goodness to accept it as our oblation, our Easter offering. 'The earth is the Lord's, and the fulness thereof'; everything that there is of beauty in sculpture, poetry, painting or architecture, everything that there is of skill in mechanical contrivance, has its religious side, has the link, if it can be found, which binds it round the throne of God and the gates of heaven. The alabaster from our Midland quarries, the marble from our Cornish rocks, mosaic colours from the isles of Venice, the porphyry from the shores of the Nile or of the Bosphorus, the jewels from the far-off coasts of Asia and America, combine as truly now in the service of Him who has 'given us the heathen for our possession, the uttermost parts of the earth for our inheritance', as did the gold of Ophir and the sandalwood of India for the temple of Solomon.

But even that was not the end; as late as 2 March 1875 the Chapter was ordering 'the Reredos to be completed'!

WARMING PLANS AND OTHER INTERMINABLE QUESTIONS

Meanwhile, but very much more speedily, work of a very different kind was being undertaken. In place of the old coke-burning stoves a central heating system was installed. The Sub-Dean had spoken to Stanley of 'warming plans' at the Dean's installation; Stanley thought such a matter a waste of time, but it fell to him not only to preside at a number of Chapter meetings at which it was discussed but also to correspond with the Ecclesiastical Commissioners on the subject. The negotiations for the taking over of the Dean and Chapter's estates were now in an advanced stage, and it was felt that the Commissioners should therefore contribute towards the cost of the central heating since they were about to deprive the Abbey of so much of its resources. In June 1865 Stanley was able to report that the Commissioners were willing to find up to £3,800 for the purpose, and a month later the Chapter were considering the respective merits of two schemes; it was minuted that 'Mr. Haden's was preferred, the plans of Mr. Woodcock presenting such objections that the Dean and Chapter would rather defer the question than consent to its adoption in the Abbey'. Messrs G. H. Haden & Sons of Trowbridge were therefore awarded the contract; it took Haden fourteen months to make the necessary survey, and to produce specifications and estimates. These were accepted by the Chapter in August 1866, and in only a little over six months the work was finished and the new heating system in operation in the main part of the church. Shortly afterwards Haden was ready with plans and estimates for its extension to Henry VII's Chapel. He backed them up with a report (entered in the Chapter Book) in which he gave tabulated columns of temperature readings taken three times a day in the first fortnight of March 1867 shortly after the 'warming' system had come into operation. They showed that whereas the average midday temperature outside had been 37 degrees and that in Henry VII's Chapel 42 degrees, it had been 56 and 60 degrees respectively on the floor of the Nave and up in the Clerestory. Further, while the cost of coal for the new boiler had worked out at 15s. a day, the old stoves had consumed 26s. worth of coke a day. The Chapter was understandably impressed and ordered the extension of the system to the Chapel right away, and in the following years it was extended elsewhere—to St Faith's Chapel, to the Jerusalem Chamber, to the Receiver-General's office. With its panelling and timber roof the Jerusalem Chamber's heating by hot pipes seemed a risky business, but the Dean and Chapter were reassured by a letter from Haden in which he begged 'respectfully to say that the system of hot-water circulation in use at Westminster Abbey is the open system and under no circumstances can the heat of the water exceed 212 degrees but generally in full work it is not more than 180 degrees. We have put Lucifer matches on the 1st flow pipe from boilers of similar design and left them there for several days uninjured.' All in all the new heating system was a great success.

Stanley had professed distaste for the idea when he first heard of it, and he was much more enthusiastic about the Sacrarium and the new Reredos for the High Altar. But if he was compelled to suffer the tedious slowness of the artists and craftsmen engaged on the latter he could not but be impressed with the great efficiency of the new heating apparatus and the speed with which it had been installed. And in his letter to Gladstone of 3 February 1872, to which reference has already been made, Stanley included a paragraph recommending the extension of the Abbey's warming apparatus to the restored Chapter House.

Central heating was not the only technological 'improvement' in which the Dean and Chapter were interested. They bought a 'mowing machine' in 1867 and another in 1875; they had the entrance to Dean's Yard 'paved with Val de Travers asphalt' in 1870; they decided to instal extended gaslighting in the Abbey in 1873, and at the same time equipped themselves with seven 'Dicks Chemical Fire Engines (*l'Extincteur*)'; in 1877 they had 'the great Tank in the South West Tower painted with Pulford's Magnetic Paint', and in the same year they granted permission to Dr Bridge to 'connect with the water main the small engine by which the Organ put up by him for Choir Rehearsals may be blown'.

But not all such 'industrial improvements' were welcomed. In 1867 the Chapter petitioned the House of Commons against a Bill promoted by the Gaslight and Coke Company on the grounds that 'the promoters have not fulfilled their promise of removing the Gasworks from Horseferry Road which are prejudicial to the Precincts and College'. The following year they gave permission to 'Messrs. Fahrmilow to set up a Steam Engine at their Premises in Carey Street', but in 1877 they successfully objected when the Royal Aquarium Society in Tothill St. made an application for a licence 'to keep 350 gallons of Petroleum in How's Patent Safety Tanks'. Equally successfully had they objected in 1870 when the Metropolitan Street Tramway Company was applying to Parliament for a Bill 'to authorize the Company to make certain Tramways'; the Dean and Chapter objected on the grounds 'that the Memorial Statue in the Broad Sanctuary will be required for the purposes of the undertaking'.

A few years earlier there had been anxiety for the Abbey when the Metropolitan District Railway obtained powers to build the underground line which still runs beneath Parliament Square and Broad Sanctuary and therefore close to the North West Tower. The Chapter consulted a civil engineer, Mr George Bidder, and were sufficiently reassured by his report in June 1864 to decide not to oppose the plan but to enter into an agreement with the Company. However, the matter came up again in September 1865 when the Company found it necessary to ask for permission to make a deviation from the original plan which would bring the tunnel a little closer to the Abbey. Provided that the Company would be 'responsible for any damage to the Abbey during construction or after' the Chapter would raise no objection. But doubts still lurked in the minds of some of its members and Bidder again was consulted. On 22 January 1866 he gave an assurance that the railway would be no danger to the fabric, cause no vibration and not interfere with the services, 'but for the greater satisfaction of the Dean and Chapter it was arranged that certain experiments should be made by Mr. Bidder and that he should submit a report at the Audit Chapter'.

The report was duly discussed on 8 February and ordered to be entered into the Chapter Book. It takes the form of two letters from Mr Bidder and his assistant, a Mr Kingsbury, describing the experiments which had been made at various places in the Marylebone Road, in Marylebone Parish Church and in the adjoining school, to test the effect of the trains passing in the tunnel nearby. Kingsbury had gone to St Marylebone Church at 5.45 in the morning of 6 February and had spent the greater part of the next one-and-a-half hours in its pulpit which

> stands upon a central pillar and is provided with the usual staircase, the whole being of wood, but, either on account of its form or because it is so nicely balanced or both, it is extremely sensitive to tremor; indeed, at first, with the delicate means employed for making the observations, I found that a very slight movement of my head even was quite sufficient to induce a vibration in the structure, and great care was needed to avoid this and similar sources of error. . . . At the time the experiments were made Vehicles passed but occasionally along the Road and I had several good opportunities of hearing the sound of the Road traffic and of the trains, the former clear and distinct, the latter dull and heavy and hardly attracting attention. . . . The vibration caused by the former was sharp, fitful, irregular, and transient, while that of the Trains was longer in duration, more uniform in character and apparently isochronous, besides which it was capable of introducing that kind of tremor which is felt in the hands and feet—this was the case in the pulpit, reading desk, and Clerk's desk, but not on the floor of the Church—in each instance the character of the vibrations reminds me . . . of that produced by the playing of the pedal pipes of an Organ in a Cathedral or large Music Hall.

Bidder himself began his letter by drawing attention to the 'leading differences which exist in the position, soil, and construction of the Marylebone Railway . . . when compared with the circumstances and modes of construction proposed for the carrying out of the Metropolitan District Railway in the vicinity of the Abbey'. He then proceeded to describe how little noise and vibration he had perceived in various places in the Marylebone Road:

> and I would specially remark that this was the case in the Counting house of a Wine Merchant situate not only within 16 feet of the Railways but also sunk beneath the level of the adjoining Street; and although the proprietor stated that his bottles standing upon the shelves at so short a distance from the Railway occasionally

jingled in the absence of the Street traffic this was not at all the case in his vaults which are about 70 feet farther off and he could not perceive any injurious action to the Wines or to the Building even in such close proximity as that first named.

After taking account of the experiments both of himself and Kingsbury, Bidder summed up:

On the whole, therefore, and even if the evidence of vibration and noise had been as distinct and marked as I am prepared to say it is not, and bearing in mind the difference of soil, the presence of water in it, the mode of construction and the special precautions proposed to be adopted in the neighbourhood of the Abbey, my confidence in the absolute safety of this venerable Edifice remains unabated, as well as the absence of all interruption and ground for annoyance in the conduct of the services—indeed, in conclusion, I would observe that so far as regards vibration it will never, in my opinion, be comparable to the effect upon the foundations which must result from the action of every strong gale of wind which has operated upon the Western Towers since the date of their erection.

The Chapter was satisfied, decided that the proposed deviation of the railway should be agreed to, and went on to the next item on the agenda—a letter from Minor Canon Flood Jones asking for the adoption of a uniform method of pointing the Psalms, for additional strength for the Bass voices in the Choir and for ten guineas a year to be spent on the purchase of 'many of the new anthems very generally in use by other Choirs'. The last two requests were 'declined' (the word customarily used when the Chapter turned down a suggestion) and it was left to the Dean to decide about the pointing.

It all sounds very tedious, part of that 'vista of interminable questions of the most uninteresting kind' for the discussion of which the Regius Professor of Ecclesiastical History had felt himself totally incapable on becoming Dean of Westminster. But the very variety of the minutiae of Chapter business must have impressed upon Stanley that if as Dean his main task was 'the enlargement of the Christian Church' then he would often have to find the opportunity to carry out that task in and through a committee discussion of matters which, though seemingly remote or trivial, were clearly of pressing importance to those who asked the Dean and Chapter to do something about this, that and the other: a Miss Winterton writes and complains of the removal of the pew in Hinckley Church 'belonging to the George Hotel'; a Minor Canon reports that 'his kitchen chimney had been on fire that morning for the fourth or fifth time since he came to reside in the Cloisters, although it was swept every 6 or 8 weeks'; an estimate for '£200 for the supply of a Tuba stop' is accepted, and as soon as the work has been done the Organist wants 'a third man to blow the bellows on Sundays'; the Head Master complains of conditions in Little Dean's Yard, and the Chapter orders that the wages of Jackson the Stoker be increased to 24s. a week and that he be 'required to sweep the Yard daily and to send away all loungers and idle boys and girls loitering in Little Dean's Yard'; a subscription is asked 'towards the expense of the proposed reception of a Statue of King Alfred by the inhabitants of Wantage'; the inhabitants of Dean's Yard want snow cleared from the roofs and fronts of their houses by the Clerk of Works's staff; the residents of Malvern complain of 'an inclosure made recently on the summit of the Malvern Hills'; a Lay-Vicar is charged with irregular attendance and 'intoxication at a public dinner at Willis's Rooms'; Canon Charles Kingsley wants nine new sash windows for the north side of his house and a water-closet on the top floor; certain 'Humanatarians'[sic] wish to erect a lecture hall in Horseferry Road; the Precentor wants an extra window for his nursery; there is a request for 'a deed of enfranchisement of a Close of Copyhold Land at Barleythorpe in the Manor of Oakham containing 2 acres, 0 poles, 20 perches or thereabouts and called Lord Harborough's Breeches'; the family of the late Canon Nepean are to have handed over to them 'the umbrella-stand in Canon Kingsley's house'; the Sacrist wants thirty kneelers for the Choir at 1s. each; there is a request that the Dean and Chapter will become annual subscribers to the Mathon Agricultural Society, and another that they will subscribe towards 'a suitable room for week-day services, etc.' at Alconbury; Mrs Stallard, 'a tenant at Belsize going out at Christmas', wants to 'remain in the possession of the greenhouse until the weather will permit of the removal of her plants'.

SCOTT, PEARSON AND THE STATE OF THE FABRIC

Such matters kept the members of the Chapter in touch with the hopes, fears and foibles of ordinary men and women—including those of themselves. But they must have seemed so many straws to a camel that was more particularly conscious of other burdens. One of these was the perennial problem of keeping the Abbey's structure sound and its fabric in good repair. It was like trying to maintain a crumbling sea wall; before one gap was fully plugged the water began to come through somewhere else at an increasingly alarming rate. Windows were a source of constant anxiety, and a Chapter minute of 22 January 1866 hints at the quantity of glass their repair required:

The Report of the Clerk of Works in reference to the damage done to the Clerestory windows on the South side of the Abbey by the late gales and the continual breakage of the windows on the North side by stones thrown from St. Margaret's Churchyard, and suggesting the purchase of glass by the Crate, being read ORDERED that the windows be repaired and that glass be purchased by the Crate as suggested.

But much more troublesome was the stonework itself. No sooner had the majority of the flying buttresses been made safe than there was trouble with the gable of the South Transept and with the Cloisters. The state of the latter became urgent when the tracery of one of the arches of the South Cloister fell down one night in March 1867. But before the necessary work on the Cloisters could be finished Scott had to report, in November 1869, 'the seriously decayed stonework of the pinnacles of the North Porch'; and the following March 'the falling of a piece of rotten stone from the lower angle of the North Porch and the probable fall of the capital' emphasized the seriousness of the new danger. And so began Scott's work on the North Transept Front. In fact, his interest was limited to the 'restoration' of the three portals, a work into which he poured all his enthusiasm and which absorbed his attention on and off for the rest of his life. But there were other matters demanding his attention also; he had many other buildings for which he was responsible, and in the early 'seventies his health was beginning to fail. The result was that much that ought to have been done on the Abbey was left undone. How serious could be the consequences of a few years of neglect became evident at the Audit Chapter in March 1878 when it was ordered that Scott's attention should be called

to the condition of the upper part of the North Front of the Transept—also to the ruinous state of the southern Clerestory windows and wall between them, part of which has lately fallen and pierced the roof of the Triforium below—also to the state of the Cloister Walls and groinings—and that he be asked whether he does not consider that the repairs required in these several parts of the building should be completed before the further repair of the North Porch.

Three weeks later Scott died (and was buried in the Abbey) and his son, J. Oldrid Scott, took on his work and replied to the matters raised at the Audit Chapter. The Chapter did not appoint him Surveyor in his father's place but ordered him to see to the more important works in the Cloisters and the Clerestory and to the removal of all dangerous stonework high up on the North Transept

Front before going on with the restoration of the Portals below. Permission to start work again on the Portals was given in July. That autumn a new matter was introduced by a request from the Assistant Organist (Frederick Bridge) that the organ should be re-modelled and the position of the choir changed. A Committee was appointed to go into this—it consisted of Gore Ouseley, John Stainer and J. E. Street as well as Bridge and the Precentor—and when its report was discussed on 24 January 1879 the Chapter asked for estimates to be obtained for the proposed work on the organ and requested Oldrid Scott to submit approximate estimates for narrowing the organ screen, rearranging the western stalls and for the raising and reconstruction of the seats occupied by the choir. However, this matter was taken out of Oldrid Scott's hands when at the Audit Chapter the following month J. L. Pearson was appointed Surveyor of the Fabric in succession to Sir Gilbert. Oldrid, however, was allowed to carry on his father's work on the Portals, but was soon in trouble with the Chapter over its extravagance, as appears from the following minute of 11 July:

> A letter from Mr. J. Oldrid Scott in reference to the contract for the Western Portal of the Abbey amounting to £3,718. 15. with lithograph drawings explanatory of the necessity of additional work etc. at an increase of cost of £190—and also in reference to Messrs. Farmer and Brindley's estimate for the carving and their application for an increase of £50—being read ORDERED that the proposed additional work etc. be referred to the Dean and Canon Duckworth, and that in regard to the proposed increase in Messrs. Farmer and Brindley's estimate for the carving Mr. Scott be informed that the Chapter are so sensible of the extreme inconvenience of altering contracts when once sent in that they are indisposed to entertain the application of Messrs. Farmer and Brindley.

Meanwhile Pearson was surveying the whole of the building; he made an interim report on that same 11 July about the most immediate urgent needs ('decayed stones on the South side of the Nave and Cloister roof . . . repair of the six Bays reaching from the South-west Tower. . . . Flying buttresses') and in the following December, after the state of the Fabric had been further discussed, he was requested to furnish a full report with estimates as to the present and future requirements of the Abbey and the Organ, while the Chapter set up a Committee of five of its own members to go into the question of raising the money that they realized was going to be needed. How much, they would not know until Pearson told them the whole story. The Audit Chapter was held on 9 and 10 February 1880, but

Pearson was not ready and said he could not let the Chapter have his report until May. In the event it was not until 15 July that they heard the worst. It came in the form of a letter which was ordered to be entered in the Chapter Book, and it was this:

To the Dean and Chapter   46 Harley Street,
Westminster Abbey   W.

               June 5th, 1880

Gentlemen,

 I have now been able to complete my estimate of the cost of the external repairs and restoration of the Abbey and it amounts to the sum of £49,000, including about £2000 for contingencies but not including the cost of any work that may be required to the buildings around the Abbey (of which I have not as yet made any estimate) nor for any work to the Western Towers.

 The estimate has been made in detail so that I can give the cost of any division of the work separately.

         Believe me to be
           Yours very faithfully,
             John L. Pearson.

FINANCIAL TROUBLES AND THEIR CAUSES

The worst fears of the Dean and Chapter were realized, and this letter made it clear that they had on their hands not only a major problem with the fabric but also a major crisis in their finances; indeed, it is probably true to say that never before had the Dean and Chapter of Westminster been faced with a greater one. Parliament was no longer in the mood as in previous centuries to grant public money towards the repair of this 'national church', and the Dean and Chapter had lost most of the resources with which they might have been able, over a period of years, to meet so large a bill. But although the full magnitude of the problem did not become apparent until this moment when Stanley was within a year of his death it had been in the making throughout the years of his decanate.

 From 1833 until the coming of Stanley the Chapter finances had been in the competent hands of Lord John Thynne, who over the years had fought to resist the proposal, and to retard the negotiations, for the taking over of the Dean and Chapter's estates by the Ecclesiastical Commissioners. Almost incredibly Thynne was still alive when Pearson's letter was received (indeed, he only failed by four months to outlive Stanley), but he was already a man of 66 when Stanley became Dean and no longer exercised the same influence over the direction of the Chapter's finances. At the Chapter Meeting which opened within a few minutes of his installation Stanley learned that a letter had been received from the Secretary to the Ecclesiastical Commissioners complaining that no answer had yet been received to a letter written eighteen months earlier about the transfer of the Chapter estates to the Commissioners. A minute records that Henry Hunt, the Chapter's legal adviser, be requested to report progress, and from that moment onwards Thynne's policy of delay was abandoned. It would seem that Stanley himself was anxious to co-operate with the Commissioners, and that he was supported by a majority of the Canons. The Canons of Stanley's period were not the sort of men to have much heart for battling for the Abbey's estates against the tide of public opinion in general and the House of Commons and the Ecclesiastical Commissioners in particular. For one thing, they themselves no longer had anything to gain or lose in the matter since by Order in Council of 1853 their incomes had been fixed at £1,000 a year. (It may be mentioned in passing that of the eight men who were installed Canons of Westminster during Stanley's decanate, five were chaplains to Queen Victoria, five had been dons, two had been headmasters and one was also Warden of All Souls throughout the time he held his Canonry.)

At all events, matters now began to move more quickly. On 11 April 1866 Hunt reported on the Ecclesiastical Commissioners Bill then before the House of Lords and he was instructed to proceed with the negotiations with the Commissioners for the commutation of the Chapter estates which would follow upon that Bill becoming law. On 23 June of the same year a letter from Hunt was considered, in which he said the negotiations

> have now reached a point which enables me to state that I have confident expectation of concluding an arrangement which is likely to meet with the approval of the Dean and Chapter and the Ecclesiastical Commissioners, the substance of it being that the future permanent income of the Dean and Chapter will be £20,000 per annum . . . these arrangements are to take effect as and from Lady Day last . . . and it is to be hoped that before Michaelmas an order in Council will have been made.

In fact Hunt's optimism was not justified in the event, and the delay from now on seems to have been the responsibility of others rather than of the Dean and Chapter. The draft of the scheme for commutation was approved by the Chapter on 14 June 1867 and ordered to be sealed on 2 July; in 1868 the Ecclesiastical Commission Act providing for the transfer of the Dean and Chapter's estates became law; and on 5 June 1869 it was minuted: 'ORDERED that our Corporate seal be now fixed to the scheme agreed upon between ourselves and the Ecclesiastical Commissioners for England for the commutation of our Chapter estates, the scheme sealed by us on 2 July 1867 not having been carried out.' The following month another minute appears: 'ORDERED that the scheme between ourselves and the Ecclesiastical Commissioners for the commutation of the Chapter estates of June 5 last to be re-sealed, adopting an Amendment suggested by the Attorney-General for extending the exception to educational and other like patronage.' With all now virtually settled the Chapter decided upon the salaries to be paid henceforth to the members of the Musical Foundation and *inter alia* they ordered that the Organist should 'have a further augmentation of £50 and that the Dean be requested to impose upon him as a condition that henceforth a short Voluntary be played at the termination of Services in the Church (Friday excepted).'

The Order in Council finally establishing the scheme for the commutation was published in the *London Gazette* on 13 August 1869 and was entered in the Chapter Book at the next meeting of the Chapter. It provided that all the estates of the Dean and Chapter (with certain exceptions to be noted shortly) were to be transferred to the Commissioners, together with all their corporate investments, being the proceeds of the sales of Abbey lands to railway companies, the General Post Office, the Westminster Improvement Commissioners and other public bodies in the course of the preceding twenty years and valued at £40,000; the Dean and Chapter were to retain certain lands in the West country (chiefly in Herefordshire and Worcestershire), together with Belsize House and property in the Broad Sanctuary and Abingdon Street, Westminster; and the Ecclesiastical Commissioners were also to transfer certain of their small estates in the same counties to the Dean and Chapter. It was estimated that the Dean and Chapter would thus be in possession of sufficient land to provide them with an income of £20,000, and that this would be enough for the payment of all salaries and wages, for 'the maintenance of the Services of the said Church, the repairs of the fabric thereof and of the Collegiate buildings' and for 'the payment of all other expenses and liabilities chargeable upon the corporate revenue of the said Dean and Chapter'. Finally the Ecclesiastical Commissioners were to set apart a capital sum of £20,000 for 'substantial repairs, restoration and improvements of the said Collegiate Church and of the buildings belonging thereto', but such works would first need to be approved by the Commissioners.

From this time onwards the minutes of Chapter meetings become very appreciably shorter, for no longer were the Dean and Canons concerned with a vast amount of legal and administrative business consequent upon the ownership of extensive property. At the same time if the Dean and Chapter were henceforth spared much tedium they were faced with increasing anxiety. Even assuming that the holdings with which they were left produced the anticipated rental of £20,000 they would have to watch their expenditure very carefully indeed. When £8,000 had been deducted for the stipends of the Dean and the six Canons, and £7,000 for the stipends and wages of all the other members and employees of the establishment, there would remain only £5,000 for the ordinary maintenance of the fabric of the Abbey and the other buildings. Because he saw no signs that his colleagues appreciated the need for the most rigid economy Lord John Thynne addressed the following portentous letter to them after the commutation had been effected:

1st March 1870

Dear Mr. Treasurer,

I am so strongly impressed with fear that we shall get into financial difficulties except some check is given to Orders in Chapter and out of Chapter without reflexion and in ignorance of the state of affairs—that I have taken upon myself to examine the Fabric accounts for the years ending Michaelmas 1868 and 1869 and to make an estimate for the current year which I now submit to your care and consideration; and if you think proper to circulate it, the Receiver will put it into the hand of Mr. Montague to copy it so that every member of Chapter may see and I hope appreciate the danger we have been in I won't say *are* if we are now prudent.

The excess of expenditure each year and the debts now contracted render necessary special communications through the Chapter Clerk (copies of a Chapter Order I hope) to Mr. Gilbert Scott and Messrs. Poole that no work will be recognized as having claim to payment for which an estimate is not presented and a Chapter Order given for execution—and to the Clerk of the Works that he is not to employ any stranger without a written Order of Chapter. We have to consider that our funds are now measured out with strict application to their respective purposes; also that we are at present unable even to feel confident that they will be sufficient for these purposes inasmuch as we have not yet come into the receipt of one year's income! The sum of £5,000 is assigned to the Fabric and its general liabilities some of which have from various

Y

circumstances (the loss of our supply of water from Hyde Park, the increased rates Metropolitan etc., the greater need of watching by the Police, the warming of the Abbey and the lighting of the Precincts etc.) been greatly increased. Heretofore we had occasional assistance from sales of timber (£1,000 and more in some years) but now we have a hard and fast line within which the expenditure must be restricted.

The School has of late been very expensive to the Chapter from increased requirements, although the number of boys is not half what old Westminster recollects. The construction of Haden's heating stoves and pipes (3 miles of pipe) has been more than we anticipated; but these charges will henceforth cease. The alarming part of the statement of accounts which I have drawn up of Audits 1869 and 1870 respectively—and 1871 prospectively—is the debt with which we start for the current year. I make no further comment upon Mr. Poole's bills which constitute so large an item, some without Order or estimate, as sufficient was said in Chapter on that particular subject. I ask you and all members of Chapter to give their serious attention to the state of the Fabric Fund in particular which whilst it is the most interesting so it is the most responsible of our Trusts.

I believe my figures are correct—if not please to correct them— if they are it is manifest that we have no means at command to provide for the contemplated repair of the West end of the Abbey and of Jerusalem Chamber.

I would suggest therefore to the consideration of the Dean and Chapter that the approval of the Ecclesiastical Commission should be asked for the outlay upon this work which comes strictly within the limited application of the £20,000 in their funds—thus the whole work (except the internal decoration of and under the roof of Jerusalem Chamber which is better referred to for further consideration) might be commenced and concluded without prolonging the dirt and dust attendant upon such works. Mr. Scott must of course produce plans and estimates of the whole including the iron railings and gates.

This will not interfere with the continued restoration of the Cloisters towards which *the interest* of the money held in reserve by the Ecclesiastical Commissioners is applicable and for which we have their continuing warrant.

I hope I have not taken upon myself more than becomes me in presuming thus to call general attention to the present state of affairs as related to the Fabric Fund.

Yours faithfully,
[Signed] J. Thynne—Sub-Dean

The Chapter ordered this letter to be entered in the Book and did something in the years that followed to heed Thynne's warning and to cut their coat according to the short length of cloth which they had been persuaded to agree with the Commissioners. But all calculations were thrown out by the catastrophic decline of English agriculture which began in the mid seventies, and as a result of which many of the tenants of such farms as the Chapter still held found it increasingly difficult, and then impossible, to pay their rents in full. At the Audit Chapter held in March 1880 the Treasurer reported that at the end of the previous financial year the Dean and Chapter's credit balance had sunk to little more than £1,000, whereas their tenants were in arrears to the total tune of £2,892. 4s. 11d.

On 21 July of the same year (a week after the Chapter had learned from Pearson that close on £50,000 were needed for the immediate repair and restoration of the fabric) a special meeting of the Chapter was held at which there was only one matter on the agenda—to hear, consider and adopt a report 'on the condition of the tenants and the state of the farms and the crops on the estates of the Dean and Chapter in the counties of Worcester and Hereford' drawn up by Canon Prothero and the Receiver-General. Such reports were made annually, but so serious was the picture presented by this one that the Chapter took the unusual step of ordering it to be entered *in toto* in the Chapter Book. At Church Farm, Mathon, Charles Oakley 'has been in difficulties and now has no stock of his own except horses' and Charles Purser, at South Hyde Farm, Mathon, 'has lost a large number of sheep by the rot'. On the Grendon and Pencombe estates 'the rental when handed over by the Commissioners was somewhat over £1,100 which has since been reduced to a little over £800. This is a cold clay country and does not suit cereals well except in a very dry year; the land is poor and full of springs; it is a disputed question whether or not it would pay for draining.' T. Orgee, at Horsnett Farm, 'has lost most of his sheep' and 'the yard is thoroughly out of order and neglected'; at Grendon Court, A. Dyke 'has lost £500 of sheep by the prevalent rot'; at Lower Egdon, John Nicholas has had 'a series of losses in sheep and also in horses, and was in great distress . . . crops have in fact been a total failure for two years . . . his arrears were remitted to the whole extent'. H. Hart, of Millards Court, Birtsmorton, 'has lost half his sheep and the remainder are not free from the disease. The crops look well, some of the wheat particularly. Mr. Hart is an industrious and very hard-working man with a bed-ridden wife and nine children. He paid half a year's rent, and was excused the other half on account of his losses.' At Manor Farm, Church Honeybourne, William Hurns 'produced his accounts to show that he had lost money by the farm for the last five years, and as he had lost this year his whole flock of sheep by the rot to the value of £1,000 he showed a total loss of between three and four thousands on the five years. It was proposed to remit half a year's rent and to reduce the rent to £550.' The report concluded with the following paragraph:

> It will be seen from the foregoing that although the prospects of the harvest are better than for some years past should the weather get a little more favourable: yet from the past bad seasons culminating with 1879, and the low prices of corn and increased cost of labour, many of the tenants, even at the reduced rents, and the liberal percentage which has been granted, have fallen hopelessly into arrears. We have thought it advisable to remit very large portions of this debt, hoping that if they can start clear with a good season, they may be able to carry on their farms advantageously. We have also been anxious to retain the old tenants knowing the great difficulty in finding others who are solvent. We are further very glad to report that the farms have in most cases been kept in a good state of cultivation notwithstanding the losses the tenants have sustained.

In view of this it must have come as no surprise when it was revealed at the Audit Chapter the following March that the Chapter's balance had sunk to £358. But it must have come as a severe disappointment that despite the many remissions and reductions of rent the tenants were still over £3,000 in arrears.

THE SURRENDER OF ASHBURNHAM HOUSE

At this same Chapter Meeting (3–4 March 1881) various small items of business were transacted consequent upon the death of Lord John Thynne a few days earlier, and this long-delayed event produced yet another anxiety for the Dean and Chapter. By the Public Schools Act of 1868 three of the capitular houses were to be transferred to the Governing Body of Westminster School as and when each became vacant, and for thirteen years the School had been kept waiting for all three of them by the longevity of their occupants. Now at last the Sub-Dean was dead, and the Secretary of the Governing Body wrote immediately to request the transference of Ashburnham House which Thynne had occupied. The Dean and Chapter viewed the alienation of this particular house with especial regret (for reasons which will shortly appear) and asked the Governing Body to consider accepting another canonical house in exchange,

(No. 20 Dean's Yard, in which these words are being written). Early in April the Dean and Chapter learned that the Governing Body had 'promised on the condition of the transfer to them of the House occupied by the late Sub-Dean to take into favourable consideration the exchange offered to them by the Dean and Chapter of the house now occupied by Canon Leighton', but the Dean and Chapter wanted something more definite than this before they affixed their seal to the transfer of Ashburnham House. On 18 May the Chapter learned that the Governing Body had formally resolved that they '. . . express their readiness to accept the above offer [to exchange the two houses] and are prepared to take any legal steps necessary either by application to the Charity Trustees or otherwise to carry into effect the proposed exchange, it being understood that the Dean and Chapter will if practicable arrange for making over to the Governing Body an adequate space of ground for the purpose of a Fives Court'. With this assurance the Dean and Chapter affixed their seal to a deed conveying Ashburnham House to the Governing Body on 1 June. But then something went wrong, and although the School now had Ashburnham House the exchange was never effected. This caused a good deal of bitter feeling at the time, and may well have hastened Stanley's death (18 July). But there seems no reason to suppose that either party were guilty of any impropriety or bad faith. The niggers in the woodpile appear to have been the Charity Commissioners who now ruled that the exchange was inadmissible 'on account of the small amount of area covered by the house offered by them [the Dean and Chapter] to the School, as compared with that of Ashburnham House and of the ground occupied by Mr. Turle's house'. The main object of the Governing Body (of which the Dean was *ex-officio* Chairman and of which two of the Canons were also members) was to obtain considerable additional space on which to erect classrooms and other urgently needed buildings, and a Mr Oakley of the Charity Commissioners therefore recommended 'the demolition of Ashburnham House in order to obtain a site for the erection of such buildings on the whole or part of the site which it now occupies'.

This insensitive proposal to destroy what was one of the finest houses in London did nothing to mend matters, and the Dean and Chapter were roused to make another proposal in the hope of saving Ashburnham House:

The Dean and Chapter are earnestly desirous to do their utmost to preserve, if possible, a House which is both interesting in itself and still more valuable as containing part of the oldest structure connected with the Abbey in the earliest stage of its history. They are still more anxious to retain the site of the Old Refectory, the northern wall of which is still in their possession, in the hope of being enabled by its retention to enlarge the very limited space that is now left for memorial purposes. They are convinced that the alienation from Westminster Abbey of the Garden of Ashburn-ham House, adjoining as it does the South Cloister, and rendering impossible the restoration for public purposes of the ancient Refectory would be widely felt as a serious national loss.

At the same time they fully recognise not only the legal position of the School, but its claims on other grounds to largely increased space for the extension of its educational and other buildings.

They beg therefore to submit to the Governing Body the follow-ing proposal:

They are willing (though not without considerable reluctance) to sacrifice a large part of the College Garden, by giving over to the School the area marked on the accompanying plan—com-prising 15,460 square feet, adjoining the School Dormitory and Sick House, and having a frontage of 250 feet or more to Great College Street—without requiring any payment whatever; provided that the Governing Body will relinquish their claim to the three houses named in the Public Schools Act, for which they are bound under the Act to pay a Sum of £10,000.

The Governing Body rejected the proposal and retained Ashburn-ham House. Fortunately they did not take Mr Oakley's advice to pull it down.

19

A New Era
1882–1901

'AS far as I understood what the duties of my office were supposed to be, in spite of every incompetence, I am yet humbly trustful that I have sustained before the mind of the nation the extraordinary value of the Abbey as a religious, national, and liberal institution.' These were among the words of Stanley which are said to have been carefully noted by those at his bedside and immediately afterwards written down by Canon Farrar on 18 July 1881. Stanley died at the end of the same day, and with his death there ended the fateful twelve months in which Pearson's report had been received, the Chapter's balance had sunk to £358, Lord John Thynne had died and Ashburnham House had been lost. It was the end of an era in the history of the Collegiate Church, for although the Public Schools Act had become law in 1868 and the greater part of the capitular property had been taken over by the Ecclesiastical Commissioners in 1869, the full effect of those measures was not felt until now. Queen Victoria's reign had still close on twenty years to run, but already the Dean and Chapter were living in a world very different from that to which they had been accustomed. The Abbey lost little of its spiritual influence as a national church which Stanley had gained for it—the preaching of such Canons as Farrar, Westcott, Charles Gore and Basil Wilberforce saw to that, albeit in very different ways. But in the 'eighties the Chapter Books reflect an institution 'in reduced circumstances', increasingly shorn of temporal power and influence (the Dean's vestigial powers as a local government authority virtually disappeared altogether in 1901, following the London Government Act of 1899), more parochial, more narrowly ecclesiastical, pinching and scraping to make ends meet and to prevent the Abbey itself from falling down; and thereafter beginning to serve the Church of England in a more modest way by making the Abbey a church in which Anglican worship was to be found at its best and all things pertaining to that worship done decently and in order.

The Dean throughout the last two decades of Victoria's reign was George Granville Bradley (he resigned in 1902). Devoted disciple of Thomas Arnold and Arthur Stanley, first boy and later master at Rugby, Headmaster of Marlborough from 1858 to 1870 and then Master of University College, Oxford, until his appointment as Dean of Westminster, he was a man of 60 when he was installed on All Saints' Day, 1881—the same year in which was published his *Latin Prose Composition* which has made his name familiar to subsequent generations of classical schoolboys. By this time the matter of Ashburnham House had gone beyond recall, and in the next two years Bradley and his colleagues saw the other two houses go to the School in accordance with the Public Schools Act as first the old Organist, Turle, and then John Jennings (who had been Canon and Rector of St John's, Smith Square, since 1837) died. Much Chapter thought and time were given to finding ways and means of building two new houses in College Garden to take the place of those that had been lost, but references to the School in the Chapter Books now became few and far between, and then generally in connexion with trivial matters such as the following:

The Clerk of the Works having called the attention of the Dean and Chapter to the state of the lamps round the enclosure of Dean's Yard, seven out of ten being more or less damaged by the footballs of the Westminster Scholars, and two entirely new Lamps required, the cost being between £6 and £7, ORDERED that the Clerk of the Works be desired to send the account to the Head Master through the Bursar. (8 March, 1886.)

Meanwhile the Chapter were struggling to deal with an increasingly desperate financial situation. Improved though it appeared to be at the Audit Chapter of 1882, the following table tells its own tale:

	DEAN AND CHAPTER'S BALANCE			TENANTS IN ARREARS		
	£	s.	d.	£	s.	d.
1880	+1,218	15	0	2,892	4	11
1881	+ 358	12	4	3,066	18	5
1882	+ 856	11	11	2,067	13	3
1883	nil			1,828	3	4
1884	− 109	3	4	1,929	6	1
1885	− 494	18	1	2,521	3	2
1886	−1,628	19	10	3,237	0	8
1887	−1,575	13	8	1,548	4	5
1888	− 536	9	8	1,260	17	11
1889	+3,626	15	9	742	5	7
1890	+3,583	14	6	nil		

On 14 July 1881, a few days before Stanley's death and with the Sub-Dean in the Chair, the Receiver submitted a financial statement to the Chapter as a result of which it was decided that the Treasurer should 'furnish a detailed statement and report of receipts and expenditure with a view to the reduction of the latter'. The Chapter Book does not record what the Treasurer subsequently recommended in so many words, but it appears that for a number of years virtually all work to maintain, repair and improve the official houses in the precincts was stopped, although an exception was made in the case of No. 20 Dean's Yard following the death of its occupant, the Warden of All Souls, Canon Leighton. The next occupant of the house, Canon Barry, reported its 'dilapidated and neglected state' at the Audit in February 1882, and the Chapter was sufficiently impressed to make an immediate order that 'the Chapter Surveyor be directed to report yearly on the condition of the Chapter's houses', and a month later the expenditure of £440 was authorized for the 'substantial repairs' needed to that particular house.

Further signs of stringency followed the Audit of 1883 when it was learned that the Chapter's credit balance had altogether vanished. When Canon Barry 'expressed a desire to hold simple services in the Abbey in Holy Week at 8 o'clock in the evening' there was some question of whether they could be afforded; it was ultimately agreed that 'the expense of gas be allowed'. At the same Audit Chapter the Chapter Clerk was instructed to take Counsel's opinion 'as to the right course of meeting any deficiency in the funds at the disposal of the Dean and Chapter under the Order in Council on the Commutation of the Chapter Estates—whether such deficiency should be made good by a reduction on all stipends or should be limited to those received by the Dean and Canons'. Four weeks later it was decided 'that the Sunday Evening Special Services this year should be at the expense of the Ornamental Fund', and it was regretted that 'in the present state of the Chapter finances' the Dean and Chapter could not make a contribution towards the restoration of Pinvin Church at Pershore. Appeals continued to come from the parishes of which the Dean and Chapter remained patron after the surrender of the estates in 1869, but during the mid-eighties such appeals were met either with a trifling donation or none at all. In July 1884, since the Dean and Chapter 'have not sufficient resources to meet their necessary expenditure' they are unable to contribute towards the Vicarage houses for Christ Church and St Andrew's, Westminster, or towards the restoration of St Mary's, Malden, or the re-roofing of the church at Stanford-in-the-Vale. In May 1885 the Vicar of Alconbury wrote to say that he had bought 'one of the eleven public houses in the parish . . . suited for an Institute, Reading and Recreation Room' and asking for a subscription towards the cost. Dear as such a cause was to their hearts the Dean and Chapter could only send £5 and an expression of regret that they could not spare more. In 1886 they refused a subscription to Holy Trinity, Bessborough Gardens, owing to 'the critical financial position·in which they are now placed'. More appeals than usual were received in 1887 as the parishes prepared to celebrate Queen Victoria's Golden Jubilee. Two guineas were sent towards 'a feast to the Poor' at Mathon, and a similar sum towards giving 'Agricultural Labourers and Women Beef, and Tea to the Children' at Castlemorton; but subscriptions were declined towards the new church clocks with which the parishes of Stanford-in-the-Vale and Otford were proposing to commemorate the Jubilee.

But less straitened times were at hand. Over the years it had been becoming more and more apparent to others beside the Dean and Chapter that the stringent arrangements made in 1869 had been rendered totally inadequate by the unforeseen collapse of England's agriculture. The position was at last remedied by the Westminster Abbey Act of 1888 by which the Abbey finally surrendered to the Church Commissioners such estates as it still possessed in return for a fixed annual sum of £20,000—an arrangement which has now been unchanged for over three-quarters of a century, despite the pious hope of Westcott that the position would be reviewed at the installation of each new Dean.

ENDLESS RESTORATION

Meanwhile the restoration of the fabric by Pearson had been going forward, though necessarily at a slow and strictly controlled rate. This was possible in the first instance by using the £20,000 set aside for this purpose by the Ecclesiastical Commissioners in 1869. At that same Chapter Meeting in July 1880 at which it was learned that £49,000 would be needed for the restoration there was a letter from the Secretary of the Commissioners stating that there was a balance of £12,801. 10s. 10d. in that Fabric Fund. Inevitably this came to be exhausted as the work proceeded, but thanks to the Westminster Abbey Restoration Act of 1886 and the Westminster Abbey Act of 1888 the Ecclesiastical Commissioners were empowered to provide or lend sufficient for the work to be maintained, and the Chapter had at any rate an instalment of satisfaction in receiving the following letter from Pearson on 16 July 1894:

Dear Sirs,

I am pleased to be able to report that the great and difficult work of the restoration of the South side of the Nave and of the West side of the South Transept with the Aisles and Cloisters begun about 14 years ago is now completed and that the Scaffolding is nearly all removed. This work includes the rebuilding of no less than 44 flying buttresses, the renewal of all the Clerestory windows of the Nave and Transept and those of the Aisles, and of the Aisle windows, parapets, buttresses, pinnacles etc., etc.

It was my good fortune upon the removal of Sir Christopher Wren's decayed Masonry to discover—most clearly marked—the original treatment not only of the Clerestory windows and buttresses of the Nave but of those of the Aisles of the times of Henry the Third, Edward the First and Richard the Second; and also the very interesting way in which the several peculiarities were connected as the rebuilding of the Western Arm of the Abbey proceeded from one period to another. A most valuable chapter has, I think, been added to the history of the Abbey. Doubtless the same features would be discovered behind Sir Chris: Wren's facing on the North side of the Nave Clerestory.

It was with a view of going on with this work, which had been interrupted during the time the more pressing restoration of the North Transept gable end was in progress, that I deferred completing the work of the Choir, and East Aisle of the North Transept; these works I now propose to resume, and also to take in hand the repairs of the flying buttresses on the West side of this Transept, and those on the North side of the Nave, some of which are in a very bad condition.

A much smaller staff of men will be required for this work than has been employed hitherto and the yearly expenditure will be very considerably reduced.

I am proposing to rebuild a portion of the thin wall over the entrance doorway into Mr. Wright's Yard which is bulging out; this wall is part of the inside facing of the North Wall of the Refectory and the South side of the small Staircase and passage formed in the thickness of the main wall. It is in a ruinous condition and requires immediate attention.

There are other works which it would be very desirable to undertake but I am disposed to recommend them to be left for the present and until those I have referred to are completed.

I desire to remain, Revd. Sirs,

Your obedient Servant,

John L. Pearson

Not all were so satisfied, however—and least of all William Morris who in June 1893 had told the members of the Society for the Protection of Ancient Buildings what he thought of the restoring works of Wren, Wyatt, Blore, Scott and Pearson; he described the work of the two last as 'architect's architecture, the work of the office' and asserted that 'a long series of blunders of various kinds, all based on a false estimate of the true value of the building, have damaged the exterior of the Abbey so vitally that scarcely any of its original surface remains'. After expressing his belief that the sole charge of the Abbey was too much for one architect and that a committee of the best practical architects, builders and engineers should report on the fabric and the means to be taken to render it thoroughly secure, he ended: 'The structural stability having been secured, the Abbey should be kept clean, and otherwise not be touched at all. That is the only thing to do, and there is no second course which would not lead to fresh disaster.' But this was critic's criticism, the work of the ivory tower. Pearson was not able to disregard so lightly the effect of London's climate upon the Abbey's stonework, even upon Portland stone which had only had to endure a mere 170 years of Westminster weather. After carrying on, as and when funds permitted, the works outlined in the letter quoted above he was compelled to send in a report which led to the emergency summoning of a Committee of Chapter in the middle of August 1896. The sole business was summed up in the following minute:

Mr Pearson having reported as to the serious condition of the West Front of the Abbey and Mr Codd his Assistant also being present, ORDERED that considering the dangerous condition of the North West Tower Mr Wright be authorized to do whatever is absolutely necessary in accordance with Mr Pearson's direction, until the next Meeting of the Chapter, and that the bells be not pealed till further notice.

Before the restoration of the Tower could be completed Pearson died and was succeeded as Surveyor by J. T. Micklethwaite, upon whose advice the Dean and Chapter were forced to adjudge that it would not be safe to ring the bells at the coronation of Edward VII in 1902. But Micklethwaite had already learned that another part of this ecclesiastical Forth Bridge was once again needing attention, and at a meeting of the Chapter on 1 August 1900

Canon Gore proposed and it was resolved that a Committee consisting of two Architects (Mr W. D. Caroe and Mr Philip Webb) and two Chemists (Professor Church and Professor Herbert Jackson) be appointed to consult with Mr J. T. Micklethwaite, the Surveyor of the Fabric, and to report to the Dean in reference to the best means of preserving the Stonework in the Cloister.

WORSHIP AND MUSIC

But while Bradley, throughout the years he was Dean, had of necessity to give much time and thought to the restoration of the fabric and finances of the Abbey—and to the long and finally fruitless controversy about building an extension to the Abbey for what William Morris characterized as 'a kind of registration office for the names of men whom the present generation considers eminent' (see supra p. 304)—he and his colleagues on the Chapter were anything but unmindful of the greater purposes for which the Abbey exists. They were not all great preachers like Farrar, Gore and Wilberforce, nor great scholars like Westcott and Armitage Robinson, but nearly all were men who as individuals and as members of a corporate body put the worship of God and the extension of his Kingdom at the top of the list of priorities. During the twenty years between the deaths of Stanley and Queen Victoria the opportunities for worship in the Abbey were steadily increased and the Chapter Book shows that the Dean and Chapter were ready to consider sympathetically all suggestions for making that worship more worthy. In February 1882, at his first Audit, the new Dean informed the Chapter that he was going to make arrangements for an additional daily service, a shortened form of Morning Prayer at 8.30 a.m., and that there would be special evening services in the Choir during Lent. Later in the same year a small committee was set up, under the Dean, 'to examine the accommodation for kneeling and worship in the Abbey' and while the Chapter Book has no further mention of that committee it records shortly afterwards the ordering of £50 worth of kneeling boards, 72 hassocks and 500 hymn books. In 1884, with the object of securing more orderly arrangements at services, a Minor Canon was appointed to a newly created office of 'Custodian' with such duties as assisting the Dean to make preparations for great services on special occasions, advertising services in the newspapers, seeing to the seating of the congregation and providing 'for the due order of precedence in procession'. Whatever the state of the Abbey's fabric and finances at this time there was no anxiety on the score of its being unwanted, though the great congregations on Sundays and the crowds of visitors on other days created their own special problems; in 1885 the Surveyor was requested to give immediate attention 'to the modes of exit from the Abbey in case of a panic, and to furnish a plan', and in 1892 restrictions had to be imposed after the Sub-Dean had called the attention of the Chapter 'to the large number of Painters in the Abbey and their Easels etc.'. More significant was the following minute of 13 May 1889:

> The Subdean having brought before the Chapter a suggestion of Canon Westcott as to the use of St. Faith's Chapel as a Vestry, and the subject having been discussed, it was arranged that the Subdean should write to Canon Westcott on the same.

Nothing was done immediately to rescue the chapel from its use as a storeroom (forty years before it had been a forgotten lumber room, but Scott had done much to restore it), nor did anything follow at once from the Chapter Meeting of 2 May 1892 when the Dean consulted the Canons 'as to an increase in the number of early Communions in the Abbey'. But in November 1895

> Canon Gore having proposed that steps be taken to prepare St. Faith's Chapel for purpose of Worship without delay and the subject being discussed It was resolved that the proposal be agreed to and that Mr. Pearson be conferred with by the Subdean, and that the disused Kneelers stored there be given away for Church purposes at the discretion of Canon Wilberforce and Canon Gore.
>
> Canon Gore also proposing that beginning with the first week in Advent there be a Thursday Celebration of the Holy Communion for which the Canons who have no Parochial Cures shall be responsible, the Dean announced after discussing the question with the Chapter that he was prepared to give notice of an additional weekly Holy Communion at 8 o'clock a.m. on Thursday to commence in Advent this year. . . .

But it was not until after the death of Queen Victoria that (again on Gore's proposal) Holy Communion was celebrated on Tuesdays as well as Thursdays; and beginning in Advent 1901 it was celebrated daily. The value of St Faith's Chapel was finally demonstrated when it was used for all the daily services during the months when the rest of the Abbey was closed in preparation for the coronation. Notices directing attention to the fact that the Chapel 'is reserved always for private Devotion' had been put up in 1898.

Not a little of the credit for the improvement of the services in the Abbey during Bradley's decanate must be given to Dr Frederick Bridge who, after seven years as Assistant to the aged Turle (who was rarely seen and even more rarely heard at the Organ), was appointed Organist and Master of the Choristers in 1882 at a salary of £300 and on condition that 'he be not absent from more than 2 weekday services in addition to those on Fridays (in which the Organ is not played) without special permission of the Dean'. Once in command Bridge lost no time in pressing for the improvement of the organ (raising much of the money by his own efforts) and then persuading the Chapter to install in the Cloister Garth 'a Gas Engine to supply wind'. Since the Gothic cases which Blore had designed in 1848 no longer fitted the enlarged and reconstructed instrument they were disposed of; on 25 February 1884 the Chapter agreed that 'certain parts of the Organ Screen not intended to be used in the alterations of the Organ now in progress and for which he could find good use in the Parish Church of Friskney, his native place, be presented to Mr. Wright' (the Clerk of the Works). For ten years there were no funds with which to provide new cases, but Bridge hit upon the bicentenary of the death of Henry Purcell as an opportunity to organize a Purcell Commemoration and thereby raised sufficient money to pay for one of the two great cases which Pearson designed and which are so fine a feature of the Abbey today. The Chapter showed its gratitude by presenting Bridge 'with a Gown and Hood of his Degree of Mus. Doc.' and a little later were sufficiently in funds to pay for the second case.

Bridge worked equally hard and successfully as Master of the Choristers, and by the 'nineties the reputation of the Abbey's music was second to none. The Chapter Book suggests, however, that its excellence was bought at a price. In February 1896 the Dean and Chapter had to order 'that under no circumstances may the Choir boys be practised or taken out of School between 11 a.m. and 1 p.m. except for the Monthly Rehearsal or by special permission of the Dean' and 'that no practice in the afternoons be allowed to interfere with the Choristers' time of recreation and that there be no practice on Sunday'. Three months later the Dean and Chapter took a further step:

> It was resolved that no Corporal punishment of any kind be administered to the Choristers by the Organist or Assistant Organist: that serious offences which seem to require such punishment should be reported to the Precentor who if he think fit should send the case to be dealt with by the Master of the Choir House: that penal detentions inflicted by the Master of the Choristers should not be for a longer space than half an hour: that a copy of this Resolution be sent to Dr. Bridge.

A further entry in December 1897 suggests that the Dean and Chapter were mindful of the needs and feelings not only of the choristers but of the less musically educated members of the congregation. After accepting the Precentor's advice—'the result of his consultations with various experts'—that the number of services and anthems sung in the Abbey should be increased, the Chapter added a rider:

> With reference to the selection of Hymn Tunes to be sung in the Abbey the following Resolution was passed and it was ORDERED that a Copy be sent to the Organist and the Precentor 'That it is the earnest desire of the Chapter that well known popular hymns be sung to the Tunes with which the Congregation are familiar'.

That it is reasonable to suppose that Charles Gore had a hand in this is suggested by the following Chapter minute of 17 July 1899:

> It was resolved on the proposal of Canon Gore, That the Chapter respectfully requests the Dean to communicate with the Bishop of London and withold his assent from the reading of any paper on Church Music in the Nave of the Abbey during the forthcoming Church Congress.

THE VARIETIES OF CHAPTER EXPERIENCE

And throughout the time of Bradley, as throughout the time of his predecessors (and successors), the Dean and Chapter were continuously concerned with smaller matters: John Hughes is appointed Wine Butler; Canon Farrar gives a report of his interview with the Head Master following 'annoyance carried on by rough boys in Dean's Yard'; the Library roof is leaking; following 'the report of the Inspector of Nuisances as to the discreditable state' of a Minor Canon's house the Minor Canon in question is 'required to put the Premises into proper condition to the satisfaction of the Inspector of Nuisances who will visit the house periodically and report'; the Protestant Educational Institute wants to know whether the site of the old Westminster Prison, on which it is 'the reported intention of certain Roman Catholics to erect the Metropolitan Cathedral' lies within the Precincts or the jurisdiction of the Dean and Chapter; a local resident suggests lighting the precincts by electricity (1885); Mrs Rush, the Porter's wife, is authorized 'to supply the six Policemen with tea or coffee every evening until further notice'; the Chapter is told that this and that ancient document has come to light in the Muniment Room or the Library; the Vicar of Eckington is given leave to remove a greenhouse and substitute a verandah; a tablet is to be placed in the Cloisters 'in memory of Roper, formerly Chorister for six years, who died of consumption in November last'; incumbents are presented to vacant benefices in the patronage of the Dean and Chapter; 'hand-grenades' are to be procured for extinguishing fires in the Abbey and an electric alarum is to be fixed at the West Cloister Gate; 'all dogs in the Abbey

Garden are to be kept in hand'; 'in reference to the pending question
of the renewal of the Music and Dancing Licence to the Royal
Aquarium' the Dean undertakes to write to the London County
Council 'to call attention to the fact that the Aquarium was the
nightly resort of large numbers of Women of immoral lives'; the
details of the statues for the upper part of the north face of the North
Transept are to be left in the hands of the Dean and Canon Westcott;
the Church House Corporation requires the possession of the Choir
House and the first steps are taken towards planning to build the
present Choir School; the Precentor is assisted towards the purchase
of a new kitchen range; the Electrophone Syndicate is refused
permission 'to use the transmission invention in the Abbey'; the
game of Lawn Tennis is allowed in the Abbey Garden; Henry V's
shield is loaned to the Society of Antiquaries; the gift of an Echo
Organ is gratefully accepted; after careful and repeated experiments
the Dean and Chapter feel they cannot accept as a gift the installation
of electric light in the Choir since it would injure 'the characteristic
beauty of the Choir when lighted as at present' (by candles); the
Archbishop of Canterbury writes to ask if the Dean and Chapter
will lend one of the copes to the Bishop of Peterborough who is
going 'to represent the Anglican Episcopate at the Tsar's
Coronation'; the window of the Choir practice room is to have
'plain Plate Glass in lieu of the present Cathedral Glass'; the Rector
of Islip wants to pull down the Tithe Barn; 'on consideration of the
Statute *De cultu Dei* Canon Gore proposed and it was resolved That
the list of attendances at the Abbey Services be exhibited every
quarter in the Jericho Chamber'; the seats normally reserved for
residents in the precincts are not to be reserved for the Three Hours
Service on Good Friday unless special notice has been given beforehand (1897); the Choir boys are to have scarlet cassocks at a cost
of £17. 2s. 6d.; 'the Subdean having called attention to the abuse of
the College Garden as a Bicycling and Football Ground ORDERED
that Bicycling and Football be no longer permitted' (February 1896);
the Dean and Chapter oppose the Victoria Embankment and St
John's Improvement Bill on this ground, among others, that 'a
great number of Dwellings of the labouring classes ought not to be
destroyed without preliminary provision being secured for the erection
of buildings adapted to the same class and in the same neighbourhood'; croquet is to be allowed in College Garden provided that 'it
be not played (except in the months of June and July this year)
on the Lawn in front of the Subdean's House'.

Small stuff, but typical. Certainly the Abbey had its share of
great national occasions during Bradley's years—the Golden Jubilee Service of 1887, for instance, and the State Funeral of Gladstone

z

in 1898—but as one reads through the annals of the Chapter
Book one is reading for the greater part of the little decisions of
mundane men and one looks almost in vain for any reference to
Almighty God. But that is a less significant fact than might at first
appear. There are still mundane men today, and we may be allowed
to think that they are not confined within the precincts of the
Abbey. And if the name of the Deity still appears very rarely in our
Chapter Book, we may doubt if that name appears much more
commonly in the minute books of other religious societies. The
purpose of a Chapter Book is to put on record practical decisions
about practical matters; it is not necessary to state the ultimate
reasons for those decisions. These are presupposed, and in Westminster's case they already exist in black and white in the Charter
and, behind that, in the Scriptures. It is fair to conclude that there
was more faithfulness to the Charter and the Scriptures in 1901 than
there was back in 1837. A wind of reform, say the breath of the Holy
Spirit, had been blowing. There was still resistance to it (there still
is) but it was a greatly diminished resistance; and to that extent
Westminster Abbey was more alive at the end of Victoria's reign
than it had been at the beginning.

But it is also fair to conclude that from the day in 1869 when the
Dean and Chapter surrendered their estates something of value
was dying at Westminster, and the Dean and Chapter as a corporate
body became yearly and inevitably more narrowly local and more
narrowly ecclesiastical. Certainly the Dean and Chapter had not
been the best of landlords in the past, and in the hands of the
Ecclesiastical Commissioners their former estates were now better
managed and put to much better use. But it remains one of the
ironies of the Abbey's history that just at the time when one of the
greatest Deans was seeking to realize his dream of the Abbey as
a focal expression of the nation's Church most of its organic links
with the nation were irreparably severed. The resulting problem is
with us still.

PART V

Within Living Memory

By The Reverend Canon Adam Fox, d.d.
Formerly Canon of Westminster and Sub-Dean

20

Portraits

SOURCES OF RECENT HISTORY

CONTEMPORARY history is not on the same footing as the history of the past. The sources of information for the period 1901–65 are partly documentary, partly personal knowledge. The Chapter minutes and the Chronicle are not very communicative. The Chronicle in any case only dates from 1925. The wars are elusive, because a good deal that was written down was confidential and not entered in any permanent record.

Of printed authorities I have used the relevant biographies and autobiographies; the various works of Dr Jocelyn Perkins, who, if not always accurate, knew a great deal at first hand which nobody else knew; *Westminster in War* by William Sansom; *The Times* and the *Illustrated London News*.

But my greatest debt is to those who have provided me with personal information: in particular to Dr Alan Don and Mr Tom Hebron; also to Mr Pullen, the Chapter Clerk; Mr Tanner, the Librarian; Mr Carter, the Clerk of Works; Mr Drake, the former Dean's Verger; Mr Greaves, the present Dean's Verger. The Rev. Gordon Dunstan provided me with useful information on a particular point, as also has Mr Paul Paget.

With one exception I have not named in the text any present member of the Collegiate Church.

*

Contemporary history and past history then are both departments of the same art or science, but they differ widely. In creating the picture of a former age we shall have great gaps in our information because the material available for the purpose is only a selection made by the casual hand of Time, but at least we know what has proved to be of lasting importance. For contemporary history on the other hand we have all too much material, intractable from its very abundance, while it is difficult to know what will be of interest to posterity.

The Abbey illustrates this very well. Many monuments have

been erected to poets of whom nobody now reads a line. Contemporary estimates have not been permanent. And as to what is being done today, the Dean and Chapter must tremble at the certainty that sooner or later some of their work will be described as absolutely wicked. They will probably be blamed for not having added anything contemporary to the fabric; yet, if they had done so, their taste might presently be judged to be as desperately awry as the taste of those who panelled the Sacrarium in the eighteenth-century manner. Likewise, although, in the records they are keeping, they are so much more history-minded than of old, or because of it, posterity may complain that they have been at fault. They tell us all about their great public occasions, it will be said, but what we would sooner be told is what they were like themselves and how they lived, just what the newspapers do not tell us and what even their own minutes and memoranda only glimpse at.

A formal history of the last sixty years is for several reasons impossible. Only a sketch will here be attempted, a patchwork, not a pattern. In this period very great changes have certainly taken place in the outward conditions and the inward thinking of the English, and in the history of the Abbey the chief interest perhaps is to discover how far it has moved with the times and how far it has stood out against them. The Christian Church throughout the centuries has on the whole avoided passing fancies or rejected them, and has gone on steadily indifferent to change, yet changing all the time both consciously and unconsciously. This must be very true of the Abbey, but can it be detected over so short a span as two generations?

The years 1800–1 would not be very convenient dates with which to close one chapter of this work and begin another. Britain was then involved in a great war which had another fifteen years before it. A long reign which was to end in mental darkness had still twenty years to run. The great revolution in English poetry was only just beginning and was as yet unnoticed except by a privileged few. But 1900–1 is no bad point at which to mark a break in the history of the Abbey. In January 1901 the memorial service for Queen Victoria was held. In July of the same year the old oligarchic government of the City of Westminster, in which the Dean of Westminster was the official Head, came to an end as the result of the London Government Act of 1899. A year later King Edward VII was crowned by the aged and very blind Archbishop of Canterbury (Dr Frederick Temple) assisted by Dean Bradley who was failing visibly and had himself to be assisted by the Sub-Dean (Dr Robinson Duckworth). Within six months both the Archbishop and the Dean had passed away, and an old order may be said to have passed away as well in Church and State, and at Westminster Abbey.

TWENTIETH-CENTURY DEANS

In the Deanery there is a Gallery in which there are numerous portraits of the Deans of Westminster. A lecture on the history of the Abbey combined with a tour of the Gallery would gain in liveliness from knowing what these men looked like and seemed like, who presided over the Abbey each in his time and directed the activities and inactivities of the Collegiate Church. So its history in the twentieth century so far may begin with a little word-sketch of what the twentieth-century Deans were like—all of them different, all characters, but generally speaking all the same kind of person.

Dean Bradley scarcely comes into the picture. He became Dean in 1881, in succession to his old Oxford tutor, Dean Stanley. His gentle reign came to an end by resignation on 29 September 1902, and he died in February 1903. His successor in the Deanery was Armitage Robinson who was already a Canon.

Armitage Robinson (1902–11) was a New Testament scholar of high reputation at Cambridge: he was also an impressive and picturesque figure. In his years in London he somewhat abandoned his biblical studies and produced several volumes of research into the history of the Abbey in the *Westminster Abbey Historical Series*. He still retained some of the eccentricities of the don. Mr Drake, the former Dean's Verger, who was his man-servant at the Deanery, reports that at 10 p.m. nightly he took to the Dean's study all the apparatus for making tea several times over and a large supply of cigarettes:

> He would then place what books he wanted on the floor in front of the fire, for he had the habit of crawling about his study from one book to the other. He rarely retired until well after midnight, and often I heard him going to his room at 5 a.m. and sometimes later. He smoked at least 50 cigarettes in the night. He would remain in bed until about 11 a.m. most mornings. I had to place his clothes in proper order for putting on and I am sure if I had made a mistake by putting his gaiters on top of the pile he would have put them on first. I had to take care that he had money in his pockets.

The Dean celebrated the Holy Communion once in the week and usually attended Evensong. He is said to have cared for the music which Bradley (it is said) did not. But his was not a period of great harmony. The Canons had the idea that he was too autocratic and exceeded the powers assigned to him, as for example in making appointments without consulting his colleagues. Eventually, after a series of committees had been set up to investigate the relations between the Dean and the Chapter, certain questions were framed for Counsel's Opinion. The Opinion seems to be wholly in favour of the Dean and maintains a number of his prerogatives unreservedly. Shortly afterwards Dr Robinson accepted the Deanery of Wells, married and left London. He returned to the Abbey several times however in an official capacity to perform his duties as Lord High Almoner at the distribution of the Royal Maundy. He was perhaps the greatest personality of all the Deans since Stanley. Canon Barnett after his first Chapter meeting (in 1906) wrote down that he 'felt very tender towards the Dean as a lot of fine china among rather coarse pots'.

He was succeeded at Westminster by Dr Herbert Edward Ryle (1911–25), son of a former strongly Protestant Bishop of Liverpool. Like Armitage Robinson he had been a Cambridge professor; then successively Bishop of Exeter and now Bishop of Winchester. He was no more than 54 years of age, and it was thought that the offer of the Deanery had somewhat shocked him, but his health was insecure and he had become lame. In any case his acceptance of the offer was by every account a happy event for the Abbey. He was a sympathetic and courtly person who made himself much endeared to the whole collegiate body. The First World War cut into his years at the Deanery very severely. It was a time of some notable events. The burial of An Unknown Warrior must be specially mentioned, because there the Dean's gifts and sympathies were manifested in a characteristic way. The suggestion came from a quite informal quarter, and affords a good example of the way in which a Dean of Westminster has to deal with offers and approaches when there is no precedent to go by and when causes of offence may easily arise. But Dr Ryle took up the suggestion with very little hesitation. He saw that the Unknown Warrior would polarize a latent sentiment in many minds and hearts, while somebody else might easily have rejected the idea as fantastic. He dealt with the whole business step by step with increased esteem. But more of this must be said later, as also of the appeal for funds for the Abbey made in his name in 1920. The woeful state of Abbey finances had called for all the administrative abilities of the Dean and the Chapter Office for many years.

The Dean and Mrs Ryle made a mark in London society, and a short digression here on dinner-parties may perhaps be in place as a not altogether insignificant piece of social history. Even in 1916, at a desperate stage of the war, this kind of hospitality seems to have been undiminished. It faded away gradually in the 'twenties, though some kept it up. But apart from becoming more difficult many came to think this rather a stiff, not to say stodgy, form of entertainment. Some had always done so. The Ryles had not been long at the Deanery when they naturally invited the Dean of St Paul's and his wife to dinner in Jerusalem Chamber. Mrs Inge recorded that it was 'very magnificent' of its kind, but she added 'my heart failed me if I thought that was how we ought to live'. Mrs Inge was a pioneer in much less formal entertainment which often had the charm of improvisation. But to invite eminent people to private dinner-parties was still the fashion. Mr and Mrs Thomas Hardy were much impressed by dinner in the vaulted dining-room at No. 20 Dean's Yard, then occupied by Canon Basil Wilberforce, the more so perhaps as there would have been no alcoholic drink. G. W. E. Russell in his memoir of Wilberforce says that the house 'became the scene of a brilliant and varied hospitality, to which nothing else in London exactly corresponded', and no one at the time knew London society better than G. W. E. Russell.

Dean Ryle died at the Deanery on 28 August 1925. He was succeeded by Dr Foxley Norris (1925–37) who came to Westminster from York, where he had been Dean for eight years. Previously he had been a vigorous Vicar of Barnsley. He was a man of stately presence and forthright, perhaps slightly alarming, manner, with a useful experience of the world. He regarded his duties as Dean as a unique kind of business which ought to be done with the dispatch and practical wisdom appropriate to a business concern. Possibly the particular duties of the Dean of Westminster did not always lend themselves to this kind of approach; the drawn-out and abortive attempt to build a new Sacristy ended in disappointment. But there was a refreshing individuality about Dean Foxley Norris. He sometimes irritated people, but he knew how to disarm them. Among other things by way of recreation he was an accomplished painter in water-colour; and was looked upon as a wise counsellor in matters artistic. At the Abbey he interested himself in the contents of the poet Spenser's tomb and the urn containing the bones of 'The Princes in the Tower'; the funeral effigies were overhauled and worthily displayed as never before; it is remarkable what great interest they excited in the Press. In 1937 a new organ was installed.

The appointment of Dean de Labilliere (1938–46) to succeed Dr Norris came as a surprise. He was believed to be a strong Evangelical and no great scholar, but very successful in his parish work and an amiable and effective suffragan bishop in the Ripon Diocese. When people asked how the Crown came to think of him, it was suggested that the Princess Royal had recommended him. But the fact is that he had an immense number of friends wherever he went, and was likely to make a success of anything he undertook. He was a success at Westminster, but in a way rather different from what might have been anticipated, for he was hardly in the saddle, or rather in his stall, when rumours of war and war itself engulfed every routine and every enterprise. But he kept the Abbey going with rare determination. He was a great patriot. He ordered the Union Jack to be flown on the Abbey flagpole when the war began, and there it was flown day and night until the war ended. He began a regime of timely parsimony in the Abbey finances which proved invaluable in the subsequent period of restoration. Although the greater part of his huge Deanery was made useless and mainly destroyed in May 1941, he refused to move into another house and did not often leave London while the war lasted.

But it was too much for him. At Easter, 1945, he was in hospital with a haemorrhage of the brain. He recovered satisfactorily, but at Easter in the following year he was in hospital again, and he died early in the morning of Low Sunday, 1946. Contrary to what some people thought, he was a very able man, with a gift for seeing things through, full of kindness, but by nature despotic, and with an irritable temper which he had subdued to courtesy. He was stubborn and sometimes appeared unreasonable, but he was generally right, occasionally wildly wrong. If of many things he appeared to be noticeably ignorant, it was because he had given himself wholeheartedly to the Ministry. His was a dedicated spirit.

The choice of Dr Alan Don (1946–59) to succeed Dr de Labilliere was so obvious that it was announced within a very few days. He was already a Canon of Westminster and Rector of St Margaret's and Chaplain to the House of Commons. He had been Chaplain to Archbishop Lang at Lambeth from 1931 to 1941. Installed as Dean on 6 June 1946, he began a benevolent reign of twelve years, marked by several noteworthy occurrences, including the coronation of the Queen, which was accompanied by all the satisfaction the nation felt at the accession of another Elizabeth; notable also for the success of the Abbey Coronation Appeal for £1,000,000; and for one or two other striking but less propitious events which will be dealt with in their place. Severe in character but mild by temperament, dignified in appearance, but cordial and most unassuming in manner, Dr Don would put up with a great deal, but some things he would not put up with at all. He did not spare himself and took infinite pains on behalf of the Abbey in bringing whatever business arose to a successful conclusion. He gained the profound respect of the whole Collegiate Church.

At the beginning of the century the five Canons were Robinson Duckworth, Basil Wilberforce, Charles Gore, Armitage Robinson and Hensley Henson. Duckworth, the Sub-Dean, had been at the Abbey since 1875; he was a Canon for thirty-six years, and during the whole period except the last year (1910–11) he was also Vicar of St Mark's, Hamilton Terrace, St John's Wood. He was very much liked: he filled the bill. Wilberforce was Rector of St John's, Smith Square, and had a large congregation, listening attentively to his exposition of what was then called 'the Higher Thought', perhaps a kind of Anglican theosophy. Henson was Rector of St Margaret's and already well-known as a fine preacher and a controversialist. Gore was writing some of his best books and deeply involved in the beginnings of a religious community which came later to be known as 'Mirfield'. Robinson, presently to be Dean, was still living the scholar's life. Not that he was the only scholar. Wilberforce was not a great scholar, but each of the other four had held a Fellowship at Oxford or Cambridge. Gore and Henson came to be really eminent, more so than any of their successors so far, except possibly Archbishop William Temple, but he was a Canon for less than eighteen months.

Charles Gore, afterwards Bishop successively of Worcester, Birmingham and Oxford, was at the height of his powers as a teacher during the period of his Canonry (1895–1902). By his preaching and even more by his methodical exposition of scripture and divinity in his books—for he was not a *great* preacher—he strongly influenced and indeed largely shaped what is now commonly thought in the Church of England. This is hardly realized, because so much of what he told us that then seemed new is now taken for granted; for this very reason his works are not much read or remembered. His book, *The Body of Christ*, published in 1901, is a remarkable reconciliation of the Evangelical and Catholic views of the Holy Communion, which has commended itself to men of very diverse churchmanship. One of his great gifts was a capacity for fusing opposites. At the Abbey, as elsewhere, he was temperamentally and politically radical, but intellectually traditional and historical. He urged the importance of clerical subscription, but was decidedly a free-lance himself. He was a great champion of the people, but he exuded aristocracy from every fingernail. He was, as it happens, the grandson of two Earls.

Henson (1900–12) was a very different kind of person. He was best known as a preacher, and secondly as a liberal churchman strongly opposed to Roman Catholic theology and apologetic. He was quick-witted, forceful and somewhat easily provoked, but always endearing. When he went to Hereford as Bishop, there were loud protests, but they died down very soon after he got there. He was firm but open-minded. He always read his sermons which were elegant as well as topical; he was said to admire the writings of Swift. His books had the same quality; they were lucid, but they were mostly occasional and controversial. He seemed even to have controversies with himself; at least he had the grace to change his mind and to announce it more than once. His ministry at St Margaret's was remarkable; he was the man for the times.

Between 1901 and 1930 fourteen Canons were appointed, and between 1931 and 1960 eleven were appointed. The lower figure is partly to be accounted for by the fact that from 1941 there were, except for a very short interval, only four Canons, a reasonable reduction after St John's Church was ruined by enemy action.

Among the fourteen Canons in the first group five had got a First Class at Oxford or Cambridge, four of whom held fellowships: one had a First Class at Trinity College, Dublin; two had been headmasters of public schools. Four became bishops, four became deans, five died as Canons without further preferment, and one retired.

Among the eleven Canons of 1931–60 four had a First Class in an Honours School at Oxford or Cambridge, and one at King's College, London; four had held fellowships; two had been headmasters of public schools. One became a bishop, two became deans, two died without further preferment, four retired; two still continue to occupy their stalls.

On the whole it may be said that the kind of person who is appointed to Westminster has not much altered. The practice of retiring has in this, as in many other spheres of life, become more frequent, but if those who retired and those who died in office be combined, the result is much the same in both periods. Only the occurrence of preferment has notably declined, but here two items have yet to be added to the reckoning if a fair comparison is to be made, and these may well do something to redress the balance. It may be also that scholars are now more specialized and bishops more workaday: academic distinction does not so obviously lead to the Bench as it used to do.

Many of these twenty-five Canons were very well known, but it is only possible, and that at the risk of seeming invidious, to name a few of them and their special gifts. R. H. Charles (1913–31) came nearest to the ideal of a scholar; his successors are often reminded that he worked regular hours. In his *Apocrypha and Pseudepigrapha* he certainly produced a bulkier book than any of his colleagues.

But he was not only a man of learning. He was a fervent and some-times a lengthy preacher, and a strong Protestant. For a single-hearted devotion to the Ministry at large and to the Abbey in parti-cular Vernon Storr (1921–40) is well-remembered and respected twenty years and more after his death. C. S. Woodward (1926–33) brought from St Peter's, Cranley Gardens, to St John's, Smith Square, his great pastoral gifts, and these became better known still when he was preferred to the bishopric of Bristol and later translated to Gloucester. One could linger over the names of Barnes (1918–24), Barry (1933–41), Beeching (1902–11) and a dozen others and the various ways in which they contributed to the life of the Church in their time, but space forbids.

Lewis Donaldson (1924–50) had very interesting links with the past. He was a chorister at Christ Church, Oxford, in 1872, and had often heard Dr Pusey and Dr J. B. Mozley preach, as well as other pioneer Tractarians. He always said (what is confirmed from other sources) that Pusey and Mozley read their long sermons with no attempt whatever at oratory. Donaldson was also notable as actively left wing in politics. He had marched at the head of the first 'hunger-march' in 1905, from Leicester to London. When he had been at the Abbey two years and the Deanery fell vacant, a dean of a cathe-dral who was given to understand that the post might be offered to him wrote down his reflections: 'though I am only moderately in sympathy with my Chapter, we have no one half so bad as the communist Donaldson'. In fact this offer was not made, and in fact Donaldson was not a communist. Canon Barnett (1906–13) was reproached by his colleagues as a 'socialist', but he and his wife, both tireless social workers, would have called themselves Liberals.

21

A New Approach to Services and Ornament

ONE Canon was well known for a special work. Percy Dearmer (1931–6) had already done this work before he came to the Abbey, though he might well have distinguished himself in a different field but for his sudden and untimely death in 1936 after only five years at the Abbey. His great achievement was to present a way of doing things in churches where the Book of Common Prayer is used which has found acceptance, and one may say enthusiastic acceptance, in every quarter of the Anglican Communion. The appearance of the churches and of those ministering in them, the place and character of the ceremonies, music, and appurtenances were laid down by him for many in a genial, unassuming, reasonable, determined and most persuasive volume called *The Parson's Handbook*, published in 1899, his earliest work.

It was also in the year 1899 that the Rev. Jocelyn Perkins came from Ely Cathedral to be Minor Canon and Sacrist of West-minster Abbey, and that event and *The Parson's Handbook* are not unconnected. Dearmer did not work in isolation. The researches and writings of St John Hope, Atchley, and the other founders of the Alcuin Club brought to the Church as 'the English Use' what might otherwise have been dubbed mere 'Dearmerism', and the movement gained strength in the early years of this century. Perkins was already with it, and he devoted his life to giving it expression at Westminster. It was not an easy task, for it may be said that in 1900 the services were as drab as in any great church in England. The Abbey was inevitably famous for the unfailing beauty of the architectural design, the number, size, and interest of the monuments, and the fine collection of silver-gilt plate (since considerably augmented). Here was the very place for dignified ceremonies and ornaments and vesture of ministers and altars, and here was almost no such thing. That has all been changed in due course, and for a generation now the services have been regarded as a model and a guide. This is in largest measure due to Perkins as Sacrist. It is almost amusing to see how the Chapter often hesitated, but in the long run were unable to check his onrush. But the full flood was only after the First World War and its immediate effects were over.

The novelties were numerous and varied, first a little of one thing and then of another, as the opportunity presented itself. Gradually the Sacrist introduced the wearing of copes in procession, and then normally at celebration of Holy Communion. The altars were vested in a sequence of frontals proper to the seasons, some of them very handsome: many of the altars had never been vested at all, nor used for centuries. A hearse-cloth was given by the Actors' Union in 1921; a Lenten Array first appeared in the same year; the huge Lenten veil over the High Altar Screen not until 1935. Benefactors were persuaded to give banners for processions, seven in all, the last the gift of Mrs Itterson-Pronk more than fifty years after Perkins came to the Abbey. In 1929 he organized among old Abbey choristers in London a Brotherhood of St Edward to carry out the ceremonies on Sundays: he was their counsellor and friend. Later another brotherhood, of St Peter, among the theological students of King's College, London, gave their services on weekdays. Both these Brotherhoods he clothed in albs and amices, and created among them a devout and devoted spirit. He drew up a Kalendar of Holy Days and provided a Book of Collects, Epistles, and Gospels drawn from many (too many) sources. In his great work on *Westminster Abbey Its Worship and Ornaments*, he reports that 400, if not more, additions, exclusive of minor items, were acquired between 1900 and 1948. In the latter year there were 52 copes and 66 albs and amices. (In 1540, however, there appear to have been 330 copes and 288 albs.)

Dr Perkins effected all this by a single-minded devotion to the Abbey and what he felt it stood for. His wife used to say that if he cut himself shaving he bled Abbey. He was sometimes held up by the Dean and Chapter, but by a wonderful mixture of perseverance, judgement, timing, and a little rough stuff he almost always got his way in the end. If some cherished scheme was turned down, that was never a cause for discouragement. It was kept for a more favourable occasion, and something else tried instead. He had the added advantage of always seeing things in black and white. The Deans on the whole appeared to him as angels, the Canons as little less than a body of demons. The kings of England, about whom he often preached with remarkable fervour, were either blessed saints or unspeakable ruffians, and in all his writings about the Abbey, which were numerous, he employed a style of vigorous and picturesque, if somewhat gothic, eloquence. When King Edward VII's coronation was postponed, he referred to him in print as 'the stricken monarch'.

Alongside Perkins it is only proper to mention the Rev. H. F. Westlake, Minor Canon and Custodian (1910–25). Of very different temperament to Perkins and with a very different approach to history, he had an equal diligence and devotion to the Abbey. As Custodian he was responsible for detailed arrangements at special services, and he carried out his duties most effectively. But the elaborate funeral of Queen Alexandra on 27 November 1925, over-taxed his strength beforehand and on the day itself; he returned to his house when the service was over and half-an-hour later he suddenly died. He was only 46 years of age, a great loss to the Abbey and to historical research. Besides other works he found time to write and had produced in two sumptuous volumes a history of the Abbey as a monastery, and this is his monument. As Assistant Keeper of the Muniments he had examined and catalogued a large number of documents.

DAY-TO-DAY IN THE COLLEGIATE CHURCH

The progress of the Abbey in the matter of rites and ceremonies can be seen in detail in Dr Perkins's three volumes referred to above; it was a notable achievement. Changes in other and more humble departments are less easy to discover, yet perhaps as well worth recording. A private diary reports that at a dinner-party in 1916 Lord Ferrers observed that 'all the details which we take for granted now—how we are called in the morning by our maid or manservant, and the cost of food and bus rides and manners and customs—are what will be so interesting a hundred years hence'. A few such details culled almost at random from the Chapter minutes and some other sources may prove of interest. And first as to the introduction of mechanisms of different kinds:

1. At the coronation of King George V in 1911 the cinematograph operators are allowed to photograph the Procession of the Regalia passing through the Cloisters, but nothing inside the church.

2. In March 1924 the Dean of St Paul's, preaching at the Abbey, inspects 'a new electrical apparatus for magnifying sound'. In 1934 a new system was completed; another is contemplated in 1944: about the year 1950 this problem was still inviting the attention of the Dean and Chapter. The building has proved intractable, but complaints have been mainly from the deaf.

3. In April 1924 the Dean and Chapter invite Mr Westlake, the Custodian, to have a telephone for official purposes. Mr Westlake

replies that he does not want it, but in the next year he has one. (The Barnetts installed a telephone in No. 3 Little Cloister in 1906, and they thought this was the first to be put into a prebendal house.)

4. At the beginning of 1925 the caretaker of No. 1 Abbey Gardens asks leave to erect a radio aerial.

5. In March 1926 a recording of some anthems is made, for 'His Master's Voice': these are on sale in the next month, a double-sided 10-in. disc at 4s. 6d., 12-in. disc at 6s. 6d.

6. In 1929 it is thought worth entering in the Chapter minutes that Canon Dearmer took a photograph of the clergy and choir in the Nave prior to a service.

7. In May 1934 the Choir School is to have a projector for exhibiting films.

8. In 1937 the coronation was broadcast almost in its entirety and was very audible at great distance, at Dakar, for example. The marriage of the Duke of Kent had already been successfully broadcast from the Abbey in 1934.

9. In June 1943 it was ordered that the Chapter minutes be typed instead of being written out by hand, and be kept in a loose-leaf cover until ready for binding. In 1950 they were ordered to be microfilmed.

10. In 1947 records of the marriage of the Princess Elizabeth and Prince Philip, pirated by transcription, were suppressed by purchase. The King gave £20 for this purpose.

11. For the coronation of Queen Elizabeth II in 1953 the Dean and Chapter wished to limit the use of television in the church to the procession, but they soon gave way, and the whole ceremony was successfully televised to the great satisfaction of the nation and the world. Since then many great ceremonies have been seen on television, and the complicated mechanisms have been remarkably inconspicuous (until 19 September 1963 when they were remarkably conspicuous).

12. The biggest machine of all, the Organ, was replaced by a new one for the coronation of King George VI, and was drastically overhauled for the Queen's coronation in 1953 when J. L. Pearson's handsome cases were replaced.

A few stray notes on some economic and domestic matters follow:

1. The Chapter minutes for 1903 refer to the College Larder and the College Wine-Cellar; the Steward is empowered to expend the sum of £25 on replenishing the Wine-Cellar, and also the further

AA

sum of £50 in laying down Port. Now both these institutions have had their day.

2. In February 1904 the salary of the Assistant Master at the Choir School is raised from £35 to £50 a year, and in the following November to £60. Presumably he lived in.

3. In 1916 the Dean and Chapter purchased 100 tons of coal at 30s. a ton.

4. In February 1916, no doubt as a result of the Dean Ryle Appeal, extra masons were to be employed ('non-union men, if possible').

5. In 1923 the salary of a new verger was £2. 10s. a week.

6. In 1903 a Pension Scheme for the Abbey staff was to be considered. In 1932 a Pension Scheme for all servants employed at the Abbey was to be considered. In 1949 a Pension Scheme was started. (The Lay Vicars had a Pension Scheme from a much earlier date.)

7. In 1947 it was thought that official houses ought to be provided with refrigerators.

8. At the same time it was resolved to retain the old gas lamps in the Cloisters: visitors now look at these antiques with great interest.

Of old chronicles and day-books those are most valued which give such details as these, and that perhaps is why since 1923 what may be called the New Abbey Chronicle has been kept with one of the Canons as Chronicler. The present holder of the office wisely keeps the current volume to himself; of his predecessors it must be said that they are for the most part sadly disappointing to the curious, though they will be very useful for verifying dates. But only Canon Vernon Storr had his eye firmly fixed on posterity. In a handwriting ever more tiny he details very carefully any points of precedence or custom that arose and many matters that would not find their way into the Press. To the end of his record for 1932 he appended a careful *Note on Inks* which he had used, four of them, beginning with 'an American ink, "Higgins' Eternal Black"'. 'Future generations,' he wrote, 'will judge of the durability of these various inks.' At present (1965) all are defying time successfully. The *Note* will be a researcher's delight at some future date.

The main activities of the Abbey, as seen in the Chapter minutes and the Chronicle, do not seem to have altered much. The daily round of services, the special commemorations and anniversaries, the visits of societies or eminent individuals, the marriages and the funerals have been of the same kind and have not varied much in frequency from one time to another. Perhaps there are rather more special occasions under Dean Ryle, and more still at the present day. But a notable development has taken place in regard to midday services. In the City of London services at such an hour have for many generations been a feature of Church life, and they answer to the needs of a large non-resident business community; now that the City of Westminster is rapidly being commercialized the same need has to be met there. A short address, a couple of hymns, a few prayers, and at certain times of the year a course of lectures is sure of a congregation. A ministry brief but significant is exercised by the clergy daily when one of them enters the pulpit at noon and invites those who are in the Abbey 'to stand or sit down, and if they will to join in a short prayer'. This is heard by amplification in all parts of the building and creates a mixture of surprise and quiet, while a Collect and the Lord's Prayer are being recited. A midday celebration of Holy Communion each Friday was begun at the end of 1963. Midday lectures which had gradually fallen into disuse have been revived and are frequent, but as a rule they do not subsequently appear in print, as those of Gore and others commonly did.

22

The Abbey's Overseas Visitors

TOURISM

ALL these changes, whether they have a directly religious importance or are primarily material, are tangible and visible, but there have been other changes not tangible or visible, changes in the feeling or atmosphere or spirit of the place, not very difficult to discern but difficult to catch and describe. Perhaps some part of this can be conveyed under the headings of Tourism, Empire, and Death, representing respectively a mainly social, a mainly political, and a mainly religious change.

Tourism is a word which has recently become common, because it sums up a group of social activities which have rather suddenly become a passion but also a problem, and among these activities a visit to Westminster Abbey is often included. This is not a new thing: in fact in another guise it is medieval. What is new is the huge number of visitors who may be in the church at the same time, and the very wide extremes of knowledge and ignorance to be found among them. They were described very sympathetically by Dean Ryle in a period piece of 1920:

> Can any sacred building in the British Empire compare with Westminster Abbey? Is it not the most unique and priceless treasure of the English-speaking race? Such was the exclamation uttered by an American friend of mine whom I was taking round the Abbey. It was not made in the tone of rhetorical compliment, but with the intense conviction of one who had quite suddenly been awakened to a full sense of the significance of this great inheritance from our common Anglo-Saxon ancestry. It is the same story if you take round friends or visitors who have just come from Canada, or Australia, or New Zealand, or South Africa, and who have never before been in the Mother Country. One feels overwhelmed and humiliated in the presence of their delighted enthusiasm, their reverence for the historic association of the building, their appreciation of its antiquity, their emotion at the

356

sight of places and things of which they have so often heard. Familiar as it is to some of us, to them the Abbey is the heart shrine of the world-wide Empire. The thought of it is intertwined with the most sacred feelings and deepest affections of brothers and sisters scattered over the whole world.

But, as a matter of fact, the case is scarcely different with our own people at home. Spend an hour or two on any Bank Holiday among the thousands who are swarming through the Abbey. The ignorance of course is often profound; but the interest is keen and insatiable. Words of explanation are listened to with delightful eagerness. The Abbey stands to the people for the Empire; and all alike, working men, clerks, soldiers, factory-hands, schoolboys and schoolgirls, who are making their holiday trip, want to know all about it. With some it is sheer wonderment over the great age of the building; with others it is delight and surprise because of the historical associations of the monuments; some are absorbed in the remains of medieval art, sculpture in stone or wood, mosaics, metal-work in iron and bronze; others want to know about the architecture, about the fan-tracery in the roof of Henry VII's Chapel, about the difference of styles, etc. Others are curious about the old monastic foundation; others are simply there perhaps to see the burial place of Dickens or Tennyson or Henry Irving; others with guide-books in their hands are going to 'do' the Abbey through and through from end to end.

Doubtless in such a crowd there is plenty of mere listlessness, unintelligent dawdling. But begin to talk about the simple facts of the coronation ceremony, about the tombs of the Kings, about the Knights of the Order of the Bath, about the statues of the statesmen, about the memorials of the Empire-makers (it is indeed an infinite theme), and your audience, casually collected from the ends of the earth, grows all around you, testifying by remark and question and comment to their appropriation of the Abbey as the Mother Church of the Commonwealth. (*The Times*, Westminster Abbey Appeal Number Supplement, p. 1, 29 June 1920.)

Twenty years before these vivid words were written the situation would have been rather different, when the great majority of the population did not often go far afield and the great churches were not usually the objective of the annual trip. It may be said that as the twentieth century has proceeded, more and more people have been qualified to appreciate the Abbey, but at the same time more and more have seen less and less. The visitors must go round the Chapels by a prescribed route, and nowhere now is there an opportunity for dawdling; all but an occasional two or three have others treading on their heels. This is partly due to the hurry of the age, partly due to sight-seeing now being so highly organized, partly to the layout of the Abbey which does not lend itself to leisurely circulation, partly to the fact that there is so much to look at, but above all to the over-crowding for many months of the year. A two-fold problem is created—to preserve the quiet which ought to belong to a great church, and for which this great church was specially built; and at the same time to do all that is possible to help the visitors to satisfy the interest which now more than ever they are capable of feeling in the architecture and history of the place, and often in the worship which is offered here. A leaflet is now available in French, German, Italian, Danish, Swedish and Spanish, as well as in English indicating briefly what is to be seen and inviting to prayer in this great house of prayer—which at times looks anything but that. The atmosphere has changed since Macaulay at the end of his essay on Warren Hastings described the Abbey as a 'great temple of reconciliation and silence'. But it is much more than ever before a meeting place of the nations. Perhaps the great task before it is to become more conscious of being so.

And here may be the place to mention the bookstall outside the south-west corner of the Abbey. This has in fact grown into a bookshop, but it is the direct successor of a trolley inside the church from which the Verger in charge sold guides of different size and scope to visitors. The demand, steadily growing for many years, increased rapidly during the Second World War, largely because the American soldiers bought so exuberantly, and since the war, even more rapidly, until Miss Pratt, who then presided over it, was often almost mobbed. So in 1953 the rather dingy Chapter Office was transferred elsewhere, and adequate and attractive premises provided for a great range of books which those who came to the Abbey might like before or after their visit. This has proved to be no small or incidental change, but a notable example of an opportunity seized for a new kind of ministry and service growing up out of altered and better social conditions. It has changed what threatened to become rather unseemly in a church into a very suitable resort outside.

EMPIRE AND COMMONWEALTH

In the extract from Dean Ryle's article given above the word 'Empire' occurs three times, and it ends with the word 'Commonwealth'. It hardly has a thought beyond the English-speaking people. It is entitled 'The Abbey and the Empire', and it would be interesting to trace the use of the word Empire in connexion with the Abbey between Queen Victoria's Golden Jubilee and the present day. The inquiry would provide within its own field quite a history of our own times. In 1887 the Queen came to Westminster to give thanks for a glorious reign of fifty years; there was not a whisper of misgiving, and the height of glory seemed to be reached at the Diamond Jubilee ten years later, though it was then that Kipling wrote his famous Recessional with its prayer:

> *For frantic boast and foolish word*
> *Thy mercy on Thy People, Lord.*

Yet for the coronation of Edward VII he wrote:

> *The peculiar treasure of Kings was his for the taking:*
> *All that men come to in dreams he inherited waking.*

The Empire was still a great sentiment in the First World War and after. As late as 1930 portrait-plaques of Lord Milner and Lord Curzon were added to that of Lord Cromer in Henry VII's Chapel, and the name of Cecil John Rhodes was put with theirs in 1953, the centenary of his birth. But it must be acknowledged that these memorials of the Empire-builders are in rather an inconspicuous position. They excite a certain nostalgia, but the names convey little or nothing to many who read them there. And now their contribution to Empire is utterly transformed: it is hard to know whether that would make them sad. Be that as it may, a different spirit has come over the nation as a whole, as Great Britain has shed much of the more recently acquired territories of what is now called almost exclusively the British Commonwealth. Services of dedication have been held in the Abbey for new nations going forward into independence and self-government. But no place but the Abbey is thought suitable for such services as these; and even if the sentiment of the Empire only haunts the place as a ghost, English-speaking people will always feel an interest and affection for the monument which a grateful nation erected to our great forbears, and not least to the 'Earl of Chatham, during whose Administration in the Reigns of George II and George III Divine Providence exalted Great Britain to a height of Prosperity unknown to any former Age'. But few will not be happy that in a Christian church feelings of pride and domination have given place to the ideals of liberty and co-existence. Certainly on many great occasions one could feel that the attitude to God and man has changed, and for the better, even though the old sense of mission and responsibility is now less easily discerned. And perhaps finally and not irrelevantly it would be well to remember, while we are about it, that in the New Testament the Roman Empire is always spoken of with respect and in places with gratitude.

HONOURING THE DEAD

It may be part of a similar change that an Abbey funeral or memorial service is now held in an atmosphere noticeably different from that which would have prevailed two generations ago. This is true no doubt of the country at large, but more easily detected when displayed on the scale of a national occasion. The ornaments and ceremony and procedure are enormously more impressive than in 1903, when the Dean and Chapter appointed Canon Beeching and the Precentor (the Rev. H. G. Daniell-Bainbridge) 'to consider the provision of proper furniture for funerals'. A further problem arose when the practice of cremation became common, and very important at the Abbey where the space for interment grows more and more limited. For a time the urn containing the ashes was concealed in a coffin-shaped chest in order that the hearse cloth might hang over it, and this pretence was only abandoned in 1963. Mourning was very strictly worn in all classes until after the First World War; the degree of relaxation has varied since then, partly, it must be allowed, as war and peace have emptied and replenished wardrobes. Black is hardly expected any longer.

But what has altered so much is the sentiment. This is due to a large extent, though not wholly, to changes in the accepted teaching about death. In consequence a memorial service is substituted for a funeral more often than not: the funeral will be private. An Abbey memorial service seldom lasts more than half-an-hour. It is a mark of respect for a distinguished man, an expression of gratitude for his services. The thought of sending him happily into another world is hardly present, unless it emerges when 'Reveille' follows the 'Last Post'. It is apt to be supposed that the chief mourners would be embarrassed by any but brief condolences; though the sending of flowers is an important piece of routine, largely managed as a trade. The descriptions of public funerals, especially Abbey funerals, in *The Times* in the 'twenties have a melting lyricism which now seems out of place and almost absurd.

And yet the services for the Dead are today really moving, and this may be because the congregation are trying to appear less rather than more sad than they feel. The Prayer Book service cannot fail to be deeply solemn when fittingly performed, and where each one present is left to his own thoughts and devices. There is a definitely religious change here; in former times a particular attitude was expected and therefore assumed; today a common purpose is in view, but not any one prescribed way of achieving it. It is achieved, if honour is given where honour is due.

The writer of these reflections may suspect himself of partiality if he offers the opinion that among the many moving funeral services of recent years that of Field-Marshal Lord Wavell in June 1950 was specially notable. At least it was notable for the fact that, the Field-Marshal being Constable of the Tower, the coffin was brought by water to Westminster, a solemnity only repeated at the funeral of Sir Winston Churchill. A large congregation awaited it. The service was very simple and straightforward. Lord Wavell would have disliked anything else. The Dean read the declaration of Mr Valiant-for-Truth from *The Pilgrim's Progress* beginning 'My sword I give to him that shall succeed me, and my courage and skill to him that can get it'. At the end of the service the coffin was carried out by the Poets' Corner door to a motor hearse which conveyed it to the appointed burial place in Winchester College. No one in the Abbey who knew Wavell but felt that these were the obsequies of a self-effacing hero.

FURTHER INNOVATIONS

In connexion with the distribution of the Royal Maundy a notable innovation has been introduced. For a number of years now the sovereign, unless hindered, has distributed the gifts in person. It is sometimes supposed that this ceremony has always been held in Westminster Abbey, but in fact it was only in 1890 that Queen Victoria sent to ask Dean Bradley if it might take place in the Abbey after the Chapel Royal at Whitehall (originally the Banqueting House) was closed. The distribution had always been made by the Lord High Almoner, and the sovereign was not present, until King George V came and himself distributed the gifts. His example was followed by King Edward VIII on the only occasion when he had the opportunity, and King George VI came regularly; he said he thought it was rather pointless, if he was not present. Queen Elizabeth, who came with her father and her grandfather more than once, has continued the practice, but she has changed the place of the service from time to time, as for example to St Alban's Abbey, Rochester Cathedral, and other great churches, an innovation of which the Abbey does not at all complain. It is desirable that this interesting and edifying ceremony should be widely known and seen in various parts of the country.

In 1941 amid the stresses of war a service of a new kind was held at Evensong on Whitsunday, a service of Christian Witness at which ministers of all denominations assembled and took part in a great procession, each wearing his distinctive dress. This has been continued every year and is valued more and more as a demonstration of the oecumenical spirit. The lessons are read in other languages than English, and the service ends with the recital of the Lord's Prayer by the whole congregation 'every man in his own tongue wherein he was born'. The Abbey and the Christian Churches owe this valuable opportunity to Dean de Labilliere.

Quite different from such occasions as these is a tendency very noticeable, and perhaps calling for review, in the diminishing number of clergy and the increased number of laymen who are engaged on the spot in the work of the Abbey. The Collegiate Church which originally had a Dean and twelve Prebendaries and six Petty Canons, as they were called, now has but a Dean and four Canons and three Minor Canons, eleven less than in 1560 and four less than in 1900. On the other hand the Chapter Office, which had in it fifty years ago the Chapter Clerk and one youthful assistant, has three men and six women employed full time and hard at work, as well as auditors who are constantly occupied on the accounts. This does not however mean that the Abbey is being secularized. Almost within living memory the clergy would have taken it for granted that they could have some other cure as well, whereas the increased claims of the Abbey now make this much less practicable. At the same time the business side of every activity grows enormously more complicated, and 'Parkinson's Law', which operates so forcibly in the world of commerce, does not make an exception of ecclesiastical institutions. What J. B. Mozley said in a sermon of 1870 is true enough:

> Religion itself is beautiful and heavenly, but the machinery for it is very like the machinery for anything else. I speak of the apparatus for conducting and administering the visible system of it. Is not the machinery for all causes and objects much the same, communication with others, management, contrivance, combination, adaptation of means to end? Religious machinery calls forth and exercises much the same kind of talents and gifts that the machinery of any other department does, that of a government office, or a public institution, or a large business. The Church as a part of the world must have active minded persons to conduct its policy and affairs.

The clergy may be such persons themselves, but the Abbey has been fortunate in having some very active-minded laymen in its Chapter Office for many years past and down to the present, leaving the clergy free to perform the extended duties which fall to them by reason of their being in Holy Orders.

23

War and Peace

1914–1918

IN the separate events, as distinct from the tendencies of this century, the two great wars must clearly occupy the first place, and although wars are liable to have a diminishing importance as they recede into the past, the interest of these wars may well prove more lasting, partly because of the unprecedented perils to which this island was exposed, and partly because of the powerful stimulus they gave to the democratic idea.

But it must be allowed that the First World War was slow to make an impact on the Abbey. It will be remembered that it began with 'Business as usual' as its battle-cry, and this note prevailed for a long time. The accustomed annual services took place; projects old and new were persevered with. Only in July 1915 were daily intercessions initiated. In the same month the Coronation Chair and Stone and whatever else was moveable in Edward the Confessor's Chapel were transported to the crypt of the Chapter House. The windows in the Apse were removed, and the old Reredos of the High Altar stowed away. In the previous month buckets of sand had been provided because of enemy aeroplanes. (The first bomb fell on England on Christmas Day 1914 at Sheerness.) In February 1916 five hundred sandbags were ordered for protecting monuments. Later there were 1,630 more. (In the next war at least 60,000 were used.) In April 1916 the effigies on the royal tombs in Henry VII's Chapel were boarded over and sandbagged. In June the lights in the Abbey were screened. But the raiding by air was not severe nor the country considered to be seriously in danger. The Choir School was not evacuated; in September 1917 it was struck by a bomb, fortunately with a glancing blow which ripped the rivets off the bomb and daubed the whole area with the bright yellow explosive. It was a remarkable sight, not easily forgotten, but the damage was easily repaired at an expense of £42. 5s. No other bomb actually hit the buildings.

In fact the war figures very little in the Chapter minutes which are largely concerned with finance. The situation, in this respect already bad, deteriorated as the war proceeded. At the beginning of 1918 the stringency had become so great that £800 had to be borrowed from the bank in order to pay a bill. This is not to say at all that the Abbey authorities were complacent or that the war was not grievous. The frightful casualties, the shortages, the weariness, were felt as they were felt everywhere, but they were not thought to call for any special action, and no special action seemed possible. Such precautions as seemed justified were taken.

But the moment the war was over great activity ensued. On 29 November 1918, eighteen days after the armistice, the monuments had been restored and the Coronation Chair was in its place. On 6 December Dean Ryle had occasion to write to *The Times* that, 'several weeks must elapse before the Abbey is entirely restored to its pre-war condition owing to the attentions of "the enemy"'. This might point to a date about ten weeks after the end of hostilities. The restoration after the next war took ten years; the contrast was in all respects striking.

One unexpected and welcome benefit arose out of the First World War. The Abbey bells had not had a full peal rung on them for many years, as it was considered that the tower would not withstand the vibration, and they were only rung for a few minutes on the conclusion of the war. This caused much disappointment and comment, and two generous benefactors made it possible to put the belfry and the bells in order. Since then the bells have rung out for many occasions of rejoicing, and sometimes half-muffled in grief.

1939–1945

The Second World War was different, and it was for those at the Abbey a period of prolonged effort not exerted in vain. The following account of it owes a great deal to personal information from Mr Tom Hebron, who, as Receiver-General, was deeply involved in everything. As early as November 1937 the question of building a bomb-proof shelter had been raised, when Canon Storr was acting Dean after the death of Dr Foxley Norris; and when Dean de Labilliere arrived he tackled the matter of precautions very resolutely, with the support of Canon Barry as Custodian. Many informal meetings led to early decisions, precipitated by the Munich Crisis of September 1938, and in October of that year a Sub-Committee of Chapter was definitely set up consisting of the Dean and Canon Barry assisted by Mr Hebron and Mr Bishop, the Clerk of Works, 'to take all steps which might seem advisable in respect to Air Raid Precautions'. The Sub-Committee worked hard. 'It was like planning a battle,' one member said. The Abbey and its precincts had been scheduled as 'an internal organisation' for A.R.P. purposes, and the persons involved, consisting of all those who lived or worked in the precincts, were 'like a ship's company'.

There were statutory requirements to be met, but also of course many peculiar to the circumstances of the Abbey. The provision of the bomb-proof shelter hitherto only talked of now came to the fore, and in March 1939 a tender was accepted for the erection of one against the east wall of the College Garden with access from the garden and ultimately from the other side of the precinct wall in the now vanished College Mews. In the same month a large amount of fire-fighting equipment was purchased, and air-raid wardens were organized and trained. A course of ten lectures on A.R.P. was arranged for all male members of the staff. The ladies led by Mrs Storr, Mrs Barry and Mrs Bullock volunteered for first-aid and casualty station work. On 25 August twenty-two boxes of muniments were removed to Northamptonshire. The Bodleian Library at Oxford took some specially valuable documents into its care. On the same day the Coronation Chair went to Gloucester Cathedral, the Stone of Scone having been previously removed and hidden privily. Already in 1938 arrangements had been made for the Choristers to be evacuated to Christ's Hospital, if and when hostilities broke out.

There was drive and tenacity of purpose behind all this, so that when war did break out on Sunday, 3 September 1939, every man on the staff of the Abbey except one had reported by noon, and the absentee hurried back at once from the country. Later on, as their numbers were depleted owing to the requirements of the armed forces, volunteers were called for and came forward from every walk of life. Some thirty to forty were usually on the strength and the various duties divided among them by rota. The wardens were directed by Mr Hebron, the fire-fighting by Mr Bishop. The Abbey owes a great deal of gratitude to these wardens.

The long work of preparation duly met with its reward. In brief the Abbey Church was saved and in the war not a single life was lost in the precincts. But the course of events was none the less fraught with danger which was met with courage, not to speak of situations that demanded a great deal of improvisation and hardship.

The main damage by enemy action was done on the night of 10–11 May 1941, when London was subjected to a particularly heavy raid; but before this there had been 'incidents' and rather more than incidents. On 13 September 1940 the great West Window was damaged and on the same day a high-explosive bomb penetrated the Choir School and made considerable havoc: fortunately there was no one in it. On 25 September the first damage to a house occurred: the garden front of No. 6 Little Cloister suffered, but not extensively. Two days later a bomb fell in Old Palace Yard. It was the one which bent the sword which is so conspicuous a feature of the equestrian statue of Richard I; the crooked blade remained for many years, an odd reminder of the war. The same bomb blew in the east window of Henry VII's Chapel and made a round hole in the masonry beneath it. The window contained some rather meagre armorial glass which was subsequently replaced by the rich R.A.F. Memorial Window, the work of Mr Hugh Easton. The hole was filled up with glass, a permanent reminder of the war. Two of the stone pendants in the roof also fell. On 19–20 October the Abbey firemen and the Fire Brigade were busy; in the evening the windows of Nos. 4, 5, 6 Little Cloister were almost all blown in by blast. Early next morning the occupants of the shelter, thirty of them, were severely shaken, but the shelter withstood the shock.

These are samples of incidents which occurred all through the winter of 1940–1. It was not beyond the resources of the A.R.P. organization to avert or reduce the damage, and experience brought much skill to the task. But the attack with incendiary bombs which began with the sounding of the sirens at 11 p.m. on Saturday, 10 May, was too severe. At 11.25 one of a number of bombs fell on the South West Tower, but it was quickly dealt with. Shortly after a shower fell on the Nave and Triforium, the Chapter Library, and Nos. 1 and 2 Little Cloister. All these were successfully extinguished except those which fell on the Library. They started a fire in the wooden roof, and here a fatal difficulty arose. Access to many parts of buildings so ancient as these is tortuous. An attempt was made to get a hose up the Library stairs, but it had to be abandoned because the water pressure was so feeble. Eventually water was obtained from a tank in the South West Tower, but the fire was not quite extinguished before the supply gave out. Such was the situation when further incendiaries pierced the roofs of six houses, the Deanery, Nos. 1, 2, 3, 6 and 7 Little Cloister. No. 6, perhaps the most beautiful of our houses, but old and inflammable, was soon ablaze. The Deanery and No. 3 Little Cloister were the next to go. Assistance from the Fire Brigade was not to be had owing to pre-occupations all over London, and at 2 a.m. when more pumps became available, the water-mains could not provide water either in the bulk or at the pressure which was needed: the demand upon them everywhere was enormous. The only chance was to run a line of hose-pipe from the river. This was done, but it was too late to be of much use. The fire at No. 6 Little Cloister had spread to No. 7, and the fire at No. 3 was involving No. 1 and No. 2. Now the Fire Brigade arrived, but in spite of their efforts only No. 2 The Cloisters and Nos. 4 and 5 Little Cloister were saved, and the small wing of the Deanery nearest to the church. No. 2 Dean's Yard had never been affected.

The church itself, however, was for a long time unharmed. Some twenty incendiaries fell upon it, which was not a great number, and all but one were effectively dealt with. But this particular one pierced the exterior of the Lantern and lodged in the timbers below, where it could not be got at. The roof of the Lantern was in fact only a temporary affair, although it was about 140 years old. It caught fire easily, and the flames leaping into the air 30 or 40 feet high made many who saw them fear that the church was doomed. But it was not so. The whole roof broke away from the stone walls to which it was attached and fell some 130 feet on to the pavement below, where it burnt itself out and burnt nothing else of importance and nobody at all. And it can be said without dispute that the replacement is more pleasing from without, much more beautiful from within, and permanent.

A long period of quiet followed these events. The 'little Blitz' from January to April 1944 and the flying bombs from June to the following March, though they fell in the vicinity, never fell close to the Abbey. So perhaps this hectic story may end with a description of the shelter on an ordinary night:

Picture an oblong structure of concrete sufficiently large to be converted (as it subsequently was) into a spacious garage for four cars. There are steel doors in a little inset porch at each end; the roof is seven-and-a-half feet thick; the air-conditioning plant makes a pleasant murmur. You enter at the north end, and on the left is a wide mattress on the floor, the couch of an old couple from the East End of London, no one quite knows how they got there. Next to them are two beds for the Dean and Mrs de Labillière; beyond them in a kind of recess Mr Lees, the Minor Canon, his wife and two children; at the end of the other side close to the other entrance is a control centre operable at all times of the night and manned by Mr Hebron or Miss Pratt in most devoted fashion; occasionally a small tinkle is heard from their telephone. In the bed nearest to them is Mrs Marshall, the Porter's wife, who will make most of the beds in the morning; then Canon Fox; he will probably fold up his blankets and be the first to leave, bound for his flat down Victoria Street. Next comes Mrs Bishop, wife of the Clerk of Works. At the end of the row Canon Donaldson and his wife, a pair some fifteen years older than any of the others. But no! Down the centre of the shelter are three beds end to end, in which Dr Perkins and his wife sleep, only ten years younger than the Donaldsons; and they have a friend with them. At 11 p.m. the Dean, ever bent on punctuality, will order the lights to be put out. Dr Perkins will continue to read and write with the aid of a torch, unless requested by others to put it out. No more talking in this dormitory. In the morning some will say they never slept better, and only rarely will anyone know whether it has been a rough night or an uneventful one.

A few more lines shall complete the picture: A holy and humble member of the Abbey congregation was once heard to describe Dean de Labilliere as a 'dressy' man, and with his tall spare figure and always appropriate habiliments he never failed to look well—even in the shelter night after night with his grey hair and the scanty flesh of his grey face, and his grey shirt and trousers and his grey tie and his grey socks and shoes. It is a pity that there is no portrait of him as he was in the shelter.

THE AFTERMATH OF WAR

The return to normal after the war was a long process. But the removal of the more than 60,000 sandbags began a few days after the war in Europe ended (officially on 8 May 1945), and this cleared the way for the return of the evacuated treasures. In September 1945 the Coronation Chair came back, and towards Christmas an exhibition of Abbey statuary was mounted at the Victoria and Albert Museum. This afforded an opportunity of seeing at close quarters works of art, many of which in their rightful place could hardly be seen at all. Particularly frequented were the small statues from below the clerestory of Henry VII's Chapel—sixty-seven of them—mainly lively figures of the lesser known saints, full of fancies only properly visible at eye level. These exhibits came back to the Abbey in March 1946, as also did the treasures which had been sent to Mentmore, Boughton, Aberystwyth and quite a number of different places. The Royal Chapels were opened to the public in the following month.

The restoration of the shattered houses was far from being so prompt, since all rebuilding was for a long time subject to regulations and official approval. But already early in 1944 the Dean had invited Messrs. Seely and Paget to make plans for restoring the Deanery, and the rebuilding was authorized by Chapter in June 1945. In the following October plans for the Little Cloister were also ready. Happily the walls of the monks' infirmary abutting on the cloister and providing a front to the ground floor of all the houses could be preserved. The architects were assiduous in dealing with the public authorities concerned, and it was a pleasure to be present at their frequent site conferences with the several firms of builders to whom the successive contracts were awarded. So by slow stages one house after another was reconstructed, though it was not until

1956 that the whole task was completed. No. 1 Little Cloister, of which a good part still remained, was re-occupied in May 1948; Nos. 2 and 3 in 1950 and 1951 respectively. The ruins of these two houses had all to be demolished and removed before rebuilding could begin; No. 3 was not even on the same site. The former No. 6 also disappeared, and was replaced by new No. 6, the Surveyor's office and apartment, and No. 7 which was first occupied in 1955. Sir William McKie took up residence in the Organist's house, now No. 8 Little Cloister, in 1956. Here it was found possible to retain the first storey of the façade.

The Deanery was rebuilt by stages. Dean Don, confined at first to the northern section (the Islip rooms) gradually extended his occupation southward until the whole was completed in 1953. The two great rooms over the entrance to the Cloisters, formerly the study and the Dean's Library, were detached from the dwelling-house and made self-contained with a communicating door from the Gallery.

All things considered the Abbey and its precincts were in better shape after the war than before it. In the church the temporary roof of the Crossing was replaced by a permanent structure, and a good deal of inferior coloured glass was removed. The houses had been getting inconvenient and some of them too large for today's way of life. For historical and aesthetic reasons No. 6 Little Cloister was a great loss, but it could not be saved. It was the house that the famous Dr Busby built in 1681; the drawing-room ceiling had the date embodied in the plasterwork.

War had done much, but it had not done its worst in the precincts of Westminster Abbey.

One noticeable difference between the two great wars is that everyone seems to have wished to remember the earlier one and everyone wished to forget the later one. In the years after 1918 elaborate memorials were erected in almost every parish; after 1945 the memorial was often only the addition of more names to those of 1914–18, or something useful to the parishioners, or possibly an improvement to the church. Perhaps it was that there was so much more damage to restore, or perhaps that the civilians had suffered so much more, and so a monument distinctively in honour of the fighting men had lost some of its significance; or it may be that after a second great struggle people simply wanted to turn away from the whole business.

Be that as it may, of all the varied forms taken by the elaborate memorials of the 'twenties none was more striking and original than the burial of an Unknown British Warrior in Westminster Abbey, none that was achieved with more solemnity, none that moved the

BB

nation more deeply. Yet it must cross one's mind that if it had been suggested after the last war, the suggestion might very well have been turned down. But this is no depreciation of its universal appeal. It has been copied in many other countries and helps to make the nations feel a kindness for one another. A Head of State on an official visit to a foreign country invariably lays a wreath on the grave of An Unknown Warrior.

Although other claims have been made, it seems fairly certain that the idea originated with the Rev. David Railton, who served as a Chaplain in Flanders. He approached Dean Ryle early in 1920 with the suggestion that an unknown soldier should be buried in the Abbey and thus be joined with the illustrious dead of many centuries. The Dean welcomed the idea and persuaded the authorities to take the necessary steps with a view to the burial being on Armistice Day, 11 November, when the permanent Cenotaph in Whitehall, replacing the first temporary structure, was being consecrated. The King was to be at the Cenotaph and agreed to come on to the Abbey for the further ceremony.

It was extremely important that the identity of the soldier should never be known. There were many nameless graves in France and Belgium, and from four different areas a body was selected and brought to St Pol. Brigadier-General L. J. Wyatt, director of the War Graves Commission in Flanders, chose one of them at midnight, 8–9 November. It was encased in a coffin which was at once sealed down, and the other bodies were buried at St Pol. In the morning the Anglican, Roman Catholic and Free Church chaplains held a short service, and at noon the coffin began its journey to the Abbey. It rested for the night at Boulogne, and the next day, 10 November, after a procession through the streets and a speech by Marshal Foch, H.M.S. *Verdun* with the body on board left about 11.45 a.m. and reached Dover at 3.30 p.m. The journey by train ended at Victoria Station at 8.33 p.m. and the body remained in the train until nearly 10 o'clock the next morning, when it was borne with a great escort by a circuitous route to the Cenotaph and thence to the Abbey, King George V accompanying it on foot with many others. The service was of a fitting character.

The inscription on the slab of black marble which covers this body of 'An Unknown British Warrior' is plain to read and the marble itself likely to endure. The poignant feeling which the stone aroused was especially felt by those whose loss and bereavement had been communicated with the words, 'Missing, believed killed'. Might not this man who had come to so much honour be their father or son or lover? That must fade, though not be wholly forgotten. What remains unimpaired is the gratitude of a whole nation and its expression here.

24

The Abbey in the News

IN a foundation so old as the Abbey it would be surprising if at the present day anything occurred which was quite unprecedented, yet such an occurrence there was on Christmas morning in 1950. The famous Stone of Scone was found to be missing from the Coronation Chair where it had rested for some six centuries and a half. It came back to the Abbey in April 1951. There was by then an amazing story to be told, more like a children's tale than a happening in the very middle of the twentieth century.

It appeared upon examination that a wooden bar which kept the Stone in place had been wrenched away, and the Stone could then be freed from the Chair without difficulty except for its weight of about 4 cwt. After being removed it had been put into a sack or some such covering, and tracks on the floor showed that it had been dragged down the Sanctuary steps, then along the east aisle of the South Transept and through the Poets' Corner door, then through the stone-masons' yard alongside Henry VII's Chapel, and so into the street opposite the House of Lords. Here it seems to have been put into a car. There was but one young policeman on duty in the area, and he reported having questioned a young couple, who, speaking with a Scots accent, explained that they were on their way to the seaside for Christmas and had stopped to look at the statue of King George V. He told them to drive on, and they did so. The Stone was presumably in their car or in some other which had already been driven away.

The success of the project was remarkable. It must have been very carefully planned, but there was also a large element of good luck about it. The Poets' Corner door had been damaged in the war and never properly restored. It required force, but not great force, to break it open. The night-watchman should have heard the noise, for noise there must have been, but he was accustomed to making himself a cup of tea in the vergers' room in the North West Tower, and someone may have been watching for this opportune moment. There were certainly a considerable number of people concerned in the

371

theft, and they had probably found out a good deal of what they needed to know. Two men (again with a Scots accent) had engaged Archdeacon Marriott in conversation early in the evening; and on the previous evening another had been found in the Abbey about 6.20 p.m. He was behind Lord Mansfield's bulky statue, and he had his shoes off. Apparently he did not excite any great suspicion, and the evening watchman let him out by the West Door. As it turned out he was one of the marauding party, but odd people do occasionally try to spend the night in the Abbey, and no doubt they occasionally succeed in spite of the routine search after closing time. The incident was reported to the Clerk of Works, but he did not think it necessary to inform the Dean. The actual conveyance of the Stone from Edward the Confessor's Chapel to the waiting car, a distance of a hundred yards or more, including the descent of nine steps, was effected without misadventure, and with insignificant damage to the Stone, if any. At any rate on Christmas morning it was gone. Coming in for the eight o'clock service the clergy were surprised to find policemen in the Confessor's Chapel. Was it an old custom which had escaped their notice?

It was a likely inference, and as it turned out a correct one, that the theft was the work of some able-bodied and probably young Scottish Nationalists, and although they had planned so successfully they had not clearly thought out the consequences. They decided to go south on the assumption that the police would be vigilant on roads to the North, so they crossed Westminster Bridge and took a random route which led them ultimately down A2 and off it to a hiding place near Rochester. The Stone remained there for five or six days, while the party went to Scotland and back with many alarms and excursions, but at last it was on its way to the North. The roads were watched for this eventuality, and it is said that the car the police were on the look-out for was actually stopped and the occupants questioned, but they got through by the innocent device of sitting on the Stone; it reached Scotland undetected. But what next? There was no satisfactory answer to this. The idea no doubt was to associate this fine trophy with a Nationalist demonstration, but the movement never came to a head, and fizzled out after a few weeks. Meanwhile some students of Glasgow University were identified as being concerned in the affair. What led to their detection was curious. Archdeacon Marriott remembered that one of the men he spoke to on Christmas Eve had said he came from Forganderry, a name the Archdeacon had come across when he was resident in Scotland. The registers of Glasgow University were combed and a student from Forganderry was discovered, and it was noted that he had been taking books about Westminster Abbey out of the library. He was shadowed and was observed to associate closely with some others, and they all wore scarves or ties of the same pattern. Thus they gave themselves away. Scotland Yard reported these discoveries to the Dean on 22 March, but they did not as yet know where the Stone was located, and, until this was found out, it would obviously be very unwise to take action. There was a lull. On 4 April, however, a Glasgow student came to see the Dean, and told him that there was a counter-plot to capture the Stone and return it to Westminster. He said he did not know where the Stone was, and even those who took it no longer knew where it was, but it was possible that this could be found out, if the Dean would agree to some committee being set up to discuss what should subsequently be done with it. The Dean of course declined to give any such undertaking, and matters seemed to have reached an impasse, though discussions began as to whether those who were implicated should be prosecuted, and it also began to look as though the matter would be raised in Parliament.

But the element of romance again obtruded itself. On 11 April the news came that three men had deposited the Stone at Arbroath Abbey in the care of the Custodian. This was a dramatic denouement, if in fact it really was the Stone of Scone. As it happened, Mr Bishop, the Clerk of Works at the Abbey, had been employed at Arbroath by the Ministry of Works. He was sent up to examine the Stone and pronounced it to be the genuine article and intact. It came back to the Abbey under police protection at 9 p.m on 13 April 1951, and was deposited underground. The Dean hesitated to replace it in the Coronation Chair for fear it should give rise to a demonstration or even a second attempt to remove it. But when responsible opinion in Scotland had been informally sounded, and the agitations in the Press had spent themselves, and a statement had been made in Parliament, and the Queen had expressed her approval, on 26 February 1952 it was returned to the old resting place which had been contrived for it so many centuries before. It is now surrounded by quite a formidable railing, the gift of the late Mr J. A. Dickins, and protected by other mechanical devices. Those who had removed it were not prosecuted.

ABOLITION OF THE FREEHOLDS

The Dean and Chapter naturally strive to avoid coming into conflict with the law, but they must find themselves from time to time in contact with it. They thought themselves somewhat hardly treated, for example, in the Public Schools Act of 1868. In this century they have become intimately concerned with Measures in the Church Assembly, and in this connexion a curious point arose over the new

Church House, opened in 1937. It was discovered that the Chapel there was built on, or rather over, land within the Precinct of the Abbey, and therefore lies within an area under the spiritual jurisdiction of the Dean. The matter was settled after consideration by the Dean delegating to the Archbishop of Canterbury and his successors the conduct and control of religious services in the Chapel. The area over which the Dean claimed jurisdiction was defined as 'within the boundary of the Close of the Collegiate Church of St Peter Westminster'. It was thought possible that some part of the Chapel was outside this boundary, in which case it was in the Parish of St John Westminster, and within the jurisdiction of the Bishop of London. The Bishop of London therefore made the same delegation to the Archbishop, in case any question should arise. The delegation in both cases was only to stand 'so long as the said Chapel is used in connection with the Church House aforesaid for the purpose of Divine Worship in accordance with the rites and ceremonies of the Church of England'.

Another case, in which an obstreperous guide was prominent, went as far as the High Court, and it was established that the public have no right of entry into the church or precincts; whether they know it or not, they only come by permission, except that residents in the Precincts may not be excluded from divine service. Again a scheme for putting the Dean Ryle Fund (raised in 1920) into the hands of Trustees required legal sanction, and a similar sanction was required whereby the Dean and Chapter kept in their own hands as Trustees the several trusts established after the Coronation Appeal of 1953.

But much the most absorbing and elaborate legal business was that which culminated in what is called the Abolition of the Freeholds. It caused a great expenditure of time and energy for nearly twenty years. The personnel of the Abbey, excluding the Canons who are appointed by the Crown and the workmen who are engaged by the Clerk of Works, are all appointed by the Dean, but almost all of them he had to appoint for life. Experience and prevailing opinion in the nineteenth century had made such appointments appear undesirable. Sir Frederick Bridge, for example, a famous Abbey organist, came to find his duties too onerous, and in 1918 Dean Ryle had the task of suggesting to him that he should retire, a suggestion which he accepted. It was specially inconvenient that the Minor Canons and Lay Vicars, whose particular duty it is to sing, should stay in their posts when they could no longer sing well enough. Dr Perkins had ceased to chant the service twenty-seven years before he resigned through other physical disabilities at the age of 88. The Surveyor of the Fabric resigned in 1951 at the age of 80 after being out of action for several years.

Difficulties of this kind had always exercised cathedral chapters, but with the authority of a relevant Act of Parliament it had become possible by means of new Statutes to effect the desired reform. It was more difficult to determine the appropriate procedure in the case of a Royal Peculiar. In 1927 a Sub-Committee of the Cathedrals Commission, presided over by Archbishop Lang (then of York), had recommended that steps should be taken at the Abbey to bring to an end the system whereby Minor Canons and Lay Vicars had a Freehold Office, and had suggested that the Dean should seek advice as to how power might best be secured to terminate appointments, if and when such termination was desirable. Dean Foxley Norris was the first to grasp the nettle. In the latter half of 1932 the Dean and Chapter discussed a proposal to regulate the relations between themselves and the Minor Canons and appointed a committee to go into the matter, and at the end of 1933 they had in mind a measure for abolishing the freehold, that is to say the life tenures, of Minor Canons. The Minor Canons had recourse to their solicitors. Over the next two years new Statutes were in view, which among other things would deal with Freehold in general, and in January 1936 Chancellor K. M. Macmorran was consulted and advised an application for a supplementary charter. This would be by way of a petition to the King as Visitor of the Collegiate Church. The intention was to abolish the freehold of 'the inferior Ministers and Officers' for the future: the current freeholds were preserved: no one already having a freehold was affected. The Offices involved were those of Precentor, Sacrist, Minor Canon, Organist and Master of the Choristers, Chapter Clerk, Receiver-General, Registrar, Surveyor of the Works, Lay Vicar, Auditor. The terms of the petition were settled and communicated to the Minor Canons who at once put in a counter-petition. Some attempts at an agreement were made without success.

Nothing more came of all this at the time. The coronation of King George VI was no doubt a pre-occupation and one cause of delay. Then Dean Foxley Norris died at the end of September 1937, and by the time his successor, Bishop de Labilliere, was in a position to handle the matter the alarms of war intervened. He did begin to take it up, and some modifications in what was asked for in the petition were offered, and by the Minor Canons emphatically rejected. There the matter rested. It was Dr de Labilliere's intention to resume the project again when the war was over, but his untimely death prevented this. It fell to Dr Don, a man of most conciliatory spirit, to begin once more. He called a fresh conference of all those concerned on 2 November 1948 in Jerusalem Chamber, and asked for joint action, if a new petition was presented on modified lines which he outlined. The petition of 1936 was still lying on the table, but was to be withdrawn. This meeting had no success whatever, but in fact two years and seven months later, on 31 May 1951, the King ordered the Great Seal to be attached to a Supplemental Charter which gave the Dean and Chapter what they required.

It would be tedious and distasteful to go into the various proceedings and counter-proceedings which ended with the granting of this Supplemental Charter. The other freeholders took no conspicuous part in the affair; but the Minor Canons carried on their opposition with a remarkable tenacity which one may legitimately suppose was mainly inspired by Dr Perkins. He would love to picture himself 'fighting tooth and nail' and undoubtedly as fighting for the honour of the Abbey and for a long line of successors through the centuries to come. Perhaps he swept his colleagues along with him. Certainly they were admirably united in a cause from which they themselves would reap no advantage: their own freeholds were to be preserved. Someone closely connected with the Abbey described them as 'outraged altruists', and their altruism seems all the greater because on a cool reckoning of the situation their opposition never had much chance of success. The controversy engendered too much heat, but they did all they could. And be it said that in the long-drawn-out contest the Dean never found himself treated with the least disrespect.

But enough of it all. A description of the final scene by a not wholly impartial observer shall close this account of the Abolition of the Freeholds:

The new petition and a voluminous counter-petition to the Visitor had been referred by him to the Lord Chancellor for his advice, and the Lord Chancellor had ordered that both should be considered together by a Committee of the Privy Council consisting of Lord Simonds, a Lord of Appeal in Ordinary, Sir John Beaumont, a former Chief Justice of Bombay, and Sir Richard Hopkins, formerly Permanent Secretary to the Treasury. The hearing was in the very gaunt and forbidding Privy Council Office in Downing Street. The three members of the committee sat together at some distance from the rest of the party, furnished with all the wisdom but not with the majesty of the Council; they wore morning dress. The hearing was in private; no witnesses were called, and their Lordships hardly said a word during the four days of the proceedings.

On the morning of Thursday, 18 January 1951, Sir Walter Monckton, with Mr W. S. Wigglesworth, and instructed by Mr G. G. Hartwright, the Chapter Clerk, opened the day on behalf of the Dean and Chapter. He spoke in a quiet voice and stated the case with lucidity and moderation. Its ecclesiastical intricacies were unravelled: a great many documents were handed up by Mr Wigglesworth. Sir Walter spoke from 11 to 1 o'clock, and again from 2 to 4 p.m. Meanwhile the members of the Chapter were ranged together on the north side of the room, and the Minor Canons on the opposite side: occasionally one of the other interested parties looked in for a short time.

The proceedings were resumed the next day when Sir Walter continued his speech, but most of the day and the whole of Monday, 22 January, were taken up by Mr Basil Nield, K.C. in presenting the case of the counter-petitioners, and dealing with those of their numerous allegations which seemed to be at all relevant to the issue. He said much that was of interest and some things that were new to the Dean and Canons. The Minor Canons must have been well satisfied. For a short time they had the support of the Dean of Chichester's presence: it was understood that he had volunteered to give evidence, if called upon. On the morning of 23 January Mr Garth Moore, who was with Mr Nield, spoke for about forty minutes, and said (what is obviously true) that Westminster Abbey is unique and not to be measured alongside other institutions which might seem to be similar. Sir Walter Monckton then replied, a question about costs was asked and answered, and the Committee rose at lunchtime, bowed and retired in silence, leaving the petitioners spellbound at the solemnity and quietude of the whole proceedings now so suddenly terminated. But Sir Walter, as he passed the Dean and Canons on his way out, broke the spell with the words, 'Well, boys, we're home.'

He was correct in his anticipation. The Supplemental Charter which the King was pleased to grant contains the provisions asked for by the petitioners. The appointment of a Minor Canon, which was all along the great bone of contention, is regulated. It is to be by the Dean for a period of seven years with the first year on probation, then for a further period of five years, if the Dean thinks fit, then with the consent of the Chapter for as many further periods of five years as the Dean thinks fit. The Charter makes some special arrangements for Lay Vicars. The other offices are put on a contractual basis. Besides recommending that the Supplemental Charter be granted, the Committee of the Privy Council made a Report to the Lord Chancellor of close upon 5,000 words, which commented upon points which arose out of the hearing. Its clear statements on some of the matters in dispute will be of permanent advantage to the Collegiate Church.

25

Paying Peter

GREAT events permanently affecting the history and existence of the Abbey are not really numerous. Great occasions there have been and still are, and the accumulation of monuments is one result of them, though the greatest of all occasions, the coronations, have very little to show for long except damage done to the fabric in ages more rough and ready than our own. But apart from the original building of the church, and its rebuilding, and the addition of Henry VII's Chapel, and Henry V's elegant chantry, and the dissolution of the monastery, and the founding of the Collegiate Church, nothing has been of more decisive effect than the handling of the Abbey endowments and finances. Sir Edward Knapp-Fisher, the Chapter Clerk, wrote in 1921: 'It is true to say that if the Collegiate Foundation of today possessed the same property as the Monastery owned a century after the building of the present Abbey Church, it would be the richest Corporation in the world,' and we may add that this could be true today, if it had kept only what Queen Elizabeth I restored to the Dean and Chapter, when the Collegiate Church was refounded. But by what seemed wisdom to those who were responsible, this prospect (which of course was not visible to them as it is to us) was gradually surrendered, until in 1888 the Dean and Chapter were content with a yearly payment of £20,000 resulting from the commutation of their estates, and this figure represented almost all their resources for the next forty years. At the time it seemed the best they could do.

The most direct result of this has been the launching of two Appeals for funds to repair the fabric, endow the Choir School, and augment the annual income, in 1920 and in 1953 respectively. The first of these asked for a quarter of a million pounds and raised £170,000, to which a little more was added in 1927; the second asked for one million pounds and raised a good many thousands above that sum. This is in a way the whole history of the matter. All appeals for funds have basically the same character, but the two efforts afford some interesting contrasts which seem worth recording.

The Appeal of 1920 was in a sense the more urgent. The Dean and Chapter were actually at the end of their resources and were in debt to the Ecclesiastical Commissioners with no means of repayment, a greater cause for alarm in those days than now, when things seem to run so much more easily on credit. In 1953 on the other hand the Chapter could look back on a number of years in which commitments had been met, but the need for the repair of the fabric and for the raising of stipends and salaries had become formidable, and action could not safely be deferred. The Appeal of 1920, though mentioned as 'world-wide', did not really reach to the most distant parts of the earth. It was inaugurated by a letter from Dean Ryle to *The Times* in the special supplement of 29 June, and the Northcliffe Press most generously undertook to run the Appeal. They reminded their readers of it constantly and published lists of subscribers. Mr Harold Child of *The Times* was largely in charge, with Mr George Curnock of the *Daily Mail* having a hand in it. But the outlook on such a project in those days was comparatively limited. Dean Ryle in his letter said, 'I appeal with a sore heart, hating having to do so.' Today anyone would ask why he should hate it, except for the great labour such things involve. At the Abbey itself Mr Knapp-Fisher (as he then was), the Receiver-General, led the effort, backed up by Mr Hebron, who afterwards received the special thanks of the Dean and Chapter. Some funds were raised by lectures and recitals, to which the Organist (S. H. Nicholson) devoted much energy, but the whole collegiate body does not seem to have been involved as in 1953, when after some preliminary set-backs the entire business was implemented and managed in the precincts, and everyone felt that he was in it.

And in connexion with the 1953 Appeal it is unthinkable not to name Mr W. R. J. Pullen, the assistant of Mr Hebron, himself by this time in charge of a greatly extended Chapter Office. Under Mr Hebron's direction Mr Pullen got together a large extra staff, thought up a great many ingenious schemes, contacted a great many organizations and eventually had the satisfaction of seeing the contributions come rolling in. They rolled in from every kind of group and association. Special approaches were made for example to the T.U.C., the N.F.U., the football clubs, as well as to the Stock Exchange, Lloyd's, and all the great concerns and public authorities. The activity rose to an astonishing height in the last two months of the year. The Press was truly alerted. A total of 1,080 newspaper cuttings, representing 5,700 in. of newsprint, were culled in November, and almost as many in December. A 'Save the Abbey' week brought in nearly a quarter of a million pounds. The staff of the Appeal Office in the Langham Room, sixteen or seventeen strong, worked twelve hours a day; 17,000 letters were sent out on the last day of the appeal (31 December 1953). A great number of helpers outside did all sorts of jobs for the good cause.

But this does not mean that the campaign had ever been easy going. For nine months it was by no means a resounding success. And it so happened that both Appeals fell victim to a mischance they could not have reckoned with; they both met with rival claims for which they had to make way. The earlier Appeal was a long way from its target when a great alarm arose about the safety of St Paul's Cathedral. Canon Alexander, for many years a regular financial despot there, rose to the occasion which became quite picturesque. It was commonly asserted, and may well have been true, that the Cathedral was descending Ludgate Hill at the rate of half-an-inch a century, and men trembled for its future. The City Surveyor served a Dangerous Structure Notice on the Dean and Chapter. They had already let it be known that they would issue an Appeal as soon as the Abbey Appeal was closed, and now the Abbey must clearly give way.

The 1953 Appeal was launched by Mr Churchill, the Prime Minister, at a representative meeting on 30 January in Jerusalem Chamber, but the very next day a great inundation of the East Coast brought nation-wide sympathy, and the Abbey Appeal was suspended, while Lord Mayor De la Bere gathered funds for those who were rendered homeless or bereaved by the disaster. This was only right, but the Abbey Appeal took a long time to recover, though it did so wonderfully in the end. In fact the two Appeals afford a contrast in that the earlier one died down and really came to a standstill, whereas the later one went from strength to strength and was only closed at the end of 1953 because that was the limit which was put to it from the first. It must be remembered, however, that in 1920–1 the national economy was weak, whereas in 1953 it was expanding. The anniversary of the launching of the earlier appeal was marked by a dinner on 29 June 1921, given to those who had helped in the promotion and management of it. It was a conspicuous gathering of about thirty people, but The Times in reporting it said that they should publish no further lists of subscribers. The sum collected to date was just short of £154,000. Finally, from one source or another it rose by some £30,000 more. The termination of the 1953 Appeal and the conclusion of the immediate business that arose out of it was celebrated with more originality on 24 May 1954, by the release of one thousand multi-coloured hydrogen-filled balloons in the Dean's Yard, each stamped with a message of thanks.

This seemed an appropriate way of showing appreciation for the widespread response to the Appeal. It was an unusual and beautiful sight to see these bright baubles rise and float over the Abbey roofs. Not many reported back: one was said to have been recovered in a metropolitan city in the North of England which had steadfastly refused to contribute to the fund. The liberation of balloons was followed by a peal on the Abbey bells. The next day Dean Don expressed the thanks of himself and the Chapter for 'the splendid way in which men, women, and children throughout the world had come to the rescue of the Abbey just in time'.

The Abbey does indeed owe an immense debt to the thousands who contributed to the fund, as it does to many others also, who throughout its history have showered gifts upon it, and not least in the twentieth century.

A decade has passed since the Appeal was closed, and so far the most obvious result has been inside the Abbey Church. Its appearance has been transformed, and the transformation has been striking. The grime of ages has been removed to show something of what even Edward I might have seen at his coronation. But there has been a change which can prove to be of much greater importance. Since 1953 there has been a new Dean, and three new Canons, and a new Chapter Clerk and Registrar, and a new Precentor and a new Organist and a new Legal Adviser. The Dean and Chapter have been described in the Press as more 'high-powered' than any cathedral chapter in the country, and one would not be surprised to hear that they have taken for their motto the words of the great missionary William Carey, inscribed on the lectern which was given in his memory in 1949: 'Expect great things from God; Attempt great things for God.' And if they are of that mind we can expect great things, the more so because they have behind them officers who can assist them powerfully in church and out of it. We may well feel that things will be different and better, though the past bids us reckon that they will also be fundamentally the same. But will they? In the immediate future, yes, but in the long run who can be sure? What opportunities will they and their successors have in the next sixty years compared with those of the last sixty years? Like most estimates, this one can only be notional, but let it be attempted.

THE ABBEY TODAY AND TOMORROW

Any sketch of events and changes in this century so far will have only a comparatively short period under review, made all the shorter by the interruptions of two wars and the return to normal after them, halting work which in an ordinary way might have gone forward.

On the other hand the earlier war undoubtedly hastened on the establishment of the welfare state, and the later war compelled progress in engineering of all kinds, and both led to rapid development after 1950. The difference in general between 1900 and 1960 has perhaps been without a parallel in a comparable .period, or only paralleled, if at all, by the sixty years immediately preceding it and corresponding closely to the reign of Queen Victoria. But as far as the Abbey is concerned the contrast between 1840 and 1900 would be greater than in the years that have followed. Dean Stanley's innovations and reform seem natural to us, because they matched so well the times he lived in, but they were drastic. In this century the Church and the Abbey with it have moved forward, but it may be that ultimately their chief business will be reckoned to have been resistance to the disintegrating forces of the age. Influences which have made for change and, it may be, for progress, in other ways, have on the whole made the Abbey, if one may put it so, only change its clothes and not its mind.

It is fairly certain that in the next sixty years changes everywhere will continue to be rapid. Consider then the possibilities for the Abbey. It may be that in 2030 it will be in a ruinous condition for want of that engineering skill that erected it in the Middle Ages; the knowledge may be there, but not the means to apply it. It might even be in ruins because the will to keep it up will be gone along with any taste for antiquity. On the other hand it may be that it will stand up a noble pile amid the ruins of twentieth-century concrete. But even so we cannot be sure how far the worship in it will be as it is now. We can reckon that whatever there is of it will be Christian and devout, but perhaps it will be ministered to the faithful entirely by machinery.

But these are the extremes of speculation. More probably things in sixty years' time will be not very different from what they are now. When a tendency looks as though it would end in a revolution, there is usually a reaction for causes nobody foresaw: the revolutions there have been, whether great or small, have nearly always ended in no more than adjustments, though these may open the way to progress otherwise barred. But under modern conditions these processes seem to be much speeded up. In the coming age it may still be the function of the Church to put the brake on a headlong rush, apart from its eternal duty to recall to God those who have forsaken him. Westminster Abbey is fitted for a leading part in this work. It has an indisputable tranquillity of its own, and correspondingly a monumental indifference to passing phases in culture and politics. This may well serve an age when there will not be any one accepted creed, but with that and because of it, a new search and hunger for a personal religion. That search may lead to the Abbey, and the Abbey may answer to men's condition. It may seem more out of the world than now, more strange, but more compelling. It may become clear that worship is the very thing it is most admirably suited to, and the best thing about it; but that it should seem so will need much work and devotion, and without that it will be in danger of becoming only a gigantic curiosity.

PART VI
Aspects of Westminster Abbey

The Architecture
By S. E. Dykes Bower

Coronations in the Abbey
By L. E. Tanner

Music in the Abbey
By Sir William McKie

The Sacristy
By The Rev. C. Hildyard

The Constitution of the Collegiate Church
By W. R. J. Pullen

26

The Architecture

BUILDINGS of age and importance become the subject of an ever increasing literature because they can be studied from so many angles. Their history can be told and retold, their design analysed, their aesthetic worth assessed, their function explained. But architecture is still something that has to be experienced. The natural response to a work of art, as to the beauty of landscape, is enjoyment, most real when it is spontaneous and least dependent on foreknowledge. Entering for the first time, perhaps in a foreign country, some building of unfamiliar character, both eye and mind form their own unprompted judgement. It may lack perceptiveness but, uninfluenced by preconceived ideas, it will at least be objective. So subtly can instruction be tinctured with indoctrination that, hand in hand with knowledge, grow prejudices that too easily linger long after reason should have banished them.

The grip they can exert, evident in much that has been and still is written about architecture, may partially account for the obsession with dates and authorship that militates against apprehending buildings in their entirety. The essence of such a one as Westminster Abbey is that it has been in the same continuous use for 900 years. Age has not fossilized it into an ancient monument or a museum. A church first and foremost, use is moulding its history all the time and the centuries telescope without such clear-cut divisions of thought and practice as may be discerned where tradition has less force.

The most valuable element in its constitution is the independence which its status as a Royal Peculiar confers. To a unique degree it has been able to think and act untrammelled by ecclesiastical authority such as governs cathedrals and churches in England. And from the time that Edward the Confessor started to build the first Abbey church in a style transplanted from Normandy it has been architecturally independent also.

By comparison with anything else on English soil at the time, the Confessor's creation must have appeared not only large but an alien importation. The precursor of a host of similar buildings erected after the Norman Conquest, it was born out of due time—an early manifestation of the paradox whereby the supremely national Church of England has been the least insular in its architectural derivations. As a royal foundation it benefited from the wide view of the world that went with kingly power, no less than from the wealth that was a perquisite of that power. And when William the Conqueror was crowned in that eastern portion of it completed and consecrated barely a year before, a precedent was set which, followed by subsequent monarchs, established Westminster as a coronation church. This privileged distinction, that necessarily belongs to only a small number of churches in the world, it has enjoyed ever since.

Because of the great events it has witnessed, history inevitably plays a great part in the interest which the Abbey commands. Yet if architecturally it were not exceptionally beautiful in its own right, this would not have made it what it is—one of the great temples of Christendom—with an appeal so cosmopolitan that today it counts, in point of numbers, as the leading tourist attraction of London.

The church, however, which so many millions come to see is the second Abbey built by Henry III. Ironically enough, to honour the first English king to be canonized, he pulled down what Edward the Confessor had built that the Saint's body might be enshrined in a larger and more glorious setting. Henry's devotion to the memory of the Confessor was deep and real: he may even have felt a certain kinship to him in temperament for both, throughout long lives, evinced an ardent piety and, as witness to it, embarked on great architectural projects that became their ruling interest.

In English history, as usually written, neither king has been ranked among the greatest. Yet Edward the Confessor, King and Saint, is still reverenced in a special sense as the patron of Westminster, his spirit uniquely identified with the life and worship of the Abbey he founded. And to Henry III, as builder of the present church, honour is due without ceasing. More effectually than those whose achievements were warlike or political, these two kings have memorialized themselves through lasting tokens of their ideals.

As well as the similarity of their character, a parallel may be noticed in their respective undertakings at Westminster. Before returning to his kingdom from exile Edward the Confessor had lived long enough among the Normans to absorb their culture and, in taste and way of life, almost to become one himself. That this was not resented by his subjects when he came back to reign would seem a tribute to his personal qualities. Henry III was equally acquainted with France and an admirer of its art. That he should have aspired to emulate the incomparable cathedrals then being built in the Ile de France is not surprising in view of his enthusiasm for architecture, though this was not for lack of awareness of what his own country could produce. He attended, for example, the consecration of the presbytery of Ely Cathedral in 1252, which demonstrated what good work English architects and craftsmen were capable of at the very time when the Abbey was being planned. His preference for French rather than English work must have been deliberate and served, by disregard of what was going on all round, to emphasize that Westminster was to be a law to itself. Among English architects this cannot, presumably, have been welcomed: indeed if, as might have been expected, it should have led to some cross fertilization in contemporary design, the evidence of its having done so is small. The Abbey remains the sole example in this country of a great church markedly French in influence. No other followed its plan, form and proportions, nor attempted to rival the height of its stone vaulted roof. Stone Church in Kent, on a small scale, has resemblances which suggest the same designer. The clerestory windows and diapering of the triforium wall in the north transept at Hereford, like the similar triangular clerestory windows in the nave at Lichfield, were probably copied from Westminster. Little else is notably reminiscent.

Yet the Abbey is not so French that, could it be lifted and set down across the Channel, nothing would differentiate it from its neighbours. Henry III might have hesitated to offend his countrymen by importing a French architect: he seems instead to have sent an English one to study cathedrals in progress, such as Rheims, Amiens and others, and then to interpret what he absorbed in his own way. As a result the execution is English and, to no small degree also, the intellectual thought, on the quality of which architecture largely depends for success or failure. A certain moderation, eschewing the ebullience which stimulated French designers to rival or surpass each other in daring, makes Westminster appear comparatively restrained by comparison with Beauvais or Le Mans. The English architect may well have distrusted the technical capacity of his masons to undertake such feats of construction: it is equally possible that he felt the results did not justify the expense or the risks. No medieval building in this country is as lofty as the Abbey: but its height is easily surpassed by many in France. The effect of height, indeed of size generally, is dependent on proportions: neither is necessarily attained by magnitude. The proportions of the Abbey are so perfectly adjusted, its actual design and relationship of parts so good, that the interior is completely satisfying and in many respects superior to that of larger ones, such as Cologne, where exaggeration of one dimension neutralizes others and huge scale yields less than its proper effect.

Coming fresh to the problem, Henry of Reynes, the Abbey's first architect, may even have perceived where improvement was possible. Many French apses suffer from looking overcrowded: not only is the rhythm of the bay design suddenly broken in turning the semi-circle, but the arches are so stilted as to look malformed. The apse at the Abbey is most skilfully managed. There appear to be only three facets, though owing to a very slight canting of the two bays to the west, the number is five. Nor is the bay spacing east of the crossing constant; but almost as though it had been calculated to look so in perspective, the variations are hardly noticeable. The eye is carried round the curve with such comfort and ease that this apse immediately reveals itself as the most fitting of all possible terminations to the interior.

In one respect it is curious to find that Westminster incorporates a feature that is not normal in its French counterparts—the repetition of the ambulatory and apsidal chapels at triforium level. What was the purpose of this provision is hard to discover, though respect for continuity may partly explain its presence. Just such a second storey at triforium level flanked the eastern arm of the Confessor's church. Then it was almost a Westminster innovation, copied at Gloucester where, behind the perpendicular casing of the Choir there is an early Norman example of three-tiered formation, with the plan of ambulatory and chapels repeated at crypt, floor and triforium levels. The chapels in crypt and triforium were, like those at ground level, vaulted and fitted with altars. In Henry III's Abbey, the triforium is only floored and ceiled in wood, the roof so constructed that use of the chapels is virtually precluded. Yet they would hardly have been built if they were not to serve some function and it may be surmised that the King's death stopped a more ambitious scheme before it could be carried to completion.

The marvel however is that, in little more than twenty years, he had accomplished so much. Structure and adornment were pressed forward simultaneously. The Shrine of St Edward, surmounted by its golden feretory, astonished all who beheld it by its costly elaboration; it introduced them also to a strange and exquisite art unknown outside Italy. Again, with far-ranging vision, Henry III brought over foreign craftsmen to enrich the Abbey with such decoration as Abbot Ware, on his return from a visit to the Pope, was able to describe as of superlative beauty.

The Abbey thus came into its unique possession not merely of the only Cosmati work outside Italy but, in front of the High Altar, of the most highly wrought Cosmati pavement ever executed.

That this has now to be kept covered with carpet is due to the disastrous use of English Purbeck instead of hard white marble for the interlacing bands. Whereas the Italian marbles have scarcely suffered, the soft Purbeck has worn away to the ruin of both surface and appearance.

Not less tragic is the deplorable state of the Shrine itself. Taken down four centuries ago and re-erected wrongly, it has become a meaningless travesty of what it could and should be.

Of the Cosmati tombs only that of Henry III gives in part some idea of the beauty which must once have pervaded the east end with a scintillating magnificence. How much glory has departed may be measured by contemplating what in Italy is still vivid with colour.

When the completion of the Nave was taken in hand after a century of inactivity following Henry III's death, fortune brought to its designing an architect of exceptional wisdom and ability. By his decision to build it in the style of the older work, with only such minor changes of detail as do not break the overall harmony, Henry Yevele perpetuated the integrity of the basic conception and gave the Abbey a unity that could easily have been lost. No irrelevant questions now arise of whether his work was contemporary or expressive of its date. The centuries have telescoped and only the rightness of the result matters.

The Nave proceeded, however, so slowly as to be still unfinished when Henry VII's Chapel was started. This grand and sumptuous addition is pre-eminently English. Yet it shows deference to the old. The eastern termination of an apse with attendant chapels echoes the older apse. The height of the new Chapel is low enough to leave unimpaired the dominance of the Choir and Transepts, and care was taken not to block light through the apse windows or that of the triforium below. The latter in fact looks into a deep walled pit, enabling the new Chapel itself to have a large west window instead of a blank west wall.

Henry VII, sometimes credited with being parsimonious, showed himself precisely the opposite in his instructions for its design. No expense was to be spared: 'as for the price and value . . . our mind is that they be such as apperteyneth to the gift of a Prince'.

His architects, the brothers Robert and William Vertue, proved worthy of their opportunity. The Chapel is a *tour de force* of construction, as it outshines everything else that can fairly be compared with it. St George's Chapel, Windsor, where the detail is no less refined, is marred by the flatness of its vault. In King's College

A Perspective View of S.ᵗ PETERS WESTMINSTER

From an engraving in the

e Towers & Spires *as designed by S.ʳ Christopher Wren*.

ibrary of Westminster Abbey

Chapel, Cambridge, the detail is coarser and too repetitive: nor is the junction of the vault and walls happy.

The elaboration and ornament in Henry VII's Chapel are controlled and consistent, testifying throughout to a first class architectural mind. In spite of profusion there is no feeling of ostentation.

Fate on the whole has been kind to it. There are not many medieval buildings in which the relationship of sculpture to architecture can be so well seen (every niche of the triforium containing its statue), or of the relationship of ironwork to glass—every window retaining its ferramenta. Though stained glass no longer fills the windows, compensation for the absence of their colour is provided by the banners of the Knights of the Bath. The stalls have been extended to fill four instead of three bays on either side. Externally the three pinnacles are an anomalous early nineteenth-century addition. But otherwise the building has almost escaped alteration and affords a rare instance of work of the finest kind still looking as it was meant to look. In it we see the culmination of the main building epoch at the Abbey, not however the falling of a barrier, separating all previous from all later thought.

When Robert of Beverley, Henry III's third architect, had charge of the work, he could not resist introducing unmistakable touches of his native Yorkshire Gothic. When it fell to Hawksmoor, succeeding Wren as Surveyor, to build the two Western Towers, he instinctively looked to a Gothic building which he had come to know professionally, which happened also to be Beverley. Since Beverley Minster is the one building in England which happens to have a closer resemblance to Westminster than any other, the coincidence was appropriate. But what is significant is that so classical an architect as Hawksmoor never doubted that the towers must be Gothic and that he knew how to make them so. Nowhere else did he succeed so well when using a tongue of whose grammar he was not master. These towers in some curious way— but really because of their latent architectural strength—seem now so natural a part of the Abbey fabric that they have become almost its symbol of identification. So familiar is their aspect that, through them, the world recognizes the Abbey.

Clearly responsive, too, to its inherent Gothic magnetism are Henry Keene's two sets of iron gates in the Cloisters. They are as attractive as the instinct behind their design was sound.

Much credit is due to Blore for his two major internal works—the west front of the Organ Screen and the stalls of the Choir. Such correct Gothic in 1830 was unusual. But Blore realized that the Abbey's architecture is based on geometry and studied so thoroughly how this influenced its development that his work, particularly in the Choir Screen, is as apt as it is capable.

Later Gothicists, such as Scott and Pearson, have had to endure criticism which the lapse of years is beginning to subdue. It is unlikely that the North Transept front will find many detractors in the future. The canopy work in Scott's Reredos is astonishingly good and Pearson's Organ-Cases masterly. Perhaps the recent decoration in colour now reveals their merit more clearly.

Works of different periods and different styles the building can absorb if they have real intrinsic worth; for the spurious there is no place. Time sorts them out in the end, even if its justice is slow. Yet it can be frustrated. Only as the result of restoration in the last few years has a vital element in the original design recovered its value—indeed been brought to sight at all. The grime which gradually darkened and discoloured the entire interior had so totally obscured the conjunction of stone and marble that these two materials were indistinguishable. In this instance it was possible to retrieve what had been lost. In others it is not, though changed circumstances may give less cause for regret. The *grisaille* glass originally inserted in the aisle and clerestory windows must have admitted a toned light, enriched no doubt by more vivid stained glass in places such as the rose windows and lancets below of the Transepts. All have perished, though beautiful old glass remains in the apse and glass of later centuries in the more important windows is nearly all good.

Yet the atmosphere of London today makes acceptable and beneficial the brighter light which clear glass now admits and, history being made all the time, war damage enabled the pattern of glazing that Wren first introduced to be renewed and extended all round the clerestory and most of the aisles. Few churches of the first rank have such even illumination; few light up more exquisitely to shafts of sunshine.

Better seen therefore is the incomparable loveliness of architecture and sculpture, of carved and moulded decoration, painting and ornament of every kind: better can be appreciated how great is the diversity within the containing unity. The Abbey is particularly rich in metalwork, both bronze and iron. From the medieval grille on Queen Eleanor's tomb, the gates under Henry V's Chantry, the grilles to Archbishop Langham's tomb and those of the Countess of Beaufort and Mary, Queen of Scots, the ironwork can be studied throughout the eighteenth century—the gates in the Organ Screen and three double sets of different types in the Choir aisles—to the nineteenth century, exemplified by Blore's window grilles in the South Cloister and the superb grille to the Daubeny tomb. How many would guess that its date is 1889? In the present century Bainbridge Reynolds is represented by the pulpit stairs in the Choir and other later smiths in the screen to St George's Chapel, the railings round the Coronation Chair and the Nave pulpit stairs.

The bronze effigies of kings and queens from Henry III onwards, the gates to Henry VII's Chapel and the grille to his tomb, are so famous as hardly to require mention. In those executed by Torrigiano the already old precedent of bringing great artists from Europe was amply vindicated, for one in particular—the recumbent figure of Margaret, Countess of Beaufort—is the most perfect in the Abbey.

Of treasures in pictures, plate, tapestries, carpets, fabrics and vestments there is no space to write. All these things contribute to a whole that is much more than the church itself.

Still wonderfully remaining in the very heart of London is the complex of buildings that comprised the Benedictine Monastery of seventy monks founded by Edward the Confessor. The Great Cloister, the Little Cloister, the Garden within the monastic wall, preserve their open spaces. The buildings, some medieval like the Infirmary Hall, some altered or rebuilt at different periods, have changed in outward form as well as in the use made necessary by the refounding of the Abbey by Elizabeth I as the Collegiate Church of St Peter in Westminster.

The past continues as real in them as the present. The same sequence of building, alteration, restoration, beautification, moulds them as it has the majestic church that towers above.

The Abbey has to be experienced because it has so much to offer. Through experience comes enjoyment.

THE MONUMENTS

When Nelson, on going into action, exclaimed 'Westminster Abbey, or victory', he gave terse but vivid expression to what for centuries has been the honour attaching to burial within its walls. It has persisted for seven centuries and is not less real today than when Henry III, having re-interred the body of Edward the Confessor in the most glorious resting place that art and prodigal expenditure could devise, was himself laid to rest close by. The precedent set continued to be followed until royal tombs occupied all seven of the bays that surround the Shrine. Edward I and Eleanor his queen lie west and east of Henry III; Edward III and Queen Philippa in separate tombs on the south. Since Edward II had been buried at Gloucester, Richard II was able to erect in the remaining space on this side a tomb for his first wife, Anne of Bohemia; here he was himself reburied when, from Langley in

71 The Cosmati pavement in the Presbytery, consisting of marble and mosaic, constructed by craftsmen of the Cosmati School brought over from Rome by Abbot Ware, *c.* 1268. The design, with its serpentine bands, was believed to indicate the time-span of the duration of the world.

72 The Choir, New Stalls and Screen. 17 June 1848.

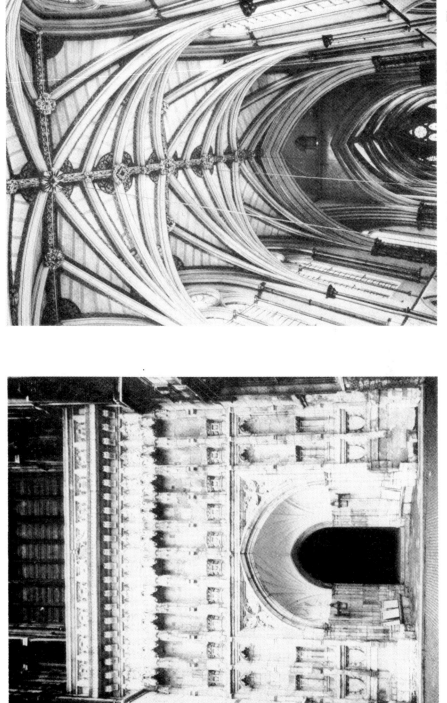

74 Detail of the vault showing carved and gilded bosses. The painted decoration is part of Henry III's work, repainted when Wren repaired the vault.

73 The Great West Door.

75 A unique photograph from scaffolding just under the crown of the vaulting, after the recent
cleaning.

76 The Shrine of Edward the Confessor as it is today.

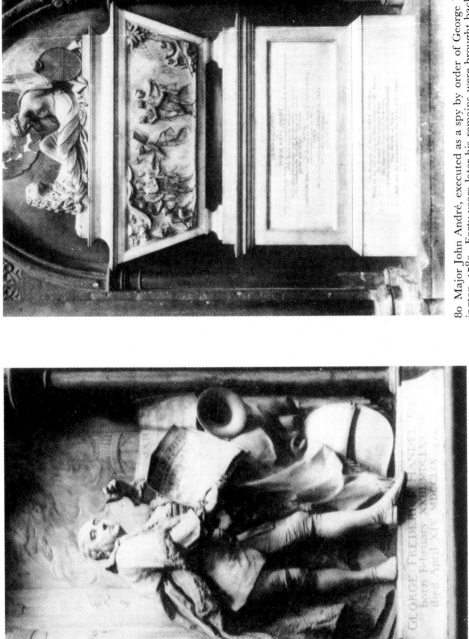

79 George Frederick Handel, d. 1759. Monument by Roubiliac.

80 Major John André, executed as a spy by order of George Washington, 1780. Forty years later his remains were brought back from America at the expense of George III and buried near this monument.

81 The Coronation Chair.

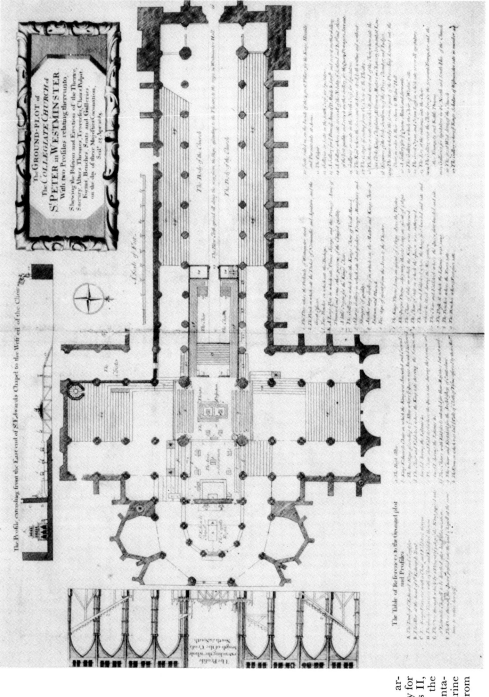

82 Ground Plan of arrangements in the Abbey for the coronation of James II, 23 April 1685. Note the contemporary representation of the Confessor's Shrine in the top elevation. From Sandford's *History*.

83 Procession of the prebendaries of Westminster delivering the Regalia to George IV in Westminster Hall before his coronation, 1821.

84 George IV in his coronation robes proceeding from Westminster Hall to the Abbey. Both pictures from Nayler's *Coronation of George IV*.

85 George IV returning to Westminster Hall after his coronation in the Abbey.

86 Dr Alan Don, then Dean of Westminster, carrying St Edward's Crown into the Abbey for the coronation of Queen Elizabeth II, 2 June 1953.

87 The Crowning of Her Majesty Queen Elizabeth II.
Westminster Abbey, 2 June 1953.

89 Children of the Choir of Westminster.

91 Gentlemen of the Chapel Royal.

88 Trumpeters and Kettle Drums.

90 The Choir of Westminster.

MUSIC AT THE CORONATION OF JAMES II, FROM SANDFORD'S 'HISTORY'.

92 Conducting the Choir during the coronation of James II.

93 Orlando Gibbons, Organist of Westminster Abbey 1623–25; a copy of the bust in Canterbury Cathedral. d. 1625. His son Christopher was appointed Organist at the Abbey in 1661.

94 John Blow, Organist of Westminster Abbey, d. 1708.

95 The Handel Commemoration Festival, 1784, showing the west end of the Abbey with the orchestra and temporary organ erected for the festival.

96 Henry Purcell, Organist of Westminster Abbey, 1680–94. From the painting by John Closterman.

97 Sir Frederick Bridge, Organist of Westminster Abbey, 1882–1924. He wrote *Samuel Pepys—Lover of Music*.

98 Sir William McKie rehearsing the choir for the wedding of Princess Margaret, May 1960.

Hertfordshire, his body was honourably transferred to Westminster by order of Henry V. Henry IV, though he died in the Jerusalem Chamber at Westminster, was buried at Canterbury and thus to Henry V himself went the last place in the east bay.

These were not the only burials in this venerated enclosure: but proximity to the Saint after death was counted a privilege only to be accorded to those of royal blood. When Richard II granted it to his friend John of Waltham, Bishop of Salisbury, the exception was viewed unfavourably, though this did not prevent Henry V from doing the same for Richard Courtenay, Bishop of Norwich, who died in attendance on him at Harfleur. Space by then was becoming limited and when, under the terms of the King's Will, the Chantry Chapel was built over Henry V's own grave a few years later, room could only be found for it by shortening the bishop's coffin and cutting off the lower part of his legs.

That the medieval tombs of the Abbey are all in the eastern part of the church is of course due to this being the earliest portion to be built; but even so their placing reflects a universal desire to be within the ambience of the Shrine. And what began from reverential motives was affected gradually by the prestige of those who qualified for a final resting place in so sanctified an environment, until burial in the Abbey was recognized as a coveted distinction. If in the sixteenth and seventeenth centuries it tended to be the perquisite chiefly of those of noble lineage, a tradition soon grew up that established commemoration in the Abbey as a fitting reward for those who had won fame in many varied ways—statesmen, ecclesiastics, soldiers, sailors, poets, artists and musicians.

In the eighteenth century and well into the nineteenth, this did not preclude a large number of memorials being erected to persons whose claims to eminence might be thought to be small or even non-existent. But in the last hundred years at least, the necessity for limiting the choice of those to whom it may appropriately be granted has served to enhance the lustre of Abbey burial. Because there is no further room for monuments, some memorials, at any rate by comparison with the standards of previous centuries, can no longer be in proportion to the importance of the deceased. The incised marble slab in the nave floor to Sir Winston Churchill is, for example, in striking contrast to the massive statue of William Pitt, towering above the West Door. Grandiloquence however in sepulchral art is no longer in favour, and it may be that the Abbey monuments themselves have in some degree influenced the change of thought.

Opinion has for long been critical of them. It is contended that their number and size have irretrievably marred the architectural beauty of the interior, to which justice will never be done while such heterogeneous incongruities remain.

Yet the monuments could only be moved if there were some other fit building to accommodate them: in view of the history they embody, few would wish to see them destroyed. No such building, now not even a possible site, exists. The idea of finding one was the subject of deliberations by two Royal Commissions in the nineteenth century and many plans were prepared for the erection of a hall or cloisters near to or actually linked with the Abbey. A measure of the care bestowed upon this project can be adduced from study of the schemes drawn up by different architects, most notably Sir Gilbert Scott and Pearson. The site favoured by the former was that which lies between the Precinct wall, bounding Dean and Chapter property, and Abingdon Street. Here Scott proposed a vast Campo Santo, in the form of two long halls under a steeply gabled roof, designed to accord with the thirteenth-century Chapter House which he had restored. Pearson's scheme, even more ambitious, was on the scale of a small cathedral. Magnificent in isolation, in contiguity to the Abbey it would have been too overpowering. An alternative, for which he also made drawings, was restoration of the ruined Refectory, which would have provided a long and noble room with the advantage of access from the Cloisters. Its surviving north wall, with a range of blocked windows, rises above the south walk of the Cloisters and there is cause to regret that, at a time when costs would have been less than half what they are now, the opportunity was not taken to carry out a rebuilding that such a master of Gothic design would have done supremely well.

But the purpose of a new building was then seen primarily as affording space for future generations to continue, not within the Abbey itself but in what would count as part of it, the tradition of memorializing national figures. It is not to be supposed that any of the architects consulted would have particularly welcomed the prospect of their Gothic conceptions having to house the more ponderous eighteenth-century monuments, nor do their designs suggest they had even envisaged such a possibility. That none of their proposals fructified may have been due to one inescapable disadvantage. However sound the essential aim of ensuring historical continuity, the timing of its execution was never quite expedient. No one minded being last in Westminster Abbey: no one wanted to be first in Valhalla.

Nearly a century has passed since what was then deemed a pressing need engaged the attention not only of the Dean and Chapter but of Prime Ministers. The position remains unchanged and the difficulty is no less. It cannot be denied that the Abbey has

The Grave of Charles Dickens in Poets' Corner, Westminster Abbey. He died 9 June 1870 and was interred 14 June.

suffered from its superabundance of monuments and mural tablets. Many, good in themselves, were inserted with ruthless disregard for the architectural design; not a few, on their merits, ought never to have been allowed a place at all. Some are of such monstrous size that the usefulness of the building for its real purpose is itself impaired. In a church that has regularly to accommodate great congregations, those in the North Transept, for example, not merely reduce seating space but render almost useless both its aisles.

Some people would like to see a sweeping clearance; others, averse from this, would prefer a moderate one. There is force in the argument that the most perfectly designed medieval building in England should not permanently suffer the disfigurement to which it has been subjected and that, however fine some of the monuments are in themselves, the parts are not greater than the whole and it is regard for the latter that should be paramount.

The contrary view is that any interference with the monuments would be tantamount to sacrilege. They are part of the history of the Abbey, a facet almost of national history. Having acquired the right of entry, that right should not be abrogated. In their variety is their charm; they provide a conspectus of sculpture through the centuries, valuable just because it is so complete. In no such concentration elsewhere can the attendant arts of lettering and heraldry be studied so effectively.

Familiarity with the Abbey, moreover, seems to engender tolerance rather than dislike of the monuments, for such is the transcendent quality of its design that the building subdues even the largest of them. The great height of the interior and its soaring lines draw the eye upwards to a level where they do not obtrude. This is more evident now that washing of the stonework, carried out in the course of the restoration that began in 1955 and accompanied by cleaning of the monuments, has radically changed the whole aspect of the interior. Previously one uniform umber shade pervaded everything, obliterating differences of material and so effectually killing light that a first impression of the Abbey was one of inspissated gloom. If the building itself suffered under its coating of dirt, its memorials suffered more. Alabaster and marble were scarcely recognizable as such; painted heraldry had either perished or became so faded as to have little significance; the pattern of lettering, faint or illegible, was no longer playing its part as integral to the design. Breakages had not been repaired, missing portions not made good.

So far as possible, in dealing with the post-medieval examples, a consistent policy has been pursued to rectify this and, though much remains to be done, the results can already be judged. Cleaning was the first step and, in the case of marble, polishing—because this is both protective and proper to its appearance. If it loses its hard surface a marble deteriorates and the more highly coloured Italian ones in the large sixteenth- and seventeenth-century monuments had in particular decayed so badly as to need extensive repair. Inscriptions, where faint, have been repainted so that their historical as well as decorative value is preserved. The heraldic tinctures on coats-of-arms, wherever required, have been renewed or restored. And the decoration in gold and colour, which is an essential element in the design of most Elizabethan and Jacobean monuments has, where authentic details of it remained, been re-applied. Paint, at once a preservative and an enrichment, is not immortal: had the real purpose of its use been realized in the last three centuries, much of the decay that has now had to be made good need never have occurred.

So long however as broken surfaces remain and the architecture is consequently disfigured, decoration is useless. The extent to which the majority of the large monuments in the apsidal chapels had been mutilated by loss of their ornaments, injuries to cornices, capitals and other features was as shocking as it was illuminating: because it revealed how wanton had been their treatment in the past and how in a large building defects can go unnoticed without constant vigilance. No illusion is more fallacious than that which ascribes to time and age what in fact is caused by culpable human mischief. Whatever the excesses of those much blamed agencies of vandalism, the Reformation and the Civil War, it may be doubted whether cumulatively the harm one or both may have done was greater than, to give one instance only, that caused by carelessness in handling brooms, ladders and scaffold poles—breaking off a bit here, another there, and never the instant urge, as in a private house, to mend what was broken. The practice of regular inspection soon shows how deceptive a superficial glance can be. When architecture is conspicuously defaced there is some chance of a protest; what it can suffer by deprivation may not even be observed.

The dividing line between essential and non-essential repair cannot be formulated, being a matter for judgement in each individual case. But wherever possible insistence upon one principle has been applied. If once the original design is allowed to disappear through failure to preserve and perpetuate it, what is handed on to posterity loses its authenticity. Restoration that acquiesces in the aesthetic and intellectual content of a design degenerating into something little better than a caricature or travesty, may end up, not as restoration, but as insidious destruction.

If it may be claimed that the enormous amount of work by skilled

DD

craftsmen in making good what through one cause or another had been lost has given a more literate aspect to the monuments, it may also be hoped that their treatment now makes possible a more sympathetic estimate of their merits. Crowding the walls to suffocation and jostling one another far too closely there is yet a fascination in the mingling of memorials so widely ranging in date, of such contrasts in size and style, and exemplifying the work of architects and sculptors from the Continent as well as England.

The most spectacular, partly because of their recent recolouring and the grouping of several together, are the great sixteenth- and seventeenth-century examples in the apsidal chapels. As architectural compositions, splendid in richness of form and elaborate ornamentation, these are a supreme embodiment of 'the boast of heraldry, the pomp of power'. Not dissimilar are the monuments which James I erected in the aisles of the chapel of Henry VII to his predecessor on the throne, Queen Elizabeth I and his mother, Mary Queen of Scots, to whom he accorded the finer of the two.

In the west aisle of the North Transept may be compared the Vere and Norris monuments, where the architecture is subordinate to the sculpture but neither show to advantage in the one area of the Abbey that a surfeit of memorials and their haphazard arrangement have really spoilt.

From Nicholas Stone in the seventeenth century, whose Villiers tomb in St Nicholas's Chapel is notably fine, interest passes to the eighteenth century, embracing, with James Gibbs's monument to John Holles, Duke of Newcastle—an outstanding masterpiece—works by the architects Leoni, Sir Robert Taylor, Kent, Robert Adam, and such sculptors as Grinling Gibbons, Quellin, Bird, Roubiliac, Rysbrack, Nollekens, Scheemakers, Bacon and Thomas Banks. The sombre black and gold Cottington monument in St Paul's Chapel is exceptional as showing the Florentine architect Fanelli in association with the French sculptor, Le Sœur.

Westmacott, Chantrey, Flaxman, Boehm, Onslow Ford and many others lead on through the nineteenth century to Alfred Gilbert, Goscombe John, Hamo Thorneycroft and finally to Epstein whose bronze bust of William Blake in 1957 was one of his last works.

Yet it is not necessarily the aesthetic qualities of the Abbey memorials that appeal most to everyone. Some will derive more pleasure from the wording of their inscriptions that mirror so accurately the sentiments of each age; or even in the evidence they supply of dress, armour, uniforms and fashion. The events portrayed range from portentous battle scenes and naval engagements to the murder of Thomas Thynne in the Haymarket and a British spy, Major André, being led to execution after refusal of a pardon by

George Washington. From such scenes depicted in marble it is a relief to find equal virtuosity more pleasingly expended on the delineation of architecture. Two buildings are so honoured—the exteriors of Westminster Abbey itself and, surprisingly, the eighteenth-century cathedral of Cashel in Ireland, on the tomb of Archbishop Agar.

It can at least be said, then, that the monuments are a very remarkable possession of Westminster Abbey, even if in some respects an embarrassing one. So indeed they have proved in the past, for one idea which needs to be dispelled is that we see them today as they have always been. In following the history of old buildings, a dearth of drawings that show them as they were at different periods is a constant handicap. Westminster Abbey, for obvious reasons, was more illustrated than most; but the discrepancies even in the works of careful draughtsmen are tantalizing and long gaps occur for which there are no pictures at all. Nor are written records always a certain source of information, though they often tell enough to show how little can be checked by visual records.

Close acquaintance with the monuments is productive of many unsolved problems. Certain architectural evidences for example that came to light when restoration of the large monuments in the apsidal chapels was in progress suggested that some of these were not designed for the positions they occupy and might have been moved from somewhere else. Even the medieval tomb of John of Eltham, which it has been surmised may once have been in the Confessor's Chapel, is a puzzle. It formerly had an elaborate canopy which was damaged and removed in 1776. If the tomb was in its present position when the canopy existed, the wooden screen (or what survives of it) could not also have been in the place for which it must have been intended. The screen is manifestly wrong now; is John of Eltham's tomb wrong too?

In the adjoining chapel of St Nicholas the little marble sarcophagus to Lady Jane Clifford has been moved and its design rendered meaningless by hanging both its inscribed marble scrolls on one side, when the original iron fixings remain to prove that they were to be on front and back. Therefore it stood free; but where? The Flaxman monument to Captain Montague, now under the North West Tower, was formerly in the Nave itself; that by the younger Bacon to Captain Harvey and Captain Hutt, now on a window ledge in the North Aisle, was also in the Nave standing between the pillars of the arcade. The seated figure of Wordsworth, now in Poets' Corner, was originally in St George's Chapel. Dr Arnold and John Keble have been moved within the last forty years and many other instances could be quoted. There has been no fixation in the past and it would be unwise to impose one now.

There is still scope for minor changes in the placing of some mural tablets, particularly in cases where it is now known that they originally had a better setting that did not conflict with the design of the building. Removal in 1960 of the more than life-sized statue of James Watt from St Paul's Chapel to a more appropriate home in the British Transport Commission Museum at Clapham evoked no expressions of regret: a small bust was acquired in its place and the inscription by Lord Brougham, formerly on the pedestal, can still be read, incised on a new slate slab in the floor. The standing figures, of which the North Transept contains so many, are perhaps of all the memorials those least easily assimilated by the building; the numerous marble busts in the South Transept are but little better. It is nothing less than ironical that there should be a massive seated figure of Lord Mansfield, that distinguished Lord Chief Justice having expressed the wish that, though he should be buried in the Abbey, there should be no such memorial of him.

Such an anomaly is of one kind: others, of a different kind, are violations of architectural propriety so flagrant that they ought not to be tolerated. Examples may be seen in the South Ambulatory where, in order to make space for tablets, blocks of Portland stone masonry have been built up against the Purbeck pillars. Within the last two years some lesser ones have been eradicated on the north wall of the Nave, where the possibility of original arcading and stonework remaining intact behind additions of brick and plaster was diagnosed and proved to be correct.

The conclusion must be that, while the monuments deserve the care that has been given to them in the last few years—and never before, it may be claimed, has so much been done to ensure a fairer evaluation of their merits—acceptance of them should not become blindly uncritical. On balance they enrich the Abbey of which they have become an inseparable part. But although English history is so fully represented in it, for future history there is now less and less room. As time passes, an unbalance may be found in the disproportionate representation of the last three hundred years: it may even be felt that a hundred or two hundred years is as long a tenure in Westminster Abbey as the subjects of certain monuments should be granted, since some at least have become little more than names, barely remembered or already forgotten. The Abbey is not a historical museum but a church. The last word can never be refusal to envisage all possibility of change or improvement.

27

Coronations in the Abbey

HORACE WALPOLE writing to his friend, Sir Horace Mann, a few days after the coronation of George III in 1761, says: 'What is the finest sight in the world? A Coronation. What do people talk most about? A Coronation. What is delightful to have passed? A Coronation.' There is, of course, an element of truth in this, but it must be remembered that to Walpole and his contemporaries a coronation was regarded, to use his own words, as 'a puppet show' of which he could and did make fun in his own inimitable way. There is no hint that he or anyone else realized that there was any deeper significance in the Service. It was regarded as a curious survival; but that there was any real meaning in its component parts—except, perhaps, the actual crowning—had been largely forgotten. William IV was only with difficulty persuaded to have a coronation at all, and *The Times* writing of the forthcoming coronation of Queen Victoria in 1838 could say, fortunately without justification, that 'the anointing is a part of the ceremony more recommended by antiquity than delicacy, and will probably be omitted altogether'.

But in the hundred years or so between the coronations of Queen Victoria and Queen Elizabeth II a great deal of work had been done on the Service from a liturgical and historical point of view. Much that was incomprehensible to our forbears was explained. It was shown that far from being a meaningless relic from the past completely out of touch with modern conditions, it was a piece of living history to which every age had made, and was still making, its contribution, and that it had a significance not only for this country but for the Commonwealth as a whole. At the same time it was shown that however splendid was the setting, the Service itself was a simple and deeply religious one in which our sovereigns dedicate themselves to the lifelong service of their peoples.

This will, perhaps, become clear if we analyse and explain the various stages of the present Service, and show that reduced to essentials it follows a logical and coherent plan.

But before doing so it may be permissible, perhaps, to register a regret. Throughout medieval and later times and until 1831, when William IV in ignorance of its significance abolished it (together with the Coronation Banquet) the morning of a coronation opened with a ceremony in Westminster Hall in which the sovereign was solemnly placed on a throne (originally this was the marble seat known as the King's Bench) by the Great Officers of State and Lay Lords. This represented the choosing of the sovereign by the lords temporal of the Second Estate of the Realm. A message was then sent to the Archbishop waiting within the Abbey church asking him to hallow the new sovereign. Thereupon the clergy of Westminster went in procession carrying the Regalia from the Abbey to Westminster Hall. The sovereign was then solemnly led in procession on foot from the Hall to the Abbey church. Within the church, at the Recognition, the Third Estate of the people confirmed the choice of the Second Estate, and the Archbishop, as head of the First Estate (the Lords Spiritual), having thus received authority to proceed, hallowed, invested and crowned the new sovereign.

This, then, was the secular side of a coronation of which only the religious side remains today. But if, as has been suggested by more than one serious authority, this ancient ceremony of inauguration in Westminster Hall could be revived in (let us hope) the distant future, it might be possible so to bring it into line with modern conditions that the representatives of the Commonwealth together with the Speaker and the leaders of all parties in the House of Commons, might play an active part in the coronation instead of being merely spectators within the Abbey as they are at present. Again, too, in the procession from the Hall to the Abbey, as it would be part of the secular ceremonies, the Regalia could be carried by representatives of all the religions within the Commonwealth who, at present, with the exception of the Moderator of the Church of Scotland, have no active part to play in a coronation. It might even be possible, after the Service in the Abbey, for the sovereign, robed and crowned, to return to Westminster Hall and there receive from the representatives of the Commonwealth, each in their own way, the testimony of their allegiance to its Head, in some form of secular Homage.

To return to the Service itself. It now consists of four distinct parts, each one leading on to the other, and forming, as has been said, a coherent whole.

1. It begins with what may be called the *Introduction*. This consists of the *Entry*, the *Recognition*, the *Oath* and the *Presentation of the Bible*.

As the Sovereign proceeds up the church from the West Door to the strains of the traditional anthem, 'I was glad, etc.', so splendidly set by the late Sir Hubert Parry for the coronation of King Edward VII, the music is broken into by the acclamations of the Westminster Scholars. This does, in fact, represent the old spontaneous shout of approval of the people. The more formal Recognition follows, when the Sovereign is led to the four corners of the 'theatre' and presented to the congregation by the Archbishop as the 'undoubted' Sovereign. Those present are thereby asked if they wish the Service to proceed, and this was formerly the ratification of the election previously held in Westminster Hall. The Recognition makes it clear that the Monarchy is based on the people's will and consent.

Assured of this, the Archbishop proceeds to administer the Oath to ensure that the Sovereign will respect and govern according to the laws of all his peoples, and will uphold the Protestant reformed Church of England and Scotland. The Recognition and the Oath together form the contract between the Sovereign and the people, and they are the foundation upon which the whole Service is based. This is ratified at this point by the presentation of the Bible (presented at the last coronation for the first time by the Moderator of the Church of Scotland instead of, as formerly, by the Archbishop) as the source of all wisdom and law.

2. *The Consecration of the Sovereign by Anointing.* The Introduction concluded, the Archbishop is now prepared to consecrate the Sovereign and begins the Communion Service. At the conclusion of the Creed the Sovereign moves to the Coronation Chair, and is there anointed with the holy oil. This, of course, and not the crowning, is the most solemn moment in the Service. All through the ages kings have been thus consecrated and set apart.

3. *The Investiture and Crowning.* It is not until the Sovereign has been anointed that he or she can be invested with the royal robes and insignia, each with its separate symbolic meaning, culminating with the actual crowning with St Edward's crown.

4. *The Enthroning and Homage.* After a brief pause the Sovereign rises and moves from the Coronation Chair to the Throne which is placed in the middle of the 'theatre' and raised on five steps. There the Sovereign (in the words of the rubric) is 'lifted up into it by the Archbishops and Bishops, and other Peers of the Kingdom'. The significance of this is that the Sovereign, robed and crowned, is now for the first time conspicuously visible to all. It is also the moment historically when the Sovereign takes possession of his or her kingdom. The Sovereign is now ready to receive the homage of the people. This is performed in person by representatives of the Lords Spiritual, and Lords Temporal, and by a threefold shout of acclamation from the congregation representing the Third Estate.

At this point, if there is a queen consort, her coronation follows.

Otherwise the Archbishop resumes the Communion Service at the
OFFERTORY and continues it to its conclusion.

Then after a brief recess the Sovereign re-emerges no longer
clothed in the crimson robes of a Peer of Parliament as at the
beginning of the Service, but in the purple robes of full majesty,
wearing the Imperial crown, and carrying the Sceptre with the
Cross ('the ensign of kingly power and justice') and the Orb, and so
passes out from the Abbey church.

Such then is the Coronation Service, and it has seemed worth
while to explain it at some length, because its essential features have
remained the same for 1,000 years. It can trace its direct descent
from the Service used by St Dunstan at King Edgar's coronation
at Bath in A.D. 973, and that Service was itself based on older models.
It has, of course, often been revised, and English has taken the place
of Latin, but it is still a service of election; of confirmation of the
people's choice; of self dedication; and of consecration. There is no
doubt, too, that it was deliberately modelled on the service for
the consecration of a bishop—anointing taking the place of the
imposition of hands—and since 1689 (reverting to ancient usage)
both these Services have been incorporated in the Communion
Service.

The connexion of the Coronation Service with Westminster Abbey
is almost as old as the Service itself. In pre-Conquest days, there
seems to have been no fixed place for coronations. Several took
place at Kingston-upon-Thames where the 'King's Stone' is still
shown. But Kingston was not the only place, for Edgar was crowned
at Bath and Edward the Confessor at Winchester. There is some
slight evidence which suggests that Harold was hurriedly crowned
not in St Paul's Cathedral but at Westminster during the mass at
the Confessor's funeral within the Abbey. It may well have been so,
for with a disputed succession it was all important to be crowned
quickly.

But if the place of Harold's coronation is doubtful there is no
doubt that William the Conqueror was crowned within the Abbey
church at Westminster. It gave rise to a remarkable scene. When
the moment came for the Recognition the question was put to the
congregation both in English and in French. The confused shout
of assent which followed was mistakenly thought to be a hostile one
by the Norman soldiers outside the Abbey. Following their natural
instinct they proceeded to lay about them and to set fire to anything
within reach. As the smoke began to fill the church the congregation
panicked in their turn and rushed out. Only the Conqueror and
the officiating clergy were left in the church and 'in the solitude of
that wintry day, amidst the cries of his new subjects, trampled down

by the horses' hoofs of their conquerors, he himself, for the first time in his life, trembling from head to foot, the remainder of the ceremony was hurried on'. The precedent, however, had been set, and from that day to this every sovereign, except Edward V and Edward VIII, has been crowned at Westminster.

Something, however, was still lacking, some visible 'link' which would inevitably connect the church at Westminster with coronations. Something like the 'King's Stone' at Kingston-upon-Thames or, on the spiritual side, the chair of St Augustine in Canterbury Cathedral. This was provided between 1297 and 1300 by Edward I when he ordered the Coronation Chair to be made in order to enclose within it the Stone of Scone which he had captured from the Scots in 1296. It had been the original intention of the King to place the Stone in a bronze chair, and work on this had already begun when he changed his mind and commissioned Master Walter of Durham to design and make the present oak chair at a cost of 100s. It was completed and the Stone set in its place beneath the chair c. 1300.

The Stone of Scone itself is a roughly hewn block of reddish-grey sandstone. It weighs about 4 cwt., and is 26½ in. long, 16½ in. broad and 11 in. thick. At each end are iron rings so placed that a pole could be passed through them to enable the stone to be easily carried. Geologists seem to be agreed that it closely resembles sandstone of the lower Old Red Sandstone age which is not uncommon in the neighbourhood of Scone.

In an account of the coronation of Alexander III of Scotland at Scone in 1249, the chronicler, John Fordun, definitely states that the young king was placed on the Royal Stone, preserved at the Abbey of Scone, in accordance with ancient custom, and this is the first known reference to the Stone of Scone. But if its authentic history begins in the thirteenth century, its legendary history goes back much further. Legend has identified it with Jacob's stone at Bethel, with the Irish Stone of Destiny and with the Stone at Iona on which St Columba laid his head and died.

But whatever may be its legendary history there is no doubt that it was a greatly venerated stone which Edward I brought back with him from Scotland. He was well aware that an object of such reverence might prove to be a danger and gather round it the traditions of a brave and hitherto independent people. He therefore caused it to be enclosed for greater safety within the Chair and placed it near the Shrine of Edward the Confessor at Westminster. Twice only has it left the Abbey. In 1657 both Chair and Stone were taken over to Westminster Hall for the installation of Oliver Cromwell as Lord Protector. Three centuries later, at Christmas 1950, some young Scottish nationalists, having concealed themselves in the

Abbey, forcibly removed the Stone by night and took it back to Scotland. It was retrieved some three months later from the Abbey at Arbroath where they had deposited it in front of the High Altar and close to the tomb of King William the Lion.

The Coronation Chair, or St Edward's Chair as it used to be called, has also left the Abbey on one other occasion since 1657, but only for its greater safety. During the Second World War it was taken to Gloucester and placed in the Crypt of the Cathedral. The Coronation Stone, however, remained buried within the Abbey throughout the war, and that there might be no doubt of its exact position, should anything have happened to the Abbey, a plan of its hiding place was deposited with the Prime Minister of Canada.

A chair so ancient as the Coronation Chair must inevitably suffer from its age and, it must be added, from the neglect and ill-treatment which it has suffered in the past. An opportunity, therefore, was taken during the preparations for the coronation in 1953 to make a minute examination of it with a view to seeing how best to conserve it and keep it in repair. It was, in fact, found to be structurally perfectly sound, but in the course of this examination some new facts came to light. It unexpectedly became apparent that very early in its history the Chair had been drastically redecorated. As originally designed by Master Walter in 1300, and as can still be seen on the exterior of the back and sides, it must have been a fine and dignified 'architectural' chair, rising at the back to a high gable with a gilded finial, flanked by crocketed pinnacles. Two more pinnacles rose from the arms of the chair, and the whole surface of the front, back and sides was enriched with tiers of carved arcading, so that it 'reflected in style the architectural idiom of the Abbey itself'.

Scarcely fifty years later, as it would seem, the whole scheme of decoration was altered. The carved arcading at the back of the interior was removed, and the whole surface of the Chair, back and front, was covered with gilded gesso offset by glass mosaics. On this gesso was 'pounced' or diapered the seated figure of a king on the interior back, while on the inside faces of the arms of the Chair and elsewhere were diapered panels containing foliage, grotesques and birds. The result must have been a chair of great splendour which was still further enhanced when, in place of the original step, it was raised on the backs of four small gilded lions which appear to date from the beginning of the sixteenth century.

Very little of the splendour now remains. In course of time much of the gesso has flaked off revealing the original surface and faint traces of lettering beneath. Considerable remains of the foliage, grotesques and birds, however, can still be seen, although only a small fragment of the seated figure of the king has survived. Much damage, too, was done to the Chair at former coronations by hasty repairs and by nailing on to it coverings of cloth of gold. At the coronation of George IV in 1821 the pinnacles were deliberately sawn off, and the last of the enamelled shields was stolen from the grille which encloses the Stone. Even worse things happened at Queen Victoria's Jubilee Service in 1887 when the Chair was painted a dark brown in order to tone it down to one uniform colour, and more damage was done when the paint was afterwards removed. Finally no special care seems to have been taken of the Chair until comparatively modern times. In the eighteenth century and later it stood unguarded in the Confessor's Chapel and anyone who would, could sit in it on payment of a small fee to the vergers. Names, initials and dates were carved all over the Chair and on the companion Chair which was made for the joint coronation of William III and Mary II and has not since been used. On the seat of the Coronation Chair itself, for instance, is boldly cut 'P. Abbott slept in this Chair 5.6. July 1800', while higher up at the back, within a roughly incised shield, appear N. Curzon, T. Lister, T. Pelham and R. Assheton, names which can be identified as those of four cousins who were at Westminster School just over two hundred years ago.

But shamefully treated in so many ways as the Chair has been in the past, no one who has been privileged to see it in the splendour of its setting at a modern coronation could fail to be impressed by the way in which this ancient chair, scarred, mutilated and now left completely unadorned, has alike by the historic memories which surround it and by its unbroken continuity with the past, dominated so many coronation scenes.

Out of those many memories some few may, perhaps, be recalled. The youthful Edward II was the first to be crowned in the Chair in 1308. Not very much is known of the details of his coronation. But the fact that the most conspicuous person present, actually carrying the crown, was the hated favourite Piers Gaveston, showed all too clearly that the ship of state was to be guided by 'Youth on the prow, and Pleasure at the helm', and foreshadowed the tragedy to be enacted nineteen years later within the walls of Berkeley Castle.

The coronation of another youthful king, Richard II, in 1377, was marked by three events: the first recorded instance of the Procession from the Tower of London to Westminster, a custom which continued until the time of Charles II; the creation of a body of young men as 'Knights of the Bath'; and the first appearance at the Coronation Banquet of a Dymoke as the King's Champion. The Dymokes (*Dimico pro Rege*—as their proud and punning motto has it), as Lords of the Manor of Scrivelsby, had inherited the office from the Marmions and their co-heirs the Frevilles and the Hillarys. The Banquet was discontinued in 1831, but it marks the continuity of history that although the Champion no longer appears fully armed and on horseback to issue his challenge, the office is still held by the Dymokes and the head of the family carried the Union Standard at the last coronation.

Richard's supplanter, Henry IV, had no great love for the Abbey, although it was to be his fate to die within its walls. Everyone knows the scene in Shakespeare's *Henry IV* where the Prince of Wales was found to have taken the crown from his father's pillow as he lay dying in the Jerusalem Chamber within the Abbot of Westminster's lodgings. It is perhaps less well known that the young Henry V spent the night of his accession with the Abbey Anchorite. There, according to tradition, he had vowed to lead a new life and, later, besides transferring the body of Richard II from Langley to a more honourable tomb within the Abbey, he made the rebuilding of the Nave of Westminster, which was then in progress, one of his special cares. It is, perhaps, no accident that his coronation is the only one commemorated in contemporary sculpture within the Abbey itself on the sides of the Chantry Chapel above his tomb. On the south side of the Chapel in the central niche is a representation of the crowning with attendant figures of peers, judges, etc., in the adjacent niches; while on the north side the scene represented is the Homage, with the King crowned and supported by two mitred figures and with two kneeling figures on either side.

Tudor coronations were remarkable in several ways. Edward VI, for instance, was crowned with three crowns, St Edward's Crown, the Imperial Crown and 'a very rich one' which was specially made for the occasion. These, we are told, 'one after another were set upon the king's head and between each the trumpets sounded'. An address was given by Archbishop Cranmer and, by a Westminster tradition, this address was delivered from the contemporary pulpit with linen-fold panelling which is still in use at Services in the Nave of the Abbey. It is sometimes said that Mary I refused at her coronation to sit in St Edward's Chair because it had been used at the coronation of her Protestant brother. She was actually crowned in 'a rich chair before the High Altar', and this is thought to be the chair now preserved in Winchester Cathedral. To be crowned thus was not unusual, but the accounts of her coronation make it clear that she was then 'conveyed' to St Edward's Chair which was some-times used not for the crowning but as the Throne for the Homage, as, indeed, it had been used at the coronation of Edward VI. The Service was of course in Latin, but at the following coronation of

Queen Elizabeth I the Service for the first time was partly in Latin and partly in English.

The omens of coming disaster which were noted by the superstitious at the coronation of Charles I were to prove but too well founded. It was remembered, for instance, that at the Recognition by some misunderstanding there was dead silence, and the congregation had to be told to shout 'God save King Charles', and that the text chosen for the sermon had been singularly unfortunate: 'Be thou faithful unto death, and I will give you a crown of life.'

Fortunately no such omens marred the coronation of Charles II so graphically described in his *Diary* by Pepys, who 'with much ado' had got himself into a place in a gallery on the North Transept where he had to sit 'with a great deal of patience' from four in the morning until eleven when the Procession entered the church. What memories must have stirred in the aged Archbishop Juxon as he placed the crown on the head of the son whose father he had attended on the scaffold. Pepys, himself, was to take a more active part at the coronation of James II when, as one of the Barons of the Cinque Ports, he supported the canopy which by ancient right it was their privilege to hold over the Sovereign in the Procession from Westminster Hall to the Abbey. The right, which dated at least from the twelfth century, passed into abeyance when the Procession was discontinued in 1831, but the Barons still attend at coronations.

The coronation of William III and Mary II was unique in as much as both had an equal claim to the throne. Never before had joint sovereigns been crowned together, and in the Procession they walked side by side with the Sword of State carried between them. A replica of the Coronation Chair was provided, and the Queen was anointed, invested and crowned immediately after the King. When Princess Anne, standing by the Chair said, 'Madam, I pity your fatigue', the Queen snapped back, 'A crown, sister, is not so heavy as it seems'!

With the Hanoverians coronations became pageants, pure and simple, without much religious significance, and they reached their climax in the gorgeous but theatrical coronation of George IV. The King, himself, rather pathetically imagining that he still possessed the incomparable fascination and grace of deportment of his youth, devised his own robes for the procession from Westminster Hall, but was almost overcome by heat and exhaustion from the weight of his immensely long train. A 'hideous auburn wig with hanging ringlets down the back of his neck' crowned by a great plumed hat made him look 'like some gorgeous bird of paradise' or, in the cruder words of a Westminster boy, 'more like an elephant than a man'. Darkness had fallen before he was eventually forced to return to his Palace by a devious route owing to the hostile manifestations of the crowds.

After the fabulously expensive coronation of George IV expenses were cut to a minimum at the coronation of William IV, the 'penny coronation' as it was called. It was only with difficulty that he was persuaded to have a coronation at all. The King himself was determined that there should be nothing theatrical about his coronation but, as he never did anything like anybody else, on being disrobed for the Anointing he revealed himself to the astonishment of those standing by and to the consternation of Archbishop Howley in the tightly buttoned up full-dress uniform of an Admiral of the Fleet.

No one who saw her ever forgot the grace and charm of the young Queen Victoria which redeemed 'the continual difficulty and embarrassment' of her ill-rehearsed coronation. No one seemed to have the least idea what was happening or what was to be done next. Even the Queen, who with the Archbishop and the Sub-Dean of Westminster (Lord John Thynne) were the only people who kept their heads, was provoked at last to turn to Lord John and say, 'Pray tell me what I am to do, for *they* do not know.' The climax was reached when two pages of the Service having been turned over by mistake the Queen was informed that the Service was over. But when the mistake was discovered the Queen insisted on returning to her seat so that the Service might be properly concluded.

If confusion marked the coronation of Queen Victoria, anxiety was the prevailing note at the postponed coronation of Edward VII some sixty years later—anxiety for the King who had but recently recovered from a serious operation, but bore the strain with a dignity, reverence and composure which won admiration from all who saw him. His own constant anxiety for the aged but self-reliant Archbishop (Frederick Temple) who, almost blind, had to have cards held up before him with the prayers printed in large letters, and even so occasionally made slips (e.g. exhorting the King to protect 'widowers'). Anxiety at the moment of the Crowning when the Archbishop, having retrieved the crown from the equally aged Dean of Westminster who had turned away with it at the critical moment, seemed about to drop it before placing it with shaking hands on the King's head.

Nine years later came the coronation of George V, and here, perhaps, a personal memory may be permitted of an unforgettable moment, when, after her own coronation, Queen Mary, crowned and carrying her sceptres with her long train borne up by her Maids of Honour, moved, as only Queen Mary could move, round the 'theatre' and 'bowed herself reverently to His Majesty' as she passed him before taking her seat on her own throne.

No one who was present in the Abbey at the last two coronations could fail to have been impressed not merely by the faultless perfection with which every detail was carried out, but by the feeling that they were personally taking part in a deeply religious and moving Service in which the Sovereigns were indeed dedicating themselves to the lifelong service of their peoples. Moreover, that feeling was communicated to the millions of people who were able, for the first time in 1953, to follow the Service on television.

Such then are some of the memories which centre on the Coronation Chair. Westminster Abbey has been rightly called the central shrine of the British Commonwealth, and of all the threads with which it is entwined with the history of the nation none have been more continuous and unbroken than the coronations which have taken place within its walls.

28

Music in the Abbey

THE MUSICAL ESTABLISHMENT

THE ideal history of Abbey music would tell us exactly how the members of the musical foundation went about their daily work in the past. There are many things we should like to know—what music was sung at the daily services, and how it was sung; when and where the choir rehearsed; how the choirboys were trained; how the organ was played. A good deal can be discovered in the Abbey records about the daily lives of our musical predecessors, and by the exercise of a little imagination it is possible to get a very fair idea of what kind of people they were; unfortunately the records are almost completely silent about the musical matters in which we are most interested. At least, however, they are very clear about a most important historical fact. Elizabeth's Charter for the new Collegiate Church of St Peter in Westminster set up a musical foundation of six Petty Canons or Minor Canons,* ten choristers and twelve Lay Vicars (four altos or counter tenors, four tenors and four basses). This confirmed an arrangement which went back to the reign of Henry VIII and probably a good deal farther still. It holds good today, except that the number of Minor Canons has been reduced from six to three and the ten choristers are now supplemented by a certain number of singing-boys who are not on the foundation.

To many people the phrase 'Abbey Music' suggests coronations, royal weddings, state funerals and the like, which may involve large choirs, orchestras, trumpeters and fanfares; the millions whom television brings into the Abbey for these ceremonial occasions may know nothing of the singing of the daily Services all the year round by the members of the Abbey's own musical establishment. But this is the real Abbey music. The daily Services are a corporate act of worship, in which the entire Abbey family takes part; choristers,

---

* The term 'Petty Canon' appears in the Foundation Charter and seems to have been generally used for some time, but from 1729 onwards the Precentor's Book uses the title 'Minor Canon'.

Lay Vicars, Organist are members of this family just as much as the Dean, the Canons and the Minor Canons, with equal responsibilities for the decent ordering of the services at which they sing.

THE MINOR CANONS

The official head of the choral foundation has always been the Chanter or Precentor, who is appointed from among the number of the Petty Canons or Minor Canons—a good custom in a society ruled by custom rather than by statute, where successful administration depends on sound knowledge of custom.

CHANTERS OR PRECENTORS OF WESTMINSTER ABBEY *

1560–9	Alexander Peryn
1569–70	Nicholas Kennam
1570–97	William Punter
1597–1623	Matthew Holmes
1623–42	John Frost
1642–	Dr Peirce
[Period of the Commonwealth]	
1661–73	Philip Tinker
1673–1711	Stephen Crispen (or Crespion)
	N.B. 1696–1711 Charles Barnes and Stephen Crespion seem to have held the office jointly with Barnes apparently the senior.
1712–28	William Battel
1728–46	George Carleton
1746–55	Edward Lloyd
1755–94	Anselm Bailey
1794–1808	Weldon Champneys
1808–46	William Whitfield Dakins
1846–69	John Clark Haden
1869–95	Samuel Flood Jones
1895–9	John Troutbeck
1899–1909	Howard Gurney Daniell-Bainbridge, M.V.O.
1909–12	Trevitt Reginald Hine-Haycock, M.V.O.
1912–33	Leigh Hunter Nixon
1934–51	Cyril Moxon Armitage, M.V.O.
1951–63	Cyril Theodore Henry Dams
1963–	Rennie Simpson

* Anselm Bailey was the last to add 'Chanter' after his signature on official documents. His successor, Weldon Champneys (appointed in 1794) always signed 'Precentor,' and so all his successors.

EE

In modern times the musical duties of the Minor Canons are limited to the chanting of Services—an exacting task, for the quality of the chanter's singing of the service can have a powerful influence for good or ill on the singing of the choir. In the past some may also have taken an active part in the singing of Service music with the choir—certainly it is a fact that many of them, before receiving formal appointment as Minor Canon, actually held the appointment of Lay Vicar. This may have been in name only, but for many years it appears to have been the custom that one of the Lay Vicars was in Holy Orders with the right to succeed to the next vacant Minor Canonry. The earliest of these was the Rev. Charles Green, who became a Lay Vicar in 1687/8 and a Minor Canon in 1696. After that there were one or two exceptions, but from 1744 to 1842 only two Minor Canons were appointed who had not previously been Lay Vicars—one of these was the Rev. W. W. Dakins.

Many of the Minor Canons were good musicians as well as good singers. The Rev. William Tucker (Minor Canon 1661–79) was a competent composer, and his anthem 'O give thanks' and a Service in F major were widely used. The Rev. Luke Flintoft (1720–8) is remembered as the composer of an excellent double chant which is still in general use (it is set to Psalm LXXIII in the present Abbey Chant Book). The Rev. E. G. Beckwith (1828–56), the Rev. William Fitzherbert (1754–77) and the Rev. James Lupton (1829–73) also wrote admirable chants which still survive. Fitzherbert and Lupton were both Minor Canons of St Paul's Cathedral as well as of the Abbey. Pluralities of this kind were frequent and were taken for granted, though this could go rather far. The Rev. Weldon Champneys, Minor Canon from 1766 to 1810, a member of a family with a long and close connexion with the Abbey and Westminster School and himself a former chorister and King's Scholar, was not only Minor Canon of the Abbey, St Paul's Cathedral and St George's Chapel, Windsor, simultaneously, but also held a series of livings—at one time five together. But this was an extreme case.

THE CHORISTERS

There is no means of discovering when boys first began to sing in the choir in the Abbey, but the first mention of an official choir master in the records is the appointment of William Cornyshe as 'Master of the Song Scole' in 1479. In 1479 Henry VII issued a proclamation giving the Chanter the right 'to take any well singing men and children'—i.e. to impress good singers from other choirs. This right was certainly used in monastic times, however harsh if may now seem, but its practice must often have been tempered with kindness. It is pleasant to read in the Sub-Almoner's accounts for the year 1512–13 of how when 'Wyllyam ffynnes' was taken for the choir he was given a 'russet cape'; his mother received a present of 'xii d.—to have her good will'—and she was entertained at the charges of the monastery when she came to Westminster to see Wyllyam. From the accounts at this time it would seem that the boys were well looked after, well clothed and well fed—such luxuries as junkets, 'comfetts' and strawberries were provided. And if the work was hard, there must have been plenty of fun too—feasts on high days, play acting and above all the Boy Bishop ceremonies on St Nicolas's Day.

When the monastery was dissolved in 1540 and the Abbey became for ten years the Cathedral Church of Middlesex, the King's new foundation provided for twelve Petty Canons, twelve laymen singers and ten 'queresters'. The Chapter made the Master of the Choristers, William Foxe, generally responsible for the boys:

> . . . it is concluded y^t Fox the M^r of the Chorustars shall haue the whole gouerning of the chorusters, to teache them, to prouide for meate & drinke, & to se them clenly & honestly apparailed in all thinges, & he to haue ther whole stipend/Also it is agreid, y^t the said M^r of the chorusters shall haue the howss ouer the gate going into the Allmery for hymself & the said chorusters rent free, he repairing it sufficiently before Ester next cummyng. And bicause the howss is now in grett Rwyn, it is agrid y^t the said Fox shall only at this time have xl s. towardes the charges of the said reparacions. (Chapter minute, January 26 1543/4.)

It was also arranged that the boys should be educated 'in ye gramer scole' (5 July 1547).

Elizabeth's Charter of 1560 reaffirmed the provisions of that granted by her father in 1540 and established ten choristers on the foundation; it also ordered that they should be educated with the forty Queen's Scholars of the newly founded Westminster School. This link with Westminster School seems to have been a very real one to begin with, but to have been gradually loosened with the passing of time; long before the first independent Choir School was founded in 1848 the boys were living at home and receiving a money allowance in lieu of the privileges to which they were entitled as members by statutory right of Westminster School.

The first 'Choristers' School for Daily Instruction' was a single room off the South Cloister; there were sixteen choristers, and their schoolmaster was the Sacrist, the Rev. William Sanders. The first boarding school came later; it was in a house on the north side of

Little Smith Street, from which it was soon moved to a specially built Choir House on the other side of the street. The present Choir School, on the west side of Dean's Yard, was opened in 1915.

The Elizabethan Charter aimed at giving the Abbey choristers the best possible education. This aim has been achieved in modern times—choir and choir school combine to offer a singularly full and varied education, and the contemporary chorister is intelligent, mature and well-balanced above the average. In the past there have been times when the boys' schooling has been neglected, but however much the standard of their general education has fluctuated, choristers seem to have had a way of doing well in later life. Not necessarily in music—some were successful in other fields, for example, Dr Drury, the Headmaster of Harrow School of whom Byron speaks gratefully in a note to *Childe Harold*, and the eminent painter Sir Augustus Callcott (1779–1844); on the whole few old choristers enter the musical profession, even though their training in the choir makes good musicians of them. But the Abbey choir has produced some distinguished professional musicians, notably between 1750 and 1850, which is not usually regarded as the most distinguished period in English musical history. Was this the result of the training or the personal influence of the organists of the time, Dr Benjamin Cooke, John Robinson and Dr Samuel Arnold? There was William Parsons, who was Master of the King's Band from 1786 to 1817 and was knighted for his services; John Crosdill (1751–1825), the finest cellist of the time; Charles Knyvett (1752–1822), one of the principal alto soloists at the Handel Commemoration in 1784, who was a Gentleman of the Chapel Royal, and later its Organist; James Bartleman (1769–1821), a splendid singer even as a boy (he was celebrated for his performance of Greene's verse anthem 'Acquaint thyself with God')—he lived to become a Lay Vicar and England's chief concert bass, famous for his interpretation of Purcell and Handel. William Beale (1784–1854) joined the Navy as a midshipman when his voice broke, but was encouraged to return to music by winning the Madrigal Society's prize in 1813 with his 'Awake, sweet nymph'. This and his glee 'Come let us join the roundelay' keep his memory green. Another minor composer was Thomas Forbes Walmisley (1783–1866), organist of St Martin-in-the-Fields and father of the more celebrated Thomas Attwood Walmisley. Later came Edward Lloyd (1845–1927), one of the greatest tenors in England's musical history; Walter Macfarren (1826–1905), a distinguished professor at the Royal Academy of Music; Alfred Hipkins (1826–1903), the authority on musical instruments; and J. L. Hopkins (1820–73), organist of Rochester Cathedral and later of Trinity College, Cambridge. In our own time we have Stanley Roper (1878–1953), eminent for his work at the Chapel Royal and as Principal of Trinity College of Music, and two who are still with us—Lawrance Collingwood (b. 1887) the conductor, and David Willcocks. We count these men as leaders in their generation; but we must not forget the larger number of those who have served music with devotion in humbler posts—as parish-church organists, in schools, as administrators, as singers. Many who have become singers in adult life have returned to the Abbey as Lay Vicars.

THE LAY VICARS

From its beginning the Abbey's choral foundation was closely linked with the Chapel Royal, which for centuries was the main driving force of English music. Its prestige attracted the nation's best musicians, and as the arrangement of its musical duties permitted its members to hold other appointments, it usually happened that the Gentlemen of the Chapel Royal were also Lay Vicars of Westminster Abbey or Vicars-Choral of St Paul's Cathedral—sometimes both.

The Abbey appointment could be attractive to a Gentleman of the Chapel Royal, both for the obvious financial reason and also because the post was a freehold, tenable for life. In theory the duties were exacting; in fact they were alleviated by laudable custom in a way entirely favourable to the Lay Vicar. If he did not find it convenient to appear at a Service, he might send a deputy. If he were obliged to go on from Morning Service at the Abbey to Morning Service at the Chapel Royal, laudable custom did not prevent him from disappearing from his place after the Anthem through a small door behind the Choir Stalls. This practice continued until well into the nineteenth century, and it was not unknown even then for the whole of the six men on one side of the choir to melt away during the latter part of Matins. If with advancing years a Lay Vicar's voice failed, he could call on the services of a deputy to represent him permanently without losing his appointment or emoluments—he could not be dismissed or compelled to resign. William Turner (1651–1740), who was a chorister at the Chapel Royal after the Restoration, came back to the Chapel as a counter-tenor singer in 1669 at the age of 18. In 1698 he became a Lay Vicar of the Abbey. He held both appointments, and also that of Vicar-Choral at St Paul's Cathedral, until 1740, when he died in his eighty-ninth year and was buried with his wife, who had died only four days before him, in a single grave in the West Cloister. Dr Turner was a musician of great distinction (he took his doctorate in music at Cambridge in 1696) and a considerable composer. As a young man he was said to have had a fine counter-tenor voice. We have no means of judging the quality of his singing in the latter part of his forty-two years' Abbey service, but no doubt he was sometimes represented by deputies—and he must certainly have known of the existence of the door behind the Choir Stalls.

STANDARDS OF PERFORMANCE

Conditions such as these would hardly make for order and good discipline in the choir, and they were aggravated by other factors which worked against good performance. Laudable custom did not impose on choir members the duty of attendance at rehearsals. The boys of the choir have always had their regular daily practices, but regular full rehearsals seem to be an entirely modern idea; and the frequent absences of the Lay Vicars were the more noticeable when their deputies were of inferior quality—there can hardly have been the most effective control of such matters if it were possible for Mr Pepys, on the strength of a chance meeting in the Abbey with Mr Hooper, to 'go among the choir' and 'sing with them their service' on Sunday, 29 December 1661.

How far was the Abbey choir's standard of performance affected by this state of affairs—probably typical of most choral foundations until modern times? In spite of absenteeism, lack of rehearsal and other abuses arising from laudable custom there must have been many occasions in the past when there was good singing, at least when the choir was at full strength, for there were always fine singers of whom some at least would have been as capable of rising to a great occasion as their modern counterparts. But good choral singing does not come without good morale. However individually competent the members of a choir may be, unless they are ready to submit themselves to the discipline of a musical personality stronger than their own the choir will not sing consistently well. Performing standards of cathedral music have varied between wide extremes in the past, especially between 1750 and 1850, often for reasons beyond the control of the organist or the singers. Samuel Sebastian Wesley's famous monograph *A Few Words on Cathedral Music*, published in 1849, describes clearly what was wrong with the system as he saw it and outlines his ideas for putting things to rights. That enthusiastic amateur Sir John Sutton, writing in 1847 about organs, takes a sidelong glance at the cathedral Service and gets in some shrewd blows at choirs and organists:

> . . . the modern Cathedral Organist scarcely ever accompanies six verses on the same stops, or even on the same row of keys, and

keeps up a perpetual thundering with the pedals throughout the Psalms, when perhaps the choir he is accompanying, consists of ten little boys, and six or at most eight men, three or four of whom are either disabled by old age, or by a long continued habit of drunkenness. . . . Where will it end? At present, in many Churches the choir might almost as well be silent, for the whole service is thundered out by the Organ, so that the voices are only audible at intervals, and those very wide ones too.

The Abbey Service does not escape comment. The Rev. John Jebb passes some strictures on its ordering in *The Choral Service of the United Church of England and Ireland* (1843), and even Anthony Trollope has something to say about it. In *The Warden*, which was published in 1855, there is an account of how Mr Harding attended Matins on a weekday morning in August 18—:

Mr. Harding was not much edified by the manner of the service. The minor canon hurried in, somewhat late, in a surplice not in the neatest order, and was followed by a dozen choristers, who were also not as trim as they might have been; they all jostled into their places with a quick hurried step, and the service was soon commenced. Soon commenced and soon over. . . . On the whole Mr. Harding was of opinion that things were managed better at Barchester, though even there he knew that there was room for improvement.

When laudable custom becomes vested interest, it is difficult to change; but it can be done. The Abbey's choir arrangements were transformed in the latter part of the nineteenth century, and they are now consonant with accepted contemporary performing standards.

ORGANISTS

No mention has so far been made of the Organist, since the Elizabethan Charter made no provision for one, possibly because what little organ-playing was called for in 1560 could quite well be shared among the Lay Vicars; but although the Precentor is the official head of the Abbey musical establishment, the executive officer is the Organist. Since the appointment of James Turle in 1831, the office of Organist has always been combined with that of Master of the Choristers; before 1831 the two appointments were often separated. The Organists have been as follow:

John Taylour	1559–70
Robert White	1570–4
Henry Leeve	1574–85

Edmund Hooper	1585–1621
John Parsons	1621–3
Orlando Gibbons	1623–5
Richard Portman	1625–44
[*Period of the Commonwealth*]	
Christopher Gibbons	1660–6
Albert Bryne	1666–8
John Blow	1669–79
Henry Purcell	1679–95
John Blow	1695–1708
William Croft	1708–27
John Robinson	1727–62
Benjamin Cooke	1762–93
Samuel Arnold	1793–1802
Robert Cooke	1803–14
George Ebenezer Williams	1814–19
Thomas Greatorex	1819–31
James Turle	1831–82
Sir Frederick Bridge	1882–1918
Sir Sydney Nicholson	1918–27
Sir Ernest Bullock	1928–41
Osborne Peasgood (Acting Organist)	1941–5
Sir William McKie	1941–63
Douglas Guest	1963–

The first formal appointment of an Organist appears to have been that of Edmund Hooper; payments to him appear in the Chapter records for 1585 and his patent of appointment as Organist is dated 1588, being renewed in 1610 and 1616. He was appointed one of the two Organists of the Chapel Royal in 1603,* and was thus the first of a line of distinguished organists who served the two foundations for a century and a half with hardly a break, and again for a short period at the end of the eighteenth century:

	ABBEY	CHAPEL ROYAL
Edmund Hooper	1585–1621	1603–21
Orlando Gibbons	1623–5	1604–25
Christopher Gibbons	1660–6	1660–76
John Blow	1669–79	1673 (Gentleman)
	1695–1708	1674 (Master of the Children)
		1676 (Organist)
		1699 (Composer)

* Until the death of Sir George Smart in 1867 the Chapel Royal always had two organists; at one time there were three.

Henry Purcell	1679–95	1682–95
William Croft	1708–27	1704–27
Samuel Arnold	1793–1802	1783–1802

[Some other musical links between the Abbey and the Chapel Royal might also be mentioned:

Christopher Gibbons, Blow, Purcell, Croft and Arnold—together with John Robinson, Abbey Organist from 1727 to 1762—were all Children of the Chapel Royal.

Two Organists of the Chapel Royal were also Lay Vicars of the Abbey:

John Stafford Smith (Abbey 1785–1836, Chapel Royal 1802–36), and John Bernard Sale (Abbey 1800–41, Chapel Royal 1838–56), who was also musical instructor to the Princess Victoria.

Three were former Abbey choristers:

Charles Knyvett (Chapel Royal 1796–1822). C. S. Jekyll (Chapel Royal 1876–91), who was also assistant to Turle at the Abbey from 1870 to 1875. Stanley Roper (Chapel Royal 1919–53), who was Sub-Organist of the Abbey from 1917 to 1919, but in fact served the Abbey in one way or another almost continuously from his admission as chorister in 1887 to his death in 1953.]

This connexion with the Chapel Royal in its great days ensured that the Abbey should always be served by one of the most distinguished musicians of the time. Many of its organists were composers—most of them, in fact, for church musicians have usually been expected as a matter of course to contribute to the repertory of the choirs they trained. It would be too much to hope that everything in this output of serviceable music is of the finest quality, but Westminster has had an unusual number of composers of distinction among its organists. Two of these have been of the highest eminence—Orlando Gibbons (1583–1625) and Henry Purcell (1659–95).

Gibbons was equally famous as composer and keyboard virtuoso when he was appointed to the Abbey in 1623 after having been at the Chapel Royal for nineteen years.

Henry Purcell was born in Westminster and spent the whole of his life in Westminster, first as Chorister of the Chapel Royal, later with his activities divided between the Abbey, the Chapel, the Court and the theatres, for all of which he provided appropriate music. There was no field of composition in which he did not excel, and it is doubtful whether any English composer before or since has been more admired or respected. Doctor Burney says of him:

My father, who was nineteen years of age when Purcell died, remembered his person very well and the effect his anthems had on himself and the public at the time when many of them were first heard; and used to say that 'no other vocal Music was listened to with pleasure for nearly thirty years after Purcell's death; when they gave way only to the favourite opera songs of Handel'.

Every English musician that is well acquainted with the works of Purcell is proud of being his countryman. He was indeed the creator of our dramatic music. As an amiable and pleasing man he has been as much celebrated as for his professional abilities. The writer of this article is old enough to remember the affectionate rapture with which he has been mentioned by those who knew him personally.

When Purcell died on 21 November 1695 his eminence was recognized and honoured by the Dean and Chapter. A contemporary journal, the *Flying Post*, gives this account of his funeral:

Mr. Henry Pursel one of the most celebrated Masters of the Science of Musick in the Kingdom and scarce inferiour to any in Europe, dying on Thursday last; the Dean of Westminster knowing the great worth of the deceased, forthwith summoned a Chapter, and unanimously resolved that he shall be interred in the Abbey, with all the Funeral Solemnity they are capable to perform for him, granting his widow the choice of the ground to reposit his Corps free from any charge, who has appointed it at the foot of the organs,* and this evening he will be interred, the whole Chapter assisting with their vestments; together with all the Lovers of that Noble Science, with the united Choyres of that and the Chappel Royal, when the Dirges composed by the Deceased for her late Majesty of ever blessed Memory, will be played by Trumpets and other Musick.

John Blow (1648–1708), twice organist and both predecessor and successor of Purcell, ranks near his famous pupil, who spoke of him as 'one of the greatest Masters in the world'. Besides an immense amount of church music—110 anthems and thirteen settings of the Canticles—he wrote keyboard music, songs, secular odes and a masque, *Venus and Adonis*. His reputation, high in his lifetime, declined after his death, perhaps because many eighteenth-century musicians disliked his love of harmonic experiment (Doctor Burney's *General History of Music* has a section headed 'Specimens of Dr Blow's

---

* When Purcell was organist the organ stood over the stalls in the North Choir aisle, in the second bay from the North Transept.

Crudities'); but in recent times his reputation has risen again with better understanding of his aims and methods. In his own day his fame went beyond England. His memorial tablet in the North Choir aisle has engraved upon it a canon (a GLORIA PATRI from his service in G major) which is said to have been sung in St Peter's in Rome, and there is a tradition that when the Emperor of Brazil came to visit the Abbey in the time of Dean Stanley, the first thing which he asked the Dean to show him was the tomb of Doctor Blow.

An earlier organist, Robert White, who came to the Abbey from Ely in 1570, is comparable to Blow in importance. His music seems to have disappeared from use and even from memory in the seventeenth century, but Morley, writing in 1597, could speak of him as the equal of Lassus, Fayrfax, Tallis and Byrd.*

Among lesser composers there is William Croft (1678–1727), whose immortal setting of the Burial Sentences is always sung in procession at Abbey funerals; Edmund Hooper, most of whose music is still in manuscript, though he was a prolific and popular composer in his day; John Parsons, Hooper's successor, now almost forgotten, yet he wrote a setting of the Burial Service which was performed at the funeral of Charles II—a copy still exists, bound in black, in the handwriting of Henry Purcell. Parsons is commemorated by a curious epitaph in Camden's *Remaines concerning Britain* (1657):

> *Death passing by and hearing PARSONS play*
> *Stood much amazed at his depth of skill,*
> *And said, 'This artist must with me away',*
> *For death bereaves us of the better still;*
> *But let the quire, while he keeps time, sing on,*
> *For PARSONS rests, his service being done.*

Past organists are shadowy figures, and those who were composers are most likely to be remembered. John Robinson (1682–1762) was a fashionable harpsichord teacher with something of a reputation as a virtuoso, and Dr Boyce thought him 'a most excellent performer on the organ'. He had been a chorister of the Chapel Royal and was Dr Croft's assistant at the Abbey for some years before succeeding him as Organist, so he knew the great cathedral tradition; but he did not choose to follow it. Sir John Hawkins speaks of him as 'a very florid and elegant performer on the organ, inasmuch that crowds resorted to hear him', but also says:

> In parish churches the voluntary between the Psalms and the first Lesson was anciently a slow, solemn movement, tending to compose the minds and excite sentiments of piety and devotion.

* Thomas Morley, *A Plaine and Easy Introduction to Practical Music*, 1597.

Mr. Robinson introduced a different practice, calculated to display the agility of his fingers in allegro movements on the cornet, trumpet, sesquialtera, and other noisy stops, degrading the instrument, and instead of the full and noble harmony with which it was designed to gratify the ear, tickling it with mere airs in two parts, in fact solos for a flute and a bass.

This statement of Hawkins has led modern critics to attack Robinson for vulgarity; but his crime, if it was a crime, seems to have been nothing more than to play the organ music which appealed to contemporary taste in the style desired by its composers. Greene and Stanley are only two of the composers of the period who wrote for the organ in two parts, giving the right hand solos for 'cornet, trumpet and sesquialtera' as well as for flute. But however that may be, Robinson's skill as teacher or virtuoso no longer matters; he is remembered only for a single minuscule composition—an excellent psalm chant, said to have been a great favourite of King George III, which is still sung in the Abbey and indeed all over the Anglican Communion.

Samuel Arnold was a great man in his own day and served music well as Organist of the Abbey and the Chapel Royal, as a prolific composer of music for the theatre, a conductor much in demand, an editor who brought out two works of major importance—his edition of the works of Handel, in forty volumes, and three volumes of English Cathedral Music (a sequel to the collection published by Dr Boyce). There is little to keep him in mind except an innocuous setting of the Evening Canticles ('Arnold in A') which is still sung occasionally in most cathedrals.

About some Organists so little is known that it is pleasant to come on any detail or comment, however slight, which will conjure up some image of the man himself. It is a mere historical fact that when Robert White died in 1574 his reputation as a composer stood very high; our feelings warm towards him when we discover from his Will that he must have been a kind, generous and affectionate man. He asks to be buried in St Margaret's Church, 'near unto my children', and besides making bequests to his father, his wife and three daughters and some relatives he left 'to every of my skollers to each of them iiijd'.

The name of Richard Portman, who succeeded Orlando Gibbons in 1625 and was Organist in the dark days of the Commonwealth, makes little impact on the modern reader, but he is brought suddenly to life—we can almost see him before us—by a few words of Anthony à Wood * which describe him as '. . . a little obliging man, a religious

* Anthony à Wood, *Notes on the Lives of Musicians*.

sober man. He wrote a book of meditations printed in 12 mo'. (It was published in 1645 with the title: *The Soules Life, exercising itself in the Sweet Fields of Divine Meditation, collected for the comfort thereof, in these sad days of destruction.*)

George Ebenezer Williams, who died in 1819 at the age of 35 after five years as Organist, left nothing at all by which he could be remembered, though he is said to have composed some psalm chants when he was a chorister at St Paul's Cathedral, and in later life what has been cautiously described as 'an innocent tutor for the pianoforte'.

But others have had enough variety and interest in their lives to make the reader wish to hear and know more about them. Christopher Gibbons (1615–76), Orlando's son, is said to have been a dashing soldier and to have served with some distinction in the Royalist army in the Civil War, his reward being his appointment both to the Abbey and the Chapel Royal in 1660. He tackled with success the task of re-forming and rebuilding the Abbey choir after the silent years of the Commonwealth. He understood the art of serving, and of commending himself to, princes—it was a personal letter from Charles II himself which moved the University of Oxford to give him the degree of Doctor of Music. It does not seem inconsistent with the character of a Restoration courtier that Anthony à Wood should speak of him as 'a grand debauchee' and assert that 'he would often sleep at Morning Prayer when he was to play the organ'. Perhaps this explains the reason for a Chapter minute of 18 December 1660/61 which, already quoted, bears repetition here:

> It was ordered that the back door of the Organ Loft be shutt upp and that the Organist come into the quire att the beginning of prayers in his surpliss and betake himself to his stall till towards the end of the psalms except on festival dayes when the Responds are to be performed with the Organ and then to go upp the stayres leading from the quire to the organ and perform his duty. And it is further ordered that neither the Organist nor any other permit any person to bee in the Organ Loft during the time of divine service and that the Organist and the blower keep themselves private and not expose themselves to the view of the people during their stay in the Organ Loft.

Gibbons may well have been a striking character; so certainly was Thomas Greatorex (1758–1831), the successor of George Ebenezer Williams, who had already reached a commanding position in the London musical world when he was appointed to the Abbey at the age of sixty-one. He came from an old Derbyshire family. As a boy he had studied with Dr Benjamin Cooke, the then organist of the Abbey; he had been a protégé of the Earl of Sandwich, a devoted musical amateur, and assisted at the oratorio performances given at Hinchingbrooke, that nobleman's country seat, under the direction of the celebrated Joah Bates. He was for four years organist of Carlisle Cathedral, but resigned in order to go and live in Italy, where he formed a friendship with the Pretender, Charles Edward Stuart, who valued the friendship sufficiently to bequeath to him some of his music books.

Greatorex came back to London in 1788 and settled there for the rest of his life. He had a large teaching practice; he became conductor of the Concerts of Ancient Music in succession to Joah Bates; he was much concerned with concert giving and directed triennial music festivals at Birmingham, York and Derby. Most remarkably, he also became a Fellow both of the Royal and the Linnaean Societies; he is said to have been skilled in mathematics, astronomy and natural science. He was obviously a man of vigour, of strength of character and of intellectual force. There is a story that George IV, when Prince Regent, once said to him, 'My father is Rex, but you are a Greater Rex.' All that could justify the repetition of such an appalling pun is that it shows that Greatorex was accepted as being at the head of his profession. It would be interesting to know how Abbey music flourished under his direction.

Greatorex's successors, James Turle and Frederick Bridge, held office between them from 1831 to 1918, and in these eighty-seven years the choral foundation was gradually reshaped to meet the demands of a new era. Turle's gifts as a composer of psalm chants and hymn tunes ensure that his name will always be remembered, and he was a master of the old cathedral school of organ-playing, noted for his accompaniment of the Choral Service. Bridge was a modern, who exemplified the best qualities of the Victorian age; he had vision, enthusiasm and boundless energy, and combined musical and administrative ability. In his term of office a proper Choir School was opened. By a mixture of firmness and tact he established the principle that regular rehearsals for the full choir, boys and men, were necessary and would take place, to the great advantage of the standard of performance at the daily Services. The organ was rebuilt under his direction and Pearson's splendid organ cases erected. He had a flair for planning and directing the music at the special Services which the Abbey was increasingly expected to provide for great national occasions; this gift showed itself in the highest degree when, as duly appointed Director of Music, he was responsible for the music at the Coronation Services of King Edward VII and King George V. He was a great Victorian and a great character, who served the Abbey with loyalty and devotion; his successors can be grateful for the excellence of the foundations which he laid and on which they have built.

CHOIR HISTORY

The history of the choral foundation has not been eventful; the routine of daily Services has rarely been broken except by occasional epidemics and by wars. During the time of the Commonwealth the Services were stopped, the organs broken down, the choir disbanded. A Puritan divine, John Vicars, in a tract with the title of *God's Ark over-topping the Waves* describes

> . . . a most rare and strange alteration in the face of things in the Cathedrall Church of Westminster. Namely, that whereas there was wont to be heard nothing almost but Roaring-Boyes, tooting and squeaking Organ-Pipes and the Cathedrall-Catches of Morley, and I know not what trash; now the Popish Altar is quite taken away, the bellowing Organs are demolish'd and pulled down, the treble or rather, trouble and base singers, Chanters or In-chanters driven out; and instead thereof, there is now set up a most blessed Orthodox Preaching Ministry. . . . O our God what a rich and rare alteration! What a strange change in-deed!

When better times came again with the Restoration the Services were sung by men's voices while new boys were being recruited and trained; until they gained experience and confidence they were given the help of a cornet player, John Hill.

The Second World War brought the next considerable interruption. The Choir School was evacuated to Christ's Hospital at Horsham when war began and the boys were kept together and rehearsed regularly until 1941 when they were disbanded, and most of them were found places in other choral foundations. Once again the daily Services were sung by men's voices; but later in the war a temporary choir of boys was formed. At first this choir sang on Sundays only, but as time went on it also sang on Saturday afternoons, on occasional high days and holy days and for special Services; it carried on until the Choir School was re-opened in January 1947. Several of the boys who had belonged to this wartime choir continued to sing in the choir on Sundays for some months after this. Others entered the Choir School, in which a large number of new boys were also accepted for training from the very beginning. The first Service sung with boys drawn entirely from the re-opened Choir School was Evensong on Friday, 6 June 1947. The boys were:

DECANI	CANTORIS
Robin Baddock (Senior Chorister)	David Cox
Michael Linsey	Rodney Ainsworth
Brian Railton	Robert Turner
Colin Gibbs	Michael Warner
Geoffrey Runnicles	Peter Leigh
Christopher Rand	Alan Robson
Peter Kirkby	David Orwin
Brian Graves	Donald Walker
David Weait	Robin Boyle
Samuel Hall	Paul Bennett
Douglas Higgins	Graham Gibbs

The Canticles were sung to plainsong with fauxbourdons by Tallis and the Anthem was Orlando Gibbons's 'O Lord increase my faith'. It was some years before the choir was fully restored to its normal standard of competence, but this time it was done without the help of a cornet player.

It would seem that the statutory Services of Matins and Evensong have been sung at 10 a.m. and 3 p.m. respectively on Sundays and weekdays alike until comparatively recently. In the present century the time of Sunday Matins was moved, first to 10.15 a.m., later to 10.30 a.m.; there is now a Choral Eucharist after Matins on the second and fourth Sunday of each month and on certain high days. Until the beginning of the Second World War both Matins and Evensong have usually been sung each weekday. Since the war came to an end the number of sung weekday Services has been reduced, and when the restoration of the interior of the Abbey was begun in 1954 the time of Evensong on the days from Monday to Friday in each week was changed from 3 p.m. to 5 p.m. At the end of this chapter will be found in summary form a number of weekly music lists which give some indication of the kind of music sung at different points in the last seventy-five years.

Special occasions in Abbey history have always been marked by greater ceremony than usual, and the observance of the 200th anniversary of the founding of the College offers a good example of this. A Chapter minute of 30 April 1760 details the proceedings:

. . . Ordered that on Monday the 2nd day of June next be kept a solemn Jubilee in Commemoration of our Royal Foundress Queen Elizabeth, upon the completion . . . of a second Century since her foundation of this College: and that the Dean, the Prebendaries, Masters, Scholars, Officers, Ministers and all others belonging to the Choir or Foundation, be invited to attend on that day in the College Hall, and to go from thence in Procession to the Morning and Evening Prayers in the Choir, and to dine altogether in the College Hall; The whole to be conducted according to the Directions, which the Dean shall think proper to give on this occasion.

The events of the great day are described in a Chapter minute of 3 June 1760:

ORDERED that the Treasurer do pay all the Expences of the Entertainment and other Charges of this day.

ORDERED that an Entry be made in the Chapter Book of the proceedings at the Jubilee kept this day, in such manner as his Lordship shall direct: which Entry his Lordship directed to be as followeth.

. . . All the Members of the Collegiate Foundation having been summoned to be present this day in the College Hall at ten of the Clock in the morning; they set out from thence and proceeded to the Choir, two and two abreast, and the Juniors preceding the Seniors. In the Choir Purcell's Te Deum was performed, and one of his anthems was sung; and when the morning service was ended, a Sermon was preached by the Dean on the solemn Occasion. After this all the Members proceeded in the same order as before, from the Choir to the College Hall, where an English Oration and several Copies of English Verses were spoken by the Kings Scholars from the Gallery in the Hall.

About a quarter after 2 of the Clock the whole Company sat down to a Dinner in the Hall, the Dean, Prebendaries and upper Officers of the Church being at the upper end of the Hall; the minor Canons, Gentlemen of the Choir, Singing Boys and inferior Servants of the Church of the Eastern side of it, the Kings Scholars on the western side, and the Almsmen at a Table placed in the middle.

At half an hour after four of the Clock they all rose from Table, and proceeded to Evening Prayers in the Choir, where another of Mr. Purcells Anthems was sung, and when the Evening Service was ended, the whole Company was dismissed, and the Dean and Prebendaries repaired to the Jerusalem Chamber, where a Chapter was then held, and the Business before mentioned was dispatched.

SOME NOTABLE MUSICAL OCCASIONS

This festivity is typical of the way in which important domestic anniversaries and occasions have been celebrated at Westminster, but the Abbey's doors have also been opened to the world at large

FF

when Services have been desired to mark great national events. There have also been many non-liturgical musical performances; probably the first of these was the Handel Commemoration in 1784. This had a number of distinguished musical amateurs as its directors, and it attracted the patronage and the active interest of King George III himself; its musical director was Joah Bates. Three performances were planned—a miscellaneous programme to be given in the Abbey on 26 May, a secular programme at the Pantheon in Oxford Street on the following evening, the 'Messiah' in the Abbey on 29 May; by special command of the King both the Abbey performances were repeated, on 3 and 5 June. The most elaborate preparations were made inside the Abbey. A staging for the chorus and orchestra was erected against the west wall of the Nave, rising up to the level of the great West Window; on it was built an organ with a detached keyboard, from which Joah Bates directed his forces. Seating was provided for an audience of nearly 3,000 on the floor of the Nave and in galleries at the side, and a splendid Royal Box was built on the west side of the Choir Screen, facing the performers. The King and the royal family came to all the performances. There was an immense choir—60 trebles (nearly all boys), 48 counter tenors, 83 tenors and 84 basses—and an orchestra of 249. Nothing like this had ever happened in England before; the performance was awaited with excitement and a certain amount of apprehension—could so many performers keep together; could they sing and play in tune; would the mass of sound be unbearably and deafeningly loud? In fact the performance gave the greatest satisfaction, so much so that similar festivals were held in the Abbey in the three years following and in 1791 on an even larger scale (Haydn was present in 1791, and had a seat near the Royal Box; this was the occasion when, as the whole audience, with the King, rose to their feet at the 'Hallelujah Chorus', 'Papa' Haydn wept like a child, exclaiming 'He is the Master of us all!').

Historically the 1784 Commemoration is of major importance, for it established the English tradition of large amateur choirs and our pattern of performing Handel's music. Here it was possibly quite wrong. When Handel directed performances of his own oratorios he had a small professional chorus and an orchestra of equivalent size; in Dublin, at the first 'Messiah' performance, the chorus consisted of the choirs of St Patrick's and Christ Church Cathedrals, with a total strength probably of between fifty and sixty. But it is still worth remembering that the promoters of this Commemoration had heard Handel direct his own works and many of them had known him personally and intimately; could it be possible that the princely scale on which the Commemoration was planned and carried through might have been inspired by some knowledge of Handel's own wishes, which he himself had never been able to fulfil?

Since 1784 there have been countless performances of great choral masterpieces in the Abbey, but two in particular must always be remembered.

On Maundy Thursday 1871 Joseph Barnby directed one of the first English performances—and certainly the first English performance in its proper home, the church—of a German work which has now become part of the English way of life—Bach's 'St Matthew Passion'.

On Thursday, 6 December 1962, was heard in the Abbey for the first time in London Benjamin Britten's 'War Requiem', conducted by Meredith Davies.

CORONATION MUSIC

The Abbey's most elaborate musical Service is certainly the solemnity of the Coronation, and something should be said about this, even though it is not the responsibility of the Dean and Chapter but comes under the control of the Earl Marshal, the Archbishop of Canterbury and the Coronation Committee, which appoints a Director of Music to deal with the musical arrangements. Since the Coronation of King Edward VII in 1902 the Abbey Organist has always been appointed Director of Music, and though he is instructed to consult with the Master of the King's Music, it is made quite plain that he has the final responsibility and full authority in all musical matters.

Information about the music of past Coronations varies in quantity and in accuracy. The best documented service is that of King James II on Thursday, 23 April 1685. For this we are indebted to a member of the College of Arms, Francis Sandford, Lancaster Herald, whose monumental *History of the Coronation of King James II* describes every feature of the Service in minute detail. The sixty-eight singers came from the choirs of the Abbey and the Chapel Royal:

8 Children of the Choir of Westminster
12 Children of H.M. Chapel Royal
16 Gentlemen of the Choir of Westminster (including 4 Petty Canons)
32 Gentlemen of the Chapel Royal (including Dr William Turner, who has already been mentioned, Henry Purcell, Dr Nicholas Staggins—the Master of the King's Music—and Dr John Blow).

Before the actual Service there was a 'Grand Proceeding' from Westminster Hall, where all those who were to take part in the Service had assembled. When the Procession entered the Abbey, the Choir of Westminster, with the Dean and Prebendaries, waited on one side for the entry of the King and Queen; the Children and Gentlemen of the Chapel Royal went on to their places in a gallery over the aisle on the south side of the High Altar, where an organ had been built by 'Father' Smith for the occasion ('a little organ for the King's choir'). The King's Band were already in place in a similar gallery opposite them. When the King and Queen arrived they

> were received by the Dean and Prebendaries, who, with the Choir of Westminster, proceeding a little before THEIR MAJESTIES, sung the full Anthem following:
> '*I was glad when they said unto me*' (composed by Mr. Hen. Purcell . . .)
> . . . The Anthem being ended, the Children and Choir of Westminster turned to the Left-Hand, to the back-side of the Choir, and went up into their Gallery * by the Great Organ.

The two choirs were therefore a considerable distance from each other and from the King's Band. Sandford specifically says that the first anthem in the following list was sung by the choir of Westminster alone, but that the other anthems were sung by both choirs together, which in the last two works were joined by the band; considering the complexity and difficulty of some of the anthems, it would be interesting to know how the performance went:

1. At the Entrance:
  'I was glad'   PURCELL
 (by the Choir of Westminster)

2. At the Recognition:
  'Let thy hand be strengthened'   BLOW
 Before the Anointing:

3. 'Come, Holy Ghost'   WILLIAM TURNER

4. 'Zadok the Priest'   HENRY LAWES

5. After the Anointing:
  'Behold, O Lord, our Defender' BLOW

6. After the Crowning:
  'The King shall rejoice' WILLIAM TURNER

* This was above the choir stalls on the North side of the Choir, one bay west of the North Transept; the organ was one bay still further west.

7. After the Benediction:

TE DEUM WILLIAM CHILD

8. At the Homage:

('. . . In the meantime the Gentlemen of the Chapel Royal, with the Instrumental Musick, and the Choir of Westminster, sang and played together this Verse-Anthem, as a solemn conclusion of the King's part of the Coronation.')

'God spake sometimes in visions' BLOW

9. After the Queen's Crowning:

('. . . The Choirs sang the following Verse-Anthem, performed by the whole Consort of Voices and Instruments.')

'My heart is inditing' PURCELL

Every anthem sung was composed by a Gentleman of the Chapel Royal, and every composer was present himself except Henry Lawes, who had died in 1662. This Chapel Royal monopoly was not disturbed until 1727, when Handel was commissioned to write his four famous Coronation Anthems (it is said at the express command of King George II). Every one of these anthems has been repeated at some later Coronation Service, 'Zadok the Priest' at every service since it was first sung. Few details are available about the other music performed or the musical arrangements, but the choir is said to have consisted of 40 singers, with an orchestra of 160; it is known that Christopher Schrider built an organ for the service, and that it was placed above and slightly behind the High Altar; it was later presented to the Dean and Chapter by the King.

No subsequent Coronation Service is well documented until we come to the crownings of King William IV (8 September 1831) and Queen Victoria (28 June 1838). For both of these the Director of Music was Sir George Smart, Organist of H.M. Chapels Royal, who left carefully annotated copies of both Orders of Service which are now in the Chapter Library at the Abbey. For Queen Victoria's Coronation no expense was spared. The Abbey organ was taken down and stored and an organ specially built farther back on the organ screen to allow room for the chorus and orchestra, whose combined numbers were nearly 500, the choirs of the Abbey, the Chapel Royal, St Paul's Cathedral and St George's Chapel, Windsor, being supplemented by a large number of the best professional singers of the day. The music was as follows:

At the Entrance:

'I was glad' ATTWOOD

SANCTUS and Responses to the
Commandments SIR GEORGE SMART

Before the Anointing:

Hymn, 'Come, Holy Ghost'	GRAND CHANT
Anthem, 'Zadok the Priest'	HANDEL

At the Crowning:

'The Queen shall rejoice'	HANDEL

After the Benediction:

TE DEUM in A	BOYCE

During the Homage:

'This is the day'	W. KNYVETT

After the GLORIA IN EXCELSIS:

'Hallelujah'	HANDEL

After the Blessing:

The Occasional Overture	HANDEL

This Service marked the end of the old Chapel Royal ascendancy. It was sixty-four years before another Coronation Service took place. By then the old ways had been forgotten, and when Sir Frederick Bridge began his work as Director of Music he was unhampered by tradition. He was able to get together a choir and an orchestra which were truly representative of England's performing musicians and to prepare a scheme of music which drew on the past and also gave a hearing to the best of the contemporary composers who were writing for the Church. At the Coronation of King George VI in 1937 Sir Ernest Bullock took the same policy a good deal further. He secured a better balance between music of the past and of the present day, and made two striking and valuable innovations. The custom of commissioning a specially composed Homage Anthem was set aside, and instead six short anthems were chosen to be sung during the ceremony of the Homage, one contemporary and specially written, the others representing English cathedral composers of five different centuries:

'O come, ye servants of the Lord'	TYE
'Hear my prayer'	PURCELL
'O clap your hands'	GIBBONS
'All the ends of the world'	BOYCE
'O praise God in His holiness'	DYSON
'Thou wilt keep him in perfect peace'	S. S. WESLEY

He also used his own remarkable gift for writing for brass by composing a series of brilliant fanfares which were played with splendid effect by the trumpeters of the Royal Military School of Music at climax points in the service.

The Director of Music for the Coronation Service in 1953 followed the lines marked out by Bullock in 1937; a list of the music performed is given below. This Service will perhaps be remembered for having given the congregation for the first time in history the opportunity of taking vocal part in the Service in Dr Vaughan Williams's noble setting of 'Old Hundredth' for choir, congregation, orchestra, trumpeters and organ.

At the Entrance:

    'I was glad'   PARRY

The Beginning of the Communion Service:

    INTROIT: 'Behold, O God our Defender'   HOWELLS
    GRADUAL: 'Let my prayer come up'   W. H. HARRIS
    CREED   R. VAUGHAN WILLIAMS

Before the Anointing:

    Hymn: 'Come, Holy Ghost'   arr. BULLOCK
    'Zadok the Priest'   HANDEL

At the Crowning:

    Confortare: 'Be Strong'   DYSON

Homage Anthems:

    'Rejoice in the Lord'   JOHN REDFORD (*attrib.*)
    'O clap your hands'   GIBBONS
    'I will not leave you comfortless'   BYRD
    'O Lord, our Governour'   HEALEY WILLAN
    'Thou wilt keep him in perfect peace'   S. S. WESLEY

The Communion Service:

    OFFERTORIUM (to be sung by all)
    'All people that on earth do dwell'   R. VAUGHAN WILLIAMS
    SANCTUS   R. VAUGHAN WILLIAMS
    Communion Motet: 'O taste and see'
                       R. VAUGHAN WILLIAMS

    GLORIA IN EXCELSIS   STANFORD

    TE DEUM LAUDAMUS   WALTON

    'God Save the Queen'   arr. GORDON JACOB

MUSIC AT SERVICES

MAY 1893

DAY	SERVICE	ANTHEM	
Sunday 21st WHITSUN-DAY	10.00 Turle in D throughout * 3.00 Turle in D 7.00 Service in Choir at 7—see Special Programme	———	
Monday 22nd Whitsun-Monday	10.00 Aldrich Creed . . . Goss 3.00 Aldrich	'Praise the Lord, O Jerusalem' SCOTT 'As pants the hart' SPOHR	
Tuesday 23rd Whitsun-Tuesday	10.00 Boyce in C Contn....* Gibbons 3.00 Cooke in G	'The eyes of all' KEETON 'O for a closer walk with God' M. B. FOSTER	
Wednesday 24th	10.00 Ouseley in B minor 3.00 Reade in D	'Praise the Lord, O Jerusalem' CLARKE 'Rejoice in the Lord' HUMPHREYS	Service for Men's Voices only
Thursday 25th	10.00 Barrow 3.00 Barrow	'Seek ye the Lord' BRIDGE 'O come, every one that thirsteth' MENDELSSOHN	
Friday 26th	10.00 Patrick 3.00 Patrick	'Almighty and everlasting God' GIBBONS 'Send out Thy light' GOUNOD	No Organ on Fridays (unless a Holy Day falls on a Friday)
Saturday 27th	10.00 Stewart in G 3.00 Withers	'Hear me, O Lord' WALMISLEY 'God came from Teman' STEGGALL	
Sunday 28th TRINITY SUNDAY	10.00 Goss in D Jubilate & Contn.* Garrett 3.00 Smart in B flat 7.00 Service in Choir at 7—see Special Programme	——— 'Holy, holy, holy' and 'Hallelujah' HANDEL	

S. FLOOD JONES M.A.
Precentor

N.B. These pages follow the lists as printed except that in the Abbey lists the titles or first lines of Anthems are not in quotes.

* 'Turle in D throughout' indicates that this Service was used both for Matins and for either Ante-Communion or Choral Communion. 'Contn.', i.e. 'Continuation' seems to mean, for the music of the Ante-Communion Service.

MAY 1913

DAY	SERVICE	ANTHEM	
WHIT-SUNDAY 11th	10.00 Harwood in A flat	INTROIT: 'With other tongues' PALESTRINA	Choral Communion at 11 a.m.
	3.00 Harwood in A flat	'The wilderness' WESLEY	
	7.00 TE DEUM—Stanford in B flat	'God is a spirit' BENNETT	
Monday in Whitsun Week 12th	10.00 Ouseley in B minor	'O taste and see' GOSS	
	3.00 Noble in B minor	'O be joyful in God' SMART	
Tuesday in Whitsun Week 13th	10.00 Turle in D Jubilate	'Come, Holy Ghost' PALESTRINA	
	3.00 Turle in D	'I will pour My spirit' SULLIVAN	
Wednesday 14th EMBER DAY	10.00 Ireland in F	'Lord of all power' WESLEY	
	3.00 Garrett in B flat	'Like as the hart' GUY	Service for men's voices only.
Thursday 15th	10.00 Hopkins in A	'O Thou, the true and only Light' MENDELSSOHN	
	3.00 Keeton in A	'Whosoever drinketh' BENNETT	
Friday 16th EMBER DAY	10.00 Tallis	'O come, ye servants.' TYE	No organ
	3.00 Rogers in A minor	'O Thou who makest souls' TALLIS	No organ
Saturday 17th EMBER DAY	10.00 Smart in F	'O come everyone' MENDELSSOHN	
	3.00 Stanford in B flat	'I saw the Lord' STAINER	
TRINITY SUNDAY 18th	10.00 Alcock in B flat Stanford in B flat	'Holy, Holy, Holy' ALCOCK	
	3.00 Macfarren in E flat	'Holy, Holy, Holy' 'Let all the angels' 'Hallelujah' HANDEL	
	7.00 ——	'In humble faith' GARRETT	

LEIGH H. NIXON, M.A.
Precentor

JUNE 1924

DAY	SERVICE	ANTHEM	
WHIT-SUNDAY	10.15 Smart in F	INTROIT: 'With other tongues' PALESTRINA	
	3.00 Wood in E flat	'When God of old' STANFORD	
	6.30 ——	'The Lord descended' HAYES	
Monday in Whitsun Week 9th	10.00 Plain 3.00 Garrett in E flat	'God came from Teman' STEGGALL	
Tuesday in Whitsun Week 10th	10.00 Selby in F 3.00 Selby in F	'O for a closer walk' STANFORD 'O God, when Thou appearest' MOZART	
Wednesday 11th St. Barnabas, Apostle and Martyr. EMBER DAY	10.00 Plain 3.00 Gladstone in F	'O come, everyone that thirsteth' MENDELSSOHN	
Thursday 12th	10.00 Boyce in A 3.00 Ley in C minor	'O taste, and see' GOSS 'If ye love me' TALLIS	Service for men's voices only
Friday 13th EMBER DAY	10.00 Plain 3.00 Stanford in F	'Come, Holy Ghost' PALESTRINA	No Organ
Saturday 14th EMBER DAY	10.00 Wesley in F 3.00 Lee Williams in F	'God is a spirit' STERNDALE BENNETT 'The Lord doth choose a holy dwelling' BACH	
TRINITY SUNDAY 15th	10.15 Stanford in A 3.00 Nicholson in D flat 6.30 ——	'Hymn to the Trinity' TCHAIKOVSKI 'I saw the Lord' STAINER 'In humble faith' GARRETT	

LEIGH H. NIXON. M.A.
Precentor

MAY AND JUNE 1936

DAY	SERVICE	ANTHEM	
WHIT-SUNDAY May 31st	10.30 Moeran in E flat	———	
	11.30 Stanford in C	GRADUAL: 'With other tongues' PALESTRINA	
	3.00 Wood in E flat (2)	'When God of old' STANFORD	
	6.30 ———		
Monday June 1st	10.00 Plain		
	3.00 Walmisley in D minor	'O Lord give thy Holy Spirit' TALLIS	
Tuesday 2nd	10.00 Wesley in F	'O come, ye servants' TYE	
	3.00 Wood in E flat (1)	'O Holy Ghost' MACFARREN	
Wednesday 3rd EMBER DAY	10.00 Smart in F	Litany	
	3.00 Bennett in D minor	'If ye love me' TALLIS	Men's voices
Thursday 4th	10.00 Plain		
	3.00 Wesley in E	'A Hymn for Whitsuntide' JOSEPH	
Friday 5th EMBER DAY	10.00 Lloyd in E	Litany	Men's voices
	3.00 Gibbons in F	'O clap your hands' GIBBONS	No Organ. Orlando Gibbons died 1625
Saturday 6th EMBER DAY	10.00 Wood in E	'Sing we merrily' READ	Men's voices
	3.00 Nicholson in D flat	'Come creator spirit' PALESTRINA	
TRINITY SUNDAY 7th	10.30 Harwood in A flat	'Blessed Angel Spirits' TCHAIKOWSKY	
	3.00 Stanford in A	'Cherubic Hymn' GRETCHANINOFF	
	6.30 ———	———	

CYRIL M. ARMITAGE
Precentor

JUNE 1954

DAY	SERVICE	ANTHEM	
WHIT-SUNDAY June 6th	10.30 Boyce in C 11.30 Stanford in C 6.30 ————	'Come, Holy Ghost' ATTWOOD ———— ————	
Monday in Whitsun Week 7th	10.00 Plain 3.00 Noble in B minor	'The wilderness' GOSS	
Tuesday in Whitsun Week 8th	10.00 Boyce in A 3.00 Tallis (Faux-bourdons)	'If ye love me' TALLIS 'Come, Holy Ghost' PALESTRINA	
Wednesday 9th EMBER DAY	10.00 Plain 3.00 Batten (Short Service)	'I give you a new commandment' SHEPHERD	Men's Voices
Thursday 10th	10.00 Plain 3.00 Harwood in A flat	'The Lord hath been mindful of us' WESLEY	
Friday 11th	10.00 Gray in E 3.00 Blow in G	'Lamb of God' BACH Litany TALLIS 'Dum complerentur dies Pentecostes' PALESTRINA	No Organ
Saturday 12th EMBER DAY	10.00 Plain 3.00 Hylton Stewart in C	'Blessed Angel Spirits' TSCHAIKOWSKY	
TRINITY SUNDAY 13th	10.30 Smart in F 3.00 Wesley in E 6.30 ————	'God is a Spirit' STERNDALE BENNETT 'O beata et gloriosa Trinitas' PALESTRINA ————	

CYRIL T. H. DAMS
Precentor

JUNE 1965

DAY	SERVICE	ANTHEM
WHIT-SUNDAY June 6th	10.30 Vaughan Williams in G	'Dum complerentur' PALESTRINA
	11.30 Stanford in G and F	Introit: 'O Lord, give thy Holy Spirit' TALLIS
	3.00 Rubbra in A flat	————
	6.30 Congregational Service	
Monday in Whitsun Week 7th	7.30 Matins said 3.00 Nicholson in D flat	'Come, Holy Ghost' ATTWOOD
Tuesday in Whitsun Week 8th	10.00 Boyce in C	'O for a closer walk with God' STANFORD
	3.00 Harris in A	'We will rejoice' CROFT
Wednesday 9th EMBER DAY	Matins and Even- song said	
Thursday 10th	7.30 Matins said 5.00 Byrd (2nd Service)	'Alleluia! I heard a voice' WEELKES
Friday 11th EMBER DAY	10.00 S. S. Wesley in F	'Almighty God' FORD Litany BYRD
	5.00 Weelkes (Short Service)	'The dove descending' STRAVINSKY
Saturday 12th	7.30 Matins said 3.00 Tomkins (5th Service)	'O beata et gloriosa Trinitas' PALESTRINA
TRINITY SUNDAY 13th	10.30 Britten in C	'Hymn of the Cherubim' RACHMANINOV
	11.30 Stanford in C and F	Introit: 'Ave verum Corpus' MOZART
	3.00 Stanford in A	'Where thou reignest' SCHUBERT
	6.30 Congregational Service	

Friday 11th / Ember Day: } NO ORGAN

RENNIE SIMPSON
Precentor

29

The Sacristy

IT is natural to suppose that in nine hundred years a building of such renown as Westminster Abbey would have accumulated a vast treasure representing the finest examples of ecclesiastical art down the centuries. But those who have read the foregoing pages of the Abbey's history will realize how sadly those treasures have been depleted by the very events which make the story of the Abbey so historically significant. Where one might have expected gold plate, the best is silver-gilt. The finest vestments, though these are superb, date back no further than the days of Charles II.

Of the two most costly occasions of spoliation of the Abbey treasure—the Dissolution of the Monastery, and the deliberate policy of the Long Parliament, perhaps the effect of the latter was the more completely devastating.

Before 1540, when the Sacristy built by Henry III stood at the angle of the Nave and the North Transept, it was filled with every kind of treasure. Of embroidered materials there were no less than 330 copes, 100 chasubles, 99 dalmatics and tunicles, 288 albs, 103 maniples and 8 mitres for the Abbott, not to speak of curtains and riddels, hearse-cloths, carpets, falls, hangings, banners, cushions and canopies and finally 85 altar-frontals. In the now almost empty cupboards, there were once gold and silver-gilt ornaments. Thirty-four candlesticks, 8 censers, 8 basons, 9 crosses, 3 croziers and 13 patens and chalices.

All those great possessions passed into the hands of 'The Most Excellent Lord Henry VIII' and from his hands to where? At this time also, the magnificent Refectory, and later the Chapel of St Katherine were destroyed for no apparent reason whatever. Before he died, Henry VIII created a bishopric of Westminster together with a Dean and Chapter of twelve prebendaries, and although this produced some measure of stability, the plunder continued.

With the accession of Edward VI, whatever had been left was soon to disappear. In 1549 two great Lecterns and two splendid candlesticks with angels of copper-gilt were taken because they were 'monuments of idolatry and superstition', and in 1550 the Dean and Chapter, like the country, was in money difficulties; the coinage had been devalued, and what we know so well today as an 'economic crisis', overshadowed the whole Kingdom. Alterations were being made to the Choir, and some remaining treasures were sold to defray the cost. A little later further possessions were sold to pay the wages of the servants of the Abbey.

On 9 May 1553 the final blow came in the persons of the Lord Chief Justice and the Master of the Rolls, who demanded, as 'the King's Commissioners for the gathering of ecclesiastical goods', a complete list of all Abbey treasures.

The unhappy Sacrist who was forced to do this heart-breaking task was Robert Crome. He had to surrender everything except a silver pot and two gilt cups with covers.

Within a few weeks Edward VI died and it must have been much to the joy of his strong-minded half-sister Mary to take action at the Abbey. Dean Cox fled to the Continent and the Chapter soon came to the end of a miserable life which had no single redeeming feature. They left an Abbey stripped bare, even the body of St Edward, its founder, was not within its walls.

Now, in 1556, Queen Mary realized one of her cherished hopes by once more restoring the old Mitred Abbey. At the head she placed her friend John Howman of Feckenham, Dean of St Paul's, as Abbot. Like St Barnabas, he was a 'good man', gentle and love-able. Within months of his appointment he restored the body of St Edward to its shrine. The tomb, once a blaze of glory, must have been a sorry sight in its shattered state, but Feckenham did what little he could to make it worthy of its holy charge. For many years experts have tried to conjecture the original form of the tomb, but all are agreed that as it stands now, it is a strange mixture, made from bits here and pieces there. One day perhaps, given the means, this famous resting place of the body of St Edward may be brought back to some of its original splendour, now that it has become possible to reconstruct the original design. It is to Abbot Feckenham—and we must couple his name with that of Mary Tudor—that we are in-debted for the return of the remains of St Edward who now lies in his time-honoured resting-place. But poor Mary's monastery had only two years of life. Deserted by her husband, childless and ill, she died in 1558.

When Elizabeth I was crowned, Feckenham, the only mitred abbot in England, performed the traditional ceremonies connected with his office. Had it not been for him she might never have sat in the Coronation Chair, but have followed Lady Jane Grey to the scaffold. Nonetheless, although tradition had it that she offered him the vacant Archbishopric of Canterbury, the monastery of Queen Mary was finally suppressed in July 1559.

In its place the Queen set up the Collegiate Church which we know today, and on 21 May 1560—a date we remember each year as 'Foundation Day', when the flag flies and the bells ring—possession was given by three Royal Commissioners to the first Dean, William Bill, who was shortly joined by twelve prebendaries.

We speak today of the glorious age of the first Elizabeth, but for the Abbey it was anything but glorious.

Dean Goodman, who succeeded William Bill, was, it is true, a generous, kindly and learned man, a pre-eminent Churchman and a fine citizen, who lived to hold his office for forty years. But it is clear from our records, which are admittedly scanty, that his Chapter had little zeal for the Abbey. (Seventy Chapter meetings were held in ten years, commencing in 1568. Of these, twenty-four had to be abandoned owing to the lack of a quorum.) One of the original prebendaries, John Hardyman, stands out from the rest, for he indulged in an orgy of altar-smashing which even in that iconoclastic age became such a scandal that it led eventually to his dismissal. Abbot Feckenham had handed over to Dean Goodman a quantity of copes and vestments which had been made or collected for the monastery of Queen Mary. These too suffered, and were torn up to make a canopy for Elizabeth, and the then Treasurer records that one Thomas Holmes, upholsterer, was paid £13. 8s. 7d. for tailoring copes into cushions.

Towards the end of the century, however, there was some improvement in the care of the Abbey under the leadership of men such as Bancroft, Lancelot Andrewes and Laud, but in 1643 under the cold eye of that rampant puritan Oliver Cromwell, 'Monuments of superstituion and idolatory' were smashed, stained-glass windows were broken, copes were burnt and gold and silver ornaments were sold. Once more the Abbey reached the depths of desolation.

By the time of the Restoration the great church had been stripped bare and nothing remained of the enormous wealth of treasure which it owned in Pre-Reformation times. Charles II was crowned in 1660 and it is from this period that the present Abbey treasures date. When, by June 1660, the Dean and Chapter of Westminster took office again, the church did not possess even the bare necessities for celebrating Holy Communion, and to provide the sacred vessels and vestments was their first task. Within two years they purchased seven pieces of silver-gilt plate. These are the Abbey's oldest and most beautiful possessions, and superb examples of the great craftsmen of the late seventeenth century. The plate was steadily added to in the ensuing forty years.

With the coming to the throne of the Georges, the Abbey became enveloped in a cloud of apathy. Little or nothing was done to make it worthy or less barren.

If any name stands out in this twentieth century it is that of Jocelyn Perkins, Sacrist of Westminster Abbey from 1899 to 1958. His zeal and drive raised the standard of Abbey worship and beauty to heights worthy of the great church. But alas, he found successive Deans and Chapters lacked his vision. True it was that copes and frontals and much other impedimenta of worship eventually found their way into the Abbey, but the money to be spent was so limited that the quality of materials and plate fell far below the finest which the Abbey demands, and the sad and inevitable result is that much which was bought then must now be replaced. A start has been made in the form of five white and gold copes, and a tunicle, woven in Lyons. It is of interest to note that the looms on which the work was done are those which were used for Louis XVI of France. These vestments have been made of the finest materials by the finest craftsmen in the world. Many such things are still required in the Abbey, but the quality must always be the finest, whether it be fabrics, metal, wood or stone.

30

The Constitution of the Collegiate Church

THE constitution of the Abbey when it was a Benedictine monastery must be referred to briefly before embarking on a survey of the legal history with particular reference to the constitution of the present Collegiate Church.

The Abbot, as head of the monastic community, spent much of his time in managing and safeguarding the estates, with the Prior having responsibility for the domestic arrangements. In Norman times there were probably up to 80 monks at Westminster. In the fourteenth century the average was 52, falling to 35 in 1355 because of the Black Death. The monks held various offices such as Almoner, Chamberlain, Cellarer and Infirmarer.

The community of monks living and working together at Westminster set the pattern for the present Collegiate Church. There are many similarities. One of the monks was Steward; an office held by one of the Canons today, although the duties have changed. The Monk Almoner may be compared with the present-day Archdeacon's Assistant. There was also the lay office of Dapifer which has waxed and waned in importance in the course of centuries. It probably reached its peak when it was held by Lord Burghley in the days of Queen Elizabeth I, but it survives to the present day in the appointment of High Steward.

There were customary duties and privileges in the days of the monastery as there are at the present time. For example, under Abbot Berkyng (1222–1244), the Monks made use of the legend about St Peter and the tithe of salmon, and in a court action obliged the Rector of Rotherhithe to pay them half of their full tithe. Flete records the Regulations (nowadays known as Acts of Chapter) which were prescribed for the reception of the tithe. The Sacrist received half the head and three fingers from the body of the salmon, in return for which he gave the fishermen a candle weighing one pound, and the Cellarer was entitled to one finger's breadth and one thumb's length from the tail of the fish. The salmon, when cooked, was carried to a table in the midst of the great refectory and all the monks were obliged to stand while it was carried in.

The community life which existed prior to 1560 was obviously intended to be perpetuated when the Elizabethan Charter was granted in that year. Although nine centuries have passed since the foundation of Edward the Confessor, and four centuries since the present constitution was established, membership of the Collegiate Body still generates a feeling of belonging to the Abbey family within the limits of changed circumstances and modern conditions.

The constitution of Westminster Abbey, like the constitution of Great Britain, is not written down in one document.

It is therefore proposed to deal with the subject by means of the following topics: (1) The Elizabethan Charter; (2) The draft Statutes; (3) The status of Royal Peculiar and the authority of the Sovereign as Visitor; (4) The Dean; (5) The Canons; (6) The Minor Canons and Lay Officers; (7) Conflict of Customs; (8) Specific legal questions, and (9) The Abbey and Westminster School and the Abbey and the City of Westminster.

1. The present constitution of Westminster Abbey stems from a Royal Charter granted by Queen Elizabeth I and dated 21 May 1560. This Charter established a College or Collegiate Church of one Dean and twelve Prebendaries in the following words:

> . . . we will and by these presents for us our Heirs and Successors ordain that the aforesaid Scite of the said Monastery of the Blessed Peter Westminster and the Church of the same may be and henceforth for ever shall be a Collegiate Church by the Name of the Collegiate Church of Blessed Peter Westminster. . . .

and granted to the Dean and Chapter the church 'and all the Scite, Circuit Compass and Precinct of the said late Convent'. The Charter also named the first Dean, William Bill, Doctor of Divinity, and the twelve Prebendaries, of which the first or senior was William Bishop. The Dean and Prebendaries were established as a Corporate Body in deed and in name with perpetual succession and the Dean was empowered to make all appointments to the 'inferior' offices and was also given powers of discipline and dismissal. Queen Elizabeth reserved to herself and her successors the right and authority of appointing future Deans, Prebendaries and 'all poor persons there living of our bounty'. The latter are the Queen's almsmen and are still appointed by Royal Warrant. The Dean and Chapter were at the same time endowed with lands in different parts of the country including Worcestershire, Gloucestershire, Huntingdonshire and as far south as Middlesex and Kent; and given the advowsons of the benefices of Islip, Turweston, South Benfleet and others, all of which exist today and of which parishes the Dean and Chapter continue to be patrons. The estates were unfortunately, as it turned out, surrendered to the Ecclesiastical Commissioners by Act of Parliament in 1888, following an earlier settlement in 1868 which proved unworkable, in return for an annual money payment of £20,000. The Charter furthermore required the Dean and the twelve Prebendaries 'to behave exhibit and employ themselves according to the Rules and Statutes to them and their successors by us in a certain Indenture hereafter to be made, specifyed and Declared'.

2. The first draft of a book of Statutes as required by the Charter is thought to have been drawn up by Dean Bill who before becoming Dean of Westminster had been Master of Trinity College, Cambridge. The draft Statutes for Westminster, not unnaturally, included provisions which were contained in the Statutes granted to Trinity College in 1552. One particular clause giving the Dean sole authority to deal with *graviores causae* was not accepted by all the Prebendaries, one of whom had also been at Trinity and probably knew the history of this particular clause which had also been objected to there. The authorities of Trinity were successful in getting the clause deleted when new Statutes were given to the College in 1560 and no doubt strong pressure would have been applied for the exclusion of the clause before the draft Statutes for Westminster were presented for Royal approval. But these draft Statutes were in fact never signed. In 1584 Dean Goodman urged Lord Burghley, the Lord Treasurer to the Queen, to persuade the Queen to sign the Statutes, but in doing so the Dean acknowledged that some of the Prebendaries preferred the existing form of constitution which had grown up, i.e. partly according to the draft Statutes and partly by decrees of the Dean and Chapter by means of formal resolutions passed at Chapter meetings.

There seems no doubt that the Statutes did not receive Royal authority as the copies still existing bear no date, hand or seal. There are Chapter minutes in 1567 and 1571 referring to a 'draught of Statutes' and a Chapter minute in 1610 mentions a 'project of Statutes'. The Queen's unwillingness to sign Statutes was not confined to Westminster. In 1582 the Bishop of Peterborough pleaded pathetically in his old age for the Statutes of Peterborough Cathedral to be confirmed and in 1595 the Archbishop of Canterbury endeavoured to get the Canterbury Statutes sealed. An Act of Parliament was passed in 1707 for the avoiding of Doubts and Questions touching the Statutes of divers Cathedral and Collegiate Churches. By Chapter Resolution dated 5 March 1709 it was decided to take the opinions of the Attorney-General and Sir Edward Northey as to whether the new Act applied to the Abbey. Each of these lawyers advised that the Act only applied to Cathedrals and Collegiate Churches founded by King Henry VIII and that it did not therefore apply to Westminster which had been founded by Elizabeth. Uncertainty regarding the Statutes came to a head again in 1905 when three of the Canons challenged the authority which the Dean (Armitage Robinson) was exercising over certain matters which he claimed to be within his jurisdiction in accordance with the Statutes. Eventually, in 1911, four specific questions were submitted to the Royal Visitor and referred by the King to the Lord Chancellor for advice. As a result it was established that the Statutes had no legal authority and that the College was governed by custom and by the authority of Royal Letters, but that where the custom was not clear or continuous the Statutes had weight as evidence of what the ancient custom presumably was. The Lord Chancellor also advised that by reason of current modern usage and a statement on the position which had been made at the time by the Dean with the approval of the Chapter, the Dean ought to be treated as the Ordinary unless further provision and regulation were made to the contrary. Likewise it was ruled that the control of interments and of the erection of monuments rested with the Ordinary as also did the control and use of the Abbey for purposes other than Statutory Services.

3. As a result of the Arbitration of the Archbishop of Canterbury (Langton) and other Prelates in 1221, arising out of a claim by the Bishop of London to exercise authority over the Abbey, it was declared that the Abbey was wholly exempt from the jurisdiction of the Bishop of London and subject alone to the Pope. Later on the Ecclesiastical Licences Act of 1533 confirmed by the Act of Supremacy in 1558 transferred to the Crown the jurisdiction which was previously exercised by the Pope so that thereafter the Abbey became a Royal Peculiar. Subsequently, it was constituted by Charter of Queen Elizabeth I already referred to, as a Collegiate Church with the Sovereign as the Royal Visitor.

A 'Royal Peculiar' is a free chapel of the Sovereign and exempt from any ecclesiastical jurisdiction other than that of the Sovereign. The Abbey is, therefore, not subject to the jurisdiction of the Bishop of London or of the Archbishop of Canterbury. Occasionally when the Archbishop or some other high ecclesiastic takes part in a religious ceremony in the Abbey a form of protest is read in which, while he is welcomed to the church, he is informed that he has no legal rights therein. Unless the Archbishop or other visiting bishop is invited to give the Blessing this is in practice given by the Dean or in his absence, by the Sub-Dean at Special Services and the Canon in Residence at Statutory Services or otherwise by the senior member of the Collegiate Body present, Canon or Minor Canon. The Sovereign is the supreme Ordinary and Visitor of the Church of England. Similarly the Sovereign has power to visit various places which are exempt from episcopal visitation, the Abbey being one such place. As Supreme Governor the Sovereign is the ultimate Court of Appeal in ecclesiastical matters, but as in civil matters, does not exercise jurisdiction in person, but through the Judges. This appellate jurisdiction is now exercised by the Judicial Committee of the Privy Council.

So far as Westminster Abbey is concerned the Sovereign has exercised such visitorial authority over the years by giving decisions when doubts have arisen on matters affecting the constitution and government of the Church. These decisions have been communicated by means of Royal Letters, and have dealt with such questions as the allocation of official houses (1667: Charles II), as to residence and attendance at Services by the Dean and Prebendaries (1746: George II), the fixing of a quorum for Chapter meetings (1836: William IV), the authority of the Sub-Dean to summon Chapter meetings and the affixing of the common seal in the absence of the Dean (1868: Victoria). The decision regarding the allocation of official houses was necessary as, according to the draft Statutes, an incoming Canon was entitled to the house occupied by his predecessor, but a custom had grown up whereby in the event of a vacancy the remaining Canons, in order of seniority, could exercise a right to move into the vacant house should they wish to do so. The Royal Letter referred to above confirmed the custom and over-ruled the draft Statutes.

A Royal Letter will probably be required at some future date to determine the procedure in the event of an interregnum in the Deanery. It is uncertain whether the office of Sub-Dean continues after the death or resignation of the Dean, or whether it lapses, in which case the Senior Canon acts until the installation of a new Dean. In the past this difficulty has not arisen because almost invariably the Sub-Dean was also Senior Canon. But this was not so at the time of the last vacancy in the Deanery (1959) when, on a proposal in Chapter by the Senior Canon, the Sub-Dean continued in office. It may be that the best solution is for the members of the Chapter to elect a Chairman to act until a new Dean takes office. Such a procedure would however be entirely without precedent and would require a Royal Letter to make it legal.

The Royal Visitor is not empowered to intervene in disputes

between members of the Collegiate Body and outsiders. The authority as Visitor comes into effect only when members of the Collegiate Body appeal in cases where they allege irregularities or unfair treatment. Such an appeal to the Crown was made by the Minor Canons and certain of the Lay Officers in 1949 when the Dean and Chapter petitioned the Crown for a Supplemental Charter to abolish freehold tenure of office. As a result the matter was referred to the Lord Chancellor who then passed it to the Judicial Committee of the Privy Council and both sides were heard at length, the proceedings lasting four days. The Judicial Committee issued a confidential report in due course and recommended the granting of the Supplemental Charter which was in fact granted on 31 May 1951. A further Supplemental Charter was granted on 25 June 1958 giving the Dean and Chapter wider powers of investment in respect of their Corporate funds.

The position of the Sovereign as Visitor has been preserved in the Ecclesiastical Jurisdiction Measure 1963 whereby under Section 83 (sub-section (3)) it is enacted that . . . 'nothing in this Measure shall authorise proceedings against a holder of an office in a Royal Peculiar'. This section, therefore, takes the Abbey clergy out of the ambit of the Measure.

4. The Dean of Westminster has unique powers. The draft Statutes require as follows:

> Let there be one Dean, the Governor of the whole College even as the mind is in the body. To his authority all the others are to be obedient. He must be a Clergyman and doctor or bachelor of Divinity; he must excel the rest in doctrine, religion, innocence of life, prudence, justice, faith and devotion to the College. . . .

The position of the Dean as the Ordinary was finally established in 1911, some 351 years after the granting of the Charter, as the result of formal advice given by the Lord Chancellor referred to above. As the Ordinary, the Dean has sole responsibility for the ordering of Divine Service and for saying who shall be baptized, married, interred or memorialized in the Abbey. In practice he almost invariably consults the members of the Chapter and on occasions outside authorities; but he is under no legal obligation to do so. The Dean has power to settle the inscriptions on memorials but the authority of the Chapter is necessary to determine the size and positioning of the memorials, the reason for this being that it is the Dean and Chapter and not the Dean alone who are the Trustees of the fabric and responsible for the finances.

It is now established (Supplemental Charter 1951) that the Dean

appoints to all non-capitular offices, other than to the offices of High
Steward and High Bailiff, but on terms and conditions agreed by the
Dean and Chapter and the person appointed. The Supplemental
Charter also specifically preserves the authority given to the Dean
in the original Charter of 1560 'not only to correct but also to depose
and from the said Collegiate Church to amove and expel any
inferior officer or minister of the said Collegiate Church'.

The Dean presides at meetings of the Dean and Chapter but he
does not have a casting vote.

The Dean is installed in accordance with the procedure laid down
in the draft Statutes and also takes the oath in Latin prescribed
therein including the undertaking to correct and defend all and
singular the Prebendaries, pupils, servants and almsmen in accordance with the statutes, and the Rules of Her Majesty ('omnes et
singulos Praebendarios, discipulos, administros et pauperes ex
statutis his, et Praescriptionibus Regiae Majestatis. . . .').

5. The Dean and Chapter consisted originally of the Dean and
twelve Prebendaries. But, by Section 1 of the Ecclesiastical Commissioners Act of 1840, the title of *Prebendary* was changed to *Canon*
and the number reduced from twelve to six. The Westminster Abbey
Act of 1888 authorized the suspension of one Canonry and a further
Canonry is now vacant and unlikely to be filled.

The Dean and Chapter therefore now comprises the Dean and
four Canons. Under the provisions of the draft Statutes they are
required to be:

> clergymen, and at the least Masters of Arts and preachers. They
> even as members of one Body, shall love and assist one another,
> and undertake together with the Dean, the care of all and singular
> the things in the Collegiate Church, and to him they shall be
> subsidiary in transacting and completing matters. They, both by
> their authority and by their solemnity and prudence, shall be even
> as chiefs and senators in a Republic whom all the rest should
> reverence and whose advice the majority follow.

A Canon at his installation also takes an oath in Latin as prescribed in the draft Statutes. The oath includes an undertaking that
he will preserve the Statutes of the College, as also the laws, liberties,
prescribed privileges, ceremonies and customs, so far as they pertain
to him. ('. . . Deinde me omnis hujus Collegii statuta, jura, liber-
tates, laudabiles, quae ad me pertinebunt servaturum. . . .')

The procedure for installation of Deans and Canons has now
hardened into custom by long usage and even though the draft
Statutes have no legal authority the fact that they may be referred to

as evidence of custom makes it not entirely inappropriate for Deans or Canons to give the undertakings set out above.

The Canons are responsible for attendance and certain duties at the daily Services and for preaching every Sunday during their months of residence. They also attend Chapter meetings which are held twice every month and carry out the additional duties of the four great offices of Sub-Dean, Archdeacon, Treasurer and Steward. The draft Statutes specify that not more than one of these offices shall be held by any Canon at the same time but this has been relaxed in recent years, other than for the offices of Sub-Dean and Treasurer which by Statute and custom are never held by the same person. This is understandable and quite proper as the Dean has no power *quae* Dean over the Abbey finances. If the Dean were ill or absent and the Sub-Dean acting for him, it would be entirely contrary to the constitution for the Sub-Dean (as acting Dean) to have any financial powers.

The Sub-Dean is appointed by the Dean as his personal deputy. Appointments to the other great offices are made by the Dean and Chapter. In recent years, the offices of Librarian and Lector Theologiae have also been held by Canons. The office of Librarian has on occasions been held by a Minor Canon and a layman.

The Dean and Chapter are corporately responsible, as Trustees, for the fabric, finances and general government of the Abbey, other than those specific matters which are within the Dean's sole discretion as the Ordinary.

6. The draft Statutes made provision for a number of 'Inferior Officers and Ministers' including six clergy (of whom one was to be Precentor), twelve lay clerks, one teacher of the choristers, one Chapter Clerk, one Clerk of the Works, one High Steward, one Deputy High Steward. The Dean and Chapter were advised by Counsel in 1914 that the Minor Canons and Organist held freehold offices. This Opinion was confirmed by Counsel in 1948 who also expressed the view that this freehold tenure extended to the other offices mentioned in the draft Statutes. This meant that once appointed, a Minor Canon or Lay Officer could only be removed from office with great difficulty and even then had the right of appeal to the Royal Visitor.

As a result, officers, once appointed, tended to stay in office for life and could do so, long after they ceased to be capable of carrying out their duties. The status of the Minor Canons and Lay Officers has throughout the years ebbed and flowed with the strength of character and ability of the office holder. Once customary duties were attached to a particular office, it became very difficult for the

Dean and Chapter to exercise the full authority which, as the Governing Body, they ought to be in a position to do. When opposing the petition for a Supplemental Charter in 1951 the counter-petitioners asserted various claims in respect of their offices. For example, it was claimed on behalf of the then Precentor that it was part of his customary duties to instruct a newly appointed Dean and other members of the Collegiate Church in the details of the constitution and customs. Objections were also submitted by the counter-petitioners to certain orders which the Dean and Chapter had passed containing directions as to the lessons, psalms, canticles, prayers and method of disposition of alms. A custom was also alleged that before the Dean appointed a Minor Canon the candidate should undergo a musical test by the Precentor or Organist or both, and only be considered by the Dean for the post if recommended by the Precentor. This alleged custom would have imposed a veto by an 'inferior officer' on the Dean's right of appointment given in a Royal Charter and was resisted by the Dean and Chapter.

By Sections 24 and 25 of the Cathedrals Measure 1931 all freehold offices in cathedrals (other than those of Deans, Provosts, Canons and Prebendaries) were abolished subject to a saving clause for those in office at the time. This Measure did not apply to the Abbey (or St George's, Windsor, or indeed to Christ Church, Oxford). In 1936 an attempt was made to obtain a Supplemental Charter to abolish freehold offices and to give the Dean and Chapter the power to make bye-laws. But because of the deaths of Dean Foxley Norris and later of Dean de Labilliere and also the outbreak of the War the negotiations had to be postponed.

The question was revived in 1948 and as a result of the Supplemental Charter of 1951, freehold tenure has been abolished other than for the High Steward and the High Bailiff and for those officers who were appointed prior to the date of the Supplemental Charter. By 1965 only one of the Minor Canons and four of the Lay Vicars held freehold offices. This resulted in an interesting situation in that when the Minor Canon still enjoying a freehold was on duty, he might have been able to claim the right to read the Lesson at the Statutory Service as being a customary duty of his office. But this would not be so with Minor Canons appointed since 1951 should the Dean as the Ordinary wish to invite someone else to read.

7. From time to time over the centuries, the Dean's powers and authority have been challenged and resolutions of the Dean and Chapter have been quoted to support a contention that the Dean has or has not the power to do a certain thing. For instance, in 1705 the Chapter minutes record that the Dean and Chapter exercised

discipline over a Queen's almsman and on another occasion the Dean and Chapter dismissed the Abbey Surveyor and the Clerk of the Works whereas in the Charter the Dean alone is given powers of discipline and dismissal. As far back as 23 June 1571 a Chapter resolution confirmed that permission should be given for Sir Richard Pexhall, Knight, to be buried in one of the chapels in the Abbey in spite of the fact that such a matter was solely within the discretion of the Dean. Again, on 2 November 1737 an inscription intended for Sir Thomas Hardy's memorial was laid before the Dean and Chapter and an amendment was made even though this was within the Dean's jurisdiction. On the other hand, on 14 May 1834 an application having been made to place a monumental bust to the memory of Mrs Siddons in the Abbey, it was ordered by the Chapter 'that leave be given for this in such part of the Poets' Corner as the Dean shall approve.' In this instance the Dean exercised a power which was really a Dean and Chapter matter.

Occasional instances such as those quoted above whereby the Dean consults the Chapter on matters where he could, if he so wished, act entirely on his own initiative cannot be maintained as constituting a change of custom binding on his successors and requiring them to continue to refer such matters to the Dean and Chapter.

Similarly the Dean and Chapter have on occasions allowed the Dean to make decisions on Chapter matters, but having allowed this to happen, they cannot have weakened the constitutional powers of future Deans and Chapters.

A study of the Chapter minutes over the years clearly shows how the strength of character, knowledge and, indeed, the interest in the constitution of various Deans or Canons, as the case may be, have, to a considerable extent, influenced the *modus operandi* of Deans, and Deans and Chapters and resulted in changes in custom. Furthermore, the Chapter minutes, although historically very interesting, cannot be relied upon completely as they are sometimes obviously loosely worded and incomplete and thereby capable of giving a misleading indication of the true state of affairs.

In Dean Bradford's time (1723–31) two important changes were made which affected the position of the Dean: (1) appointment to subordinate offices were made by the Dean and Chapter thus contravening the clause in the Charter which gave the Dean power to make such appointments; and (2) leave to erect monuments was given by the Dean and Chapter. Dr Wilcocks was installed as Dean in July 1731 and held the office for twenty-five years. He was not content to follow Bradford's surrender of decanal authority over appointments and reached agreement with the Chapter in 1732 that the Dean should nominate in all cases. The draft Statutes began to come into their own again and on 23 April 1735 the Chapter minutes record an order to the Registrar, Mr Gell, 'to prepare two exact copies of the Statute Book for the use of the College'. Dean Horsley (1793–1802), sought to carry out the Statutes rigidly. He was followed by Dean Vincent. Under Vincent (1802–15) and his successor Ireland (1816–42) there was a gradual resumption of the practice whereby appointments were made by the Dean alone. Later on during Dean Buckland's tenure of office (1845–56) three of the Canons sought to secure the intervention of the Crown as the Ordinary, but a letter from the Home Office rejected the submission and confirmed the Dean's position as the Ordinary. In the late nineteenth century the then Sub-Dean, Lord John Thynne, was known to have high views on the decanal prerogative. He was in the Chair in a Chapter Meeting when an order was made putting the strictest limitation on the consent of the Dean and Chapter regarding burials in Poets' Corner. Dean Armitage Robinson (1902–11) exercised his decanal authority to the fullest extent in spite of Canon Duckworth's opposition and endeavours to increase the authority and powers of the Dean and Chapter. The Lord Chancellor's ruling in 1911 as to the position of the Dean led to a period of calm which helped the development of the Abbey as a National Shrine under Dean Ryle (1911–25).

When the petition for a Supplemental Charter was submitted in 1950 the then Dean, Dr Don, being very much aware of the Dean's powers of appointment as set out in the Elizabethan Charter, insisted that the proposed Supplemental Charter should confirm the Dean's power to make all appointments. The Chapter's position was however preserved in that the Charter provided that the Dean should appoint on terms and conditions agreed between the Dean and Chapter and the person appointed. The Supplemental Charter also ensured that the Dean's power of dismissal given in the original Charter was retained.

In addition to the Minor Canons and Lay Officers referred to above, there are upwards of one hundred full-time employees including vergers, cleaners, office and bookshop staff, tradesmen—masons, plumbers, carpenters, marble-polishers and other labourers on the Clerk of Works' staff appointed by the heads of departments exercising delegated authority from the Dean.

8. Having traced in outline the constitutional history of the Abbey it might be worth while mentioning briefly the legal position relating to a few specific matters of general interest.

Firstly: ownership of property. The Abbey Church and its precincts were given by Queen Elizabeth I to the Dean and Chapter 'to be held in free, pure and perpetual alms', i.e. the common-law tenure known as 'frankalmoign'. This tenure imposed restrictions on the Dean and Chapter in dealing with the land which they held as trust property. The Law of Property Act, 1922, appears to have abolished the common-law tenure of frankalmoign and by virtue of the Settled Land Act of 1925 it would seem that the Dean and Chapter are thereby authorized to grant long leases of up to 999 years (for building), 100 years (for mining) and 50 years (for any other purpose) and also to exchange, mortgage and sell land. In practice, however, the Dean and Chapter do not grant leases of more than fourteen years thus continuing to follow the period laid down in the Ecclesiastical Leases Act of 1842.

Secondly: right of access and right of exclusion. The status of Royal Peculiar extends beyond the Abbey Church itself to include the precincts, i.e. the area outside the Great West Door known as the Sanctuary; Dean's Yard; Little Dean's Yard; the Cloisters; and College Garden, which is enclosed by the old precincts wall with its boundaries of Great College Street and Abingdon Street. The hours of opening and closing the church are laid down by the Dean and Chapter and the gates at the entrance to Dean's Yard are closed on one day every year, usually on 15 September, which although probably no longer necessary in order to preserve the close as private property, has the effect of reminding those who normally use the precincts as a thoroughfare, that they are only entering with the permission of the Dean and Chapter. One possible exception to this right of restricting access to the precincts might be substantiated in respect of those who are authorized to visit the Chapter House which is situated in the Cloisters and which is under the control of the Ministry of Public Building and Works. The Chapter House was not restored to the Dean and Chapter after the Reformation. It might be claimed that there is an 'easement of necessity' through Dean's Yard and the Cloisters to the Chapter House and also through the vestibule or entrance to the Chapter House which remains the property of the Abbey. This question has never been put to the test and would certainly be challenged by the Dean and Chapter. A most important decision concerning access was made in a High Court Judgment in 1943 in the case of The Dean and Chapter *v.* Cole, when it was ruled that the Dean and Chapter could exclude any person from the Abbey or its precincts with the possible exception of a resident in the precincts wishing to attend Divine Service. In permitting members of the public to visit the Abbey and its precincts the Dean and Chapter have a legal duty as the property owners.

Thirdly: monuments and memorials. As has been said previously, permission to erect monuments and memorials in the Abbey or precincts rests with the Dean as the Ordinary. The decision regarding size and position is the responsibility of the Dean and Chapter. Once a memorial or monument has been set up, however, it may not be removed at the pleasure of the Ordinary but, apart from certain very exceptional circumstances, only with the consent of the person who erected the monument during his lifetime, or after his death with the consent of the heir of the person commemorated. The same applies to the alteration of inscriptions on memorials. Furthermore, human remains cannot be moved even from one part of the Abbey to another without a licence fro n the Home Secretary (Section 25 of the Burial Act, 1857). Such a licence is not required for a change in the position of a casket containing the ashes of a body which has been cremated. Westminster Abbey (and St Paul's Cathedral) are exempt from the provisions of the Burial Act, 1852, relating to the interment of human bodies, if the Sovereign, by Royal Letter, signifies 'her pleasure' that the body shall be so interred.

9. No history of the Constitution of Westminster Abbey would be complete without mentioning the close association between the Abbey and Westminster School and the responsibilities for local government within the City of Westminster which rested with the Dean and Chapter prior to the London Government Act of 1899.

The draft Statutes, which must inevitably be mentioned frequently when discussing the Constitution, provided, *inter alia*, for the appointment of '40 grammar school boys and two instructors for educating the young'. Out of this requirement laid down in 1560, Westminster School was refounded and has now become one of the leading public schools in England. The school has grown enormously in size over the years and in addition to the 40 grammar school boys, mentioned in the Statutes, i.e. the Queen's Scholars, and the instructors for educating the young, i.e. the Head Master and the Under Master and Master of the Queen's Scholars, there are several boarding houses and a large number of day boys, totalling in all some 500 students. Prior to the Public Schools Act of 1868 the School was governed by the Dean and Chapter of Westminster. The Head Master, Under Master and Master of the Queen's Scholars, and the 40 Queen's Scholars were members of the Foundation. The Public Schools Act set up an independent Governing Body but stipulated that the Dean of Westminster was to be Chairman (*ex officio*) and that the Dean and Chapter should have power to appoint two other Governors. The appointments of the Head Master and Under Master no longer rest with the Dean *qua* Dean. The Public Schools Act also transferred to the Governing Body certain properties within the precincts, mainly in Little Dean's Yard, but did not convey to the School Little Dean's Yard itself, which remains the property of the Dean and Chapter. The Act also gave the School the right to use the 'playground' in Dean's Yard and the College Hall for the Scholars of Westminster School 'in the same manner as heretofore'. The precise extent of this right of user has never been established and could well have caused considerable discontent and bad feeling between the Abbey and the School. This has, however, been avoided as a result of good sense and mutual respect. Should Westminster School ever move from Westminster the School buildings revert to the Church Commissioners (apart from certain buildings dealt with specially under the provisions of the Church House Act 1934) and not to the Abbey as is sometimes mistakenly thought to be the case.

Prior to 1585 the control of the City of Westminster was in the hands of the Abbey and the Crown. In 1585 this control was supplemented by an administrative body of citizens, the chief dignatary being the High Steward appointed by the Abbey authorities. In time the post of High Steward became an honorary one filled by a nobleman of high rank, the duties being conducted by a deputy. In 1585 when the High Steward and the Dean were unable to cope with the overcrowding and disorder that had arisen in Westminster through the social disruption that followed the Reformation, an Act for the good government of the City was passed empowering the Dean or High Steward to appoint a burgess and an assistant for each of the twelve divisions or wards that comprised the City. The minutes of the Dean and Chapter record many decisions relating to local government affairs.

The London Government Act of 1899 established twenty-eight metropolitan Borough Councils in place of the old Vestries and a Royal Charter was granted on 29 October 1900 confirming the status of Westminster as a City. The authority of the Dean and the High Steward in secular affairs of the City of Westminster then altogether ceased. The High Steward at the time (the Marquis of Salisbury) was invited to become the first Mayor of Westminster, but quite naturally declined, because he also happened to be Prime Minister at the time. The office of High Steward is an appointment of honour without duties other than attendance on certain ceremonial occasions. In order to preserve the historic link between the Abbey and the City Council, it is indeed a very happy arrangement whereby since 1935 the High Steward has invariably appointed the Mayor of Westminster for the time being as Deputy High Steward of Westminster.

The new City of Westminster incorporating the Boroughs of Paddington and St Marylebone was constituted by Charter dated 1 April 1965.

In conclusion, therefore, it will be obvious that the constitutional history of Westminster Abbey has been interspersed with uncertainties which, in turn, have led to occasional friction. But most important, there has been that flexibility which is essential for any governing body to have the freedom of action which it must have to deal with situations as they arise, many of which cannot be anticipated or foreseen. The Sub-Committee of the Cathedrals Commission set up in 1926, reporting on Westminster Abbey, recommended that a Register of Customs be drawn up and submitted to the Royal Visitor for approval in an endeavour to settle some of the uncertainties. Also, in 1951, the Judicial Committee of the Privy Council, at the time of recommending the grant of the Supplemental Charter, urged that a Register of Major Customs be drawn up. The Judicial Committee recognized that some customs had long since fallen into desuetude and that others, in view of changing circumstances, would require amendment. They recommended, therefore, that not only should a Register of Customs be drawn up but that proposals should be submitted for such alterations and additions and for such powers of further amendment in the future as the Dean and Chapter thought right.

As the first stage in this operation, the former Registrar, Mr T. Hebron, with some fifty years' experience of Abbey affairs behind him, and in collaboration with Canons Fox and Carpenter has drawn up a document entitled 'Rights and Privileges' in which have been set out, with appropriate authorities annotated, the duties and responsibilities of all the officers of the Collegiate Body and the many other customs which have grown up over the years affecting the government of the Abbey and the conduct of its Services. This very important document will, in due course, and it is hoped in the not too distant future, form the basis of the long-overdue Register of Customs which will be submitted to the Royal Visitor for confirmation in accordance with the recommendations made in 1926 and 1951. Such a Register, when approved by the Visitor, will take its place with the original Charter, draft Statutes and Royal Letters as a document of major importance in the constitution of Westminster Abbey.

Bibliography

PART I THE BEGINNINGS

Barlow, F., ed., *The Life of Edward the Confessor*. 1962.
    'Edward the Confessor's Early Life, Character and At-
    titudes', *Eng. Hist. Rev.*, LXXX, April 1965, pp. 225 ff.
Burridge, A. W., 'L'Immaculée Conception dans la Théologie de
    l'Angleterre Mediévale', *Revue d'Histoire Ecclesiastique*,
    XXXII, July 1936, pp. 570 ff.
Chaplais, P., ed., 'Original Charters of Herbert and Gervase, Abbots
    of Westminster, 1121–57', *Pipe Roll Soc. N.S.*, XXXVI,
    1960, pp. 89 ff.
    Facsimiles of English Royal Writs to 1100.
Colvin, H. M., ed., *The History of the King's Works*. 1963.
Harmer, F. E., *Anglo-Saxon Writs*. 1952.
    'Three Westminster Writs of Edward the Confessor', *Eng.
    Hist. Rev.*, LI, 1936, pp. 97 ff.
Knowles, D., *The Monastic Order in England*. 2nd edn., 1963.
    The Religious Orders in England, vol. I, 1948, vol. II, 1955.
Legg, J. W., 'Inventory of the Vestry at Westminster Abbey, 1388',
    Archaeologia, LII, 1890, pp. 195 ff.
Pantin, W. A., *Chapters of the English Black Monks*. Camden Soc.,
    Series 3, XLV, 1931.
    'Gloucester College', *Oxoniensia*, XI–XII, 1945–7, pp. 65 ff.
    'Medieval Westminster Abbey', *Ampleforth and Its Origins*,
    ed. Dom. C. Cary-Elwes, 1958.
Pearce, E. H., *The Monks of Westminster*. 1916.
    Walter de Wenlock. 1920.
    William de Colchester. 1917.
Peers, Sir C. and Tanner, L. E., 'Some Recent Discoveries in West-
    minster Abbey', *Archaeologia*, XCIII, 1949, pp. 155 ff.
Robinson, J. Armitage,
    The Abbot's House, Westminster Abbey. 1911.
    Flete's History of Westminster Abbey. 1909.
    Gilbert Crispin, Abbot of Westminster. 1911.
    'The Church of Edward the Confessor at Westminster',
    Archaeologia, LXII, 1910, pp. 81 ff.
    'Simon Langham', *The Church Quarterly Review*, LXV. July
    1908.

'An Unrecognised Westminster Chronicler, 1381–94', *Proc. of British Academy*, III, 1907–8, pp. 61 ff.

with M. R. James, *The MSS of Westminster Abbey.* 1909.

The Rolls Series (passim).

Sayles, G. O. and Richardson, H. G., *The Governance of Medieval England.* 1963.

Schmitt, Dom. F. X., ed., *St Anselmi Opera.* 1946 ff.

Scholz, B. W., 'Two Forged Charters from Westminster Abbey', *Eng. Hist. Rev.* LXXVI, July, 1961, pp. 466 ff.

Southern, R. W., 'The Canterbury Forgeries', *Eng. Hist. Rev.* LXXIII, 1958, pp. 193 ff.

Sweet, A. H., 'The Apostolic See and the Heads of English Religious Houses', *Speculum*, XXVIII, No. 3, July 1953, pp. 468 ff.

Tanner, L. E., *Unknown Westminster Abbey.* 1948.

'Caxton's House at Westminster', *The Library* (*Trans. of the Bibliographical Soc.*), September 1957.

Thompson, E. M., ed., *The Customary of St Augustine, Canterbury and St. Peter, Westminster.* 2 vols., Henry Bradshaw Soc., 1902.

Thorneley, I. D., 'Sanctuary in Medieval London', *The Brit. Archaeol. Assoc. Journal*, New Series, XXXVIII, 1933, pp. 293 ff.

Victoria County History of London, vol. i, 1910, pp. 433 ff. (on Westminster Abbey).

Westlake, H. F., *Westminster Abbey*, 2 vols., 1923.

Williamson, E. W., ed., *The Letters of Osbert of Clare*, 1929.

Willis, J. W. Bund, 'Worcestershire and Westminster Abbey', *Architect. Soc. Reports & Papers*, XXXIV, pp. 329 ff.

PARTS II–V. HISTORY

Manuscript Sources

Westminster Abbey Muniments (W.A.M.).
Chapter Minutes 1542–1953.
Installation Book.
Precentor's Book (61228A).
Treasurer's Accounts.
Zachary Pearce MSS. 64856 A–B(Autobiography).
Other MSS.: 60004, 60013, 60016, 60045, 64451, 64456, 64457, 64459, 64460, 64461, 64466, 64467, 64468, 64469, 64471, 64472, 64473, 64474, 64476, 64529, 64536, 64543, 64594, 64601, 64602, 64607, 64624, 64625, 64638, 64699, 64705, 64714, 64723, 64725, 64773, 64775, 64822, 64846, 64890, 64856 B, 64897, 64822.

British Museum: Orde MSS.
       Additional MS. 7099.
       Harleian MS. 1498.
Bodleian Library: Rawlinson MS. D. 68.

Printed Sources

Annual Register.

Astle, Thomas, *The Will of Henry VII*. 1775.

Atterbury, Bp. Francis, *A Letter to the Clergy of the Church of England on Occasion of the Commitment of the Right Reverend the Lord Bishop of Rochester to the Tower of London, by a clergyman of the Church of England*. 1722.

Aubrey, John, *Brief Lives*, 2 vol. edn., 1848.

Baker, G. F. Russell, *Memoir of Richard Busby*. 1895.

Beeching, H. C., *Francis Atterbury*. 1909.

Bond, Francis, *Westminster Abbey*. 1909.

Brayley, Edward Wedlake, *The History and Antiquities of the Abbey Church of St. Peter, Westminster*. 1818.

Buckland, F. T., Memoir of Dean Buckland prefixed to 3rd. ed. of Dean Buckland's Paper on 'Geology and Minerology' in *Bridgewater Treatises*.

Burnet, Gilbert, *The History of the Reformation*. 1850 edn.

Calendar of State Papers Domestic: Henry VIII, Edward VI, Mary, Elizabeth I, James I, Charles I, Commonwealth and Protectorate.

Camden, William, *Reges, Reginae, Nobiles et alii in Ecclesia Collegiata B. Petri Westmonasteriis sepulti*. 1600.

Crull, J., *The Antiquities of St. Peter's or the Abbey Church of Westminster*, 2 vols., 3rd edn., 1722.

Dart, J., *Westmonasterium*, 2 vols., 1723.

The Diary of John Evelyn, ed. E. S. de Beer, 6 vols., 1955.

The Diary of Samuel Pepys, ed. G. Gregory Smith, 1925.

Dictionary of National Biography.

Forshall, F. H., *Westminster School*. 1884.

Foxe's *Book of Martyrs*, 3 vols. edn., 1844.

Fuller, Thomas, *The Church History of England*, 3 vols., ed. J. Nichols; 1868.
      The History of the Worthies of England, 3 vols., ed. P. A. Nuttall, 1840.

Gentlemen's Magazine.

Gordon, Elizabeth, *Life and Correspondence of William Buckland*. 1894.

Hacket, John, *Scrinia Reserata*. 1692.

Halsbury, *Laws of England*.

Hearne, Thomas, *Collections*, vol. 1 (Oxford Historical Society), ed. C. E. Dobie, 1885.

Heylyn, Peter, *Cyprianus Anglicus*. London, 1868.
  Ecclesia Restaurata. London, 1670.
  Aerius Redivivus. London, 1672.

Hope, W. H. St John, 'The Obituary Roll of John Islip, Abbot of Westminster' . . . with 'Notes on other Obituary Rolls', *Vetusta Monumenta*, VII, pt. iv (Society of Antiquaries, London, 1906).

Isaacson, H., *An Exact Narration of the Life and Death of Launcelot Andrewes*. 1650.

Jebb, H. A., *The Life of Bishop Horsley*. 1909.

Journals of the House of Commons.

Journals of the House of Lords.

Knowles, David, *The Religious Orders in England: The Tudor Age*, vol. iii, 1959.

Lacey, T. A., *Herbert Thorndyke 1598–1672*. 1929.

Lethaby, W. R., *Westminster Abbey and the King's Craftsmen*. 1906.

Letters and Papers: Foreign and Domestic Henry VIII, vols. 5 and 6.

Machyn, Henry, *Diary 1550–1563*, ed. J. H. Nichols (Camden Society No. 42), 1848.

Mackie, J. D., *The Early Tudors*. 1952.

Mayor, J. E. B., *Letters of Archbishop Williams* (Cambridge Antiquarian Society, vols. 2 and 3, 1864–76).

Neale, J. and Brayley, E., *History and Antiquities of the Abbey Church of St. Peter Westminster*, 2 vols., 1818.

Newcome, R., *A Memoir of Gabriel . . . and Godfrey Goodman*. 1825.
  Original Letters 1537–1558 (Parker Society, 1846/7), 2 vols.

Pantin, W. A., 'The General and Provincial Chapters of the English Black Monks 1215–1540', *Transactions of the Royal Historical Society*, 9 June 1927.

Patrick, Simon, *Autobiography*. 1839.

Paul, Dolben, *John Dolben. His Life and Character*. 1884.

Pearce, E. H., *The Monks of Westminster*. 1916.

Perkins, J., *Westminster Abbey* (Alciun Society, 3 vols. Nos. xxxiii–v).
  The Crowning of the Sovereign. 1937.

Pollard, A. F., *Wolsey*. 1929.

Rackham, R. B., 'The Nave of Westminster Abbey', *Proceedings of the British Academy*, vol. IV, March 1909.

Ridley, J. D., *Nicholas Ridley*. 1957.
  Thomas Cranmer. 1962.

Robinson, J. Armitage, *The Abbot's House, Westminster Abbey*. 1911.
  The Ancient Chapel called the Chamber of the Pyx. Pamphlet, 1903.

'The Benedictine Abbey of Westminster', *Church Quarterly Review*, April 1907.

'Westminster Abbey in the early part of the 17th century', *Proceedings of the Royal Institution*, vol. XVII, 1902/4.

Roberts, B. Dew, *Mitre and Musket*. 1938.

Rushworth, John, *Historical Collections*, Part III, vol. I, 1692.

Russell, W. E., *Basil Wilberforce*. 1917.

Ryves, Bruno, *Mercurius Rusticus*. 1685.

Sanson, William, *Westminster at War*. 1947.

Sargeaunt, J., *Annals of Westminster School*. 1898.

Selden, J., *Table Talk*. 1898 edn.

Smith, Mrs. A. Murray, *Westminster Abbey: its Story and Associations*. 1906.

Smyth, Charles, *Church and Parish*. 1955.

Snowden, H. P., *The Unknown Warrior*. British Legion. 1964.

Stanley, A. P., *On Westminster Abbey* (Royal Institute of Great Britain, 27 April 1866).
> *Historical Memorials of Westminster Abbey*. 5th Ed. 1882.
> *Westminster Abbey Sermons for the Working Classes*.

Storr, V. F. and Perkins, Jocelyn, *Historic Occasions in Westminster Abbey*. 1935.

Stow, John, *A Survey of the Cities of London and Westminster*, 2 vols. edn., 1720.

Strype, J., *Memorials of Thomas Cranmer*.
> *Ecclesiastical Memorials*.
> *Annals of the Reformation*. (*Works*), 1820–40.

Trench, R. C., *Life and Letters of Abp. Trench*. 1888.

Westcott, A., *Life and Letters of Brooke Foss Westcott*. 1903.

THE CORONATIONS

Anon., 'The Coronation and the Commonwealth', *The Round Table*, September 1952.

Legg, L. G. Wickham, *English Coronation Records*. 1901.

Macleane, D., *The Great Solemnity of the Coronation*. 1911.

Prescott, W. Percival, *The Coronation Chair*. Ministry of Works Publication, 1957.

Schramm, P. E., *A History of the English Coronation*. 1937.

Stanley, A. P., *Historical Memorials of Westminster Abbey*, 5th ed., 1882.

Tanner, L. E., *The History of the Coronation*. 1952.
> *The History & Treasures of Westminster Abbey*. 1953.

MUSIC

Anon. *A Short Account of Organs Built in England from the Reign of King Charles the Second to the present Time*. London, J. Masters, 1847.

(The author was a musical amateur, Sir John Sutton.)

Bridge, Sir Frederick, *A Westminster Pilgrim*. 1918.

Bumpus, J. S., *A History of English Cathedral Music, 1549–1889*. 1908.

Burney, Charles, MUS.D., F.R.S., *An Account of the Musical Performances in Westminster Abbey and the Pantheon in Commemoration of Handel*. London, 1785.

A General History of Music from the Earliest Ages to the Present Period, 4 vols. Vol. I: 1776, vol. II: 1782, vols. III, IV: 1789.

Clutton, Cecil and Niland, Austin, *The British Organ*. 1963.

Cox, H. B. and C. L. E., *Leaves from the Journal of Sir George Smart*. 1907.

Deutsch, Otto Erich, *Handel: A Documentary Biography*. 1955.

Fellowes, E. H., *English Cathedral Music from Edward VI to Edward VII*. 1941.

Orlando Gibbons. 1925.

Hughes, Dom Anselm: 'Music of the Coronation over a Thousand Years', *Proceedings of the Royal Musical Association*, Session LXXIX, 1953.

Grove, *Dictionary of Music and Musicians*. 5th edn., 1954.

Morley, Thomas, *A Plain and Easy Introduction to Practical Music*. 1597. Modern edition by Alec Harman, 1952.

Musical Times, January 1902: 'Music at the Last Coronation'.

January 1905: 'Mr. and Mrs. Joah Bates'.

April–July 1907: 'Westminster Abbey' four articles by 'Dotted Crotchet'.

Pepys, Samuel, *Diary (Dec. 29 1661 . . . et al.)*.

Perkins, Jocelyn: *The Organs and Bells of Westminster Abbey*. 1936.

Pine, Edward, *The Westminster Abbey Singers*. 1953.

Rimbault, E. F., *The Old Cheque Book of the Chapel Royal from 1561 to 1744*. Camden Society, New Series, III. 1872.

Roper, E. Stanley, 'The Chapels Royal and Their Music', *Proceedings of the Musical Association*, Session LIV, 1927.

Sandford, Francis, *The History of the Coronation of the Most High, Most Mighty and Most Excellent Monarch James II*. London, 1687.

Shaw, H. Watkins, 'Extracts from Anthony à Wood's "Notes on the Lives of Musicians"', *Music and Letters*, vol. XV, 1934.

Smart, Sir George, *Annotations in copies of the Orders of Service for the Coronations of King William IV and Queen Victoria which are preserved in the Chapter Library at Westminster Abbey.*

Stevens, Denis, *Tudor Church Music.* 1961.

Sumner, W. L., *The Organ.* 1952/1962.

'The Organ in Kilkhampton Church', *The Organ,* vol. XLII, no. 166, October 1962.

Wesley, S. S., *A Few Words on Cathedral Music.* Published privately, 1849; reprinted by Hinrichsen, 1961.

West, John E., *Cathedral Organists Past and Present, 1899–1921.* 1921.

Westrup, J. A., *Purcell.* 1937.

Index

II